11/93

Enjoy my book

Best Wishes
Always.

Sincerely,
Wm. E. Fitzgerald

ARENAS OF GREED

by

William Edward Fitzgerald

The Great Chicago Commodity Market Scam:

Billions of dollars stolen by
Broker groups, Bagmen and Exchange Officials.

Billions of dollars laundered by the Mafia.

AND THE MAN WHO STOPPED THEM!

DeVin Publishers, Inc.

Published by:
DeVin Publishers, Inc.
SAN 297-2786

FIRST EDITION
Copyright ©1990 William E. Fitzgerald

CIP 90-82203

PUBLISHER'S CATALOGING IN PUBLICATION

Fitzgerald, William Edward, 1941-
   Arenas of greed : the great Chicago commodity scam / William
Edward Fitzgerald.
   p. cm.
   ISBN 0-9627407-0-5

   1. Chicago Mercantile Exchange--Fiction. 2. Chicago Board of
Trade--Fiction. I. Title.

PS3556.I83   813'.54
                        QB190-31
                        MARC

FOR

Patrick, Keri, Daniel, William and Mary Carol my precious, precious Five! Who sacrificed my time and attention at home while I ate, slept, worked, lived and breathed this book.

THE AUTHOR SPEAKS HIS THANKS

Twenty five years ago, one of my English Professors told me that I had a talent for writing. I chose philosophy and psychology as my concentration instead. Twenty years ago, after reading several of my writings, my wife encouraged me to continue this talent on a professional basis. My argument was a lack of discipline, patience and most of all, a lack of life's experiences which I had barely tasted.

Twenty-three years of marriage, five children later, and decades of tasting both the bitter and the sweet this life has to offer, I now feel qualified to exercise any writing talent that may have been buried.

At the continued insistence of my wife, Carol, I began to gather information on the accepted behavior and personalities of commodity brokers (a different breed!) both in and out of the Chicago Trading Pits.

A special thanks to Carol, for her constant vigilance in seeing that *ARENAS OF GREED* did indeed become a reality. Her encouragement, suggestions, untold hours of deciphering my longhand, typing every single word in this book, editing and proof reading, all compensated for the frustration that goes along with writing a novel of this magnitude. Buried in reams of paper, many times wondering if there was an end in sight, she forged ahead.

I thank her also for helping me trudge up the mountains in our life. She has been blessed with a perseverance, strength, dedication, class and character, not commonly found in America today. This author's adventuresome spirit has not been easy to live with, yet Carol has been with me every step of the way. To my wife, I am deeply grateful and LOVE you dearly.

To my stoic Mother, Grace, and the strong spirit of my Father, Edward, I thank with all of my heart for their support in helping me when I stumbled along the way to maturity and for their positive philosophy that any goal is possible if one is willing to work hard.

Phyllis Luxem, my good friend and author of more than forty books, added the enzyme needed to continue when this author felt his own inadequacies. You have indeed been an inspiration. My deep and sincere thanks and appreciation.

Additional thanks to Ray Nugent, whose many suggestions proved to be invaluable; Edna McAlexander, final proofreader; George Walmsley, Jr., and George Christensen, my research advisors; and Robert Clausen, my lifelong friend who gave me a second chance. I thank all the Veterans of Foreign Wars, with special tribute to those men and women who struggled through the dual war of Viet Nam. Because of their courage and sacrifices, this book is able to be printed in the name of freedom.

To the friends of Bill Wilson throughout the world, who saved my life some twenty-four hours ago, I owe my love and dedication. Hundreds of individuals helped and encouraged me during those turbulent times. You know who you are.

Special thanks to the people whose belief in me, support, encouragement and qualities of friendship have contributed to the sum total of my being, which in turn was a catalyst in bringing this book to fruition: Joe McCarthy, Ben McCarthy, William Joffe, Peter Stavros, Sr., Alex and Josephine Monestero, Verlin Jackson, Erskine Adam, Charles Murray, Vito Cali, Jack Pilger and Richard Howarth, with added special thanks to Attorneys Michael Rosenthal and William Martin, and good friend Joseph Crabb. I am indebted to all of you.

Because of the possible controversy surrounding the issues presented in *ARENAS OF GREED*, many who gave of themselves on my behalf wish to remain anonymous. To those people, I offer my thanks.

My sincere sympathy to those individuals and their families who are currently undergoing government investigation and are faced with the purge of the courtroom and the uncertainty of their lives.

Grateful acknowledgment is made to the following: The City of Chicago, The Chicago Mercantile Exchange, The Chicago Board of Trade, The International Monetary Market, The Bull and the Bear Pub, The Traders Lounge, The Black Potato Pub, St. Peter's Church.

PROLOGUE

Dark and damp outside, morning fog still tumbling through the streets of Chicago, a few of the younger pups come out of their lair to sniff for the day's food. Usually the same ones show up, always looking for an early fare. Some, more bold than others, weasel around the more popular bulls searching for scraps. Frequently, the old bulls snap out at the youths, mainly to impress onlookers, to register automatic respect to those mulling around.

By seven-thirty a.m. at least ten times ten sly bulls snarl and muscle into the pit. Same thing running through the minds of all: "Am I going to eat today or go hungry?"

Seven-fifty-nine a.m.: over one hundred pit bulls crunch together in an octagonal oak trading pit with three steps up to a wide landing and three steps down into the center. The Arena.

The bell rings at eight o' clock and the battle begins. Growling, snapping, frothing, angry bulls tear each other for meat, sometimes getting a mouthful, sometimes a morsel, and sometimes losing the little they brought to the contest.

When the pit bull lacks the discipline of a champion competitor, when the pit bull doesn't keep physically and mentally sharp, when the pit bull makes too many mistakes, the seasoned bulls will tear his flesh to the bone. This is the arena of the survival of the fittest. The strong bulls rip out the financial life of the weak bulls.

Within thirty minutes of pandemonium, the animal sweat and odors of last night's carousing permeate the pit. Strong contenders are not overwhelmed. As the contest moves to mid and later morning, some of the weaker pups run from the snarling pit. The vociferous older and wiser dogs step in and out of the trading pit snapping up morsels fast. They intuitively know when to strike! Get every crumb that falls from the table.

The old bulls swagger out of the pit protecting their game from all onlookers, only to place the trophy among many others.

By early afternoon only the strongest pit masters and a few bold stragglers are left. Weaker ones prowl on the fringe licking their wounds. They spend crucial moments striving to snag some meat in a last-ditch effort to keep from going home hungry for the day. Starving isn't status.

At one-fifty-nine p.m. the bell rings again. This signals a one-minute liquidation warning. Sheer pandemonium erupts. The final surge for survival jams the pit. Hungry bulls scream, tear, rip at each other. Mad dogs. Hundreds of desperate eyes and nervous reflexes search the pit for bits of food being tossed into the Arena.

The final bell rings loud and continuous. The day is done. Contest over. This is the life of a "Pit bull," a Chicago commodity broker. An exercise in survival for some. A profile in greed for others. Longevity for few.

FOREWORD

St. Patrick's Day, 1984

A cold lake-mist pelted the financial district of Chicago as Tim O'Neal emerged from a private side door of the Exchange Building, crossed Jackson, and hurried north on LaSalle Street. He moved quickly, glancing over his shoulder to see if he were being followed. His keen senses felt eyes watching him, but he saw no one. He lifted his right hand, which held a heavy briefcase, and looked at his diamond-faced Rolex. The time read 8:17 p.m. A large manila envelope was tucked under his left arm. Shit, he thought, too much time! He had taken too much time. Too much of a chance! But there was so much incriminating information. He couldn't stop once he was into the computer. Screw it! No guts, no glory. The risk would be worth the extra time spent in the Fat Man's office. Could he now nail the bastard for killing his friend? Would he end up dead himself? The thought quickened his pace.

He spotted a mailbox in front of the *LaSalle Building*, looked up and down the street, then dropped the heavy manila envelope into the large blue container. He sighed with relief. Thank God that was out of his hands. The envelope contained duplicates of the original documents he carried in his briefcase. *Hawk* Hogan would know what to do with the documents if anything happened to him. He had a reason to shudder at the nightmare that was taking place in Chicago. His partner, Al Josephson, had been killed two months earlier for attempting the same break-in O'Neal had just pulled off. Hogan would get the job done if anybody could. He would see that the Feds received the information. That is, if the Hawk lived long enough.

He turned from the mailbox and pulled the stiff collar of his expensive suede jacket up around his neck, not so much for protection from the flailing wind and mist as for anonymity. Tonight, the weather was his ally.

His eyes studied the wet street again. Nobody seemed to be following him, but then he saw the slow motion of a black limousine. About a half block back, it crept in the same direction as he. Limousines punctuated LaSalle Street at most times of the day or night. Why did this one bother him? His auburn hair was soaked. He could feel the beads of rain mixed with perspiration run from his sideburns down his neck and soak into his cotton shirt.

Two laughing couples hurried passed him. Soaked green leprechaun caps with stenciled shamrocks were on their heads. O'Neal jumped in behind them, as if he were part of their group. He had to contact Hogan and tell him he had the information. Damn! He wished Mike Hogan was with him. He could use his rough friend now.

As the two couples turned to enter *the Out-Trade Bar*, Tim scanned the street. The limo still crept. Was it stalking him? What little composure he had left told him he was

going to lose his mind if he didn't lose his paranoia first. He tried to calm himself and wished he had brought his .38 revolver. A stupid oversight. Jesus! What a goddamn experience in horror. How many commodity brokers carried guns for protection?

On the other hand, how many straight brokers like Hogan and himself were trying to bring down the fastest-growing game of greed and laundering operation in the country? He felt a shiver of terror rock his body as he crossed Monroe and rushed toward Madison Street.

How in the hell did this thing get so out of hand? When he became a broker at the exchanges, fifteen years earlier, the markets were relatively clean. Now the whole goddamn commodity industry was feeding off customer orders in one way or another. Like most things, he guessed, the corruption began slowly. Steal a little bit here, a little bit there, then ten years later whole-scale grand larceny was the rule rather than the exception, accepted and promoted by the exchange officials. How did the Mafia's laundry operation get so strong, so fast? One day the major criminal elements just appeared and took over. Like a cancer. Like a parasite. One broker group after another fell to the temptation of easy, dirty money.

As he hustled across Madison Street, a cab slid to a stop, almost hitting him. The horn blasted, and Tim simply raised his hand apologetically. He looked back down LaSalle Street and saw that the limo still inched his way. He had taken many limousine rides in his days of wine and roses and knew the chauffeur's job was to pick up and deliver his passengers with expedience. This one drifted down a rainy street like a black log in a spooky creek. His breath came in bursts, and he could feel his heart beat like a hammer against his ribs.

The mist had turned to a driving rain, making it harder to be spotted. A phone! He needed to find a phone. He knew a safe place.

He moved quickly down Madison Street to St. Peter's Church. He knew there was a phone on the lower level next to the shop where they sold holy things. As he opened the heavy brass church doors, he looked back and searched the street. Nobody looked suspicious and *no* limo. Thank God!

He moved inside and walked quickly to the marble steps. They led down to the retail Holy Shop, washrooms, and telephone. He turned the corner at the bottom of the steps and ran a short distance to the old black wall phone that hung outside the Holy Shop. With his wet shoes, he slid the last four feet on the bright, shiny floor. He dropped his briefcase under the phone and grabbed the receiver.

As he reached for change in his left pocket, he stalled a moment. He listened. Did he hear footsteps, or was it his overactive imagination? All he could hear was his own heart beating and the far-off sounds of church services. The unmistakable scent of incense touched his memory. The Franciscans still followed a few of the old traditions. The smell of incense was as characteristic to St. Peter's as wind was to the city of Chicago. But it didn't make him feel holy or safe. He envisioned himself as being the sacrifice of the Mass on this, St. Patrick's Day. His guts churned and he felt sick. Hogan! I have to reach Hogan, he half whispered.

He wiped sweat from his forehead and looked at his hands. They were shaking. He dialed Murphy's Black Potato Pub, near the old stockyards. He knew that was where Michael was celebrating the day for the Irish, with his I.R.A. buddies, and everybody else for that matter. Tim wished he was also celebrating St. Paddy's Day drinking green beer and singing Irish songs. That's where he belonged, not in this eerie basement of a church.

He watched the dim hall with trepidation. The Holy Store was closed, and the corridor was empty and sparsely lit. His attention came back to the phone. Come on, answer the phone! Just answer the damn phone! Eight rings, nine, ten.

Finally the phone was picked up, and the blast of bagpipe music made him wince. He sighed with relief as a brogue-laced voice announced, *the Black Potato Pub*. His mouth opened to speak as he instinctively looked back down the empty hall. This time it wasn't empty. Two men dressed in long trenchcoats stood in the shadows at the bottom of the stairs holding long-barreled pistols. Their thick, ugly silencers were aimed at his chest.

Tim's mind blanked for a moment, and he felt his mouth go dry as it drooped open. The phone slipped from his hand and clanked with a hollowness against the marble wall. One man motioned with his gun toward O'Neal's briefcase. O'Neal feigned ignorance, and the larger of the two men fired one spit. The bullet passed through the briefcase, knocking it over. Tim felt his eyes squint, and he ground his teeth as the bullet ricocheted off the tile floor and lodged in the oak door behind him.

Nervous perspiration rolled in big drops down his cheeks and off his chin. His breath came in measured gasps. He hesitated with his foot, then slid the briefcase across the smooth floor to the faceless enemy. One of the men stooped, opened the case, and quickly went through the papers. He nodded to the other man, closed the case, and cradled it under his free arm. As he rose, Tim caught a glimpse of the wiry man's face. He had seen him before, and he remembered the distinct features of a rodent that could never hide him in a crowd.

Both men motioned for O'Neal to walk away from the phone. It swung on its short, chrome-covered cord. The sound of bagpipes could be heard coming from the phone as it moved like a black pendulum going nowhere. He stood motionless.

His reflexes moved faster than his mind. He reached for the swinging phone, wanting to shout a warning. The two men anticipated the move. The barrels of both pistols slammed down hard on his head, knocking him to the floor.

He watched the dangling phone begin to blur in front of him. As he tried to lift himself, he heard the bagpipes. Blood ran onto the tan tile floor from his head wounds.

He struggled to pull himself up by the brass ridge that framed the display window of the Holy Shop. His eyes focused on a flowered plaque. All he could make out were the words, "...AND THE COURAGE TO CHANGE THE THINGS I CAN!"

Another blow to the head, and Tim O'Neal dropped hard to the floor again. His consciousness faded fast, his senses familiar only with the smell of burning incense and the far-off sound of bagpipes. Within seconds a third man was walking down the hall. Tim's eyes were too blurred to see anything. A huge shadow fell across his body. He heard the sound of metal clinking against metal--soft metal--GOLD! Gold coins habitually sliding

across each other. This was an obsession like Lady Macbeth's compulsion with hand-washing. He could see the compulsive motion of the shuffling gold coins in his mind...he had seen them sliding before...twenty-dollar gold pieces...back and forth...back and forth.

He tried to lift his battered head. Now he knew this third enemy. The Boss Man. The Fat Man. Tim knew he would die soon. The burning incense had been for him. His neck lost its strength as his head splashed down into the puddle of his own blood. His mind turned dark and emptied of all thought.

* * *

On the fourth page of the Chicago *Tribune* the following day, March 18, 1982, a short, insignificant article stated that a Chicago commodity broker, Tim O'Neal, apparently despondent over recent trading losses and pending divorce, had leapt to his death from the twenty-fifth floor of his luxurious Michigan Avenue condominium. The police called the incident a suicide.

Michael "Hawk" Hogan threw the newspaper across the room and swore. He looked at the large manila envelope that had arrived in the morning mail. He knew what was in the package, and he knew the contents would reveal the men responsible for O'Neal's death. They would be the same men who were responsible for blowing Al Josephson's brains all over his dashboard and placing a .22 caliber in his hand. Hogan was familiar with their methods. Lightning had struck twice. The police had called that incident an unfortunate suicide, as Josephson was a community philanthropist, leaving four children and a devoted wife. Michael knew the killers were the men responsible for bringing poison to the Exchanges.

The feeling of icy rage flowed through Hogan's body as he felt his eyes narrow and his jaw tighten. Two of his close friends--dead. Killed because of greed. Brokers killing brokers. Insanity. Goddamn insanity, but it made sense because he and his friends were getting too close to the corruption that had consumed the commodity exchanges. At that moment he vowed to bring the assassins and their cohorts who lived by the sword to justice. Not the justice of duration through the courts, but swift justice. Street justice. If he had to do it himself, he would rid the Exchanges of the garbage that was fermenting. Maggots were spreading throughout the commodity industry.

The promise would be kept. Nobody, including Hogan, had any idea how far his personal indictments, trials, and executions would extend. Nobody realized the man called the Deceptive One had returned from the grave!

ONE

April 7, 1987: The Beginning

An explosion sounded in the distance, immediately followed by an even larger eruption. Or was it? The piercing whine of a siren mingled with the noise. Then a far-off cry stretched to him, "Michael, please." Another eruption. This one sent vibrations throughout the massive North Shore mansion on the lake.

Michael recognized the sound and the voice, but couldn't connect them. The persistence of both finally drove him to a drowsy consciousness. He felt a final shove by his wife, Maria. "Michael, please turn off the snooze."

The wife. Alarm and dreaming ceased. The banging didn't and wouldn't for awhile. The bawling winds were out of the northeast, which made Lake Michigan more angry than usual. He sat hunched on the edge of the bed. His mind could see the frigid surf bang against the concrete-and-steel sea wall. The manmade barrier would eventually yield to one of nature's meanest waters.

The clamor continued, and he liked it. He liked the power of nature. He would stand out in raging thunderstorms and windstorms. The force of the storms would nag at him until he let his will unite with Nature's. They would become one. They understood each other. The stronger and more dangerous the storms, the more he courted them. Life was no exception.

Four a.m. came too early for Michael Hogan. He reached over in the dark and swatted at the black, noisy menace whose glowing, numerical eyes glared at him. Three and one-half hours of sleep used to sustain him. His work load in the grain and financial pits had reached record proportions. The hours had been extended, and his so-called social drinking had escalated to a good quart of Johnny Walker Black Label a day.

Maria stirred and perched up on one elbow. "Honey, you okay?"

"Fine, babe. Just tired."

He lay back down, rolled to her side, and kissed her softly on the forehead, nose, and chin. She responded by wrapping her inviting arms, solid and strong, around him. He felt her tender body mesh with his own, and they kissed. The red-eyed sentry blasted its disapproval, and Michael, in one swift roll, slammed his fist down on the snooze alarm again. This time the red eyes dimmed and faded.

"That takes care of you, ya noisy little prick!"

"Break it again, dear?" The magnificence beneath the sheets cynically asked.

"It's not breathing," Michael said as he examined the dead intruder. "That's why I buy twelve at a time."

He turned on the light, rolled back over on the bed, and kissed Maria's soft lips. "Wait up for me tonight and we'll resume this discussion, okay? I have to get moving if you want your bills paid." He didn't wait for an answer, knowing she waited up for him every night until sleep nudged away her erotic anticipation.

With one swift leap, he sprang from the bed and made his way to his "super bathroom"--bathroom, dressing room, exercise room, sauna and steam room, with even a Chinese hot tub.

"Please be home early, Michael. It's Joseph's birthday. We'll have dinner and cake at seven o' clock sharp. Can you hear me?"

Standing at the doorway, with a mouth full of tooth paste, he garbled, "How old is Joseph now? Fourteen?"

"Twelve, Michael. You're thinking of Martin. He's fourteen."

He gave no answer. Goddamn, he thought, he couldn't even remember the ages of his six children, let alone their birthdates. How could he? He was gone in the morning before they were awake and back home after most of them were in bed. A kiss on the forehead in the morning and again in the evening didn't make much of a father. He hoped that his love for the commodity markets didn't work in inverse proportion to his children's love for him. Not having a solution, he forced the guilt back into his subconscious and sought the solace of his bathroom.

* * *

Maria pulled the covers up over her sleek body. Her thoughts were on Michael and her deep love for him. She dozed again, aware more of the thrashing and splashing in the bathroom than of the roaring thunder outside.

Maria Santini, born in Palermo, Sicily, March 19, 1949, daughter of a very popular and powerful building contractor, Carlo Santini. She was a bright, delightful beauty, with long hair as black as Manchester coal. With a delicate yet provocative sensuousness about her, she was slightly built and serious. Her most powerful weapon was her intuitive sense about people. She looked beyond a person's eyes and penetrated his soul. The intrusion was a quantitative and a qualitative analysis of his character. Maria was streetwise. Her early upbringing in the streets of Palermo provided front-line experience with raw life. She inherited her shrewd and cunning talents from her father.

Maria tried not to interfere with Michael's market madness. She kept personal thoughts to herself. Her obsidian eyes, the size of walnuts, never failed to reveal to him her concerns and needs. At 38, Maria was alert, astute, and intelligent. She trusted few Americans, thinking them frivolous, impulsive, and greedy. That made them dangerous. In fact, she had limited faith in most people.

At the age of eight, Maria had seen her grandfather shot to death on the steps of a Palermo bank. The killers were two Lupo-carrying Cosa Nostra soldiers dressed in dark

raincoats. She had overheard the vendetta pledged by her father. He gave the command to stalk and eliminate those responsible for the murder.

Seven members of the Trappoli/Massete families were executed in retribution. Three Santini people were killed at the hands of the Trappoli soldiers. That was a long time ago in a crude and uncultured country. They abandoned Sicily five years later for the glitter and freedom of America.

Maria followed the Italian tradition of noninterference where business was concerned. She was bold and confident enough to scold her good-hearted and gentle husband when he made foolish business decisions. His eccentric and unpredictable Irish behavior often took the place of common sense.

* * *

Maria and Michael fitted together like rain and springtime. His beautiful wife's encouragement would eventually be one of the reasons he became a powerful man in the City of Wind and Sin. Her influence as the wife of a successful, likable Chicago commodity broker, and as the daughter of a prominent New York contractor, was complemented by her own innate sense of survival. These qualities were paramount, as he would find out when tough and dangerous times entered their lives.

Michael, on the other hand, was an Irish cross between the Nordics on his mother's side and Spanish-Irish on his father's side. At 39, he resembled his father, not only in stature and complexion, but also in philosophy. Over six feet tall, lean, tough, and confident, Michael took care of people. He did not confine himself to family, unlike his wife's powerful relatives. He helped others without the expectation of future obligation or reciprocity. He considered mankind to be basically afraid, weak, and without direction. He thought people forced themselves to settle for the least, when the most was available to them.

Now he was performing his morning ritual. A cold-hot-cold shower, a shave, and a call from the bathroom phone to ask his associate, Sidney Stone, how the night markets had closed.

Sid traded the European and London markets between the hours of eight at night and four in the morning. Michael traded from seven in the morning to four in the afternoon. Their office was open almost twenty-four hours a day, three hundred sixty-five days a year. If one had the stamina, one could trade all day, all night, and on weekends. If that became dull, there were the ball games to bet or a gin rummy game. If things became really dull, one could always jump in the company Lear Jet and head to Vegas for a few non-stop days. Gambling became a constant, like breathing. If one wasn't gambling with markets, cards, drugs or broads, he was gambling with his life.

Now Michael glanced into the mirrored wall after his shower. He didn't like what he saw. Rough had replaced smooth and rugged had replaced a once-handsome visage. He

thought his face looked flushed from the heavy booze intake. His durable body was beginning to droop slightly. He looked down. Evidence of eating rich foods was showing. He grimaced at the start of a paunch. He fluffed his dark hair with a heavy terry-cloth towel, stepped back from the mirror, let the towel drop to the marble floor, and took a deeper look at his reflection. Fifteen years of heavy-duty pit trading in the Chicago commodity markets was beginning to take its toll. He pointed to the face that looked back and scolded himself: "You're going to stop drinking that poison and eating rich men's food." Moving toward his dressing room and out of sight of his red-faced image in the mirror, he mumbled, "I'll think about it tomorrow."

He dressed in his saddle colors, Italian shoes and pants, French shirt, and Swiss watch, all presents from Maria. His outfit alone probably cost twenty-five hundred not counting the gold watch. He often thought it amusing how Americans spent ten times more for foreign goods than American, just to cover their inferior bodies and souls. Weakness begets weakness.

He had become entangled in the web of the nouveau-riche game. He justified his extravagance by blaming his stylish living on his wife's regal tastes, his clothes on the fabric import business owned by his brother-in-law, and his expensive jewelry on the gold, silver, and diamond sideline of his associate, Sidney Stone.

All in all, Michael thought he looked like an advertisement for Gucci or the Robb Report. When he stepped out of his one-hundred-thousand-dollar Astin-Martin, a satisfied smile always wormed its way onto his face.

Time to call Sidney. The precious-metal markets were strong in Europe because of the anticipation of a large Japanese gold purchase. Michael had heard about this two days previous through his European Bank contact. He told Stone to sell out four hundred "long" contracts on the opening in New York, just in case he didn't get to work in time for the opening.

Two-hour traffic delays on the Edens Expressway were the exception rather than the rule. However, he did occasionally encounter these delays, another joke in Chicago. Why didn't the city do it like New York and not allow anybody to street park? Then, just the people who could afford to would drive downtown. He was feeling cynical this morning. This wasn't characteristic of him.

He remembered the early eighties, when gas jumped to a dollar-fifty a gallon. He thought it was great because fewer people were driving to work. Back then they were going in car pools and on commuter trains or doing more business from their homes in the suburbs.

He figured that for every ten cents per gallon increase in the price of gas, two cars per ten would retreat. His mind also calculated that at eight dollars and fifty cents per gallon, he would be able to propel himself to work in a swift twenty minutes. He grinned. He didn't care if gas went to one hundred dollars a gallon. He had already made two million this year just being long the oil market and petroleum stocks.

He emerged from the "super bathroom," strode around the bed to Maria's side, kissed her in the warm hollow of her neck, then gently on the cheek, and he was on his way to the city.

Quickly moving down the circular staircase, Michael entered the kitchen knowing Mary O'Mally, their faithful Irish maid, had already prepared his orange juice, a slice of wheat toast, and a concoction of vitamins and yogurt with a touch of sweetener blended in the food processor. His morning nutrition was merely a rationalization for the junk that would go into his body the rest of the day. He thanked her, kissed her on the cheek, and was on his way out the door.

The phone caught him as he reached for the heavy brass door knob. It twittered once, and he pounced on it so as not to wake the household. Probably Sidney objecting to his liquidation of the four hundred gold contracts when the market was certain to go higher. Michael put the receiver to his ear and blurted one of his favorite market phrases, "Remember, Sidney...The bulls get a little, the bears get a little, and the pigs get nothing!"

He had calculated a 250 thousand dollars' profit in two days on a no-brainer, and that was satisfactory to him. To ask for any more would be risky. Greedy.

"Mike? It's Joe Glassmann."

Michael sighed. Why in the hell was Joe calling him so early in the morning?

"Oh. Sorry, Joe. I thought it was Stone. What brings you to life so early?"

"Do you have a minute to talk, Mike?"

Michael looked at his watch. "I'm just walking out the door, Joe. Can I call you from my car phone? Are you at the office?"

"No, call me at home. I don't get to work as early as you young pups."

Young pups, Michael thought, remembering the image in the mirror.

Joe reeled off his home phone number and ended the short conversation with, "It's important, Mike!"

"I'll get back to you within ten minutes, Joe."

He held the phone for a moment, thinking about his good friend Joe Glassmann. Everything was important to Joe. He was a smart, good old Jewish fellow who was part owner of one of the largest cash grain and export businesses in the Midwest. Joe was a long-time friend of the family. He had given Michael his first job at the Chicago Board of Trade, tallying market quotes on a big chalk-board, years before the computer onslaught. Important or not, he would call old Joe and find out what was on his mind.

He hung up the phone and headed for the garage door again. This time he made it to the four-car garage that housed his jet-black Astin-Martin, Maria's Jaguar, a four-wheel-drive Jeep wagon, and the family's silver limo. He opened the garage door behind his car and took his usual quick walk to the middle of the circular brick drive. The large fountain tried with futility to equalize its spray against the heavy winds.

Michael looked into the dark sky, closed his eyes, breathed the crisp, clean morning air into his lungs. Eyes still closed, the spray of the fountain wetting his face and

jacket, he listened to the slamming surf and the wind whispering secrets to him. He bowed his head, said a short prayer to his unseen, incomprehensible God, and made the sign of the cross. Then he headed to his car and thought about the phone call to Joe Glassmann.

TWO

Inklings of Corruption

The horizon was showing signs of awakening. The black Astin squealed onto the Edens Expressway heading south into Chicago. Michael was about thirty minutes ahead of the rush hour. By the time it started, he would be close to the yawning city. Today he wouldn't be affected by the jam-ups and gapers' blocks.

He decided he had better get Glassmann on the phone before the poor old guy started to worry about him. After Michael's father died fifteen years ago, his dear and trusted friend Joe coached Michael in the art of making money.

He was like a godfather. Their daily talks often went into the early hours of the morning. Joe taught him what to watch for in the market place, how to buy and when to sell, and when to double up and when to press. He knew the difference between success and failure, running fast when you're wrong the market or even have the slightest inkling that you might be wrong. Shrewd individuals knew when to run; the general investor did not. This knowledge is what separates the amateurs from the professionals. Joseph had inculcated him with these basic rules of trading. They would be forever imbedded in his memory.

He would say, "Most Americans only know how to buy things, commodities included. Americans have a real problem selling out a position, always hoping things will improve. Few investors in the market ever know the significance of what selling short means. Reversing a long position and selling the market with the anticipation of its going lower is completely foreign to amateur traders. The real pros make their money with this knowledge. The bears, who sell the market short, can make in two weeks what it took the bulls two years to make on a long position. An overbought market drops like a rock; it goes up with the roar of a lion and down with the squeak of a mouse!

"Never *hope* a market, Michael," Joe would continue. "If you find yourself coming to work hoping it will rain or not rain because of your position in the grain market, you're a loser. If you're long the orange juice market, hoping for a freeze in Florida, you'll be the one to get frozen. Hoping means that the market is evidently not acting complementary to your position, and that means get out!

"Don't wait until tomorrow. Everybody waits until tomorrow. Just get the hell out!"

A smile eased across Michael's face as he remembered Joe's cliches and all of his wisdom. "Rain makes grain, never forget it. Sell the rumor, buy the fact. Never double up on a losing bet in order to lower your average purchase price. Stay away from a market

you know nothing about. Don't get in a market on a tip from a cohort whose net worth is less than yours. The market will tell you when to get in. And above all, know your own weaknesses. You can be damn sure the market will, as will your enemies.

"Don't buy or sell more than you can afford, and never try to influence a falling or rising market from going its own inevitable direction. The market is bigger than any one man or group of men. Sure, you can push it around a little bit, and if you're big enough, you can trigger a temporary distortion in a particular market. But if you get into the bad habit of trying to push a market around, she will slap you in the face. The market is like a sophisticated woman, she will only take so much shit before she snaps back.

"Bigger men than you or I, much bigger men, have come and gone at the Exchange because they were greedy and disrespectful and forgot humility.

"If you're a day-trader, always go home clean. Take no positions home with you. If you're a position trader, it may take you twenty or thirty tries before your opinion of the market comes to fruition. Once your timing is right, add to your position in small amounts and *know precisely where you are going to get out if you are wrong*! Don't hesitate in getting out.

"As soon as you smell a reversal, run fast, because thousands of others are thinking the same as you. But most of them will procrastinate their liquidation. You move quick enough on liquidating your position and you'll beat the amateurs. Don't worry about the profits. They'll handle themselves. If you are riding a winner, let it run. No one knows how far overdone a market can get. And, by all means, never, never let a nice profit turn into a loss."

Joe would go on for hours instructing, often repeating himself. He joked cynically with Michael that being Irish, his learning would probably take a long time.

Michael remembered the story Joe told of one of his partners, a big grain broker in the forties. He made $75 million in the soybean oil and meal markets. "That was a lot of money in those days," Joe scoffed. "He became pushy and greedy going for the last two bits and ended up killing himself because he lost all but ten million."

Joe would just shake his head in disgust and say, "In the forties, a ten-million-dollar net worth put you in the top one hundred wealthiest in Chicago. And my friend, Saul Mandel, blew his brains out because he only had ten mil left."

Saul's perception of the meaning of life had been lost as surely as his motivation to live. Money had become his God, his love, and the fear of going bust haunted him. It was a typical frigid winter morning in Chicago. There was ice in the dark air, and thick frost covered the single-pane office windows when Joe found his partner. He was slumped over his desk, a gun in one hand and a blood-soaked ticker tape in the other. A short note simply stated, "I'm sorry, Joe! Please forgive me!" The blood had partially obscured Saul's parting word, "Shalom."

At that, Joe would fade into his own dreams of days past and turn melancholy. The day's lesson was finished.

Every session with Joe Glassmann ended with, "Stay honest and stay humble, Michael, and you'll be a rich man some day. You'll keep those riches and other bonuses if you continue to stay honest and humble."

Now Michael snapped out of his revery when a squad car screamed by him at Touhy Avenue.

Better call Joe. He pressed the one programmed button with Joe's home number. He expected a "hello". Instead he heard his name, "Michael?"

A thought flickered through his mind. Jesus, what anticipation. "Yes, Godfather." He knew the endearing name made Joe feel good.

"Listen, Son. I'll get right to the point. I know you're rushed and so am I. You're familiar with and have worked all of the major pits at both Exchanges, right?"

Michael wanted his response to be accurate. "I haven't worked the Mercantile Exchange as much as I have the Board of Trade. But, yes, I'm familiar with all the pits."

"How about the Monetary Market?"

Michael knew Joe liked things precise, so he detailed.

"Yes, last year I spent quite a bit of time trading Eurodollars, Swiss francs, Japanese yen, and Deutschemarks. I also worked the S&Ps for quite awhile. Then I was called back to the Board of Trade to fill orders in the bean pit for Colonial Exports. Seems they couldn't get a decent order filled without a couple of cents a bushel dropping between the cracks."

"Michael, that's exactly what I want to talk to you about. Quarter points, half points, and full points that fall between the cracks or into the pockets of the bagmen in and out of the trading pits. My buy/sell orders are fairly large. I know those brokers are stealing at least twenty grand a day from my orders."

Coaxing him, Michael jousted, "Hey, Joe. What's a half mil a month to you big grain guys? Find yourself another broker. One who's honest. Hell, use one of your own men."

His mentor snapped back. "Goddammit, Michael. I'm serious. Your buddies have screwed this Jew once too often. I've used every broker in the pit, including my own. They're all crooks!"

In defense Michael countered, "Jesus Christ, Joe. What do you want me to do? I watch brokers steal all day long, but nobody gives a damn. I've screamed to the Board of Governors and President of the Exchange and even to the crooked brokers skimming points from each order they fill. It does no good, and you know why? Because they're all in on it. All the way up the ladder. And you know who they hit on? Yes. Me! They came into my company and checked my records. They found out I took a forty-three-hundred-dollar losing trade out of my aunt's account and put the loss into my account so she could buy new carpeting for her house. They suspended me for thirty days and fined me ten thousand dollars. You know what that's called, Joe?"

Michael didn't wait for an answer.

"That's called a warning. A warning that says, 'Don't fuck with the system, Irishman.'"

"I know all about that, Michael, and I'm sorry. Not the money part, because I know you can afford it, but the embarrassment of the suspension. The bastards made sure it hit the *Tribune* and *Wall Street Journal* too."

Now, Michael was entering the Kennedy junction, and traffic was slowing. The Astin eased to the left in order to scramble into the express lanes that would sweep him to the loop in fourteen minutes.

"Joe, you can't stop them. If they screwed you out of a couple of bucks, press the issue and threaten a lawsuit. That won't do you any good, though, because your complaint has to go to Exchange arbitration before a lawyer will get involved...it's in the Exchange rules. The Arbitration Committee is paid off by the Exchange, so what kind of a chance do you think you'll have with arbitration? You haven't a foot to stand on. The only way you'll get any satisfaction is if you threaten to go to the media. Tell the Exchange you're going to the news media. Tell them you're going to the *Tribune*, the *Sun Times*, Channels 2, 7, 9, 11, Mr. Rogers, Julia Child, and anybody else you can think of. Say you can prove your orders are being raped and points are being bagged at your expense. The Exchanges don't want adverse publicity. If you can prove the brokers are skimming, I'll guarantee you that you'll get all your money back in spades and the brokers who cheated you will get a good talking to and maybe even a small fine. If he fucked you real bad," his voice filled with sarcasm, "the brokers and their bagmen might get as much as a five-thousand-dollar fine and a thirty-day suspension. Of course, the brokers probably screwed fifty more guys just like you and slipped their bagmen a cool million each in the last twelve months. A five-thousand-dollar fine and a thirty-day suspension for a million bucks sounds pretty appealing to a lot of guys."

The blurred sign above the expressway flashed "Fullerton Avenue." Ten more minutes, he thought. "You know as well as I do, Joe, the brokers who are dirty have a perfect scam by skimming points within limits, that make them *Complaint Proof*, by you or any other customer."

Patience and understanding returned to Joe's voice. "You're not hearing me, Mike. This time we are going to be heard. These atrocities have been going on far too long, and all of us so-called big guys are guilty because we've known and haven't done anything about it. This time there is going to be a fall, a big fall, and I'm going to need your support."

Michael protested, "There is nothing you can do, Joe."

"Well, we'll just see about that. How about lunch? There is someone who would like to meet with you."

Michael watched his speedometer, 80 mph. "Who wants to meet with me?"

Glassmann spoke quietly. "I'll introduce you to him at lunch."

Michael grinned. "You cunning Jew. This conversation has all been a set-up for lunch with a mystery man, hasn't it?"

Joseph laughed and made an admission to Michael. "You're learning fast, Irishman. Ten years ago it would have taken you days to figure that out. Now you can read me in less than an hour. Not bad for a Mick." He guffawed again.

"Three o'clock is the earliest I can make it, Joe. I'm in the bond pit today doing some arbitrage work for Sam Ross and Company out of New York. I'll be finished at two o'clock and out of there about two thirty, two forty-five. Where are you going to dine me and the mystery man? McDonald's?"

"No, I thought the Union Club. We have reservations at three o'clock. I knew you were in the bonds today. You've been there for five days and will be for the next nine trading days or until Sam Ross and Company is finished with this one big deal."

Michael punched the Astin past a line of cars and screwed up his face, wondering how the hell the cunning little Jew knew that. Like a kid he had to know. "Who gave you that information, Joe?"

There was a moment's hesitation on the phone, and Michael heard the soft voice say, "Sam Ross told me."

Michael smiled but said nothing.

"Three o'clock then at the Union Club, okay, Michael?"

Silence for a moment, and then he pushed the words out slowly. "That's just fine."

The line went dead, and Michael still held the phone in his hand, oblivious to the luminous sign saying "Next five exits Chicago loop." The expensive automobile knew its own way and eased to the right lane to exit on Jackson Boulevard.

Questions swirled in his head. Lunch with a mystery man? Was the billionaire, Sam Ross, finally surfacing? Why was Joe suddenly interested in righting the daily injustices that had become a routine way of life for commodity brokers? His mind shuffled the thoughts, and the smile remained. His plan was beginning to unfold. He had been patient, but the time had finally come. The beginning of the end was at hand.

His mind reeled in an ocean of anticipation and satisfaction. The Astin-Martin pulled itself into the underground garage at 143 West Jackson. "Stay honest and stay humble and wealth will be yours," had been Joe's words.

This Irishman added, "and justice will also be mine."

* * *

Twenty-three miles north of the Chicago loop in his ten-million-dollar Lake Bluff estate, Joe Glassmann pressed his finger down on the phone button and severed the connection between himself and Michael. He pushed another button that gave him clean access to another line. He then pressed seven digits, waited for two beeps, and pressed the remaining coded seven numbers.

One ring and the phone was answered: "Agent Golden."

Joe simply stated, "Three o'clock at the Union Club."

The deep voice asked with personal concern, "Do you think he'll cooperate?"

Joe rubbed his thin, whiskered cheeks. "I don't know. He's still pissed because we didn't come to his rescue a few years back."

"That couldn't be helped. We're ready now."

Joe leaned forward in his chair. "We can't do it without him. He knows everything about everybody."

"I know the man, Joe. How can he say no to you and me? Two of his closest friends?"

"Andy, I know him better than you. He can be damn stubborn and can say no to anybody but Maria. We'll just have to wait and see. Lunch at three, okay?"

"I'll be there." The line went dead. Message delivered. Operation Skim-Trim had begun.

THREE

Patrick Hogan

Joe Glassmann sat back in his chair, leaned his head on the soft cushion, and closed his eyes. His thoughts reeled in reverse, to a time in the past when he had first met Michael's father. He and Patrick Hogan had disembarked in depression-ridden America, in June of 1932. They had become acquainted with each other while working on the docks in New York City. Instantly, Joe had been impressed with Patrick's ability to talk to employees and fellow workers. He calmed their fears and apprehensions during warring times on the docks.

Dirty snow and ice covered the dangerous working area, which made for perilous times during the loading and unloading of grain, cattle, and hog hides. As the temperatures plummeted, tempers spiraled. Frigid weather, poor wages, and apathetic employers encouraged brutal fighting and daily dissension on the docks. During one major dispute, and after a five- hour meeting with a group of faceless Anglo-Saxon owners, Patrick and Joe came away with a five-cent-per-hour raise for all employees, including the janitor.

This was like a political coup. Chalk one up for the underdog. Being able to find a job was unheard of during the depression, much less getting a raise in wages. Patrick had the eloquence of a statesman at the meeting. Joe knew that his uneducated friend had the rare ability to calm and persuade people. A subtle and easy manner. He dealt with the common element that runs through the veins of many men--the spiritual.

To Joe's knowledge, Patrick had no prejudices. In a metropolis that dictated strict ethnic-group solidarity, xenophobic reactions ran high. Patrick, however, would break down the invisible metal curtains and walk through as if they were merely clouds. His peace, generosity, sincerity, and Irish wit gave people encouragement and hope, whether they were Irish, Jewish, Italian, Polish, or American, white, black or red. Patrick spoke gently to all men as if they were his brothers. Joseph saw a spirit in Patrick that he had never seen in a man before and probably never would see again. Patrick was oblivious to the world of war, depression, greed, and exploitation. He was a mysterious spirit who exuded truth, honesty, and goodness. Joseph Glassmann wished a little of Patrick's mystique and saint-like qualities in day-to-day living would rub off on him, who knew how to win a confrontation only with his fists or a gun. Patrick's way was far less painful and much more effective. Patrick was the personification of charisma.

After several months on the job, Patrick Hogan had impressed his employers. He was offered a promotion, which meant a relocation to Chicago to buy livestock and grain at the Chicago Stockyards and nearby grain elevators. He accepted the position with the

understanding that he could take along a knowledgeable assistant, a man whose expertise was to chisel purchase prices down to the bottom penny.

When Patrick announced that he wanted Joe Glassmann as his associate in Chicago, vocal explosions rampaged throughout the docks. His employers shouted and pouted, and puffed and chomped on their expensive Cuban cigars as they paced the big warehouse office and slammed fists on metal tables. To send this pugnacious Jew with the gentle Irishman could only mean one thing--TROUBLE! Heaven knows, they had enough trouble day in and day out with the ordinary machinations of running the docks. They didn't need any long-distance problems.

During the vocal melee, Patrick remained silent and calm in his usual way, and persuasive in an unusual way. In spite of their consternation, they relented and agreed to let the mouthy little Jew accompany Patrick and his family to Chicago. They agreed with Patrick that it would be good to get rid of the troublemaker, Glassmann. After all, he was a hard-working and reliable employee. Maybe under Hogan's influence, his temperament would become more subdued.

When Joe heard the news of Chicago, he was mystified. Why did this tall, handsome Gentile with the soft eyes and wise tongue befriend him to the extent of having him as an associate? As Patrick put it, associates do not claim any dominance. Joseph Glassmann had a friend for life.

The two men combined and complemented each other's talents. Patrick's smooth salesmanship and his honesty attracted even the toughest of livestock and grain dealers. Joe's knack for hard bargaining brought them instant notoriety and success. As the big bosses had hoped, and much to their surprise, Patrick's philosophical influence was a moving force in mellowing Glassmann. The two men moved quickly into higher positions in the company. They eventually broke from the New York-based firm to form their own livestock-and-grain-brokerage company.

On a day when the orange and crimson leaves broke away from their sockets and dropped in piles to the ground below, Patrick Hogan died in his sleep during his usual late-afternoon nap. The call reached Joe at work, and he hoped, even prayed that it was all a bad dream. He knew it wasn't. Thoughts of his good Irish friend flashed through his mind as he quickly drove the short distance to the Hogan home. He reflected on the perilous struggles, the trials and tribulations, and the eventual triumphs they had lived through together for so many years.

When he arrived, he was shown directly to the bedroom where Patrick was peacefully lying. The family allowed Joseph time to mourn alone. Joe didn't know how long he sat there holding Patrick's limp hand in his own, but suddenly he was aware that his tears had mingled with the folded hands of his and Patrick's as though bonding them together for eternity. The spirit-man who had restored Joe's faith in the world was gone. He was a holy man, a man who belonged in the Bible or someplace far back in history, yet he lived today in these troubled times. His was a legend that would live forever in the souls

of everyone he touched, especially Joseph Glassmann. The man who had given him hope, who had shooed away darkness and shadows with his luminous soul, who had been so dear to Joe, was now but a memory. His spirit would live not only in Joe Glassmann but also in his handsome son, Michael Hogan.

Now Joe's thoughts of that dreadful day in 1968 scattered like wind-driven leaves when he was interrupted by domestic voices in his kitchen. He stood slowly and walked around his desk, pulled out a handkerchief from his silk-robe pocket, and wiped from his eyes the memory of the only saint who had ever entered his life.

He knew that Michael, although a maverick, possessed the same sense of truth that his father had. Joe also knew that the cunning son of his dead friend had the heated blood of his grandfather running through his veins--the blood of Martin Hogan, one of the most venomous vigilantes the Irish Republican Army had ever harbored. One of the founders of the IRA, the legendary man they called the Ghost of Kildare--the Deceptive One. What road would Michael choose? That of his saintly father--or that of his vengeful grandfather? Joe didn't know, but he prayed that Michael would walk in the footsteps of his father. Michael was a dichotomy.

Would Michael cooperate with the Justice Department in a peaceful way to set operation Skim-Trim into motion, or would he strike out on his own to employ the justice of blood as his grandfather had? Was the Deceptive One dead forever, or was his spirit dwelling patiently in the soul of his grandson, Michael Martin Hogan?

Joe wiped his eyes again and moved slowly from his study. He would know more this afternoon at three o'clock.

FOUR

Hawk Hogan

Michael surrendered his sleek auto to the garage attendant and handed him ten dollars. "Take good care of it, Charles," he said as he strode toward the elevators and his office on the forty-eighth floor.

As he stepped into the mirrored lift, his mind replayed the conversation with Glassmann. Although he had played ignorant, he was aware of Glassmann's friendship with Ross. Both were huge users and exporters of grain and spoke to each other frequently. Ross's empire of wealth and his economical, financial, and political involvement were far in excess of Glassmann's, but Joe was satisfied with a net worth of nearly one hundred million. Michael expected Sam Ross to be worth more than a billion. Sam was a major stockholder in at least eight of Fortune's Five Hundred Companies and had numerous export businesses. He also had controlling interest in many large banks throughout the country and dealt heavily in gold, silver, copper, and platinum. His commodity clearing house was set up strictly as an *arbitrage and hedge* house designed to lock in profits and prices on contracts made with European and domestic clients. His real expertise was saving failing businesses, ending up with a large share of the company once it was thriving again. Rumor had it that Lee Iacocca had spent six months with Ross in the seventies to find out how to save his failing automobile company.

Michael had never read or heard anything negative about Sam Ross, except that he was a cold businessman when it came to the reorganization of destitute companies. It was nothing for Ross to go into a company and cut the work force and overhead by fifty to seventy per cent. He would tell the unions to go fuck themselves and proceed to cut wages and benefits. He was also a personal friend of many senators and the President. He sat in on numerous domestic-affairs committee meetings in Washington as a civil advisor and had been one of Robert Kennedy's counselors on organized crime. He had a penchant for ridding America of criminal injustice.

After Kennedy's assassination, he served as a consultant to the Justice Department, where he continued his advisorship to the present day. He claimed no political preference, and his counsel was always available if requested in Washington. Any job he undertook had the backing of the government. Michael nodded his head with admiration and said to himself, you sound interesting, Ross, and some day soon I'm going to need you!

The bell rang on the twenty-third floor. End of the line for this leg of the trip. The elevator doors slid open. Michael stepped out and sought the next bank of elevators, which

25

would take him to the forty-eighth floor. Sixty seconds later he walked quickly down the wide carpeted hall to his office.

He had never met Sam Ross, never even talked to the man on the phone, just filled his orders. Today he would be trading in the treasury bond pit and knew the smallest order he would receive would be five hundred contracts at a crack. The anticipation of trading 250 million dollars worth of product in one fell swoop quickened the pounding of his heart.

Michael let the name Sam Ross slide into his subconscious as he crossed the threshold and stepped through the double glass doors that displayed the title HOGAN COMMODITY CORPORATION OF AMERICA, INC. and the golden logo of a proud, alert hawk prominently perched above the black lettering.

Margaret Dawson, his receptionist, greeted Michael as he entered the glass and chrome designed waiting room.

Her smile greeted him. "Good morning, Mr. Hogan."

He grinned back and walked over to the reception desk. "Hi, Margaret. How is your husband?"

"Much better, thank you. He's out of intensive care as of yesterday afternoon and in a private room."

"That's great," Michael said. "If you need anything at all, let me know. Our insurance will take care of most of your medical and hospital expenses. He's going to be out of work for awhile, so you'll be without that income. I don't want you to be in a panic about money, and don't be dipping into your savings. You've been with me a long time, Margaret, and I can't have my favorite girl concerned about money. I'm giving you your Christmas bonus early this year."

She sat straight up in her chair and protested. "But it's only April, Mr. Hogan!"

Michael rested his hands on her desk, leaned down, and looked straight into her eyes. "Then consider it your Easter bonus."

Margaret looked down, slightly embarrassed. "You've done so much for us already, Mr. Hogan. I don't know how we'll ever be able to repay you."

Michael reached across and patted her shoulder. "You already have, Margaret. What has it been, seven years? I wish everybody was as attentive and as loyal as you. So, consider this just a payback for a job well done." He turned again and headed down the wide hall.

Almost inaudibly, the bowed, white-haired lady behind the modern glass reception desk whispered, "Thank you, sir."

Michael strode into his office, knowing she would cry for a few minutes and then dutifully return to her job. His gift would be ten thousand dollars now and ten thousand more at a later date. That's what her husband, George Dawson, had made as a Catholic school janitor after twenty years of service, when a series of heart attacks put him out of commission a few years back.

Michael blessed himself and thanked Whoever might be listening for the ability, the opportunity, and the willingness to give. He threw in another thanks for his own health and that of his family.

Sunshine greeted Michael as he entered his black-and-white modern office. The brilliant purple-orange ball had just broken its linkage with Lake Michigan and was determined to cheer up Chicago for at least eleven hours.

Sidney Stone had already gone home and left messages about the night markets on Michael's messy desk. Shuffling through the papers, he found the gold sale.

Simultaneously, he snapped on his market quote machine and read the handwritten order stating that he had sold four hundred contracts of New York gold at $473.00 per ounce. He pressed in New York gold on his quote key board and the green screen read May gold, New York, opened at $472.00---$478.50 per ounce. High for the day was $482.30. Low and last was $462.10 and dropping. He looked at his order again--four hundred contracts sold at $473.00. Those bastards, he thought, they filled me one dollar from the low of the opening. The price should have been at least $475.00.

Some New York bagman had walked away with forty thousand of Michael's money on the opening. A good broker or an honest one would have sold the gold out at $475.00 at the very least. A good profit in spite of the thief in New York, and the market was headed south as Michael had anticipated. "Thieving pricks," he said out loud as he dropped the sell order back down onto the sheaf of papers on his desk. He grabbed his kelly-green trading jacket. The plastic identification badge pinned to the lapel read HAWK, and the lapel itself carried the company logo of an embroidered golden hawk.

Anger warmed his body. He wasn't afraid to challenge the credibility of the New York gold broker. He would call New York and bitch about the poor price he had received on the four hundred contracts. He'd ask for the broker's name, time and sales report, a faxed copy of the order to see what bagman bought the gold, and the telephone number to the Exchange's Disciplinary Action Director. By the end of the day, he would bet the low price would be declared an honest error and Hawk's order would actually be given a point or two credit--filled at a better price. They knew the Hogan name in New York and knew he wasn't to be fucked with.

The brokers involved would scamper around, piss and moan, and claim it was an honest fill. Those New York assholes would be utterly intimidated by the thought of anyone peeking at or questioning their trading ethics. By the end of the day they would finally succumb and agree to at least a two-point adjustment. Fucking thieves, he muttered.

He looked at his wristwatch. Time to head for the trading floor to execute bond orders for Sam Ross and Company. The sunshine followed him out the door, and the green quote screen read May Gold, New York, $456.88--and dropping.

On his ride down to the fourth floor where the trading pits were located, he began to psych himself for the market. Like an athlete before a ball game or a statesman before a speech, he would be ready for his competition in the arena.

He walked through the wide doors past the guard station and into the massive Exchange, which extended half a city block. The trading floor contained eight octagonal pits of various sizes and were filled with the usual spate of brokers milling around waiting for the clang, signalling the opening of the market.

He headed for the largest pit, the arena. He was oblivious to the rattling phones, the throngs of opinionated voices ranging from whispers to shouts, and the red and blue lights on the tops of unoccupied desks blinking their impatience. The green quote boards streaked pre-opening market information, as they moved horizontally around the four walls above the orange-and-black Exchange quote boards.

He wended his way through hustling runners and brokers to his perch on the top step of the bond pit near the phone desk of Sam Ross and Company. His kelly-green jacket would announce his arrival. He would immediately be inundated with buy and sell orders by his other customers.

He had instructed Sam Ross and Company to give Frank Hammer, one of his associates, their arbitrage orders. Frank, in turn, would take the order to Michael to be filled. This would assure Michael that no foreign eyes would read the order and act faster than he could.

Ross and Company orders were big enough to move the bond market a few points one way or the other. If news of the quantity to be bought or sold hit the pit before Michael had the order, the market would move. Hawk would lose his edge and would be buying or selling from the subtle brokers who had traded off the order seconds earlier.

He had one of his own men talking to New York, where the Buy and Sell orders originated. Frank Hammer, "HAMR," hand-carried or ran the order to the pit. This saved Ross and Company thousands of points in the short time Michael had been working for them. It was not uncommon to have brokers pay phone men to signal them. The signals instructed them whether to buy or sell. The phone man would simply rub his cheek with his fingers after he wrote the order. The number of fingers would give the spy in the pit the quantity. Three fingers meant three hundred contracts. If the fingers rubbed the cheek, palm in, it was a buy order; palm out was a sell order. If the phone man pulled at his nose, the oncoming order was over five hundred contracts. The coded messages were designed to beat the written orders to the pit and ultimately cheat the customer. It worked!

The signals were indecipherable to most onlookers. Michael had detected the deaf hand language six months earlier in the Standard and Poors pit at the Mercantile Exchange. His buy/sell orders were being anticipated in the market before he received them. Michael had been blessed with the eyes of a hawk flying at five hundred feet looking for a three-inch field mouse. He was able to pick out the incongruity of a few phone men and their broker counterparts in the pits. In only moments he understood what was going on. He focused on the phone man fingering his face and nose. Then he looked in the pit to see who made the market by jumping ahead of the order. Up until that time, he wasn't sure if the leak was actually coming from Chicago or New York. There would be nothing unusual for

a phone man in New York to have two phones to his head. On one phone he would give a legal buy/sell order to a phone man in Chicago. On the other phone, the illegal one, his Chicago contact, also on the trading floor, would listen quietly to the instructions. The illegal Chicago contact would use his hands to signal a broker that there was a large order coming into the pit. The crooked broker made his play in the market before the written order ever reached the pit. Michael had no control over a New York situation. He did, however, have control in Chicago.

Hawk Hogan called Jack Ellis, the floor manager and a good friend. From a distance, he watched the two cheating phone men signal their S&P broker-counterparts. Sure enough, the silent, disguised hand signals were made, and three S&P brokers scurried to the center of the pit to make their play before the written order arrived.

The phone men were fired. The brokers, to Hawk Hogan's disgust, were merely fined one thousand dollars each and given a warning by the Exchange officials.

This was not the first time the Hawk had witnessed and brought to a halt the sometimes simple skimming schemes, sometimes elaborate. He had the reputation of a trustworthy trader and order-filler who had no reservation about filing complaints with the Exchange and the government if he saw cheating going down. The word was out, "Don't fuck with Hawk Hogan. When he's in the pit, play it straight."

In spite of his keen eyes, he knew there were schemes that were so elaborate he could not see them. He wasn't a detective, and he had his own work to do. As long as theft didn't affect his best efforts in filling orders, he tolerated the disgusting skimming and cheating as an accepted part of the business. There was nothing he could do about it anyway.

Michael had received his name Hawk because of his Roman nose, which was contrary to the characteristic pug snout of an Irishman. He also had exceptional peripheral vision. Michael could see far to both sides of him when looking straight ahead. He would catch as many trades that came from his sides as he would by looking forward. His head was always in motion looking for runners bringing in orders to brokers. Michael would notify the recipient broker with a shout that Hawk was selling at seven and buying at five before the broker received the order. To the broker's dismay, Hawk would get the fill if the order was on the market. If the order was above or below the current trading price, the other broker would simply wave off Hawk, which meant the order was not important at that time.

His vision as a young man had been good as well. His friends called him Hawkeye because he could catch a sharp grounder hit to shortstop in the late innings of a baseball game. That was a long time ago when they would play ball games until they were over, without lights. The only problem was that he would have a foot race from his shortstop position to first base with the hitter because the first baseman couldn't see Hawkeye throw the ball to him.

A deep pass in a football game on a day that was overcast or raining was no exception. He would pluck the ball from the air when his defensive competitor could hardly see the Hawk, let alone the football.

Today the action in the bond pit went without incident. He filled over four thousand contracts for Sam Ross and Company, about seven thousand dollars in commissions to him. He would be back in the morning. By the time two o'clock arrived and the closing of the market, the sweat ran in rivulets down his neck and the middle of his back. His shirt and trading jacket clung to his body, drenched. He pulled a handkerchief from his pocket and dabbed at his brow and face, then spent the next twenty minutes checking trades with other brokers. At that, he returned to his office, quickly showered, and slipped into a fresh silk shirt, pants, and a blazer. He poured himself a healthy four fingers of Johnny Walker Black over ice and gulped it down. He felt instant satisfaction and relaxation from the burning liquid that warmed his insides. He then left the bright office in a hurry on his way to the Union Club to meet Joe Glassmann and the mystery man.

Michael glanced at his gold Piaget watch: 2:47. He'd be there on time.

* * *

Four blocks away in the lavish Union Club, two men sat in a private corner table as a white gloved waiter delivered Joe Glassmann his usual VO and water. The husky FBI agent, Andy Golden, dressed in a plain, inexpensive brown suit, had a cup of black coffee. They sat silently now, having spent the past two hours going over their strategies. Strategies that included Michael "Hawk" Hogan. Strategies that would change all three of their lives over the next five years. Golden looked at his cheap but reliable Timex: 2:55-- five minutes. The man fidgeted and spilled some of his coffee as he attempted to take a nervous sip. Joe sat silently thinking of his angelic friend, Patrick Hogan, and hoped against all hope that his spirit would sit in on this meeting. Joe, too, was apprehensive.

FIVE

The Luncheon

Michael paused on the threshold of the Union Club's Gettysburg Room and waited for the maitre d' to return from seating three late lunch diners. He didn't see Joe. The thick double mahogany doors stood open on both sides of him. He admired the cut-glass inserts with American flags artistically etched on each.

The room was plush and polished. A scent of lemon, mingled with the aroma of rich French cuisine, touched his senses. The thick dark-green carpeting felt good on his tired feet after standing on the hard oak steps of the pit all morning. At this time of the day most of the tables, clad with crisp white linens and ornate sterling, sat idle. Laughter from a table in one corner of the room momentarily caught his attention. His keen eyes noticed the straight-up martini glasses in front of each of the four occupants. That explained their volubility and gaiety.

Michael turned and focused on the huge chandelier in the center of the Royal Room. The late sun allowed amber rays by the thousands through the western windows. The crystal prisms of the hanging fixture multiplied the mandarin rays a million times, leaving the great room awash in a glow of light and warmth. The market tension left him, his weathered face softened, and his soul rested in the tranquil setting.

"Mr. Hogan?" Michael snapped out of his momentary meditation. The effeminate French voice announced, "Sir, if you would be so kind to follow me, I'll seat you with your friends."

He followed and said, "thank you." They both walked proudly through the regal room. There was one obvious difference: Michael walked naturally; the tiny maitre d', rigidly. They rounded a corner and entered a small nook where Joe Glassmann and the large man in the brown suit waited. Joe fumbled, trying to get up. The other man was already standing when Michael reached the table.

Hand outstretched, the big fellow said, "It's been a long time, Mike."

Michael felt a wide smile fill his face. "Andy Golden. You son of a bitch. How are you?"

Michael ignored Andy's bear-paw and with a lump in his throat, skirted around the table and gave his grizzly friend a powerful hug. He felt the FBI man's gun poke against his ribs. They broke from each other, and Michael slapped his old school buddy on his muscular arm. His smile remained as he grabbed Andy's shoulders roughly, held him at arm's length, and looked deep into Andy's alert government eyes. All he saw was friendship.

Michael looked down at Joe, who never did get a chance to stand, as he sat nervously playing with his drink straw.

Salutations over, the two men took their seats, then Michael took the old man's hand and shook it. "I'm sorry, Joe. How are you doing today? I thought you said you wanted to introduce me to someone?"

Joe looked at Michael and shook his head. "No Mike. I said someone wanted to meet with you."

Michael took a sip of water. "Sounds like semantics to me, or just plain trickery, you old scoundrel." His attention returned to Andy. "How's the Bureau treating you, Goldie? And what the hell forced you out of Washington to Chicago?"

Andy moved his chair closer to the table. "The Bureau's great. A lot of long hours, modest pay, as you know, but somebody has to protect you wealthy citizens from the criminals. Business and my godson's twelfth birthday brings me to Chicago.

Michael slowly moved his head from side to side. "Christ. You are Joseph's godfather, aren't you? I forget how old my kids are, what their names are, and who their godparents are. I have a good memory--when I remember." As an afterthought Michael added jokingly, "You've only seen your godson twice in twelve years, you prick. What's the matter with you?"

A sheepish look came over Andy's face. "My apologies, Mike. But you know a good soldier can't desert his post, not even to take a dump."

Michael's hand sliced through the air then pointed with admonishment. "True. True. I forgive you. But you'll have to get Maria's absolution first, then Joseph's. We're having dinner and a little party tonight at seven o'clock. You'll stay over, right?"

Andy cleared his throat and slipped his napkin onto his lap. "I'll make the dinner and party, Mike, but can't stay beyond that. I have a midnight flight out of O'Hare Field. Have to be back in D.C. for an eight a.m. meeting with the boss."

Michael tapped his fingers on the table. "I'll tell you what, Goldie. We'll have that little fruit-fly maitre d' bring us a phone. I'll call your boss and with all the diplomacy I can muster, I'll tell him to fuck himself and his eight a.m. meeting because you're at the godson's birthday and can't be disturbed."

Andy smiled and shook his head. "You haven't lost your way with words, Mike."

Michael looked over at Joe and saw a flicker of a smile rise at the edges of Joe's mouth. The smile faded just as quickly. He evidently wasn't in the mood for gaiety. Joe motioned for the tuxedo-clad elfin who stood motionless and attentive in the corner of the small room.

Michael had three Black Labels on the rocks with his soup du jour and chef's salad. Joe and Andy each had the day's fish special, baked salmon with a white-wine-and-lobster sauce. A nice respite from the dill sauce with which salmon was usually served.

Andy stayed with black coffee. Joe ordered two more VO's, spilled one, and had a hell of a time eating with his shaking hands.

Michael's brows furrowed and his face screwed up as good-natured cynicism tumbled from his mouth. "What the hell's the matter with you, Joe? You coming down with Parkinson's disease? Why so nervous?"

Michael sensed that an unruly feeling of disorientation prompted Joe to avoid him. Joe said nothing, but an anxious fidgeting seemed to prick at him. Michael sloughed it off and returned his attention to Andy.

Michael remembered the good times he and Andy had at Northwestern University. While they ate lunch they reminisced about the old days. Michael argued that he couldn't remember winning a football game in thirty-three outings. Andy thought they had beaten Miami of Ohio one year, and Michael said it was Miami of Florida and they got beaten 63-3.

Andy just shrugged. "I don't remember, maybe you're right."

Breaking a piece of bread, Michael responded, "You were the All-American. You should remember. Do you frequently have memory lapses? We did beat Wisconsin once!"

Andy took a drink of coffee and dabbed his mouth with his napkin. "That was basketball, thimble brain."

They both laughed and continued with their lunch.

Michael looked up from his salad. "Great memories, aren't they, Goldie?"

"We had a good time, Mike. Sometimes I wish we were back there."

Joe started to choke on his fish. Michael reached over and patted him on the back.

Michael's friendly cynicism reared again. "Jesus, Joe, you're having a hell of a time! You spill your drink! You choke on your food! How often do you go out to eat?"

Laughter rose in both Andy and Michael. He noticed that Joe dodged his eyes once again.

Michael sensed a supercharged tension in Joe today and wondered why. Joe and Andy had both been part of the Hogan family for years. Although Andy's business had kept them physically apart, and Michael was difficult to reach during the day, Andy frequently called Joe to see how everything was going in Chicago. Michael presumed that a rare visit to Chicago would certainly call for lunch among the three friends. And attending Joseph's birthday was a bonus. Still, Joe was acting weird. He realized he had to be patient. Was this strictly a social luncheon, or was it the beginning of what Michael had waited so long for? Time would tell. Patience would pay off. He would play the game cool.

A mocking voice inside of Michael insisted on answers. "Joe, what's up? Why are you so uptight among friends?"

Joe sheepishly looked at Golden as he pushed his big frame away from the table. Michael caught the split-second shadow that crossed between his two friends' eyes. Now he was aware of a cautious reserve. He felt something was about to be sprung. He motioned the waiter for another Black Label. Now the table was silent until it was cleared of the lunch dishes and until the drink arrived. Michael understood the intentional silence. He wasn't going to interrupt the quiet until he found out what was going on. Although the

booze had loosened his tongue for conversation, he knew the procedure when talking business with Andy and Joe. He would wait for them to show their hand first. His judgment was not impaired by the booze consumption. He was not irrational or careless. In fact, he was still quite sharp in spite of eight shots of scotch that he had downed earlier. Besides, he had some food in him to stop some of the alcohol from getting to his brain. Edgy but confident, his posture militant, he would wait with anticipation for the chess game to begin.

He called upon his father's spirit for insight and understanding. The two men he loved dearly were planning something. Michael reached deep into his own soul for the calmness and perception his father had implanted in him. His mind also reached for his grandfather's cunning deception.

Andy lit a cigarette and took a long drag, blowing the exhaled smoke into the air. His deep tobacco-roughened voice spoke gently, and the silence was broken. "Michael, in the past twenty-four months, the Justice Department has received over thirty thousand complaints from commercial and public investors about various forms of corruption in the commodity markets. We don't have the manpower to check out all these complaints, but most of them arrived with photostat copies of bogus trades, and they came from all over the country--from doctors, lawyers, farmers, white collar, blue collar, students. You name it. The amounts of money allegedly bilked from these people is staggering. If we received thirty thousand complaints, there must be ten times that many who have also been cheated but have not complained.

Silence. Michael wanted to know how much his teddy-bear friend knew.

Andy shifted in his chair and took another drag from his cigarette. "My boss remembers my introducing you and Maria to him in Washington six years ago during that goofy celebration the Bureau had for me when I stumbled onto and foiled that Presidential assassination plot. The man's memory is like an elephant's. He even remembers what you were both wearing. He knows you are my best friend, a Chicago commodity broker, and he knows of your reputation as a straight shooter. He was aware of the trouble you had with the Exchanges a few years back. So, the Director thought I might have an edge on my co-agents concerning my new assignment in Chicago because of our personal relationship. Thirty days ago I was called away from an arms-smuggling case and asked to take over the investigation of the criminal activity that is allegedly being carried on at the Commodity Exchanges.

"So far, I've spent most of my time reading through the plaintiffs' letters, and I've visited some commercial grain companies and banks that have brought complaints against the Exchanges.

"Originally I thought the complaints were just sour grapes. Then I received this letter from Joe, asking for the Department's help in stopping the blatant skimming and outright theft which is taking place by the brokers and their superiors."

Andy took a final puff and snuffed out his cigarette. "I want you to look at this, Mike." He reached into his left inside pocket, and as he did so, Michael saw the shoulder holster with the menacing black .9 mm handgun. He pulled out an envelope, removed the contents, and flipped them across the table.

Michael unfolded the bulky sheaf, then glanced at the letterhead: Glass-Ro Investment Corporation, Inc., whoever that was.

He looked over at Joe's eyes, riveted on him with uncomfortable anticipation. He flipped Joe a cool, silent look. He knew Joe hated his father's silence during times of agitation. With mild irritation, he was going to give this sly fox the same treatment.

Michael's eyes returned to the letter. He didn't have to read it to know its contents. Nevertheless, he obliged Andy.

The letterhead was addressed to Andrew Golden and signed by Joe Glassmann and Sam Ross. The letter contained commodity trades made by Joe and Sam. Names of brokers, companies, and the dates and times buy-sell orders were entered into the market. The prices at time of entry, the filling prices, the times the filled orders were called back to Glassmann and Ross, and the amount of money each order was short because of a bad fill. Two pages, hundreds of transactions.

Ninety-two consistent bad fills from supposedly reputable brokers in twelve different commodity pits. Four pits at the CBOT, two at the CME, two at the IMM, and four in New York.

The third page dealt with and made accusations about grand larceny. This was not only being condoned but also being protected by the prominent members and governing bodies of the Exchanges. The letter mentioned secret trading groups, with intricate and sophisticated systems of cheating the public investors out of millions of dollars a day. This practice had been going on for decades, with the blessings of not only the board of governors of the Exchanges, but also Senators and Congressmen throughout the country and in Washington, D.C.

The fourth page noted Michael's attempt, in 1984, to stop the illegal practices on the Exchange floors and his efforts being met with absolute contempt. The report stated that Hogan had been set up by those involved, which caused irreparable damage to his clean character and dramatically decreased his business. Michael's memory raced back two and a half years and remembered how Joe had to lend him a million dollars just to stay in business.

The fifth page was an affidavit swearing to the above, and witnessed by one of Chicago's Assistant U.S. Attorneys, Anthony Lorenzo, who was present during all of the transactions.

Michael studied the sixth page carefully. This, too, was an affidavit not only swearing to the above, but also affirming that Glassmann's New York grain associate, Sam Ross, the renowned billionaire, was present during the trading aforementioned, signed by

Samuel J. Ross, and witnessed by Assistant U.S. Attorney of the Eastern Sector of New York, Brian Brennen.

Michael felt his face tighten as he turned to the seventh and final page. This was simply a brief letter to the Director of the Federal Bureau of Investigation asking that a meeting be set up to discuss the alleged atrocities. An investigation of the foregoing would soon be considered. The letter was signed by Joseph H. Glassmann, Samuel J. Ross, Anthony Q. Lorenzo, Assistant U.S. Attorney-Chicago, and Brian W. Brennen, Assistant United States Attorney-New York.

Michael closed his eyes and let his mind catch up with what he had just read. The room was cool, yet beads of sweat began to break out on his forehead. He felt a little lightheaded. He didn't know how long he sat there in his own revery, but when he opened his eyes both men were looking at him waiting for some sort of acknowledgment.

He took a deliberate slow swallow of his scotch in order to gain composure and assemble some thoughts. These boys had something big going on here. He was moderately impressed. His mind was trying to computerize and categorize the situation and what was coming next. Joe Glassmann's complaint meant nothing. Even Sam Ross's bitching wouldn't fluff many feathers at the Exchanges. They knew that, so they had joined forces and called their company Glass Ro Investment Corp. Inc--for Glassmann and Ross. Then they had called in the U.S. Attorney and the FBI. About the only areas of the government difficult to penetrate with bribes and kickbacks. Pretty clever. Michael saw doom on the horizon of the commodity industry.

Joe's nervousness began to subside. The ice was broken, and Michael had just sunk one foot into a frigid lake. Glassmann decided to dispense with his patience and pushed words across the table. "Well, say something, goddammit, Michael. What do you think?"

Michael looked at Joe's wide eyes, then at Andy, who was watching him thoughtfully. He knew Golden was waiting for the conversation to begin so that he could start his subtle interrogation.

Michael leaned forward and tightened his jaw muscles. Anger was still in his soul, but he remained in control. "What do I think, Joe? I think nothing. I think you and Ross got a hair up your ass because you got some bad fills. You've both got enough clout to pull in a few heavyweight government attorneys. You even have enough clout to get the FBI involved. You've got the crass balls to call a good friend of mine from Washington to have a friendly lunch so the son of a bitch can interrogate me in his Northwestern, magna cum laude, law degree, FBI, CIA, PTA, YMCA way. No thanks--friends or no friends. I want nothing to do with this. You started it, Joe--you and Ross--you finish it!"

Joe protested. "No, Mike. You started it when you made waves three years ago. Now it's time to bring this stealing to an end."

Andy slipped in. "Mike, tell me this letter is a crock of shit. That there is no truth to it. That it's all a bunch of crap, and that it's honest-to-god just poor fills from honorable

brokers. Tell me this letter is highly exaggerated and that there is very little, if any, graft being practiced at the Chicago Exchanges. You tell me that, and I have the power to shelve this case in spite of Glassmann's and Ross's clout. If there is any truth to it, it will come back off the shelf in a year or two anyway. Then somebody else can chase down the bastards. But if it's true, and you tell me it's not true, there's going to be a lot of financial blood shed during now and the time it eventually can be proven. Do you know how many people kill themselves because they lose their savings in the markets?"

Michael leaned forward impatiently. "Come on, Andy. Don't play on my emotions."

Andy ignored Michael's comment and kept talking. "Fifty-three hundred people last year committed suicide, that we know of, because they lost their life savings--which they thought was worth more than their own life. Over a thousand of them were college kids and younger, and most of them were playing the commodity markets. We haven't even taken into consideration the poor bastards who lost their savings to crooked brokers and who have no recourse. Now you tell me, smartass, do I have a factual letter here or not? If not, it goes right into the garbage can and we can head up to the North Shore for a birthday party. If it's true, then we have a major investigation to prepare, and you and I have lot of talking to do."

Silence prevailed once again. A solemn cloud hung heavy in the small alcove where the three men sat. The spring sun had left Chicago to bring warmth to some other far-off land. There was another dimension of life in the room that couldn't be seen or heard. Michael felt the tugging at his spirit.

He closed his eyes and moved his head from shoulder to shoulder to relieve the tension in his neck. He ran his hands through his black hair, loosened his tie, and said, "The letter is wrong."

Glassmann screeched, "Oh bullshit, Mike. You know it's..."

Michael cut him off. "The accusations are grossly underestimated."

Surprise enveloped Joe. He looked at Andy, relief very much evident on his gaunt face.

Michael leaned back and nudged his chair cockeyed from the table, his feet outstretched to the side. His eyes studied the spoon he was flipping from side to side on the white tablecloth.

Andy took a sip of cold coffee and said, "What's underestimated, Mike?"

Flipping the spoon again, he picked it up and darted it into his water glass, splashing water spots on the tablecloth.

"Every thing in that letter is merely a guesstimate. Multiply the numbers and the brokers and the companies and the senators and all the rest of the allegations by one hundred or one thousand, and you'll be getting closer to the true picture. It's a way of life that is considered legal down there. They make their own rules, they protect each other,

they scratch each other's backs, and it goes all the way to the top and farther--at the expense of the dumb public investor."

Now Michael was glaring at Golden. "Andy, I want nothing to do with this. I've told you that you've got a case here. You're the investigator. You put your task force together and do what you have to do. Ridding the Exchange of some of the scum won't hurt my feelings, but I want nothing to do with your investigation. You've got my blessing. I hope you nab a bunch of 'em. I hope you get a promotion and they have another dinner for you in D.C. I hope you get to be Director of the FBI, but count me out. I've caught my last long ball for a losing cause. I asked for your help a couple of years ago, and you as much as told me to get lost. Nothing you could do, you said. So, now I say, FUCK YOU AND THE BADGE YOU RODE IN ON!"

"I need your help, Mike," Andy said. "I can't do it alone. I don't know where to start. You know the Exchanges, the people, the schemes, and you have the pit savvy. You see things and know things I could never find out even if I had five hundred men on it. I'm not on the trading floor. You are!"

Someplace in the distance a Big Ben chimed six times. Michael let Andy stew as he stood up and stretched. As comfortable as the cushioned chairs were, he still had to pull at the back of his expensive trousers and rub his behind. "You don't need five hundred men, Andy. Ten good ones and five or six mil from your boss's treasury could get the job done. Come on. We've got to go to a seven-o'clock party. Joe, thanks for lunch. I can't say this has been one of my more enjoyable outings with you. You taught me how to make money. Now you're trying to show me how to get myself ostracized, out of work, broke, and probably dead. Thanks, but no thanks. I can do all those things by myself." As an afterthought, he said sarcastically, "I do appreciate the consideration for complete self-annihilation, though!"

Joe snapped, "Michael, you can be a real prick sometimes."

All three men were standing and stretching now. It looked like a mini-aerobics class.

Michael placed his hand on Glassmann's shoulder. "No, Joe. You can be the prick. I didn't invite you to lunch and feed you a couple of Canadian whiskeys and suggest you go get yourself killed, because you blew the whistle on the biggest con game in the country. At least when I went after the bastards, I laid my cards on the table. Every Exchange and broker in Chicago knows my position on larceny."

Glassmann walked to within inches of Michael and hissed between his teeth, "Don't give me any of your pompous holier than thou crap. If you can't kill a rat by biting its head off, you sneak up behind it and bite its ass off. Then it can't shit and it'll die in its own grunt."

Michael snapped back at the tough little man he loved so much. "I've never bitten a rat in the ass."

Joe glared into Michael's eyes. "Goddammit, you're about to, Michael! You're about to!" Joe hesitated, his eyes clouded with a light mist. "I know you like my own son, and I knew your father better than you or anybody ever did. You've got the same spirit and thirst for truth and justice as he did. It's in your soul. You've already shown me that. Now you have backers, the biggest and strongest support in the United States. But they can't work without you. Just give it some thought. Talk it over with Andy tonight. Everything's going to be fine."

Michael let his hand drop from Joe's bony shoulder, turned to leave, and mumbled, "Oh, bullshit! Let's get out of here, Andy."

Andy picked up a large, beat-up briefcase and followed Michael. Joe lumbered along behind.

The Gettysburg Room was empty and would remain so for the rest of the day. As they left, the French maitre d' sat by the door in a down-filled wing-back, fast asleep. Joe touched his arm, and the pint-sized man snapped to attention. Mike and Andy walked into the ornate hallway as Joe signed his lunch bill and slipped him fifty dollars for his overtime.

They rode the elevator to the lobby in silence, all reflecting on the three-hour debate that had just taken place. On exiting the Chicago landmark building, Michael turned to Joe and gave him a hug. He held him by his slight shoulders and reassured him. "You're right, Joe. I do want to see the corruption stopped at the Exchanges. They've gotten too greedy, and now they're getting careless with their assurance of protection from a higher echelon. This will only get worse if it's not stopped. I'm not sure that Andy and his federal boys can even stop the stealing. It's a real sophisticated labyrinth. You'll get the little guys who don't cover their asses, but I doubt if you'll touch the big guys. I'm going to have to think about this long and hard. I'm not as concerned about myself or my money as I am the safety and reputation of my wife and children."

Joe hugged Mike again, the mist returning to his eyes, then they parted. Joe walked north on Clark. Andy and Michael headed south to retrieve the Astin-Martin from the garage.

* * *

None of the three men noticed the long, black limo with dark tinted windows parked across the street. A fat hand with a tight, black leather glove reached for the car phone and pressed one button, automatically programmed to dial a Barrington Hills number. A raspy, corpulent throat spoke into the car phone. "They're leaving now. Glassmann, Hogan, and some big guy I don't recognize. Do you want me to do anything?"

The voice on the other end gave orders, and the black limo crawled into traffic in the same direction Michael and Andy traveled.

39

SIX

Garage Trauma

The cool, early-evening Chicago air felt refreshing and brought life back to Andy's senses. The afternoon meeting at the Union Club had drained him. He felt the tension of the luncheon, which had brought three friends into minor confrontation with each other, subsiding. Michael had calmed down and was joking as they both walked Clark Street to Michael's waiting auto.

As they approached the corner of Clark and Madison, the light turned yellow. Impatient cabs, buses, and motorists were beginning their street-creeping, getting ready to jump out in front of them. As Andy stopped for the red light, Michael grabbed his suit jacket, proceeding to cross, and yelled, "Come on, Bozo, we can make it. Live a little!"

Squealing tires and honking horns from the oncoming speedsters had already begun. Andy tried to pull back and protested. Michael had taken him completely by surprise. "Hold it, Mike, you'll kill us." Before he finished the sentence, Hogan, with his palm outstretched against the angry motorists, had Andy in the middle of the street. Horns blasted their war cries; a bus driver yelled, "Assholes!" and a cabby would have stopped to fight if it hadn't been for the fifty cars behind him. When they reached the other side, Michael turned to the mass confusion of angry metal with its robot drivers and pronounced loudly, "THIS IS POLICE BUSINESS. YOU'VE ALL BEEN VERY KIND, AND YOU CAN GO NOW!"

Andy felt his ears warm with anger and knew his face showed exasperation. Michael began to laugh. "You need a little excitement in your life, Andy."

Andy brushed down the front of his wrinkled suit. The gesture served to restore his dignity as well. "You're still a crazy bastard, Hogan. I don't know why I like you."

Michael laughed again and continued to walk south on Clark. "Because I'm lovable, trustworthy, considerate, kind..."

Andy cut him off as he trotted to catch up. "You're a raving lunatic, that's what you are." Andy remembered Michael always taking on people and things bigger and meaner than himself. "You still like to arm wrestle with society, don't you, Michael?"

He looked at Andy and said, "Why not? Can't find out who the winner is if there isn't a contest. And I don't limit myself to society."

Andy looked straight into Michael's dark eyes. They sparkled with life, yet they were alert and suspicious. His black hair was combed straight back and boxed neatly at the neck of his expensive shirt collar. Andy decided it was his Roman nose and dark complexion that distinguished him from other Irish. His soul and spirit distinguished him

from other men. He was rough cut but handsome. At six feet three inches both men looked eye to eye. "I don't know how Maria puts up with you, Mike. She's beautiful and you're ugly. She's got class and you're a junk-yard dog. She's probably always dusting off the crude, foul-mouthed Irishman in vain, only to find more dust."

They both smiled and Michael simply said, "Touché, Apeman."

They walked a block in silence, speaking nothing of their luncheon. They both knew that street people had open ears. They appeared merely as two businessmen going home from work.

Andy carried his briefcase in his left hand out of habit in case he ever had to reach for his weapon quickly. He did it intuitively, the way he had been trained. In his line of work, even a fraction of a second could mean his life.

At Monroe and Clark Andy pulled Michael out of the flow of bustling pedestrians. Turning toward him he said, "Do you know that Lake Michigan is getting so polluted that in ten years it will be a toilet?" As he was spieling the phony lecture on pollution, his eyes roamed the street and sidewalk. He scanned their route for a shadow ducking into a doorway, or someone momentarily stopping and reading a newspaper. Some incongruity in the crowd that would give him the suspicion that they might be followed. He figured it was probably unnecessary, but he did it out of habit.

The streets had been filled with bleating horns, curious city sounds, and tantalizing aromas wafting from nearby restaurants. Now, the quickening crowd and impatient drivers in traffic had begun to subside. Rush hour was over. Andy's quick eyes glimpsed nothing suspicious. A black limo was about a half block back on the far side of the street moving slowly in light traffic. He dismissed that. There were thousands of limos in Chicago. They all moved with slow, arrogant precision. The nonsense conversation about pollution in the lake lasted less than ten seconds. Michael watched Andy's eyes scrutinize the street while he talked. He said nothing. He probably accepted Andy's actions as simple FBI paranoia.

When they rounded the corner of Clark and Jackson, moving toward the Exchange, another brief stop, short conversation about low-income housing, and the sharp eyes swept the street once again. This time the black limo, about a hundred yards behind them, cruised to their side. As Andy surveyed the rest of the street, Michael became agitated. "Come on, Andy. We're late. I'm going to have to call Maria from the garage." He hesitated a minute, and sarcastically asked, "What the fuck are you looking for? A sniper?"

Andy instantly turned his thick shoulders toward him and said, "As simple and innocent as this may seem, Mike, these tricks of the trade have kept me from getting my head blown off."

Michael flung his hands in the air. "That's a helluva guarantee, and you want me to take the same chances? Again, I say no. Fuck you, G-Man!"

Andy's voice was a near whisper. "Not here, Mike. We'll talk in the car. You call Maria. I need to check in too. Incidentally, what kind of car are you driving?"

"A black Astin-Martin."

"What exit do you use?"

Michael became curious. "Clark Street. The only way out. Why?"

Andy let his thick eyebrows rise, and he shrugged. "Just wondering. I might want to drive." He would indeed ask to drive in order to have the side and rear-view-mirror vantage point. One last inquiry. "Do you have a car phone?"

Michael cocked his head slightly. "Hell yes! You ever see a hundred-thousand-dollar automobile without one?"

He was pressing his luck with Michael now. "What's the number in case my office has to reach me?"

"Lighten up, Andy, we're only driving to Glencoe, not Peoria. Why don't they just beep you on that high-tech receiver you carry in that thing you call a briefcase?"

Andy felt his ears heat up again. "I don't need any of your bullshit. Just the number to your car phone--please!"

Michael sighed and said, "You're a real piece of work, Golden! Mobile 881-2262."

"Thank you."

"You're welcome."

They entered the Exchange building and walked past the *Sign of the Trader* Lounge. A mixture of sounds emanated from the crowded bar. Cigarette smoke escaped into the hall. The familiar smell of stale liquor, mingled with laughter, shouts of merriment, clinking glasses, and loud music wended its way beyond the open doors.

They approached the escalator and rode two floors down to the parking garage. Before entering, they stopped at a bank of four unoccupied pay telephones. Michael said, "I'm going to call Maria and tell her we're running a little late."

Andy asked with concern, "Do you think she'll be upset?"

Michael shrugged his shoulders. "I don't think so. Not since I'm coming home with a G-Man and not out boozing. You know she thinks a lot of you and will take it as a real compliment that you came all the way from Washington for your godson's birthday. Italians take things like that to heart. Besides, she trusts you about as much as she trusts any American, especially an American cop." Michael turned and picked up the third phone to make his call.

Andy lifted the earpiece from the end phone and waited to hear Michael's conversation commence before he punched in a four-digit code, then seven numbers. One ring and the phone was picked up. "Lewis here."

Andy's back faced Michael. "Pete, we'll be coming out on Clark Street exit in a black Astin-Martin. Where are you now?"

"I'm directly across the street in a U-Park lot all set to go."

Andy looked around to see if Michael was still talking. He was. "Do you have a back-up?"

"Sam--I mean--Unit Two is parked on the Kennedy Expressway someplace around Division. We're both ready."

Andy was going to break the connection, but decided that nothing was insignificant in FBI work. "Say, Pete. Keep your eyes open for a black limo. It may be nothing and this will probably be a dry run, but I noticed a limo following us earlier. Probably just biding its time for a passenger pickup, but keep your eyes open anyway." Andy replaced the receiver and turned to face Michael.

Michael had apparently heard some of the conversation. "What's this about a 'back-up' and a 'black limo'?"

Andy picked up his briefcase, and both men started for the double glass doors leading to the garage. "I'll tell you in the car. Let's get a move on."

Charles, the garage attendant, sat in the office. His legs, crossed at the ankles, rested on the desk, while he read a racing form. When he saw Michael, he quickly jumped to his feet, grabbed a set of keys from the wall rack, and emerged from the office. "Hi ya, Mr. Hawk. I had extra time so I washed your car today."

Michael reached into his pocket, removed the gold money clipped wad of bills, peeled off a twenty, and slipped it to the attendant. "Thank you, Charles."

As the two moved toward the black auto, always parked within easy reach, Charles halted their advance. "Mr. Hawk, those two men you sent down here said they really liked your car."

Andy looked at Mike, and they both shrugged. Michael moved closer to Charles and whispered, "What two friends?"

Dutifully, Charles reported the happenings. "They said they were your friends, and you was gonna sell your car, and you sent 'em down here to check it out."

Michael continued to question. "What did they look like, Charles?"

"Big, like your friend here." Charles's sleepy eyes inspected Andy from head to toe. "Not that big, but big. An' they was ugly, too. They gave me a coupla bucks and told me not to say nothin' to you cuz they was gonna surprise you and bring you a big check to buy the car. You treat me real good, Mr. Hawk, so I thought I ought to tell you. They din't look like no brokas ta me. At fust I thought they was trouble, but they was real nice."

Andy listened intently, digesting all the information. A chill ran the length of his spine. Uncertainty reflected in Michael's eyes. He asked, "Did they have trading jackets on?"

Charles's slow answer was directed toward Michael. "Ya, but they din't fit very good, and they din't have no badges on like yours that say, Mr. 'HAWK'!"

Andy broke in. "How long ago were they here, Charles?"

Charles raised his shoulders, hands out, showing pink, worn palms. "Two, maybe three hours ago."

Andy's FBI experience surfaced and said with authority. "How long did they look at the car? Did they open the doors or the hood?"

Charles stood quietly and shoved his hands into his pockets while trying to recall the incident. "They was only here about ten minutes. They wanted to see the inside cuz I always lock up Mr. Hawk's car. I told 'em Mr. Hawk would have to show it to 'em cuz I din't have no keys. Then they left."

Michael handed Charles another twenty. "You did well, Charles. Thanks." Facing Andy, he shook his head and said, "I don't know anything about this."

Andy moved toward the sleek black machine, set his briefcase on the cold cement floor, and strolled around the car slowly. Michael followed. "Stand back over there, please, Mike."

Michael obeyed and moved away from the car.

Andy circled the auto once, then went to his briefcase, pressed in a combination of four numbers, and the case sprung open. He withdrew a small silver device about the size of a deck of cards, pulled up a tiny antenna, and with the press of a black button, a faint hum sounded.

As he turned to the car, Michael inched further away, bumping into an XR7 parked two stalls away. "What are you doing, Andy?"

Running the device around the car, Andy said, "Your car is turned off, has no electricity going through it, so there should be nothing here to pulsate any current. If there is, this little gadget will pick it up."

Michael merely mustered an, "Oh...great!" Michael stepped close to the little dial on the tiny spy catcher. First the doors, then the hood, the two tires and tire wells on the driver's side, the bumper and underneath. The dim hum continued.

Andy knew Michael's curiosity was growing. He was standing a car length away now. "Anything there, Andy?" He sounded like a little kid following a friend into a dark basement.

"Nothing yet," Andy whispered.

"You do this often, Andy?"

"All the time," he lied.

"Oh, all the time. Then there's nothing to worry about?"

Continuing to move the gadget with efficiency, Andy said, "Not unless it's a remote-control bomb and Charles has the terminal with a little button on it."

Out of the corner of his eye, Andy saw Michael leap back, this time falling over the fender of the expensive Mercedes behind him. Now on his hands and knees, Michael looked to the parking attendant's office where Charles was standing wide eyed and empty handed. He crawled halfway back to his car, looking at Andy's feet while checking the passenger's side. The hum increased as he swept the rear of the car and started to go crazy as the tiny antenna entered the back wheel well.

"I think I found something, Mike. Come here!"

"Fuck you. Tell me about it in the cab I'm about to call!"

"No, it's harmless. Come here!" Michael crawled the rest of the way around the back of the car and carefully peered between the wheel and the metal frame above it.

A little black box, the size of a pack of cigarettes, with a tiny blinking, red light was attached to a metal bracket. Andy covered the rest of the car with his little scanner and returned to the wheel where Michael, still on his hands and knees, watched as the red light blinked its signals.

Andy reached in and gave a yank to disconnect the hearty magnetized pull. Michael flinched. A small, blinking light on a black box rested in Andy's big paw.

Beads of sweat fell from Michael's forehead. "What...What the hell is it, Goldie?"

Andy shook his head, disgusted because some son of a bitch was already on to Hogan and apparently had been for some time. "In layman's terms, it's a goddamn transmitter. Whoever put this here wants to know where you are all the time. Those guys today were probably just checking to make sure it was not running out of juice."

Michael's dark eyes were the size of half dollars. "Maybe they just put it on today."

Andy turned the little black gadget over in his hand looking at it carefully. "No, it's caked with mud. It would be clean if they had just put it on. Did it rain here lately?"

Michael thought for a moment and wiped the sweat from his forehead. "I think it rained last week for two or three days."

"So it's been on for at least that long. Chances are you have company following you to and from work every day and any place else you go." Andy pulled out of his memory file the black limo he had seen twenty minutes earlier. He said nothing as Michael mumbled something profane.

Surprisingly, he saw no fear in Michael's face; curiosity, maybe some anger, but no fear. Then again, he knew Michael well, and he didn't scare easily. He remembered Michael telling him once that an honest man has nothing to fear. Fear was a lack of faith in one's self. Fear and faith couldn't live under the same roof. He envied Michael for that, because Andy had experienced much fear in his life. He knew it was from his lack of self-confidence.

"Have you noticed anybody following you around? Anything unusual?"

Michael looked at Andy and ran his tongue across his bottom lip in thought. "I'm usually just looking for cops when I'm driving, not fucking goons." Andy watched as Michael's mind worked. "There have been a few occasions..."

Andy probed: "...A few occasions what, Mike?"

Michael looked at the garage floor and Andy saw his jaw muscles tighten. He spoke slowly. "There have been times when I've noticed a black limousine following me, or parked across the street from my house, or at the top of the ramp when I leave the garage...But there's a thousand black limos in Chicago."

He lifted his eyes from the floor, to the transmitter, to Andy's face. His voice was laced with anger. "What the hell is going on? Who has the right to violate my privacy, my family's privacy, by putting that goddamn thing on my car?"

"I don't know, Mike. I don't like it!"

Michael snapped back. "You don't like it. Well tough shit! I don't like it more than you don't like it." He looked down at the transmitter and spoke slowly, intently. His tone of voice made Andy more nervous than the transmitter. "We have a new game in town, Andy. We may as well name the stakes right now and not fool ourselves with euphemisms. We're NOT going to call the game 'follow or be followed.' We're talking live or die. I'll kiss your ass if you think I'm going to be the one on the short end of the shovel. Fuck those guys! Who the hell do they think they are?"

During their college days, Andy had seen Michael in action and didn't want to see his rage erupt again. Not yet. "Let's not jump to conclusions, Mike. This is only a transmitter."

He knew Michael's mind was calculating at an accelerated pace. "Andy, you don't know how big this commodity scam is. You have no idea how desperate the men behind it are. You say it's only a transmitter. I say it's just the beginning of something that will affect the international financial, monetary, and economic markets. It'll leave them scarred or dead forever."

Andy shook his head in disbelief. "You're either crazy, or there's going to be a whole lot of shit hitting the fan at the Federal Building during the next few years."

Michael leaned back on his knees. "I'd settle for crazy--but I speak the truth!"

Andy felt Michael's thoughts and words come to a halt when he saw him replace the blinking device where he found it. Michael protested. "What the fuck are you doing?"

"I'm putting it back. Let's find out who is so interested in you."

"How are you going to do that? I don't want any scumbags following me home."

"When I called in, I requested two back-up cars to follow us to your place. They'll keep their eyes open for a foreign tail. I had no idea they might earn their money tonight."

Michael spoke quickly. "That's why you asked me which exit I took and what kind of car I had?"

"Yup."

Andy noticed that Michael's moods were swinging. His anger eased. "Do you think there is a bomb in the car?"

"Nothing with a transmitter on it. Not according to my little detector."

Michael looked back toward Charles, who was standing wide-eyed near the exit door. "That's real encouraging, Andy. How about a bomb hooked up to the battery or starter?"

"I doubt it. Charles said they couldn't open the doors or the hood, and they weren't here long enough to get under the car and do the job right for a kill."

"Jesus Christ! A kill? You mean a Hogan kill? And you *doubt* whether or not there is a bomb under the car? You always were the master of understatement. Andy, I play percentages all day long, and sometimes I doubt that the market is going down, so I bet that it's going up. Sometimes the son of a bitch that I doubt is going down falls right out of bed. You *doubt* there is a bomb in my car? Fine. You wanted to drive. *You* drive and pick me up at the top of the ramp. If I hear a big bang, then I'll just figure you fell out of bed and took my car with you. You DOUBT it??? Don't you have a SWAT team you can call to remove all doubt?"

Andy continued to look over the car as he talked. "That would be nice, Mike. Then whoever is outside waiting for us would know they've been made and get out clean as shit through a tin horn. Where is your sense of adventure? Your balls? Your quest for intrigue? You're the guy who likes walking the razor's edge."

"You're enjoying this, aren't you, Andy? You like to see me a little nervous. You blimp Jew prick. My sense of adventure, my balls, and everything else I like is sitting in a warm home seventeen miles north of us. They're waiting for Dad to join them for dinner and a party....I happen to enjoy living. My wife and kids like me most of the time. My dog likes me. The gardener and maid like me. The IRS likes me. The economy likes me. We'd go into a recession if anything happened to me. Who'd buy all these cars, clothes, homes, and yachts if anything happened to me?"

Andy crooked his mouth and gave Michael an unimpressed look. "Somebody would pick up where you left off. Give me your keys."

"Oh, for Christ's sake, Andy. Call a bomb squad, or whoever checks this type of shit out."

"There is nothing to worry about, Mike. I do this every day," Andy lied again.

Michael tossed him the keys. "Here, genius. Take the keys, but I'm standing over there with Charles."

Laughter erupted from Andy as he got off his haunches and looked down at Mike on his hands and knees. "Please don't crawl over to Charles in those nice clothes. That poor guy is so scared. He's liable to shit in his pants if he sees his esteemed 'Mr. Hawk' crawling toward him like a Neanderthal."

Michael hopped to his feet, brushed his hands and knees, and stared indignantly at Andy's smiling face. He bent and kissed the roof of his car and spoke to the machine, "Remember, honey, Andy says the odds are with you. He *doubts* that you'll turn into an erector set. So don't worry, baby, okay?"

Andy put the key into the door lock. Michael quickly kissed the black, shiny roof again, cleared his thoughts, and chided over his shoulder, "I don't know who I'm going to miss more. You or my car. Hey, Charles, is there a coke machine around? You say on the fourteenth floor? Good, let's go get one. I'll buy! See ya around, Andy!" Michael shouted from Charles's side. "You're loony tunes, you know that, don't you? Step into my office for a moment, Charles, while my friend tries to get killed."

Andy wished Michael would shut up while he felt and looked for signs of entry. He was sure none were there. Goddamn, this kind of crap always made him nervous. He was a professional at this shit, but there were so many sophisticated ways to kill a man in a car. He could hardly keep up with them at the Bureau. Son of a bitch! Why didn't he stay in Washington today? This was a job for Pete Lewis. He thrived on shit like this. Pete was the designated agent for Hogan anyway. He swore again under his breath. Sweat began to roll down the side of his cheeks to his chin.

He turned the key gently and the door clicked open. It sounded like a gun being cocked. He cursed as his big hand slid its fingers into the crack between the door jamb and the door to feel for wires. He went quickly all the way around the door. No wires. He opened the door, felt under the seat. Nothing. He carefully slid his big frame into the leather seat. He frantically looked under the dash, under the passenger seat, the back seat. Nothing. He opened the other door and gave it the same routine. Then he swung it open. Perspiration was coming fast now. Tension sweat. He rubbed his coat sleeve across his cheeks and forehead. From the driver's side, inside the car, he reached for the hood release and mumbled to himself, "Here goes nothing, I hope."

He pulled the release, and the hood yawned open right in front of him. "Jesus Christ!" he yelled. This startled him. He expected the hood to open from the front like his Chevy. He began to relax a little. Slowly, he filled his lungs with air. Before he had a chance to let it out there was deafening noise: sirens, mechanical screams, bleating horns, and flashing lights.

In a millisecond the thought flashed through his mind, "I'm dead!" A thousand other thoughts collided. Andy rolled out of the car, did a somersault, and instinctively pulled his weapon, all in less than two seconds. Just what happened? He couldn't think. Michael's laughter brought him back from the grave. He looked down at himself and found that he was in a crouched position with both hands on his gun pointed at the car.

Laughter had Michael doubled over. "Andy..." Laughter..."Andy, you okay?..." More laughter..."I...I...It's just the burglar alarm."

Streams of sweat dripped off Andy's chin, and his brown hair was tousled and wet. He nearly turned his gun on the laughing baboon who was holding onto the little black parking attendant so he wouldn't fall down in his mirth.

Michael approached the car still laughing. He pointed at Andy in his ready-to-fire stance. "I swear, Goldie...believe me...I forgot all about..." and laughter volcanically erupted. This time coming all the way from his toes. "I forgot to tell you about the twenty-second-delay alarm and the hood-release alarm. I swear I'm sorry. Put your goddamn gun away. My car's going to think she's under arrest."

Andy's eyes turned red with meanness as he slowly stood to full height towering over the screaming car and his cackling friend. He screamed at Michael. "YOU SADISTIC BASTARD! I ought to shoot you...you crazy son of a bitch. I'm glad you can still laugh

at the devil. That scared the hell out of me." He decided he'd better put his gun away before he succumbed to his desire to shoot Michael in the foot.

Wiping the tears from his eyes and try as he did, Michael couldn't keep his laughter under control at the sight of his burly friend pointing the gun at the black beast. He reached in and turned off the alarms with a key he kept on the dashboard. He wiped his eyes again with the back of his hand, patted the car's roof, and said in an almost crying voice, "See. I told you, honey. Uncle Andy's gonna take good care of you." At that, he pulled out a handkerchief and wiped his tearing eyes.

Andy was furious, not necessarily with Michael but with himself for being so uptight on a simple bomb search. Michael's continued needling brought Andy back to reality. He, too, began to see the humor in this scenario. Andy checked under the hood quickly as Michael slid into the passenger seat. By this time he didn't care whether there was a bomb or not. He slammed the hood down, climbed into the car, started the powerful engine, shifted into reverse, and screeched backwards. He put it in gear and fishtailed past Charles, who was shaking his head and probably thinking he might take a few days off.

At the top of the ramp they waited for the electric door to open. The garage incident was good for both of them. Andy had made a fool out of himself unintentionally in front of his friend, and Michael's anger had been interrupted with, as he saw it, a terribly hilarious situation.

Golden mused that the transmitter attached to the car would anger Mike to the point where it wouldn't take much persuasion now to get his support with the investigation.

As the large aluminum door continued its noisy ascent, Andy reached for the fancy car phone and pushed in a Mobile phone number. Andy spoke in lingo akin to his profession. "Unit One. You're in place?" He received an affirmative. Unit Two in place also?" Another affirmative. "I'll be going south on Clark to the Eisenhower Expressway for a short distance, then northwest on the Kennedy to the Edens Expressway and exiting east on Willow Road to Sheridan. Stay close. When I get to home base, I'll call you for a report. If you notice anything amiss, call me on this phone. Incidentally, Pete, I'll be traveling at a high rate of speed so you can watch and see if we have a tail. Any cops bother us, call them off with your phone. I won't have time. And pass the word on to Sam."

The voice on the other end asked a question. Andy answered. "No, I don't think there will be any trouble, but be alert anyway. They placed a transmitter on this vehicle so they can lose us and still know where we are." Andy replaced the receiver in its tight holder and eased out into the light traffic, turning south on Clark. Once in traffic he used the mirrors. He saw only car lights reflecting at him. He would know shortly if Michael's car was actually under surveillance. He would like to know who was watching and why. Soon, he thought. Soon he would know.

SEVEN

Going Home

Traffic had thinned dramatically in the past hour. There were few delays. Andy could have made it through the yellow light at Van Buren and Clark. Michael figured he had decided to stop in order for his back-up agents to get in place.

Michael still pushed tears aside from his uncontrollable laughter over the garage fiasco. Spontaneous, choked laughter followed flashbacks of Andy sweating and squatting with gun drawn. Hell, he was ready to shoot his car.

Trying hard to calm himself, knowing Andy was back on the job, Michael glanced at his friend's huge profile. Now Andy's eyes were deadly serious as he scanned the streets, routinely glimpsing through the rear-view mirror.

The light turned green. Andy responded by flooring the Astin. A black streak of rubber a hundred feet long remained as they headed for Congress Street. Half-way down the block Michael covered his eyes with his hands. Andy speed-shifted into second, and more rubber deposited itself on the Chicago Street. Instead of slowing for the turn at Congress, he kept the precision auto in second gear and sped up. He made a sharp turn and gunned the car again. More protesting Pirelli tire rubber.

Michael's side mirror revealed a blue fog. A myriad of dim car lights entered the burned-rubber smoke. The pungent smell permeated his senses and filled the air. Another gear shift and more blue smoke. Michael swore under his breath as he snapped on his seat belt.

Arcing his arm through the air, Michael gestured at their surroundings. "I suppose you do THIS all the time too. What's it called? Escape?"

Michael saw Andy's mouth form a crooked grin. He took his eyes off the road for a moment and explained. "All the time, Mike, and it's called smoke 'em out. I want them to show themselves. We've got to see if they have a game plan."

Michael tossed his hands up in frustration. "Yeah? Well, in the meantime you just left ten thousand miles of tire rubber on the street in less than a mile. At this rate I figure you can do that four or five more times before we're riding on the rims. I'd hate to have to hitch a ride from whoever is following us, because we have a flat tire. Then we could really see what their game plan is, and that would definitely be smoking them out. It would also be called 'good-bye.'"

Andy grasped the wheel tightly, ignoring Michael's attempts at humor. He shifted down and turned sharply onto the Kennedy Expressway ramp. The rear of the auto fishtailed as he shifted back into third gear, then he punched the accelerator to the floor.

Michael felt his forehead wrinkle as he leaned over to glance at the instrument panel. The speedometer read 78 MPH. Christ, 78, and they weren't even off the ramp yet. He snapped his head toward Andy. Just inches away from his sober, concentrating face, Michael hissed through his teeth, "Jesus Christ, Batman! I paid over a hundred thousand dollars for THIS CAR, and that was a good buy. SHE'S TEMPERAMENTAL so try to keep the tachometer out of the FUCKING RED ZONE! She overheats at three hundred miles per hour."

In spite of his cynical joking, Michael was still enraged by the invasion of his freedom and privacy. Anger percolated within him, and this cynicism was his way of keeping it from erupting. "Well, at least you're only going three times the speed limit," Michael facetiously remarked as the black car sped past a blurred yellow ramp marker issuing its 25 MPH reminder.

* * *

Andy rationalized. "I figure at thirty-five miles over the other traffic speed, you can just about pick your own position on the highway if traffic isn't too heavy."

"And are you planning to do that all the way to Glencoe?" Michael wondered out loud. His question went unanswered.

Winnetka was hometown to Andy. The wealthy North Shore suburb bordered Glencoe. After college he had returned home to live. The first five years of his career for the Bureau were in the big city. He commuted by car daily. This was his turf, and he knew it well. Traffic had thinned, so he was able to keep his speed at 85 MPH. He hugged the left lane, avoiding the express lanes in case he needed to exit from the expressway instantly. He hoped he wouldn't have to do so. He shifted into fourth gear and picked up the car phone to check in with his teammates.

"Pete, you see anything?" A negative response. "Where are you located?" For Michael's benefit he mimicked the answers. "'A half mile back.' How about Unit Two, Sam?" Again, to keep Michael from his incessant vocal speculation, he repeated, "'Parked just beyond the Diversey ramp on the shoulder.' Keep your eyes open. This might be a dry run, or they may have a faster car than the limo, if indeed there is a limo involved. I'm going to push faster. Maybe I can pull some snakes out of the weeds." He hung up.

* * *

The Astin sped by a green sign which read, "Diversey Exit 3/4 mile." Michael saw Andy's counterpart, Unit Two, first. A blue auto, parked less than a hundred yards away, but beginning to move quickly along the shoulder of the road. He reached over and pressed a button. *The Cavalry Charge* blared from hidden horns under the hood.

Again, Golden was taken off balance, slapped at his hand, and sputtered. "Goddammit, Mike--what are you trying to do? That's the second time today you've scared

the hell out of me with your horns and sirens. That hasn't happened to me since the last time I saw you ten years ago. No wonder my visits to see you are so infrequent. I'd be in a mental institution if I spent more than a couple of hours in your company. How does Maria put up with your nonsense?"

Michael reached over and gently nudged the hard shoulder next to him. "Hey, settle down, partner! I just had that horn installed for six hundred dollars and couldn't think of a more appropriate time to let the enemy know we're coming. As far as Maria goes, she calls me her seventh child."

"I can see why," Andy said. "Are you just tense and releasing nervous energy with this spontaneous frolicking? Or are you actually enjoying this cat-and-mouse game? I presume the latter! Doesn't anything scare you? Aren't you the least bit afraid of the situation you may be in?"

Michael sat back. He thought of his own philosophy of life, which was based on faith in an Infinite, Protecting Power. A Power that walked him through life. A Power greater than any evil the human mind could conceive. After a while, he said softly, "Why should I be afraid?" He wasn't sure and didn't care if Andy heard him.

The phone buzzed. Andy grabbed it and listened intently. All he said was "okay," leaving Michael wondering what the caller had said.

Michael leaned forward and rested his palms on the dash. He looked at Andy. "What's up?"

Andy's eyes remained steadfast on the road. "Unit One will be passing us to take the lead, and Unit Two will take its place behind us."

Michael shifted in his seat and moved his head slightly to establish perspective of the passing "Unit One." In the far-right lane he saw a beat-up '77 gray Ford whiz by. The only giveaway was the small aerial on the back of the car. With all the sarcasm he could muster, he spewed, "*That* pile of shit is 'Unit One'?"

Andy nodded. "You got it!"

Michael let his body fall back in the comfortable leather seat and asked, "What in the hell happens to 'Unit One' if we have to barrel ass?"

Andy sat at the wheel with the confidence of one who had full control of himself. "That unpretentious 'pile of shit' has a Jensen Interceptor Chrysler engine. She tops out at 160 MPH."

Michael was mildly impressed. "You're kidding."

Andy's tone grew more serious. "Mike, are you with me now? Will you help me out with this Chicago mess?"

Michael hesitated, ideas germinating within him. Now it was time to make his move. The move he had been waiting for. He had waited patiently for this invitation, and now was the time for an RSVP. "It doesn't look like I have a choice. Whoever has tagged me will sooner or later start to cause me trouble. I'd rather get the jump on them before they get to me. I'm concerned about my family, though. What do I do with them? My kids

go to school. My wife goes shopping. I go to work. What's to prevent the enemy from kidnapping or just plain killing one or all of us?"

Andy was ready with an answer to his obvious concerns. "Whoever we are dealing with is still speculating whether or not you are trouble. Until now they have no reason to believe you are doing anything out of the ordinary. They obviously don't trust you. They know you made a formal complaint to the government about the skimming and other forms of thievery on the Exchange floors, but you haven't taken any action since then. You haven't gone back to the U.S. Attorney or taken a recent trip to Washington. They figure they stopped you with the scandal and scared you into submission. When they killed your two buddies, they probably hoped you accepted their philosophy of 'Might is right.' They don't know about me, and I doubt whether they know about Joe Glassmann and Sam Ross's recent complaints to the Government. You're in the clear as long as you don't change your daily routine. Everything we do together will be completely covert."

"You forget one thing. If they have been watching me, and we both seem to think somebody in a black limo is, then they probably saw us come out of the Union Club together."

Andy waved his hand through the air. That means nothing. You've met Joe there for lunch before, and I'm just an attorney or client who joined you for lunch."

With that statement, Andy left the door wide open for Michael to roast him again. "Not in that brown, wrinkled Sears suit and that shit box for a briefcase, are you a Chicago attorney, *or* a million-dollar client? What do you take them for? Village idiots?"

The teasing didn't faze Andy. "Who I am is pure speculation on their part, and they don't generally act on speculation."

Michael sunk into the black bucket seat as he gazed out the window. Now the auto sped through the junction and up the Edens Expressway. "I like your choice of words, Andy, 'generally don't, probably won't, might not.' I should have stayed in bed this morning with my warm, inviting woman."

Michael anticipated Andy's next words and smiled to himself. "We'll have a man near your family and you at all times. They won't be obvious, even to you. I'll have a clean phone put in your house. Yours is probably tapped."

Michael's head snapped toward Andy. "Ah, fuck! Now they're listening to me too."

"Don't worry about it," Andy reassured him. "Your conversations have probably been very innocent for a long time now. Don't change that! If your phones are tapped, whoever is involved probably stopped listening to the tapes a long time ago. If you call me, or anyone concerning the investigation, use the clean phone or a pay phone. Just make sure there is plenty of noise around and you are in a phone booth, not using a wall phone. And don't call from your office, unless you want me to put in a clean phone there too."

Rearranging his thoughts, Michael said, "I think you'd better clean all my phones, home and office, and give me some scramblers, a private line, and whatever other toys you

have so my conversations are private. When I'm at the office, I spend a good deal of time on the phone, and I can talk to you in private. It may be difficult at home with Maria. She knows and senses everything. I would only be able to talk to you late at night."

Michael knew Andy liked what he heard. He was catching his fish! "Good point, but don't be afraid to call me late. I'm up late most of the time anyway." As an afterthought, Andy said, "I think we should keep this from Maria, don't you?"

Michael shook his head. "Don't be silly. As soon as she sees us, she'll know something is up. She gets the whole story so she can also be on guard. That's her nature. She'll be okay. I doubt if she will allow you to put a man on guard at the house. She'll pick her own bodyguards, or she'll let me pull a few good men together."

Andy began to protest. "Come on, Mike. Where are you going to find qualified professionals to..."

The phone buzzed and abruptly ended their conversation. Andy's answer was instant. "Yes. Aha! They picked us up at the junction. How far back are they?...Do you have the license number?...A Canadian plate?...Check it out and get right back to me. And Sam, change position with Pete. Let him fall back before you leave your spot."

Thrusting his head forward, Michael strained to make out the old supercharged Ford in the right lane slowing to let traffic pass. He checked the side mirror. Bright lights blinked twice then an '83 blue Mercedes sidled beside the Astin. The young driver looked over and Michael did a double take. Clarifying the image in his mind, he now saw that the driver was an absolutely gorgeous blond woman. He smiled and nodded. He watched as she hesitated to smile back. He shook his head yes, trying to tell her it would be okay to acknowledge his gesture. She finally smiled back, and Michael's alert eyes saw perfect white teeth and long blond hair. All this in four seconds. He wanted to ask Andy to stop the car so he could ride with "Unit Two."

He felt his mouth open slightly as he looked over at Andy, who gave "Unit Two" a thumbs up, and the Mercedes sped forward. Michael could see only the tail lights as the Mercedes moved ahead of them. Don't leave! Michael said to himself. Who are you?

He cleared his throat. "Uh,...Andy?...WHO IS DRIVING UNIT TWO?

He watched Andy's serious eyes move from the road to the side mirror, to the rear-view mirror, and back to the road. His concentration kept him from answering quickly. "Her name is Sam. Why?"

"Sam what?"

"Sam Winters. I mean Agent Samantha Winters. Why?"

Michael had the picture of her beautiful face tattooed in his mind. "Is she as pretty as her pictures?"

As the Astin sped past Dempster, Andy looked over at Michael with a disapproving frown on his face. "What the hell are you talking about?"

"I'm talking about Unit Two, Samantha Winters. Is she as sharp as she looks, or is her face just pretty and the rest of her body built like yours?"

His eyes returned to the road. "She's one of the best. Mind, body, and spirit."

"Is she married?"

"No. Not now, but you are!"

Michael pouted. "Jesus Christ, Andy, I'm only asking a few innocent questions, and you're reminding me that I'm married. What do you think I want to do, bed her down for the night?"

Andy's frown remained. "You'd have to stand in line just to ring her door bell. Every agent we have has made a pass at her at one time or another."

"Any luck?"

"Not even a good-night kiss. She's all business, and I mean all business."

Michael laid his head back on the soft leather headrest and thought, goddamn, what an entree! He wondered if he would ever see her again, what she really looked like, and just how much business actually occupied her mind, and why?

Andy's harsh voice invaded Michael's train of thought. "The Mercedes will not look out of place in your neighborhood, Michael. Sam will have a good view of your house and the passing traffic from your neighbor's drive up the street. Unit One will be close by on Sheridan Road."

Michael kept the conversation going, not really caring about the answers. His thoughts were on the blond driver ahead of them. "How do you know the home owner won't object to having a stranger sitting in his driveway?"

A look of professionalism crept onto Andy's face. "They're in Europe for two months."

Michael shook his head. Andy's comment called for a compliment. "Shit. You guys think of everything!"

"This is a science, Michael, and we're damn good at it!"

Still shaking his head, Michael sighed as he thought to himself, Science, my ass! More like a study in politics, manipulation, and force. Out of courtesy he said to his friend, "I hope so, Pal."

As Skokie Boulevard blurred by them, Andy reached into one of his pockets, pulled out two folded pages, and handed them to Michael. "What can you tell me about these people? Anything?"

Michael switched on the little laser that lighted up his lap. He unfolded the pages, noted the government stationery, and scanned the list of brokers, badge nicknames, company numbers, and the pits in which they traded. "What's this?" he asked defensively.

"These are names that have been mentioned in the complaints we've received. They have all come to our attention more than once. Just look them over and tell me about them. We also have names of people who have had some type of run-in with the law and are now trading on the Exchange floors."

Michael looked down at the names as the car sped up the Willow Road ramp at 70 MPH. It blatantly ignored another 25 MPH ramp marker.

Michael read through the list of names, then read through them again, this time taking an engraved gold Tiffany pen from his shirt pocket, marking checks and numbers next to each name.

The phone buzzed again. Michael kept reading and checking, no longer interested in Unit One, still interested in Unit Two, though the list he held preoccupied him for the moment.

Andy grunted into the phone and answered his man still on the expressway following the intruders, "Keep checking, Pete. Call Washington and have them run it down. Have them check all bulletproof limos registered in the States and Canada. See if you can get a match-up between the two."

Now, Michael's attention diverted from his task. He sat forward and looked at the big face lighted up by the green dashboard lights. The papers fell to the floor.

This time Andy had the chance to chide. "You know anyone who owns a 1984 black, bulletproof Cadillac limousine?"

Mike brought his face closer to Andy's and with another hiss and a grimace, he said, "Yeah, my Aunt Agnes owns one. She works at Walgreen's in Bridgeport. She also carries an automatic rifle on her front seat and a couple of pineapple grenades in her glove compartment. You never know when someone's going to accost you in front of Walgreen's in Bridgeport." Then seriously he added, "Hell no, I don't know anyone who owns a bulletproof anything. How do you know the goddamn limo is bulletproof, anyway?"

Andy raised his eyebrows. "Unit One says that from his vantage point, without getting too close, it seems as though it's riding like a tank instead of a limo. A 1984 Cadillac limousine doesn't ride like a tank unless it weighs two thousand pounds more than normal."

Michael flopped back into the bucket seat and sighed to himself, "Holy Mother of God. What have I gotten myself into this time?"

Andy eased up on the accelerator, down-shifted, and turned north on Sheridan Road. Glimpses of moonlight shimmering on the inky waters of the lake shone through the North Shore trees and mansions they passed on their right. Michael lived four blocks away. Like a programmed lawman, Andy picked up the phone, punched in seven digits, and spoke softly with confidence. "We're coming in, Sam, keep your eyes open. I'll call you from this phone once inside. And remember, I have a midnight departure. You work tonight's schedule out with Unit One. Keep sharp!" He replaced the phone gently as he turned right toward the lake on Shore Drive. The auto slowed and stopped at the end of the short block. Two imposing black iron gates confronted them.

The gates slowly moved open with the touch of a button on the polished wooden dash. Beyond the gates and lengthy drive perched a large white colonial house, three stories high, hosting a welcome light in each window. A black Doberman appeared from the shadows and trotted toward the car that he knew so well. He barked once at the foreign driver. A call from his master halted any further aggression. As the car pulled forward, the

stately looking animal ushered it toward the inviting mansion. The gates automatically closed behind them.

Michael filled his lungs with air, puffed his cheeks, and exhaled with relief. He was glad to be home. Spring had laid a warm shoulder of sun upon the day, but now, almost parallel to his mood, the surf was becoming agitated. It banged against the sea wall, then rolled down the shore until another wave hit and powered its way along the path of the others.

The garage door opened from the inside. Maria stood beside her Jaguar in a stunning red shirtdress. She wore a welcoming smile, mingled with a tinge of concern. Michael ran his hand through his hair as the Astin eased in next to her. The car stopped, engine died, both doors opened simultaneously, while behind them the garage door moved relentlessly downward.

One look at Maria and all thoughts of the blond agent driving the Mercedes left him. After so many years, Michael was still glad to see Maria. Tonight her beauty was especially welcomed. He remembered this morning and her promise for tonight. That seemed so long ago. So much had happened during the day that he felt like a soldier home from a war after a year away from the ones he loved so much.

He quickly slid out of the death seat, pulled Maria close to him, and wrapped his arms around her, tightly moving his body into hers. They fit perfectly.

Maria stood on her tiptoes and pulled at Michael's ear lobe with her soft lips, then spoke over his shoulder, "Welcome, Andrew. I hope you're hungry for pasta and my black velvet fudge cake. Did you both enjoy your day together? It's nice to relieve the pressure once in a while, isn't it?"

Michael broke the clinch, his dry humor returning. "Great time, honey. We had a lot of laughs. Never a dull moment with ol' Goldie. Come on, babe. Forget about him. You saw him ten years ago and haven't seen me since this morning."

Andy was still in the car desperately trying to eject himself. "How do you get out of this thing? With a shoe horn?" Maria nudged Michael, walked around to Andy, cupped his face in her hands, and kissed him gently on the forehead. "It's so good to see you, Andrew, welcome to our home."

With that Andy emerged and hugged Maria. "It's good to see you, too, Maria. I've missed my two friends." Maria and Andy walked toward the lights of the kitchen door. Michael and the Doberman followed. Once inside, Michael crept behind Maria, again wrapped his arms around her, kissed her neck, and said, "The food smells terrific, but you smell better."

Maria turned around, looked up at her man, and smiled. It was a good smile, and it warmed him. She gave him another squeeze, and Michael knew she felt a tense body. Maria had always sensed when Michael's body was tense. His mind and heart suffered the same tightness. Later he would tell her of the crazy day, and she would love his tenseness away.

EIGHT

Library Wisdom

Exquisite dark oak paneling graced the walls and shelves in Michael's library. The bookshelves reached the ceiling, where they met ornately carved molding. This was where he came every evening to shake off his tensions. Dinner and birthday celebration over, he now waited for Andy to return from the Astin, where he'd gone to check in with his agents on the car phone. Safer, he thought, than the house phone.

Michael liked the solitude in the warm atmosphere. The sweet aroma of burning cherry and oakwood in the stone hearth gave comfort to him. It was not a large fireplace, but the detailing was exquisite. Dark wood with high-relief carvings framed the opening, while above the heavy mantel lay rich linenfold paneling. His eyes were mesmerized by the reaching orange arms of the fire. He blocked out the gay noises from his children in the other rooms to listen to the snapping protestation of the wood yielding to a power far greater than itself. He relished being in the silent company of the sage men of the ages, those who filled the shelves of the room.

The corner of a burgundy leather Chesterfield sofa now enveloped him. One leg rested comfortably on the seat, the other outstretched on the lush Oriental rug before him. A tumbler of iced scotch, loosely held in his left hand, rested on the tufted back.

He sensed the wisdom around him. Although he couldn't see their faces and names, he felt the telepathy of Aquinas, Socrates, Plato, Aristotle, Augustine, Dante, Thoreau, Merton, and the others. As if by osmosis, they gave him solace, guidance, and courage.

They spoke of truth and love and understanding, of justice, of humility, of forgiveness. What Michael had fought so hard to extract from these books seemed to come naturally to his introspective father. Michael had been a good student to his aged teachers now bound in leather. He had read philosophies of living, their realism, their idealism, their positive holy mysticism. Most common men called them all visionaries. Michael called them common-sense teachers who had the answers to life. He lived by the words he had read on the yellowed pages of these volumes.

In the midst of all these masters, in various poetic forms, a few constant laws of living flowed through each of their philosophical themes.

Michael understood that if you gave of yourself, you would be given to. If you took from the world without returning something better, life, in its own harsh way, would rebel. It would take that, and more, back. If a person was mean, arrogant, and selfish, he

would be treated the same. If a person provoked slander and cruelty on others, he too would be crushed. A braggart would be scandalized.

If a man's soul was filled with hate and prejudice, he would be hated and cursed. He learned that life was patient in handing out rewards and punishments. His father would tell him to leave a person, place, or thing better than he found it, and when it comes time to depart this world, to depart without grudge or grievance, knowing that through your efforts, you are leaving it better than you found it. His father would say that it's the growth of the soul that we will be judged upon, not the growth of our pocketbook. The material things will naturally flow to the good man if it's meant to be. If you have wealth and take care of your fellow man, good things will come to you.

Patrick Hogan frequently said to Michael that good begot good, giving begot giving, love begot love, and that happiness could not be found in books or bought with money. It was simply a by-product of a simple and holy life. No matter what blessings God bestows upon man, man is capable of losing everything by frivolous and careless living. To Michael's knowledge, his father had never read a book in his life, but his goodness was contagious.

While his consciousness was enraptured by the activity of the crackling fire lapping at the air, his subconscious was speaking to his soul of these things. He felt he was being prepared by the masters of life to take on an assignment he alone could accomplish.

A hand on his shoulder interrupted his revery. The heavy double wooden doors had silently opened. Maria had quietly ascended two stairs into the library, and she now stood next to him. The younger children had long since retreated to their warm beds. The older ones watched television in the Lake Room.

Maria held a Limoges saucer and cup of tea. Seeing Michael's contemplative mood, she sat at the far end of the sofa and faced him. The flames of the fire formed images on her face and made her black eyes sparkle. "Do you want to talk to me now or later about what's bothering you, Michael?"

He had tried to hide his apprehension after the fearsome day. He knew she would recognize and confront the unknown issue. She was calm and patient as usual.

Michael swirled the scotch around his ice. "Wait until Andy returns, and we'll both go through everything with you."

She reached over and undid his shoe on the sofa, then bent to complete the job on the other foot. Both feet were up now. She raised her own stockinged feet to meet his, toes touching. They sat in quiet for a short time, she sipping her tea, he sipping his scotch.

The door opened again, and the big frame of the FBI man filled the doorway. He stepped in and closed the doors behind him.

Andy pulled a leather wing-back around to face them both, his back to the fire. Placing his briefcase next to him on the floor, he dropped into the chair, then he flipped the lists of names he had given to Michael earlier onto the glass-topped coffee table. "Everything is okay outside. Our friends in the limo left for the night."

Michael watched his friend intently as he spoke. "Andy, I want Maria to know everything that's going down. Not only because she has a right to know, but for her own safety and that of our children."

Andy looked sheepishly at Maria, then at Michael. He straightened himself in his chair, put his hands on his knees, looked back at the silent Sicilian beauty of Maria, and slowly began to explain.

He first talked of the complaints made to the Justice Department; the luncheon conversation between Joe Glassmann, Michael, and himself; the garage incident, omitting the embarrassing quick draw on the car. Michael knew Maria listened to every word, categorizing them in her organized mind to get the full picture. He appreciated Andy's honesty, as he knew Maria did. Andy recounted the ride home and his suspicion of the black, Canadian-plated limo following them. He told her of his agents outside who would stay until they did away with any potential danger. Then he spoke to her of his need for Michael's help to bring the travesties at the Exchanges to an end.

He said, to Michael's surprise, that he wanted to bring the whole family to New York on a long weekend vacation where they would all stay at the Plaza Hotel in the manner to which they were accustomed. This would appear, to any onlookers, to be a simple getaway with the family for a fun weekend. Michael would be transported the short distance to Washington to meet with the Director and a few other agents who were going to be on the case. Both their house and their safety in New York would be assured.

Andy concluded his comments trying to leave a feeling of confidence that there was nothing to worry about. Up until today, Michael had made no recent moves to contact the authorities regarding his contempt for the Exchange larceny. "Maria, we'll keep him as clean as possible. We just need information which only he has and is willing to share."

Michael watched Maria. Her expression was hard to define. She had comprehended every word spoken by the FBI agent and knew he was playing down the dangerous aspect. He knew the early years of terror were still locked deep inside her. He also knew she would recall many years ago in Sicily how protected her grandfather had been, yet he had ended up dead on the rainy steps of a Palermo bank, a river of blood running down the cement block steps to the gutter. She had sat in the car as a young girl, waiting...watching. She had a sense for danger and could avoid many mistakes that Michael invited as a challenge.

He noticed a shiver run through her. Then she finally said, "What do you plan to do, Michael?"

He was careful with his words. "I plan to help. Andy didn't bring this on. Greed did! Whoever is out there...is following me to protect something illegal on a major scale. I'll give Andy what information I have, and then step back to let him do the investigating. Maybe we can rid the dirty elements from the Exchanges." He knew he had said enough.

Maria thought again for a long moment. "I agree with both of you. After the slap in the face they gave us, someone must pay. You may as well try Andrew's way first."

Michael smiled at her last statement. What other way was there? The three choices were the government's way, her father's way, or Michael's grandfather's way.

She stood, walked to the fire, gazing briefly at the flames, before she picked up a small log and dropped it on top of the red embers. Then she turned and looked at Andy. In a voice laced with a threatening tone, she said, "You watch my husband, Andrew. You guard him with your life. I will hold you responsible if for some reason he is left unprotected and something happens to him." Her words were soft, but both men knew the truth she spoke.

Michael watched Andy as he squirmed in his chair. He knew Maria's heritage to be a violent one with a philosophy of "an eye for an eye." He assured her as confidently as he could that they would all be protected by the best people the Agency had.

She walked to Michael's side, leaned and kissed his cheek. "I love you and don't want to lose you because of some greedy American peons. I have to get the boys to bed. You two work out your plans and let me know about the New York trip. I'll notify the children's schools, and my parents."

As she walked out of the room, she patted Andy on the head. "Take care of my man!" Michael thought it sounded like a good-wish salutation--but could it also have been another threat? He knew Andy would rather face death by hanging than the wrath of Maria Santini Hogan. She left the room as silently as she had entered.

Andy turned to Michael, who had just finished his drink and was up to get another from the small table bar in the far corner of the room. He took a deep breath and said, "Where do you want to start, Michael?"

NINE

Broker Profile; Tricks of the Trade

"Philosophy, Andy. The daily life philosophy of the commodity broker. That's what we're going to talk about first."

Michael had thought long enough. Now it was time for him to speak. He had looked over the two lists of broker names at both Exchanges and had found a number of names on the FBI hit list who were as honest as nuns. If left to themselves, the FBI could hurt many good people. With no offense to Andy, the Agency would be apathetic as all government was, not giving a damn who they ruined in their "search and destroy" missions.

"I'm going to help you, Andy, but you're going to have to tell your boss I want to know everything and everybody involved in this investigation. I want to know every detail and I want to help direct the investigation, as a civilian. Otherwise--the deal's off. No offense to you, but in many instances you guys in government are more ruthless than the people you go after. If the investigation isn't properly monitored, you'll ruin a lot of innocent people. We're looking for a minority group who controls ninety per cent of the stealing. They're not the majority! Any signs of your boss's playing with my head, or going around me, I'm out. I blow the whistle on this sting, even if it means my job. You know damn well I'll do it! I have a few lists of my own, brokers and companies I don't want touched. They're clean. I will also present other demands, nothing you can't live with, but I'll give them to you later."

Golden lit a cigar, sat back, and listened. Michael continued. "If you want authorization for this with your boss, go ahead. Call him from the car phone. I'll continue when you get back."

Andy took a drag and shook his head. "That won't be necessary, Mike. He told me to recruit you no matter what the cost."

Rearranging himself on the sofa, Michael said, "Okay, pal, here goes. First of all, you just don't go screaming into the jungle shooting at everything that moves. You're going to have to be subtle because you won't know your enemy. Remember, we all look alike. This will be like sitting in a restaurant in Saigon. You won't know who is for you or who is against you. Which ones are carrying bombs, which ones are carrying rosaries.

"You have to get into the head of a seasoned commodity broker. Remember, a lot of guys can't take the pressure and they quit. But the guys like myself, who thrive on pressure, are half crazy and have balls the size of muskmelons. We're the pros. Most of us came from nothing and had nothing to lose. We're mavericks, not thoroughbreds. Our

blood lines are not patrician. They start with us. We lived in the streets while our parents worked themselves to death for pennies to feed us. We made up our own rules for survival.

"We came into a business which suited us perfectly. It's a game of survival of the fittest. The tough ones make it; the weak ones don't. There are two sets of rules. The ones we show the public, media, government, and are window-dressing in our rules-book. Then, we have the unwritten rules that we live and trade by daily. These rules have been around for a hundred years. Whether they are legal or illegal, ethical or unethical, moral or immoral, is purely incidental. They were designed for survival. If you follow them, you survive. If you don't, you die. There is no respect for failure. The only respect we hold is for the strong and for success. Success at any cost. We need to be looked up to by our peers because our egos demand it. We gamble with our fortunes, our families, and our lives on a daily basis. We're like kids. We need attention because most of us had so little growing up. We don't need to be educated. In fact, brilliance and high I.Q.'s are a detriment in the pits. Hunger is the key ingredient in trading commodities. When we see or hear a trade in the market place, for the most part, the transaction bypasses our minds and goes directly to our vocal cords and fingers. Quick physical movements. Quick actions and reactions are primary factors to be a successful commodity broker.

"People like doctors have a very hard time making it as traders for two reasons. First, they are technical men and not quick to make judgment calls until they consult their books. I've known a few doctors who have taken on the market, and they have been miserable failures. What a blow to their ego. Everything has to go through their mind, be analyzed; then, and only then, they just might make their move in the market. By that time the trade is gone. At least the *edge* is gone. You have to buy or sell with the *edge*. The *edge* is a - ¼ or - ½ or full-point bonus on an order that's a little off the market. By the time ol' doc is ready to make his move, someone else has grabbed the *edge* and already sold it out for a profit. Hell, another broker may even sell it to Doc at a higher price.

"The second reason a doctor has trouble in the pits is ego deflation. In every circle he has ever run in, he is treated with the utmost respect. Not so in the market. Here, he is treated with disrespect. He's called an asshole, a piss ant, a prick, a son of a bitch. He's spit at and pushed around, and frankly, he can't take that degradation. Knowing his education and intelligence is superior to most of the men in the pit, he finds this totally humiliating. Outside the pit he is a god and can save lives. In the pit he is full of fear with fast and greedy animals. We run right over anyone in our path. He might be able to save lives, but he can't save his money. In fact, he usually loses big time to the vultures around him.

"Lawyers are a little different because they are basically thieves anyway. Their philosophy is based on money first, and the concept of guilty or not guilty comes second, or not at all. Losing or winning cases is secondary to most of them. Most of them don't give a shit as long as they get their fee. They come around quickly in the pits. If they can't

make it in the pits, they'll find another way to make it. You'll find quite a few of the big-time traders with law degrees.

"Whereas the doctor's philosophy is based on humanitarianism. Sure they want their fee, but their patients are important to them. The majority of them have general concern for sick people. So you can see why a doctor has a hard time. Too much analyzing before making the trade. They don't utilize. They analyze. You know the old saying, 'Analysis leads to paralysis.' And you can see why the attorneys make it, because their philosophy is monetary from the start. They know how to set legal traps and loopholes. A perfect quality for a commodity trader.

"Any analytical person has a hard time succeeding as a commodity broker, unless he's a real student of the market, a chartist, one who trades by predicting future prices from present and past prices and cycles. If he is content to stand out of the pit and analyze the market for the big moves, he can be very successful. But to enter the pit and take on the fastest reflexes in the world is financial death to the technicians."

Michael was mesmerized by the fire. He sipped at his drink. "They are up against guys like myself who have worked hard physically all of our lives. We sorted cattle and pigs in the stockyards, worked on construction, drove trucks, sold cars, shoes, tires, or clothes and did it for peanuts. We're former cops, firemen, insurance salesmen. We're not businessmen because we're not disciplined in the world's eye. We're fine-honed financial competitors. Our discipline is called on only in the pits in order to survive and win. As youngsters, the rich people were the 'other' people, another breed. Their way of life was completely foreign to us. We were told by our parents that was just the way things were. Accept it.

"As a youth I remember wishing I had a rich friend so I could ride in a nice car. Maybe I'd be invited to eat steak at his house. Maybe I'd even sleep over in an air conditioned bedroom. That never happened!

"But with all of us guys, we finally caught the golden ring and were given the chance of a lifetime. We grabbed it and were able to jump off the merry-go-round and into the fast lane. In no time flat, we're driving one-hundred-thousand-dollar cars and living in million dollar homes. We BUY our families' love, we BUY off cops. We BUY broads and we BUY cocaine by the kilo, not the gram. We BUY friendships. We BUY the biggest and newest toys on the market. No foresight. No hindsight.

"On the other hand, we help build hospitals and churches and give money to the poor. We're probably one of the most important elements in the financial lifeblood of America. Every penny we make goes right back into the economy in one form or another. We use crude language, our actions are unorthodox, and we're vocal and arrogant. We're good men--damn good men, but still mavericks and undisciplined."

Michael was on a roll and Andy just let him talk. He was painting a profile, trying to explain to Andy that here was the last of a rare breed. He continued, "Sometimes we lose our money. The cars have to go, the homes go, and usually the families go because

the whole outrageous marriage has been built on sand with a dollar sign on it. Usually it's swept away with the first or second wave. The big losers go back to picking bones. Sometimes the trauma of going from poor to rich to poor again is too much for a man to take. He blows his brains out or drinks himself to death. He overdoses on drugs to the point of thinking he can fly, and goes off a thirty story State Street building.

"Some of the losers fade into obscurity. The others, the ones who don't kill themselves, resort to skimming and bagging trades. Cheating and stealing is so easy in the pits, it goes completely unnoticed on a small scale and is totally accepted on a large scale. It's a sanctioned way of life.

"Some men refuse to go down even if it means resorting to theft. They won't give up their phony self-imposed importance. Their egos won't allow them to be beaten, even if they have to fight dirty. The pits have become like a ring of pit bulls fighting and determined to stay alive. It's not like it used to be--straight out competition--with the thieves staying in the background. Stealing *used* to be the exception. *Now*--it's the rule!

"The real winners are the ones who fall from the precipice, those who slide back down the monetary dunghill to the dregs where they came from and then claw their way back to the top. If they are wise, and can profit from their mistakes, they learn humility. Then they are usually allowed to stay at the top. They become seasoned and strong. They become master pit bulls and are around a long time, scared and torn as they may be. They now realize they are but stewards of the riches bestowed on them. They use discretion and caution. They vow never to go back to picking bones. The taste stays in your mouth a long time."

Michael leaned forward and came close to Andy. "I'm going to take one aspect of commodity theft and put it in layman's terms: Let's say you needed five thousand dollars to pay a doctor bill or your daughter's tuition or your mortgage, or even a bar bill or gambling debt, or your mistress's apartment rent, and someone handed you two orders, from two unrelated people. One order reads: 'Buy a nice automobile but don't pay over thirty thousand dollars for it,' and the other order reads: 'Sell my nice automobile, but not for less than twenty-five thousand dollars!'

"Remember, Andy, you have to have five grand to pay your bills. Your reputation is on the line, your wife is hounding you for money, your own insatiable needs have to be fulfilled. You are addicted to materialism."

Michael whispered now. "What would you do, Andy? Would you let that five grand slip through your fingers to some unknown face on the other side of that order? You don't know those people whose orders you're filling, and they have plenty of cash or they wouldn't be trading commodities. They live in Toledo, Salt Lake City, or someplace in Florida or New York, maybe even Europe. You'll never even see them. They are telling you to buy at thirty and sell at twenty five. You've got to have that five thou--so you sell at twenty-five, buy at thirty, and pocket the five thousand dollars. Legally, you should have bought and sold the car for twenty-seven-five and give each of your customers a better

price for their purchase and sale. In this case the buyer, although satisfied, should have the car bought twenty-five hundred less than he honestly paid. And the seller should have sold the car for twenty-five hundred more than he actually received. They would pay you a commission and everybody would go home happy. The broker cheated each client out of twenty-five hundred and took a commission on top of it. The same principles apply when trading commodities for customers."

Continuing to explain, Michael went on. "Of course, it's not quite that simple, because a broker is not allowed to 'cross trade' with himself. It happens all the time, but legally a broker is not allowed to take the other side of his customer's trades. So he calls his buddy out of the pit and buys at thirty from him and sells at twenty-five to him. Now the five grand is in his buddy's pocket, but because they're friends and scratch each other's back, he in turn buys back at thirty from the order filler and sells to him at twenty-five, putting the five G's where it belongs--in the broker's pocket. Now the bills can be paid and everybody is happy. That is, until tomorrow when there is another bill due. This one for ten thousand dollars, and ad infinitum."

Michael set his tumbler on the table, rose to his feet, and moved to the mullioned bay windows that looked out onto the neatly manicured gardens. The colored spotlights on the trees and in the flower beds shone brightly and lighted the path. The magnificent fountain never looked better. His eyes caught the array of crocuses, the first flowers of spring, which lined the lane. Soon there would be iris's and daffodils and tulips and a glorious profusion of color from now until fall. The garden had been planned so that flowers would continuously bloom when previous ones faded. As he stood there, he spoke again. "That is a very simple example of what happens at the arenas of the cavernous Exchanges.

"Unfortunately, Andy, these are *not* the fellows you want but will probably get. They're the little guys. The big guys are a different ball game.

"I just gave you one example of bilking the public out of five thousand dollars," Michael explained. "Multiply that amount ten times a day by only one broker. Then multiply that number by one hundred dirty brokers in Chicago, and you arrive at a meager five million a day. That's a conservative figure--for little guys." He waved his hand and pinched the corners of his face downward. "Nothing--compared to the big boys.

"There are a hundred different ways to skim money from outside traders. Bucket trading, skimming, bagging, crossing, dual trading, in-house trading, debit trading. These are merely a few. I could go on and on. The big guns are masters at all of the tricks and leave only blind alleys if you try to trace the paper. The little guys you'll get in a minute because they are careless and have no network to work with. They have been skimming and bagging trades for so many years that they think they are doing nothing wrong. In their mind, it's not illegal; it all goes with the game."

He made an analogy. "The game of the little guys skimming can be compared to a person working in an office from nine to five. This would be akin to people taking pens

and paper clips and staplers from the office. After a while they start taking copy paper and boxes of manila folders. And if they work late at night, they might even take a desk lamp, a typewriter, or even the welcome mat. Stealing becomes okay, a way of life.

"With the big guys it's a full-scale operation, one of the biggest in the country. They have actual syndicates of traders set up in the pits who skim and bag points all day long, every working day of the year. Hundreds of millions of dollars, maybe billions, stolen from the public and commercial accounts. Even more is *laundered*. Who really knows how much?" Michael asked as his eyebrows rose at the same time.

Andy, intent, absorbing all of what Michael had said, now interrupted. "Who are the big players?"

Michael leaned back again and put his feet up. "I'll name the groups, but I won't give you the king-pin names until the time is right. I don't trust your boss, and if I give him too much now, he could be in there next Monday handing out subpoenas to everybody. Then the bad guys would pull back, clean up, and show you their second set of books. They'd only come back out when you couldn't prove anything. Your boss is going to have to convince me we'll do it my way, the right way!"

Michael stared into the dying fire. "The Fed's first targets will be the most obvious and most vulnerable players. Those who are simply a group of independent brokers. Those who merely steal for themselves. Bagged money goes right into their own personal accounts. The largest and most dangerous group consists of organized brokers who represent the Mafia in a laundering program that would confuse the best intelligence. You'll have a tough time breaking their network.

"Three smaller groups who skim, mainly off international accounts, are the Boys from Dublin, better known as the Irish Republican Army. Their organization and trading techniques are the tightest and best I've ever seen. Their forte is inside trading and international rumors. You'll never get close to them! Although I'm not politically involved with these men, many of them are good friends of mine. I grew up with them in the stockyards, and mark my words, I will deny their existence if it's ever brought up in a courtroom.

"Another group of brokers have been recruited by a few Exchange officials to grab what they can for political and government officials. Their main targets are export dealers like Glassmann and Ross, and banks who use legal hedge and arbitrage programs to protect outside contracts already entered into. They pay off crooked government employees for confidential government information.

"The third group is a Jewish contingency who skims for the Israeli cause. They grab whatever they can get their hands on, but don't underestimate them. They run the Exchanges and own over half the commodity-clearing corporations in the country. I think the only group who isn't represented, in some type of bucket trading, is the Boy Scouts.

"The money which is bagged by these groups goes into the accounts of offshore holding companies and eventually finds its way to the intended source, less commissions, of course. Everybody gets rich at the expense of the customer!

"I would conservatively estimate these three groups bag as much as a billion a year," Michael continued. "They are very sophisticated--again no paper trail. Too complex! The net to the smaller groups is probably half that amount. The brokers who operate the scam usually place their money into Cayman Island and Bahamas accounts with only numbers for verification of ownership. Some native peon is named trustee and knows nothing of the accounts' beneficiaries.

"The Mafia dug their fingers into the Exchanges with the help of a German-Swede named Karl Peterson during the seventies. They have set up an almost impenetrable network similar to the Irish traders, but their interest is basically laundering money, not necessarily inside trading. Mafia money goes from one of their not-so-clean operations and washes through the market. Then it goes into another company with a big tax loss, so they don't even have a problem with taxes.

"This group is headed by an Italian guy named Salvano Ruzzo. He's brutally mean, clever, and arrogant. Both Ruzzo and Peterson are the most ruthless and dangerous in the business. They have had it their own way for so long they think they are gods and untouchable. Ruzzo has a half dozen young Mafia plants working for him, and he is expanding. Peterson gets a cut of everything they do for bringing them into the Exchange. He also cleans and clears Ruzzo's trades. In addition, Peterson's brokers are used most of the time so more commissions go to Peterson's syndicate. He is too greedy to realize that Ruzzo gives up the commissions in order to keep an arm's length from the laundering. Ruzzo reports to a man named Victor Conti, who actually runs the laundry operation.

"The broker groups who steal for politicians not only skim from customer orders but also play off of the weekly and monthly government commodity reports. The brokers establish their position in the market before the reports go public. The reports are government projections contrived through the Agriculture Department.

"The government people involved keep themselves clean because they are paid under the table. The kickbacks either go directly into their pockets or are placed in offshore numbered accounts. For a fee, they furnish confidential information to certain Exchange officials, big international grain dealers, livestock, gold, and mortgage brokers. That's called *inside trading*. They all make their play in the market just before the government information is released to the public. When it's released, the market usually reacts dramatically and the dealers get out of their positions at substantial profits.

"One fifteen-second phone call from an esteemed member of Congress, a high-ranking Senator, a member of the Securities and Exchange Commission, the Commodity Futures Trading Commission, or the Department of Agriculture, and the information is passed on to the brokers in New York, Los Angeles, and Chicago. This is when the inside brokers start to buy or sell."

Michael rose, stretched, and walked over to the bar for another refill of scotch and poured a Perrier for Andy. He continued as he served the drinks. "In one instance, there was a big meeting in Washington to determine the size of the grain crop for 1979. The Chicago grain markets were in a tremendous bull market. The report was very bearish, and three large grain companies started to sell fifteen minutes before the report came out. The next three days the grain markets went limit down. It was obvious to me that the three grain companies knew something that no one else did. I knew they hadn't made a large trade in a month, and now they were selling the shit out of the market. They probably picked off thirty million apiece on the trade. The snitch in Washington received ten per cent.

"I had a friend who worked for one of the grain companies involved. I had loaned him fifty thousand dollars in an effort to get him started in the business. When the market turned south and fell out of bed, I wanted to know how this happened. I contacted my friend and told him we were even if he told me how they did it. He was apprehensive, saying they'd kill him if they knew he told. I told him I'd call my marker first, then kill him if he didn't tell!

"He finally relented and said it was simple. The Agriculture Department held their secret meetings in the same Washington office each month. If the grain reports were bullish, a man would get up from the table of eight, stretch a little, and casually look out the window. He would nonchalantly raise the shade if the report was bullish and lower it if the report was bearish. Depending on how far he raised or lowered the shade determined the effect the confidential report would have on the market. If the report was neutral or slightly one way or the other, the shade would not be touched. No positions would be executed that day."

Michael shook his head, still in awe over these seemingly small covert actions that resulted in such large effects on the market. "That little scenario went on for years, until they renovated the office building, tinted the windows, and took the shades down. I'm sure they quickly replaced it with another ingenious formula. That's inside trading, straight from the top men appointed by the President of the United States."

Michael knew Andy was taken aback. He looked shaken. He had no idea this financial fiasco was so intricately webbed and filled with intrigue. Andy asked, almost begged, "Can you give me the government names at least, Michael?"

Slightly nodding his head, he answered. "I can give you some names, but not now. I want to meet the men you're working for. As far as I'm concerned, it may have been one of your bosses who pulled the shade up and down. I want to see the eyes of the men I'm supposed to be trusting."

Michael could have gone on, but it was getting late and he knew Andy had to catch a plane. "I've given you enough information for this session, Andy. You can chew on it on your way back to Washington. Anyway, you need to get to the airport."

Andy relighted his cigar and puffed vigorously on it. "It'll wait. It's a private jet."

Michael shrugged and walked around the room with his hands in his pockets. His eyes scanned the book-shelves.

Andy evidently needed a little more. "Michael, tell me, how do we put the sting into operation?"

Michael was quiet, thinking. When he stopped walking, he stoked the dying embers. He poked a few small flames and threw two more split logs onto the fire. Returning to the sofa, he began again. "Remember at lunch you said you would have difficulty catching the thieves even with five hundred men? I told you that you needed only ten or twelve good men and four or five million dollars. You need men in the pits--in other words--*moles*. They have to be between twenty-five and thirty years old and will need to be trained in the fine art of trading. They have to know what to look for, and they should get to know their trading partners on a social basis. They should be wired if you want conversations and inside information to study. The five million will be for membership purposes, fancy automobiles, expensive apartments, and capital with which to trade. The memberships will most likely appreciate in value, but you can kiss the trading capital goodbye.

"You'll get plenty of information on tape from luncheons, bar talk, and parties. Believe me, you'll be able to build a solid case. The traders are proud of what they do and the money they make." He corrected himself, "The money they skim. They are careless and boast about it after a few drinks."

"Will you train the fellows we pick?" Andy asked.

Michael sighed somewhat in disgust. He could see how deep he was going to have to get into the investigation, but he expected as much. "Someone has to! Your men would be lost otherwise. They may be lost anyway! I want good men. They have to be cool and quick witted. They have to be good under pressure. Market pressure, not gunfire pressure. They have to be aggressive--even arrogant--I can deal with that, so can the market. Don't send me any nitwits the Bureau is trying to get off the street." Michael's eyes bored into Andy's. "And don't think for a moment you're walking into the New York Stock Exchange. If your men are found out to be moles, the men you're after won't think twice before killing them. If you underestimate your opposition, somebody is going to get hurt. Federal agents aren't excluded. These men have killed before, and they will do it again-- believe me!"

Michael added, "When we're in New York, we don't have to stay at the Plaza. I'll send my family to my in-laws' home. They will be protected there." He cut that idea short, not wanting to bring his father-in-law's business dealings to Andy's attention. "That's it for tonight, Andy. You have plenty to start with. If what I've just told you doesn't get your bosses' attention, neither would a Communist take-over. Then you'd better look for another job. Just to set the record straight, I think your immediate boss, John Simpson, is a power-hungry asshole. He came from the CIA. Except for their three piece suits, that group is America's answer to the KGB."

Andy leaned forward and explained. "Regardless of your personal feelings for Simpson, he's still only the Assistant Director. If the Director tells Simpson to give you his backing, he will. My power comes from the Director of the FBI, not his assistant. You're putting a lot on the line, and I will too!"

Andrew Golden stood. So did Michael. As two friends they hugged each other tight and broke. Andy picked up his briefcase and moved toward the library door. He turned and said, "Incidentally, there will be a 'heating and air conditioning' man here at nine in the morning, one of our men. He will scan the house for bugs, check your phone for taps, and put in a clean phone. You'll also have an extra 'gardener' here tomorrow to treat all of your plants and trees. He, too, is one of our men. The house, your family, and you will be kept under surveillance until you tell us differently." He stopped briefly. "When do you want to come to Washington, Michael?"

Descending the two stairs from the library, Michael said dejectedly, "I'll have my own guards within a month, then I'll come to Washington. Might as well get the show on the road."

Andy patted his shoulder, then reached around his frame and gave him a squeeze. "You'll be okay, Michael. You're doing the right thing!"

"Oh, bullshit!" Michael responded, then asked, "Do you want me to call a cab?"

Andy looked at his watch, 11:33. "No, I have one of my men picking me up in an airport limo in a few minutes."

Michael walked Andy out the front door. A double honk had both men looking down the long drive to the heavy black gates. The limo waited for Andy. The Doberman sat on the drive inside the gates in front of the stretched white Lincoln. Michael whistled, and the dog came running.

Standing in the doorway, he reached inside and pressed a button on the wall, and the gates slowly moved open. The limo advanced, picked up its passenger and continued on around the circular drive, passing the lighted water fountain spewing its spray.

Michael stepped off the threshold, squatted, kissed his dog on the top of his head, and ruffled his pointed ears. The dog licked Michael's face. The limo tail lights disappeared, and the gates swung shut.

"Christ," he said to the dog. "What am I doing? This is the biggest play I've ever made, Pal, and the stakes are mighty high. You may be looking for a new master soon." The dog licked Michael's face again and shot off to his post someplace in the dark.

Michael walked to the fountain and lifted his face to its spray. The fountain was on early in the year, but he liked it that way. His mind drifted as his head turned toward Sheridan Road. His estate extended the full block. He looked beyond the coach house to the distant street lamps that lined the lake shore road and flickered through the waving trees. He enjoyed the moment, letting the fountain mist his face, as he listened to the luring surf roll along the sea wall.

He returned to the open door of his house--Maria waited for him. She would soothe his mind and body with her tenderness. She always did. Passion stirred his loins. He closed the door and headed toward their bedroom.

TEN

The Battles of Bo Lynch

The dark amber whiskey with its swirling islands of ice stared at Bo Lynch, calling to him, promising tenderness and oblivion like the sirens of Greek legend. Alcohol, to men like Bo Lynch, meant destruction. He couldn't resist the alluring beckoning of this lady that would soothe his tensions and sometimes help him forget the past horrors of Viet Nam. "Nancy Whiskey," as the Irish singers called her, would caress his body and soul. Then she would kill him. Simple as that!

He sat in a far booth of the plush Trader's Lounge, conveniently located at the Mercantile Exchange, waiting for Hawk Hogan. Unconsciously, he swirled his drink with its red plastic stirrer. Swirl one way, and the imprinted logo at the top of the stirrer showed a small clenched fist with two fingers out-stretched. Selling. Swirl the other way, palm in. Fingers were buying.

Bo took the stirrer from the brown liquid. He licked the sharp taste from it. He had gone three days without a drink, and his nerves were shot. He needed the drink, which had sat untouched in front of him for fifteen minutes. The raw edges of his nerves pleaded with his shaky hands to pick it up. His sweat-soaked shirt clung to his back. The barroom was cool, but his whole body felt hot and clammy. The irregular pounding of his heart echoed in his head. His eyes watered, and his shoulders moved spastically at unpredicted times. Bo knew it didn't take a genius to figure out what he was feeling. He'd felt like this a hundred times before--alcoholic withdrawal. He needed this drink to steady his nerves. Temptation won. Both hands moved toward the glass. He lifted it gingerly. He couldn't let one precious drop fall. Medicine, he thought, as he took a long, stinging, lifesaving swallow. Moving the glass from his lips, he picked up the table napkin. He ran it across his wet brow to rid himself of the salt beads furiously forming. He reached into his shirt pocket for a damp Camel cigarette, lit it with a Zippo lighter, and drew harsh smoke deep into his lungs. As he blew the smoke straight out in front of him, he thought to himself, now, that's much better!

John Barleycorn was doing his job. The warmth filtered through his body. He gave no notice to the acid liquor stinging in his throat. He slugged down the remaining liquid and raised his glass to the sullen, black-vested bartender. He motioned for another. Gino Corillo gave him a nod and a skeptical look. He poured another double Wild Turkey 101 on the rocks for this potential time-bomb customer.

Bo stared into the second empty drink glass and wondered why Hogan wanted him. It was 4:48. Most of the markets had been closed for hours. Most of the conversation, laughter, and lies of the broker patrons came from the other end of the long, dim bar.

Michael had told him to meet here at five o'clock in the dining section. They needed privacy. This was going to be important. Bo was negative by nature. These negative projections assumed dominance in his boozed mind. Fuck! He thought, I hope he's not going to let me go. He'd been doing a good job trading for Mike in the Standard and Poors and Eurodollars. After all, he had given a hundred and ten per cent loyalty to his Irish friend. Even though a hangover accompanied him every morning, he hadn't missed a day of work since Michael put him on two years ago. Still, after fifteen years, he felt the paranoia of Nam, a gun behind every bush, a knife in every hand; with every step, a thin ground wire, when tripped, would blow the bottom half of his body away.

* * *

Gino Corillo delivered Bo's third drink. He said nothing as he set it in front of him. He wished he would drink up and leave. The big Italian bartender was afraid of Lynch. He had seen him in action. He knew Bo had done a three-year stint in the Special Forces unit in Viet Nam. After a few drinks, Lynch saw everybody as an enemy. The only guy who could control him was Hawk Hogan.

Corillo's mind, like the pages of a calendar in an old movie, flipped back a few months. One of the young, arrogant, bullying-type brokers, Mort Weisman, a former car salesman, was working to have pledges signed to raise money for the Jewish Relief Bond Fund. He went from booth to booth, pushing his pompous weight around. Weisman gave his sales pitch as he interrupted Hogan and Lynch. Corillo could see that Weisman lingered on the edge of Hogan's tolerance level, and was already beyond Lynch's. As soon as he began his spiel, Hogan had held up one hand and explained to the man that if he wanted to be equal about raising money, he should be raising it for the Polish, the Irish, the blacks, the homeless, the Latinos, the Ethiopians, and every other group who was subjected to the cruel laws of nature and tyrannical governments.

Ignoring Michael's philosophical approach, he continued talking. When Michael asked the persistent jerk what fee he was skimming off the donations, Corillo remembered the indignant look that crossed Weisman's face. He said naturally he was collecting a small fee for his time and effort. Lynch laughed in the man's face, then called him a liar. He said the schmuck would walk away with fifty per cent or more and still look like a hero in the eyes of his Jewish countrymen.

Corillo would never forget Lynch's mean eyes when he heard Bo tell the man that he was collecting for the Viet Nam refugees. Would the Weisman like to contribute ten thousand dollars? The mouthy bastard didn't take the warning. He quickly responded about

the United States wasting enough money on slant-eyed gooks who should take care of themselves. Like a time bomb, Bo's tolerance ticked close to the number 12.

Corillo knew Lynch was a killer in Viet Nam. The word gooks was hardly out of the Weisman's mouth when a foot snapped from underneath the booth and kicked the former car salesman in the balls. As he bent in pain, another snap from an unseen foot caught the man's face. It broke his jaw and shattered his nose. Blood spewed from his face and shot over Gino and the bar. The blow was so powerful the man flew across a table. The back of his head slammed against the top of the bar. He slid to the floor.

Gino remembered looking at the senseless man lying at the foot of the bar. The grotesque figure, the twisted jaw and face full of blood. It was as if a diabolic spirit had slammed Weisman into oblivion and near death.

Corillo hadn't seen anything move from where Hogan and Lynch were sitting--nor had anybody else in the bar. Lynch hadn't even taken his hand off of his drink. The two men continued their conversation as if the con man hadn't materialized. That was the last time the Israel bond peddler was seen around the Exchange. Someone told Corillo he sold his membership at the persuasive request of Bo Lynch and had returned to selling used cars. There were rumors that an anonymous contribution of ten thousand dollars was made to a Viet Nam refugee fund.

He knew this sullen Viet Nam vet had brought the war home with him. He scared the shit out of Corillo.

He secretly wished he'd find another place to drink. Better yet, he wished he'd go back to the jungle where he belonged.

He breathed an unnoticed sigh of relief when he saw Hawk Hogan enter the far end of the bar. Their eyes met, and Corillo's head gestured that his prize was to be found in the far booth.

As Michael approached, he stopped at Gino's post and ordered a double Black Label on the rocks. Gino placed two drinks in front of Michael and pointed to one of them, "That's his fourth. He just ordered it!"

Michael shook his head in disappointment. "Thanks, Gino. Start a tab and put twenty dollars on for yourself. We won't be too long." Michael turned with the drinks and headed for Bo's booth.

Hogan was an okay guy in Gino's eyes. He tipped well and wasn't cocky like a lot of the other slime-bag, nouveau-riche brokers, though Hogan was on the shit list of many of the heavyweight traders. Corillo wondered why he was so disliked--but he also knew Hogan had powerful friends. It seemed as though there was a war going on between two strong factions at the Exchange. He wasn't sure what their differences were. He really didn't give a damn. All he knew was that he was in the bar business for tips and any other gratuities that would come his way. People paid him well for the information he heard. Corillo would sell to the highest bidder. Fuck 'em! It went with the job.

A few months earlier, Gino had been handed an envelope containing five one-hundred-dollar bills. In it were instructions and a telephone number telling him to report any of Hogan's activities in the bar. Who he met with and any conversations overheard. He was instructed to look for new behavior. Anything unusual was to be reported. The man who handed him the money was a very influential broker, not one you could refuse, not one to mess with!

Despite his respect for Hogan, he reasoned, money talks. He had his own plans, his own needs. He would call the number as soon as Hawk and his asshole friend, Lynch, left. He was too far away to hear any of their conversation. He only hoped Lynch could be kept under control.

Corillo swore he'd call the cops if Lynch made any trouble. He wasn't afraid of this scarred up bastard. He thought he could handle Lynch if he had to. He puffed up his burly Italian chest. But subconsciously, he knew he was shitting himself. He really didn't want to tangle with this potential killer.

* * *

The alcohol brought relief to Bo's central nervous system. His shaky hands still had some tremors, but at least he could hold the glass in one hand without sloshing it all over himself. He felt the cool air in the room now as it began to dry his clammy skin. He lit another cigarette.

His eyes returned to his empty glass as he played with the remaining ice cubes. He thought of himself as a beaten man. He had only one skill. Killing. He had learned so well in Nam. He was one of the best at survival in the hot green jungles of Southeast Asia. One of the worst in the concrete and metal jungle of Chicago.

If it hadn't been for Hawk Hogan, he would still be on the streets pandering and drinking cheap wine. Worse yet, dead--or better yet--dead! When Hogan found him, he was trying to stay warm in the West Side Catholic Charities dorm.

Michael came two or three times a week to see a few of his old cronies from the Chicago Stockyards. After the yards closed down, a lot of the young guys ended up on the streets. When Hogan saw these street people with no hope left, he began to help them rehabilitate themselves. Most of his efforts were in vain. When he took Bo by the arm that frigid January day in 1985 more than two years ago, a foot lashed out at him. Michael easily blocked the weak kick. Bo had wasted away to 125 pounds. The fighting weight his stocky five-foot eleven-inch frame needed edwas a good 195 pounds.

Bo remembered the morning they met. He was sleeping in an alley between two wino buddies. Their warmth had kept him alive through the night. But they were dead. He remembered shaking them and crying because they were both Nam vets. Good friends. He cradled them and talked to them. Just like he held his dying friends in the jungle--but they were dead--all dead!

He remembered covering the bodies with his coat, as if that would bring some last-second comfort. Then he stumbled onto the street looking for one of the homeless shelters. He was half frozen. The digital clock on the corner of Canal and Jackson read 6:37 a.m. The time switched off and -18º blinked on. He wished he had died with the other two lucky derelicts. He remembered leaning against a boarded-up building and puking green bile. He was bankrupt, physically, mentally, emotionally--and spiritually, if there was such a thing. He looked into the frigid air and screamed blasphemy to the Demon Creature who had created him. His scream echoed throughout the frozen city. Time slowed, making every step and thought an endless nightmare. Bo fell, sobbing as he tried to walk. He stumbled against pedestrians who pushed him away as if he were a leper. His feet and hands were numb and blue. The pain in his body was severe, but he was used to pain-- almost immune to it. The physical discomfort was nothing compared to the terror in his soul--and his need for a drink! He wanted to die. He prayed to die.

Bo remembered finding a rusty dinner knife in an dingy alley behind a Skid Row diner. He tried to cut his wrist, but his hands were frozen. He couldn't hold the knife. What irony, he remembered thinking, he couldn't save his friends' lives, and he wasn't able to kill himself. His mind dulled as he watched the knife drop in slow motion to the ground. It bounced on the frozen garbage as if laughing at him.

He didn't know how he ended up at the Catholic Charities Mission. That's where Hawk Hogan came into his life. That's when things began to change. The priest at the Mission had brought Michael to him. That same day Bo found himself at Saint Luke's Hospital. Michael had arranged for the best care and a private room.

When Bo awoke three days later, he had to face a grim realization. Acute frostbite had robbed him of some body parts. Three toes on his left foot and one on his right had been amputated. His hands, tucked between his legs while he slept, had been spared. A portion of his right ear had also been removed. Three operations and plastic surgery eventually made it appear fairly normal.

Strangely, Bo didn't miss the toes or the ear as much as he did a drink. In spite of massive shots of Valium and Vitamin B, the shakes and hallucinations persisted and jarred his soul. He thrashed in sweat-soaked sheets, and yelled and screamed for someone to get him a drink. Bo knew a drink was the only answer to what he was feeling. It did what nothing else could do every time he tried to dry out. The Valium, Thorazine, and the myriad of other drugs in his system did little to ease his misery.

He knew he had a high tolerance for pain. But because he was an alcoholic, his dosage of medication had to be quadrupled even to begin to quell his withdrawal. The dose for a normal person was ineffective on him. He wished the doctors knew this. They didn't. Bo felt as though every vein in his body was being ripped out. He had twisted and writhed underneath the heavy straps that restrained him. He felt and saw the jumbo leeches of Viet Nam crawling on his body. He remembered turning his head to one side and letting the tears gush from his eyes.

The shakes and hallucinations would eventually subside, but they would take their own patient course.

Hospitals were nothing new to Bo. He had been injured four times in his three-year stay in Viet Nam. Then he had his youth and an elusive purpose--working for a U.S. victory. He healed quickly.

When Michael found him, his youth was gone and he had no purpose. Bo came home to an ungrateful, apathetic country. Any talents he might have had before the war had been stripped away by the intense brainwashing he endured in the Special Forces kill-camp. Then, for three years, he did what he was conditioned to do--kill! He killed hundreds of the enemy, maybe thousands. His constant nightmares came from the numbers of women and children he had slaughtered. He had been used in a senseless war based on the lies and deceptions of self-serving, scum politicians.

Michael went often to the hospital. He would tell Bo that first the body had to be healed, then the mind, and then the spirit. He talked of life and living and tried to quell Bo's thoughts of death and dying.

Michael's gentle words calmed him. Bo could see the mysterious intensity and sincerity in his eyes. This man who had come from nowhere and saved his life. At first he thought Michael was some kind of preacher, but the man never mentioned God. He talked only about Nature, the sun and rain and wind, as a friend and healer. Like a poet. He talked a philosophy of peace, a philosophy of truth, and a philosophy of gratitude. Michael would tell Bo that he thought too much about the bad things that had happened in his life and too little of the good things that were about to happen. "Stay in the now" were his words every time he left Bo.

With red, watery eyes, Bo would verbally fight with Michael but the argument was always one sided. Hogan would just smile and listen to him as he spieled off the pathetic story of his worthless life. Then with a few gentle words, Michael would seem to ease the confusion that filtered through Bo's mind.

Bo remembered that after a few weeks he began to eat a little and feel better. He found himself looking forward to Michael's dialogues and simply enjoying the Irishman's wisdom. A good sleep always followed those friendly chats. Except for a few of his Viet Nam buddies, Michael was the only visitor he had in the hospital. Most of his friends were dead or in VA wards.

Now, as a glass of Wild Turkey slid across the table to him, he snapped out of his revery and looked up with disdain. He softened when he saw it was Michael who sat across from him.

* * *

Michael sat silently and looked into the ocean-blue eyes of his friend. He could tell he had been recalling the horrors of his life. That's why the drinks. Bo had thrown in the towel

again! Thank God his body was back up to 180 tough pounds. The vigorous daily workouts for the past year and a half had paid off.

Bo spoke first in the tone of a child ready to be scolded. "I suppose you're pissed off at me for drinking?"

Michael chose his words carefully. He spoke only of the positive. He wouldn't let him drift into remorse, guilt, or self pity. "I'm not pissed off, nor am I disappointed! Aren't alcoholics supposed to drink? Aren't you supposed to have a hard time psyching yourself on a daily basis to stay away from the poison?"

He stopped for a moment, leaned an elbow on the table and placed two fingers on his lips. He let them slowly tap as he thought. Then he lowered them and said casually, "Bo, if you want to drink, be my guest. I can't stop you! *You* have to stop you! And only *you* will. The question is when?" He leaned the other elbow on the table now. "What happened to Alcoholics Anonymous? I thought you were going to meetings?"

Bo crooked his head and made a guttural sound. "Ah! They're bullshit, Mike. They talk about God, and how good he is, and how he won't desert us, and how he's always there for us, and how we're not alone anymore!

"Fuck their God! He must spend all of his time in America with the rich people, because I couldn't find him in Nam or the alleys of Chicago."

Michael watched Bo take a healthy swig of his fresh drink. He looked at Michael with a scowl that quickly turned to sadness. "Joe Verdolski believed in God!" He took another sip of Wild Turkey. "I remember Joe and I were on point, one night in Nam. Joe used to wear a rosary around his neck along with his dog tags. He was a great guy and very religious. He stepped out of the way of a lot of bullets. Only that night it wasn't a bullet. It was a fucking rocket. One of those Russian Q-3, duel-ammo weapons. It blew the poor bastard all over the place. There couldn't have been more than five or six Cong shooting at us. I killed four of them and the others pulled back and became part of the jungle. When I found Verdolski, he was still alive...trying to put his guts back into his belly with the bloody stump of his blown off hand." Bo's head drooped as he ran his hand through his short, sandy hair. "His other hand clutched the rosary around his neck. He tried to say the 'Our Father,' but he choked on the blood in his throat.

"As I carried him three miles to our headquarters, I could hear something or someone following us through the jungle. I couldn't see anything. It was too dark, but I knew I was being followed. I expected to be blown away at any moment--I had to keep moving, Joe was dying. No way he could live after a hit like that. I tried to believe there was a chance, if I could only get him back to home base. The brush kept moving behind me--but no one shot. I remember wanting them to shoot...get it over with. Still nothing. Just the moving brush behind me.

"When we arrived at camp, I found out what was following us." Bo looked up at Michael with a dead, hopeless look in his eyes. "It was Joe's guts, Mike. Ten, maybe

fifteen feet of guts dragging behind us. That's what had spooked me! Joe Verdolski was dead. He still clutched the rosary."

Bo's face went sullen, and his red eyes starred into his drink. They stayed there for a long moment. Then he picked up the glass, sipped it, and began talking again. "You've got people at those AA meetings who haven't lost a goddamn thing in their life as far as I'm concerned. They cry because their wife is going to leave them, or their kids hate them, or they lost a nine-to-five job. All because of their drinking. Even the ones who say they've lost everything haven't lost shit! So, I say...FUCK THEM AND FUCK THEIR GOD!"

Michael sipped his scotch slowly. He thought he had heard all of Bo's stories, but evidently he hadn't. This was just one more horror story that the poor son of a bitch lived with.

Bo wasn't holding anything back. "Those people don't know the meaning of the word 'lose.' We would blow away villages full of people just because they were in our way. We were ordered to do it. Innocent people. If we didn't do it, the Viet Cong would. We'd walk through those smoldering villages and see what we had done. Old men and women burning and still moaning.

"Babies screaming as they lay next to a blown-apart mother. Children looking at us in a daze with only bloody stumps left for arms and legs. Their homes gone, their parents or children gone, their villages destroyed. The lucky ones were dead. We had a couple of crazies who would walk through the village and put a bullet in all the heads of those who were still living. They even shot the dogs, so the Cong couldn't eat them. I remember a little girl who was still alive. She was burned beyond recognition. She died as I carried her...I don't know how long I carried her...five hours, maybe more. Then I buried her near a stream."

He looked at Michael. His eyes had misted. "They weren't the enemy, Mike. WE were the enemy, in THEIR country, bringing them peace and freedom...while the real enemies were back in Washington. They sat around big tables at the Pentagon with world maps on the walls. They smoked their big cigars and tried to figure out how they could cover up their mistakes with believable lies. All they cared about was keeping their pompous jobs and getting more votes.

"Those people in Viet Nam...and us guys who killed them were the losers, Mike! Hell, we had nothing against them. I don't want to hear about the housewife who burned the pot roast because she was stewed, or the guy who wrecked his Mercedes and lost his license because he was drunk, or the guy who puked all over his boss's desk and lost his job. That's why I stopped going to AA meetings. They're all a bunch of crybabies who spout, '*The higher power won't abandon you...don't you abandon him*! Tell that bullshit to Joe Verdolski, and that little girl buried by a jungle stream in Cambodia."

Michael looked away. His heart ached for Bo. He knew pity would destroy him. Bo had to be with others who were filled with pain. He needed to talk about it. He turned

his attention back to Bo, and cut in before his friend sank too low. "There is more than one kind of war, Bo. The people in AA who tell you their story are at war with themselves. Just like you are. Just because they haven't seen and felt what you have doesn't mean they're not feeling pain. Do you put a barometer on pain? If a person passes a certain point, they're accepted by you. If they don't, they're candy-ass crybabies?"

Michael leaned forward, his dark eyes full of compassion and understanding. He felt the words begin to flow. "Bo, I have a sober friend in AA whose son was on drugs. The son killed himself by placing a shotgun in his mouth. He blew his head off in their basement. My friend's wife heard the explosion and went to investigate. She's now in Elgin State Hospital for the insane. She just sits, sucking her thumb all day, humming some far away tune--holding a rag doll while she rocks back and forth. Do you think my friend has been through any less than you? Do you accept him into your club of self pity because he has passed your self centered pain barometer test?"

Bo snapped his angry, mean eyes up at Michael and looked deep into his face. After a moment, Michael's gentleness took effect. Bo's clenched jaw muscles relaxed, but his nostrils still flared.

Michael continued. "Lynch, you have something to give to people. You've seen too much of life to keep it to yourself. Go help some poor son of a bitch who's sleeping in doorways and eating and drinking garbage all day. Help the guy who's wondering how **much** longer his hell on earth is going to curse him. Find the one in one hundred who really wants out of the rat hole they live in."

Michael waited for some sign of expression from Bo. It didn't come. He continued. "A little over two years ago you were one of those street people. I didn't get you better. You got yourself better. Deep inside of you something's pulling you to go on in life. Pick yourself up and pick up a few more poor bastards in the meantime. You've got it in you, Bo. I've seen you work in the pits. You're a natural competitor. The best thing about you is you gather the new guys around you. Guys who are struggling to make a buck, and you try to teach them what to watch out for and when to move."

He stared across the table at Bo's rugged face. He couldn't tell if Bo was listening, or if he was back in the jungle. A quick intake of air and Michael went on. "There are two AA meetings a week at the VA hospital. Those guys need you, Bo. And you need them. There are guys there, like your buddy Joe Verdolski, who they put back together. The only thing the doctors forgot was the heart. You can find their hearts, Bo. Give it your best shot! Here is a name and number to call." He reached for his wallet, pulled out a small, folded piece of yellow paper, and slid it across the table to Bo.

Bo looked blankly at the note, picked it up, and slipped it into his pocket.

Michael spoke again, choosing his words carefully. "Listen, Bo. You're on the upswing now, both financially and physically. You've become strong again, and you've paid me back almost half of the cash I loaned you for the membership to the Exchange. Except for your temper in the pits, you're a damn good broker. Now it's time to get your

spirit and mind healthy. The people in the VA and AA can do that for you. Don't let yourself slide backwards. Do what has to be done. Become a whole man again!"

After a while, Michael said, "Bo, I'm going to need your help on something. It might be dangerous!"

Bo frowned. The mention of "help" and "danger" had stirred his curiosity and enthusiasm. "What help? What danger?"

Michael had been thinking about Lynch all day. Not only about his problems, but also his fighting instincts. He was going to need all the help he could get to beat the unscrupulous bastards he was going after.

He wasn't sure how much danger he and his family were in, but he knew Bo Lynch would be a good watchdog. Who fit the bill better than a highly decorated ex-Special Forces commando who knew how to play the rough game of survival? If necessary--killing? He shuddered at the thought.

Out of respect for the warrior, he wanted to give him as much information as he could. Yet, he had to be careful not to give too much. He didn't want Lynch to get drunk and send out any alarms. Out of all the friends Michael had, Bo was the only man he could trust. He needed loyalty. He needed a friend who couldn't be bought, and with Bo loyalty was supreme. That was Bo's God-given tattoo. His loyalty. And that's what Michael needed now.

Bo insisted. "What danger?" He now leaned forward with his forearms on the table. Both hands surrounded his drink. His attention was total.

Michael's penetrating eyes scanned the dining area. Was anyone close by? Corillo was standing near the end of the bar drying a glass. His eyes caught Michael's, and he immediately turned for another glass. He pulled his chair closer to the booth and spoke softly. "I'm going after 'em again Bo. I'm going to try to bring the big boys down."

"What big boys? You mean the cheaters? Hell! That's a no-win situation!"

"Yeah, the cheaters. The big cheaters! All the way to the top of the Exchanges, Bo. The Senators, and the Congressmen, and the government people who have betrayed the customers who have invested in and trusted the integrity of the commodity industry."

Bo glanced over Michael's shoulder at the snoopy bartender. "You're crazy, Man. You tried it once and they buried you. You know I like a good fight, but this is insane. These guys are like the Viet Cong. They're invisible. You can see them working, but when the market closes there is no trace of anything. All that's left is financial casualties, dead clients. The bad guys escaped through a complicated maze.

"If you try to follow them, you're a dead man. They know more tricks than you and I will ever know. You have to wait for them to come back through the maze and catch them on your ground. Then maybe, just maybe, you've got a chance to nail a few of the bastards. I'm telling you, Mike, these guys are just like the Cong!"

He felt his eagerness grow. "Bo, I have help this time. Help that can cut off their supply lines--their way back through the maze."

Bo's lips twisted and he tapped his glass with his right index finger. "What help do you have, Mike?...Your old friend, Glassmann, and a few other radical honest brokers? Money won't stop these people. In the short time I've been here, I've seen their operation. You have some of the strongest men in the country stealing money every day from the asshole public. Investors just keep pumping cash into the pits hoping for the big score."

Bo leaned even closer and spoke in a whisper. "The commodity markets are the best game in the country for a crook. Over the years, you guys have created a monster. You've invited all the scum in the country--probably the world--to come to your little party each day and walk away with as much dirty lucre as they can carry--with no risk!"

Michael hesitated. Why not let Bo run out of conversation before he spoke further?

"And Mike, I'll tell you something else. If it wasn't for you, I'd probably be right in there stealing with the rest of them. Because it's so easy. I don't have your idealism. I'm not made of the same stuff as you. But I do have loyalty in this beat-up body. I'd never do anything to cross you."

Michael sat back and analyzed Bo. At least he had his attention. "Well, I'm going after them, and my big guns are bigger and stronger than Glassmann and a few honest brokers. But I'm going to need your help!"

Bo was quiet. He sat back in the booth and said, "You're nuts, Michael, but I'm all yours! I've never been in a fight when the odds were on my side. No reason to start now!"

They both finished their drinks. Michael looked into Bo's eyes. They were alert. The challenge had stimulated him. "I'm going to need your help in a few ways. First, I want you to compile all the names of the pit brokers who are stealing. They work in cliques from four to fourteen passing skim trades back and forth in the pits to throw off any possible paper trail or consistency in trading with one or two brokers. You know the game! Check out all the pits, get me the names of everybody you think smells, and the cliques or syndicates they trade with.

I want the S&P's, currencies, and Eurodollars mostly! They're your biggest volume pits, and shit can be lost forever in there. Make sure you check out the Jap yen pit. I hear there are some games going on over there with a few former S&P brokers. The volume of trading is picking up. Their action has been erratic as hell lately. Then, give me a reading on the Treasury bills, Swiss francs, Deutschemark and Canadian dollar."

Silence. Bo looked at the bar and waited for Corillo's eyes to meet his. Then he held up two fingers indicating two more drinks. Michael turned and saw a disgusted look come over Corillo's face as he slammed two tumblers on the bar.

"I don't like that prick, Mike. He always seems to be trying to hear what we're talking about."

"Who? Gino?"

"Just a feeling...but I think he's bad!"

Michael looked toward the bar again, then turned and said, "Come on, Bo. He's just a bartender who doesn't like his job."

"I sense more than that!" Bo wiped his forehead with the back of his hand and watched Michael. "You're a lunatic, and I'm a bigger one, Mike! I spent years trying to do something good for my country, trying to stay alive in the process, and all I got for it was spit and scorn. Now, you want me to join you in capturing another enemy. An enemy just as elusive as those in Nam. Shit, I might as well add America's financial institutions to my resume for trying to rid the U.S. of corruption. They are going to be after us both. You know that. Just when I started to like it here!"

Michael felt a chill run down his back. "Bo, they're already after me!"

Bo's eyebrows lowered. "What do you mean?"

"I've got somebody tailing me. They have been for awhile."

Bo's words came fast and hoarse. "Again, I say, what do you mean? You got a boogie man following you? I do too, ever since I left Nam."

Michael looked around again with suspicion. "Somebody put a transmitter on my car and knows everyplace I've been in the last few months. At least that's what I expect."

He saw that Bo was now more than concerned and didn't like what he heard. "Who do you think it is? It sounds like someone has already anticipated your move, Mike!"

Gino arrived with the drinks and roughly placed Bo's in front of him, spilling a little intentionally. He was more gentle with Mike's drink, even preceding it with a napkin, then he returned to the bar. "Well, Bo...that's the second part of my request."

He saw that Bo was relaxed now. He continued his story. "There has been a black limo on my tail for God knows how long. I just found out yesterday. Today I found out that my house phones are tapped. My sources discovered from plates on the limo that it is owned by a Canadian company, owned by a Bahamian company, which in turn is owned by an Aruba company. They're all offshore, so no prominent names can be linked to the limo.

"At first I thought it was the Italian laundry merchants. It may well be. But then, I thought, I haven't done anything yet to ruffle their feathers. Not to the extent that they would stake me out. I concluded that it might be the boys from Dublin. But many of them are friends of mine. I talked to Sean McGiven today, and he swears it's not his boys. They don't work that way. If they think they're going to have trouble, they don't waste gas and manpower to follow people. They merely blow them up. That was reassuring! I believe Sean. It's not the government people, because my complaint to the Exchanges didn't even mention them. So the only ones left are the big broker cliques in the pits. Peterson's men, the clandestine BOT, Brotherhood of Traders. They are basically the guys I went after two years ago. They are the brokers who have the most to lose. They're desperate, and they're the ones who threatened me before. But they work hand in hand with the Mafia, so I suspect it's one of those two groups."

He could see Bo was ignoring his drink. Michael continued. "I have government people watching the house for me, but their hands are tied as far as getting rid of the limo, or anybody else following me. They haven't broken any laws."

He paused to assemble his thoughts. "Don't you have a few friends you hang around with from Nam?"

"Sure," Bo said. "I know two guys in particular who came out like myself--all fucked up. Now they are getting along in society with part-time jobs."

Michael's eyebrows raised in question. "Can they be trusted?"

He knew at once that Bo had taken offense. "You're goddamn right they can be trusted. We backed each other up in Nam, and we do the same thing here. We're the only ones in our unit who came out semi-whole. Maybe I should rephrase that. We're the only guys who came out not completely destroyed. What's your plan, Mike?"

Michael unwrapped a stick of gum. He put it to his tongue and folded it accordion style as he pushed it into his mouth. Savoring the juice and compacting it to manageable size, he continued. "Well, I'm mainly concerned about the safety of my family. The people I now have watching the house live by strict rules and won't be aggressive unless something happens first. They follow the rules of 'law and order' and have taken an oath to do so. That does nothing but keep me on the defense. I want the offensive position!

"I have a two-bedroom coach-house on my property which we only use for storage and occasional guests. I'll spruce that up and you see if you can talk your boys into staying there. They can pose as gardeners or landscapers or painters, but in essence they will be keeping an eye on my family. One can act as a chauffeur for my wife and kids, and at night I want the grounds protected. You and I will spend the days together until this shit is over. I don't care how it's done, but I want the limo that's following me...eliminated. I don't want them in my backyard. They pose a serious threat to my family's safety, and to my peace of mind. I want them out of the picture. I'll pay your boys well. Tell them to buy any equipment they need. Tell them to keep a low profile. If there are any guns, keep them hidden."

Bo lit another Camel and pulled the half-filled ash tray closer. He looked at Michael quizzically. "Do you really think Peterson is dumb enough to make a move against you?"

"I don't know if it's Fats Peterson or Sal Ruzzo. And neither is dumb. They might be ugly, but they're not dumb. They both have to answer to Mob bosses, and they both think they are above the law because they have so much power. They make their own rules. I'm about the only guy who has had the balls to go up against them. As long as I'm on the street and gaining support in the pits, I'm a major threat. I'm surprised they haven't taken me out before now."

Bo took a drag and then a sip from his drink. He exhaled the smoke through his crooked nose into the drink. The smoke curled in circles as it came out of the glass as if

a piece of dry ice had been dropped into the drink. "I thought you were a peace-loving man, Michael. You surprise me with your talk of guns and killings."

He saw a cocky look on Bo's strong face. He kept his words low and patient. "I am peace loving, but I'm not as passive as my father was. His spiritual philosophy of life kept him calm and in control at all times. He could walk into a room of men ready to kill him, and thirty minutes later the doors would open with everybody smiling and patting my dad on the back agreeing with his ideas. He was a negotiator and accomplished his objectives with some type of spiritual understanding. It seemed to be contagious. I don't have the same tolerance for self-willed people as he did. I believe in the Oriental philosophy of protecting oneself. 'Don't hurt a man unless he's going to hurt you. Don't maim a man unless he's going to maim you, and don't kill a man unless he's going to kill you!'"

Michael looked into his glass as if searching for an answer. There were no more answers. He let his words sink in. Then he spoke. "Who are these buddies you intend to contact, Bo?"

A sardonic smile crossed Bo's face and with confident recall of Nam, he rattled off the names. " John 'Snake' Adams and Clarence 'Bear' O'Leary!"

Michael's sarcasm spewed forth. "That's just great. I can't wait to introduce them to Maria. 'Maria, honey. I'd like you to meet, Snake Adams and Bear O'Leary! Crazy Pete and Killer Kowalski couldn't make it." He saw his own smile reflected on Bo's face.

Still smiling, Bo said, "They can do the job, Mike. It'll be a piece of cake. Watching six acres on Lake Michigan will be a whole lot easier than half the jungle of Southeast Asia. I'll contact each of them tonight and give you an answer tomorrow."

"Do they still have the balls for this, Bo? You know a lot depends on their loyalty, alertness and proficiency."

Bo reassured him. "You can trust them with your life. They're proficient in all forms of warfare whether it's on the street or in the jungles. They seldom use their weapons to kill, but they're pros on weaponry. They have expertise from top to bottom. They know electronics, explosives, and mainly, they know how to smell the enemy. They know how to keep themselves and their friends alive!"

Michael felt relief wash over him. "Thanks, Bo. I love ya like a brother. I wouldn't ask you to do this if there was any other way."

"The feeling is mutual, Mike. Besides, I owe you! We all owe you! You've made a few friends without your knowledge. A lot of that money you gave me for the vets helped them out of some real jams. We don't forget our friends, Mike."

"You owe me nothing. Just be my friend, Bo!" Michael stood and Bo simultaneously slid out of the tufted leather booth. Michael reached over, took Bo's hand into his own, and held it firmly. "Take it easy, my friend, and get to an AA meeting before you lose it altogether."

He walked to the bar and asked Gino Corillo for the bill. Gino tallied the check and handed it to Michael. At the same time Gino gave Bo a sullen look. Mike signed the tab and turned to leave. He knew there was a real hatred between Lynch and Corillo, but there was nothing he could do about that. He kept walking.

* * *

Bo sat down for another ten minutes. As he finished his drink, he recalled the entire conversation, establishing his priorities. He was eager to act upon them.

He reached into his pocket and pulled out the yellow slip Michael had given him. He read the name, "Bill M. AA; VA Hospital, 384-8800." He tucked the paper back in his pocket, thinking he'd call him tomorrow. He had beaucoup work to do for now, and he wasn't finished drinking for the day. He pushed his empty glass away, rose to his feet, and walked over to the bar. He ordered one more double. In Gino's usual style, the drink was roughly sloshed in front of him. Again, no napkin.

Bo casually stated, "Gino, if you ever splash a drink in front of me again, you'll wish you'd never left Italy!"

Using the bar as a protector, Gino said, "If it wasn't for Hogan, I'd have your ass in jail, you son of a bitch."

Bo felt a swift stab of anger. "Yeah and if it wasn't for Hogan, I'd slam that fat, dago nose up your asshole, so when you get the sniffles you'd have to wipe your fat fucking ass."

Gino backed up and stomped to the other end of the bar.

Bo slammed his drink, placed his glass and a five dollar bill on the bar. Then he started to leave. As he stepped into the corridor, he hesitated a moment. Maybe it was just superstition, but he turned and walked back into the lounge. He saw Corillo on the phone. His left hand cupped the mouthpiece for privacy.

Gino's eyes looked up and around as he talked. At first he didn't notice Bo. Then, he immediately did a double take when Bo's menacing eyes focused on him. Pure panic stared back at him. Gino's face grew pale and Bo noticed him shaking. He replaced the phone. The conversation was probably not finished. He quickly resumed his stance at the bar sink.

Bo's instincts were correct. Even the bartender was in on it; he would use that to his advantage. He now knew where he was going to extract his first bit of information. Gino would be more than happy to reveal who he was spying for when Bo finished with him.

Satisfied that his instincts were still sharp and served him well, Bo turned and left. He went to a bank of phones around the corner, near the elevators and next to the tobacco counter. He dialed "Snake" Adams. He knew he'd be home--he was *always* home! The phone rang nine times, then it was picked up. There was no acknowledgement. There never

was. Bo knew Snake always waited for the caller to start the conversation. That gave him the option to listen or hang up. "Snake, this is Bo. We've got a job to do. Get a hold of Bear and meet me at the Black Potato Pub on the South Side at ten o'clock tonight."

He waited for a reply.

"Do you want me to bring any of my gear?" Snake asked.

"No...not tonight!"

Snake replied, "See you at ten." The phone went dead.

ELEVEN

Street Walk

Michael watched another Chicago spring day wink to a close. The cool breeze of early evening rushed off the lake and scurried tardy suburbanites to their waiting autos, buses, trains, and families.

He walked down Jackson Boulevard toward the Board of Trade and his office. He would stop briefly to call Andy Golden in Washington. He'd tell him of his plans to come to New York the following weekend. He'd stay as long as it took to get things moving.

Despite his friendship with Andy, he realized the FBI by and large was virtually bribe-proof, but they were no more ethical than the rest of government. The end justified the means. No matter who they hurt along the way, they had to get their indictments. They would lie, connive, smile, promise immunity, protection, and money. Whatever worked to accomplish their so called search for justice. They hid their deceptions behind the visible skirts of Lady Justice, but they weren't much different from the CIA. Andy was an exception. He hoped his Chicago agents were as honorable and professional.

Bo and his friends invaded his thoughts. His gut told him he'd be better off having them as guard dogs than the FBI. Bo played by his own rules. The law of survival and protection. His men wouldn't have to wait for the okay from a bureaucrat in Washington to stop the stormy trouble that was forming on the horizon of Michael's life. Bo could be trusted and wouldn't hesitate if he sensed trouble.

The strong wind cut at his face. He ignored its sharpness. Instead, he felt hot--heat brought on by the thoughts of his family being in danger, his car being tailed, his phones being bugged, and two close friends killed years earlier because of the aspirations of a few greedy men. A stalking anger intensified with every step he took. He billowed his chest and could feel a meanness enter his body. His face turned hard as his muscles contracted. His arms and chest felt tense. Oncoming pedestrians moved out of his way--this was unusual on Chicago streets. He subconsciously made a note of it. His mind felt like a raft with no paddle charging down a river of killer rapids. The raft seemed to be tipping into black, swirling waters that spoke to him. They were telling him he had entered a forbidden area!

He was letting himself be pulled into something he didn't know much about. Who could he count on for help? Should he go it alone? Should he trust the Government? They had no credibility. They were untrustworthy and unreliable. Besides, they had turned their backs on him before. Why wouldn't it happen again? Bo Lynch?...Maybe...just maybe, a group of jungle bandits could help him when the going got tough--they had the capability--

but Christ, he thought, they had so many of their own personal, psychological problems, how could Bo and his buddies be effective? What Bo had told Michael about Snake Adams was eerie. A jungle man who could "see a thousand yards" is what the Green Berets tagged men like Snake. Like a chameleon, he could blend into and become part of any environment. He could worm his way within feet of his prey without their knowing it. If his orders were to kill, he would kill. It'd be swift and clean. Usually without a sound. He used the weapons of the jungle, as all point men did. Bear O'Leary, a two-hundred-fifty pound black man, had dropped out of law school to join the Special Forces. He had the strength to pull a small oak tree from the ground, then break it over his knee. Bo told Michael not to be deceived by the man's size. Bear's quick mind could anticipate danger in the split second it took the enemy to react. Bear was more religious than Bo and Snake, so his kill rate was low in Nam. He killed when he had to, but usually his style was to inflict multiple broken bones and amputate the enemy's limbs and ears. He claimed broken bones and amputation served a better purpose than death. A man, whether he was yellow, black, or white, still had a mind and could heal. Even as a cripple, he could live again. Bo said O'Leary did kill a Cong who almost decapitated him with a machete. It was only because of extraordinary reflexes that Bear's head wasn't placed on a bamboo pole for other American soldiers to see. The machete had come from nowhere, Bo said. The jungle was dark, quiet, and as still as the graveyard it had become. Bear's sense of invisible motion made him pull his head back in time for the machete to catch only his cheek and jaw. The Cong was dead before the right side of Bear's face fell to his shoulder.

Bo had sharpened four tiny bamboo shoots and used them as make-shift stitches to hold Bear's face together until they made it back to their camp. Bear decapitated his enemy, then jammed the head on a bamboo pole for the Cong to see the next morning.

Jesus Christ! Michael thought as he lumbered down Jackson Boulevard. What the hell was he getting into? He was going to have a cast of characters who cut off heads, arms, legs, pricks, ears, and whatever else the enemy had hanging out of their pants, guarding his family. Bo said all of them were proficient in the martial arts. Although experts with weapons and explosives, they preferred to fight up close. Clean, fast, and quiet. Wouldn't wake the neighbors! Knives, hands, and feet were their main weapons.

Fuck me! Michael mumbled to himself. He had seen Bo in action, and that was when he was out of shape. He had never seen faster feet or hands in his life. Bo's rugged face told his story. A nose that had been repeatedly broken. A thick scar that cut into his left eyebrow, making his eyelid droop slightly and giving his deep blue eyes a constant suspicious look. Other smaller scars lined his face and his short, butch haircut made him look like a Marine poster. He had a thick neck, wide shoulders, powerful arms, and a tapered waist. His jaw continually tightened. Michael had never seen the man smile. He had, however, seen him cry!

He breathed deeply as he walked through the crowded street. Anger continued to heat his body. He had placed *himself* in this position. There was no one else to blame. Yet

he felt like striking out at something or someone. A week ago he was a free man who worked hard. He made good money, and he came home every evening to a loving family. He thought he was a free man. He wasn't. Some sons of bitches had taken his privacy and freedom away by spying on him for God knows how long. His steps fell hard as he pushed others out of his path. He felt light-headed and dizzy.

His anger grew stronger as he forged his way through the emotionless faces and dead eyes of the rushing suburbanites. They reminded him of a group of science fiction machines conditioned to do the same things.

The scene in his mind shifted to his family. If anything happened to them he'd be devastated. Michael knew that would put him over the edge and that the power of evil would subdue his philosophy of truth, peace, and honesty he had been taught to hold so sacred. But he would have justice, the same kind Bo and his friends fostered. The thought strengthened him. He would injure--if he had to; he would kill--if he had to! He felt a battle in his soul between his father's plea for peace through negotiations and his grandfather's vehement demand for peace through violence.

Son of a bitch! His mind was confused. Perplexing thoughts fouled it. His senses were being bombarded with cold, black clouds and hot, white clouds, forming electricity and fury, like the beginnings of a fierce thunderstorm. His muscles tightened. An oncoming man in a shit-brown suit headed directly toward him. The man's eyes were down, reading a folded newspaper. Michael's eyes trained on the newspaper. Was it concealing a gun or a knife? Michael's paranoia worked overtime. The man came on fast. Neither one moved. The man in the grunt suit slammed into Michael's chest and went sprawling. Michael kept walking. He felt like running. The pale Chicago faces of winter were a blur as they hurried past him.

"Hey, watch where you're going, Buster!" the man hollered.

"FUCK YOU!" Michael snapped in his rage.

The thought of the black limo flicked through his mind. He slowed, half turned, and glanced back at the figure on the sidewalk. His fear gone, he was ready to attack. People carelessly stepping around and over the prostrate man as he groveled to retrieve the newspaper that had been caught by the rushing wind and by now had become part of Chicago's trash.

Michael saw that the man was having a hard time getting to his feet. Passersby jostled and pushed him without conscience. Now, Michael turned and faced him.

The man looked frustrated. He glanced up at Michael. His eyes were angry, but also old and tired and sad. Michael's shoulders sagged. He had taken out his aggression on the wrong person.

He turned and pushed his way back to the helpless old form still being knocked around by insensitive commuters. He bulled the people out of the way as he did in the trading pits when he was after a broker he caught cheating. "Son of a bitch, either help the man or get the fuck out of the way!" he shouted with venomous authority.

One well-dressed man Michael had pushed out of the way from stepping over the old guy turned and walked back with an aggressive stalk. Michael's face tightened in anger. His eyes widened, and he felt a meanness he knew would turn to physical hostility if the stranger made one wrong move or dared to say one wrong word. The man must have sensed this. Abruptly he turned, cursed, and stomped on his way.

Michael reached down and gently cupped the old man's arm. He felt him resist. He strengthened his grip and pulled the man to his feet.

The eyes he looked into had lost their anger, but not their sadness. Michael felt like a real jerk. Hawk Hogan had just knocked down one of the street people. He had done it intentionally. What the hell was the matter with him? Was he losing his mind?

The old man had colored his gray hair with cheap brown dye that almost matched his worn, wrinkled, buttonless suit. His shoes were old and held together with broken, knotted laces. From a distance, and in Michael's sorry state of mind, the old man had looked much younger.

He released the wrist-thin arm and looked at the deformed arthritic hands. He stared at the stooped, tired body, and then at his sad, scared eyes. He reached for one of the gnarled hands and squeezed it gently. The man tried to pull away and began to brush off his soiled suit with his free hand.

"What's your name?" He asked with embarrassment and regret.

The man fidgeted before answering, not sure who was holding his hand--probably, Michael thought, not sure if he was going to be knocked down again. "You're a bully, Mister Big Shot! My name is Homer--Homer Jones. Not that it's any of your business!"

Michael was filled with remorse. He was considered by many a humanist, not an insensitive bully who pushed people around. "Well...Homer...uh...I am terribly sorry for hurting you. I guess I wasn't watching where I was going. Please excuse my stupidity!"

Homer looked at Michael, then lowered his head and continued to brush at his suit. "You did not hurt me. I've been knocked down before." His eyes scanned the sidewalk around him. "I am sorry I lost my paper, though!"

Michael heard intelligence and hurt pride in the response. He held Homer by his bony shoulders. "You didn't lose your paper. I'll buy you another one!"

Homer spoke with pride and conviction. "That won't be necessary!"

More pride than indignation, Michael thought. He put his arm around him anyway and walked over to a coin paper machine. He slipped a quarter into the slot and extracted a Chicago *Tribune*. He placed it under Homer's arm. "Where do you live, Homer?"

The tarnished man looked at Michael's expensive clothes and answered with hesitation, "I live at the Nickel Bag Hotel on Madison Street, sir!"

Michael knew the Nickel Bag was a dollar-a-night flop house, just short of a dirty doorway. "What kind of work do you do?"

Homer's left hand toyed with the newspaper under his other arm. "Oh...just...things. I just...work around. Here and there. Doing things, odd jobs that

nobody else wants to do. I used to be an accountant and a teacher. Now I just do what I can to make enough for a room and an occasional bottle of wine."

Michael knew he was talking with an educated man.

Homer's eyes glistened with pride when he added, "I taught accounting, philosophy, and psychology at the University of Chicago for eighteen years!"

Michael studied him and was impressed. He wondered if this was the truth. "You must have your doctorate degree then?"

Homer's chin rose and he spoke with self-esteem. "I'm Doctor Jones. I was President of the University of Chicago."

Michael's eyes wrinkled, and he felt a sudden interest. "What happened?"

Homer's pride faded; his face was death still. "Things happen...in a man's life...things that change the course he had originally charted!"

That's no shit, Michael thought. "Do you have a family?"

He spoke quietly. "I used to."

"What happened? I mean...I don't mean to pry, but..."

Homer cut Michael short. "Things happen. Unforeseen things, as I mentioned.

Michael couldn't help staring at the desolate face that less than five minutes ago he was ready to pummel.

A real amateur asshole. How did he expect to go after his enemies when he couldn't even walk down a crowded street without getting paranoid? He was a professional pit broker. But he sure wasn't a pro when it came to street savvy.

He realized more than ever that he needed a clear mind and cool temper if he was going to be counted among the living at the end of the contest. He had to sharpen his senses and his wits. Could he be on the streets what he was in the pits? If so, he would be ready for his adversaries. He couldn't let what happened to Doctor Homer Jones happen again. He could end up dead, or worse--kill an innocent man!

Bo and his friends could teach him the art of survival in the concrete jungle. The FBI could show him a few things about investigation. He'd learn to screen the streets and highways for intruders. He'd learn what to do legally. He already knew what to do illegally if he had to.

When he went to Washington, he would make some tradeoffs for his information. He would teach the Feds market procedures and show them the crooked schemes being used by brokers to skim money. He would demand that the Feds teach him their techniques. He had to learn to sense and spot real danger! But--how would he handle powerful, political men? The men who literally controlled the country?

His father was a master at dealing with powerful men, and in his calm, patient manner, he usually came out of negotiations with what he wanted. Michael hoped he had some of his father's savvy. Had any rubbed off on him? Or was it his grandfather speaking to him? If the Feds thought they were going to control the Chicago sting operation, they didn't know Hawk Hogan very well. He would soon know who in Washington he was

dealing with. One thing was clear. He had to control things in a way that would elude the Feds.

As the thought of the FBI filtered through his mind, Michael wondered where his back-up was. Andy had guaranteed there would be a man with him at all times. He looked over Homer's shoulders, sharpened his eyes, his composure regained. He saw nothing.

People walked around the two of them as they stood by the newspaper machines. He watched those walking in his direction but saw nothing unusual. He then swept the other side of the street looking for a watching figure or somebody just standing reading a newspaper. His senses were returning. He could feel eyes watching him, but saw nothing-- or did he?

In one of the doorways of the telephone company he noticed a lone figure looking in his direction. A workman's yellow hard hat shielded his face.

He felt a gust of wind bite his cheeks and ruffle his hair. His attention returned to Homer Jones. "How is your cash situation, Homer? I mean, do you have enough to get along for a few days?"

Homer swayed a bit. "I'll be okay. I have enough for a room tonight and maybe some food or wine."

Michael reached into his pocket and pulled out a wad of bills. He peeled off five twenties and cupped them in Homer's hand. "Doctor Jones, you get yourself a good meal and maybe even a nice place to sleep tonight. Then he handed him one of his business cards. "I'm giving you this because I may have some work for you. Stop in my office. It's two blocks down the street in the Board of Trade Building. My suite number is on the card. Just ask for Margaret. She will direct you."

Michael saw Homer looking at the five twenties in astonishment. His eyes were wet when he looked up. His pride was gone. "I haven't had this kind of money in my hands in over twenty years. Thank you, mister!"

"My name is Michael Hogan. I'll see that everything works out for you if you come to see me. And again, I'm very sorry for being so rough with you before."

A half-smile inched its way onto Homer's face. "Oh, that's okay, Mr. Hogan. I'll stop in early tomorrow morning!"

Michael grinned. "Great. Margaret will be expecting you." Michael gave Homer a brief hug, as he glanced back across the street where the man in the yellow hard hat had been. The doorway was now empty.

"See you later, Homer!"

"Yes, sir! I will *certainly* see you tomorrow, Mr. Hogan."

Michael pivoted and headed east again. He had turned a bad scene into one that would work out for both of them. Even though he still felt ashamed and humiliated, he had rectified the situation. His mind began to wander again.

TWELVE

Bar Talk

Michael quickened his pace. He thought the encounter with Dr. Homer Jones had taught him a lesson. It cleared his mind. He wouldn't overreact again. He shook his head, trying to relieve it of negative thoughts.

Maria now assumed a prominent place in his memory. Her face. He marveled at her. She was intelligent, perceptive, strong, and amorous. After twenty years she was as fine a bed mate as any married man could wish for.

Michael's loins tightened with the thought of their love-making. He thought of her naked body. He thought of their teasing and toying with each other on their silk sheets. She would soothe his daily stress away with her soft hands. Even after six children she maintained the body of a young woman. Her image remained in his mind as he walked into the harsh, refreshing wind.

Under Maria's beautiful facade was a strong woman. A fearless woman. Her Sicilian blood could be ruthless if anybody threatened her or her family. Maria was dealing with Michael's precarious involvement very casually. She supported him in his quest for justice at the Exchanges, but he knew it wasn't for the sake of honor. She wanted revenge for the injustice and the tarnished name the "big boys" at the Exchanges had given the Hogan family a few years earlier. He saw hatred in her eyes every time the subject surfaced. She did not want the police involved. She didn't trust them. She knew they could be bought too easily. Maria was even reluctant to have the FBI around. This was a family matter. They could take care of themselves. At any cost! Michael knew her philosophy was that of the Santinis. Nobody lasted long if they messed with the Family!

As he stepped from the curb at Wells Street, a cab honked angrily. He lunged back as it sped by, only inches from him. The driver hollered something in Spanish. He was going to give the cabby the finger and his own obscenities but he remembered Homer. Michael had made a fool of himself once today. That was enough! He was pleased that his rational faculties had returned.

While he waited for the light, he wondered if he was being followed. His eyes sharpened as he looked for a yellow hard hat. Nothing but bobbing heads. Shit! he thought--he wasn't a pro at this cat-and-mouse game. He continued to search for his own satisfaction, but saw nothing unusual.

Andy had told him he'd have a Fed with him at all times. Where the hell was he?

As the light turned green, the crowd that had gathered on the curb hustled across Wells Street, propelling Michael along with them. His thoughts inexorably returned to the

95

FBI sting he knew would be inevitable. If the truth surfaced and the Feds found out how widespread the skimming and cheating were, the Exchanges would virtually be destroyed. Maybe not at first, but Michael bet that within five years the whole concept of trading commodities would be computerized. The pit brokers would serve no purpose. Memberships would have no value, because everybody would be compelled to trade through a computer. That would eliminate most human error and greed. The buyers and sellers would get a fair fill on their orders. The archaic, Open-Outcry system would be history!

One thing for sure, it would fuck up the liquidity of the market. There was always a buyer or seller with the present system because there were hundreds of brokers in each pit trading for their own accounts. Their trades made up for much of the volume in a given day. Take away those men, and any sizable purchase or sale would take forever through a computer. Maybe! What a can of worms!

There were already rumblings on the street about bringing the Securities and Exchange Commission into the commodity industry. The watchdog was coming. But Michael knew that would only make stealing more sophisticated. They were the governing body overseeing the stock Exchanges, and the cheating on those Exchanges was as prominent, or worse, than in Chicago!

Yes, the idea of computer trading was a given. With the computer age at hand, and with a shove from the Feds, the commodity Exchanges would be forced to implement changes. What a pity that a few greedy bastards could bring an end to such a fabulous industry.

Michael reached the Board of Trade Building and decided he'd call Andy in the morning. Instead he'd go around the corner to the Bull and the Bear Lounge for a drink.

He stopped in front of glass doors brandishing the Exchange logo and looked around. Was he being watched? This time he wasn't going to dismiss the idea to paranoia! He wanted to satisfy his instincts. He would watch from inside the building.

He slid through the heavy glass turnstile doors and immediately approached the marble stairs. They were on the right side of the large atrium foyer, which led to the second floor. He would be able to get a good look at the swinging doors from a mid-landing vantage point. He wished he had a little experience in this spy business. This time of day, most people were leaving the building. He knew the two secretaries who came pushing through the doors, jabbering and laughing with each other. They worked for the Exchange in the executive offices.

A limping bag lady walked through next, stopping at the rubbish container, looking for a possible treasure hidden deep among the empty styrofoam coffee cups and the newspapers. She pulled out a small discarded hand calculator. It had probably run its course or had dead batteries. She placed her find into a large paper bag and proceeded down the hall to the south exit.

The security guard approached her halfway down the hall and ushered her the rest of the way to the other exit. Poor old gal, Michael thought. As with Homer, he wondered what her story was.

His attention returned to the Jackson Street entrance. A few businessmen. A lone broker from the corn pit. Three from the wheat pit, all laughing loudly and half drunk. Nothing else unusual! He was about to leave his position when a lone construction worker with a black lunch box and yellow hard hat entered. Hesitating a few steps inside the door, he scanned the foyer. As he directed his eyes up the stairs, Michael stepped back deeper into the shadows of a large column and froze.

The medium-sized man moved over to the tobacco counter and bought what looked like a candy bar and a pack of cigarettes. He was too clean to have been working on construction. His shoes looked new, with no sign of concrete powder. He left the tobacco stand and headed up the hall, eyes straight ahead.

Michael watched him disappear amid the crowd. He returned to his watchful stance. Relieved that he saw no one else suspicious, he left his position. But the construction worker did not leave his thoughts.

It certainly wasn't unusual to see guys in the building carrying lunch boxes and wearing hard hats, with all the construction going on not only in the Board of Trade Building but also in the buildings around the Exchange.

The lunch box could have contained the remains of a bologna sandwich or a thirty-eight revolver--but new construction shoes?

Maybe he was just a new worker. Michael's stomach did flip-flops not knowing if the man was just a man, an FBI agent, or someone out to do him harm. He only semi-dismissed the thought and headed for the Bull and the Bear, where he'd have that drink he'd been thinking about. It would quiet his nerves.

He walked out the side door and crossed the narrow street to the tavern, where he knew he would see some friendly faces. He hoped his tension would ease.

The bar teemed with activity and had the familiar stench of cigarette smoke and stale booze. It was dim inside and outside. He stood for a moment to let his eyes adjust.

There was the usual hum of activity and gaiety. Most of the boys had been here since the market closed hours ago, so the laughter, jokes, and market stories were being expelled at a high intoxicated pitch. The song being played was Bobby Darren's "Mack the Knife." He flinched. How appropriate, he thought!

His eyes fell on Jimmy Palotos and Allen Cohn at the end of the bar, two broker friends who worked his orders in the wheat pit.

As he wended his way through the pathless throng, many of the patrons greeted him gregariously with pats on the back: "How ya doin', Hawk?" "How they hangin', Mike?" "Hey, Hogan. Have a drink?"

He acknowledged their greetings with joking words of approval, continuing through the packed bodies, making his own path. When he finally reached them, he slid

onto a stool next to Jimmy. "Hi, guys. Room here for an Irishman?" Allen waved to the bartender, and seconds later, a large Black Label scotch materialized in Michael's hand.

He held the drink eye level and nodded his thanks, then toasted his friends. They all clinked glasses and drank heartily. Michael could see that Allen was getting very drunk. He must have been drinking since the market closed. Maybe earlier.

At Michael's present location, at the end of the bar, he could not only talk to his friends face to face, but also could see the activity of the whole bar. Nothing was behind him but the waitress service station and the kitchen. The dining room, off to the left, overflowed with brokers. Some eating, some playing gin rummy and pitch. Others playing liar's poker and still others just telling lies and 'can you top this?' stories.

Jimmy Palotos was a rotund man, one of those people who looked as if his extra fifty pounds belonged on his big frame. Thick, dark eyebrows nearly covered his large, brown eyes. His strong, Mediterranean face was already beginning to darken further from the sun during his early spring golf games with Allen Cohn.

Michael knew that expensive tastes ran rampant in both Jimmy and his wife, Kathy. Under their present financial circumstances, they could not afford them. A propensity for gambling propelled him into some deep shit with Karl Peterson, a common thief and leader of the biggest broker scam groups on both Exchanges. It was no secret among the brokers that Michael and Karl "Fat Man" Peterson detested each other. Michael knew the feeling among his peers was that someday there would be a showdown between the two. But when?

Jimmy's membership at the Chicago Board of Trade had been financed by Peterson five years earlier. Two hundred seventy-two thousand at twenty-five per cent interest, plus an additional fifty per cent of all of Palotos' brokerage income for the favor.

Jimmy had signed what Michael voiced was an extortion agreement for ten years with the unscrupulous Peterson.

At one time, Peterson had taken title to Palotos' car and his wife's diamond ring in exchange for two months' back payments on the membership. When Michael would complain to Jimmy about the scam, Jimmy would always tell him to stay out of it, saying he was still making more money than he could in his father's restaurant business, despite the bad deal!

A thick, red scar ran from the middle of Jimmy's lower lip to the tip of his chin. Two of Peterson's henchmen had roughed him up, kicked the shit out of his insides, and split his chin open with a pair of brass knuckles. Seventeen stitches had closed the wound. That was when the not-so-golden Greek offered his car and his wife's diamond for payment of his debt. Michael felt his body grow hot with the thought of the Fat Man.

He recalled numerous conversations with Jimmy suggesting he go to the police and voice his objection. He said he wasn't going to object. They had threatened to do the same thing to his wife if he brought the issue to anybody's attention. Jimmy's fear of the fat-ass Peterson and the entire obnoxious scene infuriated Michael.

He remembered confronting Peterson in the trading floor washroom shortly after the incident. Michael told him if the Greek wouldn't protect himself, he would take the matter into his own hands, one way or another. He would penetrate Peterson's diabolic power with the Exchanges and see that the "lard-faced piece of garbage" was brought out into the open. The trading membership would see what kind of scum they had elected to the Board of Governors.

He had lost his temper with the Fat Man and slammed him up against one of the many hand dryers in the washroom. Fat was the only thing that kept him from breaking a few ribs. Peterson was a bully but helpless without his strong-armed men. Michael let the son of a bitch slide to the floor. Then he kicked him in the face. As he walked back to the trading floor, he heard the threats that resonated off the tile walls behind him from the subhuman clump of cheap shit. The hair on the back of Hawk Hogan's neck bristled at the thought of this piece of human trash.

Karl Peterson and his band of crooks had been the main thrust of Michael's complaint to the Exchanges a few years earlier. In his career, Peterson, had bought and cheated his way all the way up the ladder to the executive branches of both Exchanges. He had the power to overthrow Michael's allegations.

Peterson had threatened the Board of Governors. If he went down for skimming, he would take the whole board with him. Most of them were involved with kickbacks, not only from Peterson but from a great number of their own cliques on the trading floors. The Board of Governors were afraid of the German-Swede and the harm he could inflict on them all. Their attention was forced back on Michael.

He remembered how the executive committees from both Exchanges combined efforts. They came down on Michael's company in full force. They brought in the Exchange examiners to audit Michael's books and discovered insignificant, minor violations. They prosecuted with heavy fines and suspensions from trading and made sure all the major newspapers got wind of the phony atrocities. Michael's ire was up, and he promised retribution.

Peterson told Hogan that if he even got word of any more trouble from the sanctimonious Irishman, he'd see that he ended up in a pine box. Michael told him he could count on it, and while he was at it, to order a piano crate for his own shit-filled body.

The incident had a definite effect on the membership of both Exchanges. There was a noticeable split in the brokers' loyalties. New alliances were formed. Some were public, most were secret. The cheaters and pawns sided with the Fat Man's group, mainly out of fear rather than principle. The majority sided with Hogan, but they didn't have the power to fight the heads of the Exchanges. So they all just waited for Michael to make the first move. Now he was about to make it. He simply told his followers to be patient--the right time would present itself to nail all of the greedy bastards. Michael thought to himself with satisfaction, "It's curtain time, boys!"

He believed that because of the incident with Peterson and his physical threats, it was probably he or Ruzzo who was following him and depriving him of his precious privacy. But, that would change shortly--with Bo Lynch on his side. If Peterson wanted war, war it would be!

Now he found Jimmy sitting quietly, peeling off the label from a Miller Lite beer bottle.

Michael opened the conversation, "You okay, Jim?"

Jimmy's face tightened. "Yeah, just had a bad day in the market!"

Michael persisted. "How much?"

Jimmy hesitated, "I lost eighteen thousand!"

"How much?" Michael probed again.

The face went limp with discouragement. "Ah fuck, I lost forty grand. And I'm behind again in payments to the Fat Man."

Michael was determined to keep his temper. "Jim, you have to get away from that loan shark or he's liable to hurt you bad. You're in a blind alley, and you can't win with Fat Man. Next year the interest on your loan goes to thirty per cent, and the year after to thirty-five per cent. You can't pay him now! What are you going to do when the prick raises his rates?"

Jimmy's head hung low. "I guess I'm just going to have to sell my membership and pay the piper!"

Michael screwed up his face and shook his head. "Jim, I've read your contract with Peterson. The only way this will be terminated is if you are fired by him, or you die, or you become mentally ill. He's got you by the balls."

The Greek lit a cigarette, leaned back on his bar stool, and nearly whispered. "Those final alternatives would be welcomed right now."

Michael stood, removed his sport coat, and folded it neatly over the back of his stool. Then he loosened his tie and rolled up his sleeves. "How much are you into him for this time, Jimmy?"

Jimmy closed his eyes and sighed. "The debt is nearly ninety thousand and climbing. I'm thirty days late with my membership payment, and today's fiasco will surely bring his boys after me again. My dad said he'd take out another mortgage on the restaurant. He thinks he can get me sixty thousand, but then the fucker doesn't just own me, he owns my father too!"

"Bullshit, Jimmy!" Michael blurted. He was angry again and he couldn't help it. "You're not going to give that motherfucker a goddamn thing. I'll talk to the slime bag and make him an offer for your debt. We've got enough criminal activity at the Exchange without adding extortion and loan sharking!"

Palotos objected, "He's connected to the mob, Mike, and they don't just let you go once they have you. They're like an octopus."

Michael slammed his fist down on the bar, drawing attention from nearby drinkers and waking up Allen, who was dozing next to Jimmy. "Listen, you asshole, you're going to end up dead if this shit doesn't stop. Next week you start trading through my company. The Fat Man will take everything from you, including your dignity. When you're in so deep, he'll propose a deal to you to wipe out your debt. And the deal will be crooked. If you stay with him, you'll end up dead or in prison. Goddammit, Jimmy, you're through kissing the Fat Man's ass!"

Jimmy looked vacant, spent, all his emotions drained away. "There is nothing you can do, Mike. I'm stuck--and I know it." Another long drag, as if it were his last, and he crushed the cigarette into the amber ash tray in front of him.

Although Michael liked wealth, he was not one to follow the insensitive rules for survival of the richest. "You hang in there for a few more days, and play dumb. That shouldn't be too hard for you!" Michael couldn't resist the slam. "If you are confronted, tell them anything they want to hear. Just give me enough time to put my plan into motion. A few days, a week at the most!"

Jimmy's spirit was infinitely sorrowful. "I don't know, Mike. I..."

Anger bubbled in Michael. "That's right Jimmy. You don't know shit! You can't see the forest through the trees, or you would have defended yourself a long time ago. Why are you so afraid of the son of a bitch?"

Jimmy grabbed his beer and took a long gulp looking for courage. "You're right. I'm afraid of the prick. That rat faced bastard, Gunter Schmidt, who worked me over last year, said he'd cut off my fingers--and I wouldn't be able to trade anymore if I didn't conform to Peterson's rules. And then he said he'd do the same thing to my wife! You'd be afraid too, Mike!"

Disgust lurked beneath Michael's words. "Well, I'm not! I'm taking over from here. I don't want to hear another word about your pussy attitude toward your personal well being. This shit has to stop, and it's going to stop now!"

Michael swiveled on his stool and faced the dining room. The tightness had returned to his face, and heat once more filtered through his body. He closed his eyes. The heat began to recede as quickly as it had entered his being. He had caught it in time. He knew he had to remain cool, or he'd be good for nothing. His plans had to be based on intelligence and deception, not emotion.

Allen Cohn was oblivious to the discussion taking place. He was, however, well aware of his empty glass that he waved to the bartender for another round of drinks.

Michael turned, grabbed his tumbler of scotch, and took a long swallow. He grimaced, set the glass on the bar, then turned back toward the loud, dead-end conversations and drugged gaiety that filled the bar. He had seen the same faces a hundred times before. Same time. Same place. Same shallow conversations.

He was about to turn back to his drink for a less intense conversation with Jimmy, when he spotted three men seated at a table in the far corner of the dining room. He

squinted through the smoke. A big man, another with the face and body of a rodent, Gunter Schmidt, and a third whose face was lost in shadows of the blue haze. Michael knew who he was. The Albino, Dieter Wolf. They were in his direct line of vision when the bobbing and swerving bodies would momentarily open up an alley of sight.

Karl Peterson was stuffing something into his fat mouth. It appeared as if the slob was talking while he ate and the other two were nodding their loyal approval.

Schmidt looked up through the crowd in Michael's direction. Their eyes met. Everything seemed to stand still. Even with the lack of light and heavy smoke Michael could see icy, empty meanness staring back at him, like a rat's eyes in a dark alley.

Michael remained cool and slowly brought his fist to eye level. He outstretched his arm, lifted his thumb from his fist, and pointed it at the ugly visage that seemed mesmerized by the hypnotic hand action. The thumb pointed high in the air, then abruptly turned toward the floor and headed south in a blur. "Thumbs down, motherfucker. The Roman Empire's death penalty!" Michael said in a whisper, directing his vendetta toward the beady eyes. "Innocent or guilty, you're a dead man!" He knew the ugly face of the sadist, Gunter Schmidt.

The rodent face twitched, as if smelling bad cheese, and nervously turned his attention back to the Fat Man.

Michael's eyes remained glued to the threesome. Schmidt leaned toward Peterson's fat face and said something. The fat, blond head slowly turned, his stare cutting through the crowd until he caught Michael's penetration. The features on Peterson's face twisted into a maddening leer as his eyes flashed out a threat to Michael.

Hawk Hogan decided to dispense with etiquette. He raised his middle finger to the Fat Man, then mouthed a "fuck you!" Peterson turned crimson with anger. Michael smiled. He had made his relentless point once again to the goddamn psycho. Peterson turned back to food. Michael hoped he had ruined his appetite.

After a few more drinks, and some light conversation with Jimmy and Allen, Michael saw that it was almost nine o'clock. He decided to call it quits for the day.

He finished the remainder of his fifth drink. Now, very much relaxed, but not drunk, he said, "I'll see you boys in the morning." He hooked his index finger in the neck of his jacket, flung it over his shoulder, and walked out.

A slurred, "See ya later, Mike," came from Allen.

Jimmy turned to Michael. "Hey Mike, try not to get me killed, will ya?"

He smiled and said, "Me first, Jimmy. I'll try to keep me alive, then I'll work on you!" He patted Jimmy on the back. "Don't worry, Pal, things are about to change around here for the better!" Michael left through the side glass doors leading to the lobby. His car was housed in the downstairs garage of the same building.

* * *

Sixty seconds later the two men with Peterson left their seats and followed Michael through the glass doors to the garage. They were unnoticed by all the patrons except one man who was sitting seventy feet away at the far end of the bar.

Within a minute the glass doors swung open again; this time a construction worker wearing a yellow hard hat, and new, ankle-high work boots and carrying a black lunch box left the bar. He hesitated in the empty lobby, looked in both directions, and walked quickly toward the stairs leading to the lower level parking area.

THIRTEEN

Pete Lewis: FBI

Pete Lewis, FBI agent, took a seat near the front door in the corner of the bar, his back to the wall so he could get an overall view of the entire establishment and its jubilant patrons. He had disguised himself in construction clothes to fit into Chicago street life.

The Bull and the Bear Pub was dim and noisy. An elaborate jukebox, which looked fresh out of Star Wars, blasted Simon and Garfunkel's song "Sound of Silence" in futile competition with the surrounding melee. The song's message was falling on deaf ears. A bar of wagging, booze-swelled tongues brought truth to the words:

> *"People talking without speaking, people hearing without*
> *listening..."*

So this was the daily routine of these nouveau-riche youths who a short time ago were selling linoleum, shoes, air conditioning, and working at department stores. They had found employment where the tap spewed gold nuggets all day long!

> *"Hear my words that I might teach you. Take my arms*
> *that I might reach you. But my words like silent*
> *raindrops fell, and echoed in the walls of silence."*

He took off his hard hat, leaned both elbows on the bar, and rubbed his altar-boy face with both hands. He raised his rather short, powerful frame close to the bar and ordered a draft beer. Pete Lewis was a man with a fiercely competitive and intense spirit. He thought that his young, fresh face worked to his advantage. He didn't look like a cop, so it was easier for him to get close to an adversary, making his assault more accurate and lethal than that of his rough-hewn peers.

His sandy hair was neat but much longer than FBI regulation. A byproduct of years of working undercover in New York. He reached into the pocket of his black windbreaker for a handkerchief to wipe the pug nose on his face, which listed slightly to the left. It had been broken numerous times.

He sneezed into the handkerchief, then dabbed at his watering eyes, cursing the city. Every time he came to Chicago, he caught a cold! He took a deep breath and began what he considered to be dull surveillance. A very dull assignment indeed. Pure punishment, in fact!

He let his trained eyes dissect the crowd like a master surgeon, cutting first one way and then another. He snapped a mental picture of each section. He thought the surroundings were infectious. He could easily get used to this folly. Leaving reality on the

streets outside for the dim fantasyland and oblivion. Booze, music, laughter, broads, and most likely narcotics. All under one roof.

> *...the people bowed and prayed to the neon god they made...*

"The idle, drugged philosophies of the buzzing bar annoyed his senses, and he sneezed again, this time into a bar napkin. The man sitting next to Lewis moved his stool slightly away from him and his Chicago head-cold. The draft beer tasted good after chasing Mike Hogan around all day. He wasn't supposed to drink on duty, and only moderately off, but he had been given carte blanche from the department to keep this guy Michael "Hawk" Hogan in one piece. At any cost! Bullshit! He thought to himself. Who was this guy Hogan? He felt out of place with his hard hat and lunch box sitting in a bar full of newly acclaimed millionaires. Although most of them weren't dressed much better than he was, with their torn jeans, wrinkled trading jackets, and crooked identification badges.

One boisterous fellow even sported a straw hat with his trading badge displaying the nickname "TITS." But no one was wearing a hard hat, plaid shirt, and black windbreaker. He felt warm and wanted to take off his jacket. The thought quickly passed. Instead he smiled. He didn't think the plaid shirt would draw any attention, but he was sure his shoulder holster housing his heavy-duty .45 would certainly be suspect. But in this joint, maybe it would be considered posh! He zipped the windbreaker to the collar.

Pete Lewis looked down the bar and was satisfied to see that Hogan had found a place to perch. He pulled down the sweat from his glass of beer with his thumb and let his mind wander. He had been with the Bureau for six years and had been assigned to mainly drug enforcement in New York City. *That* was action. Constant action. He anticipated a very boring few months baby-sitting Hogan. He knew the Chicago assignment was a punishment by the department for his unorthodox way of doing things. He never was one for following orders. He thought of the many run-ins he'd had with his superiors. Their question was always, why did Pete Lewis join the FBI, after leaving the CIA, if he wasn't willing to play the game by their rules?

He sighed and sipped his beer. His technique for extracting information from scum drug dealers simply wasn't kosher according to Bureau policy. That's exactly what he did. *Extract* information from the slime!

The ploy that worked the best, outside of blowing off a kneecap, was to place the side of a .44 Magnum he also carried within six inches of a drug dealer's ear. He'd ask questions, and if no cooperation, BLAM! He would pull the trigger, and the explosive noise would destroy all kinds of brain cells.

Lewis used heavy-load, high-compression, hollow-head shells that would shake a man if he stood within five feet of the weapon's explosion. It wasn't a shotgun but had a similar effect. If an enemy caught one of Pete's shells, the bullet would enter a body leaving a bloody pock mark the size of a quarter and exit leaving a jagged bloody hole the

size of a muskmelon. The sound was deafening, even when used outside on the streets, and ten-fold, if fired in confined surroundings.

He remembered the two big spooks he and his partner, Derrick Brady, had cornered in a dirty Queens N.Y. alley-way. They were suspected of being kingpins in the movement of large amounts of Columbian coke. While he was cuffing one suspect, the other guy broke free and stabbed Brady. He then took off down an alley.

Pete remembered taking aim and blowing half the bastard's ass off. Then he dragged the screaming prick back to his wide eyed buddy, being held by Brady, who had been cut badly on the right arm but was still functioning. Pete had lost control of himself. He pulled the half-assed bastard up next to face his squirming, cuffed buddy. Placing his gun right on the man's temple, with the barrel pointed to the sky, Pete asked one question: "Who is your boss?" When all he heard in return from the black pusher was a bunch of rubbish about "knowing his rights," Pete fired!

Derrick Brady screamed his protestation to Pete as he was knocked to the ground holding his bloody arm. It had a ten-inch slice to the bone.

The concussion of the exploding .44 blew all kinds of red scrambled gunk out of the black man's nose and mouth splashing all over the other pusher and the brick wall behind him. The big bastard's scream echoed down the alley before he fell unconscious to the ground. His bloody sinus sacs were hung along with a mass of red snot from the unconscious heap-of-shit's nose. Pete thought, say good bye to at least one eardrum, probably two, and a whole lot of other unattached head parts.

He wouldn't get anything out of the comatose man. He doubted if he would ever talk again. But his cuffed buddy was ready and willing to tell all--as soon as Pete put the side of his gun to his temple, which was dripping with his buddy's bloody sinuses. The man started to cry and mumble names, dates, places, connections. Pete smiled sardonically to himself remembering the man chirping like a canary!

He recalled looking at Brady, who writhed in pain from the knife wound. Brady pleaded with Pete not to fire the gun again. He mumbled something about following company procedure. Pete had regained a portion of his composure and told him, "Procedure stops at this point. It's time for street justice." After getting the information he had asked for, he moved his weapon about six inches from the second man's head--his usual distance for such a punishment--and fired off another round. A blood-curdling scream could be heard all over Queens.

The second man had gone to his knees missing an eardrum. Thick blood oozed from his nose and his other ear, but no small bones or organs. That was the way Pete usually *extracted* information. This always worked, but it was against company procedure!

Within four weeks both men were back on the street. The big guy, with half an ass, no ear drums, and a very distorted vision of life, would be no good to anybody anymore. The other spook pledged a voodoo curse on Pete and his children and their children. He remembered seeing the fury drain from the black man's eyes, replaced with

panic when Pete told him he'd be dead within a week--as soon as he spread the word that the pusher had ratted on his vermin partners. Their attorney pressed a criminal lawsuit against Pete and the Department. Once again he would catch holy hell from the top. Once again the law had let him down. He caught the bad guys. The courts let them go. It was the 'system'. What could he do? The judge let the men go because the two weren't read their rights--*properly*--therefore, all evidence was inadmissable in court. But Pete had his justice once again. Those two weren't the only snakes crawling around New York with hearing aids. He smiled at the unorthodox technique that always worked without completely killing his prey!

Then his smile shifted to a frown as he thought of the twenty stitches it took to put his partner's arm back together. He'd be on a desk job for a while until his arm healed. The arm never would heal completely--too much muscle and tendon damage.

Now, he sipped his beer and continued his reminiscing. His eyes roamed the crowd as he listened to the pseudo, repetitious jargon of the giddy patrons. He glanced down the bar at Hogan. He looked comfortable and, with his sport coat off, appeared as if he planned to stay awhile.

His thoughts returned to the flak he had received from his bosses in Washington after the fiasco with the two Queens pushers. They told him he acted like a maverick street cop with the forceful and barbaric methods he used on *suspected* dope dealers. He had no respect for Bureau policy, and they were seriously considering getting rid of him for his continual insubordination and disregard for procedure. A humiliating demotion was the final consequence.

Fuck 'em--at this point he just didn't care! He was disillusioned with the whole laughable American system of crime and punishment. Mother Justice had let him down! She not only wore a blindfold, she was deaf and dumb!

His superiors never bothered to commend him for busting one of the largest drug operations on the east coast by using the information he literally pulled out of the Queens pusher. Instead they concentrated on another case he was assigned to and called him on the carpet for blowing away four ruthless Colombian dealers who had rap sheets as long as the bar where he sat. Four others were taken into custody as suspected dealers. Two hundred kilos found in their possession and they were considered only suspects!

Pete felt revulsion, as his body stiffened. All the punks had high-priced lawyers, and they all eventually walked. Who said, "Kill the lawyers first"? He guessed Shakespeare!

Lewis would pick the pushers up. They would sit in the slammer for a few hours--maybe even a few days. Bail would be made, and they would walk, free as the birds flying in the air. Their court appearances were a real joke. There was always a technicality that would throw the case out.

He could see their ugly faces as they laughed at him on their way out of the courtroom. They also vowed vengeance for sending their buddies back to Colombia in

black body-bags. He welcomed the duel, saying they wouldn't have to look for him, because he was coming for them. He would add that they should all get fitted for hearing aids. And soon! Their smiles usually turned into nervous smirks; their mocking moments shattered.

Garbage--fucking garbage, he thought. The four men he had killed would have killed him if he hadn't fired first. He was a dead shot. Four head shots in less than two seconds. Four dead Colombians before they hit the ground. It was too bad they didn't have to suffer like the poor ten-year-olds who shot up with the poison the bastards pushed.

So he killed four pushers. There would be forty more to take their place, maybe four hundred more! The whole goddamn situation was out of control. The fuckers had to be dealt with, and by the same means they fostered. Pete had to use violence with violent people. It was simple. He had to blow their fucking eardrums out, or better yet--just blow them away. Ah, what's the use? he thought. Maybe he'd just leave the Bureau and go into private practice. He wouldn't have to leave. They were about to get rid of him anyway. If it wasn't for his proficiency with a variety of weapons, his photographic memory, and his ability to speak six foreign languages, he would have been gone long ago.

So instead of canning him, the bastards just demoted him. They sent him to the dull, depressing, windy city to catch a cold and baby-sit some dull rich guy. His superiors were making damn sure Pete Lewis would stay out of trouble by assigning him to some shit-ass white-collar crime investigation!

Pete had to sneeze again. He barely got the bar napkin to his nose when the three-hundred-mile-an-hour explosion completely destroyed the thin paper napkin. The man next to him looked over in disgust and moved off his stool to seek a healthier place to drink his ale.

He never liked investigating white-collar crime. Just not his bag, he thought. No action! Just watch, stake out, ask silly questions, wear funny clothes, take candid snapshots. Just not his bag! He was in for a real ass-rubbing assignment.

Two hours of watching him through the foggy room, and Pete couldn't decide whether or not Hogan really fit into this atmosphere. He wasn't going from group to group glad-handing others and spewing false wisdom. Several people, on the other hand, came up to him and slapped him on the back. He seemed to be well liked, but Lewis had been told Hogan had powerful enemies in high places. They could be dangerous. Danger my ass, he thought. The closest these guys ever came to danger was a walk in the zoo!

He wondered where Hogan had picked up the name "Hawk." Although he had a Roman nose that could have been interpreted as a hawk's trademark, he figured it was something more than that. Hogan's eyes seemed to roam throughout the room ominously as he talked with his two friends.

At one point, he looked directly at Pete, and he felt damn uncomfortable. It was as if Hogan had opened him up, seen through him, and closed him up again. But how

could he see him clearly through all of the smoke? God knows he was at least eighty feet away. Pete decided the nickname fit the man--Hawk!

He put his beer glass to his mouth for cover, and the "Hawk" eyes that seemed to pierce his soul left him to scan other parts of the pub, either for broads, prey, or danger. Most likely the latter, he thought.

Pete wondered if Hogan had picked the far end of the bar to perch, for the same reason he had chosen his surveillance station kitty corner from Hogan. Both he and Hogan had chosen a stool with a wall behind them. Was it just a coincidence, or was Hogan that smart? Was he watching the bar with nobody at his back? Pete knew there was no such thing as coincidence. Hogan must smell a threat in the air. Pete felt a distant respect for the searching eyes at the other end of the bar.

He was glad, too, he had taken off his hard hat. It was a dead giveaway, and he was sure the sneaky Hogan had seen him in the Board of Trade Building. Maybe even on the street!

He thought Hogan had pretty good street sense for a businessman. Or was he, himself, just being careless on this assignment? He had to be careful. He couldn't become complacent despite a supposed routine task. He had learned long ago with the CIA not to take on any federal venture without being psyched to the limit of his extraordinary ability!

The one thing that confused him was the incident with Hogan and the old guy on the street. He had observed the whole incident from the other side of Jackson Boulevard. First, the Irishman knocked down the man, then he picked him up and had a conversation with him. Maybe the old man was one of Hogan's contacts. Maybe something was passed between the two--but shit, that couldn't be. Why would Hogan be so conspicuous by slamming the man so violently to the ground? He'd have to ask Hogan what that was all about when he got to know him--if he ever did!

Another beer in front of him. The broker with the straw hat and the name badge "TITS" had bought the bar a drink. That round had to cost a few hundred dollars!

He readjusted his rear end on the bar stool, thinking that this could take awhile. He looked back at the "Hawk" who seemed now to be having a heated discussion with the big fellow sitting next to him. Goddamn, this was going to take all night!

He tried to connect faces with pictures he had received from Andy Golden. Men and women possibly involved in illegal trading activities. Andy had told him that most of the Feds' information would come from Hogan. That's why the protection! Andy had said that Hogan was a friend, and not to let him out of his sight. There was a definite chance his life was in danger.

Golden told him, off the record, that he had picked Pete for the job because of his quick reaction to trouble, and the fact that he didn't give a damn about bureaucratic protocol. Golden trusted him and didn't necessarily disagree with the brutal methods of law enforcement he inflicted on criminals. Andy had the potential of becoming Director of the Bureau some day. He had to play by the rules; Pete played by his own rules!

His eyes were now in constant motion and he spotted a big--no, he corrected his mind, a fat man in a corner booth sitting with two smaller men. Now...*there* was a face he had seen before!

He reached for the lunch box he had placed between his feet on the brass foot rail and set it on his lap. He opened it just far enough to reach his hand in and rummage past his .44 Magnum for an envelope of photos given to him by investigators already on the case.

He withdrew the package, which contained fifteen five-by-seven recent snapshots. He swung his stool toward the mirrored wall in an effort to claim a bit of privacy, and quickly went through the photographs. Two profiles emerged, both on the same picture. A big man, about forty, he guessed, climbing into a black-and-gray limousine with a smaller man holding the door for him.

He looked back at the table that squeezed the fat man's stomach: same face--Karl Peterson! Then he tried to get a better look at the two men sitting with Peterson. People moved back and forth in front of the three men. He finally stole a glimpse of the slender man sitting on the outside of the table. His mind snapped a picture. God, he was ugly! Eyes returned to the photograph. The same unforgettable possum face of the man opening the door for the fat man--Gunter Schmidt!

He turned the photo over and read the comments on the back: Karl "Fat Man" Peterson. Approximately 6'4", 340 lbs.. SS# 231-66-6232, D/B-12/4/44, Address: 969 Haiti Lane, Barrington Hills, IL. Clean record! A number of civil complaints. All dropped! No convictions!

Second man: Gunter "The Rat" Schmidt--5'8", 160 pounds. SS# 316-61-1654, D/B-4/1/48, Address: 1512 North Ave, Chicago, IL. Six assault and battery charges, five drug charges, four DUIs. All charges dropped! No witnesses came forward on battery charges, and police officers involved with drug and alcohol charges decided they might have made a mistake. Only in Chicago, Pete thought, as he sneezed again.

Pete's curiosity had been piqued with Schmidt--rather than Peterson. He looked like the trouble shooter, a gopher, probably taking orders from Peterson. Too small of a prick to be much trouble unless he carried a five-pound weapon. Just a little man who liked to beat up guys if he had plenty of support.

Pete shuffled through the pictures and stopped at a mean-looking man with white hair, powder face color, and what looked to be glass eyes. If the pictures had been in color, Pete imagined the eyes would be red. A fucking albino. Name: Dieter Wolf, nickname: "Wolf Man". Pete thought to himself, you have to be kidding me! "The Rat," "Wolf Man," "Fat Man," "TITS," and "HAWK." Jesus Christ, he was in Hollywood! The balance of the information was insignificant, but he guessed it was Dieter Wolf who was the third party sitting with Peterson and Schmidt. All three were German, except for Peterson. He was a half breed: his father was from Stockholm, Sweden; his mother was from Hamburg, Germany. Karl Peterson was born in Bonn, Germany. Pete scoffed. The

Third Reich revisited. He ran the names through his mind and filed them in his memory: Karl Peterson, Gunter Schmidt, and Dieter Wolf--all Germans. The Gestapo Three!

Pete scolded himself for jumping to unfounded conclusions--but he had seen this Aryan Superman attitude before! He needed more information to make a judgment, but just looking at the pictures of the Fat Man, the Rat, and the albino they called Wolf Man made Pete shake his head. He knew men just like these three who were self-declared gods destined to rid the earth of almost everybody. Still, he would give them the benefit of his doubt!

He read Golden's comments further. Evidently, Peterson was Hogan's main target during a previous Exchange investigation, which eventually backfired and turned against Hogan. Peterson, according to Hogan, was connected with the Mafia, was a powerful political figure at both Exchanges, and had the largest skim and laundry operation on both Chicago trading floors. As many as sixty brokers did dirty work in the trading pits for Peterson.

Peterson evidently had the clout to turn the tables on Hogan's complaint against him--and Michael was the man on whom the Exchanges came down. Hogan was fined and suspended excessively for misdemeanors. The Exchanges and Peterson blew this completely out of proportion, and it hit the newspapers that Hogan had been suspended for gross negligence and tampering with customer accounts, when in all actuality, Hogan had taken a losing trading out of a customer's account and swallowed the loss himself!

Andy's last comment was, "These two are arch enemies! Watch Peterson and his henchmen closely! They are dangerous." In bold letters Golden had printed, **"PETE, TAKE EXTREME CAUTION! THESE MEN ARE SUSPECTED OF AT LEAST FIVE MURDERS AND NUMEROUS BATTERY OFFENSES. DO NOT TAKE THE CHICAGO ASSIGNMENT LIGHTLY!"**

Pete replaced the pictures in the lunch box and turned back to the bar, where there was a fresh beer in front of him. Another round had been bought by one of the crazies. He puffed out a loud exhale as he thought of Andy Golden's last statement, "...suspected of at least five murders...." He felt the small hairs stand up on the back of his neck. This wasn't white collar crime. This could be whole-scale racketeering! Maybe this wouldn't be so dull after all!

He had memorized the pictures. They weren't sharp photographs. Some were only long-range shots, but he could still pick out the major features of Peterson and Schmidt holding the door of the hundred-thousand-dollar limo.

As he had noted earlier, Schmidt was half the size of Peterson, and really did look like a possum or, better yet, the rat he had been properly named after! His thin face began jutting out at his forehead and tapered to a point at his nose. His mouth and chin were recessed, and his short, greasy hair was the color of mud. He wore expensive clothes. Still, they seemed grubby, as if trying to make a snake attractive. Clothes just couldn't hide the

ugliness. He could see Dieter Wolf now--not his eyes, but his white hair and chalky complexion.

Then his eyes riveted again on Hogan, who was now sitting with his back to the bar talking to no one. The bartender asked Pete if he wanted a backup beer, another round on TITS! Waving his hand in front of him, Pete said, "Sure, why not?"

Pete decided to take a closer look at the crowd. He slipped off of his stool and dragged two quarters from his change pile on the bar. He placed his hard hat on his seat and asked the bartender to watch his place. He grabbed his lunch box and threaded through the melange of drinkers toward the blasting jukebox now playing "Bad, Bad Leroy Brown."

Passing directly in front of Peterson's table, he hesitated slightly, being held up by the damp bodies. He shot a quick glance at the table and the three men, taking a mental picture of them *and* the contents on the table. He would file it in his memory bank for later use. The high pitch of noises kept him from deciphering any intelligible conversation.

The conversation was in German. Gunter Schmidt was speaking and said something like, "...twenty million last month..." Too much noise, Pete said to himself, and not enough time to see what was on the computer sheets Schmidt held, but Pete could see red circles around a grouping of numbers. Zero in and take a picture, he told himself. Shit! Not enough time! He just saw numbers!

He said, "Excuse me" to a girl and guy standing in his way. One more nonchalant look fell on the fat man sitting in the corner of the tight table. Although his head was in shadows, he could see ice-blue eyes peering out of the dim corner. His attention shifted quickly to the rodent, Schmidt, looking and listening to his explanation of the computer read-out.

A fat hand was wrapped around a green bottle of Heinekin. The ring that covered his pinky was the size of a dime. It had to be an eight-carat-plus gem. He would take a chance--one more quick look at the face that turned and stared through the shadows at him. It was Peterson! Click--he took a memory picture of him, then of Schmidt, and another of Wolf. He had worn out his welcome, now move, Lewis!

He felt a shiver run up his back. He had stayed a moment too long. He felt Peterson watching him. He moved through a chattering couple who were oblivious to his passing between them like a ghost.

He put two quarters into the jukebox, scanned its song menu, and punched "In the Air Tonight" by Phil Collins, "The Final Countdown" by Europe, and "The Gambler" by Kenny Rogers, then returned to his position at the bar.

On his way back he glanced at Schmidt. His pock-marked face registered cold and mean. Click, click--more pictures of the plain, featureless Dieter Wolf. He did have red eyes. Jesus Christ, what a threesome!

Peterson had been served a large steak with a side order of pasta. Click, another picture of the Fat Man. Lewis felt icy eyes stare at his back as he passed by the table.

He sneezed again, this time loudly and into his hands. Goddammit, he had tried to hold it until he got back to the bar, but the sneeze was stronger than he was. Well, one thing for sure, the three pricks sitting just behind him sure wouldn't think he was a Fed. What FBI movie ever showed an agent sneeze in front of a would be enemy?

By the time he reached his stool, there was another beer in front of him. The bartender smiled and said, "It's on the house--every fourth drink!"

Lewis held up his beer. "Thanks. I'll have to come in here more often." He had three beers backed up already.

Glancing at Hogan again, he noticed that the Irishman had turned to face Peterson's table and was giving somebody the finger. He laughed. The guy had balls. He thought he was going to like Hogan. "My kind of guy," he mumbled.

Phil Collins was singing:

> *"I've seen your face, my friend, but I don't know if you*
> *know who I am. O Lord...O Lord...Can you feel it*
> *coming in the air tonight? O Lord...O Lord..."*

About an hour later, he saw Hogan turn from the bar and begin to leave. He'd give him a minute or so and follow along. He finished his beer and left a fifty-cent tip. When he saw the bartender looking at him askance, he threw down another dollar.

Pete took one more look at Peterson's table and saw that Schmidt and Wolf were leaving also, apparently to follow Hogan. By this time, Hogan had passed through the double glass doors leading to the lobby of the building. The other two were heading in the same direction. All he could see over the packed bar was their heads. They were going through the glass doors also.

Hogan could be in for some real trouble, Lewis thought. He grabbed his hard hat and lunch box and started pushing people out of the way heading for the glass doors. Peterson's men had a one-minute lead on him, and lots of things could happen in one minute. Especially if it stretched into two minutes for some reason.

One of his songs was playing on the jukebox, Europe's "The Final Countdown." He caught only three lines of the song:

> *"We're leaving ground. Will things ever be the same*
> *again? It's the final countdown... "*

He banged through the bar doors into an empty lobby and looked both ways. Shit, which way did they go? He had to act fast! The ping from an elevator came from the far end of the lobby. The garage, he thought. That's where the bastards went. Pete dashed for a steel door marked STAIRS. At the same time he fumbled to open the lunch box. As he hit the steel fire door, he had his .44 cocked and ready to fire. He had placed the pictures in his jacket pocket and flung the lunch box.

The thought flashed through his mind that Chicago might not be so dull after all, and he eased down the stairs to the garage below. Behind him, just before the door clicked shut, he could hear the beginning of Kenny Rogers's song, "The Gambler."

FOURTEEN

Confrontation

Michael pushed through the glass doors of the Bull and Bear that led to the lobby of the Insurance Exchange Building. As he looked at his wristwatch, he swore at himself for leaving the bar so late. He knew Charles would be gone by now, but his car would be waiting, gassed, cleaned, and ready to go. The night guard would have his keys. He would be home in less than an hour. Time enough to tuck the older kids in and spend a few hours with Maria. He felt like making love to her. Thoughts of her soothing, erotic touch had been with him all day. The anticipation excited and warmed him.

Through the turnstile doors at the LaSalle Street exit, Michael noticed it had begun to rain. While he had been indulging in the bar, a spring storm had crept into the tired, dark city, scourging its streets of the dirt and sin that had accumulated during the past few days. The dirt would wash through the labyrinth of sewers to the lake. The sin, like a black tattoo, would remain.

A sharp flash of lightning struck nearby, and the lobby lights dimmed briefly. The thick concrete building muffled the thunder that followed moments later.

He loved storms and was anxious to get home and relax on his lake side terrace. The cool pellets would cleanse him of the day's pressures. Then a warm shower--and Maria!

His thoughts turned to the second woman in his life--Mother Nature. Her beauty, her ferocity, her power! They held him captive. The lake surf would be fierce from the storm. He could almost hear it. Could almost feel a sense of infinity when he watched nature's children battle with each other. The storm would agitate the great waters of Lake Michigan, snapping and stinging at her shivering surface.

Michael would usually outlast these spring torrents even if they went on for hours. But not tonight, he thought. If he didn't get home soon, he would have his own tempest to contend with in the form of Maria. Not even Mother Nature would relish her wrath!

Once again, he realized the time. He moved quickly to the news stand before Abe Kaplin had time to close the metal gates around his nickel treasures. "Evening, Abe. You're here late tonight."

Abe turned in a start. "Oh, hi, Mike. Inventory time. What can I do for you?"

Michael reached into his sport-coat pocket and pulled out a few loose bills left from the bar. He placed a five on the glass counter and responded, "I'm in a hurry, so just a paper and a pack of gum tonight, Abe. Thanks."

He picked up a late edition *Tribune* and a pack of Wrigley's Juicy Fruit gum, as Abe went behind the counter for his change. "Keep it, Abe, and thanks."

He stood for a moment reading the headlines, while Abe pulled out a betting form from under the counter. "You want to place a bet on tonight's NBA playoffs, Mike?"

Mike thought for a moment. "I haven't time to study the spreads, Abe..." He looked at his watch again. "What's the spread on the Celtics and Bucks?"

Abe smiled, looked down at his bookie sheet and said, "Las Vegas is giving Milwaukee three and a half points. Game's being played in Milwaukee!"

Michael slipped his sport coat on and dropped the pack of gum into his pocket, folded the newspaper, and tucked it underneath his arm. "I'll take the Bucks for three hundred dollars...it should be a close game."

Abe put his pencil point to his tongue. "Three hundred it is. See you tomorrow, Mike. It's a good bet. Larry Bird is having trouble with his knee. The game started about a half hour ago, so maybe you're a winner already."

Michael grinned at the sly fox. Abe knew exactly what the score was, or he wouldn't take the bet--not a half hour after the game started. The Celtics were probably up by ten points. As he turned toward the elevators, his peripheral vision caught two moving figures to his right. When he turned in their direction, he saw the exit door, the one that led to the upper floors and down to the garage, closing slowly.

For a moment he thought trouble, but his senses were not as keen as they could be after eight or nine scotches. Then he dismissed any threat, thinking it was probably just two brokers going home about four hours late for dinner.

He continued around the corner and approached the night security guard, chuckling as he noticed the guard's eyes riveted to the pages of a *Penthouse* magazine. He reached for Michael's keys from the board, handed them to him, and never lifted his head from the contents for even a second. "Thanks, George."

"My pleasure, Mr. Hogan."

Keys in hand, he moved to the elevators. The numbers just above the doors indicated a waiting elevator on the main floor. He pushed the down button, and a sharp *ping* opened the two sliding doors to a plush mirrored cubicle. He stepped inside and pushed LL for Lower Level.

He opened the newspaper and glimpsed at the headline. Six more judges indicted in the Graylord investigation. Good, he thought. Judge Gorden, the good-looking female judge, would castrate the do-no-evil men dressed in black for receiving kickbacks. He began to skim the column that followed, but another *ping* told him he had arrived at the garage level.

He walked with some apprehension into the garage. Most of the lights had been turned out when Charles left at seven-thirty. Red exit lights revealed the four stairwells, and a bright fluorescent light shone in the center of the now sparsely occupied garage. He saw his black Astin parked in front of the attendant's office and fingered his keys. He

heard another sharp crack of muffled thunder outside. The garage was eerie and he had the feeling that things were not right.

He stopped for a moment, not yet in the cone of the fluorescent light. Something was wrong. Definitely wrong. He sensed it! He heard a noise from beyond his car. Was it his imagination, or had paranoia returned? He stepped closer to the light and his car. The noise came again. This time he heard shuffling feet. He remembered the two men from the lobby entering the stairwell. Should he make a run for the car, or should he just back off and get the hell out? The acute anxiety he felt earlier began to engulf him again. "Charles?" No answer. He felt sweat run down the middle of his back.

Another noise. This time from his backside. He couldn't back out now. His exit was covered. Who the fuck was playing games with him? Panic began to invade his mind and body. He knew he had to regain control, but his mind was sluggish from the booze. His thoughts were confused, and his fury blossomed. Come on, Hogan. Think. Maybe it was his imagination. He listened--another shuffle. He mumbled, son of a bitch. You dirty sons of bitches.

Bo Lynch had always told him to remain the aggressor even when the odds were against him. Never show fear! That's what the enemy wants. Now the sweat ran down his face and blurred his vision. His cheeks were wet, and he wiped his mouth with the back of his hand. The sound of rushing water overhead made him duck and quickly look up-- only a six-inch water pipe pushing sewage through from a flushed toilet someplace in the building. He was barely able to muster up a challenge. "Okay, Assholes! Show yourselves, you coward sons of bitches."

A rustle came from the shadows on the other side of his car. A figure emerged, stopping just short of the circle of light. He couldn't see the face, but he had a feeling he knew who it was. Another shuffling from behind told him someone was making a move closer.

He turned his head and saw a dark shape with a pale face. He pivoted sharply and stared at the other form still in the shadows. He could almost see as well in the dark as he could in daylight. It was Gunter Schmidt, The Rat, and paste-faced Dieter Wolf, Peterson's two henchmen. He should have known! He had challenged them in the bar, and now they were going to challenge him here. He shuddered. He had underestimated Peterson. He didn't think he was dumb enough to cause an incident on the turf they both shared. He thought he must have really riled Peterson in the bar. That was good--no, that was bad!

Now Peterson's emotions were dictating his actions. He was getting careless and would continue to do so, if Michael kept up the pressure; that is, if he lived through this mess! Then he thought, Pressure. Who was he kidding? Look who was under Pressure. He really had these pricks by the balls now! For Christ's sake, Hogan, think straight! His present situation was at best precarious. He had an 80/20 spread--and he was the 20. He had to think fast and move cautiously. These assholes weren't here to sell him Girl Scout cookies!

He could hear Bo speaking to him. "Take the aggression...Scare them!...Confuse them! No matter how scared you are, keep them off guard. Use insults and belligerence. Bullies like to see fear. Not confidence! Don't let them get in your head...you get in theirs!" Surprisingly enough, he was not totally out of control. He was sweating and his hands were wet. But his mind seemed to clear as the danger became more evident. He shouted, hoping his voice wouldn't quiver. "I suppose you assholes are looking for a ride home? Sorry, I'm not going your way, scumbags!" He didn't know why he said that. The words just came out. But he felt a rush of adrenalin push down his tension. This, too, helped his body and mind begin to recover.

His mind still raced, searching for answers--for questions--for anything! What the fuck am I going to do now? he thought. Stay offensive and calm. His shirt was soaked. Then Schmidt stepped further into the light. He pounded his right fist fitted with brass knuckles into the palm of his left hand, as though to say, this is what is going to happen to you. Probably the same steel fist that worked over Jimmy Palotos. Schmidt said something in German to his partner. Wolf responded with an affirmative.

Although Schmidt was still in shadows, Michael could see an ugly smile slither onto his face. He said with a heavy German accent, "The boss doesn't like your style, Hogan. He thought maybe we should visit you. Clean up your manners and any ideas you might have about starting trouble for him." Michael could see him clearly now. His ugly, pock-marked, rodent face grinned. A nervous twitch started as he continued to beat his palm. Michael tried to position himself so he could see if Wolf made a move. He answered Schmidt with belligerence, "Fuck you, ya ugly piece of shit!" Schmidt's grin faded, but the twitch on his left cheek intensified. He seemed hesitant to come closer to Michael.

Michael moved slowly. Closer to the scan of light as he heard Dieter move in behind him. Schmidt stepped back. Michael saw that Rabbit Eyes held a long pipe. Wolf was now standing between him and the stairwell.

Michael looked up at the numbers above the elevator doors. The elevator had been recalled to a higher floor. No fucking way out! Sweat continued to drip profusely, and now his head was pounding. He was scared for his life. Though he knew he couldn't show fear to these vermin. That's what they wanted! He *would* show aggression. Yet, he could hear the thud in his heart as he waited. Waited for what? Inspiration, he guessed!

Bo had told him if he was ever confronted by an enemy with a weapon to get close enough to look into his eyes. He had said to forget the weapon. Force everything out of his mind and place an imaginary white dot between the attacker's eyes. Concentrate. Talk trash to position yourself, and stall for time. Michael remembered the words. "Keep your eyes on his eyes and the white dot. Unless he's a real pro, there will be one short moment when the enemy will let down his guard. Then you snap the heel of your foot at the white dot. Put your whole spirit behind the kick. It may mean your life!" It was a good thing Schmidt was short. Michael wasn't sure how high he could kick. He had practiced only on punching bags before. But shit, this was the real thing!

Bo spoke to him. "If you can't concentrate, and the white dot hasn't formed, aim for the middle of the eyes. The forehead. If the blow is accurate, it will crush the bones above the nose and temporarily put the man out of commission. If the kick is hard enough, it will kill the enemy. Always go for the kill!" If there was time, Bo stressed a split second of meditation. Clearing the mind of everything except the white dot in the center of the target's head.

"If it's street conflict, the enemy will be less likely to react as quickly as in jungle combat. Force fear and pain out of your mind. The white dot is all that matters. It's your enemy...yet it's your salvation. Your way out. The white dot. Snap the foot out and place the heel on the target. Kick through the forehead with all your weight and let out a scream as you begin your attack. The scream will give you extra strength. It puts fear into the air around you, which then goes into the enemy's subconscious!

"All aggression will momentarily stop, and you'll know if you score. Turn immediately to any other opponents because fear will move them quickly. You'll only have a moment. Use it to your advantage." Now, all these instructions of Bo's were coming to him as if Bo were standing next to him.

Schmidt inched closer, showing his crooked white teeth. He was next to the Astin-Martin, about six feet away. Michael figured Wolf was maybe ten feet behind him and moving up, ready at any moment to bring him to his knees with the pipe he was wielding like a baton. Bo had said to take the closest man out first.

He tried to concentrate and clear his mind. Too much emotion, though. His brain didn't have the discipline to ignore possible death. Confusion rolled around inside him. He just didn't have Bo's experience. His natural instincts screamed out for him to leap at or tackle Schmidt. To beat the shit out of the greasy bastard, but he knew that's exactly what they expected. Something spontaneous. If he reacted like that, Wolf would jump in and have a field day beating on the back of his head with the pipe. They didn't expect anything professional--Michael didn't know if he did either.

Bo's words came to him again. "Take your time, be calm, clear your mind." All right, Michael thought, if all else fails, follow instructions. He'd have only one chance. He had to be accurate with his kick. These men were here to hurt him; no amount of talk would change that.

He closed his eyes for less than a second and shook his head to clear it. He said a short prayer to Whoever was listening, "Help me...please help me get out of this mess!" That's all he could think of. Suddenly, he sensed a presence near him.

His mind began to clear, and his body relaxed. Hypnotically he stared at Gunter Schmidt. There was no white dot. He'd have to wing it.

He took two slow steps forward, raised his hands, and shrugged his shoulders. "Come on you guys--can't we talk this over? You're reasonable men...even though you're both slime!"

Schmidt's expression went from sadistic to nervous. He stepped closer and looked beyond Michael's shoulder at Wolf. Schmidt hesitated a moment too long. Michael's reaction was quick. "I'm sending you back to hell!" Michael snapped his right foot in the direction of two astonished eyes. The kick was accompanied with a cry that came from deep within his soul, and echoed throughout the hollow concrete garage.

His foot carried 190 pounds of body weight and blurred velocity with it. His hard Italian heel caught Schmidt above his left eye. Michael lost his balance and fell to the concrete floor, but not before hearing Schmidt's agonized scream from the crunch of facial bones.

Schmidt had dropped the brass knuckles in front of Michael and banged back against the black Astin. Blood seeped through his fingers as he held his face. He rolled and slid down the side of the car to his knees, mumbling and cursing in German.

Michael's thoughts scattered, then reassembled quickly. Goddamn! It worked! Schmidt was out of action! Now, Michael had to move fast. He began to rise and turned to face Dieter. Michael's unexpected defensive move had stunned him, but he was coming on quickly. Too late! The second he had spent revelling in the damage he had done to Schmidt had cost him the time it would have taken him to rise to his feet and face Wolf. He felt the German's weapon crash down on his back, knocking him to the cold floor. The pain was like a hot, plunging knife. His eyes shut as he gritted his teeth, trying to hold back an agonized shriek. He was sure his shoulder had been broken. Another blow came down hard on his back.

He snapped his right foot out, catching only air. He held his left shoulder and struggled to his knees, leaning on his right elbow for support. Wolf was in no hurry now. He had his prey where he wanted him. Defenseless! Michael looked into the diabolical face, the color of dry ice.

The albino German twirled a three-foot pipe as he said with a menacing smile, "You're a hard man to deal with, Mr. Hogan. I don't think we'll be seeing much of you for a long time, when I get finished with you. I'm very good with this!" Michael saw the weapon stop twirling. Wolf raised the pipe above his head, ready to bring it down hard.

Dizzy and sick, as much from emotion as the pain, Michael knew he didn't want to die, not yet. But he had lost this round and would have to pay. Wolf let the pipe slide in his hands until he had a grip around one end. He worked the end of the pipe with his hands, like a baseball player trying to get a comfortable grip.

Michael tried to squeeze the pain from his shoulder, then resigned himself to the fact that he was seconds away from getting his head split in half. He lowered his blurred eyes, leaned back on his knees and shins, took a deep breath, and waited for the blow to knock him into oblivion.

Then--a deafening explosion rocked Michael's senses. His right hand went from his painful shoulder to the pain that blew through his ears. He thought the pipe had been imbedded in his skull. Still conscious, he heard Wolf cry out in agony and the pipe clang

onto the concrete. Blood covered the end of the pipe and spattered the floor in front of him. He looked down at his clothes. They, too, were covered with red and white particles of blood and human flesh.

He felt a rush of confusion. What the hell was going on now? Was the blood from Michael or from Dieter? The German's screaming told him it was from the latter. He raised his eyes to meet Wolf, now kneeling and writhing in front of him. He held a wad of blood that looked like his right hand.

Michael knew he had somehow received a reprieve and thought he'd better make the best of it. His eyes focused on Wolf's nose less than three feet away. A white dot appeared, and with all his painful might, he smashed through the target with his right fist. Teeth broke, and blood erupted from the German's nose and mouth. His face lost expression as he fell backward, unconscious.

Michael toppled to his side, recoiled in pain. Struggling to a sitting position, he cradled his left arm as if he were holding a sick baby.

What the fuck had happened? Instead of his getting his head bashed in by Wolf, Dieter Wolf was lying in front of *him* with half a hand and a broken face. Michael's ears still throbbed from the explosions.

He heard footsteps coming from the direction of the stairwell. The smell of gunpowder touched his senses, and through a blue fog he saw a dark figure moving slowly in his direction. He couldn't decipher much, squinting into the blue smoke. The man was coming slowly, cautiously into his view. Both hands were wrapped around a gun the size of a football, pointed directly at Wolf's head. His feet stepped into the circle of light not far from the moaning Wolf. Clean construction boots. Oh, no! Now he had to contend with a marksman. Blowing half a hand away was no chance shot, Michael could figure that out. But whose side was the guy on? Now he was fully visible, the construction worker. He wore the yellow hard hat, plaid shirt covered by a black windbreaker, and--new goddamn construction shoes.

Seeing Dieter lying in front of him, the blood-spattered pipe a few feet away, banished Michael's immediate fear. Not that he was content to survive with an injured shoulder. He could have been killed! He flinched in pain as the figure approached him. "Who the fuck are you?" Michael asked.

The stranger said nothing as he stopped in front of Wolf. He used his foot to turn over the semi-conscious German. Satisfied that he was out of commission, he kicked him hard in the ribs. Wolf let out another scream. He then kicked the bloody pipe from the side of the prostrate German. It clanged across the concrete and slid under a new Volvo thirty feet away.

He moved quickly to Schmidt, now back on his feet but still hunched over holding his eye. Schmidt scornfully said something in German. The stranger returned a comment in the same language, then gave Schmidt a hard kick to the groin that put him on the floor again. Another scream, and both Schmidt's hands left his face to grasp his aching nuts. He

was gasping for air. Michael saw the damage his kick had done to Schmidt's eye. It looked like raw hamburger.

For some reason Michael felt temporarily safe with this mild-faced man. First, he had the feeling of relief, but then anger began to well in his body. He scooted with the help of his right hand and legs and picked up the brass knuckles in front of him. Then, motioning to the stranger's gun, said again, "Are you going to tell me who you are...or are you going to blow me away with that cannon?"

The man took one hand off his .44 Magnum and reached for his left ear, then his right, removing ear plugs. He placed them in his black jacket, and spoke as if he enjoyed the action. "Sorry, can't hear much with those things in! You're wondering if I'm going to shoot you? Not today. Only one shot per customer, Hogan, and you're not one of my customers, so rest easy. You okay?"

Michael's chest rose as he filled his lungs with air and let it all out in a sigh of relief. Maybe the confrontation was over. Still, he couldn't help wondering who in the hell this man was. "Yeah, I'm just peachy! Now what's your story?"

Satisfied that the two aggressors were down, posing no further threat, the stranger lowered the gun to his side and came to Michael, as he struggled to his feet still holding his left arm. "I'm a friend of Andy's," he said. "How's the arm?"

Michael looked at him, fear gone, anger building. "It's my shoulder. Why didn't you tell me that on the street? Christ, I could have been killed!"

He saw a young face look at him with some disgust. "You weren't, though--were you? Then he whispered. "My name is Lewis. Pete Lewis. I'm an agent with the Bureau. I'll tell you more when we're away from these two scumbags." Michael winced in pain, as Lewis reached for his good arm.

He gritted his teeth as Lewis felt his shoulder gently. "Just separated. I'll get you to a hospital and they can set it."

Michael crouched down from the pain. "Hey...*you* set it!...I've had separated shoulders before, and I don't need a doctor to set my fucking shoulder. Just yank the arm hard, and I'll hold the ball at the top of the shoulder and try to push the bitch back into place."

He saw Lewis's grin of respect--or was it ridicule? "As you say, Hotshot. All guts. No brains!" He grabbed Michael's wrist and straightened the arm. "Ready?"

Michael snapped out. "Not yet! I'll tell you when to pull!"

Michael closed his eyes, gritted his teeth, and took hold of the golf-ball-size bump on his left shoulder. "Okay, yank away!"

Lewis said, "You sure you're ready for this?"

Michael felt his insides blaze with anger as he opened his eyes and brought them within inches of Lewis's face. He hissed between his grinding teeth, "I SAID YANK...MOTHERFUCKER!"

Lewis gave a yank, and Michael pushed down hard on the throbbing shoulder bone. He gave out a yell as the separated bone slipped home. "GODDAMMIT...THAT HURTS!" His eyes shut tight. He screwed up his face and looked to the ceiling in an effort to push the pain from his mind. He jerked his arm away from Lewis and cradled it again. Except for a bruised swelling, the knot had disappeared.

Lewis had placed his .44 between his belt and backbone. "Let's get out of here, Hogan, before we wear out our welcome. I'll drive you home in your car and have mine picked up later."

Michael's body was still heated with anger. He fingered the brass knuckles and looked over at the moaning Schmidt, on the floor by the front wheel of the Astin. He put the knuckles on and felt the sharp metal points on the front of the destructive weapon. He walked, almost stumbled to Schmidt and looked down at him. "What goes around comes around, Asshole. Now it's your turn to pay the piper for what you did to my friend, Jimmy Palotos."

Forgetting the pain, he reached down with his throbbing left arm and grabbed Schmidt's greasy hair, pulling his limp face upward. With all the strength he could muster, his eyes trained on Gunter's mouth, he slammed his fist downward into the rodent's chin. Blood spurted all over Michael's shoes, and he saw that he had laid a piece of skin open to the jaw bone that extended from the bottom lip to the chin. Schmidt's lower teeth were showing--all but two that had been broken off and were someplace in the sadistic bastard's bloody mouth. "Next time I'll kill ya!"

Satisfied, he turned toward Lewis and said, "Now I'm ready!" But he saw that Lewis was now standing near Wolf. "Just for the record, he asked, "Who sent you? Was it Peterson?" In response, the German spit blood on Lewis's new construction boots.

Lewis slowly looked down at his boots and Michael watched an almost sad expression flow across Lewis's face as he said, "You albino prick, these are brand new shoes!"

He slowly reached around and retrieved his .44. Then he pointed it at the man's head and repeated. "I already know the answer, Asshole! I just want to hear it from you-- I'll ask you one more time--who sent you; you lose if I don't find out!" Michael saw the German spit again, this time up into Lewis's face. Pete patiently wiped the bloody spittle from his face with the forearm of his Windbreaker. He grabbed Wolf by his neck and held the gun to the side of his head. "One more time, powder face. Who do you work for?"

The German's eyes widened in fear. "We work for ourselves. Free-lance." Michael watched as Lewis moved the gun. The side of the huge .44 paralleled Dieter's head, muzzle pointing toward the ceiling.

Michael heard Dieter say something curt in German, and Lewis answered him with an explosion of his .44 Magnum. The discharge rocked Michael backward. His own ears screamed again with pain from the concussion. The German's cry echoed throughout the garage, as blood poured from the his nose, ears, and mouth. Lewis let go of the man's

neck. His white hair now dripped with crimson liquid, and his head fell in slow motion to the ground, splashing in its own blood.

Lewis looked down and said. "Asshole! You made me forget to use my ear plugs! I hope your employer has good medical insurance, because you're going to need a hearing aid for your right ear. Now, if you want to keep your left ear, answer me. Who sent you?"

Dieter Wolf was a bloody mess, barely conscious, as he mumbled something in German. Michael heard the name Peterson. More questions by Lewis. This time in German, and Michael recognized only names: Conti and Ruzzo.

Lewis turned and smiled at Michael. "See how a little pressure in the right places works?" Michael shook his head and followed him toward the car. Lewis said, "Get in, I'll drive!"

Michael couldn't understand what Lewis was up to. How could he be FBI with such barbaric behavior? Not that Michael minded. The evil bastards deserved every bit of pain that could be administered, but what a maverick this guy was.

The Bureau must go crazy, Michael thought, when they send this madman out on a job. He looked at both semiconscious men, groveling in blood as they held their injured bodies. He felt sick and dizzy. What a fucking day, he thought.

Lewis pulled out his handkerchief just in time to catch two back-to-back sneezes. "Goddamn Chicago!" he said as he wiped his nose and headed for the car. "Come on, Jerkoff, I've got to get you to Washington in one piece--or my ass is grass."

Michael shook his head. "Yeah! You drive. Anything you say, hero!"

Another sneeze and the Astin laid rubber all the way to the top of the ramp. The metal door opened onto a downpour, which had slowed the late traffic to a crawl.

Michael rested his head back on the soft seat, holding his left arm. He felt himself losing consciousness. His hand came up, and he wiped blood from his face--whose blood, he didn't know. The last thing he remembered was the auto fishtailing onto Clark Street, accelerating toward the expressway. Darkness took over as he faded into a sea of confused dreams. He barely heard Lewis sneeze, but automatically he said, "God bless you!"

FIFTEEN

Meigs Field-May 3, 1987

A sharp lake wind and pelting rain slashed at Michael's face, but it felt good. At least it took his mind off his aching shoulder and body. Chicago had been under siege from cold spring rains for more than seventy-two hours. The month of May usually brought sun and pre-summer warmth to the city; this year she chose to usher herself in with three days of relentless gloom on her thirty-one-day journey.

Meigs Air Field, with its single north-south runway, was located directly adjacent to Lake Michigan near Grant Park at South Twelfth Street. Extending into the lake, it was small and was mainly used for corporations and businesses. Today, because of the weather, it was quiet.

Michael stood in the mist, leaning his back against a four-foot chain-link fence that separated would-be passengers from arriving private planes. He was flanked by Bo Lynch on one side, forearms on top of the fence, cigarette hanging loosely from his dry lips, and Pete Lewis on the other side, in the same position as Lynch, facing the field. His family waited inside the small terminal. Both Pete and Bo had been in Viet Nam at different times. Lynch had been in the Special Forces, Lewis in the Airborne--and, Michael suspected, Intelligence as well.

He half-heartedly listened to their conversation as the two men talked around him, about some Cambodian coke they had both been involved in. Michael guessed that the taste of blood and the smell of napalm had formed some type of commando bond between the two men.

Bo smelled like used booze; Lewis had on too much Old Spice, and the combination collided around Michael's head, forming a sour liniment smell.

He had been standing for ten minutes with his head raised and eyes closed. The cold mist felt good soaking his black hair and drawn, tight face. Drops of water ran down his black London Fog raincoat to his feet, joining the puddle in which he was standing. He opened his eyes and looked south. McCormick Place stood out like a giant black outer-space coordinate station with huge metal and glass doors and flashing red and white strobe lights perched high atop invisible antennas. The eerie building gave him the feeling he was in a different place at a futuristic time. This added to the dismal Chicago atmosphere that hung over the city like a black shroud, matching Michael's fatalistic mood.

He looked north to the skyscrapers, crowding the lake shore. They looked like armless ghosts with thousands of dull, gray eyes staring out into a mystic drizzle.

Visibility was, at best, two miles. A gloomy day for a gloomy mission. He was sore, and run-down, and was having trouble sleeping. A confrontation with Washington bureaucrats was not something he relished at this time. He would rather take them on when he was at full strength, both physically and mentally. He sighed and closed his eyes to the biting wind. Andy Golden was running late because of the weather. This would set back their meeting with the Assistant Director of the FBI and his entourage of "Yes Men."

Michael felt his thoughts puzzling. On one hand he was angry because he had let himself be put in this position--the middle of his co-brokers and the law. A lot of good guys and their families would be hurt with the investigation. On the other hand, there was no other way to stop the escalating corruption of men like Peterson. He and the rest of the thieves were getting careless. Bold and ruthless. It wouldn't be long before they turned the whole commodity industry into a haven for crooks.

He let his eyes roam as Lewis and Lynch jabbered on. He wished they would shut up for a minute and give him a moment to meditate. He had a lot to talk over with his father, his grandfather--and his Maker. But his two comrades insisted on describing their single handed siege of the Viet Nam conflict. It was good to hear them both laughing and joking about their exploits.

His thoughts returned to the day's coming events. He would give the Feds some information--but only under certain conditions. He was determined to maintain control, for he knew he would be dealing with men who were masters at control and manipulation. Then he thought, if all else fails--Fuck it! He turned toward the air strip grumbling to himself, "Where is Andy?"

His shoulder ached every time he moved. His left arm, in a sling, was bandaged tight to his body--Too tight--leaving him short of breath. He half turned to Pete during a lapse in his conversation with Bo. "What time do you have, Pete?"

Pete was holding a handkerchief to his nose and caught another powerful sneeze. "Goddamn Chicago!" He wiped his nose and eyes and glanced at a black wristwatch, crowded with dials. His watch resembled the instrument panel of an airplane all condensed into one. "Seven-ten--he's forty minutes late!"

Pete put his arm around Michael and spoke in a whisper. "Hey Mike...uh...I'd appreciate it if you didn't mention my blowing that guy's ear drums out the other night in the garage." He cocked his head and shrugged. "You know the Bureau. They don't look kindly on that sort of activity--even though it's terribly effective. I'm...well...I'm kind of in trouble with the big bosses now. Similar behavior in New York. They sent me out here to keep you alive, get you to Washington in one piece, and to get me the hell out of New York. They took away my Special Agent status and warned me to stay out of trouble, or I'd be looking for a new job."

Michael gave him a sideways glance. Pete's blue eyes sparkled in the rain. He waited for a response. Michael knew he was a dedicated soldier, even though he was a cowboy. He certainly didn't take any crap from his enemies and probably didn't take much

from his superiors either. "Don't worry, Pete, you saved my life! I'm not going to tell the assholes in Washington that their man saved my life, but I disapprove of the way he did it. That wouldn't show much gratitude. Besides, the way I feel now, I wouldn't have cared if you blew the fucker's head off instead of just his eardrums!"

He saw Lewis's whole body ease with relief. "Thanks. They would fire me for sure if they knew I had chalked up another eardrum job."

"Just how many ear jobs do you have to your credit?"

Pete looked toward the runway and spit. "Fifty or sixty."

Michael's eyes widened. "Jesus Christ. No wonder you're on the carpet with your bosses!"

Lewis answered as casually as if he were referring to parking tickets. "Well, the Bureau only knows about fifteen of them. Besides, I believe in street justice not court justice. If I let a guy sneak into court, it's all over. Most are back on the street within twenty-four hours."

Michael let his lips widen in a grin. "That's great, Pete. Sixty blown-out eardrums and your bosses only know of twenty-five per cent of them. Are you a good liar or do your cuffs just keep quiet?"

"Most of the pricks can't even talk when I get finished with them." Lewis pulled himself away from the fence. His stocky body stood straight as he spoke with apathy. "I just tell the bastards that if I have to come looking for them again, I'll be back to blind them. They play by my rules, live by the sword, die by the sword. Isn't that one of the unwritten laws of nature?" Pete's lips narrowed in a scowl.

"Yeah, I guess that's what this whole Investigation thing is all about. What goes around comes around! You fuck somebody, then you get fucked. And I have a feeling some of these Chicago assholes are about to get an ass reaming!"

Pete leaned back on the fence. "Well, the way I look at it...at least everybody knows where I'm coming from. The people I go after kill kids and good people. They are the garbage of the earth. No conscience, no morals, no concern for life, feelings, or the pain of others. So, I really just play by their rules. I bust a few ear drums--an ear for a life. As far as I'm concerned, I'm goddamn generous!"

Michael understood. "Whatever works for you, Pete! I don't give two shits if you blow away the whole rotten bunch...both in New York and in Chicago...What time do you have now?"

"Seven-twenty."

Michael mumbled with irritation. "Son of a bitch. Come on, Andy!"

From where he stood, Michael could see the windowed lobby of the small airport. He saw his family through the rain-streaked glass. Maria was reading to the twins. Martin and Joseph were looking through a magazine rack, probably trying to get a glimpse of *Playboy* magazine. Angela and Kelly were playing video games. They would enjoy the long weekend with their grandparents on Long Island. He wished he could join them. He spent

so little time with the kids he was surprised they even knew him. But he guessed it went with the territory. Fame and fortune--or family. Something, or someone, had to suffer when a man sought his destiny. Thank God children were so forgiving--or were they? A song filtered through his head:

> *"...Cats in the cradle and the silver spoon...Little Boy*
> *Blue and the Man in the Moon. When ya coming home,*
> *Dad? I don't know when! But, we'll get together then,*
> *Son...we're gonna have a good time then, Son! You'll*
> *know we'll have a good time then..."*

The scene in his mind shifted to Maria's family. During eighteen years of marriage, Michael had stayed away from all Santini business interests. What he knew about the Santini family business was little. He wanted to keep it that way too. Michael had spoken to Maria's father, Carlo Santini, before the wedding and told him--with no disrespect--that he wanted to keep Maria and the Hogan family clean. Michael demanded it. Carlo didn't accept rejection well, but he made an exception with Michael. After all, he was about to become family. Maria never talked of her father's business, and that was all right with Michael. He knew that Carlo was one of the biggest contractors in Manhattan. He also knew it was the result of Carlo's earlier contacts in Sicily. These led to eventual ties in New York with other influential Sicilian families.

Carlo was close to a few of the six Mafia families in New York, but as far as Michael knew, not the head of any. Carlo made huge payoffs to the politicians and mob bosses who controlled Manhattan's construction contracts and zoning regulations. Santini and Sons Construction Company always seemed to land the big jobs. And that wasn't coincidental!

He knew that Carlo admired him for his ideology and philosophy of Right is right, not might is right! He was relieved that Carlo didn't deal in drugs or broads. His father-in-law was well connected on the perimeter, if there was such a thing, of the New York Mafia. Michael was willing to accept graft and bribery in place of drugs, extortion, prostitution, and pornography.

He remembered the early days in his marriage before he made it big in Chicago, Carlo had offered him a job as a union negotiator. Michael turned him down, knowing he would have to compromise his moral beliefs for power and money. Patrick Hogan had taught his son well, not about money, but about Christian ethics.

His father left a rich legacy for his son. Moral values. Be truthful and honest to yourself. Always, and in all of your dealings with others. Don't let money dictate to your good judgment. Money wasn't bad, but it had a way of whitewashing evil!

He remembered his father's simple philosophy. *Don't hedge on the truth. Once you begin to chip away at honesty, it becomes easier and easier to chip it to pieces, leaving only half truths and deception.* He would say that most people who come to the negotiating table come with the intention of deceiving their opposition. *If you know a man is lying to*

you, the lie can be as revealing as the truth itself! Michael had never forgotten that statement.

His father spoke with a wise tongue. *Listen closely, speak little, remain calm. No matter how intimidating your opponents are, remain calm!...above all...remain calm!*

Today, in a matter of a few hours, he would be in the presence of some of the U.S. Government's most powerful men. Men of deception, greed, and an insatiable hunger for power. A few of them would be no better than Peterson. No conscience. No morals. No guilt. The end justified the means, regardless of the consequences to innocent people. These government men could ruin a man or even kill him with just one phone call or significant glance in the right direction.

Although he felt queasy, today he had to be at his peak of alertness and perception. He must keep his mind clear and *calm*. It was up to him to make sure he kept control of the meeting in a subdued, diplomatic manner. He had to be the Deceptive One today, he thought. He wasn't qualified to take these men on alone any more than he could fight the whole Exchange by himself. He looked into the gray sky. A sense of depression touched him, but then an inner voice spoke to him loud and clear, *"I'll be with you!"* He felt his body stiffen. The voice scared him.

He snapped his head first in Pete's direction, then in Bo's direction. Both were preoccupied with their own thoughts. He was going to dismiss the inner voice until he realized his depression had been replaced with a feeling of strength. It was no illusion. Some form of Higher Power was walking with him. He nurtured this thought for a few moments and felt the pressure flow from him like pus from a pierced boil.

His mind returned to the job at hand. He had two plans. One he had been preparing for years, the other would hold a hammer over the heads of the government. The plan would ensure his safety, the safety of his family, and the absolution of the honest Exchange traders who would no doubt come under scrutiny because of their large volume of business. Screw the government! If they wanted information, they would have to pay for it! Otherwise, good people would be run over by their amoral, government steamroller. His father told him, *always have an ace in the hole to play as the last card*, and after all the pissing and moaning and threats, the opposition would yield--if they wanted to make a deal--and Michael knew these men wanted his information--at any cost.

The roar of jet engines landing from the south boldly intruded on his thoughts. He saw the red and blue fuselage stripes on a white Falcon jet that was touching down. Reversing its powerful turbines for breaking brought on a commanding roar.

Michael looked at Bo. His head hung low as he held a hot cup of sugared coffee, sipping it slowly. He was nursing a hangover. "Bad night, Bo?"

Bo looked up with red, droopy eyes and a two-day growth of beard. His face looked older than his forty-one years. "Don't worry about me, Mike. You just take care of yourself. Don't let those guys back you into a corner. Remember, keep an offensive position. They need *you!* You don't need *them!* The boys and I will watch the house and

find the black limo. We'll make sure whoever is fucking with you is put out of commission for good. We'll use the thirty thousand you gave us discreetly and effectively. When you return, nobody will want to come near you!"

Suddenly he felt sorry for Bo. No matter how hard he tried, his alcoholism gripped him by the balls and wouldn't let go. "Don't do anything about the limo until I get home, Bo. Just keep your eyes open. If we take anybody out, I want to call the shots--or at least know when and where and what's going on. Fair enough?"

Bo pouted and licked his dry lips. "Okay, we'll wait for your word before we make our move."

Michael studied Bo's rough face and noticed his hands shake as he took another sip of coffee. "Did you call the guy at the VA regarding the AA meetings?" he asked.

Bo's face fell into a sheepish look. "I tried once, but couldn't get through--but I plan..."

Irritation mounted in Michael. He cut Bo short. "Don't lie to me, Bo. Just say...'No, Mike, I didn't call--and I don't intend to call.' Isn't *honesty* the basis of the whole AA philosophy? Have you ever heard struggling alkies ask the question 'HOW does Alcoholics Anonymous work?' The answer that sober alkies give is, 'It works just fine if you follow the suggestions.' And doesn't HOW stand for Honesty, Open mindedness and Willingness? Make that call, Bo, before it's too late!" He looked at Bo's scarred, blotchy face. His nose was running, but he didn't seem to notice--or he just didn't care.

Michael handed him his monogrammed handkerchief. "Here, wipe your nose." Bo wiped the dribble from his nose and the white dried saliva from the corners of his mouth. "Don't worry, Mike. I promise I'll make the call!" In a futile effort, probably to get Michael's attention off of AA, Bo said, "The three of us will guard your property. It's a piece of cake."

He felt his anger grow as his eyes looked right through Bo's. "Goddammit, Bo. Nothing's a piece of cake! I need you and your boys alert, not half drugged. And don't promise *me* you'll make the call--Promise yourself." Bo turned his eyes from Michael and said nothing. He just stared into his steaming coffee.

Lewis watched the Falcon jet enter the terminal pickup area. Michael's eyes moved in his direction, then back to Bo. He reached over and held Bo's shoulder with his right hand. "Listen, you asshole. I love you like the brother I never had. My heart aches for my brother who is hurting. We can both have the world by the balls, but we both have to be free from her thousands of luring fantasies and temptations bombarding our minds and bodies every day."

Bo took a long swallow of coffee and threw the remaining dregs on the ground in front of him. He crumpled the vending-machine cup and pitched it over his shoulder. "I'll make the call, Mike. I promise you!--I mean, I promise me!"

A lump formed in Michael's throat, and he looked into his friend's sad eyes. His arm reached around Bo, and he hugged him lightly. Bo remained quiet but returned the

embrace. "Take care of yourself, Bo, and stay alive! I need you, brother, and want you by my side during all this shit!"

As they broke apart, Bo wiped his misty eyes and runny nose. Michael could see he was wiping away emotion.

Michael turned to the Falcon now parked just in front of the terminal, its engines dying. The door opened and the steps unfolded. Andy Golden's big frame emerged, barely able to fit through the small exit door. Michael saw him wave. Pete returned a half-assed salute, and Michael gave Andy the finger. Golden caught both of the insubordinate salutations. He just shook his head as he walked toward the three men.

Andy Golden greeted Pete Lewis with a nod and Michael with a handshake. "Sorry to hear about the shoulder, Mike! How are you feeling?"

Michael chided Andy. "Just great! Couldn't be better!" He motioned toward Pete and said, "Thanks to your man Lewis, I'm still around to talk about it."

Michael dropped the small talk. "Andy, I want you to meet a friend of mine. This is Bo Lynch." Bo turned slowly to meet an outstretched grizzly hand. He grabbed and held it, gripping tightly. Michael saw a grimace come across Andy's face as Bo said, "You take care of my friend, FBI man! Understand me?"

Michael could see both hands turn white from the vise grip. Bo's eyes penetrated Golden's confused face. Andy's expression changed, and Michael knew that Golden understood this potential vendetta. "It's nice to meet you, Bo. Just remember Michael is a friend of mine, too. We're both on the same side."

Michael watched as Bo released his grip, to Andy's relief. Bo said with a meanness in his voice, "Funny...I heard those same words in 'Nam!"

Bo slowly eased his eyes from Golden and looked at Michael. He slapped him lightly on his good shoulder. "Go do it, Mike! You know where I am. Call if there is any trouble." He then turned and walked toward the parking lot into the mist.

They all watched Lynch disappear. Michael looked at Andy rubbing the hand Bo had almost broken. "Mike, just who is that friendly chap? He almost broke my hand."

Michael wiped his eyes and knew it wasn't from the moisture in the air. "He's my brother, Andy, and contrary to the song, he's heavy, mean, angry, and goddamn dangerous. We carry each other when the going gets tough."

Andy still rubbed his hand and looked a little bewildered. "It's obvious he's tough--but your 'brother'?"

Michael waved his right hand into the thin air. "Just a figure of speech. I'll fill you in later."

Andy looked perturbed. "What do you have? A mercenary working for you?"

"Bo is a goddamn good and loyal friend with nothing to gain and everything to lose. He's one hundred eighty pounds of C-four plastic destruction. He's been fucked by his government once, and he sees the same thing happening to me. He doesn't trust your lunatic friends in Washington. One wrong move from any of those bastards, and your boys

will be spending another hundred million to keep World War Three from starting right in their own back yard. Don't take him lightly, Andy! Now, let's get the show on the road before I change my mind!"

Andy nodded understanding, then his eyes trailed in Bo's direction. He had disappeared, leaving a cloud of fog and impending gloom behind him. Michael saw Andy shiver and take a deep breath. Then he said, "Okay, let's get our asses out of here before more fog sets in."

Lewis had been faking attention on his global wrist watch while the confrontation took place among the other three men. Then he spoke. "How long before we leave?"

Andy looked at his watch. "Ten minutes. We're going to refuel and off we go." He hesitated and said with a hint of embarrassment, "In spite of Michael's request for your presence, Simpson wants you to stay in Chicago, Pete--to watch the house and do some investigative work."

Pete began to protest, saying that Michael was his responsibility, but Michael cut in coolly. "Bullshit, Andy. He comes with us all the way. He sits in the meetings, he meets the big guns, and he's given a commendation for saving my life. If you think that I'm going to put up with FBI dictates even before we leave Chicago, you all can shove the whole investigation up your pompous asses. Pete goes where I go--or we don't go!"

Andy, flustered, kicked the fence that separated them.

"Goddammit, Mike, I can't do that. I've got my orders. He stays!"

Michael's thoughts whirled. He was going to take control immediately. Besides, he liked and trusted Lewis. He looked calmly at Andy and simply stated, "Then your trip was in vain. Gas up and go back to Washington without me. Tell you asshole friends that I changed my mind. There is no corruption in the commodity markets. The Exchanges are as clean as an angel's wing."

He knew Golden was frustrated. They continued to talk about Lewis as though he wasn't there. "Listen, Mike. Lewis is a friend of mine, too, but he doesn't have many friends in the Bureau. Nobody wants to work the street with him--and I mean nobody. His presence will just bring unnecessary pressure to the people at the meeting. He's a maverick cop who has damn little respect for protocol and the laws we're obliged to live with as federal agents."

Michael's mind churned. Good, he thought. Andy told Michael what he wanted to hear: Lewis would make his interrogators nervous. He was Michael's ace in the hole, and would be able to read the contents of the meeting better than himself. With Pete sitting in, the defense would move from Michael to the government. Michael spoke softly, intently. "He goes with us all the way, Andy. There is no compromise."

Golden had been trained to keep his cool. He had been trained to win, but so had Michael, and he knew he was going to win this contest of wits. "Michael, you're goddamn impossible. I hope this whole trip isn't going to be based on a bunch of ultimatums! Now, it's *my* ass on the line, too."

Michael smiled. "Good, for a minute there I thought it was only my ass hanging out to dry. Then Lewis goes along?"

Andy shook his head no, disgust filling his voice. "Yeah, he goes." Then he turned to Pete and said, "Just keep your tongue in your mouth and your gun in your holster, Pete. No mouthing off to Simpson, for Christ sake--he's the Assistant Director, whether you like it or not."

Michael glanced at Lewis, who just shrugged and raised his eyebrows as if he were ignorant of Andy's allegations.

Michael turned to head for his family in the terminal. He gave Andy a sideways look. "Just remember what you're asking me to do, Andy. I need all of the good men I can surround myself with. And so far Bo and Pete are the only two I can trust!"

Michael glanced back at Pete. A subtle grin slipped onto their faces. He turned from the two federal agents. He knew he had won the first round. They all knew he had won!

The Falcon was fueled, and the Hogan family along with Lewis and Golden were strapped in their seats. The Falcon powered its way down the wet runway and lifted into the air at 180 miles per hour. Within seconds the jet was above the black clouds that curtained Chicago.

Michael's stomach growled with nervous anticipation. He reached across the aisle to hold Maria's hand on the leather arm rest. They looked at each other, exchanging secrets with silent telepathy, the result of many close years together.

She blew him a kiss and smiled. He pursed his lips and sent an invisible kiss back to her pink, moist lips. Then rested his head on the soft cushion, closed his eyes, and began to go over the strategy he was going to use with the Washington men who virtually ran the United States Government.

The Falcon turned east and leveled off at twenty-eight thousand feet. Lewis sneezed, and from the cockpit, Golden, acting as co-pilot, answered, "Gesundheit!" Michael smiled and drifted deeper into his thoughts.

SIXTEEN

Santini Family

The flight was smooth except for a brief period of turbulence over Detroit. Michael slept as the Falcon coasted over 450 miles an hour. They landed on a small air field twelve miles east of Jericho, Long Island.

He spent less than an hour with the Santini Family at the tiny terminal. He had conditioned himself over the years to put up with the Italian tradition of multi hugs and kisses. Maria embraced and jabbered with her Mother in Sicilian dialect.

Michael thought Carlo Santini looked a little like Perry Como, but he didn't make his living by singing. For a man nearly sixty, he was trim and fit. A thin, carefully clipped mustache lined the area beneath his Roman nose and lent him an air of distinction. Thick, white hair, styled straight back, complemented his olive complexion. His clothes were casual, yet elegant. A suede jacket and a Christian Dior sport shirt open at the collar revealed a gold necklace. His khaki-colored trousers had a razor-sharp crease down the front; his loafers were hand-sewn leather. As always, he was impeccably groomed.

Carlo's charm, intelligence, cunning, and suspicious nature of a serpent had kept him alive in the hills of Sicily as well as in the streets of New York.

He had power, money, political contacts, and the soldiers to cause the major Mafia families a considerable discomfort if he flexed his muscles.

Carlo was also a simple man. His family was his first love. Building New York skyscrapers was his second. He had no major problems with the other New York Syndicate families because of his lack of enthusiasm for territorial dominion. His powerful, political strength generated respect from the other families and kept them from interfering with his business. Michael believed that the only way Carlo would coil and strike against an enemy was if his family was threatened. As far as Michael knew, that was his only vulnerability. Maria had inherited his Mediterranean olive complexion along with a bright, perceptive mind.

Mamma Santini, after spending the better part of ten minutes kissing her grandchildren, came for the second time to Michael. She hugged him so hard she almost re-separated his shoulder. An attractive woman with salt and pepper hair, she exuded beauty and class. In the twenty years he had known her, she had hardly aged. The expensive clothes and jewelry accentuated her sharp Sicilian features and beauty. She personified understated elegance.

Carlo was as inquisitive as ever. Standing with arms akimbo, he spoke with a refined accent. "Michael, what is so important in Washington that you can't spend at least a day with your family in Long Island?"

Michael felt uncomfortable. As much as he liked Carlo, he always sensed that Carlo knew the answers to his questions before he asked them. Like a shrewd attorney. Michael glanced around the small terminal while his mind formulated a believable answer.

He used the endeared title of "Papa," the same as his children. He knew it warmed Carlo and showed him that Michael, after many years, had finally accepted him as a friend. "Papa...it's business. Heavy business. You know about these things. Sometimes business comes before family."

Michael knew he had said the wrong thing and wanted the last few words back in his mouth.

Carlo's eyes narrowed, making Michael feel awkward. "The family always comes first, Michael!"

Short and sweet, Michael thought. The family, then business--God bless him! If only it were that easy. "You're right, Papa. Family, then business. But I made these commitments before the family decided to come to Long Island."

Michael watched Carlo's eyes close in on him. Then Carlo laughed heartily. "You're too serious, Michael. That market pressure is too great for any man. It's too demanding."

Michael smiled back and thought aloud, "If you only knew."

Martin had been standing to Michael's left, hiding the limp sleeve of his London Fog. When Martin moved to give his grandmother a fourth hug, Carlo noticed the injured shoulder.

Michael watched Carlo's eyes sadden as he gently touched the empty coat sleeve. His mouth had drooped slightly, and he examined the shoulder as if it were a piece of fragile crystal.

Michael thought, goddammit! Here comes another inquisition. The Italians could make so much out of nothing. He thought he had better explain before Carlo sent men to Chicago to begin blowing people away for hurting his son-in-law.

With his right hand, he reached out and touched Carlo's arm. "It's nothing, Papa-- nothing, really, just a separation. It happens all the time in the pit. Brokers get a little excited and a fight breaks out. Just a misunderstanding, and the other guys are still in the hospital. Honest!"

Their eyes met. Carlo showed a deep concern, also understanding. He was silent. Michael knew he wanted to know more. "Okay, Papa, I had a problem with some people in Chicago, but everything will be fine."

Carlo slowly took his hand from Michael's shoulder and ran his tongue across his lips. "You got trouble like you had a few years ago, Michael?"

Michael dropped his head and studied his shoes, thinking of what to say. He decided there was no use lying to him. Maria would privately fill him in on everything anyway. He felt nauseous and just wanted to get back on the plane. He didn't feel like going into a lot of detail with Carlo just yet. With an affirmative he confirmed Carlo's suspicions.

"Yes, the same type of trouble as a few years ago. But this time I think I'll win!"

He watched Carlo rub his temples in thought and look again at the shoulder. "It doesn't look like you're winning so far!"

Michael smiled a friendly smile as he looked down at the shorter man. "I play a stronger game in the second half than I do in the first." He backed up a step and said, "I have to be going. Maria will answer any questions you have."

Carlo began to protest, but Michael decided it was time to take control. He merely held up his hand to end the subject. He saw respect in Carlo's eyes and reached around and gave him a hug. "Don't worry about me, Papa, I have nine lives."

Carlo shook his troubled head and said, "You're right, son, you do have nine lives. My only concern is that you may have used up eight of them. But you're right-- enough for now. We'll talk when your trip is over. Maybe there is something I can do to help. I have many powerful friends in Chicago who are in my debt. One phone call from me and there will be no more trouble for my family--you understand?"

Michael nodded. "Perfectly, but this is something I must do by myself, Carlo. If I feel there is a threat to the family, and I can't take care of it, I promise I will call on you for a favor."

Impatience crept into Carlo's tone. "Favors are for strangers, Michael. Love and protection is for family. You have always shunned my offers..."

Feeling his own impatience, Michael cut him short. He knew Don Carlo wasn't used to abrupt endings, though. "We'll talk of this another time, Papa. Now I must go."

Mama Santini's attention was once again directed toward him. A slight accent flavored her words. "What is your hurry, Michael? We have a house full of people and food and good desserts. Can't you stay with us for at least a few hours?"

Swallowing his impatience, he instead forced his lips to pull back a little, in a half smile. "Important business in Washington, Mama. Save some pasta for me when I return." Thank God she hadn't noticed his injury.

Maria's two brothers were tending to business in Manhattan. Good, he thought. He hadn't wanted to see them anyway. He didn't trust either of them. Carlo, Jr., and Anthony were both in their late twenties. He didn't know if he was afraid of them or just disliked them. Probably a little of both. Sicilian women, especially one from a family like the Santinis, seldom married outside of their own ethnic blood.

He was sure that the resentment of Maria's marrying Michael ran deep in the brothers. The younger one, Carlo, Jr., was cocky, noisy, and very sure of himself, while

Anthony, with the black, searching eyes of his sister and father, was much more subdued and as handsome a man as Maria was beautiful.

Two other men with the family were introduced as cousins visiting from Sicily. Somber looks painted their faces but they were both polite and careful--he noticed gratefully--not to shake his hand too hard. Michael was family, and they had recognized his injury. They were present not for a reunion, but to protect the Santinis from any outside intrusions. He nodded to them and noted the slight gun bulge in each man's jacket as they shook hands.

Mama Santini handed him a box of homemade cannolis, kissed him hard on the cheek, and spoke something in Italian about the Virgin Mary being with him in Washington.

Before leaving, he glanced sideways at Carlo, who gave him an understanding nod. Michael accepted the acknowledgment and returned the nod, then took one more look at the cousins. They had stepped back to scrutinize everybody and anything that might cause concern to the safety of the family who had brought them to America.

He kissed everybody once again and turned to leave. Maria strode along beside him on his way back to the jet and spoke to him gently. "Watch yourself, Michael. You know you'll be with vultures. Don't trust their empty promises."

He kissed her soft lips and eyes and whispered, "I've lived with you too long to walk into a den of jackals without a spear!"

He put his arm around her slender frame and leaned down to kiss her again. She held on to him tightly as if she were seeing him for the last time.

She smiled at him, and they parted. He felt a pang of melancholy as he left those he loved behind. But he knew they would be safe with Carlo. That's more than he could say for himself.

Twenty minutes later the Falcon touched down at Langley Air Field, in Langley, Virginia. Headquarters of the CIA.

SEVENTEEN

Langley, Virginia

The Falcon touched down on a runway that seemed to extend far into the horizon. One hundred fifty acres of concrete buildings in various shapes and sizes surrounded the runway. His stomach dropped faster than the jet when he saw the sign announcing LANGLEY FIELD. The headquarters for the CIA. Some people called it a state within a state. A government within a government. The Devils of American Law and Order.

Michael leaned over to Andy, who was readying a brief and sipping a mug of stale black coffee. He felt his jaw tighten as he spoke through his teeth. "I thought we were going to Washington, Andy?"

Andy didn't look up. Instead, he pretended a nonchalance as he paged through the brief in front of him. "The Director thought it best to meet here not only for expedience, but also for security. Does that bother you, Mike?" he asked with FBI authority on his face.

Michael grabbed Andy's arm as the plane taxied toward the far end of what appeared to be a plain gray building. "Listen, Andy. I don't care if we meet at St. Patrick's Church in New York City, at the Washington Monument, or a Boy Scout picnic. I want to be kept informed of any changes, so don't go playing with my head. Why Langley?"

Michael saw Andy's expression resume a professional calm. He looked sincere as he said, "Listen to me, Mike. Nobody's playing with your head. I'm your friend, but you seem to forget that. You know your business in the commodity industry probably better than any of your peers. You're the only guy who has witnessed a rape and is willing to come forward to report it. You haven't closed your window, not wanting to get involved."

He adjusted his big frame in his seat for more comfort and to face Michael's perplexed anger. "I know how you feel....You're out on a limb, all by yourself. You think the government is sawing it off. Believe me, Bro--I'm out there with you. I'm not leading you down a primrose path to the end of the rainbow. What has to be done, has to be done. You're the only guy who can do it. So let's do it."

Michael released his grip on Andy's arm and unlatched his seat belt. Fury bubbling, he was about to slam into Andy with verbal abuse, but his mind told him to stay cool. He decided to drop his probe into the location change. He knew Andy didn't make decisions for the Bureau, and Michael didn't want his own demands to force his FBI friend to have to choose sides.

Andy no doubt saw the suspicion in his eyes and continued. "The people you're going to meet today--although you don't trust them--have dedicated their lives to cleaning

up crime in America. They're not meeting with you to discredit you. I wouldn't let that happen. They just want to add to the voluminous information they already have on certain individuals and companies, in an industry they view as becoming a dangerous threat to what's left of our free-enterprise system."

The wall of his wide forehead furrowed into a gully, and Andy looked past Pete Lewis to the front of the jet. Then he looked back at Michael and said, "There's something I didn't tell you in Chicago when I was there. We have been investigating all of the Commodity Exchanges, both in Chicago and New York, for close to two years. We have dossiers on most of the big players, including yourself. I'll be truthful, Mike, we can't figure out the goddamn trading techniques. Yet we know that millions of dollars are being ripped off from the public daily. We also don't know where they put their money, once it leaves the Exchange floor. Sure, we have a good idea where they hide the money, but that's not good enough for the courtroom. We would be pissing in the wind if we charged onto the Exchange floors now to subpoena records not knowing the full extent of the brokers' tricks." Andy finished his coffee and looked into his empty paper cup. With a tone of frustration, he continued. "We just haven't been able to find what we're looking for. We have found out--the hard way--that this investigation is going to take more than just a simple bank audit.

"Your buddies in Chicago are a hell of a lot smarter than we gave them credit for. They are like ghosts. We think we have something, then it vanishes. They dot their *i*'s and cross their *t*'s, yet we know they're stealing. The government is goddamn frustrated, Michael."

Michael felt sorry for him as he crumpled his coffee cup and rubbed the back of his thick neck. His agitated sigh brought out more explanations. "We contacted you for three reasons. First, you're a friend of mine, and I know you're legitimate. Second, you were fucked by your own people because you stood up for what you considered to be right and just. You wouldn't have made so many waves if you had something to hide. For two years we've watched and studied the whole Exchange investigation. What seemed to be a slap in the face to you gave us more confidence in Michael Hogan. It confirmed our own suspicions that something is being grossly mishandled by the brokers and executives of the Exchanges. And, third, we know that your knowledge of what goes on down there--not to mention your uncanny ability as a commodity broker--is the best in Chicago.

"The excellent eyes that God blessed you with can catch a thief at a hundred yards. You were born with tenacity and courage. You have guts. They're inbred. You took that inherited talent and developed it. You're a guy who knows how to take the ball and run with it.

"Your actions have impressed all of us. That includes Director Collins. I have always admired, even envied, your zealous moral behavior. You live by your conscience even if it means your loss. You're the type of bastard who tyrannical governments like we saw in Germany under Hitler--and now have in Central and South America and South

Africa--would want to eliminate immediately. You expose truth with little concern for the consequences." He rubbed his thick chin, then said, "I expect a few guys at the Exchanges would like to see you disappear, Michael, and..."

Michael put his hand up to stop Andy. He wiped beads of perspiration from his brow. "Andy, you're damn right. I do have my share of enemies down there, but until the black limo showed up, they've kept their distance. I do have great concern about the consequences of this investigation. That's one of the reasons I'm here with you today. If the truth comes out, the whole industry goes down. It will put things back fifty years, and the Exchanges will never recover. Not in our lifetime anyway. It will all but destroy the free markets and free enterprise. And that's a goddamn shame. The commodity markets are the last of a dying philosophy that made America what it is today. A few greedy bastards have brought cancer to the floors of the Exchanges!"

Michael's thoughts quickened. "I apologize for my shortness with you, Andy, but I hope this patronizing dialogue of yours is from your heart, and not from one of your FBI training sessions on how to soften up an informant."

Andy started to object, but Michael cut him short again when he raised his hand. He remembered to stay on the offense and keep control. "You're right. I don't trust the government men you have waiting to meet me. I trust their superiors even less. They've proven time and again that power and money are more important to them than truth and justice.

"You know as well as I do that their credo is 'The end justifies the means'. Always has been. Always will be. Politicians haven't changed since day one. They'll be nice to me, shake my hand, pat me on the back, offer me a drink, offer me anything I want, tell me how proud they are to find a loyal American who is not afraid to stand up for what is right, despite the odds. I know their game, Andy. At the press of a button they could turn from back-slappers to back-stabbers, and ol' Hawk Hogan would never be seen or heard from again. Your people are truthful only when it is to their advantage or political advancement. And if you think differently, you're just plain naive."

Andy shook his head. "You've been reading too many Robert Ludlum books, watching too many spy movies. You have a real attitude problem, Mike. We're all on the same side."

Michael felt his anger seethe. " Attitude problem, my ass. The government is good to me only until something goes wrong. Then I become a liability. Don't be stupid, Andy-- and don't insult my intelligence." There was silence for a long moment, then he continued. "I have a few demands I'm going to present at the meeting in order to ensure my protection and the protection of innocent brokers who are not involved. I'm going to need your support on those issues."

Andy's head tilted. Behind his patient eyes, Michael saw anger brewing. He responded curtly but respectfully. "If your goddamn demands aren't too severe, I'll back

you up, and if I back you up, so will Director Collins. The only guy you have to watch out for is the Assistant Director, John Simpson, but...you already know that."

Michael turned away from Andy and toward the small window of the Falcon. They had, by now, come to a stop. A stretched 600 Mercedes limo was speeding toward the aircraft.

Andy spoke again, this time like a penitent in a confessional. "There is one more thing you should know, Michael. I should have told you, but I had to be absolutely sure you were going to work for us."

Michael's head spun toward Andy, and he let his eyes glare at him. "More surprises, Andy? Now what?"

Andy squirmed in his seat, avoiding his piercing eyes. "Well, uh, I told you we've been investigating the commodity industry for quite awhile. We've also had infiltrators working at the Exchange for well over a year. A few are working as phone men on the floors of the Exchanges. Others, in offices, working their way into the back rooms, where the trades are processed. Others just sweep up after trading is finished. They collect all the discarded orders. These are then sent to Washington to be analyzed and filed. Our agents have gathered *some* information which has helped us to substantiate certain trading infractions. But they haven't given us much, not for the amount of time and money we've sunk into the operation."

Michael felt his body relax, and the anger left his eyes. He wasn't surprised. How else would the FBI have dossiers on brokers if they hadn't already infiltrated the Exchanges? The Feds surely weren't going to tell him everything. He said simply, "Good! That will make things a little easier for me, if you already have someone there who understands the trading lingo."

Andy seemed relieved, knowing he wasn't going to get another verbal thrashing. He unbuckled his seat belt. He struggled to squeeze his body out of his tight seat and into the narrow aisle. Michael felt Andy's eyes on him. "Our people in Chicago haven't come up with *jack shit* as of yet. So far, their reports haven't revealed any major infractions."

Michael was already on his way out of the Falcon when he turned and said, "Of course not. You're looking in the wrong place, and you think you're dealing with a bunch of bank robbers who leave trails. Forget it, Andy, you're right. You have grossly underestimated the enemy. Your men don't know what they're looking for or how to get it."

"How's that?"

"Are they able to recognize *a skim trade*, *a prearranged trade*, *a curb trade*, or *bucket trades*? Can they tell the difference between a *'bag man'* and a *'straight'*? How about a *'corner hedge'* and a *'contract hedge'*? Fuck, no, they can't! I suppose your agents have limited their infiltration and covert snooping to the companies within the Exchange buildings."

Andy followed him out the door, his hair messed and his brown suit rumpled. "Yes...basically we've confined our investigation to the companies within the Exchange buildings. That's where most of them are located. Where else would we start?"

Michael waited for Andy to lumber off the jet. He put his hand on his shoulder and looked deep into his droopy, hound eyes. "Andy...Most of the dirty trades aren't even processed at the Exchanges. The trades that are processed at the clearing houses are clean as snow by the time they reach the computers."

He saw Andy try in vain to say something professional. All that came was an indrawn gasp. In a voice barely audible, he asked, "Where are they processed?"

Michael let a smile, tinged with superiority, flicker across his face. He looked at this man who had access to billions of dollars' worth of equipment to track criminals. "Many are processed right under your nose in the Federal Building. What better place to hide a scam operation than the Federal Building?"

Andy's lower jaw drooped, pulling his lips apart. He slowly blinked his eyes as if trying to understand. Visibly shaken, he now remained silent. He finally closed his mouth, turned toward the limo, and mumbled, "Son of a bitch!"

Pete Lewis had been a disciplined, quiet passenger for the whole trip. He followed Michael and Andy off the jet. Michael looked back at Lewis, who raised his eyebrows and said, "You think you got his attention?" Michael smiled. "I think so...if I didn't, this is going to be a long trip for nothing." They both walked together, behind Andy, to the spooky, black Mercedes, which normally carried only dignitaries.

EIGHTEEN

Conference Room H-280

Standing with ramrod posture, eyes straight ahead, a uniformed Marine held the door to the black Mercedes. Andy entered well ahead of Lewis and Hogan. Michael had deliberately fallen behind to let Golden lead the way. He needed to talk to Lewis.

Pete walked with a cocky strut as if he knew exactly where he was, what to do, and where to go. Michael knew Pete had been here at some previous time, probably doing work for the CIA. He put his hand out and slowed Pete's stride, then said, "I want you to keep those photographic eyes open. Take a picture of everybody and everything. Keep your ears open, too. You understand and know these people a hell of a lot better than I do. We'll go over everything after the meetings. I'll save your ass, if you help me save mine."

Smiling, Pete put his hand on Michael's right shoulder and said, "Done." Then, as an afterthought he said, "One word of caution, Mike. Don't say anything that can come back to haunt you. There will most likely be a stenographer at the meetings. Everything you say will be recorded. The car, restaurants, elevators, the halls--even the johns are bugged. The walls have ears, and in this place so do the floors, ceilings, doorknobs, and toilet paper dispensers--just so you know."

Michael's stomach began to churn again. He felt confident with Pete and would hold on to him for security, as a child does a rag doll. "Thanks for the warning."

He and Pete climbed into the limo, and the uniformed man, who could have passed for a poster of a recruiting Marine, jutting jaw and all, closed the heavy door with authority.

The long black limo with tinted windows and black curtains masking the back window reminded Michael of a hearse. He hoped it wasn't for him. "Two-oh-seven. We're only about an hour late," Andy said.

Michael remained quiet as the car sped and weaved around wide concrete airplane taxi trails heading for a stark white building near the end of the runway. In less than two minutes the driver had skillfully maneuvered the limo off the airfield, through a narrow alley, and into the garage of the windowless fortress.

As they passed through the garage opening, Michael saw that the walls appeared to be at least four feet thick. A heavy metal door automatically began to close behind them. He pulled the black curtain apart and looked out the rear window. The metal door inched its way to the floor like an obsequious, massive servant squeezing back the outside light, which tried in vain to peek inside. It reminded him of a giant coffin lid being closed on him, leaving life outside. He let the black curtain slide back into place and turned to face

the front. He wiped his clammy brow with the back of his right hand. The battle was starting.

His agitation grew, and he felt sick to his stomach at seeing all this cold concrete and metal. He scolded himself for being pulled into this precarious situation. He should have insisted that the Feds visit him in Chicago--his turf. If that garage door didn't open again for his exit, no one in the world would know where to look for him. He wondered how many people had disappeared behind such a door. How many before him had made only a one-way trip? The sickness went through him again in small, black waves.

Why was he thinking and feeling this way? He had to get rid of these negative thoughts. Fast. It was just the pressure and fear of the unknown, he told himself. He could see how men, even strong men, in similar situations could drive themselves crazy if they let their imagination project and spiral their thoughts out of control. How did the POW's handle fear? The incarcerated? The dying? The homeless? The starving? An inner strength must come, like a second wind in a ball game. He hoped he would get his second wind-- but he hadn't remembered getting his first. He knew he was making more of this ordeal than it deserved. He decided he was not going to let the FBI, CIA, IRS, or anyone else play ping-pong with his brains or live rent free in his head. He felt color returning to his face.

Quickly winding the Mercedes downward to an underground parking area, the Marine brought it to a smooth halt in front of a bank of elevators. Before Michael knew it, both rear doors had been opened with such precision and speed that it seemed to Michael there were two chauffeurs. But on emerging he saw only the expressionless face of the one seasoned Marine, wearing smooth fatigue clothing, in the erect stance of a statue. He bet that the Marine would hold the same emotionless expression if he stuck his boot knife in a man's neck and pulled it four inches deep from ear to ear. Michael wondered if the man ever took a shit!

As he climbed out of the rear seat of the limo, he said, "Thank you." The Marine remained still and silent.

On the way to the elevators, he looked at Pete and said, "Nice guy!"

Pete smiled and said, "He's one of the friendly ones."

Andy placed an ID card in a little slot and punched in seven numbers, which opened the sliding doors. It was large, very bright, and very plain. Not even a hand rail around the inside. There were no floor buttons, just a bunch of color-coded toggle switches on the wall. Andy flicked three of them; the doors closed, and to Michael's surprise the elevator quickly began to descend rather than ascend. He knew the garage was already two stories below the ground. Before it stopped he estimated they had gone down about five more floors.

He quickly calculated they had to be about two hundred feet underground by the time the elevator came to a halt. The doors opened to a large reception area. They were

greeted by another Marine, same stature, same expression. He slowly checked Andy's security pass and nodded. He motioned with his hand to step toward the desk.

Michael looked into the black eyes of the Marine and thought that the CIA must have a section where they cloned these men to look and act alike. He felt damn strange in these surroundings.

Andy stepped ahead of Lewis and Michael. A rather plain but attractive girl sat at the reception desk. Brown-rimmed glasses matched her shiny brown hair pulled tightly into a chignon. Andy showed his pass and introduced himself. She smiled and picked up one of many elaborate phones. She efficiently announced their arrival. Then she reached into a side drawer, pulled out two laminated security passes, and handed them to Andy. He in turn gave one each to Michael and Pete. "Wear these so they can be seen!"

She pointed to two heavy metal doors where the CIA logo was displayed. In a tone of professionalism, she instructed them to follow the hall to H-280, where their party waited.

Andy motioned Lewis and Michael to follow. The steel doors opened into a wide, well-lighted hall. Tinted see-through glass, mirrored on the opposite side, shielded the comings and goings of passers-by down the long hall. But the occupants of the walkway could scrutinize the work going on behind the windows.

Michael couldn't see the other end of the hall. It had to be more than one hundred yards long with numbered doors lining the left side. On the right side, and through the one-way windows, Michael saw a massive underground network of people, machines, computers, and glass offices. All of the workers were dressed in white smocks, the kind doctors wear. Picture ID badges similar to the one Andy displayed hung from each breast pocket. Michael thought he might be impressed if he just knew what they were all doing.

Andy's explanation followed as though he could read Michael's questioning mind. "This is the largest government building in the Washington area, after the Pentagon, Michael. The grounds are over one hundred fifty acres, and the cost to build it was over two billion dollars. There are over ten thousand agents abroad and nearly thirty thousand research specialists employed here at Langley. The CIA and FBI have a combined budget of nearly ten billion dollars annually."

Michael felt his interest intensify. "What's going on with all the people in white?"

As they looked through the windows at the melee within, Andy answered in a tone of pride. "There are experts in practically every field you can think of, electronics, economists, psychologists, atomic scientists, surgeons, doctors, pilots, and cryptologists. There are experts on every major jurisprudence system in the world, on foreign naval and air-force construction, on political metallurgy, judo, physics, and microfilm. Shall I go on?"

Michael looked at Andy with the same questioning expression on his face. "All that in *this* room?"

Andy shook his head, stopped in the middle of the hall, and leaned up against the window. He and Lewis did the same as Andy went on. "The underground labyrinth extends throughout the whole complex of buildings. We're one hundred eighty feet below ground, a total of seven levels just like this one. This particular section is in charge of translating into English over two hundred fifty thousand Communist and foreign publications every month. Innocuous things such as road maps, railroad timetables, telephone directories. Also, reports of foreign medical and scientific meetings and organizations all contribute to a constant flow of information. Everything is immediately filed and cross indexed.

"Can you imagine that twenty four hours a day, seven days a week, experts in every language in the world listen to foreign radio broadcasts to analyze every scrap of information? This is also placed into our computers and cross referenced. Machine translation computers work at over five hundred thousand words an hour."

Andy pointed to a bank of glass offices filled with mainframe computers. "Over there is the agency's special international criminal division. If you've had as much as a speeding ticket, you're in that room. Over twenty million bits of criminal information are recorded daily--again, information gathered from all over the world. Next to that is a special microfilm and microfiche laboratory with ultra-high-speed duplicating and print-out machines. There are other labs that conduct laser and infra-red research as well. All of this, plus more, means the CIA has the most extensive, sophisticated systems in the whole damn world!"

Andy broke his dialogue and looked at his watch. "We'd better get moving." All three men continued down the endless hall.

Michael answered with a tone of irritation, "With a budget of ten billion dollars a year, it's no wonder the system is so elaborate. Tell me, Andy, where is the section of the CIA that's responsible for starting revolts in other countries? Where are the assassins trained? Where do you teach special agents how to lie and beat drug inducement and the polygraph machine? How about the section that promotes snuffing out your own agent if his usefulness has ceased? How do you train people to terminate their buddies? And where is the room with the picture of slaughtered innocent women, children, and old people in Central and South America all in the name of freedom? *All backed by the CIA!* Are they in your records? Or has every bit of evidence been destroyed in those high-powered shredders? The graveyards are loaded with your 'could-be', 'pull-the-plug', and 'blow-the-whistle' agents."

Michael saw Andy's disgust. "Go to hell, Mike. I don't know shit about any of that. I sure don't know where you're getting your half-assed information. It's a figment of your imagination. Keep your politics and your sarcastic remarks about clandestine government groups to yourself."

He turned to Michael and, with exasperation written all over his face, said, "These people you're about to meet aren't here to fuck Michael Hogan or anybody else. They are here simply to organize and broaden an investigation that's going to take place with you

or without you. So get off my back!" His expression relaxed, his frustration still obvious as he spoke again. "Don't worry--you'll feel much more at ease once you've met everybody, so just relax, and don't be so goddamn insulting and paranoid. Your insecurity is showing! Do both of us a favor and settle down."

Without thinking first, Michael let his angry words pour free. "Fuck you and the horse you rode in on!"

Andy forced himself to keep his rebuttal silent. He tightened his lips and shook his head in disgust.

Michael couldn't decipher the mumbling that was coming from Andy. **H-280 Private Conference Room** was printed in heavy black letters on the imposing door before them.

Before Andy opened it, he said, "Ya know, Mike. You have a real hard-on for us. We do a hell of a lot more good for this country than we do harm. I've said it before, and I'll say it again--you have a real attitude problem. I don't know if it's from the pressure you're feeling or if your Irish balls are shrinking!"

Michael grabbed Andy's jacket roughly and came within inches of Golden's face to spit out a counterattack. "Listen, Asshole. I know you're FBI, not CIA. You're just giving us the five-cent tour. But you forget who you're talking to. Stick up for the actions of the CIA with your other guests, not with me. And get your head out of your ass. There is no negotiating with morality. The right hand that pulls the trigger is connected to the rest of the body. You can't feed someone with your left hand in Angola and blow some innocent human being away with your right hand in Managua and say the day was a good one, because you fed a hungry African peasant. You also killed some poor son of a bitch in Nicaragua. Bread crumbs and blood just turn to salty paste. And don't try to impress me with those white-coated, brainwashed clones you have working behind the glass. Their minds don't go beyond the tip of their pencils!"

Michael felt Golden yank his coat sleeve from his grip, as he spoke. "Listen, hothead. We're here now. Cool it will ya...and you said it--so remember it--the FBI is a completely separate entity than the CIA."

"Bullshit! You guys work together when it suits your mutual purpose. Well, I'm going in there to tell a story about a group of American commodity brokers who steal with one hand and feed their own greed with the other hand. We're talking the same philosophy, Andy except you guys have the gold badges saying FBI and CIA on them. It's okay for you guys to bend the moral laws and interpret truth to fit your needs. It's okay for you to manipulate justice. But watch out, world--if you're not with us, we'll put the white coats on your trail--and you better watch out even if you are with us, because there are no guarantees!"

Andy just stared, not choosing to argue any further with Michael.

Now that he had that dialogue out of the way, he felt better. He knew it was mainly because of the pressure that lay beyond the H-280 door. Although his anger was directed at Andy Golden, he was using him simply as a whipping boy. He looked at Andy's droopy eyes and said, "Okay. I got that off my chest. I'm sorry for taking it out on you. Let's go see what these assholes want from me!"

Andy shook his head. "Just stay cool will you, Mike? Please?"

He cocked his own head and said, "Cool as an ice cube, Andy. Don't worry about a thing!"

Pete Lewis patted Michael on the back and as they followed Andy, he said, "Nice show, partner. Go give 'em hell and watch your step."

The heavy metal door to Conference Room H-280 closed securely behind the three of them--leaving the mile-long hall empty, stark, and listening.

NINETEEN

The Beginning of the End

Michael and Pete followed Andy into the conference room. Michael felt a sickness run through him in waves of nausea, and the urge to urinate was strong. This was the same feeling he used to get before an important football game. He knew it had just been nerves then and would go away after the kick-off. This was just another kickoff.

The room was large, probably seventy feet long and forty feet wide. The decorative accessories didn't call attention to their costliness. Antiques, with timeworn distinction, something like you would see at the Ritz, held prominent places of honor throughout the room. A conference table, long and oval, of rich, dark, cherry wood, polished with a high lustre, stood elegantly in the center. In front of each of the leather arm chairs that surrounded the table perched small, intimidating microphones and a yellow legal pad and pen. Pots of coffee and jugs of water staggered every other seat.

A large glass-enclosed world map hung on the wall at the far end of the room. Michael noticed a red circle had been drawn around Chicago and New York, evidently the topics of today's conversation. Six numbered clocks were set close together above the map giving the times in New York, Chicago, Los Angeles, Tokyo, Moscow, and London. It was 2:18 P.M. New York time.

Nine middle-aged men sat around the far end of the table chattering and drinking coffee. Half of the other chairs were occupied mostly by younger people in their twenties and early thirties. He had anticipated a caucus with six or seven men, but here he found at least twenty-five: mostly men, a few women. He didn't study the faces--he'd do that later.

To his surprise the room was not stark or a bit offensive. The pressure on him eased immediately. The temperature was perfect, fresh air surrounded him, and a clean scent of lemon polish permeated the room. A plush cocoa carpet covered the floor, and the walls held a covering of sand-colored moire. Pastoral oil paintings, historied for the past two hundred years, lined the walls in ornate wooden frames. A portrait of Ronald Reagan on another wall was centered and flanked by the American flag on one side, the CIA flag on the other.

He wondered why the meeting was taking place here instead of the FBI headquarters in Washington, but it was too late to concern himself with that now.

The chatter stopped, and all attention was directed to the three newcomers. Michael felt his ears warm and a flush come over his face. A white-haired man at the end of the table lifted his trim frame out of his chair and headed around the table toward the

guests. The other eight men who were seated with him followed their apparent leader, but with less confidence and a bit of confusion, bumping into each other as they rounded the corner of the table. It appeared to Michael that they were as flustered as he, which made him feel more comfortable.

His confidence was returning, and the temperature in the room had already begun to cool his warm body. He rolled his head slightly to readjust the tight cartilage in his neck.

Lewis took his windbreaker off and helped Michael with his raincoat, revealing the sling on his left arm. He noticed a few of the younger people whisper speculations to each other when they saw his arm.

Andy prepared for introductions, as he put his right hand gently on Michael's left shoulder and pulled him forward to meet the men coming their way.

The white-haired gentleman approached with a friendly smile showing perfect white teeth, an appropriate complement to his handsome face.

He wore an expensive, three-piece black suit and had that impeccable look that is usually reserved for the wealthy. Starched white cuffs peeking through his coat sleeves. Pocket handkerchief to match his expensive tie--Yes, impeccable! He extended both hands, and Michael noticed his gold jewelry. Wristwatch, ring, monogrammed cuff-links. Fitting for the confidence and stature of the man.

The thought flashed quickly through his mind that this man was either on the take to afford such extravagance, or he wasn't FBI or CIA connected.

Andy began the introduction. "Mr. Ross, this is Michael..."

The man cut him off. "Nonsense, Andy. I know Michael..."Hawk" Hogan. He's the best pit broker in the City of Chicago, and probably in the world, if we'd give him a chance. Michael, it's my pleasure. I've never met you formally and you've never met me, but I've watched and admired you in action. I'm Sam Ross." He grabbed Michael's right hand and held it with sincerity and authority.

Michael was speechless. He hadn't expected a billionaire supporter to be at this meeting. Maybe he wouldn't have to carry the ball by himself after all. Sam Ross and Joe Glassmann had started this whole investigation anyway. He felt a great sense of relief.

Ross waited for an acknowledgment. Michael remained silent, remembering his mother's wise words: "It's better to remain silent, Michael, and appear ignorant, than to open your mouth and remove all doubt!" He decided he had better go against his mother's warning. He couldn't keep quiet for the whole meeting. He cleared his throat and forced a smile. Hoping his voice wouldn't crack he said, "It's my pleasure, Mr. Ross. I've heard a lot about you--and I want to thank you for all the business you've directed my way in the trading pits."

Ross let go of his hand. "You deserve it, Michael. You're the best I've ever seen, and that's all I want on my team."

Michael felt his eyes tighten. Ross must have noticed also because his smile faded and he stepped back. Michael didn't want to be on anybody's team--at least not yet. He'd let that drop for now--this time hearing his father's brogue, "Stay calm, don't be intimidated, listen and watch, then speak only when you have something to say."

Andy had stepped behind Michael to take a seat by Pete Lewis, leaving an open chair for Michael between the two agents. Pete was pouring himself a cup of coffee. Sam Ross turned to the other eight men to make introductions. Clay Hudson, Executive Assistant to the Director of the CIA; John Simpson, First Assistant to the Director of the FBI; Harvey Shultz, Executive Director of the IRS; Thaddeus Overton, Chief Assistant to the U.S. Attorney General; Anthony Lorenzo, U.S. Attorney for Chicago; Brian Brennen, U.S. Attorney for New York; Marty Ruiz, Chief Investigator, Drug Enforcement; and Marvin Kaluski, Head of the Securities and Exchange Commission.

Michael greeted all of them with genuine acknowledgment, "My pleasure." Then, without warning, his tongue moved before his brain told it to and he said, "Looks like the only one missing is President Reagan."

Sam Ross led the laughter, and the room's tension eased. Michael noticed a sneer come over John Simpson's face. Fuck You, Simpson. He said to himself.

As the others returned to their seats, Sam Ross took Michael around the table introducing the others. Agent Randy Harris, stationed in Chicago; Special Agent Vern Oblowski, also Chicago; Agent Eli Hanks, Chicago; Agent Joe Fitzsimmons, Chicago; Agent Sean Patricks, Chicago; Agent Ted Tully, Chicago; Agent Vito Calusso, Chicago; Agent Barry Kane, Chicago; Agent Perry Washington, Chicago; Agent George Goldburg, Chicago; Agents Serra Brooks and Vince Martini, both Chicago; and Agents Colleen McFadden and Samantha Winters, also both based in Chicago.

Samantha Winters--that name he had heard before, and not too long ago--but where and when? He walked around the table with Ross, shaking hands with the agents and looking hard into their eyes, but Winters wouldn't lift her head high enough for him to get a good look at her face. She was blond and lovely. The hint of an alluring fragrance touched his senses. He dipped to get a closer look and said, "My pleasure...Agent Winters." Her head raised and their eyes met. For a brief second they studied each other. Her sensuous face was direct and challenging as she said with an air of professionalism, "I'm very happy to meet you, Mr. Hogan." Their eyes held for a bit longer and he remembered. She was "Unit 2"--"Sam!"--the blue Mercedes that had passed Golden and him on the expressway the night of Joseph's birthday. He felt his mouth move into a slight smile, as he shook her hand firmly. He held it for just a moment longer than would normally be fitting. He nodded politely, tried to get a better look at the rest of her, but he knew Sam Ross was waiting. He moved on to meet the agents from New York, letting her hand slide gently from his own--Damn! She's gorgeous, he thought, as he continued on around the table with Ross. He hoped his enthusiasm with "Unit 2" hadn't been too obvious

to the trained eyes watching him. He forced her pretty face from his mind: time for the meat and potatoes of the meeting--not the dessert!

Ross introduced one more Chicago agent, Dan Angeleri, then looked at Michael and with a wave of his hand said, "This is our Chicago team. Fifteen of the bureau's finest agents. All at your disposal if you so wish."

He moved further around the table to three other men. "Michael, these men are heading up our New York investigation, which is still a bit unorganized. They will, however, be working in conjunction with Chicago. Special Agents Jack Kyle, Alex Taylor, and Joe McNurtney. FBI Director Collins, although he was unable to meet with us today, has asked them here to listen to your comments, that is, if you don't mind."

Michael nodded in agreement. He said nothing, and made damn sure he showed no emotion.

Ross continued. "The pretty young lady sitting next to Pete Lewis is Sherry Nelson. She'll be taking notes on her steno machine. Everything said here today will be on the record. Keep that in mind before you speak."

At first, Michael was going to object. Hell, this wasn't a trial and it wasn't a deposition. He decided to let it pass. He just wouldn't sign anything--as if that really mattered!

Sam led him to his seat, then returned to his own at the end of the table.

Andy poured Michael a cup of coffee, and Michael added two heaping teaspoons of sugar. It was really time for a Black Label, but since that wasn't available just now, he thought the sugar in the coffee would have to do. He mentally cursed, thinking that sugar was a poor substitute for the alcohol that he really needed. He could see this was going to be a long session. His stomach had stopped churning, but the grumbling moved to his brain, and he was being bombarded with confused ideas and thoughts. He was almost at the edge of desperation. Stay calm! he told himself, as he looked at the men and women around the room. There seemed to be a pretty good cross section of nationalities represented: three black agents, a Latino, a few Pollacks, Jews, Irish, Germans, and Italians...the rest were WASPS.

He looked down at the black mouthpiece on his microphone and took a moment to meditate. His eyes closed, and his spirit asked for guidance and courage. Thoughts scrambled through his mind like a handful of BB's in a shoe box. He told himself to let the spirit rule the body and the mind. The spirit was infinite and could go back in time or into the future and find the answers he needed. He could only deal with the limited amount of space, time, and matter that made up the physical part of Michael Hogan, a mere grain of sand on a vast, dark ocean floor.

"Mr. Hogan?" Michael heard his name being called from someplace far away. "Mr. Hogan, are you all right?" He snapped his head up and saw that the whole room looked at him quizzically. "Mr. Hogan, are you okay?" He looked to the end of the table.

The words came from Sam Ross. He managed to answer. "Yes, your Honor. I mean...I'm fine, Mr. Ross."

A few of the younger agents laughed at his mistaken courtroom inference, and Sam Ross smiled. "You and I are not on trial here, Mike. You may call me Sam...and if you don't mind, let's drop all formalities, and I'll call you by your first name." He raised his eyebrows and nodded his agreement.

"You may be wondering why I'm leading off this meeting, Michael. Since you and I are the only non-government employees in the room, I thought it only fair to begin these talks on a neutral basis. And, since I'm the one who registered the complaints to the FBI about the possible illegal activities and trading practices by brokers in Chicago and New York, I will take the liberty of beginning the meeting. Fair enough?"

Michael returned the smile and shrugged his shoulders. "It's all yours, Mr. Ross."

Michael noticed all attention shift to the confident, debonair man who seemed to mesmerize the whole room. He knew Ross had the political power and influence to accelerate the investigation. Michael's adrenalin began to pump him up, and he felt good about Ross being in the room. He had expected the attention to be totally on him during this meeting. Now, to his relief, he saw that this would not be so.

Again, his mind flipped back to a football game. Ross was the quarterback. He would call the play, then flip the ball to Michael. After that, Michael thought, the game would be under way, and the heavyweights at the head of the table could give him the ball all they wanted--he would be alert, and he would be ready for their 8-3 defense!

Everyone in the room was prepared to take notes and had already begun to scribble on their legal pads. Sherry Nelson feverishly worked her silent steno machine. Michael's sharp eyes caught John Simpson (FBI) lean over and say something to Clay Hudson (CIA).

They both looked down at Pete Lewis. Simpson had an exasperated look on his furrowed, overweight face. Michael figured Lewis made him uncomfortable, but that would work to Michael's advantage. Instinctively, he didn't like Simpson. He didn't like the shadows in his eyes, the continuous sneer hovering about his mouth. And it was Simpson who had demoted Pete Lewis from Special Investigator status to a simple Agent's position-- that's like taking a Master Sergeant and breaking him to a Private.

Ross looked down at Michael and spoke. "Michael, help yourself to coffee and anything else that will make you feel comfortable. We even have some scotch--Black Label, I believe, which I will join you in after the meeting."

Michael thought, the fucker can even read minds. He was going to ask for the bottle right away, but thought against it. That would definitely impress everybody. *A bottle of scotch for the one-armed man at the end of the table, please.* He erased the mockery from his mind.

Ross shuffled and straightened some papers in front of him. He pulled the microphone closer and began. "Ladies and gentlemen. In January of this year, Joseph

Glassmann of Chicago and I began a trading scheme to see what we could find out about the execution of trades made at the Chicago Mercantile Exchange, the Board of Trade in Chicago, and the Comex in New York. We had in our presence Tony Lorenzo, who was then an Assistant U.S. Attorney of Chicago, and Assistant U.S. Attorney for New York, Brian Brennen. We entered the orders under a corporate name, Glass-Ro Investment Corporation, Incorporated, as both Glassmann and I are well known in the Commodity industry, thus the insignificant and anonymous label, 'Glass-Ro'.

"All conversations with floor brokers and phone men were taped. All orders were time stamped by us to indicate the precise time we placed buy and sell orders in the market. All orders were watched by our undercover men on the floor of the Exchanges to trace the orders. They watched the order go from the phone man, who writes up the buy/sell order from the customer, to a runner, who literally runs the order into the pit. It is then up to the broker to read the customer order and immediately execute it at the best possible price he can get. The broker is prohibited from disclosing the contents of the order. He is simply required to buy or sell for the customer--that which is written on the order sheet.

"Our men on the floor had stop watches to measure the period of time it took to fill each order. They also registered the prices at which the markets were trading during the time the order was in the pit. Our orders were basically all large--large enough to whet the appetite of a broker who would have the tendency to skim a point or two. In other words, if the broker was cheating, he would not give the customer the best possible price available in the pit--he would keep a few points for himself!"

Ross looked at the blank faces around the table and said, "I'll explain. The temptation would be to pay more for a commodity, or sell it for less than the true market price actually dictated. The difference between the low price he *could* have bought the commodity for and the higher price he actually *paid* for the product is measured in points-- which is money. The extra Points, or money, he paid for the commodity eventually finds its way back to the broker's pocket in one way or another. It's my understanding that this illegal practice is called 'skimming trades' or 'bagging trades.' Mr. Hogan will explain the procedure at length later in the session."

Ross stopped to pour himself a glass of water, and Michael grabbed the opportunity to glance over at Samantha Winters. She had placed a pair of dark-rimmed glasses on, and her head tilted as she wrote. Her lips pursed with intensity, as though she did not want to miss a word of Ross's monologue. Michael smiled to himself, thinking he would be happy to tutor her if she had any trouble understanding market lingo.

Then, he told himself to keep his mind on the matters at hand--not get caught up in dangerous territory. This was so unlike him. Naturally, he was a normal male, and he certainly always noticed beautiful women, but by the same token, he had always been faithful to Maria. Somehow, though, this was different--very different. He felt his cheeks

puff out with a rather loud exhale. Goddamn, the blond girl called "Unit 2--SAM" had a definite pull to her that Michael couldn't explain.

Andy leaned over and asked, "You okay, Mike?"

He nodded his head yes, then said, "I could handle a drink about now."

At that, Andy reached over, poured Michael a glass of water, and said sarcastically, "Whatever you want, Mike, just ask ol' Andy."

Michael looked at the clear, impotent liquid of life and said, "Thanks, Einstein...could I have that with a twist?"

Ross cut back in. "We chose three groups of floor brokers, also called order fillers, on whom we tested our theory of 'skim trading.' The first group we chose were brokers who had been mentioned in numerous complaints. The second group of order fillers we chose at random. And the third group we chose was Michael Hogan's team of order fillers and floor brokers."

Michael's attention had returned to Samantha. She sat about halfway down the table on his right side. She continued to write until Ross mentioned his name; then she looked up and caught Michael watching her. Their eyes met. He sensed she wanted to ask him a question. He gave her a boyish smile and felt uncomfortable as hell at being caught spying on her.

Ross's remark about "Hogan's team" turned his concentration back to the front of the table.

Ross continued. "Michael, incidentally, knew nothing of Glassmann's and my activities, nor did anybody else except the U.S. Attorney's Office. All three groups filled orders as they were accustomed, so we had a pretty good feel for the variety and quality of buying and selling by the different broker groups on the trading floors.

"The broker groups we chose for our investigation were stationed in the S & P 500, the Eurodollar, the Swiss franc, and pork belly pits at the Mercantile Exchange. They were stationed in the wheat, soybean, Treasury bond, and Ginnie Mae pits at the Chicago Board of Trade. In New York, we entered orders in silver, gold, heating oil, and frozen orange juice pits.

"Each day, we recorded and computerized all the trades entering the pits. Time of entry...time it took for execution...market price of the filled order. We also noted the broker and phone man taking the orders. We understand from Michael that sometimes the phone men and brokers work together in skimming operations.

"We then entered into the computer the prices the markets were trading at during time of order entry, and the prices the markets were trading at during time of exit from the pit--in other words, our computers collected the high price, the low price, and the price the order was filled at during the short period of time the order was in the pit.

"Also recorded was the time we placed the orders, compared them to the time the orders were received on the floor of the Exchange, and the time it took for the executed order to return from the pit. The Exchanges require time stamps on all orders at the time

a customer calls in an order and again at the time the order is returned to the order desk after execution. With the first group there were many discrepancies between our time stamping and their time stamping, indicating faulty or illegal timing devices. Michael tells us that some of the brokerage companies who specialize in skimming have as many as four time stamp machines hidden under their trading-floor desks, all set at different intervals, which gives them as much as thirty minutes to manipulate an order; in some cases, even longer.

"We placed our orders during active market times and at slow market times. The results were almost always the same."

Ross paused and took a drink of water, then looked down at Michael, who gave him a nod as if to say, "So far, you're right on the money." Ross went on. "After three solid weeks of trading, we found that group one, the brokers we had received complaints about, had consistently given away an average of four points on each order, two points when we entered the order to buy, and two points when we sold out our position. We allowed one full point for normal order filling, a half point in and a half point out, to be given up to fill the order. That left three unanswered lost points. As of today, we have no idea where they went. Each of our orders averaged fifty contracts. They were all market orders, not price orders. That meant the broker was to fill the order immediately, at the best price he could.

"At an average of forty dollars per point, three points per contract, each trade was one hundred twenty dollars short. Multiply that by fifty contracts, and that's six thousand dollars per trade left in the pits to be divided among what Michael coins the bagmen, the skimmers, or the bucket men and the broker who filled the order.

"We executed forty-six trades with this first group of traders, and we estimate that over two hundred eighty thousand dollars was bagged in that three-week period, by the pit brokers who filled the order and the bagmen they had working for them."

Ross stopped again, loosened his tie, and sat silently for a moment. "I'm sure you'll all have questions, but please save them for Michael. He'll be able to clarify any confusion that you may have.

"As complicated as this might sound, it's actually quite a simple, yet very sophisticated, well-organized method of corrupt trading. Losing two hundred eighty thousand dollars with no trace seems quite intriguing to me. Compound that number by thousands of outside public and commercial traders, and the amount of bagged money is astronomical. My calculator doesn't even go that high.

"We picked the second group of traders at random. They had a better track record. Not much better, but better. We're not sure if their record was better because the second group just wasn't as greedy as the first group, or if the brokers we picked were incompetent and unable to fill orders properly. In both cases the orders were filled improperly.

"Perhaps Michael can look at the names of the second group and shed some light on the people involved. With this group the number of points given away were one and a half...after the point allowance. This was still a give-away of over one hundred twenty thousand dollars.

"Hogan's group, the third group, on the other hand, gave true market fills. They not only didn't give away the full point that we allowed to fill the order, they sent back filled orders with less than the allotted point give-away. And the give-away on fills coming back from Hogan himself was less than a half point. We actually saved twenty-three thousand dollars with the third group.

"If we hadn't used all three groups at the same time, we wouldn't have known if the bad fills were because of bad market timing, or if it was just the price a customer has to pay in order to play the game. But since orders went into the same pits, at the same time, in the same amounts, and there was a continual and consistent difference in the quality of fills given back to the customer by the different broker groups, our only conclusion is that there are definitely flagrant violations on the trading floors of the Exchanges. We found similar results with fills coming out of New York.

"Michael told Joe Glassmann that skimming and bagging trades are just two of numerous ways to dupe the public trader out of money. They are the easiest, fastest, and most common violations. Millions of dollars daily are stolen from outside orders through skim and bag trading. I believe that Michael will be able to tell you of the more complex, major trading violations that occur. Corrupt practices that will boggle your mind when you hear the amounts of money involved."

Ross looked down the long table at Michael and said, "Mike, do you have anything to add at this point?"

Michael eased forward in his chair. Ross had touched the tip of the iceberg--just the tip! Enough to get everyone's interest--or confuse them completely. "You're doing just fine, Mr. Ross," he said, and then addressed the whole room. "Does everybody understand what Sam just said?"

He scanned the room and looked into a lot of blank eyes. Some heads nodded up and down, some shook negatively, and others avoided his stare, looking down at the legal pads in front of them.

"Well, let me present the same type of situation in other words." Ross nodded his approval and leaned back in his leather chair to listen. "Mr. Ross picked three groups of brokers to purchase various commodities for him. Under the same conditions--and at the same time--and purchasing the same commodity. Take soybeans, for instance: Group one paid $5.03 per bushel, group two paid $5.02 per bushel, and group three paid $5.01 per bushel--or less.

"At a later date Mr Ross decided to sell the soybeans he had bought. Again, under the same circumstances, group one sold at $5.07, group two sold at $5.08, and group three sold at $5.09. The orders went into the soybean pit simultaneously, so all three orders

should have been filled at the same price, but they weren't. Why? That is what we are all here to try and figure out. How are some brokers ripping points off orders? And if they aren't, what the hell is going on? I ask you to consider the possibility that this investigation just might uncover a drop in the bucket compared to what's actually happening.

"Theoretically, Mr. Ross made money on the example trade I just mentioned, but why the discrepancy in prices?...There is only one answer. As a continual practice, groups one and two were skimming points from Mr. Ross's orders."

He did a long, slow slide around the table with his eyes. "Does this register? Am I clear, or have I confused you even more?" Most of the heads gave a confident affirmative this time, and Michael was satisfied. They had to understand skimming and bagging trades, because it would be the cornerstone of their investigation.

He looked down at Ross and the other eight men, who bobbed their spring-held heads like car-window dolls. Michael said politely, "You're on again, Mr. Ross."

The group was now taking copious notes, as the stenographer silently clacked away non stop. Lewis sneezed a couple of times and otherwise seemed bored. Michael poked him with his right elbow and said in a low voice, "Wake up. You might learn something."

Lewis responded. "I'll remember every word said here today but I'd still rather be on a drug bust."

Michael kept a grin to himself and said, "That will come later."

He watched Ross take another swig of water and adjust his chair to a more comfortable position. He felt content in letting Ross ramble on as long as he wanted. He knew the man liked center stage like most wealthy magnates, except for maybe Howard Hughes.

Ross said, "Now I'm going to summarize a complaint that Michael Hogan filed with the two major Commodity Exchanges in Chicago two years ago."

Michael saw Ross's questioning eyes look his way, as though to get an approval. Michael waved his hand slightly, motioning his okay.

"Two years ago, the complaint that Michael filed charged a number of the brokers with defrauding customers by improper trading practices. Skimming points from orders, bagging trades, pre-arranged trading, illegal dual trading, bucket trading, cross-order trading, curb trading, low or no margin trading, and a myriad of other charges, all dealing exclusively with cheating the unsuspecting public out of hundreds of millions of dollars. He named the number of offenses that took place, the times, the pits where the offenses occurred, brokers who participated in the alleged thefts, the dates, and the approximate amount of money which was stolen. It's a very thorough fourteen-page report, and it was presented to the highest Exchange officials.

One of our inside people acquired a copy of the complaint, and it found its way through Joseph Glassmann to myself. I met with the U.S. Attorney General and the Director of the FBI. That's when we officially began this investigation. We watched

Michael's complaint get swept under the carpet at both Exchanges. We witnessed a combined effort on the part of both Exchanges to defuse Hogan and defame him right in front of his peers. Then, they initiated a counter attack on him, his company, and his entourage of loyal followers. It seems that no one at the Exchanges is completely free from some type of wrongdoing, as minor as the infractions may be, including Michael Hogan.

"It was obvious, by the scope and accuracy of Michael's complaint, that he had help in accumulating this information from his friends in the various pits mentioned in Hogan's charges. After all, he couldn't be in eight places at one time. Since the Commodity Exchanges are self-governing, they formed a task force to shift their own wrongdoing from themselves to Hogan and his men. Since he has avoided any personal political advancement at the Exchanges, he and his team were easy prey.

"Our sources tell us that both physical and financial threats were issued to Hogan's men if they persisted to back Michael. There were a number of beatings to men who wouldn't give in easy. There were a number of suspensions and heavy fines which were based on so called major trading violations. We later found these violations were actually only minor trading offenses. Hogan and his company were scandalized and dragged through the mud by the Chicago *Tribune*, *Sun Times*, New York *Times*, *Barrons*, *Wall Street Journal*, and other major city newspapers.

"One of our undercover agents, acting as a reporter for the Miami *Herald*, asked Exchange officials about the allegations made by Hogan and Company against twenty-seven floor brokers. Both Exchanges answered exactly the same, as if they had been coached. The allegations mentioned in Hogan's complaints were without merit, and all twenty-seven brokers named were cleared of any wrongdoing. It was their consensus that Hogan had fabricated the complaints to cover up his own wrongdoing."

Ross lifted his head from his notes, removed his half-glasses, and looked at Michael. "Is that an accurate summary of what happened, Michael? A few of your friends were worked over pretty bad, weren't they?"

Michael recalled the whole incident, as if it happened yesterday. Ross had some of the facts, but the guts were missing. He leaned back in his chair, slightly slouched, feet outstretched in front of him. His slinged arm rested in his lap, the other elbow slung over the back of his chair. He looked down the long table at Sam Ross. The room was stone silent.

The whole rotten mess had been brought back to the present, and it stirred an anger deep within his soul. Michael knew Ross was no fool--that was certain. He had just proved his ability to manipulate--to manipulate Michael!

He had taken over the meeting like Coach Knute Rockne, "Let's win one for the Gipper." Ross thought the mention of Michael's humiliation would fire him up, just as Rockne knew the mention of the dead George Gipp would fire up his football team. Ross was going for a win in this investigation. He wouldn't be satisfied with a tie. And *losing* was not even in his vocabulary. Yes, Ross was going for an overwhelming win. But there

were a few things Ross didn't know, and Michael knew he needed him for those precious pieces of the puzzle.

Michael recalled his vow years ago, to always go for a win--a deadly win! That was something Ross didn't know. Ross was playing the game as Michael had expected.

He knew Ross didn't like complacency or indecision, so he had fired a cannon at Michael to wake him up. He guessed Sam Ross thought he was on the fence with a "should I or shouldn't I" attitude toward this meeting, and he demanded Michael swing one hundred per cent to his side. And he did it by trying to open an old wound. He thought the recall of the past would have an effect on Michael, but Ross wasn't aware that a day didn't pass without the wound's opening. Both men's eyes met and probed each other's souls. Michael felt his own eyes narrow. He could read the secrets hidden behind Ross's cool facade as if he were inside his mind. The glint of victory on Ross's face changed to a knitted frown with Michael's deadly concentration directed at him. Ross broke the stare and reached for the glass of water in front of him.

He knew Ross had gambled with him, not knowing whether Michael would react with anger or resentment. He did neither. Michael was a gambler, a professional gambler, and was now about to be an adversary and co-conspirator with the strongest men in the country--but something deep inside told him they would be no match for him.

The room was still. Everyone waited for Michael to speak. He remained silent, letting his sharp eyes search every face in the room for emotion. His eyes came to a welcomed rest on Samantha, who had taken her glasses off and was watching him with a deep, concerned frown on her slender face. Was she feeling pain for him? He kept his eyes on her until she blinked with embarrassment and turned away. He remained calm and quiet until he felt the unrest in the room grow to a peak. An inner voice told him it was now time to speak, to carry the ball. Fuck you, Ross! he thought, and all the rest of your ass-kissing politicians--try this on for size. He felt the strength in his voice. "Mr. Ross, my applause to you for a very effective summarization of how we all arrived here at CIA Headquarters, behind the closed doors of what you people coin a Safe Room."

He hesitated as he pulled himself into a more professional posture, then pulled his microphone closer to him. He glanced at Lewis, who, like an artist in a court room, was drawing pictures of everyone around the table. He looked at Andy, who returned the look, and waved his head in the direction of Ross, indicating a needed response.

Ross said, "Tell it like it is, Mike. It's your stage now."

Michael clenched his jaw, then said, "Just so we don't underestimate each other, and with all due respect, I am aware of what you have just tried to accomplish by throwing into my face the traumatic experience I witnessed some years ago. You succeeded in opening those jagged wounds that were inflicted by that experience. You did, however, neglect to mention some salient points that I think the people in this room must know so they can assess the importance of the issues we're addressing today."

He cleared his throat and went on, feeling a fire burning deeply within him. "On March 17, 1984, St. Patrick's Day, a close and dear friend of mine, Tim O'Neal was killed. He was pushed from the twenty-fifth floor of his apartment on Michigan Avenue. He landed on a windshield of a passing cab. The police called it suicide--I call it murder. I had met with O'Neal five hours earlier, and he was in his usual good Irish humor. He had a few drinks and was looking forward to a big Irish bash at the Black Potato Pub, on the south side of Chicago. He had backed me in my complaint against the Exchanges and lashed out in particular against an Exchange warlord, Karl "Fat Man" Peterson. He told me, that afternoon, that he was going after computer information that he thought would convict Peterson of countless felonious activities, not only in regard to the Exchange, but the information would also expose him as one of the front men for a Mafia laundering operation. O'Neal was as clean as a summer cloud, and had no suicidal tendencies. He was as emphatic about nailing these larcenous bastards at the Exchanges as I was!

"Because of his siding with me in my complaint, someone had planted phony trades in one of his accounts at another company, and exposed a Miami bank account, in his name, with over sixty thousand dollars in it. As a result of this, he was reported to the IRS, was suspended for one year from the Exchange, and fined one hundred fifty thousand dollars--which he didn't have. He had to sell his membership but remained as an employee in the accounting department of the firm through which he traded. Evidently he had gathered accounting information from friends who worked for Peterson and others mentioned in my report.

"The only thing he told me was that he had account numbers of Bahamian banks, Cayman Island banks, and Miami banks. A total of seven hundred fifty million dollars from skim and bag programs conducted on the Exchange floors went into these accounts. His information confirmed that more than sixty brokers actively participated in the hi-tech scam. We were supposed to meet the next morning in my office at six a.m. He never showed. At approximately eight-fifteen a.m. I received a call from a detective friend of mine in homicide. He told me the story.

"O'Neal had numerous head wounds, not caused by the fall. And he had his tongue cut out--one of the penalties for informing. The death was written up as a suicide. According to the police, there was a typed suicide note. They casually dismissed his tongue as probably being bitten off during the fall. As far as the police were concerned, the deep gashes in the back of his head were also caused by the fall. No information was found in his apartment or office. No evidence of any wrong doings." Michael didn't mention the fact that O'Neal had sent him a copy of all the documents he had confiscated--that information was priceless and would be needed later, at the right time, shared with people he could trust.

As he spoke, he felt the heavy tide of anger rising in him. The men and women around the table looked at and listened to him like motionless mannequins. He knew he was getting through.

"A few months prior to O'Neal's death, another friend of mine, Al Josephson, was found with his brains splattered all over the dashboard of his car. Again, the police conveniently ruled the incident a suicide! Again, he was no more suicidal than my goddamn parakeet. The man had just made four hundred thousand in the bond market, and was happy as a kid at the circus. His tongue had also been cut out!"

His eyes swept the room looking at each agent. He told them things they hadn't heard before. Their young faces were creased with questions.

Michael contained his anger as he spoke calmly into the microphone. "Our adversaries waited sometime before they hit again. Then, when I began to make waves with the Exchanges one more time, a number of my friends were physically beaten. They were warned to drop me as a friend if they wanted to stay alive. Jimmy Palotos was almost beaten to death by two of Peterson's men. Jimmy was one of my key men on the floor, and he owed gambling money to Peterson. His membership was virtually owned by Peterson. Palotos never filed charges, because the two scumbags who worked him over with a hammer and brass knuckles vowed to come back. They threatened to cut off his fingers so he couldn't trade anymore. They promised to do the same to his wife and family if he squealed.

"After these incidents, my brokers began to leave my company, saying they were sorry, but they had families to consider. I understood. My company was on its way downhill until Joe Glassmann loaned me a million dollars to stay in business. He promised to send me a few good-size customers. That's when I began filling orders for Mr. Ross. Today I'm solvent again, and have as much business as I can handle."

He lifted his arm from his lap and placed it painfully on the table. "This bandaged shoulder is the result of a potential beating I was to receive at the hands of the two bone-breakers who work for Peterson, who, as I mentioned before, fronts for the Mob in a money-washing operation, not to mention his octopus skim operation. If it hadn't been for Agent Lewis, here, I would be dead today or living with mush for brains the rest of my life.

"Three other apparent and very questionable suicides occurred within a twelve-month period after my complaint against the twenty-seven members of the Exchanges. These men were also friends of mine and key figures in my allegations. Too obvious! Too coincidental! Five dead men, numerous beatings, all my people!"

He lowered his bandaged arm and placed it back on his lap. His eyes focused on the ceiling for a moment. He sensed a tone of anger in his voice, which he tried desperately to conceal. His words were slow and deliberate. "These men are brutal. They are ruthless. And they are mean. They have no conscience. *Money is their god*--and nothing, and nobody, will stand in their way. Including the United States Government!

"I dropped my charges against the twenty-seven brokers because my naive idea of U.S. justice was not as effective as theirs was for revenge. I couldn't watch more of my

people hurt or killed, because of my illusion that criminals should be prosecuted. Ladies and gentlemen--I will not make that mistake again."

He picked up the glass of water in front of him and took a long swallow. He felt good that he had captured the attention from Ross and continued. "When my friend Joseph Glassmann contacted me less than a month ago to re-open the case, I naturally balked. He said he had support, big support. He mentioned Samuel Ross and the FBI being behind us. I wasn't impressed. The first time I brought my complaints to the Justice Department, you all stood behind one-way mirrors and, through your own admission, watched as my men were beaten and killed." He gritted his teeth and glared down the table at the sour face of John Simpson. "After asking Andy Golden if there was anything the FBI could do, he told me that his superior, *John Simpson*, expressed his regrets and wished me good luck." Michael waited--hoped--that Simpson would say something. He remained quiet sitting next to Sam Ross with a perpetual smirk on his face. He continued. "Despite Mr. Glassmann's and Mr. Ross's money and power, my men and I are still the guinea pigs. We are the ones who have the most to lose. If the government had supported me when I needed help, a number of my friends would still be alive today, and my Greek friend, Palotos, and I wouldn't have had the crap beat out of us.

"After giving a great deal of thought to my conversation with my friends, Glassmann and Andy Golden..." He motioned with his head to Andy sitting on his left "...I came up with a plan that would take the pressure off of my small army, and put it on you bastards, where it belongs. You can use the FBI or the CIA or the Joint Chiefs of Staff or any other group you want involved--I don't really give a damn. If you're interested, and it is the only effective plan that will work--I'll present the plan later in the discussion."

Sherry Nelson spoke in a squeaky, naive voice. "Could you slow down a little, Mr. Hogan? I'm...I'm not catching some of the swear words."

He snapped back with a loud hiss. "You catch up, Miss Nelson! This is just getting started!" She flushed with embarrassment and almost fell from her tiny stool. He knew that he startled the occupants of the room with his boldness in front of these powerful men--and he wasn't finished. He had plenty to say before his curtain went down And plenty more for encores.

Pete Lewis covered his microphone and whispered with the motionless lips of a ventriloquist. "Atta boy, Mike!--Fuck 'em all!"

Andy heard the comment and glared across at Lewis as if to say, shut your fucking mouth.

Michael pushed his chair back and stood. He stretched briefly and re-adjusted his sling, which was becoming irritating with its tightness. He knew he had a strong voice because of his pit trading, so he didn't need a microphone. Not with what he was about to say.

He could see the nine men at the other end of the table began to squirm uncomfortably. They weren't used to having a man stand in front of them, preparing a

challenge. Evidently they could see in his taut face an obstinate attitude they did not approve of. Michael expected they were mentally preparing their objections. He could care less!

He spoke from his diaphragm, and his voice filled the room with strength and authority. "Before we go any further, ladies and gentlemen, there may be a few of you at the head of the table who would like me to leave. I must warn you my attitude about the government isn't going to get any better. I wouldn't be a bit offended if you told me to go home. In fact, it would be a big relief." He looked down the long table and saw Simpson lean over and cover his mouth as he whispered something to Clay Hudson. Hudson shook his head no, and Simpson's scowl returned as he rested his corpulent frame back in his chair.

Michael's eyes felt slanted like a cat's as he glanced at Samantha. Holding the tip of a pen to her lips, she seemed to be studying him with amusement. This time she didn't flush as he let his own eyes charm her alluring gaze.

Sam Ross broke the room's tension. "Michael, I think we all agree that you have good reason to be uneasy with us. You feel betrayed and let down by men you're supposed to be able to trust..."

Michael cut in sharply, "Betrayed? Let down? You're damn right I feel betrayed. In fact, I have sixty thousand reasons not to trust the words spoken in this room. There happens to be a little wall fifty miles from here with the names of sixty thousand Viet Nam veterans who only exist in the memories of their families and friends. Sixty thousand black bags came home from Viet Nam with only pieces of their bodies. They trusted politicians just like you; they believed the lies coming out of Washington, and look where they ended up."

Ross stopped Michael. "Okay. There have been atrocities, mistakes, made in the past; but now the Justice Department would like to make things right. Although no one can undo the harm and pain that the veterans have suffered or that you have endured, maybe we can help prevent any further lies and violence. Would you consider giving us another chance?"

Michael let what Ross said assimilate. He had won another round. They were asking him to stay. Now, he had to be forceful but cool--he needed them for the plan he was formulating. They just didn't know it. After a long moment he said softly, "Yeah, I'll give you another chance. Just too damn bad *those* guys didn't get a second chance."

Now it was time for a little bullshit, then another grand slam. His eyes swept the whole table as he spoke. "I apologize for my arrogant outburst. I was not only speaking for myself, but for the widows of my friends and a dozen kids who no longer have fathers because of all the crap that's going on in Chicago."

He stood behind Andy and noticed his shoulders sag with relief with Michael's apparent apology. Michael smiled.

"Mr. Ross, do I still have the floor?"

Ross's brows rose and he shrugged his shoulders. "I don't hear or see anybody willing to take it away from you, Michael--it's still your show."

Good, he thought. Now comes the hammer. We'll see just how bad they wanted my information and cooperation. "Naturally, being a trader by profession..." He looked over at Sherry Nelson, who was still flustered from his first thrashing. "Ms. Nelson, the word I used is trader, not traitor. Please don't screw that word up."

"I...I have it right, Mr. Hogan." She spelled it, "T-R-A-D-E-R...!" Then she looked up and smiled, as if she had just overcome a major obstacle.

"Perfect, Sherry, perfect." A number of the agents chuckled at Michael's attempt to further ease the tension in the room that seemed to be shrinking in size.

He continued his original thought. "The government is also a trader. I trade commodities, and money, and stock options--you trade information; you trade bad guys for good guys, good guys for bad guys; you trade all kinds of things: things that none of us civilians will ever know about. Since we all understand what trading is all about..." He swung his free hand around the table, "...let's make a trade. I have something you need and you have something I need." He paused for a moment, listening for objections. There were none. "I have a few requests which I want honored." Now, he felt confident, almost like walking into a trading pit, where he was greatly respected. He felt he had turned the tide. He had taken control. He wondered if, in fact, he had ever lost it. He had demonstrated to the people in the room that he had the most to lose if the investigation went sour. Now, it was time for him to hit them between the eyes with what he considered to be modest demands and certainly attainable. His life was on the line. They knew by now he was intelligent enough to realize that the government was trying to use him.

Ross spoke softly from the other end of the table, feeling his way. "Shall we take a short recess before we go on?"

Michael recognized the play. Ross was going to try to regain control of the meeting in an attempt to let Michael cool off. He snapped. "No! You just gave me the floor, Mr. Ross, and what I have to say won't take me long. I'll say my piece; then we can break if you'd like!"

The men of authority sitting next to Ross squirmed noticeably now, and avoided eye contact with him. They were usually the ones making the decisions on who would speak, and when they would speak, and what they would say. Not this time, Michael thought--not this time.

He began to stroll slowly around the table. "I want a paid-up twenty-million-dollar life insurance policy purchased for both my wife and myself and a ten-million-dollar policy for each of my children. That's one hundred million dollars in insurance. My attorney will draw up the trust papers in which the policies will be placed."

The nine men chattered quietly among themselves, no doubt wondering where this was going.

He continued strolling and talking like a progressive priest giving his Sunday sermon while walking the church aisle. "It is my contention that if you have a financial stake in Michael Hogan and his family, you will not be as likely to be lax in your protection of my family. And the information you receive, without my knowledge, will be less likely to disappear into one of those computers out there. I want to see all information gathered at the Exchanges.

"Along with my family's protection, I have one more monetary request. That is, that ten million dollars be donated to a Viet Nam veterans' trust fund, which may be drawn on for government guaranteed tax-free investments. With the proper management, this fund can grow to more than one hundred million and will eventually be able to support V.A. hospitals and other veterans' organizations throughout the country. Since the vets do not trust the government, I suggest that Mr. Ross and I be the trustees and decision makers of the fund.

"Second, I want to be in complete control of any Exchange activity that goes on in Chicago. Nothing is begun and nothing is finished without my knowledge. That's for your benefit as much as it is mine. I can't afford to have a federal agent doing something behind my back when I know it to be dangerous--or know a better way to accomplish the same thing. It's my understanding that Andy Golden will be the agent in charge of the Chicago investigation. I can work with Andy. And I'll be happy to work with Mr. Lorenzo, the Chicago U.S. Attorney. I'm generally an easy man to get along with, but I'm also aware of the fact that you people may know how to track crooks across state lines, but you don't know shit about a crook standing on the top step of a trading pit for six hours a day in a space no bigger than three feet by three feet stealing millions of dollars a year."

He waited for objections from the top guns. He had traveled half way down the table placing his right hand on each of the agents' shoulders and giving it a slight squeeze, hoping to psychologically gain their support and instill his own confidence in them. He felt good now. He was carrying the ball, and the holes in the line were opening for him. He felt the presence of his father walking with him. He said a short prayer: *"Give me some of your wisdom, Dad.*

"Third, I want at least ten good men and women to infiltrate the Exchange trading floors. I want them to buy memberships and learn how to trade. I'll teach them what to look for, how to trade, and point out the do's and don't's of pit etiquette, which is quite crude but still necessary. I feel they should be wired to record conversations in the pits...at breakfasts...lunches...dinners and social gatherings. I don't pretend to know the legal ramifications of wire tapping and entrapment: that's your job to figure out."

He felt confidence surge through him. "The ones chosen to infiltrate the pits should be aggressive by nature, competitors, have rough edges, a sense of humor, and an eye for corruption. Once again, I'll teach the traders what to look for. Others should infiltrate the various corporate offices, which I feel are the most corrupt. The most important thing to consider are the taped conversations between the agents and the brokers.

You'll be able to extract tons of information because the brokers are vulnerable and careless. They've been stealing for so long they almost consider it legal. They are not a bit shy in talking about the amount of money they make through skimming programs. There is a chance--not a good chance, nonetheless a chance--that a few of the agents can become bagmen for larger brokers, if they can worm their way into the broker--syndicate networks. The best way to get close to the big brokers who steal is to claim you have substantial tax losses, write-offs you want to sell for skim trades, or cash under the table. The big order fillers make over one million a year. If they're dirty, a few million more in skim money. They are always looking for someone with tax losses to illegally shelter their incomes. If you accept my requests and we make a deal to work together, I'll teach you what I know and what to do.

"Incidentally, your appearance should be somewhat shoddy, yet expensive. You *must* drive an expensive automobile, and live in a luxury condo. And...depending on how unethical this gets, you'll want to join in some of the dope, gambling, and call-girl parties that go on frequently. Cocaine is bought, for personal use, by the kilo--not the gram--and broads are brought in by the dozens for these social gatherings.

"You will all have to buy or lease memberships. The cost of memberships at the Board of Trade is running in the three hundred twenty-five to three hundred fifty thousand dollar range. Or, a membership can be leased for approximately ten to twelve per cent of its value. At present, the rent for a leased membership is thirty-seven hundred per month for a six-month period, and thirty-four hundred for a yearly rental. You'll need trading money. I'd say at least fifty thousand each. Preferably one hundred thousand in order not to raise concern with the clearing house you use to sponsor you. Hogan and Company, Inc. will sponsor a few, but not all of you.

"I estimate a budget of approximately six million dollars just for floor operations. If you lease memberships, the budget will be less. You can kiss your trading money good-bye because we will eat you up in the pit. Yet you have to make trades, or it will look suspicious. Right now the crooks are vulnerable and careless. You don't want to scare them off. Most commodity brokers are crazy, but we're not stupid, so nothing should be too obvious. And...ladies and gentlemen, if this investigation does get off the ground, don't be surprised if a few of you get caught up in the fast lane to the extent that you'll question your position with the government. Why should you work seven days a week, twelve to fourteen hours a day, for thirty or forty thousand dollars a year when you can easily make that amount in a month and work only five days a week for six hours a day ten months a year? Be careful not to be caught in the spider's web. Remember most of these men we are after began as simple, honest peons, just trying to eke out a living. But something happens to people when greed sets in: they change. Power and money, in the wrong hands, breeds immoral strength." Then he said, "I hope that last comment didn't make anybody in this room uncomfortable." He directed his comment to the nine men he was approaching.

Now, at one end of the table, he looked down at Hudson and Simpson, who both avoided his look. "No comments yet?" He guessed they were disciplined men. They would wait for their chance.

He now continued to move behind the powerhouse group. The government men. He sensed the hairs rise on the backs of their necks as he passed. Even Ross was agitated, tapping his Gold Cross pen nervously on the yellow legal pad in front of him.

"I also have a list of forty-six brokers and seventeen clearing houses for which I want complete immunity granted. I am on the list, along with my Company. These are people I work with and have known for many years. They are all straight, honest men, or I wouldn't be doing business with them. If they have committed any violations, they were insignificant. I don't want any of my friends hassled because of some minor rule infraction!"

Tony Lorenzo pulled himself forward in his chair and said. "What kind of minor violations are you talking about, Mr. Hogan?"

Michael turned and looked into polite, sincere eyes of the genius U.S. Attorney. "Mr. Lorenzo...when you go home tonight look in your desk drawer and see if you have any Bic pens that you brought home from the office. Also, try to remember if the paper clips in your desk came from the office or if you went out and bought them with your own money. Have you ever driven sixty miles per hour when the speed limit is only fifty-five? Those are the types of minor violations I'm talking about, Mr. Lorenzo. Violations that don't hurt anybody and that are more or less accepted."

He thought quickly, then smiled. "Now, Mr. Lorenzo, if you go home tonight and find an I.B.M. computer, five typewriters, an oriental rug, a library full of leather furniture, and a shoe box in the bottom drawer of your desk filled with hundred dollar bills that came from your downtown office--then I think you and I should have a little talk after this meeting"

The whole room erupted in laughter, and Lorenzo was embarrassed, but laughed with them. He was smart enough not to take offense where none was meant. Michael had made his point. He liked Lorenzo immediately because he could take a joke, and he had the balls to ask the loaded question in the first place.

Michael proceeded around the table. "Lastly, and I direct this to YOU, Mr. Simpson, Pete Lewis is to stay with me in Chicago. He saved my life, and I feel that I can trust the man. He's a crack shot with a gun, has a one hundred fifty IQ--which means I only have to instruct him once. I don't have to think for the both of us. Furthermore, he has courage, big balls, and an insatiable thirst for justice. Maybe not the kind of justice recommended by the Bureau, Mr. Simpson, but still...the man has dedicated the better portion of his life, trying to pull garbage bags off the streets and place them behind bars. For that you punish the man? I would like you to consider returning Mr. Lewis to a certain agency status, which I understand he lost because of some misunderstanding in New York.

Any back pay or benefits that may have been diminished or revoked will be retroactive, and any negative reports will be removed from his record."

He was now headed down the other side of the table and looked at John Simpson, who pushed his chair back. He stood, and with a fidgety hand he shook his finger at Michael, anger written all over his pink face. "Just one minute, Hogan. I've listened to enough! Where do you come off telling the Bureau who we promote and who we demote? You are entirely out of line smart guy, and..."

Michael cut him short. "Listen Simpson, if you can make deals with terrorists, communists, pimps, prostitutes, drug dealers, criminals, Mickey Mouse, and Santa Claus, you can make a deal with one of your own. Am I incorrect with my information that Pete Lewis has more New York drug busts to his credit in the past five years than any other FBI agent?"

Michael watched Simpson's blood pressure rise as his heavy face reddened, and what hair he had spilled onto his forehead. He looked around the room at his own agents' faces, then back to Michael. "You're crazy...and...and Lewis is a madman--has no respect for agency regulations, and...and I'd have to get the okay from the Director to reinstate him to his Special Agent status."

Michael stared back at Simpson. He thought for a split second, wet his lips, and spoke harshly. "Listen, Asshole. The Director didn't send you here without authority, or he would have come himself. Who do you think you're talking to? Some Irishman who just fell off a potato truck? YOU make the decision, and YOU take the consequences. If you think I'm going to be the only guy with my ass out on a limb to be shot off, you're crazy!"

Now, he let the anger blaze in his words. "Reinstate Lewis, or I walk and you can spend the next five years in Chicago trying to pin down a few crooked brokers. By that time, they will be stronger than the Mafia. So shit or get off the pot, Mr. Simpson!"

He watched as Clay Hudson pulled at Simpson's arm. Simpson sat back down exasperated and spewed a few final words, "DEAL OR NO DEAL, HOGAN, YOU'RE PUSHING AROUND THE WRONG MAN...YOU ARROGANT BASTARD!" Ross leaned over to him and whispered in his ear. With reluctance and a screwed-up look on his red face, Simpson shook his head no to Ross's request. Clay Hudson slammed his hand down in front of Simpson, and the whole room felt the authority of the CIA. Simpson's eyes rose slowly to meet Michael's. His right cheek twitched nervously as he said with curled lips. "Okay, Hogan--Lewis is yours. I'll be glad to get him out of New York anyway."

Michael added, "And re-instatement, and back pay, and benefits?"

Simpson wiped his brow with his handkerchief and groped for his glass of water. "Yeah...yeah, all that too! Now go on with your goddamn demands!" But before Michael had a chance to begin speaking, he cut in again. "Incidentally, Hogan, what are you planning to give us for all this *shit* you're throwing in our face besides a lesson in commodity trading?"

He glared at Simpson and said. "Within twenty-four months, if YOU don't fuck things up with bureaucratic red-tape, you'll have enough solid information for at least five hundred subpoenas, which will lead to hundreds of indictments, and as many convictions! You'll have enough information to not only prosecute corrupt commodity brokers, but also public officials, lawyers, Senators, Congressmen, and other major government offices! You'll have the names of six Miami banks, twelve Cayman Island banks, nine Bahamian banks, three Swiss banks, and two Canadian banks where dirty, tax-free money has been deposited during the past fifteen years. I'll give you the new banking areas around the world which have been established since Switzerland is now cooperating with the U.S. Government, as they have willingly begun to break their International Secrecy Code: Toronto, Luxembourg, Liechtenstein, Panama, Mexico--the list goes on. You probably already know about these banking areas as stopovers for dirty money and tax dodge havens, but you don't have the account numbers and the names the accounts belong to--I DO!"

He rested a moment, not wanting to give too much information too fast. He directed his words toward Simpson. "You'll have the information you need to stop the Mafia from laundering money through the Exchanges. In other words, Mr. Simpson, you will have enough evidence to uncover the largest financial scandal in the history of the United States. The result will be the destruction of the Commodity Exchanges and my business. I will be ostracized and out of a job--YOU BIG ASSHOLE!" He glared at Simpson as he now cowered deep into his chair.

Michael moved on, resting his hand unconsciously on the shoulder of Samantha Winters, who was in the next seat. She felt soft and warm, and her long, blond hair fell over his hand. She felt good to him. He gave a gentle squeeze and felt a slight shudder. He sensed the presence of a sensuous woman, but immediately dismissed her from his mind as he proceeded down the rest of the table to his seat, brushing each agent's shoulder as he walked.

His eyes caught Pete's, smiling at him. He gave a wink and returned the smile out of sight of Ross, Hudson, and Simpson, who he knew were watching him. He glanced at Andy, whose elbows were on the table, with his bear paw hands covering his face. He wrinkled his mouth, thinking he was going to drive Andy crazy before this was over. He could just hear him, *"You just don't call the Executive Assistant to the Director of the FBI a fucking asshole!"*

As he approached his seat, he forced back his grin, feeling he had come away with another victory. Now, he was ready to challenge the CBOT, Corrupt Brotherhood of Traders in Chicago. He felt exhilarated after pushing Simpson around: he was a bully, like Peterson. The only difference was, Simpson flaunted a gold badge and Peterson shuffled $20 gold pieces. He hoped he wasn't jumping the gun with his feeling of victory. He could taste it, yet he knew many a contest had been lost during the final seconds. But he had surely defused the bastards--especially Simpson, and that made his day.

Now his voice was smooth and gentle. "Mr. Ross, I think I'm ready for that break, if you are...I'm also ready for that Scotch."

Ross looked back amicably and smiled, "You're on, Michael. Let's make it a double. I've a bit of work to go over here, so go on without me. I'll try to catch up later."

He looked down at Andy still holding his face in his hands and mumbling through his fingers, "You imbecile! You absolute imbecile!

"Why?...Whadya mean?"

Andy shook his head in frustration and said, as Michael knew he would, *"You just don't call the Executive Assistant to the Director of the FBI a fucking asshole!"*

"Well, he is an asshole! And I didn't call him a fucking asshole, I just called him an asshole."

Andy groaned.

Michael turned to Lewis and patted him on the back. "Is there a bar in this joint? Let's go get a drink, Pete."

Pete shoved his chair back and rose. He looked Michael in the eyes and said with a touch of mirth, "Anything you say, boss. I wouldn't have missed this goddamn show for the world."

Michael scanned the room as he began to turn toward the door. His eyes met Samantha's, and they locked. He felt that same warmth come over him as when he had touched her shoulder. He broke the stare and headed with Pete toward a nearby VIP lounge. His mind was trying to shake the blond, blue-eyed angel. He told himself almost audibly, "later, Michael...later!"

TWENTY

Seven Continents Lounge-CIA Headquarters

The two men pushed through double-wide mahogany doors to the VIP lounge. Michael had never seen anything quite like the Seven Continents Lounge before. This could have been called the Eighth Continent. He had been in hundreds of bars, many of the finest and most expensive in the world, but nothing came close to reaching the extravagance and plush decor of this one. Seven ornate sitting rooms, each decorated in the style and cultures of the land represented. Each room resembled a museum with priceless paintings and statues. One-of-a-kind artifacts embellished each room. Exotic plants, ferns, and other appointments warmed each one beyond imagination. Each had a separate, well-stocked bar and an assortment of specialty hors d'oeuvres, displayed on opulent servers throughout the great room.

The lighting in all the rooms was dim, but not dim enough to deter document reading. The only constant in each room was the bartenders, dressed in white shirts, black vests, and robin's-egg-blue bow-ties and arm garters. The bartenders were as disciplined as robots, serving the various dignitaries who spoke in their native languages and relaxed in casual conversation in plush wing-back chairs.

The seven rooms branched from the nucleus of the lounge. A large, step-up, circular glass topped bar was surrounded by at least one hundred tufted arm chairs swathed in gaily colored floral chintzes. Waterford crystal goblets of all sizes and shapes hung from racks that encircled the top of the bar. The display of back-bar booze was Heaven for a drinker. Booze and liqueurs from all over the world rested on glass shelves of the mirrored back. Stately decanters boasted deceptive liquid that spewed the illusionary potion that would make a meek man mean, a mean man weak, a loser a winner, a winner a loser, and an insignificant politician a powerful worldly dictator--at least in the politician's own mind.

Pete Lewis and Michael sat at the bar. Lewis spoke first. "Pick your poison, friend." He waved his hand at the wealthy array of Lady Whiskey perched in front of them.

Michael looked at the sundry bottles to choose from and casually said to Pete. "They don't have my brand!"

Lewis frowned, did a double take, looking first at the massive inventory, then realized Michael was laughing. "Funny, Mike! Real funny! They have more booze here than in the whole state of Vermont. They even have Mogen David. You would be surprised how many Europeans have only heard of Mogen David and Coca Cola."

Michael shook his head and said "Do they mix them together or drink them straight?" Pete motioned to the bartender.

A handsome man, Jamaican, Michael sensed, placed a coaster embossed with the U.S. logo of an eagle circled with fifty stars in front of both new patrons. Michael ordered an Ol'Rarity Scotch on the rocks, and Lewis a bottle of Singha, a beer made in Thailand.

Imbedded in the glass bar top were coins and paper money. Gold pieces of all denominations from America, numerous thousand-dollar bills, rubles from Russia, francs from Switzerland, marks from Germany, dollars from Canada, rupees from India and Pakistan, pound notes from England, yen from Japan, pesos from Mexico, Colombia, and Cuba, and on and on all the way around the bar. There must have been three hundred thousand dollars in coin and paper imbedded in the bar top. All countries were represented.

Michael felt his eyes drawn upward to a massive stained glass mosaic of the earth, as seen from outer space, which domed the entire ceiling of the lounge.

Lighting from the other side shone through the art work, revealing the outline of the seven continents. Every color in the spectrum remotely related to blue and green sparkled through the masterpiece. He felt awe at the sight, revealed only to the gods and a handful of astronauts. It seemed so real it was almost hypnotic. The art work spread across the ceiling, terminating above the seven arched doors, and was bordered by an ornate European molding awash in the color of plum. Columns around the doors led to a thick, dark-green carpet that spread like still ocean waters throughout the main room. The only feature in the grandiose room that brought reality back to him was the red exit lights over four paneled fire doors. Exits to where? Maybe to nowhere!

He suddenly remembered where he was and felt his skin turn clammy. He imagined opening one of the exit doors only to find a black wall facing him on three sides. Open another and find no floor, just a drop off into blackness like a horror film. Open another and skeletons would appear as in a spook house. The final door wouldn't open and upon closer scrutiny would show it had been welded shut.

He shook the fearful creations from his imagination only to bring in new confusions. Christ! They probably planned revolutions, assassinations, and all sorts of covert activities in this room. Give a few Arabs a few shots of Napoleon cognac, a bit of encouragement, and the price of oil would go up or down five dollars a barrel. Give a little Bacardi 151 to the right men from Chile along with a boatload of heavy weapons, and a South American government would be overthrown. Some fine Louis V and a few bucks to a radical group of psychotic Americans--and a President would be assassinated.

Offer a few million here and a few million there to high-ranking technicians and scientists in the world, and a rocket ship explodes or a biological killer germ would be let loose in Africa and accidentally spread throughout the world. All in the name of world power and control, shadowed by the words "Peace on earth."

Suddenly the beauty in the room began to change to a charade of ghosts and secrets. Whew! He was beginning to have trouble controlling his own mind, but he had to manage this situation.

Suddenly he felt cold, and he shivered although the room's air was clean and temperate. He had to talk. Talk about anything. Just get his attention off himself and onto some outside subject. He took a deep breath and let it out slowly, tapped his fingers on the glass bar top nervously, and said, "How's your beer, Pete?"

Pete didn't look up, just played with the rim of the Waterford beer glass. "Good. Damn good beer. Used to drink it all the time overseas."

Michael took a long deep swallow of the smooth, amber scotch. "Overseas?" Michael hadn't heard that connotation in a while. That was 1st and 2nd-World-War jargon. "You mean in Nam?"

He saw Pete's frown. "Yeah, Nam and Hong Kong and Singapore and Seoul and Amsterdam and West Berlin and Madrid. Wherever I was assigned."

Michael eased back in his chair and let the alcohol warm his body. "You've been to all those places?"

Pete took a sip of Singha and set his glass back on the coaster, then ran his finger down the glass pushing the sweat together. "Yeah, I've been around, Mike. All those places, and a whole lot more!"

Michael's guts still tumbled, and his mind wasn't just right. He could feel his body pulsing from his conflict with paranoia. He hadn't realized how much mental strength had been drained from him during the meeting. Now he was determined to settle himself down. He leaned forward, placing his right elbow on the glass bar, stirred his drink with his index finger, and asked, "What was your business in all those places, Pete? You're too bright and too energetic to be a tourist. I thought you were in the Airborne in Viet Nam?"

Pete hesitated and his frown deepened. He looked a bit uncomfortable as his eyes swept the room for listening ears.

Michael rested his right hand on Pete's left arm, then held up his hand like a cop stopping traffic. He leaned over and whispered into Pete's ear. "Can we talk here?"

Pete turned the brown beer bottle around, and with his finger divided the sweat, showing the clear brown figure of a question mark. He then ran his finger down the bottle and erased the silent response.

Mike patted Pete's arm, affirming the message. "Maybe we'll watch the late movie tonight and discuss geography. Where are we staying, anyway?"

"I'm not sure. They'll probably want us to stay here, in their elegant suites. He looked at his watch. "It's four-thirty-seven now. We're over the introductions, and you made no bones as to where you stand. I wouldn't be surprised if they adjourned for the day, so they can all regroup and start off early in the morning. It's not common practice to let us out of a meeting, let us fill our tanks with booze, and then bring us back to a shouting match. And since they know you can't be pushed around, they'll probably want

to give you a good night's sleep to take the edge off, with the hope that you will be a little less demanding in the morning. They are all premier psychologists when it comes to control and negotiating, and you didn't give them a chance to even cock their guns!"

Michael leaned back and surveyed Pete's profile. He had told Michael a few things without coming right out and saying them. First of all, it was obvious Pete had been here before. He knew his way around. Knew they had nice suites. Knew the place was bugged and monitored, knew the itinerary, and had spent time in most of the heavy espionage sectors of the world. There was no question in Michael's mind that Pete Lewis had once worked for the CIA, or had something to do with them during his time in Southeast Asia. In what capacity, and to what extent, he would have to wait to find out. "What's the matter, Pete? You okay?"

He glanced over his right shoulder, then back at Michael. His altar-boy face and eyes, pale blue with a splash of green, made him look like a kid out of college, but Michael knew he was in his mid thirties. Finally he spoke, "This place gives me the creeps. Always has." Pete's eyes told stories, Michael thought. If only he could read them.

Michael looked away, finished his drink, and another was immediately placed in front of him as was a beer in front of Lewis by the handsome Jamaican. He reached into his pocket and pulled out three twenties and placed them on the bar. The bartender's mouth transformed itself into a broad smile, as he pushed the money back saying in his attractive native lingo, "No thank you, Mon. Everything on the United States Government." He threw his head back gave a loud, friendly laugh and walked down the bar. With his wide, bright smile he reminded Michael of a tall Eddie Murphy--the only non-serious employee in the joint.

Michael thought he probably recorded more information, here at the CIA bar, than the Joint Chiefs of Staff received when the country was in full conflict. That would figure. Give a naive Chicago boy a few good belts of booze and let him spill his guts out at the CIA Lounge so all of Washington could hear him--bastards!

Pete reached over and pulled the twenties closer to Mike. "Can't pay for anything here, Mike. Put your money back into your pocket, or we'll both be shot at dawn. This is on the taxpayers."

Michael laughed. "I'll probably be shot at dawn, anyway. I don't think your bosses like me very much."

Pete took a slug of beer, looked to his right, then back at Michael and said, "I can't imagine why you feel that way--running off at the mouth like you did. They'll be all right. They just aren't used to being talked to like that. You pretty much laid your cards on the table. If they have any objections, you'll find out when we meet again. But I doubt if you'll get any serious resistance from most of them. You're not demanding cash in pocket in exchange for information. You're asking for protection for your family and friends, and that will be understandable to the majority. Contrary to your own thoughts, all the people in that meeting are not amoral or without sympathy. And it seems you have

a friend in Sam Ross, which doesn't hurt your cause. He has a ton of money and even more contacts. He has a lot more pull in Washington than the rest of those department heads sitting in with us."

Michael asked, "How does a layman get the authority to lead and dominate a meeting with so many government heavyweights involved?"

Pete thought for a moment and looked blindly at the mirrored back-bar, then said, "He's a neat guy. For a civilian, Sam Ross is a very powerful government figure. His company's grain-export business is the largest in the country, as are many of his other import/export businesses--petroleum, lumber, sugar, cotton, livestock, even palm oil--not to mention his involvement in a myriad of other major American corporations. He's big-- and because of his power to make decisions as to who he buys from or sells to, he has many influential European contacts. He trades all over the world. Although theoretically, he has no official government status, he is one of the strongest financial figures in the United States--and in the Government. He's also a good friend of the President. His civil complaint, with criminal implications against the Exchanges, is valid. Criminal racketeering charges will no doubt be introduced at a later date, when we're finished with our investigation. All of our read-outs say Ross is clean. Ruthless, but clean.

"Between Ross, yourself, and your friend Joe Glassmann, you're the only three who know exactly what illegal activities are going on at the Commodity Exchanges. It's going to take the three of you to carry this off. I've never seen the government so stymied with an investigation. They just can't seem to get a solid foothold in the Exchanges. They don't understand the language, nor do they know what trades are legal and what trades are illegal. So, despite your like or dislike for the men at the meeting, it is imperative that you set your prejudices aside and work with them to help solve the problem."

Pete still played with the rim of his glass, thought for a moment, and continued. "Mike, you're sitting in a room with some of the leaders of our government. They aren't interested in Michael Hogan or Pete Lewis. Nor are they interested in Ross's civil complaint. They want criminal indictments, and they know how to go for the throat once they get their foot in the door. Money is absolutely no object, believe me. And I think that Sam Ross and Joe Glassmann have proven that, by losing a half million dollars in the market just to make a point. They want the crooked brokers in Chicago and New York, and they'll get them. Without you, it will definitely take them longer--probably five or six years, but they'll get them. They'll resort to as many scare tactics and coercive techniques as it takes to break the Exchanges, and believe me--guys like Simpson and Hudson and Lorenzo and Brennen wrote the book. You're just a name to them, and you're small potatoes when it comes to making deals. They have asked for your help and will go the distance to get your support. We can break this Commodity corruption wide open, if you will settle down a little and work with us as a team. You can't believe the support and information we will be furnished with from the Bureau, if we play the game right. We all want the same thing--to bring an end to the stealing." He hesitated as he sipped at his beer,

then said, "You are putting on a pretty good show. You've gotten your point across--but now I would walk easy with these guys. I think I can read your game plan, but now it's time to lay back and tread softly.

"And when I say this is a small-potato operation, that's exactly what I mean. You think it's a big deal, and that the government should be right in there stopping the theft. The Feds are used to dealing in billions, not millions!"

Michael watched Lewis through the mirrored glass, then decided to ignore the warning. He wasn't impressed with Lewis's whitewash. Lewis didn't know what his game plan was. Sure, the Feds deal in billions because it's not their money, it's the taxpayers' money. They weren't much different from the crooks in Chicago; they just had a license to steal from the public and the brokers didn't. He put his palm in the air. "We are talking billions, Pete!"

Pete snapped back. "Over a period of how long, Mike?"

Michael's lips tightened, and his brows raised in thought. "Does it matter? A billion dollars is a lot of money, regardless of how long it takes to steal. I know that millions are stolen, laundered, and diverted to dummy accounts each day--and that's only what I'm aware of. If you compound what I see by all the commodity markets in the country, multiply that by two hundred and twenty trading days a year, you'll have your answer. Maybe ten billion a year...maybe more, but I don't think it's less than that."

Pete swiveled in his arm chair to look at Michael and pulled his mouth in at the corners. "The Feds make billion-dollar deals in five minutes here. A billion dollars might seem like a lot of money to you, but to the government it's pocket change. The illegal drug business alone in America is well over a hundred billion dollars a year. So, a commodity scam for a few billion, although big, is not the biggest game in town. Don't misunderstand me, I'm not making light of the dirty dealing which is going on in Chicago. I just want you to know where you stand with these government men."

Michael had heard enough. "Wait a minute, Pete, don't patronize me. I know exactly where I stand with the Government. I'm expendable, but not yet. And you say the Mafia's business tops a hundred billion a year?" He leaned close to Pete and spoke softly. "Where do you think that hundred billion goes? It's dirty money. It doesn't go right into a savings account at Continental Bank with Mr. Mafioso's name on it, or in safety deposit boxes. There aren't enough safety deposit boxes in the country to hold their goddamn money. Christ, the Mob could pay off our national debt and have enough left over to renovate America!" He sat back and questioned Pete with his eyes. "Why am I telling you something you already know? You know as well as I do that the Mafia are business men-- and money makes money! Dirty cash has to be cleaned immediately and put to work, otherwise their system will break down. And where do they clean their money, Pete?...I sure as hell don't know where it's *all* washed--but I do know where twenty to thirty per cent is washed: right on the floors of the Commodity Exchanges! So why are you giving me all this gibberish about the Chicago investigation being small potatoes?"

When Pete finally spoke, it was with caution. "Mike, I guess I just don't want you to underestimate the men in that room. You pushed Simpson around pretty good, and everybody sitting in there knew you would slam into anyone who came up against you. You moved around that room like you owned it...cocky...arrogant...pushy. I thought it was great, but you don't want those men as your enemies, they're the heads of law enforcement in America. You will have enough enemies before this is over."

Pete ran his finger around his glass, pondering. "And don't overestimate your own abilities. That *could* be a mistake and *could* get you killed! I like you, Michael, and I don't want to see you get hurt. You're playing with some real dangerous shit. I was playing down the Chicago investigation because I was trying to temper you, not because it's less important than any other case. It is a big case, and the government wants it as bad as you do."

"Not as bad as I do, Pete."

"Okay, you want justice more than the Federal Government does, which is incidental--both want justice. Once we get to the bottom of this mess, we may find that it really is the largest white-collar crime ever committed in U.S. history, but as of yet, we have only your word on that. We have a lot of work to do before we come to any solid conclusions. Remember, we need strong evidence: facts--nothing circumstantial in order for our findings to hold up in a court room. Keep your personal opinions, observations, and political skepticism to yourself. They mean nothing to the government. Right now your words wouldn't hold water if you were to testify. A good...no...a lousy attorney would make you look like a real asshole on the stand, and that is why our whole sting operation has to be neat, clean, and complete. All the *i*'s dotted and *t*'s crossed. We have to cover every angle so nothing can be thrown out of court."

He took another swig of his beer and went on. "This can get dangerous, Mike--as you have already witnessed first hand. But it will get a lot more heated when the word gets out that Big Brother from Washington is watching, and you know who the bad guys will look to first for revenge. That's right, partner--Michael "Hawk" Hogan. Neither Bo Lynch, his friends, nor I can watch you all the time. If bad guys can get to the President and to the Pope, they can sure as hell get to the "Hawk"--unless you have some type of vanishing act up your sleeve. So let's nail the bastards, scare the hell out of them, threaten them, and get some of them off the streets and behind bars before they know what hit them. We won't get 'em all--we never do--but we'll get the majority."

Pete's face screwed up in thought. Then he looked at Michael and held back a chuckle. "Hell, we'll just shoot the ones we can't get."

Michael didn't return the smile. Pain shot through his shoulder as he tried to adjust his sling. "Pete, you're a real cowboy. I'm glad to have you on my side."

"Right! I'll tell you another thing. These prima donna brokers will panic. Unless they use professionals, they will be very unpredictable in the way they come after you. They are amateurs when it comes to street combat. I'm used to dealing with professional

killers and know what their next moves are going to be. A pro won't think twice about killing. Most of the guys at the Exchanges aren't really criminals. They've just found a way to cheat their way to the top of a financial empire. But when the heat is turned on, they are liable to do anything to escape the possibility of a criminal indictment--including murder. And since they are amateurs, we won't be sure where or when they plan to make their move. The only predictable thing about what action they take is that it will be confused and unpredictable. I'd rather go up against a professional. So take my advice and use all the tools the Bureau, the CIA, and the U.S. Attorney offer you. With one phone call you can acquire information that would take you months to put together otherwise, and our information is accurate, not hearsay."

Silence engulfed Michael again. Pete was telling him, in a nice way, to stay cool with the Feds, and don't push them too far. The situation was a whole lot more complicated and dangerous than he realized. If he wanted this commodity fiasco resolved, he'd better have enough sense to use the political and investigative resources of the Federal Government--especially if he wanted to stay alive. That is what Pete was telling him. What Pete didn't know was that Michael knew exactly who he was dealing with and exactly what to expect.

Wearily, he considered his existence. Walking the razor's edge had always been a way of life to him, but now he thought he might be feeling the razor's cut. A growing uneasiness settled within him. He spoke almost inaudibly. "I'm too young to die. Too much work left to do in this life. I haven't even seen the goddamn Grand Canyon yet, or the Amazon River, or Butte Montana. I'm fucked!"

Pete looked over with a frown on his rosy cheeks. "You say something, Mike?"

He said dejectedly but with volume, "I SAID, 'I'M FUCKED! BUNK, JUNK, AND TRUNK, I'M FUCKED!'"

Pete's frown was replaced with an expression of humor. "Bunk, junk, and trunk, you're fucked? You're not the guy who's fucked. Those dummies at the Exchange are the ones who are fucked. Wait till you see us in action. Believe me, you'll be impressed and goddamn glad you're on the right side. All we have to do is keep you alive, and if you stand still long enough and follow instructions which isn't your nature we'll keep you alive."

Michael looked at Pete. He couldn't get over an obsessive sense that something was going to go wrong. "Why do I feel apprehensive? Not that I don't trust your combat abilities but..." Fear of the unknown knotted and writhed in his stomach.

Lewis cut into his thoughts. "You're just shit in your pants scared, Mike. In spite of your macho image, you're scared to death. I've been there, pal. I know what you feel, like you're in a dark, blind alley. Dark...lonely...and full of demons...with no way out. Just follow instructions and you'll be fine."

Michael leaned back in his chair and clutched his tumbler of scotch for security. "I hope you're right, Gunner. I'm not ready for the next world yet. But first things first,

let's get these meetings over with and be on with it." He thought for a moment and said, "I suppose that I'll have to repeat this whole conversation I'm having here with you again at our next meeting, right?"

Pete looked up and with a nonchalant attitude said. "Not necessarily. They probably have this whole conversation on tape--video and audio."

Michael moaned. Well, he thought. They can't hear me thinking. He was still determined to control the investigation in Chicago. The government could use all of their high tech methods to uncover the scam, but Michael had to know what they were doing, and where they were going with the investigation in order to infiltrate and exercise his own plan. He had made his point with them. Now it was time to make peace with them so they could help each other. He didn't feel that would be too difficult.

He was amused with himself. He had just put on a show at the first meeting as he did frequently in the trading pit. Appear angry, but with logic, to throw off his competitors, then lay a bunch of shit on them that they weren't expecting. Cantankerous and unpredictable behavior had worked to his benefit more times than not. Pete was right. The next meeting should be conducted amicably with wit, sophistication, and cooperation. He could always fake anger and still be in control.

Pete sipped at his Thailand beer, wiped the suds from his upper lip, and continued. "How long do you think it will take to gather the information needed for subpoenas and indictments, doing things your way?"

"What are you asking me for? You're the cop, I'm the informant, remember?"

"I've been busting drug pushers for the past several years. You've made this case an obsession, and I know by all the law books I've seen laying around your office that you've been doing your homework. So you probably have a better feel for the timing of this investigation."

Michael rubbed his chin, feeling the slight stubble of dark whiskers as his mind calculated. "I'm not an attorney, but here's what I think: It's the first week in May, 1987. I figure four to five months with a group of undercover agents on the floor just to teach them how to trade and spot the invisible methods of deceit used. It should take another year, year and a half, to gather the information needed for indictments. So, figure about two years--that is, if they give us ten good agents to work with and six more to place in offices suspected of criminal activity. By the end of 1988 or early 1989 the government should have all the information needed to go to court with violations against the Securities and Commodity Act and RICO Charges. I would expect the first subpoenas in twenty months, around December of '88--just in time for Christmas! I would look for the first grand-jury indictments four to six months after that because of all the trading orders and computer sheets that will have to be scrutinized by your people. Indictments should come down sometime in the summer or fall of '89. Trials should begin within six months of the first indictments. The whole thing should be out in the open and in the court room by the end of 1990. If there are any delays, it will be the defense attorneys who ask the court for

time to put their case together. They will milk as much time and money from the brokers indicted as possible. For those brokers who don't plea-bargain or cooperate with the Feds, and plead not-guilty, and go to trial, I can see each of them paying at least a half million to defend themselves. Chicago criminal attorneys don't come cheap--and you can be sure they will clock as many hours as possible with these presumed wealthy commodity brokers.

"You can't imagine the volume of information the government will have to page through. If the investigation is going to be effective, the government will need hundreds of agents to trace the paper. They will come to a lot of dead ends because most of the trades are legitimate. But if I tell them what to look for, and who to look for, a lot of time can be saved. For instance, it's the large orders which are violated the most, because that's where the big money is.

"You noticed Ross and Glassmann whet the brokers' appetites with large orders. That's how they were able to get the information they did in less than a month's time. So I wouldn't even consider tracing trades under twenty-five or fifty contracts."

Michael had been over this a hundred times in his own mind, and had read quite a bit about pre-trial preparations from the law books he had bought. Now, his mind was racing into the future trying to forecast the timing and probable moves of the Exchanges themselves. They would also be under close scrutiny. "And remember another thing. You won't get any help from the Exchange lawyers, because any findings will reflect directly on them, and their high-paying jobs will also be on the line. Expect *no* cooperation or delayed cooperation from the Exchanges. They will barter for time, claiming they need time to gather the information requested by the government. Once you receive the information, you may as well throw it in the waste basket, because it will be worthless. The Exchanges and clearing houses will buy as much time as they can in order to destroy incriminating information and to change illegal trades to legal trades. They only hold the actual trading cards and profit-loss statements for a short period of time, then they photograph everything, just like the library, and store the information with an independent company. You can be sure the independent storage company will be notified to destroy years of records--not only the microfilms but the hard copies as well. They would rather be criticized by the government for destroying evidence than be indicted for what could be found on the microfilms.

"The Exchanges will puff up their insulted chests and try to do a major white-wash job on the whole investigation. I know them. They will inflict all kinds of new disciplinary actions on the Exchange members in order to show the world they are good guys and very interested in protecting the public from a few unethical pit brokers. They will be sure to cover their own asses and will be sure to throw a few guys to the wolves for trading violations, to protect their image. You can put the Exchange officials on the back burner, because they really won't throw one of their own out into the cold unless absolutely necessary. Remember how many of the Exchange authorities and their legal counsel made it to the top? Through kickbacks, inside trading, and cash derived from other illegal trading

activities, which they allow for a piece of the action. Their money is hidden in dead-end foreign accounts. You will have to hit them by surprise. Slam everybody with subpoenas at the same time. Don't give them time to regroup or doctor the books, or you will get nothing."

He sifted through all of his thoughts, which were now clear and beginning to accelerate. He calculated further. "Once you get into unraveling the bogus trades, it will be like peeling an onion. Just when you think you're down to the clean heart of the onion, you'll peel off another layer only to find more decay. If the government can convict just one broker of RICO charges, you'll have floor traders flocking into the U.S. Attorney's Office with their lawyers begging to plea bargain for immunity or reduced criminal counts if they turn government witness. The fear of jail scares everybody, especially those who have no criminal records and are used to unusually high social standards.

"Threaten their life style, threaten to take some of their personal possessions away, and total pandemonium will break out. You won't have to work at the last half of the investigation. The weak links will hand you all the names and information you need just to save their own asses. Then you will have your case, and you can take that to the bank."

Pete lowered his brows in question. "You really think they will roll over that easy?"

Michael knew his tone of voice underscored his confidence in what he believed would occur. "No, they won't roll easy, not at first. That's why it's so important for the government to get its first hefty conviction. That's when the real fear of financial ruin and possible jail sentences becomes a reality. At that point, you won't have enough stenographers to take down their babbling confessions. These men are only strong because of money. Take that away and you've returned them to Sears and K-mart salesmen. Threaten them with jail and you'll reduce the weak ones to vocal encyclopedias of information on who, what, where, when, why and how!"

Pete ran his hand down his cheeks, first one side, then the other, and pushed on. "How about the big shots or the stubborn ones who won't talk?"

Now exhilaration poured into Michael. He was on a roll. He had studied the handwriting on the wall for a long time and, meeting or no meeting, he couldn't contain his thoughts. "The government won't get the big guys. They are too well protected and the paper trail won't lead to them directly. It will lead to bogus holding corporations all over the United States, and eventually lead to Europe or Caribbean accounts which are protected by the International Banking Secrecy Act. All you'll get are numbers, and you won't legally be able to break the numbered accounts. If you do, you won't be able to use them in court--and any foreign bank which breaks the International Secrecy Agreement would virtually be out of business when they are found out. Besides that, most foreign banks could give a damn about problems in the U.S., except for the Swiss banks. I don't know what kind of deal the U.S. made with the Switzerland Banking Commission, but they are letting the CIA take a peek at some of their numbered accounts."

He leaned closer to Pete. "Except for the men you have planted in the foreign banking systems, you can absolutely forget about any cooperation from outside banks. Look how much Columbian drug money they harbor and hide for criminals, not to mention Mafia money, and their own criminal banking activities. The last thing they will allow is the U.S. Government coming in and checking their records. As far as you having your own contacts in the foreign banking system, I doubt they will be much help. Your information will be too incomplete.

"Some brokers will be willing to sit for a year or two in a white-collar, minimum-security jail, a country club, figuring it's worth it for the one hundred million they have stashed in the Cayman Islands or the Bahamas." He began to feel the fine edge of anger. "I know of a number of instances where men stole millions in short periods of time. They were caught by the customer, not the Exchange, fined fifty to a hundred thousand dollars by the Exchange, and given ninety day-suspensions. I'll take that any day! Let me steal three million dollars, I'll give a hundred thousand back, and punish me by giving me a twelve-week vacation."

Pete ordered another beer, and more drinks were set in front of them. The booze was smooth, and Michael felt very much at ease now, maybe because of the conversation or maybe because of the booze. He didn't know, nor did he care.

He heard Pete's pressing words. "Maybe I'm naive, but I thought if you had an interest in an off-shore bank or foreign corporation, you could only own forty-nine per cent of the stock and a citizen of that country had to own fifty-one per cent and control the business entity."

Michael pulled back his shoulders and lifted his sharp jaw. "Not so with off-shore banks. You can buy an off-shore bank out of a magazine, and, with a little manipulation, one hundred per cent control of foreign corporations is very easily accomplished, as I'm sure the IRS and your foreign agents know."

Pete persisted. "Well, explain it to me. International banking and corporate corruption is not my long suit." He was sure Pete knew the answers to the questions he was asking, but thought he was probably testing him to see if he did indeed know what he was talking about. Michael played along, "You know as well as I do that you only have to find an illiterate cab driver in Nassau or Grand Cayman and give him five grand to be your partner. Of course he has no voting rights, no signature rights, and virtually no stock because he places the certificates in escrow as collateral to the American who loaned him five thousand dollars. And the stock is held in escrow by an American's attorney who has power of attorney and proxy rights, so the American virtually owns all of the stock."

He felt increasing interest in his own conversation. "There is a man named Vergo Espenoza, a Bahamian, who is the major stock-holder of at least seven off-shore corporations. In this particular case, he has signature rights, and all the prestige and corporate privileges which goes along with being a major stock-holder. However, power of attorney has been given to an American attorney in Miami by the name of Louis

Alverez. Espenoza's voting rights are always done by proxy and executed by the same attorney, Louis Alverez.

"Alverez is also the attorney for several of Chicago's wealthiest commodity brokers, who own the balance of the stock of the seven corporations. These corporations are all off-shore holding companies and own real estate in America, Europe, England, Ireland, the Bahamas, Caymans, and have foreign bank accounts containing over eight hundred million dollars. The majority of the money came from the Chicago and New York commodity markets as a result of skimming from customer orders."

Pete leaned closer to Michael and planted his right elbow on the bar. "Outside of the money being dirty and no taxes being paid, what's your point?"

He faced Pete and heard the rich timbre of his voice rearrange itself into a whisper. "The major stockholder, Vergo Espenoza, has been dead for over twelve years. It's nothing more than a tombstone corporation--only one of many."

Pete leaned back, eyes straight ahead, took a deep breath, and pursed his lips for the exhale. "Son of a bitch. That's something I wasn't aware of. You've got some high rollers down there and with big balls. How do you know all this and who are the brokers involved?"

Michael felt his face harden, remembering the large manila envelope he had received in the mail that cost Tim O'Neal his life. "I have some key sources in the back rooms of most of the questionable brokerage houses. We help each other. The guys involved? Well--that's my secret for now. Just like your work with the CIA is a secret to you."

He had taken Pete off guard with his comment about the CIA, and Pete snapped his head, wholly surprised. He looked into Michael's eyes, then with a near frantic whisper said, "How do you know about that?"

Michael whispered back, toning his words with a touch of mock counter-intelligence. "I make my living speculating. Just like a detective...Taking information, assimilating it, discarding some and keeping some. I speculate off the information I keep, then I make a judgment...sometimes I'm right...sometimes I'm wrong. This time I think I'm right. As I said before, maybe we'll watch the late movie tonight and talk about geography. Your geography. Where you've been, when you were there, what you did while you were there. You know a lot about me--If we're going to be hanging around each other for a few years, I think I should know what kind of a nut-case you are!"

With one eye on Michael and one eye scanning the room, Pete looked for eavesdroppers. He glanced at his watch. "It's five o'clock. We'd better get back. A few of the men in the room will be interested to hear about Vergo Espenoza and Attorney Louis Alverez."

As they finished their drinks and were about to leave, Samantha Winters appeared unnoticed behind Pete. "Pete, Mr. Simpson, Mr. Hudson, and a few more of the brass would like you to join them for a few minutes. They said to plan to be back together at

eight-thirty in the morning. Apparently, a few of the men have to get back to Washington tonight, and it's a bit too late to resume for the evening. In any event the boss wants to speak with you."

Michael felt a warm excitement flow through his body at the sight of her. He tried to hide his enthusiasm, which was not exactly platonic, but when she looked at him with her striking blue eyes, he knew she sensed his inner desires. He watched her study his face and felt a jab of sexual pleasure just in her brief look.

She smiled at Michael and said, "I'll entertain Mr. Hogan for a few minutes."

Pete rose, stepped aside, and held his chair for Samantha. "I'll bet you'll entertain my handsome friend, you fox. Let me introduce you."

Before he could say anything, Michael interrupted, "Samantha Winters, I'm Michael Hogan." He extended his hand which she shook firmly and with confidence.

"My pleasure, Mr. Hogan. May I sit for a moment?"

Michael was standing now, and gestured toward the vacant chair. "Be my guest, Ms. Winters."

Pete held the chair for her, then looked at Michael. "Be careful what you say, Mike. She's probably wired and every word will be broadcasting throughout FBI headquarters in Washington."

Michael watched as she moved her blue eyes upward to meet Pete's sarcastic smile, and with a slight tilt of her head she countered, "Be gone, Satan--and don't spread ugly rumors about your favorite female agent. Now go do as you are told, and report to Simpson in the North American Lounge or your next assignment may be in Anchorage, Alaska. You'll be giving Mr. Hogan the wrong impression about me."

Michael was trying to look and act casual, but felt clumsy and couldn't take his eyes off of the pretty face sitting next to him. He felt the drum-beat of his heart. Without even knowing her, he felt as if he had been struck by lightning. What the hell was wrong with him?

He looked at Pete and saw that he had noticed Michael's attraction for Samantha. He said with a grin, "I think Hogan has already formed his own opinion of you, Sam." Pete tucked her chair in, moving her closer to the bar and also to Michael. Then he leaned down and kissed her cheek, saying, "Maybe the three of us can have a drink and dinner after I'm finished with my 'agent abuse session,' okay?"

Samantha said, "Sounds good to me, Romeo. We'll talk when you get back...maybe we can break away from this fortress for a few hours. You game for a late night meal, Mr. Hogan?"

He could hardly speak, overtaken by her sensual presence. Her voice, her smile, her scent, all combined to form waves of passion that rushed through his loins. His response was barely audible. "Sounds good to me. I'm just along for the ride anyway."

Pete slapped him on the back and headed toward the North American Room across the main area of the lounge. Michael watched until he was almost out of sight. Before Pete crossed the threshold, he looked back at Michael, winked, smiled, and disappeared.

TWENTY-ONE

Samantha Winters

The bartender placed another scotch in front of Michael, whose eyes by now were on his drink, staring as he toyed with the flag-topped red-and-white stirrer. His mind was racing again. Why was Pete called in with the man who despised him? He trusted Pete and figured he would get the scoop from him later. He hadn't seen Andy or Ross and assumed they were in the North American Room as well. Other members of the meeting were scattered around the bar, sitting in small groups of twos and threes in wing-back chairs. Most were drinking beer.

A disturbing thought entered his already perplexed mind. What if Andy and Pete were reporting all of his moves to John Simpson and Clay Hudson? Fucking traitors!--Naw--It couldn't be true! If it were, then everything he knew about people was wrong. He had more confidence in his judgment of men than did the boogie man who lurked in his subconscious. After all, they were located at CIA headquarters, not his own living room. The Brass, as Samantha had called them, were certainly exploring every possibility not only to make a deal with him but also to agree on the direction that they wanted the investigation to follow.

Samantha was served a Galliano on the rocks with a slice of lime. The few moments of silence were an eternity to Michael. He felt like he was in high school again trying to get up the nerve to ask the girl sitting next to him for a dance. Finally she broke the quiet. "Am I trespassing on your thoughts, Mr. Hogan?"

"Oh, no...not at all...I was just waiting for someone to come up and shoot me in the back of the head--and you showed up. You're not going to shoot me, are you?" She smiled and raised her glass in toast fashion. "I'm not going to shoot you nor is anybody else. Your first time here naturally brings on self-inflicted paranoia. Here's to a good relationship and a victory in Chicago, if we get that far!"

He nodded and raised his glass. Her statement was either sincere, professional, or full of double meanings. They clinked glasses and sipped their drinks. His eyes remained on her lips as she sipped the yellow Italian liqueur. He saw the pink lips, which she licked with an even pinker, inviting tongue. Perfect features, he thought. She was slightly tanned, with a clear, exciting face, blue eyes, curly, blond, shoulder-length hair. A thin, gold chain decorated her slender neck. Gorgeous, he thought again--Goddamn gorgeous!

Two top buttons of her white silk blouse were left unbuttoned to show just enough cleavage, to spur interest and stir his imagination. She wore no bra, and he could see the slight protrusion of her nipples through the silk. His libido spoke subconsciously, and the

urge came over him to plop her right up on the glass bar and make love to her in front of the bartender, dignitaries, and whoever else was watching via hidden cameras--he bet that would be a first. She was sexy and inviting.

Despite all the girls in Chicago who were in his midst everyday, he had never felt like this before. Contrary to statistics and contrary to the goings on of many of the other brokers, he had always been faithful to Maria. She was his only love, and he never desired another woman to the extent of violating his fidelity. These feelings within him now were different from anything he'd ever experienced. He was a happily married man. His relationship with Maria was good in every way. Why did this woman affect him so? What was happening?

He had this feeling in the meeting room when he first encountered Samantha face to face, but he had been able to dismiss her as a pretty and welcomed distraction. Now he was sitting next to her, and he liked the feeling that was going through him. He didn't want to dismiss her, but this wasn't right. Dismiss it, he told himself. But instead he pushed aside the guilt pangs gnawing at his soul, as a slight scent of her feminine musk touched his senses. He felt the excitement continue to grow in his body.

Again, she broke the silence. "I'm impressed you remembered my name."

He smiled. "I'm good with names and figures." A blush rose to her cheeks with the mention of the subtle innuendo.

He wrinkled his forehead and said, "I just have a hard time placing faces."

This brought a smile to her face, framing perfectly placed white teeth and a dimple in her left cheek. She spoke softly, her voice deep, sexy, and sensational, accentuating her attractiveness even more. "You know we've met before--I mean, from a distance."

He remembered--how could he forget?--but feigned ignorance, both to keep the conversation going and to retain his nonchalant image. He asked her point blank, "Was I drunk?"

She took another sip from her drink and their eyes met. Again she smiled. "No, you weren't drunk--at least I don't think you were. You were driving down the Kennedy Expressway with Andy Golden about ninety miles per hour. Remember?"

He was amused and nodded. "I remember. At least I remember the ride. Who could forget a casual ride home with that maniac behind the wheel? But did I miss something? Where were you? In the back seat?"

Her smile lasted as she studied his face. "I was in the blue Mercedes that passed you someplace around the Edens Junction."

He squeezed his lips together, giving the appearance of shallow thought. "Ah...Sure, I remember...you were 'UNIT 2--SAM!' Well, UNIT 2, you're a damn good driver--even if you were driving one of those common-man cars, a Mercedes Benz." He purposely threw the final, arrogant statement, hoping to provoke a reaction.

She looked down, then shook her head. "That was me. And that 'common man' car passed your pompous toy at nearly a hundred and ten, and I could have passed you just

as easily had you been going a hundred and fifty. That 'common man' automobile has a four-fifty-two Magnum engine, with dual..."

Michael held his hand up to stop her. "You're losing me, Ms. Winters. I just buy cars, I don't work on them." He smiled back at her. "Pleased to meet you."

She flushed. "My pleasure, Mr.Hogan." Sipping at her drink she said, "You handled that meeting pretty well. "Her right brow lifted slightly. "Are you naturally bold, or just outright arrogant?"

He swiveled his chair and took a swig of scotch. "I think the word you're looking for is *stupid*!"

She crossed her legs beneath a closely fitted straight black crepe skirt. "Well--as the philosopher says, 'Know thy self!'...But I wouldn't necessarily call it stupid to stand up in front of some of the strongest political men in the country and demand a hundred million in life insurance, immunity for your friends, money for Viet Nam vets, total control of a billion-dollar scam investigation, and the promotion and assistance of one of the Bureau's most undisciplined and unpredictable agents. I think I'd call it--crazy!"

He forced a stern look and said, "Pete's not undisciplined. He's just angry. And maybe that's the word I'm looking for. I am crazy; I've proved that just by being here. I am not naturally bold or arrogant or stupid, but I am goddamn angry! And just for the record, Ms. Winters, Pete is very predictable. He blows ear drums out of the heads of people who kill kids with drugs. We belong together, because that's the kind of *crazy* I like!"

He sought internal counsel, then carefully weighed his next words. He decided to see what she was made of and said, "I'm really not concerned about what you or the government thinks of me, Ms. Winters. My feelings go far beyond even anger." He waited for a response and none came. She seemed to be amused. He went on. "I work with a group of thieves who have forced me into a position I don't like very much. Then I have to deal with a bunch of hypocritical bureaucrats who could not give a damn about Michael Hogan, but are willing to use me as a pawn to accomplish a political end--not a moral end. My financial future is dubious. My family is in danger. A few of my close friends have been murdered. I've been followed for months by some heavy-weight assholes, and beaten up once--I don't take kindly to that sort of bullshit. Your people invited me to this party because they need me. Let's just see how far they'll go to keep me."

She held one arm on her lap, the other hand resting on the bar and around her drink. "Let's be friends. You call me Sam and I'll call you Michael...Okay? If we are going to work together in Chicago, I don't want you to take your anger out on me. I don't want you to think of me as a hypocrite or a bureaucrat--because I am neither." She hesitated with some embarrassment. "And, if it's okay with you, I would rather not debate our working relationship. I'm very good at what I do and can be a big help to you and the investigation. Just give me a chance and try not to take your anger out on me."

Michael was sure this whole conversation was being picked up on a microphone planted someplace close, but he didn't care. He wasn't saying anything he hadn't expressed in the meeting. He figured the more people who knew where he stood, the better off he'd be. He wasn't going to play their game of smiles and promises. He would, however, play their game of deceptions. That was a game he knew, and knew well.

He looked at the gorgeous specimen of woman who was waiting for his response. God, make her legitimate, he asked mentally. "I'm sorry for being so harsh. I guess I get a little carried away when I start talking about all this crap."

He looked into the searching blue eyes trained on his face. He continued to feel her warmth, her comfort. "What exactly is it you do, Ms. Winters...Ah...I mean, Sam?"

"I do undercover work for the Bureau--and I'm good at my job."

Michael's eye-brows raised. He was going to say, "I'll bet you're good at your job--under the covers?" Wow, did he bet she was. Then he quickly scolded himself for being so crude. He knew his thoughts were trite. Besides, he was sure every guy in the Bureau had tried to put the make her at one time or another, and he wanted respect from her. As much as she aroused him, he would try not to toy with her. He would give the beauty the courtesy she deserved. He posed a question, "Undercover work?"

Her lovely lips moved into a smile. "Undercover, Michael, undercover. You know, like pretending I'm someone I'm not, in lieu of the nice girl that I am, from Dayton, Ohio."

"Well, you're certainly not Army issue, that's for sure. If you were working for me, I'd think you were a sharp girl from Dayton, Ohio, not a Fed trying to get enough evidence to put me in jail. I guess being a nice looking woman does have its advantages with the Bureau."

She smiled and said. "It does! And thanks for the flattery." He raised his glass in acknowledgment.

They both sat quietly for a few moments. Michael felt that under normal circumstances he'd encourage small talk, but he hadn't come this far for trivial pursuits. "Just exactly what role are you supposed to play in this game, Sam?"

Her eyes turned deep blue and professional. She looked down at her drink and said, "It's not much of a game to me, Michael. It's serious, evidently large-scale, white-collar crime investigation, and we've being given the assignment to collect incriminating evidence against those involved. I take my job seriously and despise being patronized."

She looked up at Michael quizzically, and a ringlet of blond hair fell across her forehead. He smiled at her. He reached over with his right hand and with a gentle touch brushed the ringlet back in place. He saw her shiver slightly and wondered if it was from his touch. He hoped so. "Okay."

"Okay?" she asked.

"Yes, okay. I'll be serious about your job. I have no intention of patronizing you; I want to be friends." His words halted in his mouth. He was going to say more, but the right ones were not there.

She touched his left hand and gave it a friendly squeeze. He winced instinctively, and she let go immediately. Then she must have noticed the ripe wounds on his hand, still very much noticeable from the fight in the garage. He watched her examine the hand closely. One of his fingers was swollen and blue, and there were a number of scabbed-over cuts on the fist and knuckles. For a brief moment he was glad he had the injury.

"Have you had this looked at?" she asked.

He placed his hand around his drink, and all but the stiff, bluish finger gripped the glass. He saw her looking at his hand and unconsciously turned the drink slightly to hide the wounded hand. "It's only a broken finger and a few bruised knuckles. Nothing you can do with a broken finger except let it heal. I heal fast."

She took her eyes off his hand and peered around him. "And the shoulder?"

He hoped she didn't have a mother complex. He said with some annoyance, "It's just a separation. I've had them before and, like the finger, it will be like new in a few weeks, Sam. I didn't see a doctor--Lewis set it for me and wrapped it. I just picked up some pain pills, and that's all the doctoring I need."

"How did you get pain pills without seeing a doctor? I mean you're supposed to have a prescription to get narcotics."

He looked at her as if she were naive. "I made one phone call to a broker friend of mine, and within thirty minutes I had two hundred heavy-duty Percodan tablets, twenty vials of Demerol, and a whole bunch of other drugs delivered to the house. I could have opened up my own drug store. I only use the Percodan when the shoulder hurts. The Demerol makes me see pink elephants."

She scoffed. "Macho man, ah! No doctor, just a buddy who deals drugs to his friends and another friend who sets broken bones."

He forced a smile. That's what it's all about, Sam. It's who you know, and who owes who a favor. It works in my business as well as it does in yours. Right or wrong, that's the name of the game, and you know it. And don't call me Macho Man unless you want a little patronizing thrown your way."

She was quiet for a moment, then she said, "Okay." They both smiled and clinked glasses. She toasted again. "To a good relationship, Michael."

"To a good relationship, Sam. Let's go get the bastards!" Michael watched her pink lips sip at the yellow liqueur as she continued to study his face. Her eyes roamed from his hair to his eyes to his chin. He wondered if the physical attraction was mutual. She moved her feet under the bar, and her leg brushed his. He took that as a confirmation. His body and mind had relaxed in her presence. She had disarmed him. He felt like Samson without his hair. At this moment she could take him by the hand and lead him into the fires of hell, and he would follow like a puppy. Was she a siren or an angel? He didn't care.

He tried to shake the fantasies from his head, but they were like fish hooks, there to stay. He needed rest. A good night's sleep would restore his strength, he told himself. Until then, he would just sit back and enjoy her erotic presence.

They both finished their drink and talked until Pete returned. Andy Golden was with him, disheveled and serious as always. Pete looked at the two of them and said, "How about a bite to eat, kids? Phil's Steak House is about twenty minutes from here, greatest steaks on the East Coast."

Michael rose and pulled Sam's chair out. "Sounds good to me. This place makes me nervous, and I have to make a few phone calls without having half of Washington listening in."

He knew the combination of pain pills and booze was going to get him drunk. He just wanted to get out from under the watchful eye of Big Brother. Besides he wanted to check in with Maria, his attorney, and Bo Lynch. He hoped to god he would find him sober. Bo played a big part in his plan for survival. He was no use to him drunk.

He waved to the bartender and thanked him for his hospitality. The man smiled, waved back, and said, "My pleasure, Mr. Hogan. Come back and see us soon, Mõn." Michael knew his mind was blurred, but his senses were still sharp. He knew nobody had exchanged names--but the Jamaican knew his. Shit, he thought. Let me out of this prison.

* * *

The bartender, without his ever-present smile, watched the four leave the lounge. When they were out of sight, instead of removing the glasses from the bar, he reached under the thick glass top and pressed three orange buttons next to a blender that looked like reset buttons for a T.V. set. In a room filled with recording equipment, not far from the lounge, a number of reels stopped their slow forward motion and began to rewind at an accelerated speed. One tape had recorded the total conversation that had taken place among Hogan, Lewis, and Winters. Another had videotaped the entire stay at the bar, and another, engaged a sophisticated infrared camera, which was able to lift fingerprints from the bar top and the glasses used by the three patrons--standard procedure! The reels were all labeled, "HOGAN-7C-OPERATION SKIM-TRIM-CHICAGO. 5/4/87." The man in the white smock placed the three reels on a nearby rack that contained eight other tapes with a similarly labeled code. He then picked up the phone and dialed four numbers. One ring and the phone was answered. "Hudson here."

"Mr. Hudson? We have the Hogan tapes."

"Good. Just keep them on file. Before this is all over you're going to have a lot more taped information, so make room for them."

Hudson hung up the phone, took a puff from a long cigar, and looked across the table at John Simpson. "Well, it's started, John. I think we're going to crack this Chicago

191

thing. It appears as if Agent Winters has his attention. I don't see any real problem with Hogan, do you?"

Simpson, in his usual surly mood, waved the cigar smoke away from his corpulent face. "Not unless the broad falls for the cocky bastard."

"See to it that she doesn't, John. She's too good an agent to get involved with a wild man, and make sure Golden keeps a close rein on him--if that's possible. Now how about that drink? You look like you need one."

"Yeah...Sure, pour away."

Hudson poured two tumblers of expensive brandy and slid one over to Simpson. They both raised their glasses to each other, drank deep, and replaced them on a silver tray on Hudson's desk. They looked at each other, Simpson with skepticism on his face, Hudson with confidence. They rose at the same time and headed for the door.

Hudson said, "Don't worry, John. Hogan isn't as tough as he appears. No man is. You've seen the readout on Hogan--arrested three times as a youth for fighting, charges dropped...after that...nothing. Except a possible affiliation with Sean McGiven, an IRA sympathizer. But Andy Golden says that relationship is simply on a friendship basis--that Hogan doesn't agree with the politics of the IRA."

Simpson said sarcastically, "I wonder whose politics he does agree with?"

Hudson continued. "His father was a grain and livestock dealer, from Ireland. He was a pacifist, negotiator, peacemaker...no record...never even spit on the sidewalk as far as we can tell. We didn't check any further back. His grandparents were probably poor, Irish potato farmers. So, as far as Michael Hogan goes, he's just a street fighter...no violent background. Besides, we're not investigating him. We just want his information and the crooks he works with then he can fend for himself. Just put up with him for now. Once back in Chicago, he won't give you any more trouble."

Simpson turned the handle to the heavy door. "Don't be so sure of yourself, Clay. He's intelligent, has brass balls, has a mean streak, and can read us like a book. We just heard Golden and Lewis tell us that danger intrigues him--and that he spits at the devil!"

Hudson smiled reassuringly. "John, if a man finds danger amusing and has little fear of the devil--maybe the man doesn't know all of the facts."

Simpson mumbled out loud, "Or maybe we don't know all the facts, Clay. Did that ever occur to you?" Hudson frowned as the heavy door closed firmly behind them.

TWENTY-TWO

Meeting II: May 1987

Even with a good night's sleep and a clear, patient mind, Michael was getting tired of Simpson's insinuations that the whole commodity industry was corrupt. He allowed his anger to rise and spoke through it. "Mr. Simpson, your questions are misleading and insignificant. Everyone who drives a Rolls Royce or Lamberghini at the Exchange is not a crook. I, myself, drive a one-hundred-thousand-dollar automobile and live in a million-dollar house on Lake Michigan. And I make my money honestly!"

Simpson continued to press him sarcastically. "Well, Mr. Hogan. What would you say is the percentage of brokers in Chicago who skim trades or violate trading rules?"

Michael leaned back and propped his right elbow on the arm of his chair. He was staring a hole into the small black dot of his microphone. His eyes raised slowly to meet Simpson, who was waiting for his reply. "We're talking *major* violations, Mr. Simpson. I'd say twenty-five per cent...tops thirty per cent of the brokers are thieves. I'm not talking about the *perks* that go along with spending a quarter of a million for a membership. I'm talking grand larceny." He repeated, "Thirty per cent are stealing.

"Most of the brokers put their life savings on the line and are willing to lose what's taken them years to save. They are honest, good men. A lot of them cheat a little-- but that's just a way of life down at the Exchange."

With his thinning, gray hair slicked neatly back and fat cheeks still red from his morning shave, Simpson asked, "What exactly are the perks, Mr. Hogan?"

Michael had removed his arm brace and felt the throbbing again in his shoulder. He looked at his watch--10:00 am. Shit, he thought, only an hour and a half had gone by since they'd begun the inquisition. In that time, he had repeated his conversation with Peter Lewis about the Miami attorney, Louis Alverez, who helped set up *dummy corporations, untraceable holding companies,* and *foreign bank accounts.* He was surprised when he saw the stunned looks on the younger agents' faces as he told the story of Vergo Espenoza, the Bahamian, who had been dead for twenty years, yet owned controlling interest in seven off-shore corporations with proxy and power of attorney in the hands of Alverez. Evidently, they hadn't taught the young agents about *tombstone* corporations at the FBI Academy.

He also repeated that he estimated the combined Chicago and New York commodity scams netted billions of dollars a year, much of which went into the foreign accounts.

Simpson's impatience reared. "Mr. Hogan, we're waiting!"

Michael snapped back to the moment. "I'm sorry. What was the question?"

Simpson looked at Hudson, who sat to his right, and said, "Christ, I wish this guy would pay attention." He repeated his question. "What exactly are the perks you say come with owning a membership?"

Michael pulled himself together. His eyes glanced around the room. All heads were pointed in his direction. The question and answer session reminded him of a tennis match--heads and eyes continued to move from one end of the table to the other. Michael realized that the answers to the questions were all common knowledge to him--general trading lingo. But they were probably being heard for the first time by the people in this room.

He had promised himself he would be patient and try to be a good teacher today. That's why he was here. He answered the question. "One perk is called *curb trading* or if you're English it's called *kerb trading*. The whole foundation of *pit trading* is based on what we call *open outcry*. A group of brokers get together in the morning, a bell rings, and the open outcry system of trading takes place all day until the bell rings in the afternoon. Every broker is required to shout out his buy and sell orders so the rest of the world knows what's available at a particular price at a particular time. It is a violation to trade before or after the bell, and a violation to tell another broker what you have to buy or sell. That's called *disclosure of orders*. The perk comes when a friend or any other broker comes to me before the market opens and tells me he is in trouble and has to buy or sell *x* amount of contracts on the opening bell. I look in my *deck*, which is the word we use for the orders we are holding. Basically, a deck is a chronological schedule of buy and sell prices. If I have orders in my deck that can help the guy out, I'll tell him to stand by me on the opening. When the bell rings, I turn to him and with an open outcry sell or buy from him the amount he needs to get out of the market. Although I didn't disclose my orders to him, he pretty much knew I had the orders in my deck to get him out of a jam, since I told him to stand by me. That's one type of curb trading. The agreement was theoretically made between two brokers before the opening, *on the curb*, to buy and sell with each other. This *curbing* also can occur after the close of the market."

Michael looked around the table. Some of the heads were down, pencils scratching intently on the yellow pads. Others concentrated on him. "Most floor brokers come to the market in the morning *naked*. That means they have no position in the market. They own nothing. Their money is made or lost by trading all day long, in and out, picking up a point here, a few points there, or losing a point here and there. They are called *scalpers*. They make their living by *scalping* the market. They scalp a little bit wherever they can. This is legal. Without the scalper, the order-filling brokers would have only other order-filling brokers to go to for a trade, which would kill the liquidity of the market. However, the scalper always wants to go home naked, without a position in the market. The scalper is different from a *trader*, like myself, who makes money by taking trades home with him. I seldom go home naked."

A number of the agents got a chuckle out of the terminology. He looked down at Samantha, and she raised her eyebrows as if to say, "Interesting."

He sipped cold coffee and continued. "If a scalper has bought one hundred contracts during the day and after counting his trades he finds he missed his *count* and had only sold out ninety contracts, he panics because those extra ten contracts could cost him a bundle of money the next day. His philosophy is simply to *day trade*, as opposed to *overnight trading, naked vs. dressed.* He may come to me after the close and ask if I have ten contracts he can buy at any legal market price which I may have been unable to fill on the close. If I have what he's looking for, I sell the contracts to him. No one knows if the trade was made before the close or after the close, as long as the price is in the *closing range.* He's happy and the customer is happy. Curb trading...a border-line violation...but no one is hurt.

"The type of curb trading that's a major violation of trading rules is when another broker comes to me early in the morning and wants to buy all the sell orders I have up to a certain price. Well--it doesn't take a genius to figure out that this guy has *inside information*, which told him the market is going higher. Some brokers will make the trade right then and there, fifteen minutes or a half hour before the market opens. The orders are filled on the curb--outside of the pit--quietly. All that is missing is the price, which will be determined on the *opening*. There is no open outcry--or recording of the trade with the *quote clerk* in the pit. The scalper or trader in this instance has a definite advantage. If there's a profit in the trade, the broker holding the deck will receive the *kickback* from the broker who made the trade. This is not only called curb trading, it is also called *pre-arranged trading*, both illegal.

"The same thing can happen after the *close*. A trader may come up to the order filler and ask if he has anything to sell up to the top of the closing range. Obviously, the broker looking for the trade has received information in the past fifteen minutes that will open the market higher or lower the next day; for instance, a weather report, or a government announcement--and yes, even a rumor. Since we don't send all of our orders back to the companies where they originated until about a half hour after the market closes, because of other paper work that takes priority, there very well may be a curb trade taking place as late as an hour after the closing bell, a major violation.

"So you see, there are two types of curb trading. One is a marginal violation to help a fellow broker who is in trouble. This is also called a perk. The second type of curb trade is for the purpose of getting a jump on everyone else. These trades almost always involve kickbacks to the deck holder, or to the broker who made the product available to the other broker. Kickbacks are to guarantee loyalty and further income."

Michael picked up his glass of water and took a long swallow. As he set the glass down, he looked around and asked, "Does anyone have any questions?"

Brian Brennen, U.S. Attorney of New York, pointed his pencil in the air. He had a slight lisp or slur, Michael couldn't distinguish which. A large, rugged man with a

whiskey nose and a well-used face, Brennen had a full head of dark-brown hair graying slightly at the temples, and his face was accented with thick eye-brows that sank as he talked. "Mr. Hogan, I thought all orders were *time stamped* and had to be returned to the place of origination immediately upon execution. You state that trades are made before the market opens and after the market closes with as much as an hour lapse in time. How do you explain the difference in time stamping verification?"

Michael watched Brennen's eyebrows rise and fall as he spoke and found himself doing the same thing unconsciously, as he began to answer. "Mr. Brennen, the opening orders could have been time stamped hours before the market opens. The customer who places the order may live in Europe, or he may be a doctor in Florida, who talks to his Chicago broker early in the morning. Or the customer may just be a man who is going out of town and places his buy or sell orders the previous day. So the first-time stamps don't count for much on openings, because they can vary greatly. An illegal trade can be made before the opening. Broker identification is on the order, along with the company they trade through, and the quantity being bought or sold. The only thing missing is the price. After the opening, the *deck holder* sees what the market is trading at. He picks the best price for his friend, and they both agree. They both record the price. The deck holding broker sends the filled order back to the company who represents the customer. Then the order is time stamped, maybe two minutes after the opening. No apparent violations, as all time stamps and prices are as they should be--except the customer received a pre-arranged lousy *fill*!

"It's not so easy to cheat if the trade is made a half hour after the closing of the market." Michael posed the question, "How can a broker show that a trade was made on the close, when it actually took place a half hour later? With no time stamp to verify the transaction? Simple! There are a number of places on the floor that have time stamp machines, which are set anywhere from a few minutes apart to a few hours apart. The broker simply goes to the machine that is set back a half hour. He punches the order in, showing the trade was made on the close, rather than a half hour after closing. The actual time may be 2:37 p.m, but the time stamp on the order reads 2:07 p.m...the market closed at 2:00 p.m."

Brennen leaned his heavy body back and held a match to his cigar. "That's very interesting. Thank you."

Michael felt he had control of the meeting and was handling himself with confidence and certainty. He viewed the conference table as a trading pit and he, the holder of the deck. "Interesting? Yes, it is interesting. But that is probably the simplest of all scams, Mr. Brennen; others are downright genius. Some customer orders never even reach the floor of the Exchange. They are made in outside offices."

Brennen mumbled through the fat cigar in his mouth. "How can you execute an order, without sending it first to the trading floor? That sounds impossible but I get the feeling you're going to tell me it's not."

With a slight squint of his eyes and a sideways movement of his jaw, Michael said, "It's not only possible; it's done every day."

Waving smoke from in front of his face, Brennen exclaimed with his bar room voice, "How? For God's sake!"

Michael responded in haste. "Take this for an example. An office on the fifteenth floor of the Exchange building receives an order to buy one hundred contracts of corn at three dollars per bushel, and another order comes in to sell one hundred contracts of corn at two dollars and ninety-five cents a bushel. There is a five-cent-per-bushel difference between the two orders. The two *account executives* make a deal in the office. One buys a hundred contracts from the other at three dollars a bushel, and the other sells a hundred contracts at two dollars ninety-five cents a bushel. A five-cent profit on one hundred contracts of corn, or five hundred thousand bushels, is twenty-five thousand dollars. All the two *A.E.*'s need is the signature of the floor broker handling the order and another floor broker to accept the order. A simple visit to the trading floor to have this done results in a twenty-five-thousand-dollar pre-arranged trading profit, time stamped, and virtually filled forty-six stories above the trading floor. The trade goes into a *Granny account* (for grandmother), and the profit is eventually split among the four men involved. That, Mr. Brennen, is an explanation of curb trading, both marginal and illegal, disclosure of orders, and pre-arranged trading. All are done a thousand times a day!"

Michael settled his elbows on the table, pressed all ten fingers together making a tent, and peered out above their tips. "What's next?"

Harvey Shultz, Executive Director of the IRS, looked at Simpson for approval to ask a question. Request granted. Shultz, a wiry little man with "Mr. Peepers"-type glasses to match his thin frame, had a kind but serious face, and he was dressed in five-year-old apparel. He said, "Mr. Hogan, naturally, as head of the IRS, I'm concerned about the amount of money that is derived from trading with little or no income tax being paid. If what you say is true about billions of taxable income dollars being diverted to foreign accounts and billions more being laundered through the markets by society's criminal element, I presume that everyone involved is guilty of tax fraud or tax evasion."

Michael interlocked his fingers and brought his hands down to rest on the table. "That's true, Mr. Shultz. What's the question?"

Michael could see that Shultz was intelligent, clear in speech, but self-conscious in his fidgeting. As an accountant would speak, the little, bald man asked, "How is the dirty money laundered, and where does it go? And how come the IRS isn't aware of the funds that go out of the market and into foreign accounts?"

Michael's mind clicked clearly as if he were in the trading pit and orders were coming at him from all directions. He evaluated the questions quickly, readied his answer, and said without hesitation, "The Mafia are notorious for buying up bankrupt corporations and companies with huge *tax losses, loss carry-forward* in tax vernacular. Let's say, for example, the Mafia, or even large broker groups, buy one hundred defunct companies for

pennies on the dollar and that each company has a tax loss of ten million dollars. They then open up one hundred trading accounts, one for each company, and place a small amount of money into each account for trading, using different *commodity clearing houses*. They open up one hundred more trading accounts and place ten million dollars into each account. This money is, of course, dirty money to be laundered. In a short period of time, the one hundred accounts with the dirty money have been laundered through the markets, by special brokers, in special, sophisticated ways. The one hundred accounts of the defunct companies have each made ten million dollars, which they claim is tax free because they have a ten-million-dollar tax loss carry-forward. Ten million dollars multiplied by one hundred companies equals one billion dollars. Less commissions and kickbacks of approximately one hundred million, or ten per cent. So the Mafia has cleaned one billion dollars and given the brokers involved one hundred million to do the job. They now own one hundred legitimate companies in the United States, which are each worth nine million dollars with zero tax liability!"

Shultz peered over the top of his glasses. "I thought you said ten million per company was being laundered, not nine million."

"Ten million is being laundered, but one million per company is kept by the commodity clearing house as a fee for doing the job, making the once-bankrupt company worth nine million. That's a ten per cent commission, about what the Miami banks *charge* for holding drug money--but of course you already know that." His last remark was said somewhat sarcastically, knowing full well that Shultz didn't know that to find a home for drug money in a bank meant to *pay* interest, not *receive* it. He watched Shultz search his mind for an answer as he questioned him. "Mr. Shultz, isn't it true that the IRS checks the bottom line, the profit line, not the labyrinth of commodity trades a company makes to become healthy again?"

He felt sorry for the little man. He was the head of an organization that next to the KGB was probably the most hated group of individuals in the world, and he was probably paid only fifty or sixty thousand a year for all the bullshit he had to put up with.

"Yes, Mr. Hogan. We look at the bottom line, and at as many lines as we possibly can. If a company has a nine-million-dollar gain and the receipts to prove that the gains came from a legal source, we have no reason to delve any further. And if the company has a ten-million-dollar tax loss and can prove it, we have no reason to disallow the declaration of the nine-million profit. In fact, we are happy the company is getting back on its feet. Theoretically, the company will be paying taxes the next year."

Michael said, "As far as getting the money out of the country without the IRS knowing--that's a wrong assumption. The IRS computer does know about it, but it takes too long for the computer to catch up with the money. Thousands of *tombstone* and *holding companies* are set up all over the country. Skim money and kickback money is passed from one company to the next. The money may pass through as many as twenty companies before it gets lost and ends up in a European or Island account. Check your records, Mr.

Shultz, and find out how many holding companies you have on record that are owned by other holding companies that are owned by other holding companies ad infinitum. Your revenue officers look for addresses that aren't there, post boxes that have been closed, people who don't exist and money that has long since left the country--and is probably back in the U.S. again."

Michael scanned the room and saw only blank faces. He looked back at Harvey Shultz, who nodded his understanding. Michael sighed and thought, so much for teaching poker to robots. "As I see it, Mr. Shultz, many of the indictments that come down will eventually lead to a simple case of tax evasion--something that is traceable and obvious to the IRS. Forget the big money--you'll never find it! The methods used by the Pros in stealing money from the market are too difficult to follow. The government may have to settle for tax fraud and violations of commodity-fraud laws. If the government pushes hard enough for RICO violations, the penalties will probably be severe enough to please the public, the media, and the politicians. It will be a whole lot easier to trace blatant *backyard trades* than running all over the world looking for *capital flight money*."

He rested his head in his palms for a moment, wondering if he was making any headway. He had to continue. Even if it seemed like Greek to the agents, they could review his statements being recorded by the stenographer, Ms. Nelson, at a later date. He spoke with sharpness. "Where many of the brokers make their mistake is when they bring the money back into the country. They buy real estate, stocks, bonds, and toys, then put them in a trust or in their own name. When they are finally audited, the Government sees that they made "x" amount of money but own ten times more than "x." The real careless men let greed overpower reason and begin to write off losses that are made on losing investments made with flight money. When the IRS comes asking to see the checks written for the bad investment, the broker is caught by the balls. He can't very well tell the government he paid for the investments with cash. Nor can he pull out a handful of checks written from a Cayman or European account. If he finds a U.S. bank that will transfer large amounts of foreign funds without reporting it to the government, he'll be okay until the bank is audited. Then the government can get him on false financial statements. It's easy to get large sums of money out of the country but damn hard to get it back in...the right way. But the real pros know exactly how to bring their money back with no questions asked. If a novice does bring money back into the U.S., he had better be goddamn careful what he buys with it."

He stopped talking long enough to swig a mouthful of cool water. He looked at Samantha. She wrote as if she were taking a timed test.

He directed his next comments to the group. "Again, I'd say that most of the brokers who go down after this investigation will be nailed with tax fraud, mail fraud, bank fraud, and commodity fraud, with a few RICO violations thrown in for color. You all know better than I that those are the felony convictions that are the easiest to prove. The only

problem with that is...you are cutting the lawn but you're not getting the weeds! That is, you're not getting the Mafia, nor the broker syndicate groups, nor the murderers."

He took a long breath, eyes aimed at Shultz again to see if he was satisfied, but just like an accountant, he wanted more. "Mr. Hogan, what do you know about *parking trades*?"

Michael sighed and said, "Parking trades, Mr. Shultz, is more of a stock term for moving income into the next year by placing profitable trades in someone else's name with the understanding that the man parking the trades will take them back at a later date. This is all done in order to avoid paying taxes on the income. It's usually after the first of the year that the trades are taken back, and a fee is generally paid the man who *rented* the parking 'space' to the trader who parked his winning trades. The same thing goes on in the commodity markets, but we call it spreading: *butterfly spreads, tax spreads*, or *dead-head spreads*."

Shultz persisted. "Would you mind giving me an example of these spreads, Mr. Hogan?"

Michael was getting tired of talking. He looked at his watch. Time oozed so sluggishly that he could hardly notice any movement. Cynically, he thought, wow, another minute went by. But, since John Simpson had agreed to all of his requests, with the prompting of Sam Ross and, he presumed, Clay Hudson, he now had the obligation to tell everything. His eyes roamed the table and stopped at Samantha again. The black silk blouse she wore contrasted strikingly with her blond hair pulled back today. She looked up from her notes to catch his gaze and gave him a sensuous smile. He felt the warmth flow through his body but forced his attention back to Shultz.

He began to speak. "Before the 1980 Tax Reform Act, tax spreads were legal. That means that if I made one million dollars in a given year, I could negotiate what we call a tax spread. A spread is the simultaneous buying and selling of the same commodity, but different delivery months. For example, I may buy February gold and sell April gold. By doing this I would be sure of a loss on one side or the other. If I bought one hundred contracts and sold one hundred contracts at four hundred fifty dollars per ounce, and the market goes to five hundred dollars per ounce, by the end of the year I have a large profit on the Gold I bought. I also have an equally large loss on the Gold I sold. On December thirty-one, I take the loss and let the profit stand. If the loss is one million dollars, I break even for the year, because I haven't taken my profit yet. On January two, I take my profit, thus moving or *rolling* the income into the next tax year. The spread actually didn't make or lose any money, but I protected the million I had made during the year by the million-dollar loss on December thirty-one. I do that year after year, paying no taxes, because as far as the government is concerned I break even or have little or no income. When the Tax Reform Act of 1980 was put into effect, we were screwed, because we had been rolling our income for years. Now we had to pay taxes on all that income we had moved forward. Butterfly spreads are similar, a bit more complicated, but similar. As a result of not being

able to roll our money into the next year to avoid taxes, dead head spreading began. Know the saying, 'Where there's a will, there's a way'? Although illegal, the profiteers found a way to continue to put off paying taxes by placing profitable trades, via dead head spreads, into the account of a friend who had large losses. On the first day of trading of the new year, those involved would take back their profit from the previous year and give the friend his losses back, plus fifty thousand dollars for doing the favor. I know that sounds complicated, and I didn't explain the complexity of it all because there's so much involved. This is illegal, and it is widespread, but illegal spreads shouldn't be one of your primary areas of investigation."

Shultz held up his hands in a "That's enough" pose and said, "That's okay, Michael. We'll go over it later. There is too much ground to cover without me taking up the whole session."

Thank God, thought Michael. He was getting bleary eyed and weary; his eyes felt sandy and his bones ached. Time was passing with tedious monotony. He looked at Simpson, who seemed to be anticipating more from him.

Simpson's corpulent face pinched with his usual look of impatience. "Mr. Hogan, there seem to be many aspects to this thing, and the web of corruption flows into almost every area of the commodity industry. Rather than take a shotgun approach to this investigation, it might be wise to consider directing our attention to the areas which are thé most likely targets for corruption."

Michael tapped his neatly manicured fingertips on the heavy wooden table and for the first time thought that Simpson was finally talking some sense. "I think you're right, Mr. Simpson. The most obvious target and easiest to attack are the *broker rings* or *syndicates* that are made up of from five to fifty brokers working together, sharing expenses, profits and losses. With groups of this size, *skim trades* can be passed from one broker to another, all the way around the pit, and eventually end up in an account designated for the *skim money*. The original broker pays too much or too little for a customer's order and gives the skimmed points to one of the ring members. That broker in turn passes the profit to another ring member next to him, who passes it to another, and on and on around the pit until the last ring member takes the skim trade. He then places the profit into any one of a number of private accounts. The profit goes into XYZ, or *no name accounts*, and are shared at a later date by the members of the broker rings. Millions a day go into these accounts, both in Chicago and New York."

Tony Lorenzo, U.S. Attorney asked, "What other targets should we concentrate on, Michael?"

Michael shook off his fatigue and answered with clarity. "There are three other areas which have unlimited access to customer orders and customer funds. The first group are the account executives, mentioned earlier, but I'll go over it again, because it's important if you're planning to have undercover agents in the offices all over Chicago. The A.E.'s receive orders to buy and sell all day long. Many times they will compare orders

in the office before they call them down to the trading floor for execution. On numerous occasions, they will give their customer the wrong information and tell him over the phone that the market is trading higher than it actually is, and the account executive recommends buying before the market gets away from them. On another phone he tells a customer that the market is trading lower than it actually is, and he should sell before "the market falls out of bed." Both customers trust their broker's judgment and both give him their orders: one tells him to buy; one tells him to sell. On large orders there may be a ten-, fifteen-, twenty-, or even a fifty-thousand-dollar difference in where the order is filled, compared to where it should have been filled. Of course, the profit difference goes into the A.E.'s account or a no name account controlled by the A.E!"

Lorenzo pushed further. "An example, please."

Michael poured himself a fresh cup of coffee, loaded it with sugar, and drew it into his mouth slowly. "Mr. Lorenzo, say you're a customer of mine--an attorney from Kankakee, Illinois--and you want to buy one million bushels of soybeans. That's two hundred contracts. The market happens to be vulnerable and has had a trading price range for the day of five-fifty to six dollars, a fifty cent swing. The market is actually trading at five seventy-five per bushel when you are on the phone--but I tell you it's trading at five-eighty per bushel. You say, 'buy the million bushels at five-eighty--or better.' You don't have a ticker tape, so you don't really know the true price. You take my word. I then call my doctor client in Flint, Michigan, and tell him the market is headed lower, and the price is five-seventy per bushel, and that he should sell. Again, he takes my word for it and tells me to go ahead and sell a million bushels at five-seventy per bushel. Now I have a million bushels to buy at five-eighty and a million bushels to sell at five-seventy--or better. I have just talked you and another naive customer into giving me discretion with a hundred-thousand-dollar difference. I turn to my partner in the same office and tell him I'll buy a million bushels of beans from him at five-eighty and sell him a million at five-seventy. "Done," says my buddy. I call my associate broker in the soybean pit and tell him the story. He writes up the order, time stamps the order, and fills it on the curb with another associate broker, then time stamps it again...Voila! One hundred thousand dollars goes into a mutual account to be split up between all at a later date."

Michael thought Lorenzo could pass for a middle-aged male model. Tall, cool, not a hair out of place, and dressed as well and as expensively as he, himself, was. All Lorenzo needed was a pipe and an ascot. He figured that Lorenzo must have come from money. A man can't buy clothes like that on a U.S. Attorney's salary. His face was serious and dedicated as he said, "What happens to the customers, Michael? Don't the losers catch on?"

Michael's shoulder still throbbed. He winced and took his left hand from the table and placed it in his lap. "Eventually...but hear me out. Say the market closes that day at six dollars per bushel. I look like a hero to one customer, the lawyer, and a chump to the other customer, the doctor. But I feed poor ol' Doc a line of crap that the Japs came in

unexpectedly and started buying up everything in sight. It was Pearl Harbor all over again. If the Japs hadn't surprised the market, with their rash of buying, the market surely would have fallen out of bed. Although upset, the doctor in Flint, Michigan, wants to believe his broker and comes back the next day for more."

Lorenzo's sharp eyes squinted a bit, and he merely asked, "Why?"

Michael said, "Because both the doctor and the lawyer are hooked. They need the action of trading commodities to fill in their dull lives, or some other void in their lives. Maybe they're compulsive gamblers. Maybe they like pain. Maybe they don't like their day-to-day routine, or have a divorce pending and don't care. And maybe...they're just hooked."

Michael pulled himself up straight in his chair. Adrenalin began to pump through his veins just thinking of the fast phone conversations with the doctor and the lawyer and the quick hand movements of the brokers that would go undetected. He heard his own voice rise. "Now, the best part comes. The next day the tables are reversed and the doctor gets the good trade *and the lawyer gets screwed!*...This goes on and on until both are out of money." He slowed down, pulling himself back out of the pit and into the CIA meeting room. "Oddly enough, it's not impossible for both parties to make money despite the dirty dealings of their broker. However, at the end of the year, the doctor may have a profit of a half million dollars, but has paid four hundred seventy five thousand in *commissions*, leaving him a net profit of twenty-five grand, and the broker, a gross profit of four hundred seventy-five thousand dollars.

"I remember when I first became a broker back in the sixties, the pork bellies were going crazy. It was a new game in town. A little Jewish broker who befriended me showed me how he *churned* his customers. He was a good broker and had a excellent feel for the market, especially the pork bellies. He told me he had seventy-five customers whom he divided into three groups of twenty-five each. On a given day he would make a few hundred trades in the market. The first group would receive the winning trades, the second group would receive the losing trades, and the third group would remain stagnant--out of the market. This would go on for a week or so, then he would rotate the groups. The losing group would begin to receive winning trades, the stagnant group the losing trades, and last week's winners would stay out of the market. The next week he would rotate his customers again using the same process. These were all called *discretionary accounts*. These accounts gave the broker power of attorney to trade the account without permission from the customer. At the end of the year, although he had actually made a lot of money for his customers, the commissions generated had taken all of the profits, plus some or all of the invested money. This man today is one of the Exchange's most powerful executives, and has one of the largest discount brokerage companies in the country."

Without warning Joe Fitzsimmons, the young Chicago agent, yelled out, "You mean this goes on and nobody complains about it?"

Michael was glad to have Harris finally break the ice. Maybe the younger agents would get involved now. They had to learn these things if they were going to know what to look for. "Agent Fitzsimmons, it's very common, and there are a lot of complaints covered up by the Exchanges. If the heat from the customer becomes too intense, the Exchanges will make a move against the broker who had the complaint filed against him. That broker will usually pay back some of the churned money to relieve the heat. He is told to do so by the Exchanges or they will really come down on him. The Exchanges don't want any bad publicity for fear of what an investigation may turn up. As far as my other example, regarding the account executives pre-arranging trades in the office, nobody ever finds out that the trade was made in the office, and that the order to buy or sell wasn't actually executed on the trading floor. If there are enough complaints from customers against certain office brokers or account executives, the Exchanges may call the crooks on the carpet and mildly scold them for churning their customers. That happens rarely, because it's not really illegal, and is usually forced on the Exchanges by a second party, such as the Commodity Futures Trading Commission."

Thick red hair topped Fitzsimmons's head. He looked like a middleweight Irish boxer. His professional interest was intense, as he asked, "What does *churning* mean?"

Michael rubbed his sore shoulder and quenched his parched mouth with the pleasant lemon-water in front of him. He picked up a pencil and began to tap it on the yellow legal pad. He thought he had just explained churning, but he would explain again. "Churning is a word we use when we find that a broker or account executive places his customers in and out of the market excessively, merely to generate commissions. 'Turn 'em, burn 'em, and churn 'em!' is the way we describe the practice."

"Is that legal?" Fitzsimmons asked.

"Sure!" Michael responded. It may not be ethical, but it is legal at least to a certain extent. If the customer is dumb enough to give complete *discretion* and power of attorney to a stranger and entrusts him with a couple of hundred thousand dollars of hard-earned money, his only right when the money is gone is to say, 'I made a big mistake!' If the brokers or account executives are as smart as they purport to be, why wouldn't they risk their own money and trade the market themselves? As far as the Exchanges are concerned, and if there is an investigation into allegations of churning customer funds, then it all depends on who you are. If you're one of the men and women who serve on the Executive Boards, you'll get away with a warning. If you're a nobody or have caused the Exchanges grief, like I have, then you can get a fine and maybe a suspension. There is a dusty rule, seldom imposed, which states something about improper use of customer funds being subject to disciplinary action. The rules are by-and-large window dressing to cover the Exchanges' ass."

"I thought you said it wasn't illegal?" Fitzsimmons asked again.

Michael felt that the blood was slowly seeping from his brain and his thinking was slowing down. "If the Exchanges' hierarchy thinks it will enhance their public image to

come down on someone, they will. When that happens, there isn't much a broker can do, guilty or innocent. Remember the Exchanges are autocracies, self-governing. If they want to close early or open late or shut down for a day or two, no one can stop them. If a market is going up and they want it to go down, they can force you to liquidate your position to force the market down, so they can protect their own investments."

"Does that ever happen?"

"Yes. In nineteen seventy-nine and eighty when two brothers in Texas pushed silver from ten dollars an ounce to fifty dollars an ounce. This was an obvious *squeeze-play*. Many of the powerful members were *short* the market...wanting it to go lower. The Exchanges, both in Chicago and New York, where silver is traded, called emergency meetings and raised the *margin*, or required money for owning a contract of silver. They raised the margins so high that nobody could afford to keep their long contracts including the Texas boys. This panicked the market and drove it down from fifty dollars an ounce to near twenty dollars an ounce. Eventually, it went into the teens, and today it is trading at six-fifty an ounce. The brothers in Texas and all the traders who were *coat tailing* them received a good fucking, because they had to sell out their positions. Exchange executives, plus the outside political cliques, who have great influence in decision making, bought in their short positions, and the dynasty became stronger."

Another voice was heard from--Agent Randy Harris, who looked fresh out of Harvard Law School, shook his head in disbelief as he said, "You mean the Exchange officials along with these outside cliques can start and stop trading whenever they feel like it to protect their own position? Can't they be sued by the Texas men?"

"The goddamn Exchanges can do anything they want, whenever they want, and to whomever they want, regardless of their supposed government watchdog, the CFTC."

Now, questions were coming at him from all over the room. Fitzsimmons and Harris had opened the door for the rest of the agents. Marvin Kaluski, Securities and Exchange Commission Representative, spoke with a guttural voice. "You may or may not know it, Mr. Hogan, but the SEC has been pushing for legislation which would enable us to join with the CFTC, or completely do away with the CFTC, because we don't feel they have adequate control over the commodity markets. We just want a foothold, and we'll take it from there. Do you think that's possible?"

Michael watched as Kaluski leaned his heavy frame back into his soft chair. Michael snapped out his answer. "What makes you think, Mr. Kaluski, that the SEC could do any better at the Commodity Exchanges than the CFTC? You have people in your organization taking kickbacks, just as the CFTC does. You caught six SEC investigators just recently who were on the payroll of one of the top stock houses in New York. You made sure it didn't hit the papers, but I found out about it. You're bigger and you have more authority than the CFTC, but that doesn't make you more effective. So you caught Boesky and a few others, trading off inside information--big deal! My kids could have figured that scam out, and from my information, Boesky could have been stopped years

ago." Michael watched as Kaluski's big ears reddened and his face tightened. Good, he thought, now I have his attention--and if the man is a professional and has an open mind, he'll listen to the rest of what I have to say, rather than close his mind to resentment. Michael continued in a softer tone. "However, and in spite of the holes in the SEC, the Chicago Exchanges are scared to death of you. The SEC *does* represent a higher authority than the CFTC, and that is a big threat to the people who run Chicago. The Chicago Exchanges have full power over the CFTC. If the SEC is given a foothold at the Merc and the Board of Trade, that's a big threat to the autonomy the Exchanges now enjoy. Now that I've given you my opinion, I'll try to answer your question. If this investigation goes as planned, and if the full magnitude of the corruption is identified, and the crooks are exposed, the SEC will be in Chicago by early nineteen-ninety-two. Not necessarily to protect the customer, but because Washington politicians and lobbyists will swing your way. Why? Because it's an election year, and the political pressure put on them by the media and their peers will be tremendous. You're in, Kaluski, just be patient."

Kaluski's face showed his dislike for Michael, or was it what he had just said? Michael didn't give a shit. He was going to lay his cards face up on the table, whether the pricks from Washington liked it or not. Kaluski's tight face relaxed, as he thought over what had just been said. Now his look of anger was replaced with one of acceptance, even respect. Michael liked working with men from Polish backgrounds. Of all the nationalities he dealt with, the Poles seemed to be the most reliable. By and large, they held no secrets, they were honest, tough, damn hard workers, and could get the job done. For that, they were rewarded and subjected to a million jokes made about them. If Michael put together a football team, he'd pick eleven Poles.

Now another voice made an entry. Michael looked to his right as Eli Hanks, a black agent with a smooth face and short cropped hair, asked, "How can the CFTC stand by and not interfere with some of the Exchanges' decision making?"

Fuck, he thought, how much longer? "First of all, a number of key CFTC people are owned by the Exchanges. The dedicated CFTC officials try their best to do a good job, but they are blind and find that any efforts to control the commodity industry is virtually impossible. It's like trying to keep an elephant from moving by attaching a yo-yo string around its neck. The Exchanges are just too powerful, and by the end of the century, if things keep up the way they are, the men who control the Exchanges will be the government!" Michael watched the agents. Hanks continued to shake his head, but was evidently satisfied. Thank God! Michael thought.

Colleen McFadden spoke next. She was a pretty girl, slightly overweight, with short, straight auburn hair and big tits. She sat next to Samantha, who was still busy writing. Colleen's voice cracked when she spoke. "Mr. Hogan, you mentioned squeeze-play. What is that exactly, and is it legal?"

Michael smiled at her, hoping to help her feel more at ease. "Contrary to popular belief, Miss McFadden, a squeeze-play isn't anything sexual!" Light laughter spread

through the room, relieving the intensity that veiled the interrogation, and Colleen blushed. "There are two types of squeeze-plays. One is not legal, and that's when one man or group of men get together and buy up enough contracts of one commodity to force the market prices substantially higher than the actual value. That's a *forced squeeze*. The other is a *natural squeeze*, and is not only legal but, in essence, is the purpose for the Exchanges. A natural squeeze is when a processor or user of a commodity buys up futures contracts for his business commitments, such as corn, wheat, soybeans, hogs, cattle--even silver and gold. He actually wants to take delivery of the product, because he's going to sell, or use the commodity to promote his business and our economy. Remember what a futures contract is: *an agreement to buy or sell a specific amount of a commodity at a predetermined price within a given time period.* It's a legal and binding contract. Let's say the date is November fifteen, nineteen eighty-seven. Our man, the user, buys a large amount of nineteen eighty-eight July soybeans on the futures market on November fifteen, nineteen eighty-seven, because the price is right. He needs the beans eight months later, in July of eighty-eight, to fulfill his customer commitments. Let's say again that July approaches on the heels of a drought year and the price of beans is much higher than where he bought them in November, eight months previous. That is what the market was originally designed for, to *hedge* and buy products for the purpose of future use and delivery. But someplace along the way the user accumulated more contracts than are available for delivery. The result is a *legal squeeze*, and will probably drive the prices even higher. Today, ninety-five per cent of the Exchange volume is based strictly on speculation, not hedging by the user. It's not uncommon to find that the speculators, who wait until the final days of trading in a particular delivery month, find themselves running around looking for product. Many times the legal and binding contract that has been entered into turns to crap and the Exchange has to deal with making things right with both buyers and sellers. If they are in a dilemma on what to do, they just change the rules, and somebody--usually the user--gets screwed. The Exchange will justify this by saying the user or customer forced an illegal squeeze."

Her red lips pursed. "Can the Exchange force liquidation and drive the prices down if a user has a legal squeeze position on?"

"Sure can! God forbid a processor of beans ever owns a large amount of product and the Exchange officials or other processors who have clout on the Exchange want the price to go down, not up. The Powers That Be could and would force liquidation and make the company who bought in November sell out a large position of their bean contracts. This could break a small processor, because he wouldn't have the beans to fulfill his commitments. Further, it would make a large processor damn mad. There are large commercial users who trade big volume on the Exchange floors. Over the years they have developed tremendous influence at the Exchange and can force emergency action to avoid having to deliver the product on termination of the contract. If the price is too high, they would have to buy at an inflated price from the farmers or cash market. These grain

conglomerates refuse to take their losses like everybody else, so they maneuver to force all big traders or hedgers to sell, thus driving down the market to where they want it. This is inside trading, if I've ever seen it. They change the rules that have stood for a hundred years, for their own benefit--and the honest traders, who are struggling daily to make a buck, get it right in the ass!"

He stopped for a moment then continued. "Sorry for the crude description, Ms. McFadden, but that's the way it is."

Questions continued to be fired at him. "Couldn't the legitimate hedge company who bought in November and was forced to liquidate by the Exchange changing the rules, sue?"

Michael's eyes were drooping, and his mind was weary. Was he ever this tired? he asked himself. How much longer? "Sue the Commodity Exchange? Sure, you can sue after a long process of arbitration. Of course, they have their own men as the arbitrators. I've never seen the customer come out on top. Then you can take your case to an attorney, who can present it for breach of contract on the part of the Exchange. That would be like trying to sue Russia. Everybody has a right to take legal action in the United States; that is, if you're willing to wait five to ten years to find out the results. And as the attorney gets richer, you'll probably go out of business, and be worse off financially than if you had just walked away from the mess. Remember, you are trying to sue a group who has the power to change the rules in midstream. If the U.S. Government can't break the Exchanges, what makes you think one company or small group of honest brokers can?"

He leaned back and sucked in all the air that was around him--or so it seemed. He had been talking non-stop since the meeting opened and was more than uncomfortable. He knew it showed. His ass hurt, his head hurt, and his body and eyes were tired.

Clay Hudson from the CIA finally said, "I think we'll stop here for lunch, ladies and gentlemen. We've heard a lot so far, and I think we could all use a break before we get too overwhelmed. This afternoon, I would like to hear Mr. Hogan tell us more about the different techniques used to cheat customers out of their money and the way clearing houses cheat the customers and use the excess funds to trade for themselves. We've heard about the powerful broker syndicates which operate on the Exchange floors. About the powerful commercial companies who have the clout to change the rules for their own benefit. We've heard about Peterson, Ruzzo, and Conti and how they skim and launder money into defunct companies. About Alverez in Miami and how he sets up foreign corporations and holding companies. About the awesome power of the Exchanges and their corrupt executives. And we've heard about their fear of the SEC as a possible watchdog. We've heard a lot--certainly enough to give Messrs. Golden, Simpson, Lorenzo, Shultz, and Brennen a good start with this investigation."

Michael saw Hudson's cold, dark eyes. "Mr. Hogan, you may have wondered what my purpose here is as head of the CIA. What interest would I have in commodity fraud? My sole purpose in being here is to ascertain if any international laws are being

broken, what you know about illegal drug trafficking on the Exchange floor, how much skim money flows in and out of the U.S., and what part the IRA, Irish Republican Army, plays on the Exchange floors. These are international affairs, and while John Simpson and Thad Overton are responsible for national security, I am responsible for international security. If there is heavy drug infiltration into the New York and Chicago Exchanges, it's coming from outside the U.S. If we have a terrorist group living among us, such as the IRA, I want to know about it."

Michael went cold with anger, and he thought Hudson knew it. He didn't care about divulging what he knew about the Exchange activities, the Mafia's involvement, the drug dealing, which wasn't much, and the tricks of the trade. But he sure as hell wasn't going to speak against his good friend Sean McGiven, who headed Irish International Trading Corporation, Inc., and was the IRA Representative in Chicago. Sean and Michael had been through too much together. Michael didn't agree with Sean's political philosophy, but they had been close friends for over twenty years. Sean had helped him out of numerous scrapes and had saved him from a terrible beating once in the stockyards when he had been cornered by four tough rednecks over some insignificant squabble.

Michael knew his face had drained of blood. He saw the sly smile on both Simpson's and Hudson's faces as if they had an animal almost in the trap.

Hudson, with an arrogant, half-hearted compliment, said, "Thank you for your informative eloquence...up 'til now, Mr. Hogan. Let's hope this afternoon's meeting is just as fruitful. We will all meet back here at one o'clock."

* * *

Michael walked into the long, cold hall that connected the main complex with the auxiliary building where the meetings were being held. He had been one of the last out of the conference room and now leaned his back up against the white block wall resting his head against its cool surface.

Pete Lewis passed by and said, "Let's get some lunch, Mike."

Michael, closed eyes pointed toward the ceiling, said, "I'll meet you down there. Let me catch my breath for a minute."

Lewis stopped and came closer. Michael opened his eyes to look at him. His crooked nose gave him a kind of rugged geniality with a durably boyish face. Michael said, "What?"

"What?...What the fuck are ya doing...that's what!"

Michael leaned his head back and shut his eyes again. "I'll be along, just have to sort a few things out, that's all."

"I'll bet you do. Don't think too long, or you'll go crazy."

"I'm already crazy! Paranoid as hell!"

Lewis chided, "I hear paranoia is just heightened awareness."

209

Michael shook his head and said. "Go fuck your horse, Tonto."

Lewis laughed, and Michael heard his footsteps fade away down the hall. His thoughts were on Sean McGiven. The two of them had literally grown up together. Sean, an Irish orphan, had lived with the Hogan family for many years. They had worked in the stockyards together, drunk together, fought together and with each other, and finally went to the Exchange together. They were like brothers.

Michael, an only child, had always had friends, but never anybody quite like Sean. He knew Sean was on the run from the British, that's why he ended up in America at age sixteen. He had tried to recruit Michael into the clandestine IRA, but Michael refused, saying he wasn't into killing people who weren't trying to kill him, even if the British had subjected his forefathers to poverty and cruelty. Michael argued that every society had its sinister, ruthless men who stopped at nothing for power, money, and territory, including America. But that didn't make the whole of society. Besides, the IRA made too many mistakes, and had killed too many innocent people.

He would become angry with Sean's persistence and say, "You just don't blow away women and children at your own discretion--Limey or no Limey!" Michael recalled asking Sean many times how an Irish Catholic could have so much hate in him. Sean would just sneer and walk away. Michael didn't have to reach far back in his memory file to recall the night he and Sean fought four black guys in a junkyard near the stockyards. The two "brothers" won the fight, but not before Michael had separated his vulnerable shoulder, and Sean had taken a razor slash across his chest. Sean was a wild man when he fought, and beat the black kid, the one with the razor, to death with his fists. The other three ran at the sight of their buddy and crazy Sean. Michael would never forget the picture in his mind of the black kid's face...it looked like a watermelon that had been run over by a car. After the fight Sean showed Michael how to reset his own shoulder, and Michael taped Sean's wound closed with his shirt and electrical tape. They headed for Murphy's Black Potato Pub and drank Irish beer and shots until they were falling-down drunk. That was the night Sean told Michael the reason for his hatred of the British. As if it were yesterday, Michael could see Sean's pitiful face as he told him a horror story.

Sean told of that day in Belfast and his vain efforts to pick up the scattered pieces of his brother Liam, who had been blown apart by British machine guns and grenades. Merely killing Liam wasn't enough satisfaction for the British. As he lay dead, the giddy, laughing soldiers placed a grenade in his brother's crotch and another between his limp chin and chest. The explosions rocked the whole warring neighborhood, leaving Liam a headless, legless burnt torso, smoldering on a cobblestone street of Belfast.

Michael remembered the tears streaming down Sean's face, as he told how beautiful and idealistic Liam was. The pity of it all was that he was only fourteen years old. Sean told how he went crazy and came screaming from the empty building he was hiding in, and killed the four soldiers with a handgun. Then, sobbing, he tried to piece his brother back together so his mother wouldn't see Liam in a thousand parts. Sean told

Michael he was on his hands and knees, crying, as he tried to figure out what body part belonged where. He said all he could think about was that he couldn't let his Mother see her son like that.

Michael remembered Sean crying and saying, "Mom...Liam, I'm sorry...so sorry! I'm sorry, so sorry." He, Michael, was crying too.

Sean said he didn't remember much after that, except friends pulling at him, and gunfire from other British soldiers coming for him. Shortly after that he was hustled out of Ireland to the States.

Sean had made Michael promise that he would never tell anybody that he saw him cry. Michael vowed his allegiance to the simple request, and they never talked of the Belfast atrocity again, both remaining close friends, both fighting different wars.

Sean was as tough and as lucky as a horseshoe. Shortly after the incident, Joe Glassmann asked Michael if he wanted to work at the Exchange for him. He told Joe yes, but only if he could bring Sean with him. Glassmann said no; Sean was a roughneck, a troublemaker, and had no class. Michael quickly reminded the elder Joe that if his dead father, Patrick, had thought that way, Joe would still be handling hog hides on the New York docks. He knew Joe was disgusted with Michael's clear logic, saying he was just like his father. Joe hired both him and Sean to work as board markers, which quickly turned into phone jobs and eventually a membership on the Exchange.

Sean had not only stopped Michael from getting numerous thrashings in the stockyards, but years later he came to his rescue during the Hogan Scandal. He not only was a terrific influence in the major markets, but also had a strong influence with Chicago and New York Irish politicians. He told the officials at both Exchanges if they persisted in slandering his friend Hogan, they had better hire somebody to start their cars and open their mail--and to keep their families away from the windows in their homes. They all knew Sean, who always spoke quietly and precisely, was nobody to fuck with. The Exchanges backed off--but not until a two-hundred-thousand-dollar Rolls Royce, which belonged to the Chairman of the Executive Committee, was blown up in his locked garage. A car bomb went off at 3:00 a.m. one winter morning in December of 1985, in Lake Forest, Illinois, a well-patrolled and wealthy suburb of Chicago. That incident curtailed any further problems for the Hogan family--but not before the intended damage had been done.

Sean had eleven IRA men working for him on the floor of the Exchanges. All U.S. citizens, all dedicated to the Irish Cause. They called themselves The Dublin Twelve. They were cool, friendly, helpful, excellent traders--but ruthless if need be. They had the ability and conditioned temperament to snap at an enemy faster than a viper and with twice its venom. They had the discipline of soldiers and wouldn't strike unless provoked to the limit of their durability. They had only one purpose: to send money to Ireland for the Cause. Michael knew they pulled large sums of money from the markets, both legally and illegally. He knew The Dublin Twelve didn't make the same careless moves as the other brokers who would soon be coming under investigation. He had never seen them skim,

curb, bag, or pre-arrange trades in the market, and he had watched them carefully for years trying to figure just what their game was. Their methods of larceny were far more sophisticated than any Michael had ever witnessed. They always seemed to be the first ones to make large plays in the market even before national or international news broke. This was the only indication to Michael that they had a jump on the news before anyone else had it. He figured they had set up an elaborate information network throughout the world that fed them inside information before it was common knowledge. It figured--the IRA had woven its way into all the major governments and corporations in the world. They were as persistent in their cause as any radical group. Michael knew the IRA was far more powerful than anybody gave them credit for. One of their greatest assets was their low international profile. Although their battleground was the British Isles, their strategy was planned from all over the world.

Sean's affiliation with the IRA, their American counterparts, and his own determination allowed him to grasp political power early in his life in the United States. After he left the stockyards and entered the world of finance, many doors were opened to him, and over the years he had been groomed to perfection. Sean had developed the charm and charisma of a statesman, and had the intelligence and cunning of a Philadelphia lawyer, the strength and stature of a long distance runner, and the spotless presence and enthusiasm of a novice priest. He was Michael's best friend.

Because of Sean's international and corporate connections, the millions he extracted from the market were based more on inside trading rather than downright pit theft. He would establish a position based on corporate takeovers and rumors that Sean himself would create to move the market.

Despite their political and philosophical differences, their brotherly spirit never diminished. Michael wasn't out to nail Sean to the cross for the sake of a few megalomaniacs who ran the country. Michael knew he rationalized his ethical beliefs when it came to Sean McGiven, but that was tough shit. He wasn't perfect and didn't purport to be. He had a right to keep a few things to himself: his knowledge of Sean's illegal actions, and his thoughts of Samantha Winters, they were personal. If an investigation brought down a few hundred blatant thieves, McGiven was no stranger at covering his tracks. How Michael was going to get around the issue of the IRA with the clever Clay Hudson and the politically aspiring John Simpson was going to be difficult. Somehow, he would keep Sean's name clean. He didn't know just how. He would have to weigh his words very carefully, and he must remain in control. He would ask a higher dimension of life for help--it never failed him!

He felt a hand on his arm. Startled, he looked down to see Samantha. "Anything wrong, Michael?" Her face was firmly set in deep concern with a delicate dimension of sensitivity. Her brow was furrowed, her scarlet lips pursed in question.

A feminine fragrance intoxicated his mind momentarily, and he said, "Oh...hi, Sam. I'm just organizing my thoughts for this afternoon, trying to categorize the things we went over this morning."

She gently scolded him. "Enough thinking for awhile. Let's have lunch. She placed her arm through his and nudged him away from the wall. Then, thinking it was a bit too forward, she withdrew it. They walked quietly toward the North American Room, where lunch was being served. He liked everything about this woman. Her warm, beautiful presence relieved the frustration and uncertainty he had been engulfed with only moments before. Maria and the children seemed a million miles away.

The door swung open to the Seven Continents Lounge and closed quietly behind them, leaving the stark hall silent. Another video tape had been recorded and filed. The tape would be on Clay Hudson's desk within minutes.

TWENTY-THREE

Sam and Michael

Lunch and the enigmatic charisma of the man called "Hawk" came as a welcome relief. Samantha was happy that she and Michael were able to sit alone. Lewis had struck up a conversation with Andy Golden and the agents assigned to the Chicago investigation. They sat together at a corner table of the North American Room dabbling with a platter of fresh fruits and cheeses. Joviality rang from their table.

She and Michael ordered soup du jour and a shrimp salad. For over an hour they talked in quiet communion, as if they had known each other for years, hardly touching their food, relenting to the tides and the sensual undertow that pulled them farther from shore and deeper into the green waters of passion. They bathed each other with temptations and encouragement to explore the erotic waters further. She felt herself faltering helplessly as he continued his gentle vocal caressing.

Her body was warm and comfortable in his presence, and she wished he would hold her tight. He had the insight of a priest, and with his questions, she felt him break through her fortified soul, stripping away the armor she had so carefully sculptured over the years. God, what a loving man, she thought. He reminded her so much of Jonathan. She missed him fiercely. There had never been another man like Jonathan, and she desperately needed him. But he was gone--and so were all their dreams and the love and passion they had shared. Now she looked at Michael and wanted him to hold her and tell her that everything was going to be all right. Her senses were unraveling like a ball of yarn. His penetrating eyes looked deep into hers, and he asked, "Have you ever been married?"

She played with her shrimp salad, moving morsels of food from one side of the plate to the other. Her acknowledgement was hardly audible. "I was once married to a fellow agent, three years ago, who was much like you, Michael, fearless, bold, strong and handsome. He lived by the unrealistic philosophy that right is right, not might is right. He had been assigned to work with the DEA and led an investigation that took him into Mexico. While undercover he was labeled as an informant and was shot to death. He was found six months later, buried in a shallow grave near Vera Cruz, Mexico...decapitated." Her racing heart seemed caught in a vise and she could hardly breathe. Her eyes misted over and a tugging pain of sorrow had gripped her throat.

Michael dropped his fork on his plate and said in a whisper, " Sam, I'm so sorry! It must have killed you too."

She managed to push her words out. "I loved him very much. He was a wonderful, caring, kind and gentle man. I had never met another guy like him. In fact, there was no one serious before him, and there has been no one since." Until you, she thought. "We had a wonderful relationship, Michael."

She tried to hold back signs of emotion. She had conditioned herself to that. But she knew he sensed she was vulnerable at this place in time. Her heart still ached, and she needed warmth--there would only be one Jonathan, but now he was gone and she felt she needed Michael's warmth. She almost felt guilty for wanting him, though.

What if she had encouraged him last night to take her home after dinner instead of insisting she drive herself? Would they have made love? She would never know. "Since then I have lost myself in my work, day and night, twenty-four hours a day. Up until now, I haven't wanted any male companionship around me for fear that I might get involved again, and the same thing could happen, which would put me right over the edge." Her eyes trained on his rough, hawk-like features. His eyes were deep and searching. He strategically placed his knife and fork at four o'clock on his plate, as did she. The waiter eyed the cue and immediately removed the finished dishes.

He reached over and touched her hand. She felt warm strength flow into her from his touch. "Samantha, I've known you for less than twenty-four hours. My heart skips a beat every time I see you, and it skips two beats every time I touch you. I haven't had this feeling in twenty years. I'm confused, and I'm frustrated. We have a lot to do and we'll be spending quite a bit of time working together in Chicago. We don't have the answers right now, but that doesn't mean they aren't there. Let's give things time. Okay?"

She nodded, but knew he really wasn't free. They both knew what they wanted. Time wasn't going to change the fact that he had a wife he loved. He leaned over and kissed her forehead and briefly held the side of her face close to his lips--neither cared who might be watching. "It's ten minutes to one, Sam, we'd better be getting back."

She dabbed her lips, then the corners of her eyes, with the plum cotton napkin. Don't let him go yet, she told herself, hold on as long as possible. Then she spoke. "I wish this could have lasted longer, Michael. I've enjoyed every minute we've been together, especially last night's dinner, once we got rid of Andy and Pete. Besides Jonathan, I don't think I've ever met anybody quite like you--I know I haven't--and I also know this isn't right." His eyes were calm and comforting. "I mean, you're married and all, so do you really think we'll spend time with each other in Chicago?"

She felt a warmth of passion streak through her body as he began to rise. "We'll just make it a point to see each other as often as possible. I want to get to know all about you...who you are...what you're made of...your likes...your dislikes...your philosophy of life...and I would also like you to get to know me. You don't really know me--you may not like what you find!"

He smiled at her. "I am truly sorry about the horror you experienced with Jonathan's death--but that's over, and now it's time for this butterfly..." He pinched her

cheek "...to flutter her wings and get on with life...her beautiful life. Let the past go, Samantha." He cupped her face with his strong hands. She felt like melting. "I'd like to be more than a friend to you...I'd like..." He didn't finish his statement. When he spoke, his words were gentle..."Life, Time, and Nature will heal your wounds and allow us to peek at some of the answers that will affect us both."

She sensed that he felt he might be getting into something that could turn into a mess. She imagined the thoughts of Maria and the children that must be flitting through his mind and whispers from the proper little elf on his right shoulder saying, "Better not, you'll be sorry!" While the lively imp on his left shoulder cackled, "Go ahead, you deserve it!"

God knows she desperately wanted to see him again and be with him--intimately, too. He gave her a promising smile and said, "Sam, you've been the only bright spot on this trip." She blushed, feeling the warmth in her face.

He pulled out her chair and as she rose, her fragrance imbued his senses. "You smell delicious," he said.

She smiled, and the blush brightened. "I hope the scent stays with you!"

He kept his thoughts to himself, and placed his arm around her shoulder and they strode toward the lounge door and the final meeting.

TWENTY-FOUR

Last Session with the Chiefs

Sam Ross returned to New York, but before he left, he told Michael if there was anything he needed or if anybody gave him trouble, to call him on his private line, which would be answered twenty-four hours a day. He would be in his Chicago office the following week and would meet with Michael and Joe Glassmann at that time. As friendly as Ross had been, Michael wasn't sure he trusted him. What was in this for Ross? Was he using Michael to get something? If so, what? He had no reasons to believe that Ross's intentions were anything but honorable.

It was just a feeling--maybe it was because Ross was so accommodating. But that was no sin. Yet, a man like Ross hadn't made billions by being accommodating without an ulterior motive. Sure, Sam Ross was one of the largest users and exporters of grain in the country. He had a right to bitch about skimming--but why wait until now to come forward with legal action? Skimming points from customer orders had been going on ever since Michael could remember and probably for a hundred years prior to that.

Michael had been straight with Ross and asked him why he had waited until now to take action against the Exchanges. Ross told him it had been Glassmann who prompted the action after being cheated out of a few points in the wheat pit. Ross said Glassmann had called him and proposed the plan to see just how much was being stolen from their orders. Joe suggested they use Michael and his men, for a period of time, to compare the quality and efficiency with that of other brokers. Ross's grain companies traded hundreds of millions of bushels of soybeans, corn, and wheat a year. Ross knew his own brokers had been ripping off points, but considered it the price one had to pay if they wanted to play. So he had let the petty theft slide until it wasn't so petty anymore. After hearing Glassmann's suggestion, Ross said the timing was right to reorganize his trading-floor operation anyway. When he and Glassmann compared Michael's prices with those of their standard brokers, they couldn't believe the consistent difference in Hogan's better fills. That's when Ross made his move by talking to his government contacts, only to find out that they too were investigating similar complaints made by smaller investors. Could Ross be trusted or not? Michael thought so, but, he'd know more later. Besides, Michael knew that his ultimate plan demanded Ross's allegiance.

His thoughts continued. Harvey Shultz had received the information he needed on illegal tax schemes practiced at the Exchanges and had left for Washington. Thaddeus Overton, Chief Assistant to the Attorney General, had also picked up enough to report to the Attorney General and the President. Marvin Kaluski, Head Investigator for the SEC,

had returned to his office in New York, after hearing what he had come for: the ineffective and impotent activities of the CFTC, the supposed government overseer of the Commodity Exchanges. Before he left, he had stopped to thank Michael for all the information he had brought to the meeting. Although he was angry at first with Michael's criticism of the SEC, Kaluski realized that the truth hurt. The SEC, the giant watchdog of Wall Street, had its shortcomings in more areas than one. He also told Michael that a new man, Walter Bollin, would be running the SEC after Reagan's term was finished. Bollin, a no-nonsense guy, wouldn't accept the position if he didn't have the guarantee that he would oversee the Chicago stock-index futures. Bollin would demand that the SEC and the CFTC be merged. Then the whole Chicago and New York commodity gamut would fall under the jurisdiction of the SEC. As far as Kaluski knew, he, would remain as head investigator for the SEC.

That left five big chiefs: Hudson-CIA; Simpson-FBI; Lorenzo, U.S. Attorney-Chicago; Brennen,U.S. Attorney-New York; and Marty Ruiz of Drug Enforcement. The rest of the agents had remained for the final session, except for a few who had been recalled to their Manhattan office. Special Agent Joe McNurtney would be heading up the New York commodity investigation, working directly with Brian Brennen.

Michael watched the chiefs as they filed in and found their places at the large table for the third and final session. Hudson reminded him of an Englishman, with his plain, unreadable face, superior attitude, a propensity to be forever right. He figured Hudson's biggest fear was making a mistake. Of course, if he did make a mistake, he had the power to shift the blame. He looked a little like Margaret Thatcher wearing a jockstrap, straight and proper. Outside of an occasional sneer, his face was devoid of any sign of emotion or recognition. In appearance, Hudson and Simpson could have passed for brothers. Simpson, however, showed his anger too easily, which detracted from his professionalism: Hudson had complete discipline.

Tony Lorenzo was another Elliott Ness, without his hat. A determined man, in a cool, calculating way, and stern, but easygoing. Nothing seemed to surprise him. He'd been around the block a few times, Michael thought. Of course, he was just coming off the Graylord investigation, where he was involved in putting over thirty judges in jail for taking kickbacks. He had pronounced cheekbones, and sharp, clear eyes, and a pencil-line mustache accentuated his thin lips, capable of a smile here and there. Michael liked this man and knew he would be working directly with Lorenzo and the U.S. Attorney's Office in Chicago.

Brian Brennen, a typical Irishman, looked like many Irish politicians-bulbed whiskey nose with a battlefield of red booze-veins running through his heavy face. A haughty man with craggy features: thick eyebrows, puffed, pouting lips, and a deafening voice that sounded as if it were coming from the bottom of an amplified, fifty-five gallon drum.

Marty Ruiz, a strong wiry Latino, had jet-black hair, a thin face with evidence of acute teenage acne, and suspicious dark eyes. Michael sensed he really didn't give a rat's-ass about this investigation unless he could bust up a drug ring.

The Chicago investigators had been chosen. Fourteen, in all. They sat together and compared notes. The conference table was one sided, with everyone sitting on the right all the way down to the chiefs. Michael thought this was to his advantage. From this point, he was able to watch all expressions.

He heard the opening call come from Simpson. With his beefy face hovering over the microphone, he said sarcastically, "Mr. Hogan, are you with us today, and do you mind if I start the meeting?"

Michael stayed cool and let the sarcasm slide. "Yo, I'm here, and it's your show, Mr. Simpson."

Simpson looked down at him with his usual sneer and said, "We have chosen the men and women you will be working with in Chicago. They are all sitting together to your right so you can remember their names and faces. We will expect you to train these people so they will be able to walk into the pits and not be eaten alive. We've decided to buy six memberships and lease others if needed. Our budget will allow for that. The agents assigned to the trading floors will all have between twenty and fifty thousand dollars placed into their trading accounts, and they will submit applications for membership at different times, so as not to arouse suspicion. Fifteen agents will be assigned to the Chicago sting operation. At this time, we have yet to decide which agents will be working with you on the floor, which agents will be working in offices suspected of fraud, or which agents will be working with Mr. Lorenzo and his men at the U.S. Attorney's Office."

Now, he said with venom in his voice, "At the suggestion of Director Collins, Andy Golden will be in charge of the Chicago sting...and...and..." Simpson almost choked on the words. "*Special Agent* Pete Lewis will be responsible for seeing that the trading floor operation runs smoothly. He will work directly with you, Mr. Hogan." Pete had been reinstated to his Special Agent status. Michael felt a grin slice across his face.

"Lewis, your men will be Agents Randy Harris, Vern Oblowski, Eli Hanks, Joe Fitzsimmons, Sean Patricks, Ted Tully, Vito Calusso, Barry Kane, John Perry, and Vince Martini. The people I want placed in offices are Samantha Winters, Colleen McFadden, and Serra Brooks. Perry Washington and George Goldburg will work directly with the U.S. Attorney's Office and Andy Golden. You will all meet at the Federal Building twice a week to touch base. Lewis, you and Hogan will correlate all information with Agents Winters and Martini, who will pass everything on to U.S. Attorney Lorenzo, Andy Golden--and myself. We'll take it from there."

The thought of working with Samantha excited him on one hand. On the other, he wasn't pleased with the thought of her working in a dangerous office with men like Peterson, Conti, and Ruzzo. He felt the sharp edge of panic cut through him. He felt his brow narrow like an angry hawk, and he spoke loudly, without the use of his mike.

"Simpson, you're placing a lot of confidence in these three girls and putting them in a dangerous situation. A better idea might be to let the girls work on the Exchange floors. There it would be safe and when the shit hits the fan, they would be the least suspected as possible informants."

Simpson's face and ears reddened, and his jowls quivered with anger. "Goddammit, Hogan, this happens to be your idea, not mine, so just pay attention. Worry about yourself, and hope that your family doesn't have to collect your insurance money prematurely. I make the decisions around here. I decide where and when my agents work. Don't you forget it!"

Michael remained calm, but he let everybody in the room know how he felt about Simpson. "Okay, it's your call, Asshole, at least for now!"

Simpson's face ignited in anger with the disrespect Michael had shown him in front of his peers and subordinates.

Michael quietly sat back. He brought his fingers to his chin and reflected. It had been his idea to have agents in Peterson's, Ruzzo's, and Conti's offices, but that's when they were just faces. Now he knew the face and mind of Samantha Winters and didn't want it to change into hamburger, which is what would happen if she were found out. He saw Simpson's look of disgust slowly move from him to the other agents. "You'll all meet next week in the Federal Building to begin the training sessions." His anger returned, and he challenged Michael. "That's my final word, Mr. Hogan. Any problems with that?"

Michael calmly raised his palms and shrugged his shoulders, not accepting Simpson's challenge. His face was confident, not showing the apprehension he felt. He thought, fuck you, scumbag, I'll give you this round, you prick--but I'll take it back later.

Tony Lorenzo was keen enough to hold his question until the right moment. Breaking the tension, he asked, "Michael, maybe you can tell us a little more about the trading abuses both on the floor and off the floor. I don't think we've covered everything. For instance, *dual trading*, which seems to be an obvious violation."

Michael's eyes left Simpson's angry face reluctantly and looked at Lorenzo. With a nod, he acknowledged Lorenzo's question. He thought, just a few more hours, and this shit would be over. Simpson was still on his mind. He leaned over to Andy and whispered, "Andy, do you think when the meeting is over, I can call your boss 'shit-for-brains'?"

Andy looked up, almost expecting such a comment. With the eyes of a tired hound-dog, he said, "You've already done that, numb-nuts. Now just answer Lorenzo's question and try to keep it clean."

He pulled his chair closer to the table and leaned back feeling for a comfortable position. As in the pits, his voice traveled with authority. "Mr. Lorenzo, to my knowledge, dual trading is not allowed in the stock market, but is legal in the commodity markets. This simply means that floor brokers--order fillers--are permitted both to execute orders for their customers and to trade for themselves in the same commodity. Dual trading has been under attack for a number of years by critics. They say it gives brokers the opportunity to trade

in front of a customer order, retaining a portion, or all, of the customer's order for themselves."

"Would you give us an example, please?"

Michael began to speak slowly and methodically. "Sure! I'll give you a number of examples because it's such a controversial issue. Let's say, theoretically, you are a large investor. You give me an order to buy four hundred contracts of Gold at four hundred fifty dollars per ounce. The market is trading at four-sixty per ounce. The market begins to fall. When it hits four-fifty per ounce, I bid four-fifty for four hundred contracts. Let's say a broker sells me one hundred contracts and the price rebounds to four hundred fifty-five dollars per ounce. I keep the hundred contracts for myself, sell them out at four-fifty-five, and make five thousand dollars. I then tell you that I couldn't buy anything at four-fifty. I was *unable*! If I was a little smarter, and a little less greedy, I would at least give you fifty contracts, keep fifty contracts for myself, and make twenty-five hundred dollars. Then I would tell you that I was able to buy only fifty contracts and unable to buy the balance of your order. In trading lingo, I would report to him that I bought fifty contracts and was still *working* the balance of his order, or three hundred and fifty contracts. Legally all one hundred contracts that I was able to buy should have gone to you.

"If I want to personally and legally trade the market, as a broker, I must fill my customer orders first. Then I have the right to buy or sell for my account. Otherwise, I am stepping in front of my customer order, or *front-running*, which is illegal. Front-running is one of the by-products of dual trading, which simply means, a broker steps ahead or trades ahead of a large customer order. The sole purpose of front-running is to personally profit from the large order, rather than letting the customer profit.

"Another by-product of dual trading is the broker using the customer order as a cushion for his own trades. If the broker is long four hundred contracts and the market breaks through four hundred fifty dollars on the down side, the broker can lay-back, by not bidding for his customer. He then sells his four hundred contracts to the customer. He is assured that his loss will be minimal, if he even takes a loss, simply by keeping the customer's order a secret.

"Yet another case. If the market breaks through four hundred fifty dollars hard and fast, the broker may just sell the customer's order himself and go short the market, hoping to make his profit while the market goes south.

"These are three instances where dual trading is considered illegal. In the last two examples, the broker needs an accomplice broker with whom to swap trades. His accomplice does not even have to be in the pit at the time--the broker will give his accomplice the information later.

"Now listen closely. What I have just said about dual trading is common. This goes on all the time, and is seldom a cause for disciplinary action by the Exchanges. The critics of dual trading have highly over-rated its evil effect on the market. The only reason you see any criticisms about dual trading is because it's the easiest for the novice and a

newsman to understand. Naturally they'll run that into the ground. Believe me, it's okay with the Exchanges to receive so much bad publicity about dual trading, because that takes the focus off of the more sinister schemes. When the heat is put on the Exchanges, they will agree, as if it were their idea, to do away with dual trading--hoping nobody looks beyond the obvious."

Lorenzo pressed further. "Then I take it, Michael, you're for dual trading?"

Michael said, "Mr. Lorenzo, I'm neither for it nor against it. I personally don't take a trading position in a commodity where I'm filling orders. There are twenty other markets I can trade--if I wish--while I'm filling orders for customers in a given pit. I'm saying it doesn't matter if you allow dual trading or if you ban it. It is totally irrelevant. The crooks have a hundred more ways to kill the customer and will always find a way to beat the system. You know that better than I do! If dual trading is banned, what's to prevent the broker holding your four-hundred-contract order from leaning over to his brother-in-law and telling him to bag or buy one hundred contracts at four hundred fifty dollars? He then sells out at a profit, giving the broker a cut. One way or another, banned or not, legal or illegal, it exists at the Stock Exchanges and the Commodity Exchanges and always will."

"Thank you!" Lorenzo sat back and gulped a drink of water.

Michael looked down at his notes and reviewed them in a glance, then said to the whole group, "Dual trading, front running, skimming or bagging trades by using bag men, curb trading, pre-arranged trading, off-floor trading, forced squeeze plays, parking trades or dead-head spreading, and churning customers, these are most of the on-floor violations which take place on a daily basis at all of the Exchanges, including the Stock Exchanges.

"I might also add that over and above the violations mentioned, many trades are made between brokers in the bars, restaurants, and coffee shops before and after market hours. These trades are pulled out of thin air. The brokers just have to be careful to card their prices within the actual price range, and to make sure the time stamp coincides with the prices on their trading cards. These trades are *phantom* trades and are indistinguishable from legal trades done competitively through the open outcry system.

Brian Brennen, twitching his thick Irish lips, said in his deep voice that sounded as if he were talking from an amplified drum, "Mr. Hogan, why would somebody want to trade before or after the market?"

Michael felt his thoughts organize quickly. "It's called collusion, Mr. Brennen, just like inside trading is collusion. It's done for personal gain. Greed, if you will, at the expense of someone else. In these cases, it's generally done between a *bagman* and the broker who feeds him. These are kickbacks. If I have a bagman to whom I've given a hundred thousand dollars of skim money, he owes me fifty thousand dollars or one half the skim, or whatever we have agreed upon. Instead of taking the time in the pit with the possibility of being seen, we make a fifty-thousand-dollar trade after hours and turn the recording cards in later.

"Or, another example of after close trading is for the purpose of parking trades, or hiding income through dead-head spreading. This type of spreading, once again, is the selling of a profitable commodity position to a friend. The seller can retain effective ownership of the commodity, showing a loss on paper for tax purposes. By doing this, the seller can also evade requirements that he publicly disclose his commodity holdings. This is tax fraud!"

He heard Brennen clear his thick tobacco throat and grumble again, "Mr. Hogan, uh, what's a bagman again?" He could see the sweat forming on Brennen's forehead. He thought that he probably needed a drink--poor bastard.

Michael looked down at his folded hands. For the third time he would explain. "A bagman is a friend of an unscrupulous broker who is fed skim money by using the customers' orders to pay above current market prices or sell below current market prices. As long as the prices are within a certain range, no one will ever catch on, especially on market openings and closings when prices often travel much of the daily price range in a matter of minutes. A bagman can act as a middleman also. Trades can pass between the broker and the middleman to a granny account, which is mutually shared between the two. Or, money can pass through a bagman--and instead of giving the broker back money in the form of a trade, he may pay for the new car the broker wants, or buy him a condo in the islands, or a new home in the mountains, or he may just give him *cash*...which is the safest way for the broker to take a kickback."

Lorenzo came back alive. "Michael, you mentioned that you thought the main crux of our investigation would end up with indictments based on bank fraud, tax fraud, mail fraud and consumer or commodity fraud. Is that correct?"

He nodded. "Yes, sir, that is correct."

Lorenzo spoke smoothly and clearly, a complete contrast to his New York counterpart, Brian Brennen. "Can you think of any other avenues to cover where we can target our investigation to expedite the entire process?"

Michael rubbed his chin and felt a dark, mid-day stubble forming. His mind was clear and racing, trying to pull something from his subconscious. He looked over at Andy, who was lost in a brief he had been preparing for his boss, Director Collins. He remembered something Andy had told him in Chicago a month earlier. "Mr. Lorenzo, a few months back, Andy Golden mentioned to me that the Justice Department had received over thousands of complaints concerning commodity fraud in the past two years. I would pull those files and check the names of brokers who the consistent complaints are directed at, then compare the names to the list I plan to give to *Special Agent Lewis*. For Lewis's sake, Michael's words were loud and clear, and directed toward Simpson, rubbing the prick's nose in his own shit. Back to Lorenzo, he said, "You can also subpoena the Exchange records and find out who has been charged with major violations during the past five years. You can piggyback those cases with your own findings to help build your case against a given broker or group of brokers. When you computerize the names and cross

reference their trading records along with the customer complaints, I'll bet you a box of Fanny May candies you will find enough to keep twenty agents busy for six months. Other than the ways I've mentioned, you're on your own."

Lorenzo nodded his understanding, jotted a note on his legal pad, and sat back.

Agent Joe Fitzsimmons shook his head as he spoke. "Mr. Hogan, I'm sorry, but I still don't get it. Why do people continue to play the game, if it's virtually impossible to win and the market is so crooked?"

Without moving his head, his eyes moved around the room as Fitzsimmons's question germinated within him. To establish perspective and to bring attention back to the subject, Michael said, "Joe, have you ever seen a clean businessman hooked on drugs? I mean a pillar of the community--a doctor or lawyer, or your parish priest, or mayor of the city, or even a nun? You know they're on something. You can see it in their eyes. Hear it in their voice. Watch it in their work--and if you can't smell it, you know it's narcotic: uppers, downers, snow, grass, ludes, M, dust, mushrooms, and God only knows what else. These people are hooked! They deny it, fight it, and live and die with their addiction. Joe, many speculators are just plain hooked--just like the junkie, they are hooked! They're looking for the pot-o-gold at the end of a rainbow. And just like the kid on acid who thinks he can fly, the gamblers' dreams turn from the bright colors of delusions of grandeur to the dark colors of cold reality.

"Even if their broker informs them of the risks involved, which are all explained on a *risk disclosure form* the customer has to sign, the customer believes that the pot-o-gold is well within reach. Remember, the broker is a salesman. He wants the customer to open an account with him. If he doesn't get his money, somebody else will. The customer expects to win the Lotto, that his horse will come in, that he will finally be looked up to by his friends and family, because he has been blessed with financial wizardry. Eventually, his dreams are shattered, he goes home empty handed, and usually without the money he started with. The compulsive speculators are trying to fill a void in their lives. They either have a gambling disease, or something is wrong with their day-to-day living which needs to be replaced with excitement--with chance. If the speculator has the misfortune of winning the first time out, his dreams escalate, his ego inflates to a dangerous level, and he is set up for a traumatic let-down. When the crash finally comes, he is devastated, and the problems that originally led him into a game of chance come back more severe than before. God only knows what goes through the poor bastard's mind after that. If he doesn't kill himself or die from stress, he'll probably come back for more, and more, and more. Win or lose, the man cannot, cannot win!"

Fitzsimmons said, "So you're a firm believer that an outside speculator, sick or otherwise, has no chance whatsoever of making money in the commodity markets?"

Michael answered quickly. "A very small percentage make money consistently. There are exceptions, but by-and-large, ninety to ninety-five per cent are losers. It's like

any game. You have to learn how to play it. Then, it takes a terrific amount of discipline to continually play it well. Like most professional games, very few make it to the top."

Fitzsimmons persisted. "Aren't the odds fifty-fifty? I mean--you either buy or sell; it **either** goes up and you make money, or it goes down and you lose money--or vice-versa!"

Michael ran his fingers through his thick black hair and squeezed the back of his neck to relieve the tension that was pulling at his muscles. "Your concept is correct, but your application is wrong. I'll give an example. You're the speculator and you open an account for one thousand dollars. Your broker tells you Treasury bonds are headed higher, time to buy a contract. That's okay with you, your broker should know. You put an order in to buy one contract of Treasury bonds. It's not unusual to lose thirty to sixty dollars to a bagman in the pit. A very common occurrence! Then you'll pay a commission on one contract of at least sixty dollars. That's over one hundred dollars on a thousand-dollar account. You've lost ten per cent of your money before the order even hits the pit. Let me tell you of a poker game I was in early in my career at the Exchange."

Brennen rumbled a question. "A real poker game?...Something I can relate to--or is this more market lingo?"

Michael laughed. Brennen looked funny, talked funny, and was funny. "Yes, Mr. Brennen, a real live five-card-stud poker game, something you can relate to. A friend of mine wanted a group of us to open up our own Clearing House. He wanted to give us an example of how lucrative it would be. We all started the poker game with a thousand dollars, and when the thousand was gone, the player had to drop out. The only catch was that we all had to give the house five dollars to play each hand. Five of us played for about six hours. I knew I was a winner at the end of the evening, but when I counted my money, I only had three hundred fifty dollars. I figured I should have about sixteen hundred, but I forgot about the house taking five dollars a hand per player. The house came away at no risk with over three thousand dollars, and the rest of us went home losers. Six months later we opened our first clearing house."

Michael had been watching the faces around the table and noticed Marty Ruiz, the rough-looking Latino from the DEA. He had hardly been paying attention. He realized Ruiz's only concern was how much drug use and trafficking was going on at the Exchanges. Michael decided he would relieve him of his misery by bringing him into the discussion. Hudson would eventually hit on the drug issue anyway, so why not get it over with?

A sharp stare caught Ruiz off balance, and before he could recover Michael said, "Mr. Ruiz, maybe we should try to address a few of your questions at this time."

Ruiz stammered for a moment, then caught himself. "Um, well, yes, Mr. Hogan, I'd appreciate that. Thank you!"

Michael reassured him. "Where would you like to begin?"

Ruiz's deep, black eyes were cool and alert like a lightweight boxer waiting for the bell to ring. "Mr. Hogan, I am here primarily to find out how extensive the illegal drug problem is at the Chicago Exchanges. Can you give me any information concerning this issue?"

Michael toyed with a button on the sleeve of his beige suede sport coat. His tongue traced his upper lip while he mentally reviewed the question and quickly formulated his answer. "Wherever you find big money in young hands, you're going to find drugs, Mr. Ruiz. The Chicago Exchanges are no exception. I'm sorry I can't give you a whole lot of information. My attention has primarily been on the illegal trading activity rather than illegal drug use. I can tell you that the men who are heavy users buy cocaine by the pound, rather than the gram. Many of the younger brokers, who are less discreet, carry and use drugs visibly in the washrooms or wherever and whenever they get the urge. At some of the more aggressive parties, there is usually a pile of cocaine on a table in the restrooms for the guests."

"Who are the major pushers?"

"There is a young fellow by the name of Tony Zitello who works for Karl Peterson who moves quite a bit of junk. This is just a sideline, but he's a heavy user himself. He makes most of his money skimming and laundering for Peterson in the S & P pit."

Ruiz kept pushing. "Anybody else?"

"Joseph Conti is your major supplier. He's a nephew of Victor Conti, who has been mentioned earlier in the meetings and is one of Chicago's Mafia kingpins in charge of laundering dirty money at the Exchanges. I think the kid, Joseph, has a record for drug dealing, so you probably have more information on Conti than I do. Between Zitello and Conti, they have a small band of men who push whatever drug anyone wants. There is never a problem picking up a pound or two of coke if you need it in a hurry. Of course, top dollar is paid. But the brokers in need have no qualms about paying fifty grand a kilo. They don't even know what the street value is, and they don't care. Actually, though, I think there is more of a booze problem than a drug problem at the Exchanges. Not because it's a legal drug, but because there is more camaraderie in drinking than there is in drugging. After a hard day at the market, the pressure is relieved by talking and drinking with fellow brokers more than it is by sneaking into the toilet and snorting a white line of powder. Maybe it's because I don't use the stuff that I don't pay attention to it. I'm sorry if I'm a bit vague, but I'm just not up on the drug business. I have given you two of the major suppliers."

Ruiz's words came quickly. "Thank you, Mr. Hogan. I'll run the names through our computers. With a few cross references and other information I have at my disposal, you'd be surprised what I can come up with."

John Simpson took the floor once again and spoke with his full lips set in his perpetual, arrogant sneer. "Mr. Hogan, what do you know about the commodity group out of Boston presently under investigation for commodity fraud?"

Hogan shook his head in disbelief and thought, what an absolute moron. Why would the asshole bring up such an insignificant, small-change operation like the Boston group at this meeting, where they were talking billion-dollar larceny? Simpson's stupidity almost outdid his worthlessness. He used his title to make ignorant statements seem profound. A typical politician who spoke to hear himself speak without thinking first, and who had limited knowledge about everything. He surely didn't follow the philosophy of Michael's mother, that it is better to remain quiet and appear ignorant, rather than open your mouth and remove all doubt. He was more the "open mouth, insert foot" type. Didn't Sister Nora always say, "Empty cans make the most noise"?

He let his voice rise in direct proportion to the anger that was also rising. "You of all people should know that the Boston group are mere parking attendants, compared to what is going on in New York and Chicago. Two men, tops, can break that *boiler room* operation. It's going to take hundreds to break Chicago. The money stolen from the Chicago Exchanges is enough to bring most other global governments to their knees, so let's not pollute the waters with insignificant scam operations like the Boston group."

Simpson's face turned beet red, then he stammered, trying to regain the offensive. Michael knew he was in his own back yard when talking commodities. Neither the FBI, CIA, IRS nor anybody else knew the things about the corruption in the futures industry as he did. His eyes shifted to Samantha, and she gave him a wink of encouragement. This simple wink excited him. But he couldn't afford to think about her now; he'd blow his concentration. He told himself to come back to earth, but...goddamn, she was nice!

Tired of sitting, he pushed back his chair, rose from it, turned his back on the group for only a second; then he pivoted and pointed his finger at Simpson, more for show than anger. "Mr. Simpson, you bring up a rinky-dink, boiler room operation going on in Boston when I'm laying out all the cards in front of you, one by one, for a Chicago sting. Why are you bothering me, or any of us, for that matter, with trivial pursuits?"

Simpson's jowls quivered. Michael presumed he was having trouble finding words that might help him gain a semblance of authority. "Well, I...we've got files a foot thick on all the men involved in that operation. I thought it would be a good place to start."

Michael tried in vain to contain his impatience. "Start?...Start, my ass! I'm giving you the place to end, not start. I've already started, years ago, long before you even knew the snake was in the barn. If you want to chase down a bunch of commission merchants in Boston, that's your business, but don't bother me with your 'foot thick folder,' and don't dilute this investigation with a bunch of nobodies, who, if indicted, will get a maximum of two years. For God's sake, man, we're after elephants, not rabbits!"

Simpson was stunned, as were the rest of the people in the room. Michael sat down and feigned annoyance. He was going to try to keep Hudson off of the IRA subject as long as possible. Besides, he liked picking on Simpson.

He looked over at Hudson, who didn't seem impressed with his outburst. A grayish pallor masked his skin, and a vein in his forehead swelled like a thin, black worm. Michael thought nothing was going to move that son of a bitch. He was like stone!

He had to push his offense for one more drive, this time against both Hudson and Simpson. He had to hit them with something they didn't already have. "Mr. Simpson, if you want to go after boiler room operations, go after the hundreds who are set up all over the country without the knowledge of the government. They have no license to trade commodities, stocks, or securities. Yet they display signs saying they are licensed and members of all major Commodity and Stock Exchanges. They have lavish offices with ticker tapes and fancy quote machines, nice-looking secretaries, bars and toilets in the executive suites, and on and on. But not a goddamn one of them has anything more than driver's license, let alone a securities license."

Hudson finally spoke, Michael thought, probably to get Simpson off the hook. "How can that be, Mr. Hogan? That sounds pretty far-fetched. I think you're getting a little carried away."

"Far-fetched...bullshit, Hudson. You know what the percentage of public winners in the commodities is? Less than ten per cent! So what happens when this fact is finally realized? A group of con-men get together and decide to open up shop--and they book the trades themselves. They don't go through the aggravation of putting up a bunch of money for customer security and licensing, which they probably couldn't get anyway, because most of the guys running the scam operations are crooks and have felonies against them. And that's exactly what they do. They set up shop, get a bunch of hotshot salesmen who can sell a Jamaican long underwear, and they book the trades within the office. It's better than bookmaking. It's the best game in town, and they seldom get caught."

This bit of information woke Brennen up again. "What happens if one of their customers turns out to be part of the ten per cent winners and hits it big?"

He looked at Brennen's ruddy complexion and said, " If the customer hits big, and the con-men don't have the money to pay off, they just pack up and move out of town, Brian--set up shop elsewhere."

Brennen smiled back and nodded. "Neat...goddamn neat!"

Michael listened to the silence, which prevailed in the room while everybody took copious notes and tried to put together what had just been said.

He felt sweat begin to form on his brow, but refrained from wiping at it. He didn't want to give Hudson the notion that he might be losing his cool. He thought, I'll give them one more piece to chew on. "One other thing you might be interested in."

He watched all heads rise in unison and focus on his end of the table, as if they were waiting the outcome of a roll of the dice at a craps table. "One of the largest

skimming operations in the country is coordinated and cleared from an office in Chicago. The office was leased to a federal judge, and when the judge had a heart attack, it was subleased to a Chicago attorney."

Hudson calmly and sardonically said, "So what, Mr. Hogan?"

Michael leaned forward in his chair, came close to his microphone, and spoke with the same calm as Hudson. "So what, Mr. Hudson? That office happens to be located in the Dirkson Federal Building on the corners of Jackson and Dearborn in the City of Chicago, Illinois, right under your nose. That's so what, Mr. Hudson!"

He sat back. The room was as quiet as a crypt, and the attention had now turned to Hudson, whose face had lost its sneer and had, instead, turned to a cold piece of granite.

He finally recovered from the shock, shuffled a few papers in front of him and said, "Simpson, that's your area. Check it out and see if there is any truth to it--which I doubt there is."

"You think I have nothing better to do than to sit at home and fabricate stories, Mr. Hudson?"

There was no response. Michael watched Hudson with amusement, as he scrambled through his papers attempting to divert attention from the eyes around the table. Eyes which seemed to be saying, "How come Hawk Hogan, a Chicago commodity broker, knows about a major scam operation being run from a Chicago Federal Government building and the heads of the FBI and CIA have no idea it is going on?"

Hudson's stony eyes met his. "Mr. Hogan, what do you know about a man named Sean McGiven?"

Here it comes, Michael said to himself. He had to stay cool; he had the ball and he didn't want to give it to Hudson--the blow-hard with the glass eyes. "He's a large international trader, probably one of the biggest in the country." He figured Hudson knew that and he also probably knew that Sean and he were long-time friends. He would try to give him back the information he already knew.

He listened carefully as Hudson spoke. "To your knowledge, does Mr. McGiven have any affiliation with any groups other than the Exchanges?"

Michael gathered his lips and reflected. "Yes, I think he does."

He saw a glimmer of hope flash across Hudson's hungry eyes.

"He's a Catholic, and I think he goes to St. Peter's Church every Sunday, and I think he's a member of The Knights of Columbus."

A few snickers filtered through the room, but Hudson ignored them and tried to zero in on his prey. "You've known Sean McGiven for a long time, Mr. Hogan?"

He chose his words carefully. "Yes. We worked together in the stockyards and started about the same time at the Exchange." Nothing to sink your teeth into there, Asshole, he thought.

"Then you must know that Sean McGiven is a key American representative for the Irish Republican Army?"

He knew he had to be careful now. The prick was after blood. "When I first met Sean, he was pretty hyped on the IRA. Wanted to kill all the British, because they had mutilated his younger brother--that was when he was in his teens. But I think as time went on, he became Americanized and his anger subsided. Now, as far as I know, he's just a successful businessman."

"You know nothing about any further affiliation McGiven may have with the IRA?"

"Hudson, I see McGiven only once every few months. Who his affiliates are is none of my business. I'm here to discuss corruption on the floors of the New York and Chicago Commodity Exchanges. If we're going to talk about political philosophies, we're going to be here for a long time because we're going to have to talk about the Jews and their so called Israel Relief Bonds, the Italians and their charity drives, the Catholics and their Bingo games, and my tainted ideas about a once-clean United States Government that has become very dirty in the past thirty years. You're the investigators, not I. I don't know anything about international bullshit!"

Hudson's face had gone sullen. His eyes were mean, like a mad animal who had just lost his food to a stronger animal. Those were not the answers he wanted. Michael had him by the balls, but only for the moment, and both men knew it. He felt as if he had just escaped a bad trade seconds before the market collapsed. He was not going to sit around and wait to try his luck again. He was going to get the fuck out. Time for a graceful exit. A strategic retreat, he thought.

Before Hudson or Simpson could combine thoughts, Michael looked at his wristwatch and said, "It's getting late, and I have a plane to catch. I'll be in touch with Andy Golden, and Pete Lewis will be with me during the day. Mr. Simpson, you can contact one of them to receive and forward any information. I would like to meet next week with the whole Chicago team." He stopped for a moment and felt his jaw tighten. His eyes burrowed deep into Hudson and Simpson. "You boys want to play ball; I'm willing to play too. If I find that you're trying to fuck me, I'll see to it this investigation is set back ten years, and that--my friends--will mean your jobs! See ya'll next week. Until then, ladies and gentlemen, it has indeed been an experience and a pleasure. Good day!" Quick and sweet, he thought, now move your ass, Hogan.

He was holding his breath. He wanted out, before Hudson recovered. He started for the door just as he sensed Hudson was about to say something. He pivoted quickly to see the man standing, mouth open, ready to speak. He beat him to it. "Incidentally, Mr. Simpson, what's the name of this sting operation?"

Simpson, off guard, fumbled through papers in front of him.

Brennen popped up. "Mike, It's called Operation Skim-Trim!"

Michael nodded an okay and said, "Thanks, Brian," and out the door he traipsed before the thoughts could clear in the room.

He heard a round of applause as the door closed behind him. He pressed his forehead against the cool wall in the hall and mumbled out loud, "Operation Skim-Trim. What an imagination. How asinine! It should be called 'Operation Let's Fuck Hogan.'"

As he heard the applause wane, he quickly dismissed the thoughts and headed for the Seven Continents Lounge and the friendly Jamaican Bartender for a double Black Label. Then he had to catch his flight and get away from this nightmare. As he walked, the hidden cameras followed.

TWENTY-FIVE

Mother's Day: May 10, 1987

Bo Lynch tossed in his bed, half naked, his body soaked-in sweat. He drifted in and out of the deranged nightmares that had harassed him nightly for fifteen years. They seemed to be intensifying with horrible accuracy. Hogan had set him up in a once-nice efficiency apartment on Lake Shore Drive, but he had let it deteriorate as he had everything else, including himself. Even in his dreams, his keen senses picked up the stale smell of dirty clothes, unlaundered bedding, and his own booze-soaked body. But in his semi-conscious state of mind, he related the foul smell to the damp jungle through which he was running. Curtains shaded the windows, pushing even the predawn darkness away. This made the room seem like the dark, humid caves he had remembered from so many years in Viet Nam.

He woke with a start. The shriek of the phone sounded more like a fire alarm. He swung his legs from the bed, ignoring it. He wiped the perspiration from his face with both hands. How long had the phone been ringing? Eight? Ten? Twenty times? He reached for his sweat-soaked pillow and wiped his face again, then flung the pillow across the room, knocking over a small lamp on an end table still lighted from the night before. The lamp fell to the floor but remained aglow, filling the room with distorted shadows. He stared at the walls with watery, drooping eyes and a bone-crushing headache. The phone blasted again, cutting into his nervous system like a sharp electric knife. But he didn't care. He looked at the menace next to the bed shouting its persistence. The clock radio read 5:07 a.m. "Who's calling at this time on a Sunday morning? Well, fuck'em!" he shrieked.

His hand shook as he reached for the phone. Mid-way he decided to grab the half-empty bottle of Stoley's vodka next to the clock radio instead. He took a healthy swig, grimaced, and shook his aching head as the Russian poison burned his throat. He knew, that for him the silent, clear liquid was a killer, as sure as a bullet though the head. The only difference was that death came slower. But his body craved it for the immediate relief it gave him. The AA's called this maintenance drinking. An early-morning drink just to keep the parts oiled and intact.

The phone screamed half a ring and died. He looked at it with contempt as he took another swallow of vodka, then fell back onto the mattress. His head hit the Smith & Wesson .38 Special always tucked under his pillow. But the pillow had been flung into the corner of the room. He rubbed the back of his head and shoved the gun to the other side of the bed, drifting back into semi-conscious delirium.

Black-and-white dreams controlled his mind again. This time he found himself running through a dense jungle, making his own trail. He could feel thorns from the heavy foliage slash deep into his face. He felt the blood from the wounds drip down his cheeks and off his chin as he plunged ahead. He was carrying a child who had been burnt black from U.S. napalm. She was smoldering but still alive. He could hear a far off whimper. Running feet thumped behind him and to his sides as he raced through the black forest. More thorns, like razors, cut his face. Vines were alive, trying to trip and hold him back. His legs wouldn't move fast enough, and he heard the enemy coming closer. He stopped. In one motion he placed the dying child on the ground and whirled with his automatic rifle, ready to fire at the footsteps. His rifle wouldn't fire. He reached for a grenade on his combat vest. The grenades were rigged to automatically pull the pin as he ripped them away from the vest. But he couldn't pull the grenade free. He tried another. Same thing. Why couldn't he free them from the vest? Why? His rifle wouldn't fire. Why? He couldn't run. Why? The brush was moving all around him, and a snake slithered across his heavy boot. He reached for his boot knife. The snake moved quickly to strike. He couldn't pull his knife. Why? He watched the snake coil. Its head was the size of a softball filled with venom. He heard enemy rifles snap into a firing position and imagined a thousand rounds being pumped into him at any second.

He looked down at the little girl who had started burning again, her arms outstretched toward him. Everything happened at once. What the fuck was he going to do? The snake struck out. The enemy guns fired. And the little girl exploded, covering Bo's face with pieces of burnt flesh and black blood. He screamed and flew off his bed onto the floor of his apartment. He was on his knees and elbows, hands covering his ears. He could hear the drum beat of his heart pounding as it pushed blood through his throbbing head. His body was drenched again. He trembled as his breathing came in heavy spurts. Like a puffing locomotive. He rolled over onto his back. Ever so slowly he came to the realization that he was in Chicago, Illinois, not someplace in Laos or Cambodia. His body now shook from anger as much as from the nightmare and morning withdrawals.

Bo looked around the dim room, still questioning reality. He lay on the yellow pile carpet. His eyes moved slowly to the mint-green ceiling. To his left, he saw his burgundy Lazy Boy recliner and a brown coffee table. He looked down his chest, past his toes, to the red-and-white label of an empty bottle of Stoley's lying next to the recliner. Over his right shoulder, he saw the red digits on his clock radio. They read 5:18 a.m. The black-and-white nightmare was over, and he, Bo Lynch, was still alive. The dream had lasted less than ten minutes--probably less than ten seconds.

He rolled again, pulling himself up on the side of the bed, and wiped his wet face across the sheet. He reached for the bottle. As his fingers made contact, the phone blasted a warning. He pulled back quickly, as if someone had caught him doing something wrong. It screamed again. And again. He looked at it. Finally, on the fourth ring, he picked it up and yelled, "It's five fucking thirty in the morning. This better be good."

At first there was no sound. Then he heard Hogan's voice. "Hey, numbnuts . Where've you been? I've called twice before." The Hawk was one of the few people who had the privilege of kidding with him.

"I went to early Mass. Why are you up so goddamn early and bothering your so-called friend?"

"Shit!" Hogan said. "You haven't been to Mass since you were baptized. It's Mother's Day. Time for all good dickheads to be out shopping for their mothers."

Bo sat on the edge of the bed and ran his hand across his face. First one way. Then the other, feeling a two day's growth. "My mom's been dead for eight years, but I think I'll just go out and buy her a couple bottles of booze and drink them here with her spirit this afternoon."

He heard Hogan ask, "Are you drunk?" His eyes fell on the quarter full bottle of Stoley's. No use lying. Hogan could always tell.

"Not yet."

"Get drunk last night?"

Bo's eyes traveled over to the empty bottle on the floor. He remembered yesterday beginning with a few shooters when he woke up, then meeting with "Snake" Adams and "Bear" O'Leary at Hogan's coach house, where he downed a bottle of Wild Turkey 101. He must have drunk a bottle and a half of vodka. That was two and a half bottles of booze before he passed out. No wonder he felt so bad. "Yeah, I guess I did." Bo listened to a dead phone. He knew Michael was quiet on purpose. Waiting for more from him. "I was sober for three days this week. Uh...then my nerves couldn't take it. Mike, I had to have a drink or I would have fallen apart."

"You cretin. You need a hospital where you can dry out the right way. Obviously you can't go 'cold turkey'. You just can't quit on your own. If you're playing on my team, it's either AA or re-hab. Goddammit, Bo, I need you sober."

Bo ran his fingers through his matted hair, then reached for a Camel cigarette and lit it. He'd agree with Hogan just to get him off his back. "Yeah, I guess you're right, but not now, not until we get some of the pressure off you."

"You can't get the pressure off me if you're drunk, Bo. You'll just add to the danger."

Bo shook his head dejectedly. He wasn't in the mood for a common sense lecture from Hogan. Whatever this booze addiction was, it was going to take more than common sense, will power, prayers, or hospitals to get rid of. Sure, the Higher Power would relieve his addiction...Fuck the Higher Power. The bottle was his Higher Power and probably always would be. "Well, forget my problems. Let's just concentrate on yours. Then we'll work on mine, okay?"

He heard Michael sigh and say. "All right, Asshole. Have it your way. But you're no good to me drunk or dead, and I've got a lot riding on you and your Nam buddies' abilities to keep my family safe."

Bo rubbed the back of his neck, trying to relieve the pain in his head, then he remembered his meeting the previous day with Snake and Bear. "Okay, listen, Mike. I was going to call you at seven this morning to give you some instructions for the day. I met yesterday with Adams and O'Leary, and we plan to get rid of your limo friends today. This should have been done when we first came on the scene, but you held us off thinking the Feds would get rid of the bastards. They haven't done anything, so we'll have to do the job. Lewis tells me the FBI won't move them because they're not doing anything wrong and they don't want to let them know that anything is changed in the Hogan household. You're just supposed to be coming and going as usual. Well, we think they could be dangerous. Time to clean the area of any problems we don't need. We'll play by our rules, and believe me, you won't have any more worries with people following you. We'll take them today. Whoever is in the limo must have a mother complex and want to stay close to you, so we're going to give them a Mother's Day gift."

Bo heard Hogan's voice take on a sharp edge. "I don't want anybody killed, Bo. We're not at war yet. I just want you to scare them enough to stay away. I don't care if they follow me to Europe, but now they're beginning to follow Maria when she shops and Mary when she goes for groceries. Just get the pricks out of my hair. The Feds may not think they are a threat, but I agree with you. We're not working for the Feds. They're supposed to be working for us. They don't give a damn about me or my family. All they're interested in is taking their pictures and writing up fancy reports. Then when the shit hits the fan, they can take everything back to Simpson in Washington and sit around a big, fancy desk and show off their investigative abilities. They'll say these are the men who killed Hogan and his family. I can just hear Simpson: 'Arrest them and we'll use them as informants or to testify with immunity against their boss. Too bad about Hogan.' Fuck them, Bo. They have overstayed their welcome. They need to know who is running the show. Get rid of them."

Be felt himself begin to lose his temper and said, "What do the Feds think those bimbos are doing every day sitting up the street waiting for somebody to move from your place? They're watching you for a reason, and there's no way you can take the bastards lightly. It's like a sniper sitting in a tree outside your house and the Feds tell you there is nothing to worry about. Bullshit!"

Michael's voice was agitated. Bo knew the presence of the intruders was beginning to get to him too. "The Feds think it's a scare tactic and that Mob boys sitting outside my front door will keep me from causing any trouble. According to their so-called 'experts,' the people who sit in noticeable stakeouts do it to put the fear of God into people. This is a frequent ploy used by the Mob in court cases with witnesses and jurors who plan to testify against one of their bad guys. Once a witness sees a big black car out in front of their house, they suddenly lose their memory. The message is clear. Either lose your memory or your life. There is only one group who pulls these scare tactics, and that's

Ruzzo and Conti. Bo, they are mean sons of bitches. They represent a whole boatload of Mob laundry at the market place. So be damn careful."

Bo took a deep drag from the harsh cigarette and flopped back down on the bed. He felt a sneer ease onto his rough face. "They underestimate you, Mike. You don't scare easy--at least I've never seen real fear in your eyes."

"Yeah, well you don't have to wash my undershorts. You might not see it in my eyes, but I sure as hell feel the devil's touch in my guts. I get plenty scared, especially if it concerns my family. I get goddamn scared when I think of the people we're fighting. They've got all the money in the world and the political clout that helps them control the Exchanges. Their control leads all the way to Washington. They'll stop at nothing to keep their dirty operations going." A silence fell. Then he continued. "Christ, Bo, you and your buddies are the ones who seem to court danger as if it were the Sunday funnies."

Bo felt a sense of pride from Hogan's compliment. "Mike, were you aware that another car is parked a half block down in a driveway on the eight hundred block of Sheridan? Could that be the Feds?" Michael didn't answer, so Bo continued. "One man. Two shifts. Twelve hours each. They look like cops. Anybody you know?"

"Probably Feds. They're supposed to be watching me. But to be honest with you, I think they sleep on the job."

Bo shook his head to himself in agreement. "Assholes! You'd think with the amount of money they're putting into this operation, and you being the cornerstone, they'd have two men on, three shifts, eight hours each. Anything happens to you, your family, or even your dog, they blow everything. And I make a lot of government people pay with their goddamn, incompetent blood." He heard his voice rise. "Believe me, Mike. If they fuck up this operation and anything happens to the Hogans, I'll go after them first--then I'll get Ruzzo, Conti, and Fat Man Peterson."

He heard Michael laugh. "Take it easy, Bo. The Feds are supposed to be on our side even though they have a very nonchalant way of showing it."

Bo rubbed his bloodshot eyes. They felt like open wounds. "Mike, this is going to get pretty heavy in a few months. Neither of us can afford to be in partnership with a bunch of bumbling Federal jerkoffs who are going to sit in their cars with their suits and ties, drinking coffee and eating McDonald's hamburgers. Hell, they have to call Washington and ask permission to investigate an explosion or automatic gun fire."

"That's why I'm counting on you, Adams, and O'Leary to keep my family safe."

Bo took a drag from his cigarette, exhaled, and watched the smoke cloud the stale air above him. "Your family will be safe at the house, but we have no control when they leave unless you want us to blow our cover. When the shit hits the fan, your government friends aren't going to be worth a damn."

He heard Michael sigh as he answered, "Don't worry about it. I know how the Feds work. Or don't work. They won't be around when the real trouble starts. When the time comes, we'll change our strategy. Besides, I'd hate to pull Adams and O'Leary away

from their chores around the house. My goddamn garden has never looked so good. O'Leary looks like a big, black bear standing in the middle of my flower patch. I see where he gets his nickname."

Bo rubbed his feet together. His amputated toes were aching. Phantom sensations. "He didn't get his nickname from talking to flowers and swiping honey from bees."

"What did he do in Nam?"

Bo closed his eyes, not wanting to remember. "You wouldn't want to know, Mike."

"Try me."

"Both O'Leary and Adams can kill ten men in ten different ways before lizard shit hits the ground--faster if the enemy's confidence level is up. The three of us were point men in Nam. We took turns. When I say point men, I mean *point*. We would go as far as two, maybe three miles ahead of our outfit--not just fifty or a hundred yards. Snake was the best. He blended into the jungle like a chameleon. He had that thousand-yard look they talked about in Nam. Bear would go into the jungle wearing only a G-string and his boots so his clothes wouldn't get caught on branches. The boots protected him from snakes. He looked like a big, black rock--until he threw his knife into a VC's neck. Bastard's a bullseye with a knife. We did the dirtiest jobs in the war and it took something out of all of us. I think it's called a heart. The war also left us thinking and living like jungle animals. We're always on the defensive, ready to strike out at anybody or anything at anytime."

Michael fell silent for a moment then said, "I think you guys came out okay. Both your men are gentle and good with my family. Maria likes them and the kids love 'em. We've got six acres of ravines and overgrowth that have been here since the Indians. They've never been touched except for a wide clearing from the house down to the lake. Adams has cut narrow paths through the brush for the kids. He even made them a number of tree forts...one for each child. They love your guys."

Bo shook his throbbing head. Michael was in tune with life. He had a whole lot of street and business savvy. But he was goddamn naive when it came to survival. "Mike! Adams and O'Leary didn't do that work for the kids. Even though it might appear that way. They did it to fuck up any assholes who might try to hit your place from the lake side." He went on carefully. "If you take a close look, you'll see the paths go in circles and S's leading into each other, and the tree huts are directly over the paths. The grounds are covered with grid pressure sensors. If anyone comes at you from the side of the house, it will probably be at night. They will naturally follow one of the paths, and the sensors will pick up their movements and location. The grids are set to pick up foot pressure and the weight of anything over one hundred pounds. Messages from these grids will be transmitted to the coach house. The wrist watches we all wear will begin to vibrate when the transmission comes in. Within sixty seconds, the intruder is identified. The only thing you have running around here over one hundred pounds are a few deer and maybe a dog

or two. If it's a deer, it lives. If it's not a deer, it's not welcome, and will be eliminated."
Bo listened to silence once again, almost as if the phone had gone dead.

Michael was quiet, then said softly. "Let's hope it doesn't come to that."

"It's going to, Mike. I have a feeling in my gut this whole thing is going to get real dirty before it's all over."

He could almost hear Michael thinking. "Are you sure you're not just suffering from some type of morbid, post-war syndrome?"

Bo sat up. He put his cigarette out and looked at the bottle of vodka. "I hope so, for your sake. But don't count on it."

Michael sounded a little unnerved. "How about Adams and O'Leary. What do they think?"

Bo's head felt like it was going to blow apart. He wished Michael would end the conversation so he could get some pain pills into him for his aching head. "They're just doing a job. They like you a lot because of what you did for me and the help you've given to the vets. When you opened the half-way house for our Nam guys, 'Hill 112,' you made yourself a lot of friends. Those vets were just like me. Bums with no reason to live. Now they have a place to go, to live, and to be with their own kind. Right now, you could recruit one hundred guys like Snake and Bear if you needed to."

"Bo, you're the guy who inspired 'Hill 112.' Don't give me the credit. I just had the real estate. You set it all up."

"Sure I set it up, but you have to remember how a vet thinks. Nobody including the Government has given a two-hundred-thousand dollar gift to us without a long, drawn-out fight." Bo could sense Michael's humility. He would always take the blame for something but shunned the credit. He wasn't a politician and would never be mayor. That was certain. Too humble, Bo thought.

"You think we'll need more men?"

Bo erupted in anger at Michael's statement and he almost threw the phone. "FUCK NO, I DON'T--anybody crazy enough to come on your property unannounced with Adams and O'Leary there, will be dead in seconds. Those ravines are just like Nam. Especially this time of year. Even in winter, the brush is so thick an enemy could walk within inches of one of those two killers. The intruder's eyes would watch the rest of his body standing as his head hit the ground. I don't know how long it takes to die, but in Nam I saw headless Viet Cong stand for thirty or more seconds, waiting for the detached brain to tell the body what to do. The head would be on the ground blinking and wondering why the torso wasn't carrying it anymore. You put a few heads on a few bamboo sticks, post them along a trail, and that trail would be safe for a day or two."

Michael spoke with irritation. "You're making me sick, Bo. No wonder you have nightmares. Your jungle ways are a little barbaric for Chicago."

Bo needed his usual four Alka Seltzers, six heavy duty pain pills, and a vodka chaser. "Mike, just a minute. I have to get a few aspirins in me or *my* head is going to be on the floor wondering why *it's* not attached."

"That's okay," Michael said quickly. "I just wanted to check in with you before I go to Mass. I'll talk to you later."

Bo rubbed his head. His hands were beginning to shake out of control. "Just a minute, Mike." He had things he had to talk about with Hogan. He grabbed the Stoley's from the night stand and took a long gulp, retching at its burning descent. A small price to pay for the relief it would bring. He caught his breath and said, "You asked about the nightmares. My nightmares aren't caused from the dismemberment of a North Vietnamese, Mike. My nightmares come from the kids and families who were killed in our wake of destruction. Men, women, and children we used to give candy and cigarettes to, we eventually ended up killing because we were *following orders*. As far as being barbaric, we knew that many Viet Cong had a superstition about dying without their body parts. Especially if inflicted by the enemy. I guess it was all right to be blown apart, but to have your hands cut off, then your feet, then your head and your ears and prick, this was absolute voodoo to them. Something about not being able go into the next world without their body parts. Some religious gibberish. This worked in Nam, and Snake and Bear were the best. Snake had a gunny sack full of shriveled-up ears and pricks. Our C.O. was ordered to give us ten dollars for a set of ears and five dollars for a prick. Snake and Bear were wealthy men according to the Vietnamese economy. This was a better business than dope in some areas. So, a simple gun shot to the head won't satisfy those two. If they do cut somebody up, they'll let whoever sent them know what the penalty is for trespassing on Hogan property. Your enemies will probably send out teams of four to eight men at a time. As long as they don't know we're here, they're dead men and don't know it. We usually try to capture one or two to get information. But believe me, that's not a priority."

"Then what?" Michael asked.

"Then nothing. If we happen to take a man alive, we destroy both knees first so he won't give us any problems. If they know anything, that's usually enough persuasion to make 'em talk. Whether they talk or don't, the same thing happens to all the intruders. We take a mini-grenade, slightly larger than a golf ball, and jam it in their mouth. Tape their hands to their face and take 'em down to the lake for a boat ride, about ten miles out. If they're not dead already from suffocation or fear, we pull the pin and push them overboard. No head for dental records, no hands for finger prints. The fish take care of the rest of the body...That's who you have working for you, Michael, whether you like it or not. They're the best, and I guarantee you'll be safe at home. Just watch your family's asses outside, where we can't keep an eye on them."

Bo tried to shake the pain from his head. He knew it wouldn't leave until the wires in his body were cauterized with a coating of booze. He felt he had to tell Michael about Snake and Bear and how savage they could be, especially if someone pissed them off,

which wasn't hard to do. He knew that Mob violence had to be met with fierce violence--brutal violence. The Hogan family would be victims of not only the criminal elements that would be stalking him, but also the corrupt government people he was dealing with. Bo didn't really believe that Michael trusted the Feds. They were using each other simply as a means to an end. He shrugged his shoulders. He was worried for his Irish friend.

"Incidentally, Mike, I think you had better take some judo lessons from Adams."

He heard the righteous indignation. "Why? I can take care of myself just fine."

"Man, it's just a goddamn precaution. You can take care of yourself if it's one on one and maybe even two on one without any weapons involved. But you'd be worthless if somebody who knew what they were doing came at you with a knife. Snake will show you how to defend yourself, not how to kill. The Snake is the best I've ever seen. He'll get you in shape and teach you some very simple defensive moves. He won't teach you the things that will allow you to kill your adversaries. Killing a man in a second with your hands or feet is privileged information. This takes a lifetime to learn properly. Besides, you're getting fat and could use a good workout."

"Okay, but I don't think it's necessary."

"You don't think it's necessary because you think you're as good on the street as you are in the pit. Start working out with Adams tomorrow. Okay?"

"Yeah, okay."

"One more thing, Mike. Do you know how to use a gun?" He heard nothing. "Well, do you or don't you? I haven't got all day."

"Hell yes, I know how to use a gun. Remember, I came from the South Side of Chicago. The stockyards. Almost everybody carried a 'piece.' Especially on pay day."

"Bear is going to give you a Mauser C96 or a Walther PPK. Whatever feels good to you. They're small, powerful, and very accurate at close range. He'll also give you an ankle holster so it will be out of sight and won't be conspicuous. Keep it in your car or locked up at home when you're around the house. Put it on every time you leave the house. He'll give you a few extra clips just in case you get into a real battle."

"That's horseshit, Bo. I need a gun like I need a longer nose."

"Goddammit, Mike. Just follow instructions, will ya?"

No answer came at first, and then the words. "Yeah, sure, give me the fucking gun. Give me judo lessons. How about a cyanide capsule in case I get captured?"

Bo ignored the question. "What Mass are you going to?"

"Nine-thirty at St. Edwards in Winnetka. I should be home by ten thirty."

Bo thought for a moment. "Does the whole family go?"

"The house will be empty," Michael said. " Everybody will be at church except for the dog, and it's Mary's day off."

Bo reached for a pad of paper. He had jotted a few notes on this the day before with Adams and O'Leary. He glanced at them quickly. "Why don't you take the family out

to breakfast for Mother's Day and come home about noon? The limo will be gone. Guaranteed!"

"Michael said, "Done."

Bo snapped his fingers. He had almost forgotten a very important point. "Mike, use your own limousine today to go to church."

"How about the Jeep wagon? An eighty-thousand-dollar, silver limo is a little pretentious for me to go to church in. This just seems to be a contradiction."

Bo felt sick and was getting pissed off. "Fuck the hypocrisy, Michael. Your goddamn limo has tinted windows. If the assholes we are after won't be able to see you, they'll stay put. You take the Jeep wagon, and they'll follow you to church. That will really fuck up our plans, not to mention nine-thirty Mass."

"Okay, okay. Don't get your balls so tight. I'll take the limo."

Bo rubbed his forehead and closed his eyes. "Okay, nine-thirty Mass, in your limo. Back home after twelve noon. I'll talk to you later, Mike."

A silence fell. Then Michael said. "Bo, don't kill anybody."

Bo felt he was about to go over the edge. "Jesus Christ, Michael. Stop worrying about the enemy getting killed, will ya? We're just going to give them a warning. Just a warning. I can't guarantee your last request, but I'll mention it to Snake and Bear."

"Okay. Get your aspirin. I'll talk to you later."

The phone was nearly back on its cradle when Bo heard his name. He exhaled with frustration. "What now?"

"Where did Bear, a black man, get the name O'Leary?"

"Jesus Christ, Mike. How should I know? Maybe his father was Irish. You know, like Ella Fitzgerald. Maybe the street he lived on was O'Leary Street. You know how the black families from the ghetto name their babies. After presidents and movie stars. Grocery stores. Street signs. Game shows. They just pull a name out of the air and evidently O'Leary was the first name his Mama saw after his delivery."

"Thanks. Just wondering."

"You're welcome...anything else?"

"No, that's it. Go get your medicine."

Bo hung up the phone. Fast. Before Michael thought of anything else to say. He went quickly to the sink and grabbed a handful of pain pills. Then he returned to his bedside and slugged them down with a mouthful of Stoley, emptying the bottle. "Fuck the Alka Seltzer," he said out loud.

He lay back down and reviewed the plan that he, Snake Adams, and Bear O'Leary had gone over the day before. He let his eyes close. He waited for the drugs to relieve his aching head and body. The image of a little child burning and melting cropped into his mind again. He jerked himself up and said out loud, "Fucking kids. Why can't I get them out of my mind?"

He reached for the phone and pressed seven digits. After one ring, it was picked up. There was no answer. He expected that. "Snake?"

"Yeah, Bo?"

"Hogan's going to nine-thirty Mass with his family. Nobody will be around until noon. I'll be there in about forty-five minutes. You have everything ready?"

"You bet. Don't I always?"

"See ya soon." Both lines went dead.

The combination of vodka and pills was finally relieving Bo's pain. Reaching for his thirty-eight Special, he looked to see if he had fired any shots during the night. All shells accounted for, he slipped it beneath his mattress. Piss-ass gun, he thought. A cop's gun. This was accurate and easy to use in close quarters, though.

He ambled over to the desk drawer, pulled out an Army Issue forty-five, and checked the clip. With a pair of clean underwear he found in the same drawer, he wiped bits of oil from the gun and two extra clips. He slammed one clip back into the gun with the palm of his left hand and pulled out a homemade silencer the size of a roll of quarters. Both he took to the bathroom with him. A cold shower would feel good.

* * *

Thirty minutes later, Bo was speeding north on Lake Shore Drive in his black, four-speed '79 Firebird. The oversized Havana shirt he wore would cover his weapon well if for some reason he had to go into the open. He didn't think the gun would be necessary on today's mission. The weapons he and his Nam buddies used were generally silent. No noise. Little blood. Just death. There would be noise today, though. Grenades made noise. They hadn't designed a silencer for grenades or plastique or blasting gelatin yet.

A smile crept onto his face as he thought. Now we can start to ease the pressure on Hogan. He owed at least that much to Michael. Plus a hell of a lot more. Adrenalin began to pump through his body. He felt he had a sense of purpose again. This time they would win the war. He started to reach for a chrome flask in his glove compartment but decided to light a cigarette instead. The smile remained. The gun was uncomfortable but felt good tucked into his belt. He flipped on the radio, and a soft-rock station was playing John Denver's "Rhymes and Reasons":

> *...you wonder where we're going, where's the rhyme*
> *and where's the reason? And you cannot accept it is*
> *here we must begin...*

Bo pushed the car faster. As the sun broke its morning mating with Lake Michigan, he put on his dark glasses.

> *...To seek the wisdom of the children and the graceful*
> *way of flowers in the wind. For the children and the*

242

> *flowers are my sisters and my brothers their laughter*
> *and their loveliness would clear a cloudy day.*

The Firebird climbed to ninety m.p.h. He fought the curves around Winnetka and handled the auto like a professional race driver. Behind the shaded glasses, his eyes had taken on a meanness.

> *...In their innocence and trusting they will teach us to be*
> *free.*

His mind saw the innocent faces of the bewildered children in Nam. They hadn't taught him to be free. He had wiped away their trust by killing their parents. But now he had a chance to go after bad men, evil men. Maybe he could make up for some of the evil he had done in 'Nam by helping Hogan out.

He hit the snake turns, which were cut through the ravines leading into Glencoe, at eighty m.p.h. He slowed to sixty-five, still forty over the limit. He came to the top of the hill entering Glencoe and accelerated again. He passed the black limo parked on a side street just off Sheridan and mumbled, "Adios, Assholes."

Twenty minutes after he'd left his apartment, he pulled into the back entrance of Hogan's property. The gates opened automatically from a control inside the coach house where Snake and Bear waited for him. He said again, this time audibly, "Happy Mother's Day, Motherfuckers." The limo would be gone when Hogan returned from church.

TWENTY-SIX

No Pasta For Joey

Joey "The Gorilla" Grollo sat in the driver's seat of the heavy, black Lincoln limousine, the usual frown pasted on his rough, Italian face. He pulled at his black mustache with his thumb and forefinger. First one side, then the other. The mustache, the downward curl of his lips, and his deep-set, dark eyes gave him a sinister, cruel look. He was thinking how nice it would be if he were with his mama and papa on Mother's Day. That's where he belonged. Not sitting on Shore Avenue looking down Sheridan Road waiting for some Irish son of a bitch to make a move from his house. How long was this goddamn job going to last? He and Eddy "Cheeks" Lopatta had been on this guy Hogan for more than three months. Except for a fast ride home one night, Hogan had done nothing unusual, saw no one unusual, went no place unusual.

Lunch with a friend named Glassmann sure didn't mean the prick was talking about Ruzzo's laundry operation at the Exchange. Hogan never went near the Federal Building, and that's what he and Eddy were supposed to watch for.

He looked at his wrist watch. Thick, black hair from his muscular arm covered the crystal. He moved the hair away with his right index finger. 8:52 a.m. Fuck! His mama already had the pasta sauce on the stove, and would simmer it for hours, until it was nice and thick. She would add meatballs and pork and a chunk of beef and probably some sausage. He could smell the tantalizing aroma of garlic and spiced tomato sauce cooking. Goddamn, he could almost taste the hot spaghetti.

Joey looked over his shoulder at the fat, sleeping figure in the back seat. "Hey Eddy?" No response. "Hey, Eddy. You awake?"

There was movement in the back seat. Eddy sat up and said, "Whadya want now? I'm trying to get some sleep and you're asking me if I'm awake. You're like the damn nurses in the hospital. They wake you up to ask you how you're sleeping. What the fuck you want, Joey?"

No goddamn appreciation, Joey thought. I pick him up at four in the morning, drive him around all day, sit for days watching some rich Irish prick, and "Cheeks" talks to me like I'm garbage.

He weighed his words as he spoke again. "Hey, Eddy. I was just thinking. Maybe a little later...me and you can sneak away from here for a few minutes and go over to Mama's house for some good pasta with sugo. You know, meatballs, sausage, hot bread, good wine--just long enough to get a good Mother's Day meal. How 'bout it, Eddy? This Hogan prick ain't going no place today 'cept maybe to church. How 'bout it, Eddy?" Joey

knew that food was about the only thing that could make Eddy break the rules. He hoped this time was no exception. He strained his neck until it hurt, trying to see if his suggestion was getting any approval.

Eddy mumbled, "I don't know, Joey. Sure sounds good. But we already got in trouble with Ruzzo for fucking up an assignment. If he ever found out we left Hogan on his own for five minutes, he'd tell Conti. We'd get it up the ass again, an' I don't want any more shit like this. Just watchin' some broker prick do nothin' ain't my idea of fun."

Joey dejectedly turned to the street. "Hey, Eddy. Fuck Hogan. We been watchin' the prick for a long time. We deserve a little break. Whatcha say, Eddy? He could hear the fat bulk grunting as he moved around in the back seat of the heavy car. The car moved gently with the shifting of Eddy's weight.

"What time ya got, Joey?"

He looked at his watch again. "About nine." Joey knew the fat man was thinking about the pasta and warm bread. "My mama lives right over on Devon, Eddy. We could be there and back in an hour. I'll just call her from the car. She'll have two big plates of pasta and a half a loaf of warm bread waitin' for us." No answer came from the back seat, but Joey knew he was making "Cheeks" hungry. "Eddy, whatcha say?"

Joey moved the rear view mirror. He watched Lopatta as he rubbed his shaved, bald head and said, "Let's sit until eleven o'clock. Then ask me again. I'm gonna sleep for a few hours. Now don't bother me no more, okay?"

Joey felt his lips turn upwards into a smile. Fuck Ruzzo and Conti. His mama was more important than this job. "Yeah, sure, Eddy. You just think about those meatballs and sausage, ol' buddy."

He wished they would let him do what he did best. That was breaking bones and heads with a ball bat. He clenched his fist and looked at it with pride. These knuckles had pummeled many a face. These hands had collected lots of juice and numbers money. His smile faded as his lips turned down again. He felt his face grow cold and mean, as he remembered how much he did for his bosses. Just because he had killed a South Side baker who wouldn't make his weekly payment, this was how they repaid him. It was an accident. Joey had hit the guy too hard. He hadn't known the old man had a heart condition. He remembered Conti scolding him like he was a child instead of a loyal soldier. "You were supposed to break the man up. Not kill him. How's he going to pay us now, Joey? Now that you killed him? I'll tell you. *You're* going to pay us what the old Jew owed us, Joey. Twenty three hundred dollars."

Joey hated to be talked down to by anybody. His mama knew that. She never talked down to him. She told him what a good boy he was and how good looking he was, and how smart he was. Fuck 'em all, he thought, as he pulled down the visor and lifted the cover to the mirror. He checked his teeth and examined a few pock marks on his olive face. He could hear Eddy snoring in the back seat. Then he thought he saw a movement in the rear-view mirror. He squinted as he studied a white van parked about fifty yards

behind him. Watching the van closely, he could see there was no sign of movement. How long had the van been there? He hadn't actually seen it pull up, though he knew it wasn't there when he parked earlier. He looked toward Hogan's house. His attention was taken off the van when he saw Hogan's limo pull off of the side street next to his mansion. As it eased with confidence onto Sheridan Road, he leaned forward. Holding the top of the black leather steering wheel, he squinted as the limo passed in front of him. Tinted windows, he thought. Was Hogan in the car? He couldn't tell. He leaned back in the seat and thought for a moment. He could hear Eddy sawing logs behind him. Should he follow or stay put? Should he wake Eddy and let him make the decision? Fuck 'im. Let 'im sleep. He'd make the decision himself. One thing was clear. He wasn't going to follow Hogan's limo around all day and miss Mama's pasta. As far as Joey was concerned, the nigger chauffeur could be going to fill the car up with gas.

He looked on the dashboard where a small tracking monitor had been installed. This was about twice the size of a radar detector. The four inch screen depicted a tiny, white dot halfway down on the left-hand side. The transmitter on Hogan's car hadn't indicated any movement. He adjusted a few dials and tapped the top of the monitor with his stubby fingers to make sure it was working. The little white tracking dot shivered and became elongated as he tapped and adjusted the machine. Hogan's auto hadn't moved-- that's all Joey cared about. He would stay put and pretend he didn't see the limo leave.

As he leaned back into the driver's seat, he looked at the white van in the rear-view mirror. He felt uncomfortable as he adjusted the mirror trying to get a better picture. The van, too, had tinted windows. He couldn't tell if it was a Chevy, Ford or Dodge. There had been work done on the old junk, and it had no grill. He pulled at his mustache nervously. The sun played havoc with his vision. The van was positioned where the early morning sun reflected off its windshield, shining directly on Joey's vehicle.

He looked at Hogan's place again. No action there. His eyes moved alertly back to the van. His body tightened as the driver's door opened. Through the glare of the sun, he squeezed his eyes to see a figure emerging. The body was tall and lean. The man wore an open shirt, a baseball cap turned backwards, and sunglasses. He watched the man stretch, glance in Joey's direction, and head to the back of the van. He saw the back door open and swing out toward the street. Joey felt the hair on the back of his thick neck nervously prick to attention. He cracked the driver's window to see if he could hear anything unusual. A warm gust of air rushed passed his face. This was going to be a hot day in Chicago.

A small compression motor started, and Joey watched the tall man wheel a lawn mower out from behind the van. He leaned back and sighed with relief. Only the lawn man, he thought. He was getting jumpy, too jumpy. After months of watching this guy Hogan, Joey had a funny feeling he was the one being watched. Hogan was no dummy. Ruzzo had told both him and Eddy not to underestimate the Irishman. Joey could not imagine that Hogan hadn't noticed the black limo. Why didn't he do something about it?

He had to know somebody was following him. Maybe he just didn't give a shit. Or maybe he did give a shit and was planning something of his own. His instincts told him that something was not right. As the lawn man passed by the limo, mowing the curb side, Joey could see him clearly. He wore a loose-fitting Hawaiian shirt. And he knew the big red *C* on the hat stood for the Cubs. He's a loser, he thought. He probably bet his whole salary on the Cubs. What a great job--cutting lawns at nine o'clock on a Sunday morning. Then he thought it odd that the man would be working in a rich neighborhood on a Sunday. On Mother's Day, no less. He would think the rich asshole neighbors would bitch about the noise. Maybe Friday's rain set the guy back a day and he took Sunday to catch up. He dismissed any anticipated threat by the lawn man. He continued to watch as he mowed down to the corner of Sheridan and disappeared around the brick wall.

Joey reached for the Sunday *Tribune* on the seat next to him and began to browse. He could hear the old lawn mower puttering along on the other side of the brick wall. His eyes moved up from the newspaper and fell on the man pushing the mower. As he moved closer, Joey sensed a ferocity to the man. There seemed to be a meanness in his face. He was tall, maybe 6'4", thin, and unshaven. In spite of the bright early sun, there was a shadow of savagery in the man's tight face. The man stopped. He was parallel to Joey. He glanced through his dark glasses at the limo. The mower sputtered and died. He was expressionless as he leaned down, apparently to fix the machine. Joey grinned. Fucking loser, he thought again, and returned to his reading. When Joey looked up again, the man was gone. He looked in the rear-view mirror and saw the tall fellow heading for the van, probably out of gas. What a mentality, Joey thought. Can't even start a job without checking his equipment first.

He made a mental note of the man's face and knew there was something he didn't like about him. He felt the nerves on the left side of his face twitch. When the tall workman had looked at the limo, it was as if he looked right through the black windows, directly at Joey. He ignored the chill that ran down his spine at the man's challenging, crafty look. Well, he thought. That son of a bitch better think twice about fucking with a guy like Joey Grollo. He ate guys like that for breakfast. His thick fingers squeezed unconsciously together crumpling the sides of the newspaper, eyes flicking from the black print of the *Tribune* to the rear-view mirror and the van. But now the sun was at such an angle that it was impossible to see anything of the van except a bright, glaring light. Almost as if it were planned that way, Joey thought. An intuition of coming trouble dampened his forehead and palms with sweat. He didn't know why he felt so uneasy. He guessed he just didn't like anybody standing behind him, sitting behind him, or parked behind him. He especially didn't like the ugly look of the man who had been pushing the lawn mower. A real fighter's look. Like one who had taken an awful lot of punishment at one time. Oh, fuck. What was he concerned about? Nobody was going to touch Joey Grollo and Eddy Lopatta in the metal-plated fortress that enveloped them. Once again, his eyes dropped back on the newspaper.

He heard a light thud. The heavy auto quivered as if a tennis ball had bounced off the car. His head jerked from side to side, looking for the cause of the thud. Nothing. He looked at Eddy snoring. Maybe he had kicked the door or seat. There was another thud. What the fuck? He listened. No noises. But something was happening to the heavy limo. He sensed the back end rising gradually. Was this his imagination? He looked in the rear-view mirror. As he saw the white van moving in reverse, he felt a sense of panic. He saw it make a 180 degree swing in the middle of the narrow side street and turn left at the first corner.

"What's going on?" he said out loud. "The goddamn guy didn't even take his lawn mower."

From the back seat, Eddy's voice droned. "Hey, Joey. What are you mumbling about? I'm trying to sleep."

Joey felt the rear of the car continue to rise slowly as if it were being lifted hydraulically. He kept his own words low as he listened. "I dunno, Eddy. Something strange is happening here."

Eddy sat up, yawned, and scratched his shaved head. "What the fuck you mean? Is Hogan making a move?"

"I dunno. It's not Hogan. Some asshole left his lawn mower on the other side of that brick wall, and I feel, or I think I feel, the car rising. You feel anything?"

Eddy was quiet for a moment. "You're nuts. A guy leaves a lawn mower, and the car is rising. Jesus Christ, your biscuits aren't done. I'm going back to sleep. Wake me if you see any U.F.O.'s."

Again came a suspicious jab of intuition. "Hey, Eddy. This isn't funny. Something is going on. This car is rising in the rear."

"Yeah, sure. A six-thousand-pound bulletproof car is lifting right off the ground. A Volkswagen, yes. A three-ton limo, no."

Joey put his hand on the door handle. "I'm getting out to take a look."

Eddy protested. "We're not supposed to leave the car, Joey, unless we're instructed to."

"Fuck it, Eddy. There's something strange happening."

Eddy was quiet, then said, "Hey, the back of the car *is* rising."

Joey turned around and looked at the bald creep. "No shit. Whaddaya think I been tryin' to tell you, dummy. I'm gonna take a look."

He pulled the handle and gave the heavy metal door a push with his shoulder. He almost fell when he got out of the car. What used to be an eight inch step down to the ground was now more than a foot. He felt for his gun in his shoulder holster. It was ready. If he only knew what the fuck he was going to need it for.

He walked slowly to the back of the car, eyes on the street and yards around him. Perspiration broke out on his forehead, and he could feel a bead of sweat run from his armpit down the side of his rib cage. The neighborhood was quiet except for a slight hiss

coming from under the car. His eyes came to rest on the back of the limo, then around at the left wheel. He felt his mouth drop open when he saw the thick back tire. It was twice its original size and rising. "Holy Jesus Christ, what the fuck's going on?" he said out loud. He dropped to his hands and knees and peered under the car. He wasn't ready for this shit. He looked cautiously at the tires. They had both been penetrated in almost the exact same spot with some type of metal darts. No, they were metal arrows. He knew that the tires were bulletproof, but also knew that with enough force a sharp object could puncture the tire. The hiss was coming from inside the tire. Instead of the tire deflating, it was inflating. Joey leaned back and rested on his knees and calves. Goddammit, what now? The arrows must have some type of air-compression tube on them. He had never heard of such a thing. Those tires were going to both blow any second.

He jumped to his feet, disjointed thoughts colliding with each other. He turned a complete circle, not knowing whether to run or get in the car and drive. Drive fast. Maybe he could make it to a safe place before the tires went. The hiss continued. The rising continued.

He heard himself scream. "Eddy. Goddammit. Edddyyyy." Joey turned to get back into the car. As he did so, he caught a glimpse of the handle of the old mower on the other side of the brick wall. "That lawn guy did this," he said out loud. He bolted to the wall and looked at the mower. Christ! He felt his eyes bulge and his body go cold beneath his perspiration soaked clothes. He wiped sweat from his eyes with the back of his shaking hand, as he saw what looked like a kitchen timer on top of a gray mass of mud. Wires ran from the mud. Mud? This was a plastic explosive, and there looked to be plenty of it. Between the lawn mower and the brick wall was an over-sized red container of gasoline. His eyes narrowed when he noticed that the timer faced him. The ticking was loud. He saw the dial moving methodically and patiently toward the number twelve. There wasn't much time. He had to get the fuck out of here. At most, he figured, sixty seconds to get the hell away. He turned and ran to the car as the back door opened on the parking side and Eddy began to emerge.

"Joey. What the fuck's going on? You're running around like a lunatic. What's happening to the car? You want pasta? Let's go get some pasta!"

"Lunatic my ass. We're about to be blown away. And fuck Mama's pasta. Let's just get the hell out of here or we won't be eating any food ever again. Haul ass, Eddy."

Eddy's face was a mirror of questions. "What the fuck you talkin' about?"

As Joey ran to the driver's side, his leather shoes slipped on the street grit, and he went down on one knee. Just as quickly, he recovered and grabbed the door to slide in.

"So the tires are big. That doesn't mean a bomb," Eddy said.

"Look at the lawn mower on the other side of the wall and you'll see the bomb," Joey said. "No, Cheeks, don't look--just stay in the car. We're getting the hell out of here."

Joey could hear Eddy thrashing and grunting to get his heavy body out of the back seat. "Bomb, my ass. Who's going to place a bomb on a lawn mower? Who's going up against us?" Eddy grumbled.

Joey yelled through his fear: "The guy in the van, Asshole. And you can bet the orders came from that sleeping Irishman Hogan--who you said was a piece of cake. Now stay in the car. We only got a few seconds."

"Fuck you. You're losin' it, Joey."

He yelled again, feeling his breath catch in his throat. Fear squeezed his lungs. "STAY IN THE CAR, EDDY--THAT FUCKER IS READY TO BLOW."

"I'm taking a look for myself. Just cool it."

The limo had been running, to keep it cool. Joey slammed the car into gear, ready to gun it. But Eddy had the back door open, about to hoist himself out of the car. "Hold on, Peabrain, I'm going to look..."

Eddy was half way through his sentence when the deafening explosion came. Bricks from the three-foot wall smashed the auto like mortar shells. The concussion blew Eddy into the back seat and slammed him against the far door. The three-ton auto lifted off the ground and settled down sideways in the middle of the street. Joey tried to shake the horror from his scrambled mind. He looked at Eddy, who was crunched into the corner of the back seat. His eyes were open, and a deep purple gash ran diagonally across his face where a flying brick had hit him. Blood oozed from both eyes. What was left of his fat nose had been pushed back into his sinuses, leaving the image of a hog nose. Flat. With two huge bleeding nostrils. He looked dead, but Joey thought he was probably just knocked out. He didn't have time to check. He had to move ass. And now! Shattered bricks rained like shrapnel onto the crippled limo. The velocity of one brick had been so strong, it had disintegrated the passenger-seat window and was lodged, half in and half out. Joey thought, if the explosive had been a little stronger he would have had that brick embedded in his skull.

The car was still settling into its new position in the middle of the street when Joey punched the accelerator. He heard a loud snap, and the right-rear tire exploded. Then, another snap, and the other tire exploded, lifting the rear of the heavy auto off the ground. The side mirrors told him both back tires were in flames. Joey was scared. Scared to death. In his wildest dreams, he never imagined anything like this happening to him. What was going on? Panic shook his body, and sweat ran down his face. Vulnerable and completely defenseless, he knew he had to get moving. He pushed his foot to the floor and turned south on Sheridan. The car moved slowly, at 20 mph, on flat, burning rubber and bare rims.

"Son of a bitch. Go faster," he said out loud. The limo defied speed with its destroyed back tires. He had gone a half mile and was going to turn north on Lakeview Road to avoid the dangerous snake turns on Sheridan. No way was he going to be able to control the car through the steep, treacherous ravines. As he began his turn off of Sheridan,

he slammed on the brakes. Directly in front of him, in the middle of the road, was the same white van with its lights on and no grill. Goddamn, what now? Joey could see that the van's windshield had been modified and was cocked open like a jeep's. The long, thick barrel of a high powered rifle, held by two huge black hands, was aimed directly at the limo. He realized there were at least two guys in the van.

Guns wouldn't hurt the limo. For a split second his fear subsided, and in this brief moment of renewed confidence, he thought of ramming them. Fire a few rounds himself, and be on his way. He pulled his revolver and set it on the seat next to him. He could smell burning rubber. There must have been an explosive in the arrows for the rubber tires to be burning out of control.

Joey was ready to push the pedal to the floor and ram the van when he saw the driver's door open. He was less than one hundred feet away. The baseball cap came into view first, and his insides flooded with panic again. What is the prick up to now? Joey noticed that the cap had been turned back around and that there were no sunglasses. He could see the deep, mean eyes beneath the red *C*. They were piercing and cold, yet the face was expressionless. Who was this guy? A pro, yes--but who?

Joey felt his jaw tighten. Now it was his turn. He would kill the bastard. Hit the accelerator, then the van door. Crush the motherfucker. The tall man anticipated the move to the second. Just as Joey began to flex the muscles in his right leg to punch the heavy machine forward, the lawn man lobbed what looked like a black racquetball toward the limo. Joey watched the round object hit the street, as if in slow motion. It didn't bounce-- just rolled toward Joey. "What's this shit?" he asked.

Racquetballs bounce. He didn't know what it was, but it sure as hell wasn't a racquetball. Then, he had never seen metal compression arrows loaded with explosives, either. This much he knew. The rolling ball meant trouble. He yanked the car into reverse and gunned it backwards. The smell of burning rubber was overwhelming as he backed into black smoke and turned back onto Sheridan to follow the road through the ravines. He'd have to take his chances with the dangerous corkscrew turns. He had no choice. Sweat was running into his eyes, but he didn't have time to wipe it away.

He yanked the gearshift hard into drive and gunned the smoking automobile. It stalled. "Son of a bitch." He fumbled for the starter and turned the key. Nothing. Why nothing? Put it in park, Asshole, he thought, it won't start in Drive.

As he fumbled to get the car started, his eyes moved from the black rolling ball, to the van, to the Cub hat, to the black hands holding the rifle, and back to the starter. His eyes lifted to see the black ball disappear under the car. "MOVE IT JOEY--MOVE IT!" he screamed. The car engine turned over, and he jammed his right foot down hard on the accelerator. The car was riding solely on the smoldering rims and would hardly move carrying its load of weight. He took one more look at the van. Sweat had soaked his body, and a combination of fear, terror, and panic screamed through the hollow halls of his mind. The guy with the Cub hat had thrown another black ball. Or whatever the hell it was. The

thought flashed through his mind that he had always been the hunter; now he was the hunted, and he didn't like it. Before he had time to analyze the revelation, another explosion ripped the front of the car. Joey covered his eyes. Automatically, he ducked his head, but not before he saw the front bumper go flying into the air. From the first black ball, he figured.

He knew he was being forced to take the ravine road, but he didn't give a shit. "Just get the fuck out of here, Joey," he muttered to himself. The other black ball was rolling off course but in front of the car. He thought it would roll across the street. Suddenly, though, as if planned, an explosion erupted twenty feet in front of the struggling limo, covering the car and windshield with a thick oil that evidently came from the contents of the black ball.

Joey's foot was pushing down so hard, trying to gain speed, his leg was throbbing and beginning to cramp. The big engine worked feverishly to reach twenty miles per hour. Gunfire erupted from the van. Joey could see that whoever was shooting was trying hard to break through the right passenger window where the brick was imbedded. The bullets were forming webs on the glass around the imbedded brick, weakening the passenger window.

Almost out of range, he heard the sound of the high-powered rifle again. The bullet shattered the brick and finally blew out the window. He screamed with pain as razor-sharp brick sliced through the right side of his face. He saw his own blood spatter on the windshield, while more poured from his mouth. He spit out a piece of jagged brick that had cut through his right cheek and lodged in his tongue. When he looked at the blood on the inside of the windshield, he saw that the outside of the window was still covered with oil. He could see nothing through the dense film.

The speedometer struggled to reach thirty miles per hour as he topped the first hill leading out of Glencoe and into the ravines. Now he could pick up speed going down the hill--if he could only see. He flicked on the windshield wipers and squirted the cleaner button. The water turned the oil to glue, and the wipers stopped in mid-motion. Eddy groaned in the back seat. He wasn't dead after all.

With a mouth full of blood, Joey's speech was muddled as he yelled back to Lopatta. "Hold on, Eddy. We're going for a ride."

The limo labored down the hill and around the first turn at forty miles per hour. Joey's peripheral vision could see the sparks, flames, and smoke still pouring from what remained of the back tire rims. He had to roll down the window to see where he was going. Gawking at a deep ravine, he stretched his head out the window and could see he was in the wrong lane. The black limo careened off a guard rail and back into its own lane, then worked its way up the next hill and began to roll again at fifty miles down the second hill. He was having trouble controlling the car. Now his face and body were completely soaked with blood and sweat. He knew fear and panic had total control of his scrambled thoughts, and he was trying in vain to muster some sort of reasoning. Everything had

happened so fast. His mind couldn't handle the onslaught; it turned to panic with the overload. No feeling was left in his hands, and his vise-grip slipped and slithered on the steering wheel because of the sweat and blood.

Eddy was now conscious and delirious with pain as he bounced around the back seat like a two-hundred-fifty-pound medicine ball. The dial climbed to sixty by the time the limo hit the bottom of the hill. Then the road turned abruptly to the right and up another hill. His eyes caught the curved *S* on the yellow sign, which read 25 mph. He turned the sharp curve, and the back end began to fishtail. The metal guard rail across the road was coming at him fast. He was in the oncoming lane and thought he had the car under control when he saw a Mercedes approaching. He instinctively turned left to avoid it but knew immediately that he had made a mistake. He was headed for the guard rail and a deep ravine that lay beyond. The sun shining through the trees off of Lake Michigan momentarily blinded him. He pulled his head back inside the car window and covered his eyes with his forearm. He felt the Mercedes clip the rear end of the limo, giving it the extra push it needed to plunge through the rail and start a two-hundred-foot roll down the ravine.

Joey cried out, "We're going over, Eddy, hang on. Shhiiittt." He remembered hitting the steering wheel and feeling a sharp pain tear through his chest. He tumbled around the front seat like a punching bag as the auto plummeted down the steep hill. Head first, the car hit the bottom of the ravine and landed with a sick thud. The crunch of dead branches echoed through the ravine and the auto slowly rolled onto its side. Joey's mind reeled. Was he dead? Was he in shock? The strong odor of burned rubber mixed with gas told him he was alive. Goddamn. I gotta get out of here before she blows, he thought.

He felt warm blood on his face. Fresh blood, oozing from his mouth and head. He reached up from the passenger's side for the open window. This framed a picture of tall trees with spears of sunlight cutting through smoke and fog. As he tried to move, he felt the pain in his chest intensify, and he wanted to scream out.

He gritted his teeth, and grabbed the steering wheel and then the door, pulling himself to a standing position with his head pushed out the window. The gas fumes were strong. He looked back at the smoldering tire. His head was clearing. Son of a bitch. I got to move fast or I'm fried, he thought. Then he thought of Eddy. "Eddy?" No answer. If the explosion and wild ride hadn't killed him, the fall into the ravine must have. He looked into the back seat. Eddy's face was a mass of blood, but he saw that his chest was heaving spasmodically. How was he going to get the fat bastard out? He had to save himself. The damn car was going to go at any time, and he was no hero.

He yelled. "Eddy, can you hear me?"

He heard a groan and painfully pulled himself out the window and stood up on the side of the car looking down into the back seat. He tried the back door. Surprisingly, it opened with only two painful tugs. He looked down into the blood-filled back seat. Lopatta

was crumpled in a heap at the bottom of the car, lying against the door. "Eddy. You got to get out. The car's gonna blow."

He saw that Eddy's eyes were trying to open but were matted shut with blood. One fat hand reached out to him, and he leaned down and took it, but "Cheeks" Lopatta was too heavy. Joey didn't know what to do. Blowing people away was what he was supposed to be doing, not vice versa. "FUCK!" he said out loud as he looked around the damp ravine. "Come on, you fat bastard. Help me to get you out of this death trap."

Joey swore to himself and climbed down into the back seat. He tried to hoist Eddy up through the open door. "Come on, Peckerhead. Grab the goddamn door and pull--or we're both dead."

Both of Eddy's arms reached out. Screaming in pain, he grabbed the rocker panel of the back door with his fat, bloody hands. Joey saw him up close now. What a mess, he thought. That brick must have broken every bone in his face. He pushed and Eddy pulled weakly, but finally the fat mass tumbled out head first. He landed in the thick brush and screamed again as his bald head hit the ground. Joey followed but let his strong arms do the work. Gently, he set himself down on the ground next to the undercarriage of the smoldering auto, and his fat partner. Blood had been running profusely from his own head wounds, and he knew he had some broken ribs. "Come on, Eddy. We gotta get away from the car." He pulled on Eddy's arm, and they both crawled. Like blind men. Feeling their way and stumbling through the heavy brush. About eighty feet from the car, they rolled down into a drainage ditch. Exhausted, they sat in about six inches of running water. Joey leaned his head back, closed his eyes, and held his chest. Each labored breath assailed him with pain, like barbed wire binding his lungs. His mind was near delirium. He could hear sirens in the distance. His eyes, half closed, looked up in the direction of the road. There must be people at the top of the hill. They would get help. Thank God!

His eyes adjusted to the top of the ravine, and he froze. Now he didn't feel any pain. Panic gripped him instead. He could hear and feel his heart thumping. His mouth went dry. The sirens were getting closer, but--standing at the top of the ravine was the tall man wearing his Cub hat. He held a black ball in his hand, flipping it from one to the other. His shaded eyes stared down. Even from the distance, Joey thought he detected a sinister smile. He watched the man as he turned his head in the direction of the approaching sirens. Then he did something strange. He looked back at Joey and motioned with his hand to stay down. At least that's what Joey thought he meant. The man turned his Cub hat around characteristic of a SWAT team and flipped the black ball in the air one more time. As he caught it, he casually tossed it underhanded toward the gas soaked limo.

Joey screamed, "Fuuuck," and dove face down into the drainage ditch, pulling the unconscious Eddy along with him. The explosion sounded like a sonic boom. The earth around him trembled like an earthquake, and remnants of heavy metal, automobile parts, and tree limbs slammed into the ground in all directions. Joey's head was buried in the running water. He pulled his head from the water, gasping. His body shook with pain as

he pulled air into his aching lungs. Then he pushed Eddy over with his foot so he wouldn't drown. As he brushed his long, black hair from his eyes, he looked up to see if the next black ball would be pitched into the drainage ditch. The man was gone. Red and blue lights flashed at the top of the ravine. He pulled himself up to look at the limo. Not much more than a burning metal skeleton left. He felt a tug on his leg. Eddy had forced one eye open. Between the blood and mud, Joey hardly recognized him.

"You okay, Eddy?"

The voice cracked. "I dunno. What the fuck happened?" Joey laid back down in the cool water. This felt good running over his body. "I dunno what happened."

"I think I do, Joey."

"Yeah? What?"

"I think Hogan got pissed off, Joey. I told you he was too quiet for too long."

They fell silent for a moment, then Joey said. "So much for letting sleeping dogs lie."

Almost unconscious but able to mumble, Eddy asked, "Who was the fucker in the van?"

His own words rasped from his tight, dry throat. "Beats the hell out of me, but he had three opportunities to kill us and didn't. He's a pro, and I think he would have killed us if he had it his way. I could see it in his face. Hogan must have told him to just get rid of us."

Just before Eddy passed out, he said. "The boss is going to be pissed off."

Joey didn't answer, just let his mind wander. Fuck the boss. If those were the kind of guys Hogan had on his side, he wanted nothing to do with them.

A voice startled him and pulled him back to the moment in a flash of panic. "Hey, you guys okay?" He reached for his gun that wasn't there.

A paramedic stood over them looking down into the drainage ditch.

"Yeah, Asshole. We're just great. Get us out of this shithole."

* * *

Bo watched John "Snake" Adams lower his hand, palm down, to warn whoever was in the ravine to cover their ass. He did it only once, then lobbed the baseball grenade down the steep hill at the demolished limousine. Adams turned casually and walked to the van as if he had just tossed out stale coffee. He half smiled as he strolled. Bo heard the sirens getting closer.

Clarence "Bear" O'Leary perched in the passenger seat and said, "Hey, Snake, get a move on." Adams stopped just outside the van by the driver's side, looked in, smiled, and said, "One...two...three."

At that moment a frightful explosion shook the quiet hills. Then the gas tank blew, and Bo saw the sky behind Adams flash into flames as he climbed into the driver's seat.

Debris from the explosion fell onto the van, and what was once the trunk of the limo slammed down fifteen feet away. Now it looked more like a three-hundred-pound crushed accordion than an automobile trunk. Bo saw a few trees lift into the air and fall back into the deep crevice. Flames licked at the top of the trees. He said out loud, "Jesus Christ! That plastique is strong."

Bear turned around in his seat and smiled at Bo. "That's just a little C-4, Bo. Mixed with some of the Snake's special ingredients. A little bit like the booze you drink."

Adams started the van and Bo heard the powerful 460 engine grumble perfectly. "Snake" put one hand out, palm up, toward "Bear." The Bear slapped the hand hard. Bo slapped the hand and said, "Do you think maybe we should roll now, John?"

Snake looked over his shoulder and said, "Bo, we're eyewitnesses. The cops will probably want a statement."

Bear leaned over, his big black face full of sarcasm. "Move your ass, you stubborn son of a bitch."

Adams gunned the van. Gravel shot out from the tires, mixing with the falling branches, dirt, and pieces of automobile. Just as they reached the top of the same hill the limo had been unable to negotiate, three squad cars and a paramedic mobile raced down the hill past the van. Bo looked at the speedometer. Adams was going about five miles over the speed limit--not too slow, not too fast. The job was completed. Now, as unobtrusively as possible, get back to home base, clean your weapons, and wait for further instruction.

The van turned west on Tower Road, took side roads through the posh suburb, and came back to Sheridan Road north of Hogan's house. Bo watched as two fire trucks raced south on Sheridan. Adams pulled out behind them, followed two blocks, and turned into the side street that led to Hogan's back entrance.

O'Leary pushed a five-button combination on the remote control, and the back gates opened. He pushed another button, and one of the garage doors to the coach house opened. Adams eased the van into the garage. The door closed behind them. Bo put away the explosives: glue, oil, C-4 plastique, blasting gelatin, and a variety of other materials he used to fill the grenades.

He looked around the back of the van. A mini arsenal. A gun rack was attached to one wall with all the newest weaponry available. Bo feasted his eyes on the handguns: Smith & Wessons of all sizes and calibers, Brownings, Mausers, three Walthers, a Makarov, various size Berettas. Magnums: 357's, .44's, .22's, .41's. His eyes scanned further back where more rubber holders secured the automatic and semiautomatic machine guns: two AK 47's, two Uzis, two Colt AR-15's, a number of Savage shotguns, a Kar 98k, machine pistols, and modern guns Bo had never seen before.

The other side looked like a small section of safety-deposit boxes all different sizes and marked accordingly. Wire, detonators, transmitters, batteries, shells for every weapon in the van, six different types of grenades, terminal switches, acid, medical supplies. At

the mere push of a button under the dash, all of this could be hidden by an electric wooden shade housed in the roof of the van.

Bo said to Bear, "Give me your cross bow and I'll put it away." Bear obliged and handed Bo the miniature bow, a magnifying scope attached to its top. Three razor-sharp metal arrows were attached with a hard-rubber holder. Bo touched the tip of one of the arrows, and instantly it brought blood to his finger. He put the cross bow in the rack next to an AK-47. "Johnny Boy, you have anything to put away?" Without looking, Adams flipped a small black grenade over his shoulder. Bo almost fell out of his seat trying to catch it before it hit the floor.

"You crazy bastard. I wouldn't drop a bottle of whiskey, but I'm damn likely to drop one of these." Bo shook his head, and the two in front laughed.

"What are you doing with an extra, anyway?"

Snake looked back at Bo, as if he were talking about adding more ketchup to french fries. "I wasn't sure if I was going to kill those two guys or not. That grenade was for them."

Bo looked at the black "sleeper" grenade, eight times more powerful than the standard. Detonation time: six seconds after it hit the ground. "When did you decide to follow Hogan's instruction and not kill them?"

Snake turned his Cub cap back around, pushed open the van door, and stepped out. He shut the door, turned, and leaned his elbows on the open window. "I just decided a few seconds ago." Then he laughed out loud, as did Bear. The long, pink scar wrinkled on Bear's black face. Bo smiled and thought to himself that these two guys were his life blood. They had been to hell and back together and knew each other's thoughts and actions before they themselves did. If Hogan were to get into trouble, it wouldn't be because of Snake and Bear. Another siren screamed down Sheridan past the coach house.

Bo caught Snake looking at him. He knew the look. "What's the matter, John? Everything went smooth."

Snake shook his head from side to side. "Yeah. Everything went fine." He thought for a second. "You should have let me kill the bastards. You know they'll be back. Maybe not the same two guys, and probably not for awhile, but they'll be back--and probably in numbers."

Bo nodded his head in agreement. "Yeah, they'll be back, but we'll be ready for them. And we won't be nice guys next time." Bo placed his hand out in front of him, and both men slapped it in friendship and brotherhood.

* * *

Michael looked at his watch. Nine forty-eight. Msgr. McFadden had just finished another lethargic sermon on the Holy Eucharist and what an important part it played in our daily life but especially on Mother's Day. So many sheep, so few shepherds, he thought. And

the shepherds the Church had were so inept he didn't know how they stayed in business. He seldom let his religious feelings be known to others. He would follow the traditions of his heritage only out of respect for his dead parents because it wasn't really a big deal, going to church once a week. Though he found it much more comforting and far easier to pray and meditate sitting in an empty church after work than it was sitting at Mass on Sundays with hundreds of people mouthing rote script. He thought of the cheerleader chants. "Stand up. Sit down. Fight. Fight. Fight." The only thing missing was the football.

Common sense told him there was a God. Intelligence told him there was a God. And often in his life, he had experienced the feelings of a spiritual presence. But he didn't believe that God was as complicated as the Roman theologians would have their flock believe. In fact, it was man who was complicated, with his confounded emotions, prejudices, and self-deceptive rationalizations. God was simple and quiet and peaceful. It didn't matter to him if Christ was the Son of God or just one hell of a Great Guy. Christ said it all, and so simply: "Love God and your neighbor." Unfortunately, Christ added, "as you love yourself." Michael thought, therein lies the problem. Many people not only did not love themselves. They despised themselves. Therefore, they despised their neighbor. The more perceptive statement by Christ was, "Do unto others as you would have them do unto you." Much more just, he thought. He was a Christian. He believed in the simple words of Christ. He did not believe the complex interpretations that man had given Christ's words. He did not believe an Infinite God would condemn a finite being to eternal punishment. The bad guy might get the basement in the mansion of Heaven. If there was such a place. But to send somebody south forever didn't seem to be God's *modus operandi*. He often wondered about the poor Catholic bastard who knowingly ate a hot dog at a Cub game on a Friday and died of a heart attack in the bottom of the ninth. Having committed a mortal sin, he was on his way to everlasting fire. Then, forty-five minutes later Rome decided it was no longer a mortal sin to eat meat on Friday. *No longer a mortal sin!* No longer would a soul burn in hell for eternity. Talk about bad timing for the guy who ate the hot dog at the ball game. What nonsense!

His thoughts were interrupted by Msgr. McFadden. "Let us all pray now for those who are sick and who have gone ahead of us, for our special intentions, and let us not forget the mothers of the congregation."

Michael bowed his head, put his arm around Angela on one side of him and Martin on the other, and prayed to himself: "Whoever is listening, I implore you to protect my family." He held his two children close, and at that instant there was a not-so-far-off explosion. He visualized a black limousine on fire.

The Msgr. looked up from the altar, at first unsure of himself. Then he smiled and said, "That's either a sonic boom or somebody in this church hasn't been to confession for awhile." The congregation chuckled respectfully. Michael could sense Maria's eyes on him, but he feigned meditation by lowering his head and closing his eyes.

Fourteen minutes later, after the consecration, the congregation stood to say the Our Father, "Who art in Heaven, hallowed be thy name...Give us this day our daily bread, and forgive us our trespasses as we forgive those who trespass against us..."At that moment, the unmistakable sound of an explosion, closer this time, shook the church and cracked two stained-glass windows on the Virgin Mary's side. Msgr. McFadden looked a bit shaken. He just stared at the two cracked windows, then said, "I hope that was an act of God, my children."

Michael smiled to himself and thought, in a way, it was. "Do unto others as they have done unto you. Live by the sword, die by the sword."

"Let us offer each other the sign of peace."

He leaned and kissed his children, then turned to Maria on the other side of Angela and Joseph. He reached for her hand. Her eyes searched deep into his. Smiling, he leaned over and kissed her on the cheek. "Peace be with you, Honey. Happy Mother's Day."

Her eyes, dark and perceptive, moved slowly away from him, showing no emotion but total understanding. As she knelt for the preparation of Communion and closed her eyes, he watched her profile. What a wonderful, beautiful woman, he thought. Now maybe the house would be safe. Getting rid of the limo was only the first step in his plan. Now the hard work would begin.

After Communion, the Msgr. ended the Mass with the words, "Go in peace, my children, and God be with you all." The Msgr.'s eyes swept the crowd and seemed to lock on Michael, who was a head taller than those around him. At first the priest seemed a little nervous. Maybe it was the look he saw on Michael's face. They both nodded, and Michael genuflected, blessed himself, and followed his family from the church.

Outside, Michael couldn't help noticing the strong, acrid stench in the air that mingled with the smell of burning wood. Parishioners were pointing down Tower Road toward the lake and the billowing black smoke that was surrounded by blue sky. The early morning eye of the sun was also curious to see what foolishness mankind was now doing to his beautiful earth. Michael smiled and blessed himself.

TWENTY-SEVEN

Devil or Angel

After a long, weary trading day in the bond pit, Michael fixed himself a scotch. In his plush office, he would relax until the next contest began. He sensed this would be soon. A mellow creation of his favorite classical music played softly in the background, Tchaikovsky's 1812 Overture. He leaned his head back on the cushion of the comfortable leather desk chair. His eyes closed as he let the music soften the hard attitudes that flowed deep in the black, canyon rivers of his mind. The amber, iced scotch gently rolled from side to side in a cut-glass tumbler as he swiveled his chair slowly back and forth. He enjoyed about fifteen minutes of rest before the receptionist's buzz interrupted his semi-conscious state. He pivoted to reach for the end button on the fourteen-button phone.

"Mr. Peter Lewis is here to see you, Mr. Hogan. Shall I send him in?"

Michael smiled to himself, "I've been expecting him. Yes, thank you. Send him in, Margaret."

He set his drink down on his paper-strewn desk. Turning off the green screen of his Quotron, he swiveled to look out one of the large windows housed in two walls of the expensive modern office. The setting sun reflected off the gray buildings across LaSalle Street and painted them a dying, molten-rock color. The sun's last kiss of the day would give way to the chilly caress of the late spring air accompanied by the natural chill of the heartless city.

He heard the office door open quietly. The voice tone came in a soft question, "Mike?" When he turned quickly, Pete Lewis was standing in the doorway, attempting in vain to conceal a look of trepidation. Michael reached for his scotch and raised the glass to Pete. "Come on in, Pete. Good to see ya. Want a drink?"

Pete closed the heavy door gently and headed for the bar. The newspaper, clutched under his arm, he now flipped on the couch, as he set his briefcase next to a leaded-glass-topped coffee table. "Yeah, I'll have a beer. Do you have any Canadian brew?"

Michael let his eyes wrinkle in cynicism. "I buy American, Pete. There's Bud and Miller in there, and maybe a few bottles of Michelob."

Pete opened the cooler and grabbed a Bud. "Yeah. You buy American. Everything but your clothes, cars, and jewelry."

Michael pushed his chair back and flung his legs atop his desk, crossing his ankles. "All my wife's choices, Pete. Maria sets my clothes out in the evening, makes sure I put them on in the morning, hopes I keep them on during the day, and helps me undress

at night--that part I don't mind. If it was up to me, I would come to work unshaven, in jeans, a comfortable cotton shirt, and a dirty pair of sneakers."

Pete took a long swallow of beer and plopped onto the white tufted couch. "She has good taste in clothes. Can't say much for her taste in men."

Michael saw that any apprehension Pete might have had disappeared with his claim to the Budweiser, the comfort of the couch, and the warm atmosphere of the office. He crumpled up a loose-leaf paper on his desk and threw it at Lewis. "I intrigue her, Pete. She never knows what I'm going to do next. She says the only thing predictable about me is my unpredictability."

Pete picked up the newspaper, then looked up with clear, perceptive eyes. "Speaking of predictability, have you read the newspaper today?"

Michael knew exactly what Pete referred to. The next contest had begun. Michael snapped his mind and senses to an alert state without changing his expression. He knew Pete was a master at perceiving mood changes and drawing information from facial expressions and body movements. He had been trained to watch for a blink, a sigh, or an unorthodox move at the wrong time by a man he was ready to quiz. Their eyes met, and Michael answered casually, "I read the sports page and the markets. The rest of the paper depresses me. Why? Did I miss something?"

Pete's eyes searched his face for a moment, probably watching for some sign of guilt or acknowledgment. But Michael remained in complete control, showing only curiosity. Pete looked down, licked his thumb, and opened the *Sun-Times*. Michael took a silent breath.

Pete's eyes snapped quickly upward, "You wouldn't happen to know anything about this, would you?" His head bowed again, and he began to read out loud:

> *"Mother's Day, in the peaceful, affluent suburbs of Glencoe and Winnetka, started off with what many residents described as the beginning of World War Three. At approximately ten a.m., an automobile driven by Joseph Grollo lost control while trying to negotiate the sharp ravine curves that lie between the two wealthy suburbs along Sheridan Road. The automobile, a large limousine, crashed through a metal barrier and exploded at the bottom of a ravine just north of Tower Road.*

> *"Grollo and his passenger, Edward Lopatta, were rushed to Evanston Hospital. Both men are in the intensive care unit, in stable condition. Both are suffering from internal injuries, and facial and neck wounds.*

"A police spokesperson said that Mr. Grollo of Chicago was apparently driving his passenger, Lopatta, of Northbrook, to O'Hare International Airport when his brakes failed.

"There were, however, conflicting reports from two eyewitnesses. Adam Silvers said he was doing yard work at his home when he heard an explosion. Silvers stated that at first he thought nothing of it, but five minutes later he saw a black limousine pass his home and head down into the winding ravines going south on Sheridan Road. Silvers said it reminded him of a scene from a movie. The rear of the car was on fire, as were both rear tires, and it looked as though the auto had already been in an accident as the whole right side of the car was smashed in.

"Another witness, Dr. Sidney Levine, whose two-day-old Mercedes struck the rear of the limousine driven by Grollo, stated that there was nothing apparently wrong with the car when he approached it near the bottom of one of the hills. Levine stated that the other auto was traveling at a high rate of speed and crossed directly in front of him. Levine said that he swerved to miss the large car but Grollo's auto was in the wrong lane when the two cars collided. The crash was evidently enough to push the limo onto the shoulder of the road, through the barrier and down into a deep ravine. Levine stated that there was absolutely nothing wrong with the limousine when he hit the rear of the auto except that it was going quite fast, refuting Silver's statement.

"According to Levine, a green pickup truck stopped to help but drove off after the woman driver of the truck probably assumed there was nothing she could do. Levine called it a miracle that anyone was able to survive the crash and explosion.

"Police officials are investigating another explosion that occurred six blocks away from the crash at approximately the same time. North Shore Police Captain William Johnson stated that the two explosions were merely coincidence. Foul play did not appear to be a factor in either case."

Michael felt his face flush with the inaccurate information, but forced his mind to remain calm. He swung his legs down from his desk and propped his arms in front of him, cupping his scotch with both hands, sipping at it slowly, keeping the glass in front of his lips so Pete couldn't read his expression. Both men's eyes met and drilled at each other like lasers. The office was as still as a graveyard except for the classical music, which now brought on the sound of suspense rather than calm.

Michael's mind quickened, and his senses sharpened. In spite of the phony information the press had received and the fact that Pete intuitively knew that Michael's men had taken care of the limo, so what? He still wasn't sure if Pete Lewis, former CIA, present FBI agent, was on his side or if he was a plant by the Assistant Director of the FBI, John Simpson. He didn't read things that way, but Lewis could be an FBI pawn reporting all his actions and attitudes. Michael knew Simpson didn't trust him, any more than he trusted the two-faced bastard.

He set his drink down next to the Quotron and broke the silence. "That's why I only read the sports page and markets, Pete. The rest of the news is depressing."

Pete surprised Michael. Casually, he leaned back and rested his left arm on the back of the expensive couch. His young altar-boy face remained expressionless. Michael knew they were playing cat and mouse. "You know all about this, don't you, Mike?"

"I heard the explosion while I was in church. Everybody in church thought it was a sonic boom, including the priest."

Pete's words came fast. "Except you! You knew exactly what it was." Then his voice gained volume. "Sonic boom, my ass. You knew Lynch and his boys were going to take out the limo as sure as you knew I'd be knocking on your door ten minutes ago. Why the fuck didn't you let me in on it? Were you afraid I'd tell Simpson? Remember, I'm the guy who saved your ass from the Fat Man's men in the garage."

Michael picked up a number-two chart pencil and pointed it at Pete. He felt like a hawk ready to swoop up a field mouse. "You saved my ass, Pete, because you were instructed to. Not because you were my friend. You didn't even know me then. I have asked you and your FBI gurus in Washington to get rid of what I considered to be a danger to my family. Despite a hundred-million-dollar life-insurance policy on myself and my family, your organization treats a dangerous situation as if it's a fishing trip. Well, fuck your casual methods, Pete. I'll ask once for help from the Feds. If I don't get it, I'll take care of the problem myself." He hesitated a moment, then popped the question: "How do I know I can trust you, Pete?"

Pete slowly removed his arm from the top of the sofa and sighed. "Mike, you're right. We haven't known each other very long. I don't blame you for your hesitation in trusting me because I am a federal agent. But you're the man with insight; you can tell if I'm bullshitting you. I care about you. I care about me, and I care about the investigation. You've got to trust me. I can get you information that you are going to need. It seems as if we're running two investigations here. Yours and the government's. I don't give a shit--

that's okay with me. But goddammit, man, we have to trust each other. If that's the case, and you are doing your own thing, I have solid friends in high places where we can get readouts, records, and cross-references on anybody you wish. I can tell you what the bad guys had for breakfast, lunch and dinner, and how many times they fart each day. Without me you are nothing but a flea on the tail of a mean, government bear."

Michael snapped the pencil in two and threw it on his desk. "You didn't answer my question, Pete. How do I know I can trust you? You could feed me information that's worthless, and I wouldn't know the difference. What do I know about government readouts? The Feds print more lies than they do truth. We've been through this before. Your Washington prima donnas speak with forked tongue."

He saw Pete's face turn crimson and his lips an angry gray. His eyes narrowed, and his jaw muscles tightened. "Listen, Asshole. I don't speak with forked tongue. Why do you think the story in the newspaper about Sunday's explosion is so distorted?"

He listened to Pete correct the distorted news article. "An eyewitness, Dr. Levine, said the black limousine was completely intact when it actually looked like it had been through a war. The same eyewitness, Dr. Levine, said the other vehicle that stopped was a green pickup truck when it was actually a white van carrying Lynch, O'Leary, and Adams--and that the driver of the pickup was a woman when it was actually Snake Adams. And good ol' Doc Levine said nothing about anybody lobbing a black-leather 'sleeper' grenade down into the ravine to finish the job."

Michael felt his defenses loosen, and he sat back in his chair and studied Pete. He wondered how he knew so much when he wasn't even there. Pete spoke curtly. "How about the police chief saying the two explosions weren't related? Do you think your local law-enforcement agency is stupid?"

Michael pushed some papers away from in front of him and leaned forward. He felt his eyes blink nervously now. He knew Bill Johnson, Captain of the North Suburban Police Department. A sharp, clean cop. "Okay, hot shot, why did Johnson tell the press there was no correlation between the two explosions when it was obvious they were connected?"

Pete hissed out like an angry snake. "Because I talked to him before the press did. I showed him my badge and asked for his cooperation in a government investigation that involved North Shore drug trafficking. The man's a real gentlemen. He asked no questions, didn't pull any bullshit about trading a favor for a favor or trespassing on his jurisdiction. Said he would be happy to help out in whatever capacity he could. He just wants to be kept informed."

Michael stared back at Pete for what seemed to be five minutes, but was probably only seconds. He analyzed Pete's eyes and face. Even his anger. He looked for and found sincerity when Pete continued. "One more thing, Mike. Do you want me to tell you what the Snake was wearing? A Hawaiian shirt to cover his gun; jeans, old tennis shoes, and a Cub baseball cap."

Michael felt his lower jaw grow heavy. His mouth would have fallen open had he not been in control. He forced his teeth together to tighten his jaw. He had seen Adams before he left for church, and that was exactly what Snake was wearing. "How did you know that?"

Pete downed his beer and threw the can, with disdain, into the corner by the bar, where it clanked and spun on the Italian tile floor. He glared at Michael. His look was challenging and angry. "Because I'm Dr. Levine, Mike. Do you hear me? I'm Dr. Levine, the good doctor who smashed a nice, new Mercedes against the rear end of the limo, giving it the extra push it needed to go over the embankment. Do you think those orders came from Washington? Do you think I'm going to have fun explaining to Simpson that I leased a fifty-thousand-dollar automobile and smashed it up two days after I leased the goddamn thing? How do you think he's going to react when he finds out that the guy I'm in charge of took it upon himself to blow the front of his neighbor's house off in order to move a car? Did you take a good look at that house? All the windows in the place--gone. All the trees in the yard--gone. A three foot brick wall in front of the house--gone. Simpson can't stand me as it is. This will really cap it. Just another fuck-up for Pete Lewis!"

He watched Pete's anger turn to frustration, as Pete laid his head back on the couch and covered his face with both hands. Michael's head bobbed approvingly. Pete had proven himself. He could be trusted. If he was telling the truth, Simpson would have Pete's ass in a sling. And just after he got his Special Agent status back.

Michael rose, picked up his glass, and walked over to the bar. He leaned down, retrieved the beer can Pete had thrown, and tossed it into the nearby wastebasket. He poured himself a Black Label and grabbed another beer from the refrigerator for Pete. He walked over to Pete, who was breathing heavy between his hands, still covering his face. He looked down at his long, blond hair that just touched his black windbreaker and said, "Hey Doc Levine. How about a beer?"

Pete lowered his hands. Michael saw the sincerity in his eyes. His face had returned to its natural color except for a few white finger marks, which were quickly filling with a healthy pink. He reached up and took the beer from Michael. "Does this mean I pass your trustworthy test, Asshole?"

Michael felt himself smile, and he clinked his glass against Pete's raised beer can. "Ya pass, G-Man. You do nice work. But you don't look much like a doctor to me." Michael felt a friendship forming. He sensed a man he could now trust.

* * *

Pete felt that he had finally made it through to Michael. He could sense that Michael didn't know exactly how Bo and his boys got rid of Grollo and Lopatta. He only knew that the job was done, and that was all that mattered to Michael. He was strange to Pete. He was

usually full of warmth and concern, helping street people, people in trouble. Black or white. Color didn't matter to Michael. He knew he had a soft spot in his heart for Viet Nam vets--all veterans, as far as that went. He must feel they could be trusted among other men. He showed no prejudice, and he gave with no expectation of return.

But now, Pete saw another side of Michael. A rare but truly cunning coldness ran through his eyes. This scared the hell out of Pete. As much as Michael tried to remain in control, and he was good at it, Pete was learning to read him like a book.

Pete saw that even with his extraordinary discipline, Michael assumed an attitude and outer visage of a competitive animal ready for the challenge of talents. Michael had been blessed, or cursed, with the intrigue of danger. Whether it was financial or physical. He felt a high by walking the razor's edge. The expression on Michael's face wasn't fear, and it wasn't anger. Rather, it was cold indifference. Deep-seated revenge that had been lying dormant for so long had probably turned Michael's internal blisters to callouses. Pete had seen it before, but never in a man like Michael. This was the kind of attitude characteristic of a man who could kill another human being with ease--no remorse. Then walk to the kitchen, eat a ham sandwich, go to bed, and sleep like a baby. Pete knew that if Bo hadn't taken out the limo, Michael would have. The job might not have been as effective, but he was a man called intrepid when it came to protecting his family.

Pete also saw the challenge in Michael's face. A contest. A new game in town. Gambling with life was the ultimate game--it always had been. Now, this new friend of his was ready, willing, and able to gamble the limit: his life.

Pete spoke softly: "Watch yourself, Michael. Killing is addictive." With cold eyes, Michael ignored the remark.

Pete reached over for the newspaper and opened it to page five. "Mike, do you know a bartender by the name of Gino Corillo?"

"Sure, he's one of the bartenders at the Trader's Lounge at the Mercantile. Why?"

"Well, it seems he was found in the elevator of his apartment building on Clark Street last night with his ears cut off. He's in the psycho ward at the Martha Washington Hospital, in shock. Nearly dead from fright, and won't speak to anybody."

Michael's face went blank. Pete couldn't read it. That cold look again, Pete thought. "I know nothing about poor Gino's ears." Michael said it with no compassion--a "so-what" attitude. Most people would have shown some sort of emotional response, but not Michael. Pete thought this was one of those times Michael's soul was cold. All that was missing was the ham sandwich. Pete let the newspaper rest on his lap, and he looked at Michael. "Cutting ears off was a Viet Nam hobby of some of our hard core troop. And you have a few of those men working for you. I just thought maybe this Tony guy might have pissed you or one of your boys off."

Michael shrugged and took a swallow of scotch. "Do we have business, Pete? Or are you going to read the rest of the newspaper to me?"

Pete sighed, looked down at page five of the *Sun-Times*, and raised his eyebrows. He folded the newspaper and placed it on the couch beside him. "We have business, Mike, but not before you shoot straight with me. Who cut up the bartender?"

* * *

Michael felt the chill run through him, but he was a determined man now. A man in a contest with professionals. He would be damned if he'd let his inside feelings show on the outside. But Pete was right. He needed him. They needed each other. "Pete, I honestly don't know who de-eared Corillo. He and Lynch hated each other. Bo said the prick was spying on us and listening in on our conversations at the Merc bar. That's where I usually meet Bo when we talk business. Bo saw Tony make a phone call every time we finished a meeting. He swore he'd find out who Corillo was working for."

Michael finished his drink and set it on the heavy glass coffee table that separated them. "I would expect we have that information now. I guess Bo persuaded Corillo to tell him who his contact was."

"That's a pretty cruel way of extracting information from someone, don't you think?"

Michael's body tensed slightly, then relaxed. "No more cruel than blowing a man's ear drums and sinus bags all over the street trying to get information."

Pete meshed his fingers together, then leaned forward. "No, I guess it isn't. But I deal with hard-core drug dealers. This was a simple-ass bartender who was probably just making a few hundred extra a week to keep an eye on you."

"That was his mistake, Pete. I'm sorry, but we're dealing with high class crooks and killers. The sooner they learn that I'm not a guy to be fucked with, the easier my life will be."

He watched Pete lower his head and shake it with futility. "Mike, these guys are like the Chinese. You kill one hundred of them, and one hundred more come...You kill them, and one hundred more come, ad infinitum."

Michael allowed a sardonic curl to ease onto his lips. "Then I'll hire a few more men. There is no just war that can't be won. Manpower doesn't win wars anymore. Nor does technology. We've seen that in Viet Nam with the Americans, and we're seeing it in Afghanistan with the Russians. Purpose, Pete. Unadulterated purpose, patience, and intelligence wins wars now. Power and money give goons a false sense of security. We plow into Viet Nam with all our powerful weapons and our strong, handsome men. The Viet Cong dig five thousand miles of tunnels, kick our ass with pea shooters, kill over sixty thousand of our guys, and send us home mentally and physically crippled. We were in somebody else's backyard and didn't belong there. We can't force our way of life on another culture any more than the Russians can force their culture on us. Democracy is a philosophy of attraction, not attrition. This would have caught on all over the world years

ago, if our politicians would have allowed it. Now, the American way is catching on, despite the politicians. Pete, I'm trying to make a point."

"That is?"

"Stay out of my back yard and off my property. As small and unimportant as I may be, don't threaten those I love, or I'll expose my unadulterated purpose. Then I'll kill you."

Pete said, "I follow what you're saying, but you're getting off the subject, Mike. Right now, I'm not interested in international democracy. I'm interested in putting some bad guys away and keeping you alive in the process, not starting a goddamn war in Chicago, let alone Glencoe, Illinois."

He wanted out of the argument. Pete was on his side, and that's all that mattered. Pete was a tough, intelligent cop who would watch his back when he was away from home. That's what he needed.

He spoke into the tense atmosphere of the room. "Incidentally, Pete. Don't walk around my back yard without letting Snake or Bear know about it. The whole forest is covered with pressure-detecting grids and sensors. Your weight will signal an alarm in the coach house, and you'll be back in Viet Nam in thirty seconds."

Pete's eyes widened, and his forehead turned into a mass of wrinkles. "Are you crazy, Mike? What happens if some doped-up kid wanders onto your property some night and thinks he's a kangaroo? You going to kill him? We don't need a murder charge pinned on you along with destroying the neighborhood."

Michael was calm but stern. "He won't be killed. He may lose his ears, but he won't be killed. If I have trouble at the house, they will come in numbers, not one at a time unless it's a one man hit. It would be a lot easier to hit me away from the house than inside the house."

Michael could see that his coolness about death and dying was confusing Pete. Pete just stared at him with a look of disbelief in what he was hearing. He didn't know if Pete was trying to think of something to say or if he was trying to sort out what had just been said.

Finally, Pete threw his hands into the air and said, "I thought this assignment was going to be dull, white collar--catch the cheating commodity brokers. Instead, I end up with a lunatic. His coach house full of killer mercenaries, his back yard wired for intruders, and his best buddy cutting ears off of bartenders. Is your back yard mined too?"

Michael pursed his lips in thought and cocked his head slightly. "I don't think so, but don't take any chances!"

Pete sat back, exasperated. "You're beautiful, Mike. You know, the first kill is the hardest. After that it becomes easy. I'd hate to see you turn into a killer. You're too good of a human being."

Michael watched him for a moment in silence. He'd never really thought about actually killing anybody. Commodity brokers weren't physically dangerous. The men they

worked for, though, would be trouble. The men with the money. But he knew he could kill. And would--if he was forced to.

Pete rubbed his lips and chin in thought, then looked at Michael. "Okay, Tarzan. Have it your way. What will be, will be. Kill or be killed. I can see you've got your ass pretty well covered at home. I'll stick with you on this. But you know if Washington finds out I allowed this or even had any knowledge of you forming your own little army, I'm out of a job."

Michael finally let himself show a little emotion and grunted with a smile, "Thanks, Pete. You're the guy I want on the outside."

"Oh, you're a real charmer, you are. How can I ever thank you?"

Michael turned serious again. "Just watch my back, I'll take care of my front. If you lose your job, you can always come to work with me. You'll make ten times what you make with the Bureau."

Pete took a final swig of his beer and said, "I don't know if you're devil or angel, Mike."

Michael finally laughed, and it felt good to him. "Probably a little of both. Aren't we all?"

TWENTY-EIGHT

The Victims

The soft music brought a sense of calm back into Michael's office. He went to the bar, refreshed his drink, and pulled out another beer for Pete. Pete had moved to a small antique conference table near one of the large windows that looked out onto the steel city. "Where do you want to start first, Mike?"

Michael placed the beer in front of Pete, went to his desk, retrieved a legal size manila folder about two inches thick, and brought it to the table. "I want you to work with me, Pete, on the trading floor--in the pits. You'll have to buy a membership, which is three hundred sixty thousand. It'll take you about a month to become a member and pass through the different committees. In the meantime, you have an orientation class to attend and will work as my phoneman and runner until you're cleared for membership. Then we go to work."

Pete moved nervously in his chair. "Mike, you're forgetting those two jerks in the garage who saw me. If they don't know I'm a Fed, at least they'll know I'm a bodyguard."

"Fuck them! First of all, I don't think they had that good a look at you. Even if they did, they'll expect somebody to be backing me up after that little ruckus. You're perfect for this job. It's not uncommon for a big broker to have a heavyweight stand alongside him, both in the pits and out. If they remember you, the word will spread fast that you blow hands and eardrums away. Nobody will come at us head-on."

Pete sighed. "Yeah, that's what I'm afraid of. I don't like amateurs coming at me from any direction."

Michael felt intent now. All business. "I'll clear you tomorrow as an employee of mine, and you start the next day. Application for membership is in this folder. Fill it out and give it back to me tomorrow with the application fee. All I have to know is what name you're going to use."

He watched Pete as he wiped the sweat down the can of beer with his thumbs. "Pete Alexander is my undercover name."

Michael's eyes lifted in sarcasm. "As in Alexander the Great?"

Pete grumbled. "No, as in Alexander the Asshole."

Michael opened the folder and read from notes he had been jotting down since he left his meeting at Langley. "How many agents are going to be involved in our day-to-day operation?"

Pete's response came slowly. "Simpson said he would give us six agents to use on the trading floor and in the offices of suspect offenders."

Michael's back stiffened, and he reared back. "Six?? I said I needed ten good men to get the job done."

Pete shot words back defensively. "Simpson's a prick, Mike. He said the payments on your insurance policy prohibited him from giving us any more than six agents, and two of them are women. He's placing six agents at the New York Exchanges also, but he doesn't have an inside man--they're going in blind."

Michael said with angry determination, "I don't give a shit about New York. Who are the agents coming here?"

As Pete began to speak, he avoided Michael's eyes. "Well, Randy Harris. Young, but a sharp kid; Joe Fitzsimmons, also young, just so-so with the smarts; Ted Tully, he's about my age, sharp guy who has been around. And...uh...Barry Kane..."

Michael felt anger warm his body and knew his face was turning red. "You hesitate with Barry Kane. Why?"

Pete dropped his hand to the table, raised his left eyebrow, and said, "Kane is soft as mush. He's screwed up more assignments than I care to think about. The dummy even forgets what alias name he's using."

Michael exploded and stood up, knocking the chair back against the heavy glass window railing. "And the women. Who are they?"

Pete didn't hesitate. "Colleen McFadden and Samantha Winters." Michael's hawk eyes narrowed with indignation as he watched Pete bring his left hand to his chin and cup it as though to ward off a punch. He shot his words out. "That son of a bitch. What are we supposed to do with them?" Pete's answer was again defensive. "You knew the girls were going to be on the job."

Michael slammed his fist down on the table, sloshing his drink over its side and moving Pete back in his chair. "Goddamn it, Pete. I asked for ten good men, and that was the deal. Five to go undercover at the Board of Trade and five at the Mercantile. The girls were to be extras to help coordinate information. They sure as hell aren't going to work the pits."

Pete added with hesitation, "Simpson...is...uh...counting you and me as two more of his men, bringing the total to eight. He figures..."

Michael snapped out. "I can count. He figures I asked for ten good men. He's giving me eight, counting you and me and two women. Well, I don't work for the bastard, and he's not about to live rent free in my head and play ping-pong with my emotions, let alone my life."

He turned abruptly to look at the dark city with the secret white eyes of neighboring windows staring back at him with apathy. He tried to clear his mind of anger and sort out the players quickly. He leaned his forehead against the window and watched the night traffic pass slowly below him. The scene looked like a huge video game. His unconscious mind turned to Samantha. God, it would be good to see her again, he thought. A picture of her tan face, her soft, blond hair, her silk blouse with the protruding nipples

flowed like clear spring water through his mind. In less than a second he was making love to her, deep love, passionate love. He felt bad because he had been ignoring her, not answering her phone calls, answering her curtly at meetings. The last thing he needed was to have the Federal Bureau of Investigation realize their key civilian had fallen for one of their key agents. He didn't want to hurt the blond beauty, but he would try to explain later.

"Mike? Hey, Michael, come back to earth. Simpson's not our only resource." He turned and heard the music first, then saw Pete looking at him quizzically. "What...what did you say, Pete?" He felt calm beginning to return.

"I said Simpson is not our only source of manpower. The U.S. Attorney, Tony Lorenzo, said he'll give us back-up, but we have to break the ice and get the ball rolling first."

Michael sat back down, reached for his scotch, and looked into the amber liquid. "He's working directly with Simpson, isn't he?"

"In a manner of speaking, yes. But I don't think he likes the prick any more than we do."

He swirled his drink until it almost touched the rim. Then he looked at Pete. "He might not like Simpson, but he needs him if he wants this sting to go into his political portfolio. That means we can't completely trust him. And if we can't completely trust him, we can't trust him at all."

Pete nodded his head. "True."

Michael continued. "But neither one of them gets jackshit unless we give it to them, do they?"

Pete had relaxed proportionately with Michael's mood. "True again."

"Then maybe we should just give them some jackshit until we have hold of some of the big fish."

Pete took a deep breath, cocked his head, and asked, "Mike, am I missing something here? Aren't we all after the same thing? To get the bad guys?"

"Yeah, Pete. We're all after the bad guys, but I'm not after the good-bad guys."

Pete's face showed his confusion. "I am missing something."

Michael considered for a moment, reassembling his thoughts, then spoke quietly. "There are a lot of guys who steal on the trading floor. Most of them are guilty of minor thievery. You know, they steal a few hundred here, five hundred, a thousand there. That's like taking the paper clips and staplers from the office. Those are the good-bad guys. They not only are allowed to steal, but they have also been taught to steal by their superiors who have total knowledge of what's going on. They give their unquestioning absolution to this day-in-and-day-out practice."

He ran the back of his hand over his chin, hearing the day's growth. This reminded him that it was getting late. "Pete, these guys are literally going to be the innocent victims of this investigation or this sting operation or whatever you want to call it. They steal because it's okay to steal here. The rule book doesn't say that 'you can steal.'

But the Exchange officials say," his voice turned sarcastic, "it's okay to steal because we make the rules, and we steal, and it's the only club in the country which allows stealing. However, if a customer from the outside complains because a broker is caught stealing, then we're going to have to warn you not to do it again. And if you do it again, we, the upper echelon of the Exchange, will have to warn you again and maybe even fine you a few dollars. Maybe even suspend you a few days, to appease the outside customer--so our image won't be tarnished. So, steal if you want, but try not to get caught.' That's the philosophy of the leaders of the U.S. Commodity Exchanges. How do you think they got to the top--by picking off a quarter and half cent here and there? All of 'em aren't dirty, but the leaders with the most power are. They control the rules, regulations, the voting, and the others. The clean executives are merely marshmallows being molded and squeezed as the criminal elements dictate."

Pete said, "Jesus Christ, what a system. You're afraid we're going to grab too many little fish and Simpson and Lorenzo are going to hang their hats on them, right?"

Michael clamped his lips together in dejection and nodded his head. "Right. They'll be satisfied to bring into the open the easy prey. The guys who are swiping the paper clips, the guys who are guilty of double parking, the guys who steal two, three hundred dollars a day, rather than the guys taking twenty-five thousand per day. And believe me in these markets twenty-five, fifty grand is easy to walk out with each day by doing a little fancy footwork. Believe me again when I tell you that the hand is faster than the eye. Most eyes that is, not my eyes, and hopefully not yours."

"Mike, with the exception of those broker friends of yours the government granted immunity, a lot of little guys are going to go down whether you like it or not. They are right in the middle of the whole mess. There is no discrimination in this sting. We can't single out a few guys because they're not stealing enough or because they are friends of yours. The list of brokers you don't want touched--they'll be left alone."

"There can be discrimination," Michael answered, "if we control the operation. That's why I'm upset with the four agents Simpson gave us to work with. Two out of four of them are going to tell on every little misdemeanor they see, in order to get their name on Simpson's 'job well done' plaque. Those misdemeanors will be translated into felonies by Simpson and Lorenzo. They'll be the first to go to trial, the first to have to spend a half million for legal counsel, the first to have their families turned upside down. They'll live a nightmare for years--and for what, paper clips?"

Pete slouched back in his chair. "Well, nevertheless, a lot of small guys are going to catch their lunch. This can't be helped!"

Michael pulled his right leg up and hung it over the arm of the chair. "I know. A lot of them are acquaintances of mine. I'm leading them right into the mouth of the lion."

"That bothers you, doesn't it?"

"You're goddamn right it bothers me. These guys have families, go to church on Sunday, give to the poor, help each other out. They're just good guys. They're the victims. The sacrificial lambs."

Pete finished his beer. "Well, if it makes you feel any better, Lorenzo will use them strictly as bait to get the bigger fish. This will be humiliating for them and their families, but most will plea bargain, admit to one or two felony counts, maybe a few misdemeanors. The most they will get is one year, maybe. Most likely just five years probation and a few hundred hours of community service. That won't kill them. What might kill them is the torture of their own imagination. The possibility of a few years in jail. Lorenzo will tell them if they don't cooperate with the government he'll see that they go to jail for ten to twenty years. Try to carry that around with you for a half a day. You're liable to head straight for the local gun shop. A few of the weaker ones will crack, Mike. You play the odds every day. Out of one hundred victims, paper-clip thieves as you call them, how many will break under the pressure of a possible jail term?"

Michael fell silent. He took his leg off the arm of the chair, planted it firmly on the floor, and looked Pete straight in the eyes. "We're going to keep as many small guys clean as possible. Even if we have to cover up, erase tapes, destroy trading cards. Whatever it takes."

He could see that Pete was beginning to get a little agitated and that his mind was working fast. His jaw muscles were noticeably tight, and he began to tap his fingers on the table.

He said as unruffled as he could, "Mike, the fuckers are still breaking the law whether it's paper clips or typewriters. They're still stealing, and they are the ones who will lead us to the big guns. As I said, some of them are going to have to be sacrificial lambs. I'm sorry, pal. But that's life. You stretch the rubber band of morality just so far, and it gets tired and snaps back. We'll cover as many minor infractions as possible, but we're going to grab a few. Percentages again. If a thousand of these guys are stealing, we'll get three hundred of them. We'll get a hundred more that we can sweep under the rug, and we'll probably miss the other six hundred. That's just the way it is, Mike. You knew when you took on this assignment that this was going to happen. Some little guys are going to get hurt. Those are the facts."

Pete stopped for a moment, then went on. "Mike, you know human nature. First you steal fifty bucks, then a hundred, then a thousand. Before you know it you are into big-time grand theft. Human nature isn't satisfied with the sweet fruits of the Garden of Eden. They want that damnable red apple--and have since the beginning of time.

"In my business I have to bust well respected, good men with families for buying two to three grams of cocaine. If they have over five grams, I scare the devil out of them for possession and pushing. Tell them what the maximum penalty is and remind them what will happen to their families when I turn them over to my superiors and they make the newspapers. You know what happens? They melt like hot butter and can't wait to tell me

who they deal with. Then I go get that guy who sold the shit to the first guy and do the same thing. Then to the next guy. And the next guy. All the way down the line. It's usually the third or fourth pusher who gets me close to the top. Those are the mean bastards who kill for a living. Those are the guys who lose their eardrums and head parts when they start preaching their rights to me--that really pisses me off. I seldom get to the top man. The point is...the first-time thief, especially white collar, usually learns his lesson and is able to get treatment. Then, he is able to go back to living a normal life if he wishes. So what if he's humiliated, and he loses a few unworthy friends, and maybe a few worldly possessions? If it saves his life and any further criminal activity, it's worth it. Nobody is above the law, Mike. Nobody." He considered before he spoke his next statement. "And that includes you!"

Michael downed the rest of his drink. He noticed that Pete was content to sit in silence for a few minutes, probably to let what he had said sink into Michael's mind.

He finally spoke, but almost inaudibly. "Pete, tell Tony Lorenzo I want to meet with him."

"When?"

"As soon as possible."

As Pete stood, he said, "Anything else?"

Michael didn't look up. "You get your application for membership tomorrow. I go back to work in the bond pit on Thursday. Make sure you've got your little spy camera and recorder with you, and have our so called 'sting team' here on Wednesday. It's time to get them ready. I want four membership applications ready to be submitted on Friday."

Pete's forehead furrowed into a valley of crevices. "Friday's a little early, Mike. Simpson was expecting this to happen next month." Michael merely looked at Pete and felt his facial muscles harden.

Pete almost tripped in turning. "You'll have six agents here on Wednesday and four applications ready for submission on Friday. I have to tell Simpson about the wrecked Mercedes anyway. I may as well tell him I need two million for memberships by Friday. That should make the prick's day."

Pete started for the door and Michael stopped him. "Pete?" He watched Pete turn in his tracks grimacing, expecting more bad news.

Michael felt his face soften, his eyes clear, and his mind relax. He knew these meetings were not easy for either of them. "Thanks, Pete. Thanks a lot. If you're who I think you are, we're going to make a good team. Forget about telling Simpson about the Mercedes. Give Terry Miller a call at North Shore Imports and he'll take care of the car. I'll take care of the bill. He'll do a good job, and nobody will know you were even on Sheridan Road last Sunday."

Without waiting for Pete to respond, he said, "Hold on a second." He leaned over and opened up a manila folder, then pulled out a long, sealed envelope. "Take this, Pete. Look it over. This is for your eyes only. I think you'll find it interesting. There is enough

information in that package to get your mind in tune with the scope of what we're really about to begin."

Pete walked back to the conference table with a question on his face. "Would you like to elaborate a bit more?"

Michael haphazardly flipped the envelope to Pete. "Bo pulled most of the names out of trading pits at the Mercantile. These are the people who skim big bucks. They are either members of the so called clandestine broker syndicate groups or the organization called the B.O.T--Brotherhood of Traders. There are also names of floor brokers who work directly for the Fat Man, Ruzzo and Conti--washing money. I did the same at the Board of Trade. You'll find most of the heavyweight thieves in there. Those are the brokers who will lead us to the top. I don't have all the Mafia or government names involved. Most of them are well covered and try to stay hidden from the Exchanges on the surface. But they are connected and call the major shots. They reap most of the money which comes from skimming and laundering. The trail leads all the way to Washington. There is a Senator. I'll give you his name later. Anyway, this guy swings heavy influence in DC. He also hands down plenty of inside info to the cheaters. Consequently, he receives the largest kickbacks from these criminal groups."

"You don't know his name?"

Michael's eyes were tired. "I know his name, but if he is the man who's responsible for killing a few of my buddies, I'm saving him for myself. He calls all the shots for the Mob from Washington. He's in on every agriculture and monetary move Washington makes. He has a group who lobbies for the independence of the Commodity Exchanges under the guise that it's the last bastion of free enterprise in America. You've got enough to keep you busy here. I'll tell you later who the mystery man is. If anything happens to me, Bo will give you the name. If anything happens to Bo, Maria will give you the name." He looked down at the file in front of him and said, "and if anything happens to Maria, her father, Carlo Santini, will take care of the man himself."

He felt his mind float into other areas of life, but forced himself to continue. "The man will show his hand when push comes to shove. Then--maybe sooner--you'll know who I speak of."

Michael watched Pete's lips turn down and his blue eyes sparkle with patient approval. "Nice work, Mike. Maybe we should trade places. You be the investigator and I'll be the trader."

Michael smiled. "Not on your life, pal."

Pete turned to leave, holding the envelope in his left hand. "Call me on the car phone when you're ready to leave. I'll pick you up in front of the building."

Michael rose and said, "Give me a half hour."

The door closed gently. Then he walked to the bar and poured a heavy scotch without ice. He drank deep, leaving the glass a third full, and poured to the brim again.

Setting the drink on the bar, he cupped his face in his hands, then ran his fingers through his thick hair. What a deal I got myself into, he thought.

He walked to his desk, and set his drink down, spilling a little on insignificant pieces of paper. Flopping down into his desk chair, he turned it toward the window and the depressing blackness. He closed his eyes and forced his mind to drift with the music. The booze was doing its job. Without his realizing it, the soft violins in the background had conjured up the image of Samantha. He let his fantasies flow with the tide of the strings. His soul was hers at that moment while he imagined all the colors of the rainbow wrapping their gentle ribbons of light around the two lovers who twirled in space exploring each other, teasing each other, becoming one with each other. A pure, white beach held their rolling bodies as they caressed and longed for a closeness. A oneness, as the warm waters washed against their bodies. The fantasy plunged deeper and deeper, and the rolling and lovemaking became so fierce that they were hurting each other but relishing even the pain that brought them together. The waters subsided gradually, and colors disappeared. The intense loving dissipated, and he opened his eyes to the black, ugly eye of the office window. What had interrupted such a wonderful dream? He looked around the room. The music had stopped. The three-hour tape had come to an end, and for this day, so had Michael.

TWENTY-NINE

Hard Evidence

Pete Lewis returned to his hotel after dropping Michael off at his house. He felt the night chill prick his face as he walked across Lake Shore Drive. The demon wind off the lake was biting. A cold mist had invaded the city, bringing with it a sense of impending doom. Autos hissed by on the wet pavement as oblivious to Pete as he was of them. His mind was occupied with Michael. He zipped up his jacket and pulled his collar around his neck trying to convince himself that it was nearly summer in Chicago rather than mid-winter. He thought of Michael and felt bad for the tough Irishman who was fast becoming his friend and whose life was changing by the minute--not for the better. Things would get worse, far worse, before they would finally settle. He hoped Hogan would survive. He'd seen strong men break in half with the pressures the government put on them, not to mention the pressures of their peers. Hogan was physically strong and mentally quick, but what was the man really made of? How durable was his spirit? Would pain break him or make him stronger? The thought gave Pete an extra chill.

He pushed through the swinging door of the hotel, heading for the elevator. As he walked, he shook off the cold and wet. Out of habit, he looked around the lobby of the hotel to click a picture in his mind of anything out of the ordinary. The place was empty except for the yawning desk clerk and one security guard slouched in a lobby chair, eyes at half mast. He held on his thigh a styrofoam cup of coffee that was ready to topple into his lap.

His thoughts returned to Hogan as he rode the elevator to the eighth floor. He knew Michael was an honest man and sensed he was spiritual or mystical. Or, believed in something other than the obvious. He remembered the cold, unforgiving look in Michael's eyes for the men who threatened his family. The look of an executioner. Pete shivered and felt the nerves in his spine send an electric warning to his brain. The man confused Pete. Could Michael turn from peace to violence? Would he--Could he kill? As the doors opened on the eighth floor, Pete concluded that Hogan wouldn't break as long as nothing happened to his family. But God forbid anybody who might think to touch them. There would be war.

As he stepped off the elevator and moved down the plush hall, he squeezed his left arm against the side of his chest. The heavy .44 Magnum had become so much a part of him over the years that he checked periodically to feel if it was still there. He came to his room. Again out of habit he opened the door quietly, and quickly stepped inside. He switched on the light, plopped his briefcase on a nearby chair, unzipped his windbreaker,

again feeling for his gun. He looked around the room. The picture his mind had taken earlier in the day when he left the room was the same one his eyes were now recording. He had left orders with housekeeping not to make up or touch his room. He was satisfied. He sucked in a long, slow intake of air and gradually let it seep out between his pursed lips. He thought that if a bullet didn't kill him, the paranoia he had acquired over the years with the CIA and undercover law-enforcement work surely would. Suspicion, doubt, and a constant state of alertness ate away at his body and mind like an infected, black tattoo. After taking a warm shower, he flipped the television knob to a cable music station, then moved over to the small refrigerator, where he kept a supply of European beer. He reached in for a can, popped open the top, and gulped down the refreshing cold brew.

His hair was slicked straight back, touching the nape of his neck, and he felt the shower water dripping down the middle of his spine. His exhausted body began to relax. The music was soothing. "Dust in the Wind" played softly. The beer tasted good. He was tired, but before he went to sleep, he wanted to review the information Hogan had given him.

Hogan didn't do anything that was unimportant. So Pete decided it was a priority to scan whatever documents were in the long envelope. He walked back to the chair by the door, grabbed the handle of his briefcase, and tossed it on the bed. Then, as he rubbed a four-digit combination beneath its handle, the top popped up, and he withdrew a 9mm Beretta. Carefully, he set it on the night stand next to the digital clock radio. The time was 11:48. He hadn't realized he and Michael had talked for so long. Now it was late, especially when he knew he had to get up in four hours.

He pulled out the long, sealed envelope and said out loud, "Now, let's see what Señor Hogan has for Uncle Peter."

He took a long, thin knife from his briefcase, sliced open the envelope and pulled out a thick sheaf of legal sized paper. A note from Michael was clipped to the front page. It read:

> *"Pete, two men have already been killed for helping me obtain this information. I know who the killers are...I will deal with them. They don't realize I have this evidence...or I would be dead. I have the original documents. BE CAUTIOUS. These copies have been sprayed with Benzine Oxide 12-X. Attempts to reproduce the papers by any mechanical means will cause an explosion. Any attempt to photograph the papers will be evident when you return the copies to me. My friend...beware of the jackals to whom you answer.*

> *Signed: Hawk*

> *P.S. FOR YOUR EYES ONLY!*

Pete felt his insides stir nervously. He smelled one of the pages. His nose wrinkled--
benzine oxide. The fucker wasn't kidding. He was glad he didn't walk through a metal
detector on the way home. He raised his head to the hotel window and stared at the
distorted images of light from outside reflecting on the rain streaked glass. He ran his
tongue across his lips, looked down again, and began to pull the pages apart one by one.
He went through the documents quickly, at first taking a mental picture of each page. He
then returned to the beginning to study in detail what his mind would forever hold.

The first few pages were merely a history of Michael's tenure at the two
Exchanges, which began in the mid-sixties. He stated that he first noticed trading
infractions taking place in the pork belly pit in 1967 when the bellies had become very
popular among high-flying speculators.

The name "pork bellies" became a glamorous name for many who had made
millions off the radical, undisciplined market. Who had ever heard of people speculating
on the price fluctuations of a twelve to fourteen-pound slab of frozen, uncured bacon?

Michael stated further that a handful of men with certain inside information
controlled the wild swings in the virgin bacon market. Because of the fast-moving, wide
swinging market, the lack of computer technology, and lax Exchange policing, many
customer orders were filled at prices far above or below the actual market cost. The
customer was on his own. There was no way he could check the validity of the price he
paid, or the price he sold at, because trades were not recorded immediately by computers.
They were recorded on chalk boards by Exchange employees. Michael witnessed many
illegal price changes on the chalk boards before they eventually went to be photographed
for record keeping. Then a bull market broke out in the egg pit. Michael witnessed similar
violations, all at the expense of the customer.

The next big bull market was in the cattle pit. However, by this time, Michael
worked with a large hog and cattle clearing house, having gained respect, prestige and
money. He was on an Exchange "pit committee," which allowed him to monitor trading
more closely. Oddly enough, he stated, the cattle pit was much cleaner than the pork bellies
and egg pits. Although the swings in the market were fast and wild, there was always
plenty of volume to keep trading civilized. He attributed the discipline in the cattle pit to
the fact that much of the trading volume was from cattle and livestock companies who
knew what the price should be. They kept the prices in line. Several of the men who traded
livestock for a living had come from the stockyards. They were used to shaking hands on
a deal and not getting screwed by the broker. Cattle men were poker players by nature.
Like men, they took their losses with their gains. They told the brokers if they caught them
stealing or skimming money from their orders, they'd stick a cattle prod in their asses.
There were only a few instances in the cattle pit where he found brokers cheating. When
Michael and others pounced on them, they skittered to the belly or egg pits to play their
illegal games.

Michael felt that although people ate bacon and eggs everyday, there were a few speculators who knew where eggs came from, but damn few who knew that bacon came from pork bellies. The actual pork producers and users who played the belly market also made the prices swing higher and lower than their actual value by squeezing the market or laying back while the prices dropped, making it a haven for thieves. On the other hand, the cattle traders knew if the price dropped below a certain point, they could make money and would buy, firming up the market. If prices rose too high, they would sell the market, knowing cattle weren't worth that much. That would stop an uncontrolled runaway market.

During these early years, Michael found out many tricks of the trade. He learned in the cattle pit from the best and biggest brokers in the country. Honesty, stamina, competition, and quick reactions were all prerequisites to becoming a class-A broker.

One friend had told Michael not to think about a trade. To react instead to the motion and mood of the market. "You can think after the market is closed. If you lost money trading for yourself or gave your customers bad fills, your actions and reactions are not fine tuned. You must be like a champion boxer, able to look into your opponent's eyes. Anticipate his right or left jab coming at you. Too, you must be a champion of the pits by looking into your opponent's eyes and telling whether he has a big order, a small order, and if it's a buy or sell order. Watch his eyes and watch his hands. Then make your move before him, or with him, but not after him. Or you'll be knocked out."

Pete read on with interest, sipping at his beer and learning more about his Irish friend. During these early days, Michael was shown how to steal customer money. In an almost infallible way. Legally. One story especially interested Pete. Michael had become close friends with a fellow by the name of Ira Holtzman. Holtzman's customer business was growing rapidly. With his ability to generate customers, he reasoned, and Hogan's talents and reputation in the pits, they would be a good team. Hogan considered a fifty-fifty partnership and was going to join with Holtzman. Holtzman said that with Hogan as a partner, he could do ten times the business he was already doing.

Before he agreed, Hogan asked his partner-to-be how he generated so many customers. And how successful was he in making money for them? After some hesitation, Holtzman explained that he had twenty men doing telephone solicitation. To hook customers. He paid them a small salary at first. Then, after a few months of training, the salesmen received ten per cent of the commissions that Holtzman generated when trading their new accounts. None of his salesmen were registered with the Exchange as account executives. They were registered as phone men and runners. Although this type of selling was against Exchange rules, the Exchange seldom checked the activities of clearing-house office activity. Thus, Holtzman had free rein on his "boiler room" operation.

Michael asked if his customers made money. Holtzman laughed. Said there was no way on earth a customer could make money in the commodity market. He went on to ask how he was able to keep his customers. Holtzman took out a legal pad of paper. On it, he drew three columns. He said he had about seventy-five customers. Each day after the

market closed, he would look at his list of customer names. Then he would check the hundreds of trades he had made in the market that day. One week the first twenty-five customers would get winning trades, making them happy. The second twenty-five would get the losing trades. The third group would lie dormant: that particular week they would not trade.

The next week, the second group would get the winning trades. The third group became the losers. And the first group, the winners the previous week, would not trade. Each week the groups would move from column to column: always a winner. Always a loser. Always a non-player.

Holtzman, a better-than-average trader, made more winning trades than losing ones. This very fact helped his scheme to work. He said he averaged two hundred trades a day for customers. Two hundred, times fifty dollars each trade for commission, was ten thousand dollars a day income, less ten per cent to his salesmen. Ira Holtzman was averaging nine thousand dollars a day in commissions. Or forty-five thousand per week. One hundred eighty per month. This young flim-flam man was taking in over two million dollars a year in commissions.

Michael pointed out to Holtzman that his scheme was simply a method of "churning" customers. "Churn 'em, burn 'em, and turn 'em," was the terminology. Holtzman was nothing more than a commission merchant. Holtzman laughed and agreed. He told Michael his customers were going to trade with somebody; it might as well be him. Besides, he wasn't doing anything illegal. The customers had given him power-of-attorney, complete discretion, to trade for them. He said there wasn't any mystery to his methods of handling customers. That "everybody was doing it". Michael said that didn't make it right. He told Holtzman that he was deliberately deceiving his customers. Letting them think they could make money in the Commodity Markets, when he knew from the beginning they couldn't, under the method he was using. Michael told him it was wrong to use people and their money simply for personal gain with no intentions of trying to help them come out winners.

Ira called Michael a visionary if he thought the marketplace was a clean place to work. He had to become more realistic if he was going to be successful--really successful. Michael told him on the contrary, he was quite realistic. He told him, too, that he realized Ira just wanted him as a partner because it was well known that he was an honest pit broker. And that Ira wanted to connect with a clean name. This fact would further enhance his ability to entice customers to trade through him. Holtzman agreed and said that an Irish-Catholic name would break down barriers with some wealthy Gentiles he was trying to win over as clients. He offered Michael a million dollars to join forces with him. At the time, the money was tempting. But something inside Michael told him the two men were coming from different camps. He told Holtzman his name was worth more than a million dollars. Further, he told him his morality ran deeper than a lead pencil and three columns of doomed customers on a legal pad. He said he held no disrespect for Ira, just because their

two financial philosophies were contrary. He wished Holtzman luck and said he'd be happy to fill his orders in the pit. But wanted nothing to do with his operation.

He remembered standing to leave and Holtzman making the comment that every man had a price. What was Michael's? Michael said he didn't believe that every man had a price. If they did, he hadn't found his yet. At that, he left Holtzman's office. That meeting occurred in 1968. Today, Holtzman runs one of the largest commission businesses in the United States. He has hundreds of salesmen, is one of the wealthiest men in Chicago, and is one of the key officials at the Chicago Mercantile Exchange!

Pete flipped the papers on the bed, rubbed his eyes, finished the last of his beer, and walked to the hotel-room window. There was still a mist in the air as he watched the sparse traffic move along the shiny, black pavement of Lake Shore Drive. His thoughts were forming a conclusion to what he had just read. The corruption in the market had evolved, from the unscrupulous handling of customer funds in the sixties to the full-fledged theft characteristic of today's market. Since the men at the top, like Holtzman, made their money by feeding their greed from naive customers, how could they condemn the actions of the pit brokers, especially if they were getting cash kick-backs? Twenty, maybe fifty years of corruption in one of America's largest financial institutions, and no government monitoring of any consequence. There was one difference today that wasn't around in the '60's: the Mafia was now involved.

Shaking his head in disgust, he stared briefly into the inky darkness. Then he returned to finish the rest of the documents. Picking up the material from the bed, he decided against another beer. He moved to the chair at the table to continue his reading.

What he found on the following eighteen pages astounded him. Michael's obsessive crusade had produced hard evidence against the men who were destroying his industry. He had to have friends in high places to obtain this incriminating information.

The first few pages listed sixty-eight floor brokers who worked for skimming and laundering syndicates. Names he and Bo had compiled from each Exchange. A note stated that these men worked for broker syndicates, Exchange officials, politicians, and Mafia families. They were merely the front-runners for hundreds of underling brokers who worked for the clandestine syndicates. Many of the broker syndicates were formed for personal gain, merely skimming from outside customer money. The two largest syndicates were formed by criminal organizations to launder dirty money. The four main men connected to the Exchange who ran the laundering were Karl Peterson, Victor Conti, Salvano Ruzzo, and Jake Edwards. All four men controlled numerous trading companies, each responsible for four different sections of the United States.

Peterson controlled the laundering for Chicago and the Midwest; Conti controlled the West; Ruzzo, the East. They spent most of their time in Chicago in their respective offices. Conti also had an office in Los Angeles. Ruzzo had one in New York. Jake Edwards worked Florida. Came to Chicago only in emergencies. He set up all of the connections in Tampa and Miami and oversaw the domestic and offshore holding

companies that received the laundered money. All four men reported to Mob families in Chicago, New York, Miami, and Los Angeles. They also reported to a number of government offices in Washington, one of which was the Agriculture Department, Washington politicians; that is, those who received kickbacks and lobby heavily for the autonomy of the freewheeling commodity markets.

Pete returned to the previous page and reviewed the names Hogan and Bo had compiled. These were the floor brokers who bagged and skimmed trades for the various syndicates. Included were their given names, their badge names, and their trading pit:

CHICAGO BOARD OF TRADE:

Robert L. Travis (RLT)	Treasury Bonds
Lawerence M. Jamall (JAMS)	Treasury Bonds
John P. Edwards (JED)	Treasury Bonds
Christopher W. Cullus (CUS)	Treasury Bonds
Charles Q. Cullus (CQ)	Treasury Bonds
Arnold H. Schwarts (ARN)	Treasury Bonds
Wayne A. Olson (WO)	Treasury Bonds
Paul M. Sinclair (PMS)	Treasury Bonds
Jason P. Cooper (JASE)	Treasury Bonds
Aaron S. Weinsenstein (WINE)	Treasury Bonds
Thomas M. Smith (TOM)	Treasury Bonds
Morris L. Franko (MOFO)	Soybeans
Puls S. Monrowe (PSM)	Soybeans
John M. McGee (JMM)	Soybeans
Anthony B. Rennery (TONY)	Soybeans
Charles A. Nicolelli (CAN)	Soybeans
Theadore I. Terrin (TITS)	Soybeans
Alberto Alverado (SUNY)	Soybeans
Tami W. Briggs (BRIG)	Silver
Scott W. Bradley (SB)	Silver
Burt S. Razowski (SKI)	Silver
Edward P. Allano (ALLO)	Ginnie Mae
Sidney O. Burns (SOB)	Ginnie Mae
Barry J. Rosen (BJR)	Ginnie Mae
Saul S. Mandell (DELL)	Ginnie Mae
Jeffory E. Weisen (JEW)	Corn
Richard J. Janson (JJ)	Corn
Sallie E. McKan (SALY)	Corn
Jerry R. Goldsmith (GOLD)	Corn
Peter W. Tollend (PETT)	Wheat
Noel C. Brown (NCB)	Wheat
Wm. V. Murphy (MURF)	Wheat
Frank L. Murphy (FLM)	Wheat
James X. Hoolihan (XXH)	Wheat

CHICAGO MERCANTILE EXCHANGE AND
INTERNATIONAL MONETARY MARKET:

Raulf M. Hoge (HOG)	Standard and Poors
Alvin C. Allen (ACA)	Standard and Poors
Anthony W. Zitello (ZITO)	Standard and Poors
Daniel O. Gallow (DOG)	Standard and Poors
Edward Q. Millano (EDDY)	Standard and Poors
Jasper A. Pozzi (JAZZ)	Standard and Poors
Allen J. Rowner (ARO)	Standard and Poors
Calvin G. Levin (CAL)	Eurodollar
Anthony C. Conti (CONI)	Eurodollar
David E. Devine (DEAD)	Eurodollar
Samuel A. Kahn (SAK)	Eurodollar
Robert B. Sillva (ROBR)	Eurodollar
Aaron L. Cohen (JLC)	Eurodollar
Henry N. Shulman (HEN)	Treasury Bills
William H. Stein (WILL)	Treasury Bills
Allen L. Spellman (SPEL)	Treasury Bills
Xavier P. Randholl (XFF)	Swiss Franc
Anthony S. Hardy (HARD)	Swiss Franc
Alexander O. Nelson (ALON)	Swiss Franc
Jerome F. Finkle (FINK)	Japanese Yen
Lawrence L. Price (LAP)	Japanese Yen
Joseph S. Paminski (PIN)	Japanese Yen
Allen C. Issies (AI)	Deutsche Mark
Leo Maxwell (MAX)	Deutsche Mark
Judlo K. Manelli (JUD)	Canadian Dollar
William S. Cash (CASH)	Canadian Dollar
Edward P. Montgomery (MONY)	Live Cattle
Herman L. Linn (HELL)	Live Cattle
Lawrence J. Stone (STON)	Pork Bellies
Harvey M. Mieney (HMM)	Pork Bellies
John J. Flynn (FLYN)	Live Hogs
John C. Fitzpatrick (JFIZ)	Live Hogs
Jerry M. Jakobson (JMJ)	Eggs
Harvey H. Reinhold (HHR)	Eggs

Pete sat back, yawned, and pulled at the back of his neck to relieve a cramp. He thought with this kind of head start, keying in on the sixty-eight brokers Hogan had placed in front of him, along with the four men they reported to, the investigation could turn into an avalanche. Once Pete had some hard evidence of his own from the pits, which he would

get in the next twelve months, he knew he would have a good case. These guys would fall like dominoes. Rolling over on each other in order to save their own asses. He also knew how to scare people into talking. Being a Fed, he had authority to do things that local law-enforcement agencies didn't have. He could scare the shit out of a novice crook by walking into his home at three a.m. and threatening the man with imprisonment, confiscation of all material assets and bank accounts, and a complete audit of taxes, bank statements, pension plans, etc. He figured it would take twelve to eighteen months to get to that point. He would pull every trick in the book to make these bastards sweat.

His eyes went to the final pages of the document. Michael had written him another note:

> *"Pete, the following information is not only accurate but also dangerous. The man who furnished this information to me is dead. He knew too much and was silenced. Thrown off his Michigan Avenue apartment balcony. He was a friend of mine. A good friend. I want justice. I want his killers. (Signed) Hawk.*

Pete looked in awe at the profit and loss statements of various holding companies. There were lists of deposits, all in excess of five hundred thousand. Photostat copies of bank statements from banks in Miami, New York, Chicago, Los Angeles, London, Cayman Islands, Bahamas, Hong Kong, Munich, Luxembourg, and Switzerland. No account had less than fifty million in it. The Geneva account had 350 million in it. All of the numbered accounts had the names of the beneficiaries. Pete recognized the politicians who were mentioned--all pillars of American Democracy.

Hogan stated that there was a labyrinth of sophisticated accounting that took skim and laundered money from the Exchanges. The money eventually made its way to the accounts mentioned, real estate, and legitimate businesses, both in foreign countries and in the U.S..

Pete turned to the last page and closed the file. He looked at the documents in front of him. He spoke out loud. "Jesus Christ. No wonder they would kill for this information. Too late now, Assholes. Uncle Pete has what he needs to break your backs, and I'll blow your goddamn heads off if you try to throw me off a balcony."

He went to the bathroom, relieved himself of the last beer, and splashed cold water on his face. Time for bed. His thoughts returned to Hogan. He had balls, nerve, and something else he couldn't put his finger on. Michael was cunning and patient. He had information like this and waited until the time was right to bring it out into the open. The man was indeed an enigma. Gentle and kind in some respects. Hard and calculating in others.

Pete crawled into his bed, turned the light off, and let the rolling fog of exhaustion and sleep slowly nudge Hogan out of his mind. His last conscious movement was to reach for his weapon on the nightstand and tuck it under his pillow. The outside mist had turned to a hard-driving rain, purging the city of its evil. Deep waters of sleep swallowed him quickly.

THIRTY

Sean McGiven: IRA

The famous, lake-front landmark, Buckingham Fountain, sprayed its mist on Sean McGiven's bearded face. He stretched his thick neck and moved his blue eyes upward, then breathed in the sweet smell of the nearby flower gardens. Warm southern winds had swept into the city and Grant Park earlier in the day. He watched the tumbling clouds as the tropical breath attempted to force away the gray skies that had veiled the city for more than a week. The setting reminded him of Dublin, where sunshine and warm winds were a luxury any time of year.

Sean nudged his left sleeve to check the time. He was twenty minutes early, but he had planned it that way. He needed to get away and relax for an hour or two, and the lake setting satisfied the poet in his soul. The splashing water drowned out the mechanical noises of the afternoon traffic. Sean reached down, ran his hand through the clear, churning water, then stood and wiped his neatly trimmed auburn beard downward from his cheekbones to his chin. His sharp eyes, shaded by the wrinkled brim of his Irish cap, swept the Grant Park area for his partner and bodyguard, Shamus Flaherty. He found him about seventy yards away, on a park bench. His back to the lake, he was pretending to read a newspaper. Sean knew that everybody in the park was within Shamus's sight and that his own back was well covered.

He hadn't seen his impudent friend, Michael Hogan, for months. He looked forward to meeting him today. By the tone of Michael's voice on the phone, he knew this meeting was not social. Usually they met for drinks at Murphy's Black Potato Pub down in their old neighborhood by the stockyards. He figured Hogan wanted someplace open to talk, probably to keep foreign ears from listening. After his own many years of trying to recruit Michael for the Irish Republican Army, maybe, just maybe, he was finally seeing the justice in the Irish Cause. But he doubted that.

The last time they talked, Michael had said that if he forced himself, he might be able to justify some of the actions of the I.R.A. He would never, however, be able to convince his spirit that their violent philosophy was morally right. For Hogan, Sean knew, the injustices the British imposed on the Irish were behind him. And now, too many innocent people were being killed by unscrupulous rebel off-shoots of the I.R.A. The left and right wings had lost all sense of purpose; they had become fanatics and were killing just for the sake of killing.

Michael just didn't understand. If he only knew the suppression the Irish people had been subjected to. But, he always argued that the war had changed from a religious one

for his people, to a political war of violence. Only to satisfy the sick whims of a few rebels--terrorist rebels.

Michael hadn't been there like Sean had. He didn't know the pain, the hunger, the degradation. If only Michael had more of the soul of his grandfather, Martin Hogan, who had been one of the cornerstones of the I.R.A.. He was a legend in Ireland. Sean remembered well the things he had read and heard about Martin Hogan. A man the British called "The Ghost of Kildare--The Deceptive One." The Irish called him "The Savior." Martin Hogan helped form the secret Irish Republican Brotherhood (IRB) in the early 1900's. This daring leadership is what earned him his name. The organization wanted a completely independent Irish Republic. At a rally in Dublin on Palm Sunday, 1916, Martin screamed his rage to a huge crowd, "It is time to cut the umbilical cord from Mother England, the evil British witch. Unlike a mother from God who nourishes her children, she instead sucks love and life from Ireland, leaving only poison and decay." The next day, Easter Monday, Martin led a rebellion in Dublin. British troops finally defeated the rebels, after more than a week of fighting. In order to allow their beloved leader to escape, fifteen IRB leaders were executed. They all claimed to be Martin Hogan. Martin fled to the green hills of Kildare, where he pulled rebel bands together from all over Ireland. This meeting gave birth to the Irish Republican Army (IRA).

During the next five years, Martin and his peace-loving son, Patrick, organized and trained a clandestine group of rebel forces. Later, these same forces ravaged British patrol troops, compounds, and government buildings. His dual name, known throughout Ireland and England, was "The Ghost of Kildare--The Deceptive One." He would be seen in many different areas of the country at the same time, and he was claimed to have been killed by the British, on more than thirty different occasions. Yet, he lived, and continued to manipulate the overwhelming power of his enemy with cunning and baffling ruthlessness.

Finally, in 1921, Great Britain and the Irish rebels agreed to a treaty that allowed southern Ireland to become a self-governing country. Martin's twenty-year-old son, Patrick, met with members of the British Parliament to negotiate the treaty for freedom in Dublin. Even at twenty, Michael's father, Patrick, had the wisdom of an eighty-year-old Chief Justice. With soft, prophetic words, he conquered the British.

Sean understood Michael better than he understood himself. They had grown up together, and although Michael purported to follow the non-violent beliefs of his father, Sean knew that his grandfather's blood flowed furiously through Michael's veins. When they were teens, Sean would see a brief fury in Michael's black eyes. Unmistakably, this was the spirit of Martin. The rage would leave him as quickly as it came. Michael continued to this day believing that injustice is to be dealt with through peace and intelligent negotiation.

Sean told Michael that the day would come when the rage of his heritage would show itself to the world. He knew that the fury of his grandfather's restless soul would not

sleep in him forever. God help the man, the institution, or the government responsible for waking Martin Hogan's spirit and unleashing his violent justice through his grandson. But Michael didn't live in the real world. He was a poet, a mystic, a lover of nature. He belonged in a monastery with his foolish beliefs about the basic goodness of mankind.

A swoosh of warm air pulled Sean's cap from his head. He grabbed it just before it flipped into the fountain. He ran his fingers through his thick, wavy hair before replacing the plaid cap. He calculated that in the past fifteen years he and his hand-picked band of fine-tuned Irish brokers had moved more than a half billion from the Chicago markets into European bank accounts. The moneys were then transferred from country to country, eventually ending up in numerous Dublin banks owned by the upper echelons of the IRA. And that money was a mere pittance compared to some of the greedier broker groups at the Exchanges.

Sean lowered his head and let his mind turn the pages of time to years past. His deep-blue eyes filled with the waters of sorrow, remembering holding the smoldering torso of his younger brother, Liam. From the abandoned building where he hid, Sean saw and now recalled the cruel laughter of the Black and Tans as they tied grenades to Liam. He could hear the pins from the deadly explosives hit the cobblestone street of Belfast, then the deafening explosion. He remembered the unrecognizable, burning body of what was once his innocent, sweet brother. Liam's death also killed his mother. Cause of death: broken heart. She never forgave Sean for Liam's death.

Sean gritted his teeth and cursed the killers under his breath. His fists tightened at the recall of the fierce insanity that had run riot through his mind and body as he saw his brother lying in the filthy street. Screaming from his hiding place, he had killed all four unsuspecting soldiers with a simple hand gun. Sean had killed many more British after that incident. This was eventually the cause for his exile to the United States. His American IRA counterparts had placed him in Chicago at the stockyards. Here he had met Martin Hogan's son, Patrick, and Patrick's son, Michael. The Hogan family had taken him into their meager home and treated him as their son. Michael, an only child, had accepted him quickly as an older brother. The two had been inseparable as they worked together sorting cattle and hogs in the yards. Today, that same love and respect was shared between them despite their different views.

A voice pushed into his thoughts. "Sean? Hey, Sean? Talking to the spirits again?"

Startled, he turned quickly from the fountain and his calloused dreams. There he greeted Michael's smiling face. A feeling of exhilaration flowed through him as he opened wide his thick arms. "Michael, lad, it's good to see you. I was just talking about you with your grandfather." He watched Michael's smile widen knowingly. They walked a few steps toward each other and embraced as brothers. He held Michael by the shoulders, looking into his strong, handsome face. Then he said in a cynical, soft tone, "I see lines--crow's feet, Michael. My young brother isn't showing his age, is he? Or have you been worrying too much about ol' Sean?"

Michael's smile slowly vanished, and his eyes looked beyond Sean to the fountain. The soft wind played with his black hair. "We're both getting older, Sean, and even the persistent angels in Heaven have had their pinions clipped because of their futile success with you."

Sean let a loud laugh erupt. At the outburst, pigeons scurried away from their feet. "Ah, lad, you've always been quick with tongue, and almost as quick with mind. Remember when you used to say, 'Here's my head, Sean--my feet will be along in a few minutes'?"

He let one hand drop from Michael's shoulder as he looked into the tired, taut face. "You've lost weight, lad, and I sense your spirit is weary."

Michael bowed his head, then moved his right foot around in small circles on the tiny pebbles on the walkway. "You've always been the perceptive one, Sean." He raised his head and breathed in deeply, then said matter-of-factly, "The air is fresh today...the mist from the fountain feels good."

His eyes returned to Sean's. "Money doesn't make life easier, does it, Sean?"

He patted Michael on his arm and said, "on the contrary, Lad. With wealth comes hardship and responsibility. Sometimes that responsibility makes us wish we were poor again. Maybe 'Less is best.'"

Sean looked to the parking area. He saw that Michael had brought his own man with him. The young-looking fellow, with longish, blond hair, wearing worn out jeans, dirty tennis shoes, and a black windbreaker. He had strolled into a garden area and was feigning interest in the newly planted rose bushes spotted neatly throughout the area.

He saw the man hunch down and play with the petals of a young rose, but his eyes scanned the park. He knew that the backups weren't out of fear for each other. Rather a protection from the possibility of outside interruptions. Both of them walked the razor's edge and in the process, had made their share of enemies.

Now he said with a roughhouse grin, "I see you have reached that unenviable status of being accompanied by a strong-armed lad to watch your back."

Michael snapped too quickly, too defensively, "He's just a friend--along for the ride."

Sean stood back and observed Michael, taking in his austere face, his expensive clothes, and his Italian shoes. Then he bellied another guffaw and said mockingly, "And since when did my little brother begin wearing a gun around his ankle? I'd guess it's a Mauser, a Walther, or a Beretta."

Michael looked down at his ankle. An ever-so-slight fold was in the left leg six inches above the ankle. Michael wore a three-hundred-dollar pair of pants that should fit perfectly. But Sean could spot a hidden weapon at thirty yards.

Michael looked back up at Sean and gathered his face into a pout. "You son of a bitch. You're probably the only guy in town who would notice. Yes, it's a Mauser. And

yes," he waved his hand toward the rose garden, "...my friend over there smelling flowers is my back-up. I learned everything from you, Sean."

Sean spoke carefully. "Not everything, Michael." I've been playing this game for over thirty years. You are just beginning. You only have to watch out for local bad guys. I'm an international figure. My enemies come in all different shapes and colors. Why all the precaution?"

The question hung unanswered. They walked to the splashing water, and Michael put his foot on the tile steps surrounding the fountain. "I'm not here to talk about my problems, Sean."

Sean felt his forehead furrow at his friend's serious tone. He sensed there was something wrong. Michael was not his usual jovial self. "What is it, lad? Can I help you in any way? You name it and it's done, Michael." Michael looked over at Shamus Flaherty and gave him a nod. Sean saw Shamus return the nod and continue his scanning of the park. "What's the problem, lad? What kind of trouble could my pacifist friend have that would inspire him to wear a gun and have a bodyguard? And...what has turned you from a competitor to a hunter or maybe even a predator? Or...are you the hunted?"

Michael stared into the water as if he didn't hear the words. He didn't answer Sean's questions. "I'll get right to the point, Sean. There is something coming down. Something really heavy."

So this was it, thought Sean. He took his cap off and let the lake breeze tease his face and hair. "What could be so heavy, Michael? What kind of problem could anybody present to us that we haven't handled a hundred times before?"

He waited patiently for an answer. Michael reached down for a beer cap and skipped it across the fountain water. Sean saw that Michael's eyes had lost their usual warmth. They were strange--they were cold. "Sean, we've been like brothers for most of our lives." He stopped and kicked at the ground. "I have to tell you that unfriendly eyes are going to be watching the Exchanges. That could affect us both, but you more than me."

Sean winced and shook his head. "I don't understand, lad. You're confusing today. Whatever affects you affects me. What affects me affects you--always has."

Michael closed his eyes and wiped the fountain mist from his face as he spoke. "Not this time, Sean. There's...well, there's going to be problems, big problems."

"What kind of problems? Come on, out with it."

He watched Michael take a deep breath and sigh. "There is going to be an investigation at both Chicago Exchanges as well as the New York Exchanges. Everybody has become too greedy. The customer complaints are finally being listened to in Washington."

Sean ran his right hand down his beard and felt his thick eyebrows lower while he took a second to think. "Are we talking Feds?"

"I'm afraid so."

"You're involved?"

Michael turned his head away. "Yes. I'm into it up to my ass."

The flowing water seemed to splash louder as silence quelled the conversation momentarily. Sean looked up and saw the gray clouds give way to the southern wind. He felt Michael's frustration. He also saw his sincerity. He placed his strong hand on the back of Michael's neck. "How much do they know?"

Michael sighed again. "They know about the Fat Man, Conti, Ruzzo, the broker syndicates. About the line of corruption all the way to the senators in Washington. They know very little about your operation. They asked me about your affiliation with the IRA. I told them I had known you a long time and was sure any sympathy you had for the Irish Cause has long since been resolved."

"Did they believe you?"

Michael bit his lower lip and shook his head. "I don't think so. I'm sure they have you in their computer as a sympathizer, if not an organizer. You've been clever. Your IRA code of secrecy has pretty much protected you. I really don't know how much they know or don't know about you. You've pretty well covered your tracks so you won't be noticed like the others. But, you're going to have to watch who you trade with. Tell your boys not to accept any bargains from new guys in the pits. They plan to clean up the industry, and...they are going to have my support, Sean."

Sean tightened his cap on his head and said, "Well, let them come, Laddie. They will never break my network. Our methods are far more sophisticated than most of the obvious skimming and laundering brokers. Their trades can be picked up easily with a little paper chase."

"Don't underestimate the bastards, Sean. They're political puppets and assholes. They're not stupid. If they have the slightest suspicion that an Irish terrorist group is reaping millions from the markets, they'll cause you a whole truck load of grief."

Sean felt his ears grow warm with anger, but he kept his temper. "We're not terrorists, Michael. Terrorists have no international network. They work independently. They all have different, undefined causes. There are hundreds of terrorist groups...there is only one Irish Republican Army. I have no intention of changing my business dealings because a few Feds are looking over my shoulder. I've been stalked by far tougher men than the Federal Government. You know how our operation works. We don't steal from your precious customers. We just trick them and take their money. We have no prejudice. We trick our fellow brokers and take their money as well. We receive national and international information twenty-four hours before the rest of the world. If the market's dull, we even make up false information and run that across the tapes of the world. We buy on Monday. Put the information out on Tuesday. Let the public run the market up, and we sell on Wednesday. We take our profits and let the others fend for themselves."

Michael looked straight ahead, resting his elbow on his knee, his foot perched on the fountain step. "Yeah, I know. You make your money with inside information. You have sympathizers in high places who feed you information from all over the world. You

make your play in the market. Then you make sure the information is released immediately. You sell out at a profit to the poor bastards who trade on what they read in the *Wall Street Journal*. Which is all last week's news to you."

He felt the sharp dig of irritation. "What's wrong with that, Michael? We do our homework before our competitors do. Reading the *Journal* or trading off the six o'clock news is strictly amateur trading. They read and hear what we want them to."

Sean saw Michael's eyes turn critical, like a scolding father's. "What's wrong with taking confidential information from your sources in Washington, New York, Europe, and America and trading on that? Come on, Sean. You pay heavy for that information, and take advantage of the market to exercise your inside knowledge. And, if you don't have information, you make it up. You spread rumors throughout the world-market community that corn has root worm, or the cocoa or coffee crop has been destroyed by beetles, or the Russians are going to buy a large amount of gold. Then you sell the shit out of the market when it starts up, because of the rumors your people start."

He kept his voice patient. "Michael, what was one of the first rules we learned when we came into the business? Sell the..."

Michael cut in. "Yeah, I know. 'Sell the rumor; buy the fact'."

"Right. So what's the big deal? A trader is ignorant if he thinks beetles can actually destroy coffee or cocoa beans. Or that root worm could destroy more than a few thousand acres of corn. Anybody who trades corn and doesn't know that farmers use pesticides to protect against insect damage deserves to lose money. And what in the world would Russia want with fifty thousand contracts of gold? They're exporters of gold, not importers! They have trouble paying their light bill at the Kremlin, let alone speculating in the gold market."

Sean wasn't about to be intimidated by Michael's sanctimonious philosophy. He had always been on the side of Early American morality, as obscure and tainted as it had become. Might was not right with Michael. The end did not justify the means for him. He had gone too far with his quest for justice this time. In his naivete, he thought that Mother Justice in the U.S. protected the innocent and prosecuted the guilty. What folly. Mother Justice had decided to look the other way while lawyers, politicians, judges, criminals, and everybody else fucked with her scales. If she ever lifted her blindfold, she would scream at what she saw.

He finally said with a tone of depression, "Michael, Michael, Michael. What have you gone and done to yourself? You are the only one taking a risk here. Nobody can stop our Irish Cause. Our network is too well entrenched. Don't concern yourself about ol' Sean and his lads. You may be able to stop the greedy brokers and their greedy bosses. They've all become careless. But you know as well as I do, they will pull all of their political strings and call in all their markers if the Feds give them a little sting. It takes more than a bee sting to bring down a dinosaur. You watch, lad, the first big guy you go after is

going to get support from the biggest names in the commodity industry. And in Washington. They will come running to his defense. You know why?"

Michael stood, pitched another beer cap into the flowing water. "Yeah, I know why. Because they're all on the payroll--and in a big way. If the Feds are able to take down one big trader, the whole deck of cards could fall. The Exchanges will lose their self-governing privileges. The Washington supporters in Congress and the Agriculture Department will not only lose their huge pay-offs but could also end up doing a little time. The scandal will bring down everybody from the officials of the Exchanges to some of the most influential men in Washington. The commodity markets, as we know them today, will be dead in a few years."

Sean wiped his brow with the back of his hand. The southwest breeze felt good and was finally ushering summer air into the city. "You're right, Michael. You'll have Senators, Congressmen, and that hot-shot agriculture fellow from Washington break their backs to curtail any blemish to one of their insiders. Not to mention the Exchange attorneys and board members who have made an impressionable dent in Chicago's philanthropic society. How far do you think you'll get trying to fight people who are stronger and have far more money than the people investigating the fight?"

His voice stormed with concern. "It's *your* ass, Michael, not theirs. How long do you think it'll take them to find out that Michael 'Hawk' Hogan was the man who instigated the investigation and caused them international embarrassment? When they find out it was you, how long do you think it will take for them to kill you? That's what they will do, lad. There is no middle ground with these men. You, above others, should know that."

He watched Michael sigh and roll his head to relieve the building tension. "I'm protected."

Sean snapped out. "By whom? Bo Lynch? He's drunk by mid-day. My grandmother, God rest her soul, could out-fox Bo Lynch if he's using liquid courage. Is that fellow over there smelling the roses going to protect you? He looks like a Boy Scout. He's probably never used a gun to kill anybody. Who is he, anyway?"

A smile eased onto Michael's face and the sparkle returned to his eyes. "I'll take care of Bo. He's one of the best when he's straight."

Again Sean felt his own irritation. "But he's seldom straight, Laddie. You need somebody reliable not a sometimes-man. How about the other lad over there?"

Sean sensed the words came quickly--too quickly. "He's just a friend from New York who has done some backup work before. His name is Pete Lew...Pete Alexander. He starts brokering tomorrow. He'll watch me close. I trust him".

Sean bore into Michael's eyes. He had begun to say the man's real name, then gave an alias. Who did Michael think he was talking to? Some novice? Either the man was on loan from Carlo Santini or he was a Fed. He looked over at the man who was admiring the flowers. He wasn't Italian. He must be government. But he didn't look the part, even

if he was a Fed. He knew that most Feds weren't equipped physically or mentally to go up against a professional killer. They considered confusion as protocol. Anger blew his words out. "Goddammit, Michael. This is your army? A drunk and a panty-ass federal agent who's probably fresh out of law school? And how about your family?"

But he saw that Michael wasn't a bit flustered. In fact, he seemed to radiate confidence. "My family is taken care of."

Sean took his hat off and slapped it against his thigh in frustration. This always happens, he thought. The bastard would only give him half the story and let him try to figure out the rest. While Michael remained in complete control of himself.

A gust of wind fluffed his hair again, blowing it around his forehead. Sean's words were furious, filled with frustration. "So your family is taken care of? Is somebody taking the kids to school? Your wife shopping? Checking your mail for a letter bomb? Checking the UPS man? The milk man? The telephone man? The garbage man? How about your car? And does somebody check the restaurants you go to? The telephone booth? Under the table? Under the chair? The guy who sits next to you with a brief case? How about the trading pit? Do you think a gun is the only way to get rid of a man? How about a tiny prick that you hardly notice, and in minutes you're dead of a massive heart attack with no sign of the poison that caused it? Jesus Christ, Michael. I'm the twins' godfather, so I have a vested interest in their safety, and in you, and in Maria, and in the rest of your family. You're my family too. Can't the Feds find some guy who's single and just as crazy as you to do their dirty work?" He stopped, out of breath. He felt defeated, angry. In a millisecond he saw the clumps of Liam's flesh spread on the streets of Belfast. His mother had died blaming Sean--blaming him for Liam's death. He had to live with that. Now, his other brother, Michael, wanted to test his wits with the stronger enemy.

Michael flipped a rock into the fountain water. They watched the ripples circle out until they were caught in the current caused by the splashing, then disappeared.

"I'm the best man for the job, Sean. I can tell the bad guys from the good guys. The hand is not faster than the eye with me. I know all their tricks. Seen 'em a thousand times. Besides, I've taken the fuckers on once before and lost. I don't intend to lose this time."

Sean was desperately trying, unsuccessfully, to hold his Irish temper. "Is that what this is all about? Your goddamn ego. They beat you once and now you're going back to teach them a lesson?"

He heard his own voice rise in mocking anger. "Oh, don't fuck with the likes of the proud Hawk Hogan because I'm going to get the honorable Federal Government on your ass all in the name of Truth and Justice. Then we'll see who is King of the Trading Pits."

Sean's exasperation shackled his anger. He turned and sat on the wide, tile-border wall surrounding the fountain. When he looked up into Michael's face, he saw the sparkle

in his eyes change to dark ice--which meant danger. "You're a maniac. Do you know that, Michael? You know nothing of survival..."

Before he could finish, he saw Michael's face muscles tighten. Just as quickly, he felt the jab of calloused, closed fingers, just below the right shoulder bone, sending a sharp, paralyzing pain down his arm. He realized in an instant that somebody was coaching Michael in the use of his hands as weapons. The blow was quick, unexpected, and placed perfectly in the fatty area below the shoulder where a conglomeration of nerves met. This certainly wasn't a lethal area, but it was enough to keep an opponent from reaching for a pistol or retaliating quickly.

Sean looked over at Flaherty, who had put the paper down and was now standing. Shamus seemed confused, knowing the two men were good friends. Sean waved him off with his left hand, and Flaherty took a step back. He then looked over at Michael's man, who was facing Flaherty with his hand inside his black windbreaker. He waved him off also. Both men resumed their original, watchful positions.

"What the hell did you hit me for? Did I touch a nerve, Lad?"

Michael's eyes remained cool, his voice, strong. "I'm sorry, Sean. I can't afford to have you underestimate me. Maybe you are right. Maybe I do have some of my grandfather in me. All I know is that I'm tired of living with and accepting a corrupt situation. The Mob and brokers are playing with morality and honesty like steel balls in a pin-ball machine.

"What the crooks forget is that all the balls eventually fall into a small, black hole. Since I'm dealing with a dangerous situation, I have to become dangerous. I am carrying a gun, and I know how to use it. I have been forced to carry a gun because my adversaries carry guns. I have learned to use my hands out of self defense because I have already been pushed around by two of Peterson's men. I was lucky to get out of that situation with my life. That man behind me, smelling the roses, *could* and *would* put a bullet in Flaherty's head before he had time to blink. The men I have covering the house are professionals who use unorthodox methods of discipline to dissuade unwelcome visitors." Once again, his eyes took on the color of dark ice. "You ask for *The Ghost of Kildare*, Sean. I'll show you *The Deceptive One*. I'll give you Michael Martin Hogan. You have to be careful what you pray for, Sean...your petition may be answered."

He hesitated for a moment before he spoke again. Sean felt a chill run the length of his spine. He had never seen or heard his brother so intense, so convincing, so matter of fact about taking on some of the strongest men in America. His father's peaceful philosophy was on the wane within him. In its place, the cunning ferocity of his grandfather was beginning to rise.

Michael made a half turn, reached up and picked a piece of lint from Sean's sweater. The sleeve of his white silk shirt flapped with the warm breeze. "And our mutual friend, Bo Lynch, will be sober one day soon. Until then, he will be given the responsibilities of a soldier. Not a general."

Sean's mouth felt parched. He nodded his head with acceptance and respect. Jesus, Mary and Joseph, he thought. The bad guys had finally lit the Hawk's fuse. Sean had no doubt that Michael meant what he said. The balance had tipped. Events would soon be out of control at the Exchanges. One leader would emerge.

"Let's walk, Michael."

They began to stroll across the fountain square toward a path perfectly manicured and laced with rows of freshly planted flowers. Impatiens, petunias, pansies, begonias, and hundreds of rose bushes. Sean couldn't help thinking that the park gardeners indeed took pride in planting their splendid parade of colors. "Beautiful, eh, Michael?"

Again the eyes were cold, the voice cool. "What? The flowers or the two gunmen behind us and the subject we are talking about?"

"Don't be cynical, Lad. You're talking to your friend who loves you like a brother. The only thing separating us is our philosophies. And they aren't really that far apart. Just different countries. I'm concerned for you and your family. I don't want you to get hurt."

Michael sighed as he kicked at the gravel path. "I'm here today so you won't get hurt, Sean. Not me. I'm asking you to back off. Back off completely. Your men are good enough traders to make money without violating..."

Sean put his hand up, cutting him short. "Michael, Dublin has upped our commodity quota to four million a month. I intend to fulfill that need. With or without the Feds. With or without you. I've never had your blessing, and I don't give a shit about the Feds. They can't touch my companies or any of my men. Our sources and techniques are well covered."

They stopped by a lush red-rose bush, and Michael leaned to pluck one of the flowers. He held it up to Sean. He looked at the perfect red petals and noticed the numerous sharp thorns on its stem. "Pretty, isn't it, Sean?"

"Aye. It's beautiful!"

Michael twirled the flowers between his fingers. "Don't you think the rose is a little bit like life, Sean?"

Sean felt his brow furrow in question. "How do you mean, Lad?"

Michael's eyes slanted in thought. His face was calm, as the flower stopped twirling. "Life can be beautiful like this rose. But everything isn't as it seems, is it?"

Sean didn't answer, his eyes on the rose. Michael whispered, "Who would think that such a beautiful creation like this flower--and like life could do this to a careless man?"

Sean watched Michael grasp the full length of the thorny stem in his palm and squeeze it hard. Sean winced and felt his teeth tighten at the pain Michael must have felt. There was no sign of discomfort on Michael's face, though. In fact, he showed no emotion whatsoever. As his fist tightened around the thorns, it turned white with pressure. Blood began to drip onto the white stone path where they stood.

"What are you trying to prove, Michael?"

Michael slowly opened his hand, and Sean saw a blood-filled palm punctured by the thorns. "The rose is beautiful; the commodity industry was once beautiful." A silence fell for a moment. "But if you try to squeeze the life out of something beautiful..." He didn't finish the sentence, just looked with a sense of sadness at the flower. "Surely this rose will die prematurely now that I have cut it from its life line. But look at the message it leaves before it dies." Michael flipped the rose to the side of the path and held his hand out in front of Sean.

Sean waved his hand toward the fallen rose. "Am I supposed to feel guilty at your poetic analogy of right and wrong?"

In spite of the gusting wind, everything in the park seemed to be standing still. The whispering trees seemed far off. The sparkle had returned to Michael's eyes almost as if the pain of the flower's bite had rejuvenated an inner belief of righteousness.

Michael spoke softly. "We're all guilty, Sean. We have all taken advantage of good people, places, and things. It's almost as if wealth dictates an ultimatum that we must destroy and deceive in order to *get*. We don't believe that 'less is best.' We believe that 'more is better.' We get so wrapped up in the acquisition of money and material goods that we forget, or block out, the unwritten fact that we can't continue to take and strangle beautiful things without their turning mean and ugly before they die. In the end, they will hurt us before they take their last breath."

"What's your point, Plato?"

Michael reached into his back pocket for a handkerchief and began to wipe the blood from his right hand. "My point is simple, Sean. I'm going after the people who are squeezing the life out of our industry. I'm part of that industry, and my thorns are sharp. I will not die easily. I know who is responsible for turning a healthy, financial community into a plague ridden institution of black, internal, festering pus."

Sean shifted his weight to his left leg and pushed his hands into his pockets. "And you're going to be the doctor and cut out the poison!"

Michael shrugged as he turned toward the fountain. He finished wiping the bloody hand with a linen handkerchief and returned it to his back pocket. "No, Sean. It's too late for a doctor. It's even too late for a mortician. I'm just the grave digger. I only hope that my grave isn't among the ones I'm digging."

As they approached the fountain square, Sean said, "You say we have a dying industry, Michael. That certain greedy people are squeezing the life out of it. Yet, our business continues to escalate. Our volume grows larger. We set new trading records. The prices of memberships go higher by the day. We even have communist countries interested in trading our commodities. That's not what I consider death, Lad. I think our markets thrive on greed, get healthy on greed. Take the greed away and the markets die."

Michael gave no immediate response. Just walked slowly toward the fountain, head down. Sean wasn't even sure his last comments were heard, but then Michael spoke. "Sean, you've surely seen a potter's field. I mean a real one, where there are no pine

boxes? Where they just wrap the corpse of a poor man in a dirty sheet and throw him into a shallow grave, then cover him with a foot or two of dirt? There are hundreds of them in Ireland."

Sean felt the hair rise on the back of his neck. His body tightened with anger. "You know goddamn well I know about potter's fields. My whole family is buried in a field north of Dublin." His lips quivered. "Except for my brother--because we couldn't find enough of him to bury."

He breath came in pants. His palms were clammy. The flashback to Ireland had unnerved him. He looked with harshness at Michael for purposely bringing up a subject that he knew lay at the root of Sean's insatiable furor for the Irish Cause.

Michael didn't look at him. He didn't seem to care about opening the wound that would never completely heal. Michael had shocked him on purpose, the bastard. He felt like slapping his self-righteous pup friend.

Michael spoke right through the resentment. "You know how beautiful and green the grass is on top of the grave and how well flowers grow there? Seedlings from wild flowers attach to some of those mounds making the fields look more like gardens than grave yards. Right?"

"Aye. Right. I can't stand your analogies, Michael. Never could. You're just like your father. From him, I could accept them. From you, they're a pain in the bum."

He shook his head disgustedly as Michael continued. "The reason for those beautiful graves, Sean, is because of the decay--the food that lies beneath them. Dig one up sometime. See the paradox. Just inches away from beauty lies ugly, stinking death."

Sean grabbed Michael by the shoulder and turned him abruptly. His hand moved in a half motion backward to slap him, stopping in mid-air. Michael made no move to stop the oncoming blow. His eyes were calm. They stopped Sean, instead. His hand fell to his side. His heart fell, too. Michael's expression was unreadable. Sean felt himself shaking. He yanked his other hand from Michael's shoulder and turned away.

"Am I touching a nerve, Sean?"

"It's a good thing I love you, or you'd be dead, Michael."

"I'm trying to make a point, Sean. As healthy and busy and aggressive as our industry may seem, it is only a covering for decay and ugliness. Things aren't what they seem, remember?"

Now he was quiet, his back to Michael, as he watched a group of sailboats scud with the wind on the lake. Michael had dredged up the memory. Cruel circumstances. The death of his parents and brother in Belfast. Michael was a brilliant strategist, like his father. He knew the only way he could make an impression on Sean was to hit him in his only vulnerable spot. That was forcing him to recall a few small, flowered mounds in a Dublin potter's field. He felt an arm reach around his shoulder. Its strength pulled him close to Michael.

"Hey, brother. Time to come back from the old sod. I'm sorry for opening old wounds, but it's the only way I could get your attention. You had to know what I'm up against. You had to know what you're up against. I had to at least warn you to cover your ass. Whether you do or not is up to you. I'll do nothing or say anything to implicate you in any wrongdoing at the Exchanges. If the Feds want you, they'll have to come after you on their own." Michael's strong grip pulled him tighter. "Are you okay?"

Sean felt a mist in his eyes. The Hogan family was all that he had when he came to America--they still were. Michael was younger than he, and carried the same dreams as his own brother, Liam. Sean loved the roughneck, but he was afraid for him.

"Yes, Michael. I'm fine. You're determined every so often to impose your complex ideals of morality on me, aren't you?"

Michael smiled and turned to face him. Saying nothing, he took hold of Sean's shoulders. His eyes were gentle and had regained their spark of life and goodness. The eyes said all that had to be said. They embraced. The sound of the flowing water calmed them both.

"You take care, Sean."

"You, too, Lad. Anything I can do? If you need Flaherty or any of my men, just speak up."

Michael nodded. "I'll be fine. Just be sure you're covered."

He shook his head in agreement and watched as Michael turned and walked toward the parking area. His man, Pete Lew...Alexander joined him, and they disappeared behind a tall hedge.

Sean sat on the edge of the fountain for a few minutes reviewing the meeting that had just taken place. He reached back and ran his hand through the clean, flowing water, then wiped his wet hand down his beard. He smoothed and groomed it as he squeezed his face in a downward motion. He stood, wiped a tear from his eye, and took a deep breath of the warm southern air.

He walked back to the path he and Michael had traversed, bent down, and rested for a moment in a squatting position. He picked up the rose Michael had purged himself with. Its petals were already beginning to curl. Death would be soon. He examined the bloody thorns and took the stem into his own hand and squeezed it with his powerful grip. He felt his left hand twitch with the pain of the needle thorns being forced into his hand. As blood oozed, it mingled with Michael's on the stone path. He said out loud, "No, my brother. Things are not at all the way they seem, are they?"

He tucked the rose into the lapel of his suit jacket as a reminder of Michael's simple, clear philosophy. As he stood, he looked to the sky and said out loud, "Patrick Hogan, you have a stubborn, infuriating son. You taught him well--but I'm afraid your own father, Martin, has control of him now." He wiped his eyes, turned, and walked away from the garden toward Buckingham Fountain and his gray Rolls Royce, which Flaherty had retrieved. As he strolled, head down, he noticed his body throwing a shadow. The south

winds had overcome the gray skies, golden straws of sunlight lanced the hungry earth. Sean stopped and raised his head to a brilliant, blue Heaven spotted generously with white cotton clouds. He sensed the presence of a Protective Power. He made the sign of the cross and stepped into the back seat of his two-hundred-thousand-dollar automobile.

THIRTY-ONE

Tony Lorenzo - US Attorney

Tony Lorenzo sat at his large mahogany desk contemplating what Michael had just said. Michael watched him toy with a yellow pencil. A tall, handsome man, he wore a three-piece, dark pin-striped suit. A thin, closely trimmed black mustache gave him an air of distinction. This also detracted from his receding hair line. His dark hair was cut short and combed impeccably to the side, college style. Black rimmed glasses framed his alert, brown eyes. The American and state flags stood at attention behind him, guarding a large circular government plaque on the wall.

"Michael, I think you're overreacting a bit. What good are Miss Winters and Miss McFadden, if they don't work in the offices of the men we know to have criminal links? If they are going to work in the Federal Building, merely compiling and sorting commodity-fraud information, they might as well go back to Washington. Hell, I have hundreds of government people to do the paper work. And only two federal agents to retrieve the information from the companies in question." He looked for approval from Pete, who was leaning quietly against a bookcase filled with leather-bound law books. Pete said nothing.

Michael adjusted himself in his chair. His eyes still ached from his abrupt awakening after two hours' sleep, and too much booze the previous night. He tried to rub the irritation from them, then glanced at his watch: 6:18 a.m.

He covered his mouth with the back of his hand to smother a yawn. This conversation was going nowhere, he thought. He knew the decision had been made despite his protest. "Well, Tony. It's obvious to me that you and Simpson feel this is just another white collar investigation. Danger is incidental to you people."

Lorenzo looked bored as his eyes moved from the pencil he held in his hand, up to Michael. "Danger is not incidental to me, Mike. I just don't happen to agree with you regarding the risk involved. We had to pull a lot of strings to place these girls in the two companies--besides, they have been trained to see danger coming and to get the hell out."

Michael felt a warmth flow through him as he thought of Samantha, the shadow woman in his life. At the same time, he felt uneasy about the position she was in. Too dangerous, he thought. For obvious reasons, he could only indicate to Lorenzo a professional concern for her safety. He leaned forward and rested his forearms on his legs. "You have Samantha working as a receptionist for Peterson. A man with no conscience. He doesn't give warnings. You have Colleen working as a trade checker and out-trade clerk for Conti and Ruzzo. Two men who represent the strongest criminal elements in the

country. They don't give warnings, either. You can't train moral men and women to sense danger when it appears out of nowhere. These men we're talking about are beyond the morality of this world or any other world. The only predictable thing about them is that they'll do something nasty."

Lorenzo was patient. Michael could see the conditioned, government training in his controlled eyes. "Come on, be reasonable, Michael. Even if their cover was to be blown, these jerks aren't going to go after two female federal agents for monitoring phone calls and compiling trading information. They both did a terrific undercover job on the Graylord investigation. They'll do just as well with this sting. For Christ sake, we're talking fraud, not...not *murder*."

Michael's guts tightened with Lorenzo's last word. He pushed himself back in his chair, shaking his head. "You are dead-ass wrong. Both you and Simpson are wrong. These guys don't give a shit about people whether they're bakers or grocers or pawn-brokers or FBI agents. They're killers. Killers of the free markets, the economy, and...of people who get in their way. They have no respect for anybody or anything."

He rubbed his temples. The throbbing behind his eyes remained. It was too early in the day to be arguing with the government, he thought. He'd have a better chance of winning an argument with Maria than with Lorenzo. And he was zero for twenty years with her. His words were firm as he looked through the dark-rimmed glasses. "Who takes the responsibility if something goes wrong? Simpson will say it was your idea, and you'll say it was his idea. Then you'll both..."

Lorenzo cut Michael short. "Nothing is going to go wrong with my investigation. The decision has been made, so let's drop it."

Michael pushed further, wanting a commitment. "So, you'll take the responsibility, Tony?"

Lorenzo returned his stare with an icy look of his own. "I'm responsible for my men, not Simpson's, and I don't have to account to you. The orders have come from Washington, and those are the orders I follow. Not yours. Is that clear?"

Michael snapped back. "Clear, yes. Acceptable, no. If anything happens to either Winters or McFadden, I'm holding you and Simpson personally liable. You have me into this investigation up to my balls. I talked to you a month ago when I found out about this. You feigned ignorance, but said you would try to move them into a safer position. Now, I find out you gave your blessing, going along with Simpson. What I've told you about the Fat Man, Ruzzo, and Conti doesn't mean jackshit, does it? I've agreed to help the government. In doing so, I've got my life on the line for no personal gain. Don't you think one target is enough?"

He knew Lorenzo was listening, but not hearing. As he flipped his pencil on the table, then smoothed his thin mustache, Michael thought he noticed his hand tremble slightly. The U.S. Attorney wasn't used to being talked to like this by a civilian. There was no 'Yes Sir,' 'No Sir,' 'Let me kiss your ass, Sir,' in this conversation. Lorenzo put both

hands, palms down, on his pompous desk. Looking over at Pete, who had been listening in silence, he asked, "Pete, what do you think?"

He's just asking Lewis for his opinion to pacify me, Michael thought. Tension was building between them. Michael knew that Lorenzo was blowing a little smoke Pete's way only to take a breather from him.

His eyes locked with Pete's for a millisecond. His message was clear, Trust me.

Pete pushed himself away from the bookcase and walked the large room, thinking. Michael watched him. In spite of damn little sleep, he looked fresh for his first day of trading on the Exchange floor. His hair had been trimmed but still fell over the collar-edge of his black windbreaker. His young face and semi-grubby apparel gave no clue to his federal agent status.

Pete stopped and took hold of the back of a conference chair near Lorenzo. The fact that he stood, looking down at the U.S. Attorney, gave Michael another clue to Pete's rebellious attitude toward his superiors. "I have to agree with you and Mr. Simpson. The girls have been trained for dangerous duty, so let them get their feet wet. The information they retrieve could cut the investigation short. We're going to need names, addresses, account numbers. They'll be able to furnish a whole lot more once they tap into their employer's computer."

Michael felt his face flush with anger and frustration. He began to rise. "Pete, you know as well as..."

He was cut short by a curt warning from Pete. "Sit down, Mike, and shut up."

Pete looked back at Lorenzo. "We all have a big job to do, Tony, and we have to work together. Sometimes we don't like the arrangements or the assignments we're given, but that's life. Besides, you and I are bound to follow the instructions of others. We've taken an oath to do that, whether we like it or not. I feel that certain decisions have been made, and that's it. You and Simpson are the bosses--not Michael Hogan."

Michael was going to protest but decided against it. He saw the relief in Lorenzo's face as he removed his horn-rimmed glasses and placed them on his desk. Tony was obviously surprised with Pete's show of support. "Well, Pete, I'm glad there are a few of us left who still believe in the chain of command."

Michael sighed and leaned back in his chair. He looked around Pete to a floor-length window that framed a wall of early-morning fog. What a bunch of bullshit, he thought to himself, but he remained quiet and seated. His headache was getting worse. Lewis hadn't agreed with his superior's wishes for ten years. Why now? Then Michael remembered the quick look from Pete that said, "Trust me." He must be blowing smoke himself to win Lorenzo's confidence. At least he hoped so.

Lorenzo cleared his throat, his confidence regained. "Mike, I like you. You're a very sophisticated and courageous man, but you know nothing of law enforcement. We know exactly what we're doing. As far as the girls are concerned, we will review their

progress and talk to them daily. We will also have a man close by if they need help. If we think there is any problem, we'll pull them out immediately."

Lorenzo's thin mustache lifted with a reassuring smile. He perceived a victory, now that Pete had sided with him. Michael raised his face to meet Lorenzo's. Drilling his hawk eyes into the U.S. Attorney, he said, "Over a nice dinner and a glass of wine I think I could get to like you, Lorenzo."

He used his last name to take the friendship out of what he was about to say. His peripheral vision told him Pete was giving him the "shut up" message again. Sidestepping Pete's glance, he continued anyway.

He kept his voice prophetic and cool. "There is nothing social about our relationship. You sit behind that big, shiny desk surrounded by impressive flags, plaques, and framed citations. You're just like most other government officials, a pawn representing an oblique group of indifferent, power-hungry jerks in Washington. Don't you make the mistake in thinking you and I walk the same path--*we don't!* Maybe our paths go in the same direction, but yours is shadowed with obtuse angles and diversities, all brought on by self-indulging politicians. I don't have those obstacles hanging around my neck like an millstone--you do."

Lorenzo's face flushed, but he remained in control. "Your point is what?"

Michael's eyes narrowed further. "My point is, I still hold you and Simpson responsible for the well-being of those two women. If you are the man who is heading up this investigation, and if Pete and I are reporting to you, then the buck stops with you-- whether you like it or not. Leadership requires responsibility. Most powerful men forget that when the going gets tough."

Lorenzo tapped his fingers nervously in front of him. His face took on the cold seriousness of the cunning attorney he was. He replaced his glasses. Michael sensed he didn't feel fully dressed without them. "You have a real attitude problem with our government, Michael, and not a hell of a lot of respect. Now you're taking on the role of judge and jury, and I don't like it. You just..."

Michael cut in curtly. "Mr. U.S. Attorney--there will be no trial. You will be judged on your actions and your ability to perform quickly in a dangerous situation. I'll hold up my end of the deal. I expect...no, I demand, the same from you." Michael felt his body go cold. "If you fuck with me, Tony, you won't have to worry about me becoming judge and jury. I will become the executioner. You can count on that."

Color drained from Lorenzo's face. Michael's impudence was more than he could take. He was just short of losing it when Pete broke the silence.

He moved quickly around the chair and held out his hands. "Hey, come on, you guys, loosen up. We're all on the same side. The enemy is out there." His left hand motioned to the fog-covered windows. "Enough about your professional hang-ups. We have a job to do, and it begins in about an hour and a half."

Michael's eyes still penetrated Lorenzo. The attorney seemed relieved to hear from another country. Avoiding Michael's glare, he fumbled to straighten an already impeccably neat desk, and without looking up he said, "You're right, Pete, we do have work to do. Today is the agents' first day in the trading pits, right?"

Michael clenched his jaw. He was ready for a fight, and he knew they felt it coming.

Pete would lead the conversation away from the war of stubborn minds. He picked up his briefcase next to the chair. Gingerly he set it on the glass-top coffee table. While he ran the combination with his thumb, he talked. "Today's the day, Tony. Michael has been a good instructor. We'll have Fitzsimmons and Harris trading with Bo Lynch at the Mercantile Exchange. They'll be working the S & P and the Eurodollar pits. Michael will work with Ted Tully, Barry Kane, and me at the Board of Trade in the soybean pit this week. The bond pit next week. After next week, the agents will begin to roam from pit to pit, but most of our attention will be in the beans, bonds, S & P's, and currencies."

The briefcase popped open, and Michael watched Pete remove a black handgun. He set it on the glass top. Then he pulled out two small packages wrapped in bubble paper.

"These are the toys our men will be carrying into the pits with them." He quickly unwrapped one package. In it was a shamrock-shaped tie tack. Imbedded into its center was a light-green eye that concealed a miniature, wireless camera.

Pete held it in the palm of his right hand. "This little devil is state-of-the-art. These cameras were designed by the CIA and used for undercover work all over the world. Sophisticated criminals might spot them, but I assure you nobody at the Exchanges has ever seen anything like this."

Pete placed the tie-tack in front of Lorenzo. He asked, "How do you take a picture, and how does it focus?"

Pete removed another small object from the protective wrapping paper. About the size of a Bic lighter, it was flatter and had two tiny black buttons on its side. "This is the actual camera which we will be carrying in our trading jackets. The eye of the shamrock has an automatic focus with a combination battery and microchip half the size of a BB."

Lorenzo seemed impressed. "The shamrock is innocent enough, but what happens if one of the agents inadvertently pulls this little control mechanism out of his pocket while paying for something? It's thin enough to fit comfortably between a few dollar bills."

Pete, enjoying the espionage toys, continued. "If one of the guys drops it, or pulls it out while paying for a cup of coffee or something, which is unlikely, he merely takes out a cigarette." Pete followed his own instructions and produced a filtered cigarette, and pushed one of the tiny buttons, and a flame appeared at the top of the fake lighter. He pulled smoke deep into his lungs and blew it across Lorenzo's desk past a small, bronze desk sign which read, *Thank you for not smoking*. "Just like Jimmy Bond."

Pete continued: "The other button is for taking the pictures." He demonstrated. There was no audible sound to the camera except for a slight whine that moved the film along.

"There are seventy-two prints to each roll of film, which is about the size of a tiny spool of thread. After each trading session, I will collect all the film from the agents, then pass it on to Andy Golden for processing. Each morning the agent will open the camera by removing a little screw at its base, put a new roll of film in, and set the time and date which will appear on each photo. The tiny battery has a lifetime of at least twenty-four months, but will be checked frequently."

Pete handed the items to Lorenzo. He examined both objects and looked up at Michael. "You see these?"

Michael decided to be friendly and forced enthusiasm. "Yes, I saw them. The pictures are exceptionally clear. You can count a man's eyelashes at fifty feet or see the teeth of a flea at three feet. Should be very effective if the man using it knows what he's doing."

Lorenzo sat back and began to swivel again. He rubbed his chin and said, "Terrific."

He returned the camera and shamrock to Pete. "What do you call it?"

Pete looked back at Michael, blocking Lorenzo's view of him. Michael held his two middle fingers down with his thumb, leaving his little finger and index finger exposed, meaning "bullshit" in sign language.

Pete threw him a frown and turned back to Lorenzo. We call this baby 'Hawkeye.'"

Lorenzo peered around Pete and said, "That's appropriate." The color had returned to his face as he concentrated on Pete. "What other toys do you have?"

Pete withdrew another package similar to the first. "This little gadget, gentlemen, is a recorder. We call it 'Rabbit Ears.' As you can see, it's about the same size as the camera, but instead of being manually operated, it will be built into each agent's trading jacket with a zipper so new tapes can be inserted each day. This should be programmed each morning with the time and date, which will later show up on the tape. Unless the agent shuts it off, it will run continuously for eight hours."

Lorenzo turned the thin recorder over a few times in his hand and·said, "Is there an on-off switch?"

Michael watched the ash from Pete's cigarette fall to the floor and saw Lorenzo wince. Pete took another long drag and blew smoke into the air over the U.S. Attorney's head. He looked around the room. Where can I put this out?"

Lorenzo coughed, looked for an ashtray, and said, very much out of character, "Shit…just put it out in that dirt." He motioned to one of the many potted plants in the room. Pete took another quick puff, then snuffed the cigarette into the soil around a large

philodendron gracing the center of the coffee table. The butt sizzled for a moment and died.

Michael smiled, "Atta boy, Tony. Loosen up." He watched with satisfaction as Lorenzo grimaced, as if he had just tasted a rotten tomato.

Pete continued. "Each agent will be wearing two recorders, one on each side, just below the shoulder. That's to pick up conversations on both sides of him. These shoulder patches..." he produced two square patches that read ALEX, "...are made of tiny wire mesh with built in audio receptors. At least one will be going all the time. If a conversation starts up on the left side of the agent, he merely runs his hand down the patch on his right shoulder. The heat of his hand will automatically shut the right recorder off. If the conversation is on his right, he rubs the left shoulder, and that recorder turns off. To turn the recorder back on, he repeats the process by rubbing the patch. The heat from the hand will activate the recorder both on and off."

Lorenzo asked, "Why arm patches instead of hidden microphones? And what does ALEX mean?"

Michael watched Pete with amusement. Pete knew all there was to know about spy work. But how well was all this going to work, with three hundred guys crammed into a trading pit the size of a back-yard swimming pool shouting, spitting, moving, jumping, punching, swearing? Michael shook his head and listened as Pete continued.

"Pete Alexander is my alias, and the trading symbol on the floor that I'll be known as is ALEX. The patches will be in place next week. The reason for the shoulder patches is simple. The Louis Gonzalez case was thrown out of federal court in Dallas. For four years, federal agents used hi-tech microphones to tape conversations between Gonzalez and drug kingpins. The judge said that the tapes were based on conversations that the human ear didn't hear, so were inadmissable. The court considered it entrapment and a violation of dear Louis Gonzalez's rights. So he walked."

Lorenzo looked up at Pete, sucking in his top lip before he spoke. "And six months later, you blew his ears off."

Pete stood straight up in front of Lorenzo. He glanced back at Michael, who just waved his hand in front of him, indicating he had the floor.

Pete objected. "No, I didn't blow his ears off. I just made it difficult for him to hear again."

Michael looked at his wristwatch. "Let's get on with it, Pete, we've a market opening to catch."

Pete took the patches, recording device, and camera from Lorenzo. "So, Tony, the patches are within five to six inches of the agents' ears. They produce an exact replica of the sounds and voices around, no higher pitch, no lower. The sounds the patch-microphones catch can also be heard by the agent. Samantha and Colleen will also be armed with these, and other equipment to install in their work place."

Lorenzo sat back in his heavy chair and swiveled to the left again. "Please, Pete, let's not bring the girls up again. Michael, what do you think of these fancy gadgets?"

Michael stood and stretched. "I think they will be totally inept in the pits. Too much noise, confusion, motion. The human eyes can't see, nor can the human ear hear what's happening in the pits. Same goes for these toys.

"I think the equipment will come in handy down the line when your agents are invited to breakfast or coffee or cocktails with the brokers. They should get plenty of info then because the surroundings will be more confined and quiet. One, two, or three guys in one conversation. The trading pits are going to be difficult."

Lorenzo pushed himself up from his chair and walked around his desk to show the two men out. "Are you going to be wearing these gadgets, Mike?"

Michael stopped in mid-stride and felt heat flash through his face. He made a half turn and just looked at Lorenzo, who put both hands out as if to stop a slamming door.

"Just curious, Michael, just curious. We'll do the spying. You just point out the bad guys." He put his hand out to shake Michael's.

Michael took the hand and squeezed it firmly, then held on to it. "As I said before, I'll hold up my end of the deal, Tony. You just remember what I said. You're the one I'm reporting to. I expect your support." He squeezed Lorenzo's hand and heard a finger joint crack.

"If I don't get your support, or if you try to pull my chain, or if your decision about the girls is wrong, I'll be a real nightmare for you. Please don't take me lightly. I'm not one of your checkers you can push around on a black-and-red board." Michael released his grip, and Lorenzo said, "We'll work good together. You and I aren't all that different."

Before Michael could counter, Pete had him pushed through the door and down the narrow halls of the Federal Building.

They were alone in the elevator as it descended quickly. Pete tugged at Michael's pastel sport coat. "What's with you today?"

Michael said, "I'm in a bad mood. Not enough sleep, unshaven, and no shower. I stepped in dog shit. I might be killed. I'm hung over. Nothing I can't live with. Oh, and by the way, why did you side with Lorenzo?"

Pete pulled him around so they were face to face. "One of us has to be the go-between--the good guy. They *know* they can't handle you. They only *think* they can't handle me. If I show a little loyalty, we'll have a much easier go of it. We need their information, their manpower, and their technology. So let's try not to rock the boat too much. Besides, Lorenzo isn't a bad guy, and he's not the enemy. I don't think he'll lie down on us if things get rough."

As the elevator doors opened eighteen floors later, Michael looked at his watch. "That whole conversation was a waste. Now let's do something positive and see how good a soybean trader you are. We've got forty-five minutes to opening. Are you ready, Pete?"

"For what?"

"For your first day of trading?"

Pete's lips turned to a sneer. "A piece of cake."

Michael was through the heavy glass door first, thinking to himself, "Piece of cake," eh. We'll see, Pal, we'll see.

THIRTY-TWO

Pit Toys

A warm summer breeze had entered Chicago during the night, forcing the cool lake air to vacate the city and return to the dark womb of Lake Michigan. Early morning fog cloaked the Loop area like a shroud of gray cotton.

Michael listened to the echo of his and Pete's footsteps as they clacked in unison on the granite plaza of the First Chicago Bank. He took a deep breath, pulled back his shoulders, and let the warm, moist air exhale slowly.

Pete was quiet, looking over his shoulder on numerous occasions to see if they were being followed. "Goddamn I hate the fog...hate Chicago...can't see the streets."

Michael was beyond worrying about being followed. In fact, he loved the fog: its secrets, its hiding places, its tumbling, luring mystique. "Don't worry, Pete. The streets can't see you either."

Michael knew Pete was full of apprehension. Everyone was on his first day of trading in the pits. He smiled to himself as he watched Pete practice buying and selling with his right hand, holding his briefcase in his left.

Michael's smile widened, and he said, "Palms out, you're selling. Palms in, you're buying. One hand up, you're buying or selling five contracts or less. Both hands up, you're buying or selling six contracts or more. *Don't*...I repeat for the fiftieth time, *don't*...put two hands up. *Don't* pick your nose. *Don't* scratch your chin or run your fingers through your hair. If you do, one of those smart Jew Boys or Quick Micks will lay a hundred-thousand bushels of soybeans on you so fast you'll feel like a turtle on its back in the middle of Lake Shore Drive."

Michael watched Pete's face pale, and through the fog, he looked almost dead. His long, messed hair was damp from the wet air, as was his black windbreaker. "I...I think I have it. Don't worry about a thing. I'm a fast learner."

Michael checked the time again and quickened his pace. "You're right. You and your agent buddies are all fast learners, but you are all handicapped."

Pete came to an abrupt halt, and Michael looked back, not breaking stride. "Come on, G-Man, we have a market opening to catch."

Pete came running up behind him and pulled at his sport coat like a little kid saying indignantly, "Hey, Jerkoff. Whadaya mean, 'We're handicapped'?"

Michael stopped. He looked down Jackson into a wall of wet fog. He kept his humor to himself and waved his right hand in front of Pete. "Well, for one thing, your I.Q. is what? A hundred and fifty or sixty?"

Pete looked at him like a cocker spaniel tilting his head. "So what?"

Michael bobbed his head and screwed up his face as if he were analyzing Pete. "Too smart, Pete."

He turned and began walking again. He knew Pete was annoyed. "What the hell do you mean, too smart?"

He shook his head. "You're just too intelligent. You could shave fifty to sixty points off your I.Q., and you would fit right in. You're going to over-think the market. I can just feel it, Pete--too analytical. You have to be able to act and react in seconds, without using your mind. Like an animal--plain ol' instinct! You have to utilize, not analyze. You have to sense, not think. You think before and after the market. You use your reactions in the pit, not your brains, like an all-pro middle linebacker. He senses the way the ball is going and makes his move before the quarterback even gets the ball. You're just too smart."

"My ass, too smart. Since when has being an idiot been a prerequisite for making money?"

Michael crossed Clark Street ahead of Pete, against protesting traffic. "Pete, I've been working with you and your agent friends for months. All you guys are brilliant. You're all well trained, disciplined, and follow instructions to the letter. Look at you, Pete. You have a law degree, speak six languages, top intelligence man in Viet Nam, traveled the world spying for the CIA, and for the past three years you've been doing dirty work for the FBI. Randy Harris and Ted Tully both have Ivy League law and accounting degrees and speak numerous languages. Joe Fitzsimmons has a Master's degree in Business and Accounting from MIT. And Barry Kane. I don't even want to think about him. I think he'd fuck up a car wash. Yet, he'll probably fit right in."

He stopped again before entering the Board of Trade Building and looked at Pete. "How did Kane ever get into the agency, anyway?"

Pete shook off his cynicism and responded, "Hey, forget Barry Kane. Do you really think we're going to blow it? I mean, everybody has read the books you handed out. We've all taken the courses required by the Exchanges, and we've spent a lot of time on the trading floors answering phones and running orders. I think we're ready, including Kane. Don't you?"

Michael couldn't help showing a crooked grin. Standing in front of him was a man who was far more intelligent than he, knew the streets of America and Europe better than most people know the inside of their homes, had a photographic memory, and could kill a sparrow at one hundred yards with a hand gun. And he was asking if he thought he was ready to do a little trading and catch a few bad guys.

He ran his fingers through his hair with both hands, feeling the moisture as he raked it straight back. "Pete, I'm just shittin' ya. You're ready to take on every pit bull and bagman in Chicago. So are your men." He thought for a moment and couldn't resist the

slam. "Why is it so difficult for you geniuses to remember what way to hold your hands when you're buying and selling?"

"You Asshole, Hogan. You're playing with my head again."

Michael laughed and began to push through the glass doors, then looked back at Pete. "How did Kane get into the Bureau?"

Pete's eyes had gone from cocker spaniel to German shepherd, keen. alert. Michael saw his brow pull back. "Politics! His father was an aide for Nixon and still hangs around the White House mopping up after the President."

Michael continued through the doors and spoke over his shoulder. "The government has no middle ground. It has an affinity for loading one side of the scale with brilliant, egocentric sons of bitches and the other side with stupid bastards."

He waited for Pete to follow him through the flapping door. He put his arm around his shoulder and said, "You're going to do just fine. Just remember to put your hands out if you're selling and hands in if you're buying."

"Right. That's the easy part. What happens if somebody sells me something?"

Michael's laughter echoed through the large, marble foyer. "If somebody sells you something, and the market goes up, you sell it, put the profit in your account, and make some money. If the market goes down you sell it, take the loss, and put it in Barry Kane's account or the government account. Fuck'em. You're not planning to take any losses, are you?"

Pete's face settled into a frown. "Jesus Christ, Michael. Be serious, will you?"

He led Pete into an open elevator and pushed one of the top buttons. "Penthouse, next stop."

Pete's color was still a nervous gray. "Penthouse, my ass. Let me off at the toilet. I have to throw up."

Michael's smile left his face as the chrome doors closed. Now it was time to go to work. Time to place his mind into the powerful gear that made him one of the best pit bulls in the business. Time to place his team of five FBI agents in the Arenas of Greed. He hoped they would cut out the cancer that was eating away at the markets.

He thought of Maria and the children. He hadn't spent thirty consecutive minutes with them since this operation had begun months ago. He thought of his futile conversation with Lorenzo, and the danger Samantha was in. He thought of Samantha. Somebody innocent was going to be hurt bad. He felt it in his gut.

He thought of the smile he'd left behind the elevator door on the first floor. His spirit told him it would be a long time before he smiled again. Was this the price he had to pay for wanting to play life fairly, honestly, competitively, and with some semblance of integrity? He had to compromise with phony politicians, neglect his family, cover up the passion he felt for another woman, find no humor in life, no enjoyment. This was the price he had to pay? If it was, then others were going to pay for his discomfort, and they would pay with their wallets, their prestige, and--their lives if it came to that.

A bell dinged in the distance, and the doors opened in front of him. He felt a nudge and looked at Pete. He felt no expression on his face, just a cold anger.

Pete's color and confidence had returned, and he must have sensed Michael's turmoil, his anger. "Come on, Hawk, we have a big job ahead of us. Let's go nail the bastards."

THIRTY-THREE

A Day in the Pits

Bo Lynch smelled the pre-opening market adrenalin in the buzzing S&P pit. It was the same every day, his own stench from the previous night's carousing and the body-odors of his fellow brokers. Booze, drugs, and stale perfumes gave off an unmistakable and disgusting afterburn that permeated the octagonal gambling arena like polluted steam.

The air conditioning on the modern Exchange floor fought in vain to cool and disperse the animal smells. He wiped rolling beads of sweat from his brow, then looked up at the large red letters of the digital wall clock. 8:25:12. Less than five minutes to opening.

Most brokers, in their rumpled clothes and disheveled, unkempt looks, were already perched in their daily spots. Others pushed and squeezed their way into the packed pit, jockeying for position. The noise of a thousand ringing telephones began to dissipate with the acceleration of pit-talk.

Bo wiped his forehead with a shaking left hand as he reviewed his opening orders. One hundred forty-eight contracts to buy and only fourteen to sell. The market would be sharply higher--how much he didn't know. It was 8:26:10.

Goddamn, he thought. How did Hogan expect him to conduct his business, teach a few panty-ass Feds to trade, and point out the bagmen at the same time? 8:27:32...two and a half minutes.

He looked across the pit to find Matt Leahy standing in his usual position, first step down into the pit at two o'clock from where Bo stood. He always had an accurate opening call.

He shouted over the crowd. "Hey, Matt. Matt Leahy." Leahy's eyes were down, focused on and reviewing his orders. He looked frantic, but he always did just before an opening.

Bo sighed as a drop of sweat rolled into his right eye. He tried again, this time louder. "Matt LEAHY." An associate of Leahy's looked over, then tugged at his partner's orange-and-white trading jacket. Leahy snapped back with an irascible snarl, then looked up to catch Bo's questioning eyes.

"IT'S OPENING HIGHER, LYNCH!"

"NO SHIT? HOW MUCH HIGHER?"

Leahy's pumpkin hair matched his jacket, both dark from sweat. He yelled back in a tone of panic, "SHIT, LYNCH, I DON'T KNOW. SEVENTY, EIGHTY

POINTS...MAYBE EVEN A HUNDRED HIGHER. I HAVE NO SELL ORDERS." He dropped his head again to resume his count.

Leahy's assistant motioned to Bo with one finger, then his thumb pointing up. The market was going to be at least 100 points higher. Probably more like 150, Bo thought.

Six orders were passed over his shoulder. He scanned their contents and just as quickly placed them in his deck chronologically.

He glanced to his right where Agent Joe Fitzsimmons was standing. His trading badge read SIMS; his alias was printed in black letters at the bottom of the badge, Joseph Simms. Bo didn't like the preppie prick. Not that he had done anything to bother him. He just didn't like any type of authority--especially government people.

He brought his face close to Fitzsimmons's ear. "SIMS! Just keep your eyes open, your mouth shut, and your hands in your pockets. Watch what I do, who I trade with, and remember what I told you. During the next few weeks I'll be forcing arguments with various brokers in the pit. They will be the guys to keep your eyes on. They are the reason you are here. They are all on the 'Hit List,' and everybody around them are bandits as well. You break into those groups, and you'll get all the information you want."

He had only seconds for last-minute instructions. "If I go after somebody physically, that broker will be one of the leaders. I plan to hit on the Fat Man's key laundry and skim coordinator shortly after the opening."

He moved his face closer to Fitzsimmons's ear. "His name is Tony Zitello...badge reads ZITO. He's standing a quarter of the way around the pit from you with a big bastard named Raulf Hoge; badge name, 'HOG'. Both are cock-eyed with cocaine. They bag and skim trades all day long, then they move the stolen money to their men in the pit so the paper can't be traced. They also launder large amounts of cash and only trade with each other. The money comes into the pit dirty from one account and goes out of the pit clean, into a virgin account. Zitello and the men around him are your main targets. Just keep your eyes open."

Fitzsimmons's blue eyes gave away nothing. He looked more like a scholar than a cop. "Don't get in any trouble for my sake, Lynch."

Bo's mouth curled with impatience. "Listen, Jerkoff. Everybody thinks I'm crazy anyway. Besides, not fighting in the pit would be out of character for me. I'll only go after Zitello today--unless somebody else pisses me off. So stay sharp! When you learn who's fuckin' who, start to move into the areas where the major bagmen stand. After awhile you'll get to know them. Then your work begins and I'm finished with you. Understand?"

He looked through Fitzsimmons's phony, wire-rimmed glasses that shaded his eyes. About the same height as Bo, he was not nearly as broad. His oversized trading jacket gave his wiry frame an even slighter look. The brokers wore ties because they were a requirement, but being the renegades they were, the ties on many of them were loose and askew. Fitzsimmons didn't fit the mold. His blue polka-dot tie had been pulled tight to his neck; his hair was neatly combed and his clothes were pressed.

Bo looked up at the clock, then back to Fitzsimmons. "One more thing. Loosen your goddamn tie, unbutton a few buttons, and don't shave for a few days. This isn't an interview with IBM, and it's not Wall Street. It's a contact sport held in a sewer. So start to look like a sewer rat, not a flamingo, Dickhead."

Fitzsimmons's face, calm and disciplined, reddened with embarrassment, as he began to pull at his tie. It was 8:29:00, one minute to kick-off. "Go do your thing, Lynch, and I'll do mine."

Bo felt a tug on his left sleeve, and a hand full of orders was thrust over his shoulder. He grabbed the orders and read them quickly. Another sixty-two contracts to buy. Only eight to sell. Another tug and two more orders. Buy eighteen and sell six at a price four hundred points higher. He stuffed the sell order in the right breast pocket with other orders that were of no immediate concern.

A large drop of sweat dripped from the tip of his nose onto the last order in his deck, which he used as a crib sheet. He ignored the sweat and wondered how Hogan could remember every order in his deck without writing it down on a crib. 8:29:19. He mumbled aloud, but to himself, as sweat began to soak his collar. "Get your count, Lynch. Get your act together."

The shout came from Matt Leahy. "Lynch...Bo Lynch."

Bo looked up to acknowledge Leahy. At the same time he was calculating the net amount he had to buy. Two hundred twenty-eight buy contracts; only twenty-two sell orders...net 206 to buy...plus the buy stop-orders which would kick in if the market opened more than 150 higher. Son of a bitch, he thought. Was a large income worth this type of pressure? Goddamn right it was, and he kept counting.

Leahy yelled again. "At least one fifty...probably two hundred higher."

Bo nodded and waved him off. The market was seconds away from opening. "Son of a bitch. Two hundred higher. That means thirty-eight more to buy on stop-orders; net 244 to buy."

Again he looked up at the clock. He was as ready as he was going to be. His hands were wet and shaking. The time was 8:29:56, four seconds to the bell.

Leahy opened the market with a scream the whole pit heard. "I'LL PAY THREE-FORTY-EIGHT-SIXTY FOR SEVEN HUNDRED." There were no offers. The whole pit erupted in a bidding war. Now, Leahy could hardly be heard. He shouted again. Louder this time. "PAY 'FORTY-EIGHT-EIGHTY FOR SEVEN HUNDRED." Still no sellers. The noise drowned out the 8:30 bell as buyers pushed and shoved, looking for scarce sell orders.

Bo was almost ready to panic and join in the frantic search for offers. Sweat oozed from every pore in his body.

His mind was like a dried, stiff wishbone being pulled in two different directions by the frenzy around him. Ready to snap, he then remembered Hogan telling him not to

join in a bidding war. "Keep cool. It's only money. Look for the big traders and order fillers." He could hear Hogan's voice. "And for Chrissake, don't panic!"

Bo's nerves settled. He looked to his left and saw Danny Holmes from Merrill Lynch, getting ready to do something. "I'll sell 500 at..." Before Holmes said the price, Bo's reflexes snapped his body into motion and he pushed four traders out of the way thundering, "SOLD, SOLD, I'LL TAKE TWO HUNDRED FIFTY." He didn't even know what price he was bidding for but Hogan had told him never to hesitate. Good brokers were always close to the true market price.

Holmes looked over and in a split second acknowledged him while selling the balance of his order. "BO LYNCH, YOU OWN TWO FIFTY AT THREE FORTY-NINE EVEN." Bo checked the trade with a hand signal.

Leahy screamed over the pit frenzy, "SOLD DANNY, I'LL TAKE ALL YA HAVE." Holmes responded. "I'M SELLING YOU SEVEN HUNDRED FIFTY CONTRACTS AT THREE FORTY-NINE EVEN." With hand signals, both men checked the number of contracts traded, then each raised a fist in the air meaning the price was EVEN MONEY. Holmes did the same with Bo. One thousand contracts had changed hands in less than ten seconds. A couple-hundred-million-dollar transaction. The Podium Chief picked up the trade, immediately entered it into the Exchange computer, which would then send the opening quote throughout the world.

The market shot up to 349.40. Bo breathed a sigh of relief. He had filled the orders well. Thank God, he thought. This is terrific. I love it. His mind had gone from frustration and panic to relief and exhilaration in one fell swoop. He wrote quickly, as he felt his right hand tremble under the pressure of the pencil. His writing was almost indecipherable. He needed a drink, but he felt good.

As he endorsed the orders, he shoved them into the right pocket of his trading jacket, as he kept a close eye on the orders his left hand held. Stale booze and used energy pushed its way through his pores, drenching his body and his clothing.

A broker to his right yelled, "THREE FORTY-NINE SIXTY FOR SIXTY. Bo yelled "SELL YA THIRTY, SAM." Sam Stein acknowledged the trade without looking at Bo. "I've got thirty left. FORTY-NINE SIXTY FOR THIRTY."

"SOLD!" came a cry from across the pit.

Bo peeled off three orders from his several-inch-thick deck. Each order read, 'Sell 10 September S&P's at $349.60 or better."

Orders were being shoved into his face and held over his shoulder by runners. In one quick grab, he snatched them all and held them in his right hand like a bouquet of flowers. His deck had nothing imminently close to the present market price, so he stuffed it into his left breast pocket and went through the new orders. Five were market orders: three buys, two sells, totaling twenty-nine to buy and eighteen to sell.

He pushed the trader in front of him and yelled in order not to be criticized for an Open-Outcry violation. "SIDNEY, I'M BUYING TWENTY-NINE AT THREE

FORTY-NINE SIXTY AND SELLING YA EIGHTEEN AT THREE FORTY-NINE FIFTY." He looked up at the quote board. The market was trading in that range.

Sidney Wertz, WRTZ, turned and looked over his half glasses and acknowledged, "DONE. I SOLD YOU TWENTY-NINE AT SIXTY AND BOUGHT EIGHTEEN AT FIFTY." Sidney turned and immediately bought eleven contracts at 349.60 from a broker five people away, making him even.

Bo had just given $900 to Sidney Wertz, but he justified his actions because it was efficient. The fills were on the market. He gave an *open outcry* when he made the trade, and Sidney had taken some real *hickeys* from him on a few occasions when a *fast market* ran through his orders. Bo was just reciprocating.

Hogan would disapprove. He would have tried to buy and sell both orders at the same price. But then, Hogan was a master. He knew when to press, when to pull back, when to add to a position, when to liquidate. He knew every broker in the pit and what they were capable of buying or selling. He had a sixth sense and lightning-fast reactions, which enabled him to move seconds before the market moved. He wasn't a pro. He was a artist. The best in the business. Bo wasn't in Michael's league. Not many were. He needed guys like Sidney Wertz to *lay off trades*. Both good and bad trades.

An hour into trading, Bo had filled over 1000 contracts. The closer the Dow-Jones came to 2500, the faster the S&P's moved, bringing in more volume. He was at his peak. Business boomed. In an hour's time he had made about $1500 just filling orders.

The first two hours went by fast. The market slowed. Undertow had taken over, and filled orders were being thrown out of the pit by the hundreds. Bo saw that Tony Zitello was trading with his own men; no open outcry, no bidding, no offering. Just washing, bagging, and skimming.

Despite the profuse sweating, now he felt a different type of heat fill his body. The type of heat that always brought him into conflict with somebody or something. He brought his eyes back to Fitzsimmons, who was watching him with questioning reserve. He looked back at Zitello, his head down as he wrote frantically on filled orders. Bo watched as an order came over Zitello's shoulder. He read the order and touched the man next to him, Raulf Hoge (HOG), with four fingers, meaning he had just sold four hundred contracts to HOG. Hog then sold one hundred each to the two men in front of him and two hundred to a broker on his right. All three men in turn sold those contracts to other brokers in the syndicate who wrote the trades up on bogus order sheets then passed them out of the pit. They would be timestamped and verified later. Seventy million dollars of paper had just passed between two different companies. One dirty. One clean.

Once Bo's mind zeroed in on an enemy, it was almost impossible to pull back until after a confrontation. His thoughts raced back in time, and he heard mortar shells and the whiffle sound of helicopters. For a brief moment, the screaming in the pit confused his mind, and he was reliving the horror of Viet Nam, his friends delirious with pain, bodies half blown apart, crying children, explosions, the smell of burning flesh. Insanity. He

shook the memories from his head and watched Zitello. His arrogant, Italian face was quickly taking on the characteristics of an Oriental enemy.

He rubbed sweat from his eyes, trying to free his mind of the old war. Control was necessary for this mission. He was doing it for Hogan. Bo could care less how much money Zitello laundered or stole for the Fat Man, or Conti, or Ruzzo, or anybody, for that matter, but Hogan did, and that's all that mattered. Besides, he just didn't like the heartless fuckers. Theft wasn't beneath Bo's standards; arrogant manipulation was. Like politicians, ZITO'S group had no honor, no courage. They'd destroy the mother who bore them if it meant a step in the direction of more money and power.

At the thought of confrontation, his nerves became steady and his palms dried. A recall of his old training cleared his mind of the havoc around him, and his senses were totally on Zitello and his men.

Zitello received another order. This time he hit the man in front of him with three fingers. Bo's angry voice rose above the volume in the pit. "Hey Zitello." He knew his voice could be heard throughout the pit, but Zitello kept his head down, looking at his Deck. HOG looked up with a mean scowl. Bo kept it going. "HEY ASS-HOLE. I'M BIDDING TOO. CAN'T YOU SPLIT UP THOSE ORDERS AND GIVE SOME OF US POOR GUYS A LITTLE GRAVY?"

HOG, with his large, animal eyes, gave him a vicious look, as if his territory hád been violated. "FUCK OFF, LYNCH!"

Bo pushed two brokers apart and stepped down into the pit. Now he was on the same level as Zitello and Hoge. Pit turmoil slowed, as Lynch pushed for a show down. "WHO'S TALKING TO YOU, PIG FACE? I WANT TO KNOW WHY THE FUCK THE PRICK NEXT TO YOU DOESN'T TRADE WITH A FEW OF US PAUPERS."

Bo saw HOG make a move toward him, but Zitello's hand grabbed his trading jacket, and Hoge stepped back. ZITO finally looked at Bo. Zitello's once-handsome face was blotchy from booze. Bo knew the look well from seeing it in the mirror every morning. Zitello's heavy use of cocaine showed in his empty eyes. "WHATCHA WANT, LYNCH? YOU GOT A PROBLEM?"

Bo cut his way through brokers and persisted loudly. "YOU'RE RIGHT I GOT A PROBLEM, SHITHEAD." Brokers moved out of his way; they knew what was coming. Bo felt his own face go sullen. "YOU GOT FIFTY GUYS BIDDING IN THE PIT AND YOU BUCKET ALL YOUR OWN ORDERS."

Zitello's eyes drooped, showing no emotion. Then Bo thought, why should the prick show concern? Outside of being half dead from dope, he had all the political and financial power on his side. Bo thought, nobody had ever challenged the big boys, except Hogan. Well fuck 'em. Let's unnerve 'em a bit.

Bo was within three feet of Zitello and decided to force his hand. He might as well get the ball rolling for Fitzsimmons.

"YA KNOW WHAT I THINK, ZITELLO? I THINK YOU AND YOUR SCUMBAG FRIENDS HERE ARE ALL A BUNCH OF THIEVES."

Although Bo's eyes were on Zitello, his attention was on HOG. Hoge grabbed for Bo's neck. He was too slow. Bo grabbed his wrist in mid air and with a quick twist, a loud snap echoed throughout the pit. HOG screamed in pain and dropped to his knees. Bo released the limp wrist and drilled his eyes deep into Zitello's blank face. "I'M COMING FOR YOU, ZITO...AND I'M GONNA HANG YOUR GINNY NUTS OUT ON THE LASALLE STREET FLAG POLE."

Zitello crooked his mouth and looked down at HOG. When he looked back up, Bo saw that his lips had paled. His glass face held no expression as he said softly, "You're a dead man, Lynch."

Bo moved his face close to Zitello. "You come and get me, loud-mouth. And you better bring plenty of help, cuz I ain't your everyday, phony suicide that you boys set up when somebody gets wise to you."

Zitello's face looked as if it had just been exhumed. He said nothing. Noise could be heard from the other pits on the trading floor, but all action had momentarily stopped in the S&P pit. Bo looked down at the moaning HOG and said with emphasis, "FUCK YOU AND YOUR WHOLE CARTEL." Then he said softly to Zitello, "and another thing. If I get a fine or suspension for this little incident, I'll be back and break every bone in your body."

Zitello's face held a smirk, and his tone was mocking. "Hey scarface? You going to cut my ears off like you did the bartender?"

Bo felt his jaw muscles tighten, pulling his lips against his teeth. "No, ZITO, I think I'll leave your ears. I just want your head and balls."

The smirk erased from Zitello's face. "You're a crazy man, Lynch. Get the fuck away from me."

Bo let a sinister smile cross his face. He came within inches of Zitello's face. "YOU DON'T KNOW HOW CRAZY I AM, SWEETHEART."

He turned and moved through the crowd back to his original position. The noise increased as brokers resumed trading. To most of them, this was just another incident brought on by the pressures of pit trading.

To Bo, it was war. His mind raced for a few minutes, then he tugged at Sidney Wertz. "Sid, watch my deck for ten minutes. I'm going to the can."

Sidney made a partial turn and looked over the half-glasses that hung on his pawnbroker nose. "Sure, Bo. After that show, I don't blame you. Those bastards have had that coming. Take your time."

Bo's shirt and trading jacket were drenched, and he could feel the sweat running off his short hair and down his neck until it was stopped and blotted by his saturated collar. After standing at attention for nearly three hours, Fitzsimmons had stepped out of the pit after the confrontation. Bo saw him leaning against a desk that held red and green blinking

phone lights. He was watching the quote boards, which lined the walls of the Exchange. His expression was unmistakably one of a timid kid on his first day in school not understanding a damn thing, including the spat that had just taken place.

Bo was slightly amused, thinking back to his own first days of trading and how helpless he had felt with the paradox of organized pandemonium.

Bo pushed his way roughly down three steps and moved through running bodies to where SIMS was standing. Fitzsimmons saw him, but avoided his eyes as if he were going to be scolded. "Come on, let's get a cup of Irish coffee."

SIMS followed him off the trading floor like a puppy. Bo took a terry-cloth towel that hung from his belt and wiped his face, hair, and around the back of his neck. He looked at the red-numbered clock on the wall. It was 10:52:30.

His hands were shaking again; it was time for a quick drink to steady his nerves. Time to teach two federal agents to spot a bagman. That wouldn't be hard because half the brokers in the pit were cheaters. Zitello wasn't the only thief, merely the largest. It was so easy to steal in the commodity markets. He probably would, too, if it wasn't for Hogan. You were considered stupid if you didn't take advantage of all the money that ran through your hands on a daily basis. Contrary to most other U.S. industries, theft was allowed and promoted at the Exchanges. He said to himself, fuck it. I'll never turn on Hogan. The man saved my life, gave me another chance, and was responsible for helping me make more money than I ever dreamed of making. Hogan was right. There was plenty of money here to be made legally without fucking some dumb investor out of his life savings.

He turned to Fitzsimmons walking beside him. "Hey college boy. Where is your ass-hole friend, Tully?" Simms was frustrated. "Lynch, his name down here is Tollan. He's been in the Eurodollar pit and said he'd meet us in the coffee shop when you were finished with Zitello."

"Well, I'm not finished with that prick yet."

They were walking by the security guard station when Bo said, "and remember something, SIMS. Just because I'm nice to you, doesn't mean I like you."

Out of the corner of his eye, Bo saw Fitzsimmons shake his head as they headed for the coffee shop.

* * *

Pete watched Michael file incoming orders into his folded deck like a Vegas dealer played with cards. He had three decks, all about four inches thick. One in the left hip pocket of his trading jacket, one in the right breast pocket, and the third in his left hand. As the orders filed in, they were first looked at by one of Michael's associates, Frank Hammer. If the order was important or close to where the market was going to open, he would pass it over Michael's shoulder. Michael would snatch the order and file it in the appropriate deck.

Pete looked at his wristwatch: it read 9:25. Five minutes to the soybean opening. Michael stood on the top step of the huge pit wearing a bright, kelly-green trading jacket with a white collar. The yellow badge pinned to his left lapel read "HAWK", and his profile actually looked like the head of a patient, waiting hawk. His eyes pierced every inch of the trading pit without any head motion: only his eyes moved.

Pete watched the confusion and frenzy of the other brokers, who had just a third of the business Michael had. Michael was cool, calm, organized. He knew exactly what he was doing.

To Pete's right, a broker snapped at a young female runner. "Get that order out of my face." The man wore a wrinkled, olive drab trading jacket, with the name tag "TITS." His reddish hair hadn't been combed, nor had his face been shaved. He looked as if he hadn't slept in days. This was the same fellow who had bought a $200 round of drinks at the bar some months ago when Pete had first met Hogan. He was also one of the men on Hogan's "hit list" of skim traders and bagmen.

From across the pit came another loud voice. "HAWK! HOW'S THE OPENING LOOK?" Michael put his thumb in the air, then clenched his fist and opened it twice, showing five fingers both times. Pete knew that meant ten cents higher on the opening.

Pete was being squeezed by bodies pushing into the pit. He felt as if he were in one of those college contests to see how many people could fit into a Volkswagen or telephone booth. His body moved from side to side with the swaying human pressure. The clock moved relentlessly toward the opening. Two minutes to the bell.

He looked back at Michael. Hammer whispered something to him over his shoulder, then handed him an order. The "Hawk" cupped the folded order and opened it slightly to read. Just as quickly, he placed the order at the back of his deck and wrote something on it. He looked up at the clock, then back down. He hollered into the middle of the pit: "HEY, JAKE! HOW'S IT LOOK DOWN THERE?"

Jake Kuzak looked up over half-glasses and yelled back, "MAYBE TEN CENTS, MIKE. HOW ABOUT THERE?"

Michael answered. "I'M A SELLER FIFTEEN HIGHER, A BUYER TWELVE HIGHER."

The market tone was set. Pete took out his trading cards, about twice the size of a deck of cards, and pushed down the tip of a ball-point pen. He wasn't planning to trade today. He just wanted to fit in. He didn't want to look like a new guy.

Barry Kane stood about ten feet away, close to "TITS." Pete wondered if he was going to pass out; his face looked as if it had been dusted with flour. One good thing about it, Barry sure didn't look like a federal agent. He didn't think he did either with his longish hair, three-day beard growth, and scruffy clothes. Harris, on the other hand, was dressed like an attorney, standing next to Charlie Nicolelli (CAN), one of the brokers Michael had labeled as working for Conti.

The market had closed the previous day at $5.33 a bushel. Ten to fifteen higher would open the market around $5.50 a bushel. One minute to opening.

Pete looked up at the green quotes sliding across the black screen and saw that the stock market was twenty-two points higher and the S & P's were two hundred higher. He wondered how Fitzsimmons and Tully were getting along with Lynch. Bo was one ornery son of a bitch and hated the Feds. Fitz and Tully were no pussies, but they were no match for Bo's wrath.

Thirty seconds to go. For a moment the mass of humanity became so intense, Pete felt claustrophobic, and the pushing was enough to force the breath from his lungs. Fuck 'em, he thought, and began to push back and stake out a solid position of his own. He planted his feet firmly and resisted any further abuse to his body. Considering the circumstances, his mind told him he had learned his first lesson, "Stake your claim in the pit, or you'll be standing on the outside looking in."

Twelve seconds to go. Hands were already held high over the brokers' heads. Pete looked at the pit and took a mental picture. It was a kaleidoscope of colored and moving jackets. For a moment the picture roamed through his mind in search of a storage compartment that had never been used before.

From his left side he heard an eruption from "the Hawk" that could be heard throughout the Exchange floor.

"FIVE FORTY-FIVE FOR TWO MILLION. SELL AT FIVE FIFTY." Michael opened the market six seconds before the bell rang. The automatic and immediate explosion of noise was something Pete would never forget. His eyes flinched, and a sense of fear ran through his body. For a moment he thought he was in a panic situation.

Pete watched Michael. He looked seven feet tall, both hands out holding the thick order deck in his left hand, a black pen in his right. His eyes were intense as they searched the pit for buyers and sellers. He wrote quickly as brokers came to him to buy and sell.

The bell finally rang; the noise intensified. A total of thirteen trading pits were now in full gear on the mammoth trading floor, and the noise was beyond human understanding. What in the world was going on? How the hell did anybody know what was going on? Screaming bodies were pounding on each other, snapping, growling, pushing, cursing. Yet there seemed to be a semblance of chaotic organization that guided the melee.

The bid went to $5.48 a bushel. Pete was knocked off his feet and would have ended up on the floor, if there hadn't been so many bodies to hold him up. He tried to keep his eyes on Michael.

A red-jacketed broker emerged out of nowhere; "I'LL TAKE TWO MILLION AT FIVE FIFTY, HAWK." Michael flipped two fingers out and down. That was all the recognition the other broker needed, and he was off again into the middle of the pit.

Almost simultaneously, another broker took one million from Hawk. As he checked that trade with one finger, he pointed across the pit and sold two million bushels to another broker. Pete looked but couldn't see who made the buy.

Everything was moving so fast he had no idea what was going on. A man next to him yelled out, "SELL TWO HUNDRED AT FIFTY-TWO." A broker behind him screamed, "SOLD," as he pushed Pete out of the way to get the trade.

Pete lost his balance again and pushed hard into a broker in front of him who wore a black-and-white checkered coat. The broker jabbed an elbow backwards, which caught Pete in the chest. Automatically Pete's reflexes reacted quicker than his mind, and he slammed the palm of his hand into the back of the broker's head, knocking him into two other brokers.

All three men turned and glared at Pete. The two in front returned to their business; the other held the back of his head and shouted at Pete. "YOU DUMB SON OF A BITCH. Go over to the lumber pit and learn how to trade, Asshole." Pete remained quiet, but there was an automatic dislike for the man whose name badge read MOFO, Morris Franko, another name on Hogan's "Hit List," a broker syndicated trader.

Somebody to his right made an outcry, and without further confrontation, Franko took his attention off Pete and hit the other broker on the shoulder yelling, "SOLD."

Franko looked like a twerp, but Pete scolded himself for reacting as he did. He didn't want to be labeled a troublemaker his first day in the pit--or did he? The thought crossed his mind that this would give him an opportunity to apologize to Franko later, and eventually work on getting a little information from him.

He returned his attention to Michael, who was taking orders over his shoulder from Frank Hammer. His hands were going both ways, out--selling, in--buying. A quick scribble on the orders, and back over his shoulder they went, where his assistants gathered them to be reported to the customer.

The market was bid at 5.54 and offered at 5.56 when "The Hawk" offered five million bushels at 5.55. Brokers on the other side of the pit began to race each other on the down side. They were all long and wanted to cash in before Hogan let five million hit the market. "SELL AT FIFTY-FOUR, SELL AT FIFTY-THREE…SELL TWO MILLION AT FIVE FIFTY", screamed a heavy-set broker hysterically. In just seconds, the market had gone from all bidding to all selling.

Jesus H. Christ. How could things change so fast? Pete was utterly confused. At the same time, it was exciting. He felt a peculiar type of exhilaration in the midst of the noise, hysteria, and beaucoup money floating through the pit. An unseen energy emanated throughout the arena, and Pete felt it.

Although the offer was 5.50 by the heavy-set broker, Hawk matched his offer, yelling, "I'LL SELL FIVE MILLION AT FIVE FIFTY." Pete didn't understand what Michael was up to.

The broker with two million to sell at 5.50 looked with scorn at Hogan, then offered at 5.48. Others joined in until all offers went to 5.45.

Pete watched to see if Hawk would offer his five million lower than the others. But to his surprise, his hands were in. He bought everything up at 5.45, quietly, just using

hand signals to buy and confirm the trades. He bought the two million from the frantic, corpulent broker, another million from someone else, five hundred thousand bushels from a broker in the middle of the pit. He continued to make numerous hand signals to brokers across the pit. Again, Pete missed who those trades were made with.

Michael was cool. No expression. No emotion. He merely wrote on his orders and passed them back to Hammer, all the while continuing to scan the pit with his sharp eyes. Hammer whispered again in his ear, and both hands came up. "I'll pay five forty-eight for three million."

He had just offered at 5.48 before the market dropped to 5.45, where he bought up everything. Now he was bidding 5.48. What was he going to do with the five million he had to sell at 5.48? Brokers jumped all over him. "HAWK, I'LL BUY EVERYTHING YOU HAVE AT FIVE FORTY-EIGHT," bellowed a tall, handsome kid wearing a royal-blue trading jacket. Michael waved everybody off. "I'M EMPTY. THE BID IS FIVE FORTY-EIGHT FOR THREE MILLION."

Because of the noise, Pete could hardly hear Hogan. He was reading lips more than he was hearing words. The bid went back to 5.50, and Hawk just stood back. He filled no orders for a moment, just endorsed the previous order. He wondered what in the hell Hogan did with the five million he had to sell.

Then it dawned on Pete that before the opening he had told the pit he was a buyer at 5.45 and a seller at 5.50 or higher. That bastard filled his sell orders on the opening, then finessed the brokers by offering five million, driving the market down so he could fill his orders at 5.45. The son of a bitch never had five million to sell.

Goddamn, Pete thought. Everything he had heard about Hogan being the best was understated: he was world-class! There wasn't a broker in the pit holding customer orders who didn't continually keep a nervous eye on the Hawk. If they weren't sure what his next trick was going to be, they damn well weren't sure if he was watching them cheat. Guilt was a byproduct of questionable behavior, and it seemed to Pete that the pit reeked of questionable behavior, even though he couldn't detect it--yet.

Pete looked up at the wall clock. 9:48. Only eighteen minutes had passed. Pete's jacket was already saturated. He felt as though he'd been standing for hours. How the hell do these people keep up this pace all day long?

He looked around at the pandemonium. It was beyond the normal range of understanding. How did they keep everything straight? Customer orders flying over brokers' shoulders and landing on the trading floor. Eventually they were picked up by a runner and reported to the client, but what an archaic system, he thought. Millions of dollars floating around on little pieces of paper dropping to the floor, later to be picked up by runners, to eventually be returned and reported to the customer.

He couldn't tell who was buying, who was selling, or how much of whatever they were doing, were they actually doing. It was a enigma. No wonder it was so easy to shave and skim and bag points. No outsider could ever begin to understand what the hell was

going on. He sensed that with over a hundred years of trial and error, the system was now perfectly designed to confuse outsiders. And according to Hogan, the soybean market was the mildest of the markets they were keyed to investigate.

Michael was right. The Fed's hi-tech equipment apparently would be useless in the pits. Maybe the "Hawk-Eye" cameras would catch pictures of the brokers involved in bagging, but the "Rabbit Ear" recorders would have to be geared down to a less-sensitive frequency to pick up short-range conversations rather than general pit rage. They would, however, come in handy off the trading floor during casual conversations with suspects.

A burly, gray-haired broker reeking of stale booze pushed Pete aside on his way to the center of the pit to make a trade. Pete almost knocked over the slightly built broker next to him. "That's the third time you've pushed me, buddy."

Pete was going to say something nasty to the little man named "MAX," but he pushed down his temper and decided to remain cool. "Sorry, pal. I'm not used to crowds."

"You a new guy or did ya come from another pit?"

Without looking at MAX and pretending to be concentrating on the market, he said, "Uh, I'm rather new."

"First day?"

Was it that obvious?, Pete wondered. "Yyyaa...first day."

Max spoke as if he had found a new friend. "Hey, good luck to ya." he pulled at Pete's badge to see his tag. "ALEX, nice to meet you. My name's Max Leonard." He forced his right hand free from the packed bodies around him, and Pete shook it.

"Pete, Pete Alexander. Nice to meet you too, Max."

He poked him with his elbow. "You have trading cards, Pete?"

Pete looked into a young but gaunt face. "What?"

Max's dark eyebrows lifted, along with his thin shoulders. "Do you have your trading cards? You know the ones that have BUY on one side and SELL on the other, and your trading name at the top?"

Pete looked down into his left hand. He hadn't realized it, but he had unconsciously squeezed the thin trading cards almost into a ball. They were of no use--too bent. He could hardly read his name that had been stamped at the top of the cards. He tore them in half and dropped them on the floor, then reached into his left pocket and produced a few fresh cards. "Ya, Max, I have a few left." Max smiled and began to write on one of his own trading cards. He nudged Pete again, moved his face closer, speaking quietly but loudly enough for Pete to hear. "ALEX, I'm going to buy ten thousand bushels at five fifty from you, and I'll sell you ten thousand at five forty-nine."

He looked back up at Pete, who wasn't sure what to do. "Go on. Write it on your card. You bought ten at five forty-nine and sold ten at five fifty. You just made a hundred bucks. Not all that much, but enough for lunch. Congratulations! Your first trade was a winner, compliments of Max Leonard. I do it with all the new guys. *Shalom* and good luck, I really mean it. I like to see everybody do well down here."

Pete began to write down the trade. "*Shalom*, Max, and thanks. I appreciate it, but is this legal?"

Max was a likable little fellow with a matter-of-fact sort of friendly acceptance. He gave a sarcastic grunt. "Legal. That's a word I haven't heard for a long time. Sure, it's legal. I can give away my own money if I want. Even if it wasn't legal, who'd give a shit down here?"

Pete had installed his own arm-patch recorder. He hoped it was picking this up. Pete edged the conversation further while he finished writing down the trade. "What about all those rules I read and heard about in orientation?"

Max grunted again. "You can leave all that crap outside. We make our own rules down here to suit our needs."

Pete felt Max studying him closely. He didn't know if it was caution, curiosity, or amusement. Then, Max exclaimed. "You can make a whole lot of money, ALEX, if you know the right people--and no risk."

Pete coaxed Max humorously. "You're shittin' me! You mean it's not inevitable that I lose my life savings before I finally catch on? Christ, I already have two New York companies in financial trouble. I don't really need to complicate my financial posture any further if it isn't necessary. I came down here to try to save my companies."

Max volunteered quickly. "Hey, pal. Your days of losing money are over. You stick with me, and I'll lead you to a few fellows who are looking to invest in some tax losses. They'll be happy to meet you. And if everything works out for ya, just remember ol' Max in your will."

A broker near Hogan offered 50,000 bushels, and Max yelled, "SOLD." As he stepped away from Pete to check the trade, he turned back. "I'll talk to ya later, ALEX. Maybe lunch some day."

Pete couldn't believe how candid this guy was. How careless. The man talked openly about breaking the rules and tax evasion to a complete stranger, so matter-of-factly. Jesus Christ, what an operation. "We make our own rules down here," Max had said. A sense of nervous excitement began to build in him. He had his first lead. As insignificant as it was in itself, Max had just given him a starting point. A lead that could well be the cornerstone of the investigation. You're damn right I'll have lunch with you, Max.

Pete looked over at Michael as he glanced up and caught his eye. With a slight grin, Michael mouthed something. Pete felt his brow furrow in question, and Michael mouthed his message again. Pete read the sarcastic lips, "a piece of cake!'

He remembered making that comment to Michael on the way to the Exchange floor earlier in the morning. He mouthed his own message back to HAWK, "fuck you."

The first hour passed quickly, but he needed a break. The stench of broker sweat, used adrenalin, and the excretion of the previous night's heavy consumption of booze and drugs combined to give off a caustic fermentation that made Pete gag.

Sweat dripped from his chin. He licked his dry lips and tasted salt. He could feel drops of perspiration running down the middle of his back. A young blond boy, a runner, forced his hand between Pete and the broker on his right side, trying to pass an order to the broker in the checkered coat. Franko, the one Pete had cuffed in the back of the head earlier.

"Hey Mister." He looked at Pete's badge. "ALEX, would you please hand this to Mr. Franko?"

Pete took the folded order. "Sure, kid."

His curiosity momentarily overruled the directions of the runner who had sucked himself backwards out of the pit. As he took a step down to hand the order over Franko's shoulder, he pinched it open enough to take a quick picture in his mind. *BUY 2 MILL NOV. BEANS: MKT*. Franko didn't look back. Just grabbed the order.

The market was trading between 5.45 and 5.46 a bushel. Two million was a pretty good-size order, and the market had slowed while everybody regrouped for the next attack. There were a few small offers around the pit at 5.46. The market turned thin as Michael had said it would about this time of day.

Pete could see Franko was nervous with the order, and his head began to jerk in different directions, looking for large offers. There were none. He ignored the small offers and bid 5.46 for two million. Pete glanced at Hogan. He was watching too. The HAWK bid 5.47 for 500 thousand. Franko bid 5.48. Hogan yelled back, "I'LL SELL YOU AT FORTY-NINE".

Franko hesitated for a moment, looking around the pit for a better price. "SOLD, ASSHOLE...TWO MILLION AT FIVE FORTY-NINE," said Franko with disgust.

Hogan took an order from his right breast pocket and wrote quickly, "FRANKO, I SOLD YOU TWO MILLION AT FORTY-NINE."

Franko checked the trade with a simple flick of his finger in the air and yelled with frustration, "YA STOLE THAT TRADE, YA FUCKER."

Pete saw a slight smile cross Michael's face as he retorted, "BETTER ME THAN YOU. NICE FILL, BOZO."

The market immediately moved back to 5.46 bid, 5.47 offer. Franko, with the help of Hogan, had paid at least two cents higher than he should have, because he panicked. Pete calculated quickly: two million bushels was four hundred contracts at $50 a cent per contract, $100 for two cents times four hundred. Jesus Christ, the jerk just gave away $40,000 to the HAWK.

Pete looked over at Michael, whose eyes were scanning the pit for who knew what. Their eyes met briefly, and Michael gave him a quick wink. Pete felt a sense of pride in knowing him. Michael's body, mind, and spirit were strong. He spoke his mind, and he spoke the truth. He was a leader, both in and out of the arena.

Pete spent the next half hour memorizing all the badges in the pit and placing them with the faces. He picked out as many names as he could find that were on the "Hit List"

and watched them carefully. He saw nothing unusual. They were basically conducting business like everybody else in what Pete considered a complete state of confusion. But he knew that many trades were tainted. He did notice that six brokers he picked out as being suspect traded only with the brokers around them, and didn't search for bids and offers from any body else in the pit. They must be what Hogan called a broker-group or syndicate, who skim and bag trades. Pete was surprised Franko hadn't given the two or three-cent profit to one of his cronies. He was also surprised how much money had changed hands in such a short time. In seconds, Franko had fucked a customer out of forty to sixty thousand dollars just because he was inadequate, and he panicked with the large order--with the help of Hogan's intimidation.

It was 11:09, and brokers were leaving the pit either to count their winnings or lick their wounds. The market was trading at 5.45 per bushel and slow. It hadn't really moved much all day, staying in a rather narrow eighteen cent trading range--5.42-5.60--but an enormous amount of money had changed hands. Pete saw Michael hand Frank Hammer, **HAMM**, his two largest order decks. Then he motioned to Pete, with a flick of his finger, to step out of the pit.

He had enough of this bullfight anyway and squeezed past a half dozen sweaty bodies to emerge. The thought of a cup of coffee and a breath of fresh air would feel like a cold shower at this point.

They met outside the pit, and Michael said, "Come on, ALEX. I'll buy you a glass of orange juice."

Pete followed him off the trading floor, away from the noise, the confusion, the smell, and the greed, but he loved it. There was something addictive about the fast lane, the razor's edge, the panic, the exhilaration, the financial chess-game. Then, his thoughts returned to his purpose for being there, and he knew it was indeed a game. His mind told him the game would turn into a death-sport before the smoke cleared.

Max Leonard's words rang in Pete's ears. "We make up our own rules down here."

THIRTY-FOUR

Summer, 1987 - No Guilt, No Regrets

Michael took his handkerchief from his pocket and blotted the rivulets of sweat from his face as he zig-zagged through the streets on his way to the annex, adjacent to the Federal Building. The meeting with the agents was scheduled for five o'clock. Lorenzo and Andy Golden would be there, and the asshole, Simpson, was even going to show his face.

Chicago loved warm weather, but this was ridiculous. The temperature had hovered near 100° for nearly a month, one of the hottest summers in the history of the Midwest. Hottest in more ways than one, he thought. The city was not only gasping for breath from Mother Nature's heated kiss, but the Exchanges were also experiencing the wildest bull markets in their history.

The grain markets had moved sharply higher from no rain and legitimate drought conditions. The stock market and all of the stock indexes were in raging bull moves, and the federal agents were taking advantage of the wide swinging markets. They knew, the wider the swing, the easier it was to skim and bag money from customer orders. They continued to gather evidence.

Lewis, Tully, Harris, Kane, and Fitzsimmons already had over a hundred tapes, and a few of those carried blatant conversations of criminal activity taking place on the trading floor. Michael had heard them all. Many of the voices and the pictures of the brokers incriminating themselves were not on his "Hit List." These were men he had known for years, good men, with families. Some of them he had helped get started in the business. The fuckers, he thought, they had to take the easy way. A few hundred thousand dollars a year the honest way was evidently overridden by the enticement of five hundred to a million a year the illegal way. But, he thought, why not? Up until now, there was no reason not to take advantage of the opportunity. It had been as easy to steal as it was to take water from Lake Michigan.

Michael shook his head in disappointment as he entered the Union Club. He nodded hello to the bellman, continued through the lavish interior lobby, and strode out the back entrance. He made his way briskly down an alley, crossed Dearborn Street, and reached another building with an underground walkway.

He waited just inside the building on Dearborn, and out of sight, to see if he was being followed. They had agreed that Pete Lewis should stay away from him for a few months, as everyone at both Exchanges knew Michael was on a pilgrimage to clean up the Exchanges. If they were seen together, Lewis's ability to get close to Max and Franko and Ted Terrin would be futile.

The only man who should be following him was a new agent by the name of Charlie Taft. But Michael figured he had lost him blocks ago. Besides, the real danger for him wouldn't come until later, when the investigation became obvious to Peterson and the broker groups. It wouldn't take them long to figure out that he had played a part in the "sting" operation. Then the shit would hit the fan, but by then Michael would be ready for their wrath--he was ready now.

No one followed him, so he continued on his way, thinking of his friends that the Feds had on tape. Jesus Christ, the sirens of greed had lured damn near everybody into her clutches. Maybe Sean McGiven was right. Greed made the markets the success they were. More money poured into the Exchanges every day, record amounts of money, record volume, record membership prices, and--record theft.

He entered the long underground hallway linked to the Federal Building and took an offshoot hall that led him to the annex and the clandestine operation center for the FBI. The cool hall began to dry the sweat on his face, but his shirt still felt cool and wet.

He approached a single elevator and waited briefly for the doors to open. The cage, which looked as though it normally carried freight, was empty, and the walls were padded with heavy, green moving blankets. This was the designated elevator for Michael and the agents to take to the secret meeting place. He pushed button nineteen. The doors closed, and he moved slowly upward. The elevator stopped on the ground floor, and the doors yawned open. He expected to see one of the building maintenance men or a telephone man. His heart skipped a beat, then immediately began to race at double pace when he saw who stood there waiting to enter.

She carried a genuine leather bag under her arm, her attention focused on a notebook she held in her hands. She stepped forward into the elevator, eyes still down.

His heart kept up its frantic beat, and a chill ran through his warm body. God! She was gorgeous. Absolutely gorgeous. He hadn't seen her up close since they first met. Even though he and the other agents met weekly, he had avoided her. He had almost forgotten what beauty she carried, but not really. He had half-heartedly nudged thoughts of her out of his mind whenever they pushed their way in, but she always managed to creep back. He had been a real prick to her since the investigation had begun.

He knew the difference between love and passion. He loved Maria. He didn't trust the passion he felt for Samantha, because it could be the seedlings of an intimate and dangerous relationship.

If a relationship was trying to develop, he was doing his best to postpone it. His gut and mind told him to stay away. His heart sang a different song. The avoidance of close contact with this precious angel was the only way he knew to dissuade any advancement on her. Being a prick, he thought, was his only defense.

But here they were again. Face to face. He and Samantha. The goddamn tugging in his body gnawed menacingly. He wanted to pull her to him, hold her tight against his aching body, smother her with kisses, and never let her go.

Instead he said, "How are you, Sam?"

She looked up abruptly from her notebook. He felt awkward, like a shy kid. His stomach was flipping around as if it were filled with marbles. He saw a faint, innocent smile cross her face, but when she saw who spoke her name, she immediately stepped into place next to him, turned, and stared straight ahead, her lips taking a turn downward into a pout. "I'm fine, Michael, and you?"

He thrust his hand into his pockets, not trusting himself. "I'm hot, like the rest of the city," he said slowly.

She looked magnificent. Even her pouting lips stirred his imagination. Her hair was pulled back in a loose French braid, golden wisps framing her face. Her tanned skin complemented her golden hair even more. The soft, not quite sheer, fitted cotton blouse she wore accentuated her round, firm breasts. The blouse was tucked neatly into a straight, black-linen, side-slitted skirt that outlined the curves of her shapely hips. Her attire lent an air of professionalism, while at the same time gave off a sense of sexy, feminine mystique.

She looked over at him and said coolly, "You've been working hard?"

He tried to break the ice with a smile, but the ice was thicker than he expected. "About fourteen hours a day."

Her look turned cynical. "You should lighten up. It's affecting your charming personality."

He looked deep into her eyes. Behind the ice he saw the same enticement and yearning he had seen when they first met. She was trying to play the woman's game, and he didn't blame her. He had been a bastard.

He looked at the numbers above the elevator door. The light was on Floor Six. His eyes shifted to the control panel. Instinctively, he took his hands from his pockets, moved his right arm out in front of him, and found his fingers flipping the on-off toggle switch. The freight elevator jerked to a stop between the seventh and eighth floors.

She reached to turn the switch back on, but his hand moved faster, and he grabbed her wrist before it reached the controls.

She squirmed to pull herself free, but his grip tightened around her soft skin. Quivering slightly, she whispered, "Michael, turn the elevator back on and let go of me." Then she sought to discipline her voice, to maintain complete control. "On top of being aloof, cynical, bold, and arrogant, you're a bully too."

He said nothing and grabbed at her other wrist as he pushed her back against the padded wall. Her leather bag fell to the floor, as did the notebook she had been reading.

She struggled for a moment, then gave in to the pressures of his body and strength that pressed her to the wall. She looked away from him and bit her lower lip as if about to cry.

He raised her arms and placed them around his neck, released her wrists, and brought his hands to cup her face. He turned her face to meet his eyes. The ice had broken, and her eyes welled up. He knew that beneath the tears, behind her blue-green

eyes, lay a whirlpool that would swallow his soul. He knew her professional toughness was only skin deep and that she was as vulnerable at this moment as he.

Her arms were limp on his shoulders. "Now what, Michael? Are you going to tell me you are sorry for not returning my calls? For ignoring me? For making me feel like a fool? And shooting down any suggestions I made at our meetings?

"Or are you just going to remain quiet and act macho?" She leaned her head back against the elevator wall. Tears rolled down her tanned face to the corners of her pink lips.

Michael pressed against her and brought her face close to his. "No apologies. No guilt. No regrets, okay?"

She pulled her head from against the wall. Her look questioned his statement, as he framed her face with his hands and wiped the tears with his thumbs. He barely brushed soft gentle kisses on her velvet cheeks, then her eyes, her forehead. His mouth moved to her ears, her neck. Then his hands swept to the back of her neck where they met at her braid, and he pulled and guided her face gently toward his. Their lips parted and met, softly, barely touching. Not kissing, just brushing. Lightly, ever so lightly, a tantalizing invitation for more. Their passion escalated, and as he pulled her toward him, she shifted in closer. She ran her long fingers into his hair and tightened her grip. Breathless and urgent, their lips pressed together--and then they *really* kissed. All the pressures of his life were exploding into oblivion with this sudden onslaught of erotic kisses, hugs, caressing and exploring.

She responded with sensual vehemence, pulling at him, trying to get closer, trying to mesh. Her breath was warm and sweet and fast; her body soft, fresh. Her blond braid had unraveled, brushing his face, sending quakes of desire through him.

His pent up appetite for her took on an urgency. Their frenzy for each other increased to the highest octave. He reached to his side and ripped a protective blanket from the back wall of the elevator and flung it to the hard wood floor. He dropped to the blanket and pulled her to him, on top of him, holding her tightly, trying to get closer, smothering her with kisses. Her blond hair swept over her shoulders, brushing his face, heightening his excitement.

He rolled her over and gently placed her on her back. As anxious as he was, he wanted to be gentle with her. His head was void of all outside thoughts. He was safe, in a small metal box with a woman he had desired from the moment he first saw her. He had been caught in the whirlpool that pushed and pulled him deeper and deeper, and the ever-mounting crescendo of ecstasy engulfed them both. Their hot bodies were screaming for each other as their hands explored, pulled, pushed at clothing and passion filled flesh.

He pressed his body close to hers, and, well beyond the point of no return, they yielded to each other. Her hips arched and responded rhythmically to the entrance of his male hardness. With the reverence of tender love and the passion of seduction, he thrust deeper and deeper until the torrents of love rose with shattering intensity and rushed

through them both. The lightning of intoxicating union struck them both simultaneously. Warm turquoise waters of the sea rushed through their bodies.

Entwined as one, they had finally reached that place of rapture, where the hunger they had felt for each other had been gloriously satisfied. Clinging, content, neither wanting to let go. They lay there, quietly, closely, for what seemed like hours, utterly and totally consumed with each other.

Finally, Michael whispered, "No apologies, no guilt, no regrets. Okay?"

She merely nodded and pulled him closer, deeper. He responded.

* * *

Michael let Samantha off on the eighteenth floor so she could freshen up. He smiled to himself at her girlish embarrassment when a wiry, unappealing little maintenance man, standing akimbo, met them as the doors opened.

"Hey, you two, what's going on here? I suppose you're going to tell me there was a power failure!"

Michael patted the angry little gray-haired man on the shoulder and said, "No, as a matter of fact, there was a power surge."

Beautiful but disheveled, Samantha said she wasn't going to the meeting and scurried away from them both toward the Ladies Room, but not before Michael had told her he would see her for dinner after the meeting. She was to meet him at his boat, the *Orison Tryst*, which was docked in Belmont Harbor. They both agreed that their fantasies about each other had never included an elevator.

He rode the extra floor with the angry little maintenance man, who still grumbled under his breath as he checked the control panel. Michael stepped off at the nineteenth floor.

He stopped at the Men's Room and splashed cool water on his face and hair, then let it run down his neck to his chest. He closed his eyes, tilted his head back, and stood quietly for a moment. His heart whispered to his soul, 'Til *Orison Tryst*, Sam, 'til *Orison Tryst*.

THIRTY-FIVE

The Sting: Phase One-Complete!

Michael tucked in his shirt as he left the rest room and walked quickly down a bright, utility hall, around boxes and pieces of furniture, to the main hallway.

Double chrome doors opened to a long, plush corridor. Looking first one way, then the other, he pivoted left and strode to the meeting room. He was late, but late with a smile on his face and a sense of relief and relaxation in his body that had been missing for a long time.

Having been here twice before, he now stopped in front of a fancy, dark, wood-carved door. There were no titles on it, only the brass numerals *1910*. He tried to shake the satisfaction of Samantha's intoxicating sensuality from his bobbing, lethargic mind. His brain was working, but it was in park. He had to shift into a controlled gear for this meeting.

Fortifying himself with a deep breath, he turned the brass handle and stepped into a small waiting office, where he met a heavy-set receptionist. She greeted him with the no-nonsense demeanor of a head nurse. "You're twenty minutes late, Mr. Hogan. The meeting has begun. Sign your name and go in. You know the way."

The black-and-white plastic name sign on her metal desk read *Hilda Beatlebaum*.

She reminded him of a sea lion out of water, but not as nice. As he signed in, he quickly looked at the list of names. Andy Golden had been the last one to sign in. Colleen McFadden and Samantha were the only two agents who hadn't arrived. He knew Colleen always stayed at Ruzzo's office as late as possible in order to appear as an over-zealous worker. In fact, she was tapping telephones and trying to break the complicated codes to Ruzzo's elaborate computer system. Christ, he thought, they'd kill her if they ever caught her.

The woman at the desk began her usual, incessant, bitchy remarks. She was a reincarnation of Lady Macbeth, a self-proclaimed watchtower of righteousness. The voice was nasal and strident. "Mr. Hogan, what are you dilly-dallying for? I'm sure the Assistant Director and U.S. Attorney will not appreciate your tardiness."

He looked up into her horse-face, his temperament still smooth and calm with subconscious thoughts of the blond beauty he had just left. "Hilda, is your last name pronounced *Beatlebaum* as in '*bomb*' or *Beatlebaum* as in em*balm*ing with formaldehyde?"

Her face gathered into definite indignation. Her head and her thumb simply jerked toward a thick metal door to Michael's right.

"Have a great day, Hilda." In his giddy state of satisfaction, he opened the door wide and stepped into a dim room. His eyes adjusted quickly. A bright alley of light ran the length of the room from the open door and dulled a picture of Tony Zitello on a slide-projector screen.

Heads turned to see the intruder. He quickly closed the door behind him, dimming the room once again. The lights were about one-third their output, so it wasn't hard to see the profiles, heads, and expressions of the agents. The room was solemn. John Simpson's voice thundered from the far end, "Hogan, is that you?"

"Yo, 'tis I, your Honor." Michael was surprised at his own mirth. It was out of character for him not to be serious at these meetings.

Simpson's loud, arrogant voice countered his jovial response. "You're twenty minutes late, Hogan."

He thought he had good reason to be late, so he didn't answer. His face still wore a smile, and he felt flushed, and his clothes were wrinkled. Good thing it was dark in here.

The room was arranged in rows of chairs, theater fashion, to afford a view of a movie screen at the end of the room. Michael saw Andy Golden sitting in the back row, and he moved past Tully and Harris to sit next to Golden. He patted both agents on the shoulder as he slid quietly past. They responded with friendly acknowledgement. "Hi, Mike."

Andy, dressed in his usual brown suit, greeted Michael with a smile and a bear-paw grip, whispering, "how are ya doing, Mike?"

Michael tried to hold back the word, but it came out anyway: "Terrific."

Andy's bulldog head rolled a bit. "Terrific? You *are* being sarcastic, of course?"

Michael stretched out his legs and crossed them at the ankles, then folded his arms in front of him and sighed with satisfaction. "No, everything is fine. How about with you?"

"Everything seems to be on schedule."

The authoritative voice rolled once again from the front of the room. "Let's keep it quiet back there. Lewis is trying to conduct an investigation here."

Pete was evidently running the slide projector and narrating, as pictures of brokers came on the screen. Michael couldn't see him, but he was sitting someplace up front and using a hand control to move the slides along. He must be sitting next to Simpson. They couldn't stand each other. Michael found that amusing and smiled to himself.

The slide of Tony Zitello stood still. The time and date of the "Hawk-Eye" snapshot was in the left-hand corner of the slide, Zitello's name at the bottom. The clarity made him seem almost alive. Fitzsimmons had taken a remarkable closeup shot. Remarkable to the point of almost being able to count the whiskers on the pale, unshaven face. Michael felt his mood change. The drugged eyes of the crook stared out at him, and he felt his body and face grow tense. Heat replaced the momentary solitude and serenity he had just been feeling.

"I'll repeat," Pete said. "This is a picture of Anthony Zitello. He works the S & P pit directly for a man named Karl Peterson and indirectly for Victor Conti and Salvano Ruzzo.

"The man is a drug addict. Cocaine, booze, pot, and LSD are his drugs of choice, and it is estimated he launders and skims more than five hundred million annually for Peterson's cartel. According to Hogan's sources, he receives a percentage on everything that passes through his hands. That percentage is placed in off-shore accounts set up by Jake Edwards, an under-boss for the Mob, and Louis Alverez, an attorney in Miami. We'll speak more about Edwards and Alverez later.

"Zitello is a rich man by our standards. Our closest estimation is that he has over a hundred million stashed in off-shore and foreign accounts. He's thirty-seven years old and lives in Bannockburn, a wealthy northern suburb of Chicago. In the seventies he was arrested six times for various charges. The charges were all dismissed. In March of eighty-two, he was arrested for possession and distribution of marijuana and cocaine. His attorney cleared him on a technicality. In August eighty-two, he was arrested for assault and battery. Charges dropped at request of plaintiff. Four witnesses refused to make positive ID's. In July eighty-three, he was arrested for discharging a firearm in a public place and threatening the life of a restaurateur. Fined five hundred bucks, suspended sentence, battery complaint dropped by restaurateur. Two years later, he allegedly shot a man to death because the man wouldn't pay up on a loan. Two of Zitello's fellow bagmen swore he was with them at the time of the killing. The investigation ended, and the death was recorded as a suicide. There have been other infractions by Zitello, but his attorney always manages to find a way out for him."

Lewis stopped for a moment then added, "The man is a psychopath, but until recently has had some semblance of control over his emotions. Joe Fitzsimmons has been trying to work his way into Zitello's syndicate operation. He hasn't had enough time to be trusted as a bagman, but he has befriended a few of Zitello's men, and he has also watched Zitello's mood swings becoming more obvious."

Lewis stopped again, and Michael heard a click. Now a picture of Bo Lynch, nose to nose with Zitello, replaced Zitello's lone picture. Both profiles clearly etched across the screen. Bo's finger was on Zitello's chest, and the protruding veins in Lynch's neck obviously painted him mad as hell. Zitello's eyes were wide and confused.

Pete called out, "Joe Fitzsimmons, do you want to take it from here?"

Michael heard a metal chair move in front of him and saw the back of Fitzsimmons's head bob up as he began to speak. "Thanks, Pete. This picture was taken a few weeks after we came onto the trading floor, but it is characteristic of what takes place almost daily. The man on the left is Bo Lynch, a friend of Hogan's, a Vietnam vet, hard as hell to get along with, but a damn good teacher and one mean son of a bitch. He is determined to crack Zitello through intimidation. It's almost an obsession. Lynch is on the bastard every day for cheating. He has Zitello so paranoid that his eyes are constantly

looking over to where Lynch stands in the pit to see if he's watching him. Lynch is taking a very direct approach by yelling out, 'thief, crook, skimmer, scumbag,' etc. There is no doubt, Lynch is shaking Zitello and his group, but I think it's having a negative effect on Lynch also."

Simpson spoke loudly from the front of the room. "Anything else, Joe?"

Michael watched as Joe looked around the room and said, "Yes, sir. If these men are who you say they are and they are connected to the Chicago crime syndicate, I would be a little concerned for Lynch's safety. I mean, he's a roughneck, and I'm sure he is able to take care of himself in most situations, but I heard from one of Zitello's men that Lynch wouldn't be around too long. I don't know if he meant he wouldn't be around because he is an alcoholic or because he is going to be contracted."

Michael bristled at the last sentence. He unfolded his arms and leaned forward to hear what else Fitzsimmons had to say.

When he heard Simpson tell Lewis to move on to the next slide, he said, "Hold it, Pete. Leave the slide where it is."

Simpson turned abruptly to protest, throwing Michael an icy stare. He remained silent when he saw Michael's glare.

Then Michael said to Fitzsimmons, "Fitz?"

The redhead turned in his chair and looked back. "Yeah, Mike?"

Michael felt an edge of alarm creep into his voice. "When did you hear this?"

"Just yesterday. Last night, as a matter of fact. I had drinks and dinner with Danny Galloway. He told me Lynch wouldn't be around long. He didn't elaborate, said it very casually. I didn't want to push it to the obvious, so I dropped it."

"Did you mention it to Bo?"

"Yeah, I mentioned it to him before the opening today."

Michael's agitation shook him. *Come on, man, what did Lynch say?*"

Fitzsimmons glanced at Simpson, then back at Michael. "He said...'Fuck 'em in the butt'."

Barry Kane laughed out loud.

Fitzsimmons continued. "And that's about what Lynch did today in the pit."

Michael felt his heart racing again, this time with a different type of passion. "What do you mean, Joe? What did Bo do today?"

"Mike, he went crazy about halfway through the trading session. He caught Zitello selling five hundred contracts on the sly to Jasper Pozzi, and Bo raced across the pit calling him a greaseball and a commie son of a bitch. Then, with the palm of his hand, he slammed him in the chest and sent him airborne out of the pit, into a phone desk. If Bo would have had better footing, he would have broken Zitello's sternum. I've seen the punch before, Mike. It's a killer punch meant to break the sternum and push the ribs into the lungs. Bo was crazy. He tried to kill Zitello. It was almost like..." Joe stopped for a moment.

Michael pushed. "Like what, Fitz?"

"Well, if you'd have seen the look in Bo's eyes, you would have thought he was back in the Viet Nam jungles."

Michael knew that's exactly where Bo had been. He spoke sharply, impatiently. "What happened then?"

"Zitello had to leave the floor. Security guards were all over the place, but nobody had the nerve to go close to Lynch. He looked like a caged leopard walking--pacing on the top step of the pit. Finally, he just gave his deck to a broker named Sidney Wertz and left the floor."

Michael's anger blazed like a flash-fire. *"Why wasn't I told about this?"*

Fitzsimmons answered defensively. "Mike, I called Pete this afternoon, but he evidently couldn't find you."

Michael remembered that he had taken a long walk down to the lake after the market closed. Pete was probably going to tell him before the meeting started, but since he was late--shit, he thought.

Simpson finally sounded off. "Let's get on with the slides. We've got over fifty more to see, plus the recordings. Lynch can take care of himself."

Michael stood abruptly, his eyes riveted into the heavy face of Simpson. Heat permeated his head, and he slammed his hand down on the empty chair in front of him. The room was deathly still. "You shut the fuck up, Simpson."

He felt Andy grip his arm. "Settle down, Mike," he said. But Michael ignored him.

He let his anger continue to fever the room. His eyes blazed at Simpson, and his words shot through the air like lightning. "I have a man who is busting his ass for your men, who may have a *contract* on his head because of his involvement, and *you* say, 'Let's move on, Lynch can take care of himself.' You are a complete and utter *asshole, Simpson,* and I don't give a damn if you're the Assistant to the Director of the FBI, the Pope, or the President. How the fuck does the government find guys like you? Did you have to go to school to learn how to be an asshole--or is it inherent?"

Simpson stumbled with flustered rage as he stood to face Michael. He spat back. "You...you're...you are an impudent, disrespectful son of a bitch, Hogan. You're..."

"AH, SHUT THE FUCK UP." Michael looked down at Andy and scoffed. He was angry but in control. Andy loosened his grip on Michael's arm.

He looked back up at Simpson's flushed face. He spoke matter-of-factly. "Yeah. You're probably right. I'm impudent and goddamn disrespectful to callous bastards like you."

He glanced quickly around. Even in the dim room he could see the concern on all the faces. Tony Lorenzo watched him with question and concern. Lewis looked casual, as if he had expected the angry outburst, and Simpson was finally silent, frustration and anger written writhing in his face. But he remained quiet.

Michael shrugged his shoulders and raised his palms in front of him, elbows close to his sides. He spoke to the whole group, quietly at first. "Don't you see what Lynch is doing?" He stalled a moment. "He's going to make things happen. He's not going to spend two years taping conversations and snapping pictures and listening to wire taps and sniffing out foreign accounts. He is going right to the source and telling the whole world that Zitello and his entourage are thieves."

He stopped to let the words sink in, then he rubbed the back of his neck, keeping his eyes on the men in the room. With emphasis, he began again. "Everyone else on the trading floor is either syndicate involved, on the take, or are too afraid to do anything about Zitello and Peterson and Conti and Ruzzo and God knows how many others...*Lynch doesn't give a shit*. He doesn't have to call Washington and ask permission to fart."

He let his voice become loud and more emphatic. His words shot out like steel arrows. "Lynch is flushing out the bad guys despite the dangerous situation he is putting himself in. Can you book-learners understand that? Zitello will crack. So will Franko and Terrin and Nicolelli and Pozzi, the whole goddamn bunch. When they crack, the dominoes will start to fall and they will lead right to Peterson, who will lead to Conti and Ruzzo, who will lead to their national bosses and their political contracts in Chicago, New York, and Washington."

When he scanned the room, he saw most eyes were looking away from him. He felt like leaving but knew if he did, Simpson would take over the meeting. Michael had worked too hard for months to win the allegiance of these agents he had trained.

His eyes leapt up to the picture on the screen and saw the thick veins of anger protruding from Bo's neck, then he moved to Zitello's eyes. The picture was extraordinarily clear. The eyes told the story. Eyes that generally had the cold, gray look of dirty snow were lit with fear. Bo had shaken Zitello, and he would surely go to Peterson for a solution.

Peterson would kill Bo. Bo, who was doing a job that Michael had asked him to do. Because of his loyalty, he could die for his efforts. That would be Bo's second losing battle he had fought for his government--for men like Simpson who called the shots in Washington: cold-blooded, ruthless, power hungry sons of bitches.

Simpson spoke, trying to muster an authoritative voice. "Hogan, we have laws in this country, and whether you like it or not, everybody is innocent until proven guilty. And, another thing, the government is not supporting a sting operation that caters to or works with a bunch of vigilantes who go around punching in chest bones on pure speculation that a man or group of men are skimming money. We have no hard evidence yet. This is pure speculation, and until we..."

Michael broke in sharply. "PURE SPECULATION? Listen, Jerkoff, your way will always be pure speculation, as far as I can see. Your Federal laws suck when it comes to stopping crime. Did you count the number of times Zitello has broken the law and beat the rap on technicalities and dropped charges? Furthermore, he is only one man in thousands

every day who are guilty of criminal acts but walk because of your fucked-up laws. You handle the investigation your way, and I'll handle it my way. We'll see who gets to justice first. Just stay out of my path, Simpson."

Michael felt a trickle of sweat run from his sideburns to his neck. "Another thing, don't give me that shit about your not supporting vigilantes to do your dirty work. Your whole goddamn CIA organization is nothing more than licensed, government-approved vigilantes, so cut the shit with me, Simpson, and let's get to the bull."

He felt a tugging at his pant leg and looked down at Andy, who motioned with his head for him to sit. "They got the point, Mike, and I'll make it clear to the Director about what's going on."

Michael sat down reluctantly and said with a chill in his voice, "Go on with your sideshow, Simpson."

He watched Simpson's eyes as they roamed the room looking at his agents. Michael sensed loyalty from the men. Loyalty that had swung his way. He knew Simpson sensed it too.

Simpson's voice mellowed, probably trying to maintain what little control he had left. But his anger continued to show in his cynical reply. "Thank you for your epistle AND your permission to continue, Mr. Hogan." He turned abruptly and sat. "Go on, Lewis, next slide."

Michael felt Andy's arm rest on the back of his chair, and a pat on the shoulder indicated his support.

Lewis continued with the slides and his read-outs on each photo. Raulf Hoge (HOG), bagman for Zitello and strong arm man for Peterson, or was until Bo Lynch broke his wrist during a skirmish in the S & P Pit.

Alvin Alden, Edward Millano, Jasper Pozzi, Samuel Kohn, Robert Silva, Jerome Finkle, Joseph Paminsi, Morris Franko, John McGee, Charles Nicolelli. Pete clicked off more than fifty candid shots of pit brokers, all bagmen for one group or another. All worked to move dirty money into clean accounts for the crime syndicates or steal virgin money from unsuspecting customers. All worked on a percentage of the capital they handled plus whatever they could steal on their own.

Michael had given Pete all the information he was showing the agents except for the criminal read-outs that went with each photo. Most of the brokers were clean--no police records--that is, until the present sting operation. The whole industry would be tarnished when the truth finally came out. At this point, the Feds had enough information to indict seventy-three pit brokers for security fraud, which opened the door to mail fraud, tax evasion, bank fraud, and a whole raft of other criminal charges. Further, the seventy-three targeted brokers were just the front runners. There would be more. Many more. The investigating would go on for months. Maybe another year before it came out into the open.

Michael slouched. His thoughts of Samantha and Bo collided with each other. The separate passions he felt for each of them were not mixing well. He didn't have the answers. He knew he had to contact Bo. Fast. Maybe he'd have him move into the coach house with Adams and O'Leary. At least he'd be safe and with men he trusted.

When Lewis was finished with the slides, he stood up and stretched, then faced the group. The lights were turned up a notch, and the screen was blank. "I have prepared a dossier for each agent to study. The same information which I have just gone over on each pit broker is in the dossier. I know it's getting late, and you're all getting tired, but I have a few more shots to show and one recording I want you to hear. Maybe I'll just tell you about it and you can listen to it on your own. It's important that Mr. Simpson, Mr. Lorenzo, and Mr. Golden receive this information today. They won't be meeting with the group for a while, and I feel it's necessary that everybody is brought up to date at the same time. That way, if there are any questions, they can be answered, and if there are any differences in opinions, they can be resolved.

"The next photos are of the men we feel are the criminal under-bosses and the responsible leaders of the various broker syndicates who work illegally on the Exchange floors. These men are seldom seen on the trading floor. They run their businesses from offices which are located at each Exchange and in the Sears Tower. Believe it or not, one of the offices is in the Federal Building, not two hundred yards from where we sit."

Pete stopped his narration, looked back over his shoulder, and said. "Mr. Lorenzo, do you want to say something about the group that is working out of the Federal Building?"

Michael looked over at the U.S. Attorney, and Lorenzo spoke softly but with authority. "Thank you, Pete. When we first heard from Hogan that there was an office in the Federal Building being used to clear illegal trades for a group of brokers, frankly, we didn't believe it. This seemed so far fetched and a very stupid thing to do. But on the contrary, A&P Commodity Clearing Corporation, Inc., has a very unique set-up. The attorney, Harvey Mann, who represents A&P, and who was sharing the office with Judge Redmond, took over the lease when the judge retired. The judge agreed to leave his name on the lease and his name on the door. Don't ask me why. I know Judge Redmond, and it wouldn't be unlike him to be a nice guy and allow Mann to keep the lease in place. Redmond is getting old, and his decision-making was not at its best near the end of his tenure. Despite their sophisticated computer and phone systems, we have them under tight scrutiny. The phone is always answered by a male receptionist as 'Judge Redmond's Office.' Coded language is used on all conversations; we have broken the code, and A&P Commodities is in violation of at lease forty RICO violations. When we make the sting public knowledge, A&P will be the first ones to have their door kicked in. Using the Federal Building for a cover, and a judge's office for illegal trade clearing was a gutsy play, to say the least. Thanks to Hogan's tip, though, I think we have A&P by the short hairs. Without that we probably would have missed them. They are well covered, have no

direct contacts with the brokers on the trading floors, and we never would have thought to look for or trace their operation in the Federal Building."

Michael paid no attention to the compliment. He just wanted to get the hell out of the meeting and go to his boat. He yawned and leaned forward. He felt an uneasiness flow through his guts when Pete clicked the next photo. The large body of Karl Peterson filled the screen. Michael hadn't seen this photo before. Peterson was standing in the doorway of an office talking to two men Michael recognized as Gunter Schmidt, the Rodent, and Dieter Wolf, the Albino. His eyes dug into the screen like a burning laser, and his mind exploded with hate for the three men.

Pete interrupted his growing rage. "This photo was taken by Agent Winters." Michael's body went limp when Pete said those words. He felt his hands turn clammy and cold. Jesus Christ, he thought. She was supposed to be the receptionist and had stepped into the den of the devil to take a photo. Goddamn her! She didn't know what she was doing. He wouldn't be surprised if she used a Kodak Instamatic with flash cubes. The woman thought she was dealing with a judge or a lawyer or a priest when, in fact, she was taking a picture of Lucifer and two black angels.

Now he looked to see if by chance Samantha had changed her mind and come to the meeting. She was not there.

A sense of panic engulfed him. First of all, at being so close to Peterson and his killers, and secondly, she was out of his immediate sight. His mind sped. She was too clever to be caught by Peterson so early in the game. But Michael knew the progression of risk takers, being one himself. They always took one more step, one more chance, just a bit closer, inching ever nearer to the edge of the precipice, until the earth began to crumble from under their feet. He hoped Samantha had enough street savvy to know when the blade was ready to fall.

He sat back and folded his arms as Pete read off all the criminal activities the three men on the screen were purported to be involved in. From his right he heard a whisper, "You okay, Mike?"

He looked over at Andy, concern obvious in his furrowed look. "Yeah, Goldie. I'm okay. I just don't like the idea that you've got two beautiful girls working undercover for the scum of the city."

He didn't want to single out Samantha, so he included Colleen in his statement. Andy was a friend, but he was also a professional detective. He could detect mood swings, innuendoes, dropped names, sudden interest or disinterest, and he knew Michael well. But he didn't know Michael Martin Hogan, The Ghost of Kildare, The Deceptive One.

He had to hold onto what little control he had left. He was sure Andy had expected his outburst with Simpson. He also understood his dislike for Peterson and his group of bandits, but he would sense something if Michael showed too much interest in Samantha, even behind the camouflage of Colleen McFadden. His relationship with Samantha was personal, sensitive--a little bit of secret pleasure he had left in his life.

"What are you worried about, Mike? Those girls are pros. They've done this type of thing a hundred times before."

Michael couldn't help turning to look at the door, hoping to see Samantha walk in. He turned back to the screen and looked at his three enemies, then glanced at Andy. Andy's eyes had taken on the sharpness of a federal agent looking, smelling, sensing something.

Michael shrugged and dismissed further conversation. "Dumb broads could blow the whole operation if they happen to drop their Kodaks on the floor."

Andy smiled. Michael saw he had thrown him off the scent. "Don't worry. They won't drop their Kodaks. At least not in the presence of the enemy."

Now his guts were churning, and the sick feeling wouldn't leave until he saw Samantha and made sure she was safe. He looked at his watch. Nine twenty-three. She would be at the boat by ten. He wanted to be there as well.

Pete rambled on for ten more minutes, telling the group about Peterson's network. He showed separate pictures of Schmidt and Wolf and mug shots of previous arrests. Then he went through the same thing with Conti, Ruzzo, Jake Edwards, and Louis Alverez, the Miami attorney for the group.

Michael checked the time again. Nine fifty-two. Pete had shut off the slide projector and turned up the lights. "You can all pick up your dossier on the way out. In each folder, there is a tape between myself and three other brokers, Max Leonard, Ted Terrin, and Morris Franko. Please listen to it. All three want to give me a profitable trade in exchange for a large tax loss I supposedly have with two fabricated New York textile companies. I'm to receive fifteen cents on the dollar, cash under the table, in exchange for the tax loss. I'm negotiating now and told them I needed twenty-five cents on the dollar. Lunch with them and a few other brokers next week should finalize the deal. I told them there was enough for everybody. It's all on the tape. The tapes are to be returned to me day after tomorrow. Do not lose the tape or make a duplicate. If you try to duplicate the tape for any reason, it will explode."

Michael nudged Andy. "I'm splitting, Goldie. I've had enough. If I stay around after the meeting I'm going to beat the hell out of Simpson."

Andy frowned and whispered back. "Then get the hell out of here. I'll be talking to you on the phone. Who is your back-up?"

"I don't know. Some new guy by the name of Charlie Taft. I think I left him holding his dick in front of the Union Club five hours ago."

Andy smiled and shook his head. "Charlie's a good ol' boy from Tennessee. Great at catching bank robbers and kidnappers, but get him in the big city to back you up, and he'd lose you in an elevator.

Michael smiled at the remark. "That's exactly where I think I lost him, in an elevator."

He shook Andy's hand and stepped out of the conference room unnoticed. He glanced at the wall clock on the way out. 10:07. Son of a bitch. Be there, Sam. Be at the boat.

THIRTY-SIX

Hot Summer - Cool Water

Michael lurched from the Reception room. He needed to get to a clean phone. Mrs. Beatlebaum's desk was neat and cleared of all papers, looking as if no one had occupied the space for months. She was nowhere in sight.

The black touch-tone phone perched on the desk looked inviting, but he felt certain it was tapped into the Federal Building recording system, and he wanted his conversations kept private.

He carried himself with vigor to the same elevator he had come up on, knowing it would bring him out a side entrance. He didn't want Charlie Taft or anyone else following him. Where he was going was also personal business. He had to move fast. His guts churned at the photo Samantha had taken. Shit, he thought, he also had to find Lynch. Time--he needed time.

Heat gushed into his face as he left the building, and he immediately began to perspire. He skirted across Dearborn Street and found an empty phone booth near the entrance to the subway. He dialed Bo's home number, not expecting him to be there but hoping--ever hoping with that crazy bastard.

Twelve rings. No answer. The bum must be dead-ass drunk by now. Michael decided to call Snake and Bear.

He pushed in another quarter and dialed seven digits. A recorded voice came on the line and asked the caller to leave the number from which the call was being made. Michael examined the instruction panel and found the phone number to the pay phone, punched it in, and hung up. He waited less than thirty seconds, and the phone rang. Halfway through the ring, he trounced on the ear piece. "Snake?"

The voice on the other end was deep and sounded educated. "No, Mike. It's Bear. John's walking the grounds. What's up?"

Michael looked up at the dull night light that shone down on him. "Damn," he mumbled. Out of fifty thousand phone booths in Chicago, he had to pick the only one with a working dome light. He opened the door a third of the way, and the light went out. He sure as hell didn't need to be trapped in a lighted fish bowl.

Again from the other end Bear inquired, "What's up, Mike? You okay?"

"Yeah, Bear. I'm okay, but Lynch may be in some trouble."

Bear didn't appear to be alarmed. "Like what kind of trouble?"

Michael relayed the story to Bear about the confrontation between Bo and Zitello in the S & P pit and about a contract being placed on his head by Peterson.

He knew Bear O'Leary was a man of total discipline and patience, and his easy voice confirmed it. "Bo can generally take care of himself, Mike, drunk or sober, contract or no contract. But if you want me to go fetch the baboon, I can probably find him faster than you. I'll bring him back here and put him to bed. He'll be at one of three bars on North Clark."

Michael knew the area. Rough territory. Redneck territory. This was no place for Bo or anyone else who valued his life. But then he realized, Bo didn't give two shits about his life.

"I'll leave as soon as John gets back, Mike. About five minutes."

Michael hesitated before issuing a warning. "Watch yourself, Bear. That's redneck land, and they don't much cotton to big, black bucks."

Michael heard silence. Shit, he thought. He'd hurt Bear's feelings. He had insulted the man's ability to handle himself in a dangerous situation, and he was on Michael's payroll for just that.

He let his words roll carefully. "Sorry, Bear. Go get the drunk bastard and kick anybody's ass who gets in your way. You have any problems with the cops, call the number I gave you to reach Pete Lewis. It'll take less than ten minutes, and the cops will receive a 'hands off' order. You can come and go wherever you please."

Bear's voice was low. "Even if I have to kill somebody?"

Michael looked at the dead light above him and rolled his head. "You guys always think of the worst possible end result, don't you?"

Again came the deliberate words. "Have to if we're going to stay alive. The bad guys can make lots of mistakes, we can't afford to make one."

A bus roared by the phone booth, and Michael closed the door for a moment so Bear could hear him. The light flickered and went on again. "Even if you kill someone, you're a 'hands off' person as far as the cops are concerned. For Christ sake, though, try not to kill anybody just to fetch Lynch."

"Well, I had to do it in Nam, and some places in Chicago are worse. I just wanted to know if I was sanctioned for killing in self-defense."

Michael cracked the door again to kill the light. Even the hot air from outside felt good to him as he stood in the glass oven. "No offense, Bear. Just be careful. You're sanctioned all the way. I'll check in about two a.m. to see how you made out."

The calm voice reassured Michael. "I'll get 'im home okay. Always have before. Had to go sixteen miles through the jungle for him once. God, we left a lot of dead V.C. behind on that dog run."

"Keep the dead men to a minimum on this dog run, will ya, Bear?"

"Talk to you in a few hours, Mike."

The phone went dead, and Michael just as quickly had another quarter in the machine and dialed his boat. Six rings, seven, ten, fourteen rings. He slammed the phone down. Son of a bitch! It finally dawned on him that Samantha wouldn't answer the phone

for fear it might be Maria or anybody else, for that matter. She wouldn't disclose her presence.

He opened the door and stepped outside. The air was still and hot. A cold shower, or better yet, a swim in a cool lake with a gorgeous blond...

Before he completed his thought, he marched quickly through an alley that led to State Street. He crossed the mall area in front of a few buses and advanced quickly down the block and into the Palmer House.

There was a stalking, purposeful intent in the echo of his walk as he made his way through the fancy hotel and exited on Wabash, where he met four yellow cabs parked at the curb. He bent and peered into the first in line. A little Oriental driver smiled and said what Michael thought to be his only word of English, "Airport?"

"No. No airport."

He went to the second cab and poked his head inside to hear a Spanish song playing on a portable radio. "Habla Inglés Señor?"

"Sí, Señor."

"Do you know where Belmont Harbor is?"

"Sí." The Mexican reached for a street guide on the seat next to his blaring *Chimichanga* music box.

Michael lifted his hand off of the door window. "Sorry, pal. If you have to look it up in the book, you're history." He felt his impatience and irritation begin.

The third cab was indeed yellow but looked as if it had just fallen off the "El" tracks. He wondered if the fucker even ran.

Again he leaned his head into the open window. The dome light was on, and the *Sun-Times* newspaper covered the cabby's face. Michael looked at the man's ID picture and name next to his meter. It read 'STANLEY WALINSKI,' and the face filled the picture.

Breathing hard from his brisk walk, he said. "Hey Stanley? You American?"

The voice behind the newspaper graveled. "All my life. South Side. Who's askin'?"

Michael felt the tide of irritation lessen. "Stanley, would it be too difficult to get me to Belmont Harbor-quick?"

The newspaper came down, revealing a rough, unshaven, thick face. He clenched half an unlit, cheap cigar between his teeth and looked at Michael with droopy eyes. His big face jerked when he said, "How quick?"

Michael shoved his hand in his pocket and pulled out a bill. "Here's fifty bucks that says you can't get me there in eight minutes. Fifty more if you can."

Stanley looked at his watch. "It's ten thirty-eight and ten seconds. That means..." Stanley muttered as he started the cab and Michael bounded into the back seat.

Michael grinned while he figured out the equation for him. "Ten forty-six and ten seconds, Stanley, and you get the other fifty."

"You're on, pal. Don't mind if I play a little speedway music, do you?" The last words Michael heard as the beat-up cab bolted into scratching traffic were Little Richard's "Good Golly, Miss Molly" screaming from Stanley's cassette player.

Michael flopped around the back seat of the cab as it took two quick lefts and headed north on Michigan Avenue. Then a sharp right, and onto Lake Shore Drive. Red lights meant nothing to Stanley Walinski. Michael wondered if Stanley might be color blind. He attacked all red lights as if they were blue. His beat-up cab showed the results of quick trips prior to this eight-minute, fifty-buck wager.

Michael yelled over the blaring rock'n'roll, through the half glass that separated the front from the back, "ALIVE, STANLEY. ALIVE. You only get the other fifty if I arrive alive."

Stanley pounded the steering wheel in unison with the music and punched the accelerator, kicking the cab into a groaning overdrive. The junker picked up even more speed. He yelled back at Michael. "Alive! Now you're hedging your bet, partner. Eight minutes, hmpf! I'll do it in six and a half."

As he hurtled and banged around in the back seat, Michael could see only a big neckless head sitting on wide shoulders. Occasionally he would get a glimpse of the half-cigar as the bald head turned at intersections.

At one point, he saw some relief in sight, an upcoming stoplight where cars were backed up. Stanley merely gunned the cab, ran the red light, left the Outer Drive, and went up onto the pavement, knocking over a no-parking sign. Honking horns and screeching tires added to Little Richard's piercing voice. Stanley's large head rocked from side to side with the beat of the music, and he zeroed in on a walkway that led to the beach. The cab went airborne as it hit the curb at the wide concrete breakwater. Michael's head hit the ceiling. His stomach felt as if it were up around his neck until the cab slammed back to earth. For the first time in his life his stomach shook hands with his ass.

Stanley jumped another curb and sped along the twenty-foot walkway that separated Lake Michigan from Lake Shore Drive. For a good half mile, the cab dragged the no-parking sign, scraping and sparking from underneath. Two cyclists headed directly into the lake at the sight of the crazed cab. Late-night joggers and strolling hand-holders sprang from the walkway as the cabby sped on.

"Hold on, pal," Stanley warned as he headed off the walkway and up a steep, grassy embankment back toward the street.

For a moment Michael thought the cab would tip over, but once through a flower garden and a few hedges, Stanley had the cab back on Lake Shore Drive with the speedometer quivering at eighty mph.

The husky voice said, "Ninety seconds to touchdown, partner. Get the other fifty out."

Michael looked through the rear window to see if there were any squad cars following. No flashing lights. Just a trail of mud and torn-up bushes littered the Drive.

He watched the green overhead street signs flash by. Then down a ramp at seventy mph, a quick right on squealing tires, a rolling hub cap, another right, a left, and the cab drew to an abrupt screeching halt. Little Richard was silent!

His breath came in a sharp gust as he vaulted out of the back seat and handed Stanley a crisp fifty-dollar bill through the front window. "You're an ace, Stanley. You sure know how to take a man's mind off the pressures of the day!"

Stanley examined the fifty, snapped it twice, and tucked it into his breast pocket. Michael noticed that his short-sleeved shirt was unbuttoned to the waist, and it revealed a large, hairy, beer belly. "Want me to wait, partner?"

Michael smiled and patted the cab's roof. "No thanks, Stanley. I'll take it from here." He pivoted and began to walk away, then turned back. "Stanley?"

"Yeah, man?"

He grinned at the big Pole. "You're okay."

Stanley's head tilted, and his eyes drooped. "What da ya mean, partner?"

Michael gave him a serious look and said, "You're a man of your word. You do what you say you're going to do."

A big smile almost lost the cigar, but a quick snap of the teeth caught it. "Hey, partner. All us Pollacks are that way. Just like Lech Walesa. No bullshit. Just get the job done."

Michael felt his own admiration at the cab driver's simple wisdom. He nodded in agreement. "Peace, Stanley." He turned and was off through the parking lot headed for his sloop, the *Orison Tryst* and the blond angel he prayed would be there.

The words of the simple, beer-bellied cab driver rolled through his head as he hurdled a four-foot fence with one hand. "Just like Lech Walesa. No bullshit. Just get the job done." The world needed more Lech Walesas. More Stanleys. The whole damn globe would be a better place!

He raced down the walkway and turned onto Pier H. The wood planking thundered under his feet as he bolted the length of the pier toward the forty-two-foot sloop.

The tall mast of the *Orison Tryst* was easily spotted as it was near the end of the pier next to smaller luxury boats. He saw that the lights glowed in the cabin, and his heart and breath pulsated in unison. "Be there, Sam. Be there," he said out loud. He leapt the last ten feet over one of the taut stern ropes onto the deck. As he landed, he squatted and pulled the Mauser from his ankle holster, releasing the safety.

He called out sternly. "Samantha?" There was no answer. The louvered cabin doors stood ajar. He could hear music playing Neil Diamond--*America*! He pulled the doors open and glanced quickly down and inside. One light shone in the galley and it appeared as if another was on further up in the sleeping area. This time with impatience, he spoke louder, "SAMANTHA?"

Still no answer. He felt the hair begin to rise on the back of his neck. Son of a bitch. Where the fuck was she? He looked quickly around the deck. Nothing out of place.

Then he eased down into the cabin. His right hand was wrapped tight around the ready-to-fire Mauser as he moved cautiously down the steps into the cabin.

The thought crossed his mind that if he had to use the weapon, he wanted to be certain of his target before firing. He knew his reactions and reflexes were fine tuned from his years in the pit, but this was no trading pit. He'd rather take a bullet than fire at the wrong person. He lowered the Mauser to his side and turned on a master switch that lighted up the outside of the boat. "SAM, GODDAMMIT. WHERE ARE YOU?"

Still no answer.

He pushed open the door of the head. Empty. Two closets, nothing. He eased himself nearer to the sleeper.

The door to the small stateroom stood half open. He slowly pushed it the rest of the way. Simultaneously, as if planned, two of his senses were alerted to her whereabouts. His eyes zeroed in on her skirt and blouse neatly folded on the bed and next to it a note that simply read: I'M SWIMMING. His ears perked like a Doberman when he heard melodious words come from outside: "Michael, Michael. I'm out here."

He leaned back against the door and closed his eyes. Goddamn you, Sam. Suddenly he realized that he was dripping with perspiration, both from the heat and the tension.

He took a long, deep breath to ease his anxiety and pulled himself away from the door. He wiped drops of sweat from his face with the back of his hand. Then he looked at the Mauser and shook his head both in relief and disgust. He was becoming attached to the gun, and in this case it could have been a dangerous attachment.

"Michael?" The soft voice called.

He hurried back through the cabin, ducked his head, and was up the six-step ladder in one leap. He reached for the outside light switch and flipped it back off so he could see into the lake. "Sam, where the hell are you?"

"I'm out here about fifty feet from the boat."

He stood on the bow and scowled. "What the hell are you doing out there for Christ's sake?" He could see her blond, beautiful head as it bobbed closer.

She said defensively, "You were late, and it's eighty-eight degrees outside. I decided to cool off."

"Jesus Christ, woman. You..." He sat down on the deck. "Aw, fuck it." He thought he said the words to himself.

"What did you say? Is that a gun you have?"

Then his words filled with sarcasm. "I said, 'forget it.' And yes, it's a goddamn gun, but I'm going to put it away now that I know you are just cooling off."

Her voice was innocent, clean. "Were you worried about me?"

She was within ten feet of the boat by now, and he could see her tanned face and shoulders just above pure white breasts.

He replaced the Mauser in its holster and said honestly, "As a matter of fact, I was damn concerned."

She teased him. "Why?"

His answer was tense: "Never mind, Samantha. Let's just drop it."

She splashed water up on the deck. "Come on in. You look exhausted, and the water is beautiful."

He looked down the alley of boats. Loud music and laughter. A party two piers over. His eyes moved back down to Samantha. She was treading water and studying him in silence.

He knelt down on the deck, stretched out on his chest, and reached over the side of the boat for her arms. He held them and pulled her out of the water far enough for their lips to meet. They kissed and rolled their cheeks together and kissed again until Michael's shoulder muscles burned from holding her. He slowly lowered her naked body back into the water. She smiled with her mouth and her eyes. "Are you going to join me, my bold darling?"

He stood trying to relieve the tension that was becoming a way of life. He grinned down at her and undid the last two buttons on his shirt. "Sí, Señorita. Sí." He peeled off the rest of his clothes and dove in just inches from her. They swam and played as young lovers. Splashing and dunking and kissing and drifting and hugging, for nearly an hour.

When they were exhausted, they retreated to the cabin and made love for another hour. They molded themselves against each other, just holding, for yet another hour. They gave and received. They slept and woke and loved again. The storms and tempests of both their lives had temporarily calmed. Michael didn't know if this was the eye of the storm or if there was such a thing as lasting peace and tranquility in life. He supposed this was the former, and strong winds would soon blow again.

A new dimension of life, of passion, of love, had captured them both. A dimension that was completely foreign and exciting to them.

They lay naked, rested, under a thin sheet, her head snuggled against him. He stroked her hair. She, in turn, traced circles and hearts on his chest and stomach.

Samantha finally spoke, whispering close to him in the dim stateroom. "What are we going to do, Michael?"

He rolled over on top of her and said, "We're going to love each other, Sam." He had more to say. But for now he just looked at her and said nothing for a long while.

Her lovely face mirrored a question. "What?" She asked. "What is it?"

He studied her soft face for a moment and continued. "You are in love with two men--except that one of those men is dead." He paused again, just watching her, stroking. "I'm in love with two women, and they are each very much alive. If you can live with that..."His voice trailed off.

She pulled him close and kissed him gently. Then she let out a long, frustrated sigh. Holding him tightly, she said, "I can live with it. I know I'm being selfish, but I can't help it--I need you. I need your warmth. Let's just take it a day at a time, okay?"

He kissed her neck, her ears, then her mouth. "Okay, a day at a time. But remember. No regrets, no guilt. Just something special between us."

She smiled up at him and nodded. She spoke softly, "I don't think I've ever met anybody like you."

He was leaning on his elbows, rubbing her nose with his. "How do you mean?"

She rubbed back, slowly pulling her legs up under the sheet, wrapping them around him, feeling the raw warmth of their bodies pushing against each other. She continued. "Your mannerisms are so rough, yet you are gentle. You're vulgar, yet you're polished. You are bold and conniving, yet you're honest and good. You think clearly and have self-discipline, yet we get involved in what seems to be more than a casual affair. You are after peace, yet I see in your eyes you could kill if you had to. What else is there about you I should know?"

Michael loved her voice, her softness, her smell, her taste. He tightened his body against hers once again and kissed the hollow of her neck. Then he broke for a moment and said. "I think you should know that I'm a little stupid, and *you* are hallucinating."

She slapped him on the shoulders, then hugged him. "It feels so good to hold you. I've wanted this for so long."

She curled up in the crook of his arm and snuggled contentedly. He wrapped both arms around her and held tight. They couldn't get any closer.

Samantha spoke again. "What does *Orison Tryst* mean?"

"My boat's name?"

"Yes."

He spoke gently, with sensitivity in his voice. "*'Orison Tryst'* is a poem written by Francis Thompson and simply means a prayer rendezvous. When two lovers can't be together, their thoughts of each other are carried to God in the form of a prayer, where they are joined spiritually. The lovers' last thoughts at night and first thoughts in the morning are of each other, and they 'beat to Godward, like a carrier-dove, their thoughts of each other beneath its wing.'"

She sighed and dragged out her words "Thaaaat's beauuuutifuuul. Do you know more?"

Michael's mind drifted in pleasure as he recalled a portion of the poem:

> *"Now, when light pricks at my lids I never rouse but*
> *think - It's Orison time with her...I drop my Message in*
> *the hollow breast of God. Thy name is known in Heaven:*
> *Heaven is weary with the reverberation of thy name. 'Tis*
> *Orison time, 'Tis Orison Tryst with Her."*

Samantha kissed him gently. "And you are a romantic, a poet, a philosopher, an idealist and..."

He stopped her. "And I have to make a phone call. It's nearly two o'clock."

She doubled up a pillow and propped up her head. Her mouth pursed in a pout. "A phone call? At two in the morning? What are you checking? The Tokyo markets?"

"Not this time. I'm checking the Clark Street market." He pulled the sheet off the bed, leaving her naked body exposed. He looked her up and down as he wrapped the sheet around his waist. She watched him look and made no attempt to cover herself. God, she was gorgeous. "Don't move. Stay just as you are. I'll be right back."

Her eyes looked blissfully happy, fully alive. "I'll wait for you. I'll wait a long time for you." And then as an afterthought, "Besides, you owe me a dinner--breakfast now!"

He just smiled as he threaded his way through the cabin to the galley and picked up the phone.

THIRTY-SEVEN

The Blue Grass Saloon

Michael punched seven digits into the portable phone, and a recording directed him to identify the number from which he was calling. He pressed in the phone number of the sloop, turned off the phone, and waited. In less than thirty seconds it rang. He pressed the "on" button and spoke quickly. "John?"

A cool, calm voice answered. "Yeah, Mike, you're at the boat?"

Michael looked toward the state room where Samantha waited for him. "Yes, I'm staying here tonight. Maria's at the lake with the kids. What's up with Lynch?"

"Bear found him at the Blue Grass Saloon on Clark Street."

"Any problems?"

Snake was always direct and seldom showed alarm. This time was no exception. "Bear called about a half hour ago just to tell me he found Lynch. Said he would be home when he gets here."

"With Lynch!" Michael made it a statement rather than a question but it still needed verification.

"Yes."

He pulled the white sheet tight around his waist. "No problems, then? The Blue Grass is a mean saloon. The cops won't even go in there."

He could tell by Snake's voice that he was alert but bored with his concern. "I'm sure Bear can handle the situation with his usual cool temperament. And we won't take the Zitello situation lightly. If Peterson or Zitello or anybody has taken a contract out on one of our brothers, namely Bo, we'll have to make them understand that their threats have a tendency to boomerang. They don't know who we are, but we know who they are."

Michael understood Snake's meaning very clearly. "John, we'll talk about Zitello tomorrow. Just make sure Lynch is read a good night story. Okay?"

"Okay by me." Snake hesitated for a moment then said, "Mike, you just keep doing what you're doing and bring down the bad guys your way. Don't concern yourself with us. Believe me, we take care of our own. You should know that by now."

Proud men, Michael thought. They really did only have each other. "I know that, but *you* remember, if we're going to be effective, we have to think and act like a team, not independent of each other. As fucked up as they are, it was the Feds who gave us the information on Bo's run-in with Zitello today, not one of my pit men. Fitzsimmons gave us the word on a possible contract. When you make a move or even think of making a

move, I want to know about it. We shoot straight with each other and can't afford not to keep it that way. Understand?"

Snake's voice was firm, but Michael sensed a tone of resentment. "I understand. We'll do nothing without you knowing about it first. We always welcome your blessing Mike, but we won't ask your permission."

Michael rubbed his eyes. They were getting heavy. "Well, let's hope we continue to agree on our methods of doing things. Remember, your first priority is to protect my family and my home. Your second priority is to help me break down the criminal organizations at the Exchanges. Don't forget which comes first, John."

"You're the one signing our pay checks, Mike, and even if you weren't, we would honor your priorities. Honor and loyalty are probably the only two things we understand. We consider you one of us."

Michael let the last words sink in. Snake had paid him quite a compliment. " I appreciate that John, thank you. See you first thing in the morning."

He heard the determination in Snake's voice. "We'll take care of Lynch and see you in the a.m. at the coach house." The phone went dead.

He turned and ejected the Neil Diamond tape from the cassette player and slipped in a Frank Sinatra tape. He immediately began singing, *"My Way."* Michael mumbled to himself, "My Way too, blue eyes, my way too!"

He returned to Samantha. She had dozed off. He covered her naked body with the sheet and slipped in quietly next to her. His arm reached around her, pulling her close to him as he cupped her firm breast. She moaned with satisfaction and nestled close to him.

His eyes closed,and he drifted into the poetic world of Francis Thompson. "'Til Orison Tryst, Sam..."

> *...like a bubble from a water-flower released as it*
> *withdraws itself up-curled into the nightly lake, he*
> *sighed her name, "Samantha." His prayer for his love*
> *beat Godward.*

* * *

Bear's huge frame filled the open door of the Blue Grass Saloon. He looked back to the street, where there were a half dozen black hog motorcycles parked on the diagonal. He took a deep breath of hot air and turned back to the bar. The inefficient air conditioner was laboring in vain to cool the 100-degree room. Two large, upright fans fought to move the stale air around the dark, narrow bar.

Outside he felt the steamy summer heat at his back and it collided around his dripping face with the sick smell of the saloon. The outward draft gave off a toxic waft of cigarette smoke, spilled beer, human sweat, urine, sewer gas, and sundry other offensive smells.

Despite the heat, many of the patrons wore cut-off leather jackets and vests. A few were in dirty tee-shirts, and a few more wore no shirts at all. Arm tattoos, leather, dirty jeans, heavy boots, and a general filthy, low-life appearance seemed to be their common bond. Bear thought, "I spent four years in Viet Nam for these assholes. What a waste!"

He saw Bo sitting on a stool at the far end of the bar. His eyes searched the room for trouble spots. There were about twenty shoddy hillbillies. A few rough looking broads lingered at small tables. Two big uglies were shooting pool at the far end of the bar beyond Bo. Lynch was holding court with some sleaze-bag broad. Six men slouched, heads down, at the old wooden bar. A large Confederate flag hung on the far wall.

Bear had heard that alcoholics eventually sink to the dregs of society if they keep drinking. Bo had gone beyond that point. The Blue Grass was a cesspool, smelled like one, looked like one, and felt like one. Filth surrounded the place in both atmosphere and characters. He estimated the patrons' chronological age to be about forty. He estimated their mental age to be about seven.

Bear stepped into the saloon. He moved cautiously down the narrow bar. His eyes roamed as he walked. After spending two hours looking for Lynch, he wasn't in the mood to have some prick hillbilly try to slap him upside the head.

A bellicose voice blazoned from behind the bar, "HEY, NIGGER. YOU'RE OFF LIMITS!"

Bear shot a look at the bartender, who had made the comment. A big, unshaven man, in a filthy half tee-shirt and enormous beer belly, glared at him with curled lips and mean eyes. Puffs of gray hair billowed out from underneath a trucker's cap. "YEAH! YOU! NIGGER. OUTTA HERE!" Heads turned and the conversations dulled, then came to a tense stop.

Bear's disciplined mind stopped a hot flash of anger. Raising one hand up in peace he said, "I'm leavin' right away, man. Just here to pick up a buddy."

Again came the bellow. "You got no buddies in here, nigger!"

Bear heard a few chairs behind him protest against the wooden floor. He could see in the back-bar mirror that two of the leather-vested kings had moved from their thrones, naturally showing their girl friends and the bartender they agreed. "Did ya hear, burrhead? NO NIGGERS ALLOWED!"

Bear made his way down the bar against the words of protest. His mind controlled his body, but he felt his jaw tighten against the hate he felt in the room.

The voice boomed now. "OUTTA HERE, NIGGER!"

Bear heard Bo laugh heartily at something the girl had said. He seemed completely oblivious to Bear's presence and to the tension that had filled the room. But he knew Lynch. As drunk as he might be, he was never unaware of danger.

By the time Bear reached Bo, his female partner was planting a red kiss on Bo's sweaty cheek. The lip marks stood out like fresh graffiti on a dirty wall.

Bear grabbed Bo's shoulder and turned him around on his stool. With his own grizzly paw, he caught Bo's fist in mid air. He knew the blow would be coming. Nobody touched Lynch without warning.

Bo's slurred his words: "Bear, wha da fug you doin' here?"

Bear released Bo's fist as his eyes continued to watch the patrons through the back-bar mirror. "Come on, Asshole. Time to go home."

Bo licked his lips slowly, then objected. "Naw, na yet. He yelled to the bartender, who was now standing in front of them. "Hey Tennessee! Wan ya ta meet my buddy, Clarence C. O'Leary. Just call 'im CC or Bear. Hey, buy 'im a drink."

The big body behind the bar tensed. "Lynch, get your nigger friend outta here before these guys take you both apart."

Bo waved his finger in front of him and said almost sweetly, "Nooooo, we don' wanna be taken apart, do we, Bear?"

His head bobbed. Bear knew his mind might be drugged, but as long as he wasn't passed out he was still a lit fuse. His senses and reflexes would be slowed, but they still worked in spite of his dead brain.

He watched the room as he let his own words coax. "Bo, let's just get the hell out of here. Orders from Hogan! You're to stay at the coach house tonight."

But Bo would have none of this. "Nooooo. Les' have a liddle dwink. TENNESSEE! Two Wild-Ass Turkeys. Straight up. For me and Bear. Oh! And don' forget Gloria. Bear, meet my good friend Glori...Gloria? Yeah, Gloria. She's a hooker but only goes out with nice guys." He gave Bear an exaggerated, drunken wink.

Gloria gave him a big smile and said in a whiny voice, "Nice to meetcha, Mr. Bear." Black roots showed through thick orange hair and a missing tooth on the right side of her smile disturbed any appeal she might be trying to foster.

Again came the loud, coarse voice of the bartender. "No more drinks, Lynch. You're enough trouble in here by yourself. Now you're bringing in a King Kong nigger." He had evidently seen Bo in action, and his voice took on more of a plea than a demand.

"Come on, Lynch. Give me a break. Go someplace else and drink. I don't want my place busted up again, especially because of a nigger."

Bear raised himself to full height and caught the bartender's eye, then said softly but with ominous sincerity, "Mr. Tennessee, don't call me a nigger again."

He watched as the warning cleared the bartender's angry face. When he looked into Bear's eyes, the anger was replaced with alarm.

Tennessee took his trucker's cap off and scratched his head, then brushed his matted hair and replaced his cap. Bear watched his eyes move to the pool table. The two big men had stopped their game of eight-ball and were leaning on the pool table about ten feet away. Tennessee backed off, mumbling defensively. "No more to drink, Lynch. Just go. Get the fuck out--while you can."

Bo stood away from the stool and leaned back heavy against Bear. "Ah fug you, Tennessee." He swept his hand around the room, bumping Gloria's forehead in the process. "And fug all your butt-slammin, hillbilly, faggot friends."

Bear raised his head to the ceiling and closed his eyes for a split second. He knew what was going to happen. "Shit."

Bo leaned back, laid his head against Bear's chest, and looked up with a dumb grin on his sleepy face. "We're gonna be in a fight, Bear."

Bear pushed his words out fast. "Let's get our asses out of here, Bo."

Bo shook his head and waved his hand around the room again. "Fug 'em all. FUG 'EM ALL!...FUG..."

Out of the corner of his eye, Bear saw motion to his right, and sensed motion behind him. More chairs pushed across the wooden bar floor. Willie Nelson sang, "Mamas, don't let your babies grow up to be cowboys."

Bear looked at the two men who had unleashed their butts from the pool table. They walked toward him. "Hey, nigger!" You best move your ass, boy. Bartender said ya'll ain't welcome here."

He put his hand up reluctantly. His guts told him to strike. His mind said not yet. "We're leaving right now. Don't want any trouble. Just come to pick up my..."

Before he could finish his sentence, the largest man, bearded and bald, swung the heavy end of the cue stick around to catch him in the face.

He caught the stick within a foot of his head and snapped it in half like a wooden match. In the same motion he swung the cue stick back in a blur and caught the bald ape just below the ear. The unmistakable sound of a snapped jaw echoed throughout the bar, followed immediately by a painful scream. The man didn't go down. He spit blood and red teeth onto the floor and looked back at Bear.

He hissed out his words with dripping blood. "You cocksucker. You broke my jaw." He charged Bear like a bull and accompanied the charge with a loud attack-growl.

Bear stepped to one side, swung the cue stick in a full circle, and came up hard and quick. He caught the bald head at the forehead, snapping it back hard. So powerful, the blow sent thick globs of blood to the filthy ceiling. The bull's body hovered for a moment. His eyes had the look of soapy water, and he fell in a heap to the dirty floor, face down. In a split second, Bear's right foot came down hard on the man's back, just above the waist, destroying one of his kidneys. Another scream pierced the room. Two inches to the left, and the man would never walk again. Bear was tempted but decided to spare the trash for possible recycling.

He could have broken the guy's back. He certainly wanted to. His soul screamed to kill the man, but Hogan's words flashed through his mind, and he stepped back from the moaning pile of puke.

Bo laughed, trying to coax Tennessee into giving him another drink.

Bear didn't see the cheap wooden chair coming, but it had little effect when it slammed and shattered onto his left shoulder. He turned quick to see one of the leather-vested greaseballs staring, waiting for Bear to fall.

Bear stepped over the remains of the chair and grabbed the hillbilly by the vest, pulled him close, and said, "I really don't want any trouble." He hoisted the thin piece of human slime in the air and threw him like a medicine ball over the bar and into the mirror that housed a few shelves of cheap booze. The crash of glass brought the whole bar to their feet. Hoots, hollers, and curses filled the saloon.

Bear saw the bartender run to the far end of the bar and open a drawer. His instincts told him there was a gun in the drawer. Before the glass from the body hitting the mirror stopped falling to the floor, he turned to ward off the other pool player.

The tattooed son of a bitch had thrown in a cheap shot with the cue stick across Bear's head, dazing him momentarily. He was beginning to get angry. He ignored the pain that rushed through his head and down his shoulders. The man was tall, taller than he. He brought his foot up hard and caught the assailant in the stomach, knocking the wind out of him.

He grabbed a handful of greasy hair, walked him back to the pool table, and slammed his face down on the slate top, destroying his nose and cheek bones. Blood immediately began to cover the green felt top.

His reflexes were sharp, and he felt the adrenalin flow fast with the beat of his heart. He had to put the bartender out of commission quickly. He picked up two pool balls, the 14 and the 8-ball. He whirled to find the bartender raising a .38 revolver in his direction. Bear let the Number-14 fly. Missing him by inches, the ball crashed into the cash register and a few bar bottles.

In the second that Tennessee ducked to avoid the deadly ivory, the 8-ball was on its way with the velocity of a heavy ball bearing shot from a sling. This caught him in the middle of the forehead, and he went down like a sack of potatoes.

Bear saw two others had joined in and were on their way toward him with broken beer bottles. He prepared himself to take a gash on his left arm. As the brown, deadly glass slashed its way toward his face, a blur from Bear's right kicked the lethal weapon from the hillbilly's hand. Another blur caught the second man in the face. Bear heard the snap, and a shower of blood splashed across the barroom.

Bo's kicks had broken the first man's arm, and his second kick might have killed the other man. Both kicks were meant to destroy. The second man lay on the floor twitching. Around his limp head crept a circle of dark blood. His eyes were open but glassy.

He heard Lynch's laugh. "Whad ja do without me, Bear?"

"Probably live longer, Asshole."

Bo's words cut through the tense air. "Hey, Tennessee. How 'bout another WILD TURKEY? Tennessee? Where ja go, Tennessee? Fug ya then!"

Bear knelt down and examined the man Bo had kicked in the head. The pulse in his bloodied neck was faint but still there. Jesus Christ, he thought. Bo nearly ripped the fucker's head off. Outside of a skull fracture, God only knew how many bones were broken in the man's head. Blood spewed from the ears, nose, and mouth in gushes.

He looked around at the limp, moaning bodies and decided they had spent too much time at the Blue Grass Saloon.

He grabbed Lynch around the waist and pulled him from the bar stool. "Come on, Shit-for-Brains. We're out of here."

"Aw, Come on, Bear. I'm jus stardin' to have fun."

Bear carried him like a knapsack, with little effort, toward the door. Bo yelled back to his girl friend, "Gunite, Sweetbird. Some other time, ma dear."

Bear saw two men block the exit. One held a knife, the other a heavy chain. "Son of a bitch, these bastards, just don't give up."

He stopped four feet away, patient but explicit. "Boys, I've been given instructions to try not to kill anybody here. If you two don't move out of my way, you're going to piss me off, though, and I'm going to forget my instructions and kill you both. Is that clear enough, fellows? You've got three seconds. Live or die."

The men looked at each other, shrugged, and moved aside, letting him pass with his limp, singing luggage. Bo was mumbling a song. "Am I heavy, Bear?"

He was silent, as Bo continued to mumble his version of Willie's song:

> *"Mama, don' le' your son grow up ta be a Cowboy, or*
> *a Cowgirl, or a Girl Scout, or a Dike, or a Pimp, or a*
> *Wimpy Broad, or a Commodity Broker, Dum de dum de*
> *dum de dum."*

Bo passed out with the last dum de dum.

Bear opened the back of the white van and laid Bo comfortably down on a blanket. "Naw, Lynch. You're not heavy, man, 'you're my brother.' If we can't carry each other, who's going to help us through this jungle?" Bear realized he was talking to himself, but he also knew that if there was such a thing as brotherhood among men, it had truly been spawned many years ago in a land far away between men like Bo and himself. All they had left in life was each other. He decided that was enough for which to live and fight.

He felt his eyes narrow as he closed the van doors and looked back at the Blue Grass Saloon. He whispered an oath. "Nobody is going to hurt us again, brother, nobody."

THIRTY-EIGHT

Storm Warnings

Michael had been talking to Joe Glassmann for nearly an hour, filling him in on the investigation. He pulled the hot phone from his ear while Glassmann was still talking and tried to rub the numbness away.

He switched ears and cut in on Joe. "Okay, Joe, enough. Lately, every time we talk you head off in the same direction. My heritage and your observance of me taking on my grandfather's 'die by the sword' philosophy rather than my father's 'live by the cross' philosophy. Besides, you're one to talk. How many times did my dad have to keep you from shooting some bastard?"

The phone went quiet, then Joe said softly. "Times have changed, Michael. You have support we didn't have in the old days. You have backing from the government, the courts, the..."

Michael flipped a piece of rolled-up paper into a wastebasket on the other side of the room. Two points, he said to himself. "Joe, times change, people don't. Greed and violence run through us all. Some more than others. Most people are afraid they'll get caught stealing or killing, so they don't do it. My grandfather wasn't afraid, and my father was unique. I think he was in constant conflict with his own father.

"As far as the Feds supporting me, that's hog-wash. They can't do anything without first calling Washington and the isolated sections of government that aren't corrupt move too slow to be effective. You seem to think I'm enjoying a cat-and-mouse-game with them, that I'm playing hard to get. I've never shut the door on them. I welcome their help. I have a good rapport with Lorenzo and Golden and report to them weekly. What else do you want me to do, for Chrissake?"

Joe's voice was tired but harsh. "It just seems to me that you're forming your own little army. You have strong armed men protecting you day and night. You have won the allegiance of Pete Lewis and apparently most of the agents, including Samantha Winters and Colleen McFadden. They all report to you rather than Simpson or Lorenzo."

"That's not exactly the way it is, Joe. The agents report to Pete Lewis because he's in charge of the sting. Pete and I go over the findings and organize it for Andy and Lorenzo. We leave nothing out. Golden and Lorenzo are the top guns."

He listened to Joe rant about his hard-core bodyguards, and what did he have to hide, and who was he afraid of, and on and on.

As Joe lectured, Michael skimmed the front page of the *Wall Street Journal*. One paragraph on the left side in the condensed section of Business and Finance stood out.

"Economists say public optimism for stock and financial markets at all-time high. Outlook very bright through first quarter 1988!"

Joe's voice was impatient. "Michael, you there?"

He put the paper down and placed his feet up on the corner of his desk. "Joe, I've done exactly what I agreed to do. I have opened the Exchange doors to the Feds, trained their men, showed them how to spot bagmen, pointed out the laundry merchants, given them lists of crooked brokers, under-bosses, attorneys, politicians, and Exchange hierarchy who *are*, not *might be*, involved in the whole corrupt commodity scheme. I've laid out the whole network to them, how dollars go from black money to gray money to lily-white money, to capital flight out of the country. I've given it all to them, cake on a silver platter, and I'm about to give them the frosting."

He heard his own voice become strident. "What the fuck else do you want me to do, Joe? I won't start any violent behavior, but I'll provide it if needed. My men are professional in their own way but merely a protective measure for my family and myself. Look at the position I'm in. It's not what you call cloistered."

"I just want you to stay the same sweet Michael Hogan I've known for forty years. I've only personally known two men in my life who have made their point through peaceful negotiations: your father and yourself. You can't, you must not, exchange that peace for violence. Don't take on your grandfather's deceptive, vicious characteristics. Please, for all of our sakes. You are too important. The world doesn't need another 'Ghost of Kildare,' another 'Deceptive One.'"

Michael's mind strengthened at the thought of his grandfather's legend, but he countered Joe. "You've been talking to Sean McGiven. He's the only one who has brought the Ghost of Martin Hogan alive. And don't tell me Sean is concerned about me becoming a violent man. He's been trying to turn my attitudes of quiet persuasion into grinding attrition since I've known him.

"As Popeye says, 'I am what I am, and that's all that I am.' Joe, I'm just like Popeye. I am what I am--and that's all. The next time you talk to Sean, and when you are referring to my grandfather, tell him it's been a long time since anyone brought anyone back from the dead or changed water to wine. Martin Hogan is dead and has been for fifty years."

Michael's grip had unconsciously tightened on the phone. His hand was white and began to ache. Why was he getting flustered with this old friend? Was Joe touching a tender spot in his soul with the contrary philosophies of his father and grandfather? And exactly who was Michael Martin Hogan? Did he know himself? Was the pull he felt in his guts a battle between his father and grandfather? If so, who would win? He wasn't sure he gave a damn.

Joe's voice interrupted his thoughts. "Okay, Michael. You win for now. You're doing what you said you would do, and you're doing it well. Nobody is complaining except Simpson, and that's only an ego problem. It seems you go out of your way to call him a

fuckhead every chance you get. The agents look up to you. The U.S. Attorney, the Director of the FBI, and I presume the President of the United States all admire your big balls--and Sam Ross wants to go into business with you when this is all over."

Bullshit, Michael thought. He cocked his head and frowned. "What kind of business?"

"He wants to buy up floundering commodity clearing houses and turn them into computerized trading companies. This is inevitable, Mike. The day of the floor broker will go the way of the dinosaur. You have made your mark with Ross," Joe reflected. "I just hope it's the mark of an Irish harp and not a time bomb."

"Ross is a scoundrel, Joe. A likable one, but still a scoundrel, and my ship's flag displays the Irish harp, not a skull and cross bones. Not yet, anyway."

Joe sighed and slid onto another topic. "What's the frosting you have for the Fed's cake?"

Michael was back at what he knew best, the market. He lifted his feet from his desk, placed them firmly on the thick carpet, and leaned forward. "Okay, Joe, here's the play that puts the government in the driver's seat and takes me off the hot seat." He reached over and switched on the speaker phone, placing the hand set back in its cradle. "Can you hear me okay? You're on the speaker."

"Clear as a bell. Is anyone with you?"

Michael looked around the empty office. "Not that I'm aware of."

Impatience grumbled from the speaker. "Go on. The frosting, please."

Michael rubbed his chin and swirled in his chair, correlating his thoughts. "Listen closely and don't argue with me. In October of eighty-two, the Dow Jones broke through the one-thousand mark on the upside and held. That was five years ago. After consolidating for eighteen months around the twelve-hundred area, it began its move on the upside. The stock market has done virtually nothing but bull its way straight up since that time with minor setbacks and short periods of consolidation. Financial history has been made almost on a monthly basis for the past three years.

"In August of this year, it pushed through twenty-seven hundred. Since then, the market has attempted to bull through that high point and has fallen short every time. What happens, Joe, when a bull market tries three or four times to take out a historical high and fails?"

Joe's unimpressed voice came through the speaker: "It falls out of bed."

"What five per cent of professional traders always make money in a down market?"

Again no emotion. "The bears."

Michael pulled harder. "Why?"

"Because what takes two years to build can be broken down in two weeks."

"Exactly. So what's the next move, Joe?"

The speaker was dead for a moment. Then Joe asked, "down?"

Michael pushed himself out of his chair as if he had just been called by the coach to go into a ball game, and walked around his desk to lean down toward the speaker. "You're damn right, DOWN. For the first time in years, all technical indicators have stopped their movement upward and have turned down, moving averages, chart rhythms, and high-low close patterns. All my chart readings are showing that the market is getting heavy."

Joe's harshness eased. "A little heavy or real heavy?"

Michael's excitement grew. He knew in his guts he was on to something. "Just listen to me. The Contrary Opinion Poll shows the vast majority of investors and traders are long at relatively high prices. The Gann Theory says a break is coming on or around the twenty-first of October. Elliott says the market is a sand castle. And get this. Major Wall Street companies just spent four billion dollars in advertising to get small investors, and have recently invested ten times that amount--buying junk bonds, penny stocks, and over-the-counter stocks with the claim that the bull market of eighty-seven would blast through the three-thousand mark by year end."

Blood rushed through Michael's body as if he were living his premonition. He picked up the small, ivory speaker from his desk and held it to his mouth, then yelled. "JOE, THE DOW IS GOING TO HELL. IT'S GOING TO BREAK A THOUSAND POINTS."

Joe's pitch matched Michael's. "JESUS CHRIST, MIKE. TAKE THE SPEAKER AWAY FROM YOUR MOUTH. YOU ALMOST BROKE MY EARDRUM!"

"Sorry. I got a little excited."

"Mike, I know about bear markets, and this hardly looks like a bear to me."

Michael set the speaker back on his desk and picked up a Dow-Jones chart. He scrutinized it, then traced a line he had drawn on the chart with his index finger. His mind computed numbers he had written in. "Joe, the market is a major bull market, a historical bull market, but every bull runs into a red flag, and that's what I see."

Joe protested, and Michael could almost see him scratching his sparse, gray-haired head in frustration. "A one-thousand-point break would turn the bull into a bear market."

Michael reacted quickly, retracing the lines on the Dow chart with his eyes. "No, it won't, Joe. Take down these numbers. The market pushes through one thousand in October eighty-two, on the upside. Five years later it breaks through twenty-seven hundred. Seventeen hundred points higher, right?"

"Right!"

"We know that a healthy market can break as much as sixty-six per cent of its entire move and still be a good market. If you take sixty per cent of seventeen hundred points, the market can break all the way to sixteen hundred without violating its prestige as a major bull market. That's eleven hundred points in the Dow...AND TEN TO FIFTEEN THOUSAND POINTS IN THE S & Ps!"

Indignation ran through the speaker phone. "NEVER! That's utter nonsense, Michael. You might talk me into a four or five hundred point break, but not a thousand point Dow break. *And ten thousand points in the S & Ps...never!* You're losing your mind."

"Jesus Christ, Joe. You're like talking to a novice. You're the one who told me 'never say never' with the market. You're the one who taught me about Gann's Date Theories, and Fibonacci percentages, and just the general feel for the market. Can the market break sixty-six per cent on eleven hundred points and still be good?"

Joe answered slowly. "Well, yes. But it won't."

He backed his way to his bar and poured a scotch as he talked. "Sounds to me like you are long the market, Joe. Am I correct?"

Silence. Then Joe mumbled, "I'm long a little bit."

Michael grinned and took a slug from his drink. "How much you long, Joe? Ten, twenty million?"

Defensively, Joe argued, "all in blue-chip stocks and low-risk bonds."

Michael set down his drink, clasped his hands behind him, and paced between the bar and his desk. "There's no such thing as low-risk bonds, and your blue chips won't be worth a bag of potato chips when the shit hits the fan."

The room filled with Joe's growl. "And what does your astrologer say, Michael?"

He stepped to the bar, finished his drink, and poured another. Then he hustled back to his desk and picked up the phone.

"My astrologer said the break should have come last month, but four billion dollars in advertising for new accounts and forty billion in new stock buying delayed the break. Money can even fuck up the stars."

Victory came from Joe. "Ah ha! I also taught you not to rationalize. Not to use excuses. Not to alibi..."

"Joe, listen, Joe. In September there was forty billion in new buying from new customers plus another fifty billion from Japan, England, and Europe. Ninety billion greenbacks in new buying. My feeling is, that after a huge break, the market will recover, but not quickly because of the undermining of the whole economy by the S & L's and fast talking 'junk bond' dealers. We're also talking about hundreds of billions of dollars in 'leveraged buyout' debt--all financed by the country's largest investment institutions. S & L's, insurance companies, and pension funds mostly."

Joe's mood was still indignant. "So what's your point? People want to invest in America."

Michael spoke slowly, softly, and precisely. "Sure, people want to invest in America, but you know as well as I that timing is everything. A hundred billion dollars of new money flows into the market in September, and the market can't even take out the high made in August. So far in October we haven't been able to take out September's high." He toned his voice down to a whisper. "Joe, I'm telling you the stock market is

going to break one thousand points within the next thirty days, probably sooner. The S & P's will break over ten thousand points. Call your broker tomorrow...NO, CALL HIM TONIGHT!" His voice rose as if in victory. "AND TELL THE SON OF A BITCH TO SELL EVERYTHING YOU OWN...PLUS MORE!"

"I think you've lost it, Michael. Maybe it's the pressure you've been under, but you've definitely lost it."

He took the phone from his ear and looked at the mouthpiece, raised his eyebrows, and shook his head. Was he being that nebulous? "You're the one who is going to lose it, Joseph. In thirty days you will be asking me for a job if you don't move on those 'no risk' blue potato chips you own."

Joe was silent again. Michael sipped his scotch and turned his chart book around to look at it from the front of his desk. He looked at the S & P chart and recalculated the figures he had written in the margins. He pressed in a group of numbers and percentages on his desk top calculator. "You there, Joe?"

"Yeah, still here. You sure about this break?"

"I wouldn't bet my life on it. You taught me that. But I'm goddamn convinced the market's in for a blowoff that will shake the country."

"Then you don't see the market going through three thousand?"

"Yes I do, but not unless there is a blowoff first. A good one. A sixty-six-per-cent blowoff. If that happens, the Dow has a good chance of eventually going through three thousand, probably even thirty-five hundred--if the Arabs don't do something to fuck up oil prices."

Joe spoke one sharp word. "When?"

Michael was serious about the subject matter. The surge of adrenalin gave him a confident high. He was also having fun with his old teacher. "Jesus Christ, Joe. I'm telling you about the break, and you are fighting me on that. I've spent my time calculating the break, not the next up move. I already told you if the break comes, it will take years to recover, not weeks or months. You don't have major surgery and expect to play golf the next day."

He heard a weak sigh. "Okay. I halfway believe you. You've done your homework. I'll study the situation tomorrow. Now, when do you think the Dow will go through three thousand?"

Michael dropped his head on his chest and closed his eyes. "I don't know. You're not listening to me. You're mind is conditioned to think *buy*, not *sell*, because the market has been going up for so long. You're thinking like ninety per cent of the rest of the current investors. If the break comes, and if it's a severe break, you have to give the country a good two to three years to get over the shock. Let Europe open up its trading doors, let there be peace on earth, and you'll get your Dow Jones into the three-thousand-plus mark. Hell, Joe, I don't have a crystal ball."

Joe said sarcastically, "and this is the frosting for the Feds?"

This was all so clear in Michael's head. Why was it so difficult for Joe to figure out? He was exasperated but patient with him. "Joe, you've seen markets go up slow and down fast. You know the saying, 'up with the roar of a lion and down with the squeak of a mouse.' Answer this, Joe. What happens to the volume on a big down market?"

"It could double or even triple."

Michael held out his hand as if Joe were in front of him instructing, as a teacher would pull answers from a student.

"Right. What happens to the market when the volume gets so overwhelming?"

"The market has wide swings and races out of control."

He agreed with a nod of his head. "And what happens to customer orders and market discipline when the market is out of control?"

Joe said quietly, "The customers buy at the top and sell at the bottom and the brokers fill their pockets, and..."

Michael finished Joe's statement. "...and the opportunity for skimming, and bagging, and laundering runs rampant. The enthusiasm for bagging big bucks is so great that any caution a crooked broker may ordinarily use is abandoned. Brokers become careless and carefree in their thirst for giveaways. Obvious, careless, and *very* traceable greed overtakes a disciplined complex system of theft. The Feds will have a field day."

"If the break comes, as you say, in the Dow Jones, it will also come in the S & P's."

"Hell yes! All of the financial markets will be affected. Everybody will be scrambling. The opportunity to steal will be a once-in-a-lifetime for those who are already stealing. In addition, the federal boys will be taking pictures, taping, recording, and tracing paper as the market continues to blow off."

He walked around his desk and plopped back down in his chair. With the phone to his ear he said, "I think you have the picture, Joe. There won't be much of a paper chase. First of all, there is not going to be enough time to push millions of dollars around the pit from broker to broker. The market will be moving too fast, and everybody will be grabbing as much as they can. Secondly, the amount of money will be so great that the bagmen aren't going to want to share their 'take' with anybody. They'll put the trades directly into their own accounts or an account they control. The confusion and floating money on the trading floor will be so great that psychologically a crook will feel safe in taking the risk of not following his usual routine. It's a perfect opportunity for the Feds--if it happens."

Joe was more receptive now. "Have you told anybody about your theory?"

Michael picked up a red pen and circled the number 200 near the bottom of the S & P chart, then drew a red line from where the market closed that day, 321.80, down to his objective of 200. Over 12,000 points, son of a bitch. Sixty thousand dollars per contract.

Joe spoke again. "Mike? Talk to me! Have you told anybody else?"

He put the tip of the pen to his mouth, eyes concentrating on the chart. "Yeah, Joe. Sorry, just figuring something out. Pete Lewis and I met with Lorenzo today. He agreed to give us four more men to act as clerks on the Exchange floors for the next sixty days. He was reluctant, thinks it's a long shot, but said he can't afford not to speculate on my theory. He wants this sting to work while he's still U.S. Attorney in Chicago. This could make his whole career."

Joe probed weakly. "Where are you going to be if the break comes? In the bond pit or the S & P pit?"

He took the pen from his lips. "The bonds have already started to break, and Pete is pretty well established there. I'll roam the currencies, but mainly I'll be in the S & P's. I want to keep the pressure on Zitello. He's about ready to fall apart with Lynch's constant intimidation. Half the guys in the pit are all over the bastard's ass when he makes a phony trade. After watching Bo push him around, the fear has subsided and a few honest brokers with balls are finally putting their foot down."

Michael turned his desk chair toward his office window, which boxed a portion of the city. A much-needed rain had begun to fall, and the large window became a frame of rolling tears. He could almost smell the dampness.

As he cleared his throat, Joe's aging voice took on renewed confidence. "Well, Michael, it sounds as though you have everything in place. Your theory sounds good. Lorenzo is behind you. Lewis is covering the Board of Trade. Bo has Zitello on the run. Your agents are in place, and if your feeling for a run on the market is correct, it could make you a wealthy man, and more importantly, tie up the deal you have with the Feds. You would be a free man again."

A brief silence prevailed, and Joe continued. "All you need now is to have the Dow break one thousand points, the S & P's ten thousand points, and you're home."

Michael sipped his scotch as he watched the tears on the window run together. He spoke quietly. "I can smell it coming, Joe. As clear as I can smell the rain outside."

"Are you trading your own account, Mike?"

Michael waited to answer. He wasn't sure he wanted to divulge his market strategy to anyone. But then, he thought, Joe Glassmann wasn't just anybody. He had been his teacher; he was family. "I'm selling five contracts a day on the opening. If I'm wrong and the market takes out its highs and stays there for three consecutive days, my short position is history. I figure it could cost me five hundred thousand dollars."

"And if you're right?"

Michael felt a cunning smile form on his face, and a shiver of victory rolled through him. "If I'm right, I'll sell five hundred contracts and buy them back ten thousand points lower."

Joe calculated. "Jesus. That's two hundred and fifty million dollars!"

"Two hundred and fifty million the honest way, Joe."

He knew Joe's interest was more than piqued. "Have you mentioned this to Sam Ross?"

"No, no, I haven't, but if you want to relay our conversation to him, go ahead. Just make sure he realizes it's only my hunch and it's not any type of inside information. It's pure speculation.

"No, tell him it's pure common sense. The market is going to go down ten thousand points, and *soon*!"

"Well, Michael, I can't say your conversations have ever put me to sleep. This particular one will keep me up all night. Now, I've got to figure out what to do with my blue chips."

Michael smiled to himself. "Just call your broker and tell him one word, Joe. *Sell*!"

He could feel the dismissal in Joe's voice. "Good night, Michael."

"Good night, Joseph."

He let the phone rest on his shoulder a second and sighed. A brief sense of uncertainty flowed through his mind. Then he leaned forward and hung up the phone. Fuck it, he thought. He had sold himself on the market break because he had done his homework, not because he had flipped a coin. There would be a break, and it would come soon, he reassured himself.

In days gone by, he had lost millions when he hadn't studied the hazards of a bull market. He bought the market along with everybody else for what appeared to be a 'no brainer.' There were no free rides, no free lunches, no guaranteed trades. Now it was time to capitalize on an intelligent, well-deduced study, to take advantage of past mistakes.

Joe was right. If the break did come, and the agents did their job, his responsibility would have been fulfilled. He would be a free man again. A comforting thought. A damn comforting thought! They would have the hard evidence necessary to pull their whole investigation together.

He picked up the S & P chart from his desk, cocked his head, and studied the vertical and wavy lines that ran through the page. He flipped the sheet and looked at the bond section. Already headed south, he thought. He turned the page back to the S & P's. The market was trading around 325. A ten-thousand-point break would take it down to 225. That's where he would buy in his short position.

He flipped the charts on his desk, grabbed his scotch, and turned in his chair to watch the rain wash heavy on the window. A flash of mighty lightning illuminated the outside sky, giving a brief glimpse of the ghost city. Maybe I'll sell one thousand contracts, he thought. One for each point down. A profit of over five hundred million--a once-in-a-lifetime shot!

Another flash, and the rain fell harder. He closed his eyes and rested his head on the soft chair cushion. Mother Nature and spirits from the past spoke to him. Encouraged him. Reassured him. He felt his body and spirit fill with strength as the outside storm

intensified. He reached to his right and turned a dimmer switch, which softened the lights in his office. His mind drifted into a shallow meditation as the heavy rain on the windows crackled like popcorn, and lightning stung the black October night.

THIRTY-NINE

October 14, 1987-Ashen Wednesday

Michael used the wet sleeve of his trading jacket to wipe drops of sweat from his eyes as he looked at the bright-red numbers on the wall clock, then compared that time with his wristwatch. They matched: 2:58:03. Seventeen minutes to closing, but more important was the date. Wednesday, October 14, and the market was down again. Not a lot. But definitely down.

For ten days the S & P market had not been able to sustain a rally and had dropped over two thousand points. He could smell the depression in the pit. For three years the bulls had their way and held all the money. He knew the majority of the pit traders were long up their asses, along with the rest of the world.

Michael watched as a few brokers tried to bully the market by bidding on large numbers just below the market price. This was an old trick, but you couldn't trick the market. Nobody could. The market was King, was God. As with life, you went where it went, or you died--alone, lonely, and broke. The market was pushing the brokers to the edge of the precipice. They had made millions on the move up. Now, they were holding onto straw, trying to find footing. The wind would blow harder. He could feel it in his guts. The tempest was just beginning.

Three o'clock. He was already short 250 contracts and was about to sell fifty more. If the market did close higher for the day, he would buy the fifty back, take the small loss, and leave his high sales intact.

A broker to his right bid for seventy-five contracts. "Blake, I'll sell you fifty at 309.20." The noise in the pit was beginning to pick up for the closing.

Three hundred contracts short, that's enough for now, he thought. If the market started its rollover, he would give 'em both barrels. Financially, this could be a once-in-a-life-time shot--if he was right.

He felt a tug on his sleeve and looked left. It was Bo. "Hawk, you have a phone call. Your private line."

Michael looked at the wall clock. "Who is it, Bo? We don't have much time."

Bo leaned close and whispered, "It's Sam Ross."

Michael looked at the clock again. "Okay. Here...you hold the deck. I've got one hundred sixty-three to sell at three-oh-nine eighty and sixty-two to buy at three-oh-nine even. Those are your closest orders. I'll be right back."

He looked into Bo's eyes. They looked nervous but had cleared of the redness. To his knowledge, Bo hadn't had a drink since Bear's rescue mission at the Blue Grass Saloon.

"Hey, you look pretty good for an ol' drunk." He slapped Bo on the shoulder and said, "No fights! I won't be long."

Michael pushed his way through brokers who were oblivious to his passing. He could tell by the worried looks on their gray faces that they were hoping a savior would come to their rescue and move the market higher. *"Never hope a market..."*

He felt a sense of humility flow through him as he forced his way through the confused, frightened eyes. How many times had he stood on the steps holding a bad market position in his early days, waiting for a miracle, waiting for the market to turn? Even a few up ticks would give renewed confidence--but not today. He knew the sick feeling well, but he also learned fast. To go with the Money-God, to go with the Market.

Three desks back he grabbed the waiting phone. "Hogan here."

The voice on the other end was jovial as usual. "Michael, Sam Ross."

"What's up, Sam? I only have a few seconds."

Confidence flowed from Ross. "How does the market feel to you?"

Michael looked back at the pit. There was a roar. Lynch had been filled at 309. Somebody had just broke the market forty points.

"It's thin and heavy, Sam. I think I know how Christopher Columbus's men must have felt when they couldn't see land, but in this case I think the world really is flat."

"You think the rollover will come this week?"

Michael responded quickly. "Sure smells like it, Sam. Down two thousand points in a couple of weeks, can't hold a rally, and it keeps making new lows."

He looked up at the wall clock and wiped his wet face with the back of his hand: 3:06:07.

The voice came firm and cold. "Michael, sell me two thousand contracts!"

Michael looked at the clerks sitting at his order desk. They were all busy on the phones. Still their eyes were on him.

His face must have changed color. The fact that Ross wanted to sell two thousand contracts wasn't the problem. Michael had handled much larger orders--but with less than ten minutes to go? And the market tipping? He knew two thousand contracts would swamp the boat. "You sure, Sam? Are you going to give me a price limit? Two thousand contracts this late in the day could drive the market down a hundred, maybe two hundred points or more." He hesitated a split second while a thought shot through his mind. "Don't get greedy, Ross. You're already short a couple thousand contracts."

Ross's voice remained calm, but cold. "This has nothing to do with greed, Michael, it's strictly business. When it's time to press, it's time to press. Don't let them catch their breath. If you have to sell five thousand contracts, do it. Break their backs, Mike. NOW!" The line went dead.

Hawk hung up the phone and casually looked at the wall clock:3:06:50. He had eight minutes. He could feel eyes watching him from the pit. Brokers watched him to see what move he was going to make. He took a deep breath and sauntered slowly through the

running crowd. They were hustling to get closing orders to the pit. He climbed three steps and moved in next to Bo, who was offering twenty December S & P's at 308.80. Eyes were still on Michael. 3:07:22.

Bo screamed. "Sell twenty at '8.80."

Michael looked around the pit, giving no indication he had been given a big order. "What do you have, Bo?"

Bo showed him the order to sell twenty S & P's at the market.

Michael whispered, not changing his calm expression, "Just sell 'em. Don't squeeze the order or you'll eat it."

A broker in the middle of the pit was bidding $308.60 for fifteen and another broker 308.60 for five. Bo yelled out, "SOLD, NICK--FIFTEEN. SOLD, KENNY--FIVE CONTRACTS AT 308.60."

Michael knew Bo sensed what was coming. He didn't know how much "ammo" Michael had, but his senses were keen, and he wouldn't hesitate on any other orders during the final minutes of trading.

Three-oh-eight. It was time. Michael pulled himself up to view the brokers. He looked for key men. Big traders. Brokers who handled big clearing houses. Spreaders who could lay off trades. He knew the eyes of other brokers were still on him.

"LEAHY, WHAT DO YOU HAVE DOWN THERE?"

Leahy looked up, his trading jacket dark with sweat. "What way, Hawk? Buying or selling?"

"A LITTLE OF BOTH." He lied to the watching eyes and ears of the brokers who would try to race him.

Leahy shouted back. "I'M A BUYER FIFTY LOWER--NOT MUCH, BUT A BUYER. I'M A SELLER THIRTY HIGHER."

The Hawk looked to his left. "HOLMES, WHAT DO YOU HAVE?"

Holmes handled big wire-house orders. "I'M LIGHT, HAWK, NOT MUCH EITHER WAY...FOR A HUNDRED POINTS EACH WAY."

This was going to be bedlam, he thought. He raised both hands in the air with his palms in to buy. He heard his competitors' voices shouting to buy up close offers. Bo filled orders as fast as they came into the pit.

Hawk's lungs expanded; his palms took an about-face and turned outward. This was the time. This would be history. He screamed louder than he had ever screamed in his life. "I'LL SELL EVERYTHING IN THE PIT ONE HUNDRED POINTS LOWER--THE OFFER IS 307.60, 307.60 OFFER."

He had taken the pit by surprise. They thought he was a buyer and he turned into a seller. Brokers came from all over the pit to get in on the masquerade bargain:

"I'LL TAKE FIFTY, HAWK."

"HUNDRED 'N THIRTY, Hawk."

"TWO TWENTY-FIVE, MIKE."

"SIXTEEN, HAWK."

"HOGAN, I'LL BUY THREE HUNDRED TWELVE."

"TWELVE, HAWK."

"THIRTY-NINE, HAWK."

His hands were moving outward in all directions as if he were swatting at bees. Sweat ran like a faucet down his face, his mouth felt dry and he tasted salt. He calculated quickly. He'd have to hit the market harder if he was going to fill Ross's order. "I'LL SELL A HUNDRED LOWER, 306.60...THE OFFER IS '6.60."

Another onslaught of brokers came at him. As his mind raced to keep his count, he heard, "THREE-OH-SIX FOR THREE THOUSAND CONTRACTS." Zitello! Their eyes met. An electrical challenge was in the air, and the whole pit knew it. Was Zitello faking the move, or did he have the order? His bid for three thousand contracts brought momentary strength into the pit, and Michael filled the remainder of the two thousand contracts for Ross at 306.60.

Zitello's eyes flamed. They had lost their dullness and had turned mad, like a rabid animal. He screamed at Michael, "COME ON, FUCKER. YOU GONNA SELL ME THREE THOUSAND CONTRACTS OR NOT? JUST HOW BIG ARE YOU, BIG-MOUTH?"

Michael laid back. Stay cool, Hawk. The voice of years in the pit spoke to him: Let the bastard come to you. Watch his eyes. He saw the hate in Zitello's face, the meanness--the madness.

Michael knew he only had seconds to the closing one-minute warning bell. He also knew that a man in Zitello's state of mind was vulnerable. His emotions had taken over his mind. He was probably long up his ass and faking the big order at 306.00.

Michael felt a competitive smile ease onto his face, and he began to bid just above Zitello. "THREE-OH-SIX TWENTY FOR FIVE HUNDRED."

Zitello responded with a sardonic grin, "THREE-OH-SIX FIFTY FOR THREE THOUSAND."

The bell rang the minute warning. Michael spoke softly to himself: "A little bit more, sucker," then he yelled, "THREE-OH-SIX SEVENTY FOR FIVE HUNDRED." His bid brought renewed hope back into the pit. Meager but loud bids erupted.

Zitello threw his head back and screamed, "THREE-OH-SEVEN HUNDRED FOR THREE THOUSAND DECEMBERS."

Michael jumped on the bid like a cobra. "SOLD! SOLD! SOLD! YOU ASSHOLE, THREE THOUSAND AT 307.00--CHECK YOUR TRADE." He yelled so the whole pit could hear. "I SOLD YOU THREE THOUSAND AT 307.00--EVEN MONEY. YOU WANT TO BUY ANY MORE? Now it was his turn to play games. "YOU WANT FIVE THOUSAND MORE, FUCK FACE?"

The pit quelled for a moment, brokers' eyes on both men. The Hawk's face felt like stone. Determined, he felt his cheek muscles stand out as he clenched his jaw.

Zitello's face had turned ashen. Except for his mouth hanging open, his face had lost all expression. He had made a mistake and knew it. He was bluffing; he had no order. Zitello was challenging the Hawk. It had all been a power play. Michael had just hung Zitello with three thousand contracts he didn't want. Now he would have to pay for it.

Every broker in the pit realized Zitello didn't want the three thousand contracts. Selling erupted throughout the pit. Michael knew the market was going south--and fast. He wanted Zitello to eat the contracts, so he pushed his way quickly through crushed bodies and grabbed Zitello by the trading jacket. "I sold you three thousand contracts at three-oh-seven hundred, asshole. Make sure it clears, or I'll have you in court in twenty-four hours." He pushed the limp body away from him. "You make me sick to my stomach, Zito. You're on your way out." The bell rang loudly. The market was closed.

Michael was unable to reach his original position because of the mass of bodies, but his eyes and ears told him all he needed to know. Zitello had no buy orders, he had bluffed once too often, and the market was trading at 305.80 when the final bell stopped clanging. Michael forced his smile back. In less than a minute, Zitello had lost close to two million dollars to the Hawk and Sam Ross.

Norm Wilson, the best spread broker in the pit, patted Michael on the back and said, "Nice move, Hawk. Never saw anything like it. The way I figure it, you just fucked Zitello out of a million eight, not counting what it'll cost him tomorrow. And just 'cuz the asshole traded with his ego. Peterson's going to love that, especially losing the money to you."

Michael looked at Wilson and said, "Yeah, Norm. This is no place for ego or anger, is it?"

Norm had learned the hard way, but now had a fine tuned sense of market wisdom. He spoke with reflection. "I learned that a long time ago. You remember. My ego and my temper were very costly to me." He patted Michael's shoulder, turned, and threaded his way out of the pit.

Michael reached the phone and dialed a private number in New York City. Ross picked it up on the first ring and spoke in an exuberant voice. "Hawk?"

"Right."

With excitement Ross asked, "How'd we do?"

Michael shuffled through his trading cards, counting his trades as he talked. "You saw the market close?"

"I sure did. Right on its ass."

Michael undid three buttons on his silk shirt. "I sold about five thousand contracts, three thousand at three-oh-seven hundred. The rest between three-oh-six sixty and three-oh-seven sixty. Your average is right at three-oh-seven hundred and it closed at three-oh-five eighty."

Ross shouted through the phone with an excited, fatherly tone. "What do you mean my average, PARTNER? *Our* average is three-oh-seven hundred. If this goes where you say it's going, we are in at the top, and we share this trade fifty-fifty."

Michael was silent, not really digesting Ross's words. He tried to make Ross understand. "Sam, I can't afford the margin on twenty-five hundred contracts, let alone the risk. If a fly farts and this market goes up, I'm busted."

"Don't worry about it, Son. I have the margin money already in the account. Think big. We're going to make over five hundred million on this trade."

Michael was dumbfounded. His mind, usually working faster than, and preceding his speech, was blank. "Sam, I don't know if I can do that. I mean, I appreciate the offer, but I'm not sure if it's legal or not. And I don't want Fitzsimmons taking any close-ups of me. I don't photograph well."

Ross guffawed. "Son, I haven't had this much fun in a long time, and I've already checked with SEC and CFTC regarding a joint account. You were acting on my instructions. You were filling no other customer orders. You made the trade clean and obvious. MATTER CLOSED, PARTNER!" He hung up the phone before Michael could protest further.

He looked at the phone and said to himself, maybe honesty is the best policy. Then he turned and went back into the buzzing pit to check his trades.

FORTY

October 15, 1987-Gray Thursday

The bell rang. The market was closed. Michael looked at Bo and they exchanged a smile. Bo had been a difficult man to convince that the bull market was temporarily over.

Michael saw his trading cards every day and knew Bo was an emotional trader-- reacting to pit noise rather than his head. Even being a bull in a bull market was no guarantee you would make money if you violated basic trading techniques. Bo lived by no laws and traded by no rules. He was stubborn, would fight the market, and he took losses personally.

Michael had told him two weeks ago to cover his long position and get short. Bo finally did it on the opening bell today.

Michael yanked Bo's terry cloth towel from his belt and wiped his soaking face, then flipped it back. Bo did the same. "Thanks, Bo. You did a great job today."

He looked at Michael with questioning eyes. "You're thanking me? You get me out of a loser and into a winner and let me fill eight thousand contracts and you're thanking me? The market is down over three hundred fifty points; I'm short twenty-five contracts making thirty-seven thousand dollars, and you are thanking me?"

Michael looked at his own trading cards, counting, to make sure he was even on both the buy and sell side. He had sold seven hundred more than he had bought, making him short and even one thousand contracts, all with big money made. He estimated a paper profit of over twelve million dollars just for today. That didn't even count the twenty-five hundred contracts he had with Sam Ross that was making over eighty million in twenty- four hours. And the rollover had just begun.

What a feeling, he thought. There was no other game like it in the world. His heart pumped fast as he thought of his phone conversation with Glassmann a few weeks earlier. The ol' bastard must think I'm a genius.

He cautioned himself not to get carried away with his own good fortune. Better men than he had let their egos run wild after being right the market. He must never forget who was who in this financial relationship. The market was God, and he was the disciple. If he ever duped himself into thinking he was God and the market was his prodigy, financial death would be certain--slow and painful, but certain. He had seen it happen to the best of traders whose heads grew with their wealth.

He heard Bo's one word. "Mike?"

"Yeah, Bo?"

"How far down do you think this thing will go?"

Michael put his trading cards in his breast pocket and undid the top two shirt buttons, then looked up at Bo. "I don't know. It's just starting. It won't last long, but it will be devastating. All the smart traders who were long should have liquidated today, and should get short tomorrow. The computer and program traders haven't even begun to get out. When they go, the whole dam will cave in."

Bo's hard face was full of questions. "How did you know the market was going to break?"

Michael looked through the steamy haze of the pit and reflected. He rubbed his eyes, clearing away sweat, and said, "I guess it just made sense to me. Too many fundamentals pointed to an over-bought, air-filled market."

He grabbed Bo's arm and led him down the steps of the pit. "Come on, let's go over by the currency pits. They're all closed, and it's less congested. I'll finish answering your question over there. Besides, I need to sit for a minute and catch my breath."

He looked at the Dow-Jones quote board. Green abbreviations of stocks shot across the black background like a video game. Most were prefaced by minuses. "How much is the stock market down? You heard?"

Bo fanned his soaked face and body with his trading cards. "I talked to Lewis about an hour ago, and it was off one hundred thirty points."

Michael stopped and sat on the steps of the Swiss franc pit. "By the looks of those green minus quotes up there, it must be down a hell of a lot more than that by now."

He watched Bo as he sat down next to him. His short, sandy hair glistened with sweat. As tough as Bo had been on his own body, he exuded a rough, physical strength. "Now, back to your question. How did I know the market was going to break? I guess it was a combinatiom of homework, some common sense, a little inside information, and some luck with the timing."

"Like what?"

Michael would make this as simple and concise as possible. Bo wasn't one for details, just a quick explanation, and he'd take it from there. "I'll give you the fundamentals first--the facts about today's financial market.

"Wall Street pumped billions into the stock market in September and couldn't push it into new high ground. Most of the billions was weak money, Ma and Pa money, coming from a tremendous advertising push along with huge financial incentives to brokers for opening new accounts. Since all the big guys were already playing the game, the brokers and account executives went after smaller accounts. Middle, even lower-income investors were sold on the idea that the Dow-Jones would be at three thousand by Christmas and a new car would be in their driveways. Most of the new accounts were first-time, high-price buyers.

"Prior to that, computer and program traders added an additional few hundred billion to the market when it made new highs in August. They bought virtually the top of the market raising the break-even points and their stop-loss orders. That made for a very

bearish situation if the market was to rollover, which it's doing now, both in the stock and commodity markets.

"Second, and this is confidential, Lewis confirmed information I had received from another source. That besides the commodity market investigation, the Feds are placing two other major money industries between their cross-hairs for various degrees of fraud."

Bo looked straight ahead but moved closer and rested his elbows on his knees. Michael went on. "Remember, this is confidential."

He knew any information Bo heard from him was as good as sealed in a vault. "For years, a no-name, pseudo-investment company has been promoting junk bonds for junk companies, and that's exactly what they are, total junk--both the bonds and the companies they represent. The bonds offer high rates of interest and are extremely risky. The companies offering the bonds have no credit history and work on leveraged capital from investors. The investment company who offers the junk bonds to the public charges exorbitant commissions plus a lot of under-the-table hanky-panky."

Bo interrupted with placid indifference, "What's all this 'junk' shit have to do with our market?"

Michael rolled his head to relieve the tension in his neck, then looked at Bo. "As of this date, there is over one hundred fifty billion dollars' worth of those bonds outstanding, and most of the companies who back them couldn't get a car loan, let alone pay the interest on the bonds without further borrowing. Yet, over *eighty per cent* of this worthless paper is owned by mutual funds, insurance companies, pension funds, and savings and loan associations. These are institutions that are supposed to be the trusted, secure cornerstones of the United States economy. Do you see how much *air* this one area of 'junk' investing has pumped into the market?"

Bo's eyes roamed the trading floor; then he looked down at his feet and said, "I thought all that security shit had to have some type of government rating, and why would anybody buy 'junk bonds'?"

"You can sell anything in America, as long as the reams of paper-work look good to the government. You don't have to sell the truth, you just have to be able to sell. Most of the 'junk bonds' fall well below so-called investment grade, and if they were gradable they wouldn't get above a 'C' rating. 'C' stands for 'Can you Catch us?'."

Michael wiped rolling sweat from his cheek. "And why do sophisticated institutions like insurance companies and mutual funds invest in 'junk bonds'?" He answered his own question. "Incompetent investment trustees of the funds, greed, getting double the interest on invested money, kickbacks, and one hell of a sales operation by the fake investment company who's selling the bonds.

"Essentially, it has been a one company operation. One shady investment company sold people and institutions on the idea of placing billions of dollars into junk-yard, dog-shit, absolute swamp land. The investment company naturally realized hundreds of millions

of dollars in commissions. Many of the companies backing the bonds have a fifty-to-one debt ratio--at best!"

Bo leaned his chin on one fist, like Rodin's sculpture, *The Thinker*. "So who gives a shit, Mike? What does that mean and what does it have to do with us?"

Michael pulled back his shoulders and lifted his sharp jaw. "Just hear me out. It means that for every dollar the junk companies have borrowed, they only have the capital capacity to pay back half of that money. Many of them can't make the high interest payments and will go belly up at the first signs of economic weakness. Many of them already have filed for bankruptcy."

Bo weaved his head back and forth, slowly coming to the conclusion, and said, "If the market takes a trip south, way south, the investor gets nervous and tries to cash in his bonds or at least pick up his interest money. He finds an empty piggy bank, which puts additional pressure on an already sick market. The bogus American dream. Invest a dollar into a company that's not worth a quarter, and the investor is guaranteed fifteen per cent on his dollar. It's just an illusion, a mirage."

Michael nodded his head yes and finished the pattern. "It is bogus but not illegal. If you're dumb enough to give me fifty thousand dollars because I offer you fifteen per cent on your money, and my credit is lousy, but I tell you I've got a product that will grow corn on the moon, and you sign all the papers--shame on you! Nothing illegal about that if it's disclosed properly. But the Feds are finding that the stench is with the executives who have duped their clients into believing that fancy stationery, Caribbean trips, and high-flying parties are only mirrors being used to magnify the invested dollars, and the party is on the investor. An expensive executive life style, high salaries, and a high commission rate is the scam--there is no corn on the moon.

"When the investigation goes public, there will be a run on the 'junk' companies. The high-yield companies won't be able to pay up. Then the investors will hit the marketplace to recoup other invested capital."

Bo yawned and said, "I've heard enough about 'junk bonds.' What's the second bit of confidential info you have?"

Michael rubbed his hands together. "The next one is a doozie, and it has already hit the press, but nobody knows or wants to believe the national effect it will have on the economy. The government will only let bits of information seep from Washington, or there would be a real panic.

"Prior to the eighties recession, interest rates were low and the savings and loans in America were caught up in making long-term fixed loans at low rates. When interest rates went up, and the S & L's had to borrow money at twenty per cent, they panicked and began to play all kinds of games trying to recapture some of the money they were losing on the spread. Poor executive decisions and graft crept into the picture, and the S & L's invested more than their quota of savings-account funds into high-yield, high-risk situations. When the recession hit and interest rates soared to twenty-two per cent, many savers called

for their savings-account money to place in better cash investments. The problem arose because the S & L's had borrowed against low-interest passbook accounts and put the money back on the street at higher interest rates. When the passbook holders came for their money, they didn't have it to pay back to the depositors. That's when the S & L's had to go to the government to help bail them out of their problems. That's when this can of worms was opened up, but by then it was too late. You can only borrow so much money from the Federal Government before they smell a rat.

"Loan defaults, bad loans, even good loans at low rates began to cause the demise of the savings and loan institutions. Then the Feds found more corrupt activity within the framework of the savings institutions. S & L executives have been playing all kinds of shell games trying to cover up their mistakes."

Bo was getting impatient and bored. "Once again, Mike, what does that have to do with the market?"

In an exasperated move, Michael placed his hands out in front of him and said, "Bo, the whole thing undermines the markets, blows air into the markets, makes things seem what they aren't. Investors have been cheated, lied to, and brain-washed into thinking things are great in America. You can dress up a hog, but it's still a hog."

Somewhat anticlimactic, he said in a softer tone, "Besides that, technically the market was due for a break. All the indicators pointed to a big break in September or October. And when new highs can't be accomplished with a few hundred billion dollars, then a storm is brewing on the horizon and the apocalypse is right around the corner."

He stood and stretched. "As boring as it was, that's your economics lesson for the day, Bo, and it's just a portion of the story. The rest you can read in the paper. I've a lot of phone calls to make. Give me a call tonight about eight o'clock. I'll be in the office. Tomorrow we should see the rollover intensify. Be in early."

Bo stood and smiled. "Ya know what I say, Mike?"

Michael gave him a crooked grin. "I can imagine."

"Yeah, Fuck 'em all."

"That's what I figured you say. Incidentally, Bo. I took one hundred contracts the other day and put twenty each in your account, Bear's account, and Snake's account. With the other forty, I opened an account for your half-way house--'Hill 112.' If everything goes right, you'll all have a few hundred grand to start your own business and 'Hill 112.' You can buy and build a nice halfway house in the country where your Viet Nam boys will feel comfortable."

Bo's tough face softened. "What did you say?"

"You heard me. You guys are going to be rich men if this goes where I think it's going. We'll know more tomorrow or the next day."

Michael saw Bo's expression turn solemn, and his eyes misted over. He began to say something then turned his head and looked away. Out of respect for privacy, Michael turned too.

"Mike."

He looked back at Bo, now standing in a slouched position. Bo's arms reached out in front of him and flipped his palms up questioning. His lips were quivering. "Why?"

Michael felt good. He felt sad. He felt humble. Slowly he said, "You guys deserve a break, and so do your buddies at 'Hill 112'. If we can't make something good come out of this money, what's the use in having it?"

Bo looked beyond Michael. "Anything else, Bo?"

He pressed his lips together and shook his head no.

"Hey Bo? Don't drink--go to meetings, and maybe we can win this conflict." He turned and stepped from the pit. He left Bo standing on the top step of the Swiss franc arena. His body stance was erect, but his face was shadowed with wonder and a touch of humility.

Yes indeed, Michael felt good. Money would have a healthy effect on his men. *They* would feel good--rewarded in some way. What he didn't tell Bo was that he had set up over a hundred accounts for other people who needed money. Men and women who had no way out of their personal financial plights. He wished he could do more and would as soon as he was financially healthy himself. Then he thought, if the rollover didn't occur and the market stopped here for some ungodly reason, the big money wouldn't materialize, and they would all be back to square one. Bo was right. The market was headed south, and the next seventy-two hours would prove it. He took a deep breath and walked from the trading floor.

FORTY-ONE

Black Friday, October 16, 1987; 6:00 a.m.

Pete Lewis sat in Michael's office across from him reading the *Wall Street Journal*. "Listen to this, Mike."

Michael looked up from a complex fifty-year market chart on which he had drawn red lines. He was comparing prices on the chart with computer read-outs that gave him percentages, prices, moving averages, time sequences, and numerous other technical figures. He frowned in his concentration. "What, Pete?"

"Wall Street is trying to find a reason for the break, and this writer says:

> *"...the recent down trend is looked upon by most market analysts as long overdue and healthy for the market. Most agree that the sell-off occurred because of a fear of inflationary reports that came out of Washington this week. Economist and senior vice president of Dax Woods Investment Corporation, states that 'the sell-off is merely a technical correction and the Dow should find support between 2200 and 2300.' He states further that, 'the market is still strong and is recommending to his clients to buy the market on a scale-down program.'"*

Michael watched Pete fold the paper and place it on the coffee table as he said, "No one seems to know what caused the break. A lot of speculation but nothing solid."

Michael explained, "Pete, those guys who write in the *Journal* have to write something. They're journalists, not students of the market. The guy from Dax Woods Investment Corporation says it's a technical correction. I would call it a 'testicle' correction. The bears have the bulls by the balls and are going to squeeze until their horns droop. The so-called economists who make those blatant statements are being paid a few hundred grand a year to say something. Anything. Even if it's wrong. Most of those big Wall Street companies are smart enough to have at least two economists on their payroll, one saying the market is going up, while the other insisting it is going down. Then, no matter what happens, they can publicize the credits of the jerk who guessed right and conveniently place the guy who guessed wrong in the back room until the next prognostication arises.

"The whole street advertises the philosophy of, 'See, we told you so. Our economists predicted the move, so call ONE-EIGHT HUNDRED-PIG-SHIT for your free trading manual.' None of those over-paid charlatans have any idea why the market does

what it does. If they did, they'd be trading the market for themselves instead of talking about it."

The trading floor phone buzzed, and Michael pounced on it. "This is Hogan!"

Bo's voice was nervous. "Mike, I already have over seven hundred contracts to sell and only thirty-eight to buy, and we still have two hours to the opening."

Michael brought the phone close to his lips, his eyes scanning the computer read-outs in front of him. "What's the early New York call for the Dow?"

"Lower. No points yet, but lower."

With his red marker he circled the trading days on one of the computer sheets, Friday October 16th and Monday the 19th, then assured Bo, "It's going to be a lot lower, Bo. Believe me."

A hesitation prevailed, then Bo asked defensively, "Do you think we should cash in today? I mean, fifty grand is a lot of money to me. And I...*

Michael felt his irritation rise as he shouted into the phone, "FIFTY GRAND IS NOTHING. There is another five hundred grand sitting on the table. Be patient and act like a pro. A novice would take a quick profit. Don't let me catch you buying a goddamn contract."

"Okay. I just thought..."

He cut Bo short again. "Don't think. Leave your brains in the washroom and pick them up after the market closes. If you do anything, sell five more contracts for yourself, only five. This is a million-dollar move for you and Bear and Snake. When this is over, you can all go buy a thousand acres in Northern Minnesota or Montana or Washington and set up a mercenary camp. It's your retirement, man. Don't blow it. I'll tell you when to get out."

"Okay, my brains are out. You're in charge."

Michael looked up at Lewis and smiled. "No, the market's in charge. Anything else, Bo?"

He caught the rising emotion in Bo's voice. "Yeah. Don't take your time getting down here. I'm going to be swamped."

"I'll be there in an hour. I'm going to have you handle the stop orders and price orders. You won't have to worry about the panic orders. Just keep cool. It's only money." He replaced the phone in its cradle and took a swig of black coffee. To Pete he said, "Help yourself to more coffee."

"Had enough, thanks."

Michael leaned back in his chair and watched Pete skim the front of the *Journal* on the table. He had his jacket off, and Michael looked at the large, black gun holstered under his arm and wondered just how good he was. He liked Pete, liked him a lot. He had become a good friend, intelligent, quick witted, unorthodox, and even funny. "When do you figure the government will bring down the ax, Pete?"

Pete's head remained still, but his eyes peered up. "In about a year."

Michael's brow furrowed. "Why so long?"

Pete shrugged and bit his lower lip. "These things take time, and Lorenzo wants a tight, neat case that won't be thrown out of court. We still don't have enough information. It's pouring in, but a lot of it is no good. Although it's painting a true picture of corruption, it's not all incriminating."

Pete leaned back on the couch and rested his hands behind his head. "We figure after this market move we'll have a lot more hard evidence. At least we'll have the people and the illegal trades we need for indictments. A lot of work has to be done before subpoenas are issued. Then we can go after corporate books and records. There will be more work sifting through hundreds of thousands of corporate paper, and broker accounts, and chasing down trades. We'll present the indictments, do more work, then the trials will begin. The trials will go on for years. The government is never in a hurry to do anything except collect taxes."

Michael asked, "So you figure a year before you subpoena trading records from the brokerage houses?"

"Twelve to fourteen months," Pete said. Your own prediction is fairly accurate. About Christmas, 1988, we'll hit the first batch of brokers. I figure the way things are shaping up we'll subpoena a few hundred clearing houses, and shortly after that we'll issue indictments. Then, within another year, more subpoenas, more indictments, trials, plea bargaining, deals made, and on and on for at least five years."

"How many guys do you think you'll hit the first time around?"

Pete released his hands from behind his head and crossed his arms in front of him. "First time around?" His mouth gathered in thought for a moment. "Probably thirty, maybe fifty."

Michael inched forward on his elbows. He felt his eyes widen in surprise. "That's all?"

Pete's head tilted as he saw the disappointed look on Michael's face. "That's a shit load, señor. More will follow. We'll see how cooperative your broker buddies are. A lot of them will turn federal-evidence when we tell them they are going away for five years if they don't give us what we want."

He felt a sharp prick of curiosity. "And if they don't?"

"Oh, they will. These guys aren't crooks in the true sense of the word. The majority are just men who got caught up in a web of greed. The spider wasn't home, and they used the web for a trampoline for a long time. Then the spider came home. They certainly don't want to trade their fancy homes and cars and vacations for a six-by-eight cell."

Michael placed his head in his hands and rubbed his face. "The thought of spending time in prison would scare the hell out of me."

Pete picked up a commodity magazine and paged through it. He said casually almost to himself, "That's what I'm counting on. They'll talk like parrots."

The floor phone rang again. It was Bo. "You better get your ass down here, Mike. The phones are ringing off the hook, and we're being flooded with sell orders."

Michael pulled open the left-hand drawer of his desk and pulled out a thick stack of trading cards. "Be right there, Bo." He hung up, finished his coffee and said to Pete, "Time to go to work, G-Man."

Pete put the magazine down and raised himself easily off the soft couch. He grabbed his black wind-breaker and slipped into it. "I'm heading for the bond pit. Supposed to have lunch with a half dozen brokers today to discuss the sale of my tax loss to them. They're going to give me twenty cents on the dollar under the table for the phony company losses. They're all dead meat, and I rather hate to see it. I kind of like a few of them."

Michael walked to a leather chair near the door of his office and slipped on his kelly-green trading jacket. "Doesn't that bother you, Pete?"

Pete moved over close to him and looked him in the eyes. "Yeah, it bothers me. They're good guys, but it goes with the territory. They're breaking the law, and I can't forget who I am and why I'm here. Yes, it bothers me a lot. The only good thing about it is they'll suffer more from embarrassment and their nightmares of prison than from the actual punishment. The wives will suffer most."

Then he said casually, as if he were reading a bed time story, "What bothers me most is that some of them will probably blow their heads off or jump out of a building because of the worry."

Michael felt his own face turn calm, but there was a sadness in his guts. "They aren't the bad guys, Pete. You are hitting on the wrong brokers."

"I know that. But they're involved up to their necks in a criminal situation, and they are the ones who will lead us to the bosses."

Michael watched Pete's eyes. They were stern. They were government. He really didn't have much to say to his friend, so he didn't say anything.

As they walked down the short hallway to the reception area, Pete said, "This'll be over in a short time, so don't worry about the outcome. It's out of your control now; soon you can go back to living a normal life."

Michael pushed through the glass door to the outside corridors and thought to himself. Normal? Buddy, my life will never be the same again.

Pete had said, "Too bad, but a few guys would blow their brains out, because of the worry, the fear, the embarrassment." Jesus Christ, he thought, who would shoulder that guilt? How many families would be crushed? How many guys would just turn their backs and run?

Yeah, my life will be normal again all right! Solid as a rock. Bullshit. His life would never be normal again, and he knew it. It would be like walking on a beautiful winter lake, frozen, snow-crusted, and looking back to see that his foot prints were filling with water. That would be normal; that's what he could look forward to. The deadly waters of life's reprisal lie inches away from its beauty.

* * *

The final bell rang, and Michael looked up at the quote board. His hair and body were soaked with perspiration, and every nerve in him tingled from the intense seven-hour adrenalin push. Men and women continued to push and scream, trying to sell unfilled orders. The market was down 1600 points, eight thousand dollars a contract.

He saw Matt Leahy pushing through the crowd in a panic. "Hawk, Hawk. You got to help me. I know you're short and I'm stuck on fifty. There are no buyers anywhere, and I can't take fifty contracts home with me. This could cost me a million dollars on Monday. Maybe more."

Bo was standing next to Michael, writing fast and furiously on a stack of orders. Michael reached behind him and pulled the terry-cloth towel from his belt, then wiped his face. "A million dollars is a big favor, Matt."

Panic etched every crease in Matt's face. "I know, Mike. Even if you could help me out on a few contracts, maybe I can lay off the rest someplace else. I just can't afford to be long this market. Not fifty contracts. Please! Whatever you can do."

Michael saw the fear increase in Matt's eyes and heard the urgency in his voice. He was a good broker. Just got stuck, probably trying to squeeze the order for a better fill. He knew how Matt felt. The same thing had happened to him before. "Let me see the order, Matt."

Leahy produced a wrinkled, gray piece of paper folded in half. He opened it up and read: "SELL 50 DEC. S & P's MOC (MARKET ON CLOSE)." He looked at the time stamp: 10:04:16 10/16/87. Michael wanted to make sure the order was not a fabrication and that Matt just wanted to get short for himself. He had sold another hundred contracts for himself so he could afford to buy fifty from Leahy, million dollars or no million dollars. "Okay, Matt, you're out. I'll buy fifty at the closing price."

A huge sigh of relief came thrusting from Matt's mouth as he rolled his head back and his eyes upward. "God, Hawk! You are a saint. Jesus Christ, Man! Anything I can ever do for you...anything, just let me know." He was off again. Back to the center of the buzzing pit.

Bo had been listening as he wrote and finally asked, "What'd you do that for?"

The question angered Michael. "I did it for the same reason I put you and your friends short--to give you a break, Jerkoff. Sometimes we need each other. Or haven't you noticed?"

Backing up and shrugging his shoulders, Bo said, "Sorry...sorry I mentioned it. It's just goddamn generous."

Michael let his face harden. "You help people when you can. If you can't help with money, then find another way to help." He turned and walked from the pit. He was tired. A bone-crushing tired. He was becoming a wealthy man, but his guts were tense. With money came danger. Not from outsiders but from one's own mind and soul.

From behind him, Bo shouted, "Hey, Mike. I'm, sorry, Okay?"

Without turning, he waved a finger in the air meaning he checked Bo's statement as he would check a trade. Everything was okay.

FORTY-TWO

Blood Monday October 19, 1987

Today we cover our short position, Michael said to himself as he finished his shower and wiped his body with a thick, aqua bath towel. He looked at his naked body in the full-length mirror of his streamlined bathroom.

His workouts with Snake, his running, and long lake swims were all paying off. The small paunch that had been obvious six months ago had turned to ripples of taut muscle, and he had lost three inches from his waist. His arms and legs were lean and getting stronger. He looked at his hands and felt the rough layers of calloused skin on his palms, fingertips, and knuckles and on the cutting edge. His neck had grown at least an inch. He could tell when he wore a tie, which was seldom, and he needed to secure the top button on his custom shirts. His ability to defend himself with his hands and feet had become professional, thanks to the strenuous teachings of John "Snake" Adams.

His thoughts turned to Adams. Even though Snake appeared calm and in total control at all times, the man was full of hate. The war had done a job on all three of his protectors, but this was especially noticeable in Snake. Michael could see it only in his eyes, the windows to his soul. They told the hidden story. The resentments and scars had been branded deep into Snake's mind and guts. He never smiled, and he wasn't happy. Michael sensed Snake Adams considered this job baby-sitting a rich kid who lived in a mansion on Lake Michigan. He wondered if Adams felt about him as he did most other Americans, as just another piece of human shit, part of the establishment who had sent him to kill people in a foreign land. He would be a hard man to bring back to life. Michael wondered if it was too late. Reluctantly, he shook the deadly shadows of Snake's eyes from his mind.

He breathed in deep and held it. He felt good. He felt healthy. He felt accomplished both physically and mentally. Spiritually, the most important aspect of a man, was another subject. He did good things, but was he good? He helped others, but did he help enough? Did he help himself? He talked of the great Spirit, the Infinite, Higher Power of Life, but did he follow the road of the Spirit? Or did he follow his own self-indulging road? He didn't know. Would he ever truly know his God? Would he ever know himself?

He picked up his watch from the vanity and looked, not at the time but at the date. October 19--Blood Monday. All weekend, orders to sell had been coming into every stock and commodity office in the country. A world-wide cry was heard on the radio, in the newspapers and more important, in the commodity saloons, "GET ME OUT, SELL--AT ANY PRICE!"

He smiled and read the time, 4:08 a.m. In four hours he would know just how bad it was going to be. Today was the day to cash in. Don't press it any further, he told himself. The down move had made him a rich man. He recalled Joe Glassmann's words from years past, "Stay humble. The market can give and the market can take. Stay humble, Michael, and some day you'll be a wealthy man."

He brushed his teeth, combed his hair, and dressed in five minutes, then strode from the bathroom. A flash of lightning brightened the room as he turned off the light. The fall storms had come too late for the summer drought, which had killed the soybeans and corn, but just in time to wash the blood off the streets and into the sewers from the October market crash.

A sleepy voice interrupted his thoughts, "Michael?" Maria had rolled over and he could tell she was watching him. "Did I wake you?" he asked softly.

"Sort of. I think the storm woke me."

He sat on the edge of the bed and stroked her silky, black hair. "I'm sorry. I tried to be quiet. The storm's sorry too." He smiled to himself. She spoke mostly with her eyes. Through them he saw her distrust for others, her scorn for hypocrisy, her concern for the poor, and her love for him. Because she was a Santini, her blood automatically carried suspicion and violence, and God forbid the person who struck out at her children, her husband, or the Santinis. If she couldn't cut them apart with her sharp tongue, she would find a more lethal way. He loved the sensual tiger in her. Her spirit, her strength, her fearlessness, her allegiance.

She reached up and held his hand. "Everything sounds louder at night. What time is it?"

He leaned down and kissed her forehead, feeling the soft satin of her skin. "About four."

She squeezed his hand and pulled him closer. "Do you have to go so early?" Her voice was inviting.

He hugged her back and kissed her cheek. "I have to go early, babe. Today's the big day."

She yawned and asked, "Roll-over?"

He smiled at her market jargon. "Roll-over on you, or the market roll-over?"

She wrapped her arms around his neck. "Both," she answered.

He could see her black eyes, like a tame panther's, shining up at him in the dark. The fragrance of her body tugged at him. He pulled her to him and hugged her tightly. "I love you, Maria." The words came from his heart, and he meant them with every ounce of sincerity. She had been his confidant, his friend, and his lover for many years. She was a part of him, body, mind and soul. She meant the world to him. But the realization that he loved another woman as well was all too evident, and for a moment self-hatred trounced on him.

Her next words pierced his heart. "Try not to hurt me, Michael."

He hugged her tighter, then eased her back down on the bed gently. Her beautiful black hair spread out on the white pillow. "I'll try not to hurt either of us, Maria. Just know that I love you."

He stood beside the bed and looked down at her. She knew him like a book. She sensed the good and bad in him. She sensed his vigor for life. She sensed his anger, his happiness. And--she sensed his love for another woman. That last thought was the knife that cut deep.

Another flash of lightning revealed black eyes full of tears. He bent and kissed her on the mouth. "I'll call you after the market. Sleep now. Everything will be fine." He opened the bedroom door to the long, plush hall lit with dim, amber lights. Before he moved through the doorway, he heard her call.

"Michael." He looked back, but said nothing. She spoke softly. He sensed a heart-breaking pain in her throat. "When you win your race, come home to me."

He hesitated, about to say something, wanting to say something, but instead left the bedroom. Another bolt of lightning lit up the whole house. He wasn't sure if the heavens were angry with him, just flexing their muscles to remind him who was boss, or if the storm was a warning to those who walked the razor's edge. Then he decided it might just be a thunderstorm.

He stopped in six separate bedrooms and kissed each of his sleeping children, pulled the covers up around their necks, and made the sign of the cross. He asked his God to protect and guide them, then made his way down the long, wide hall and circular staircase to the front door.

Bo waited outside for him in the Astin. He walked around the car to the fountain. The wind blew its spray across the drive. Pulling his black London Fog up around his neck, he looked into the pelting rain. An angry but cleansing rain. He felt a part of it. White veins of electricity chased each other across the black sky, trying and succeeding in impressing him. He said a quick prayer and hopped in the passenger side of the Astin.

Bo looked refreshed. He was sober and alert and listening to one of Bear's cassette tapes by the Hollies, "He Ain't Heavy, He's My Brother."

Michael looked at Bo, nodded, smiled, and said, "Vamanos, Amigo!"

His head snapped back as the car jolted forward down the brick drive, slowing as the gates yawned open, then sped onward to the city, the city where rain would turn to blood before the day ended.

* * *

Sam Ross chewed nervously on a long, black cigar. His eyes were glued to the green numbers on the quote machines that surrounded his desk. Nearly lunch time for most people but not for those trading the stock or commodity markets. The Dow-Jones was down

over three hundred points, and the S & P's were off over four thousand points. The quote machines were running a good half hour behind, and he couldn't get through to Hogan.

He looked up at Joe Glassmann, who was sitting on the edge of his seat watching the S & P screen. "The man's a genius, Joe. A goddamn genius. I haven't had so much fun since I stole my first watermelon in the Bronx fifty years ago." He looked at the Dow screen.

"The Dow just broke nineteen hundred, Joe." Now he looked at the S & P screen. "Jesus Christ! The 'Spoos' just broke another one thousand points as we talk." He mumbled to himself, "a fucking genius. Hogan's a genius." The S & P screen read, "DEC S&P's--242.50--LAST & LOW, down 4200 POINTS." He looked up at Glassmann, whose thin, gray disheveled hair spilled down on his forehead. "What do you think, Joe?"

Joe sat back in the leather chair, eyes still glued to the green screen of the S&P's. "Sam, I don't know what to think. Hogan said the stock market could break a thousand points from its highs in August, and that would put it someplace around seventeen hundred. He said the S & P's would break over ten thousand points, and that would put the December contract around two twenty. If I know Michael, he's planning on buying in his position today. Thank God I listened to the young pup and liquidated my stocks."

Sam felt his eyes enlarge and his teeth clamp down hard on the cigar. He felt giddy, out of control. "Look at that son of a bitch drop. I'm going to sell more."

Glassmann's head snapped back and away from the screen. "*Sell more*! Didn't you hear me? I said Hogan would probably be covering all short positions today."

He felt his eyes widen. "Screw it, Joe. It's falling out of bed. It's nineteen twenty-nine all over again."

Joe leaned on Sam's desk. "No, it's not nineteen twenty-nine all over again. The market is still good if it stops where Hogan suspects."

Sam loosened his hundred-dollar tie and unbuttoned his vest. "Son of a bitch. He's a genius. Never seen anything like it. Over a half billion dollars in four days."

Joe reared back in his seat, almost falling over. "A HALF BILLION DOLLARS? How many goddamn contracts are you short?"

Sam looked up at Joe with a smile and said slowly and with diabolic pride, "Thousands."

Joe jumped to his feet, circled his chair, and sat down again. "Does Hogan know that?"

Pieces of Sam's mangled cigar began to fall on the papers in front of him, but he hardly noticed. "We're partners on a few thousand contracts that he knows about..." He spit a piece of tobacco onto the plush burgundy carpet, "...but I added a few thousand more to our partnership. We're short ten thousand contracts with over an eight-thousand-point profit."

Joe's eyes rolled back in his head. "Holy God in Heaven! TEN THOUSAND CONTRACTS! ARE YOU CRAZY, YOU...YOU OLD FOOL?"

Sam chewed and smiled as he punched in numbers on another computer showing him the ten thousand sales, the prices at which they were sold. The calculated profit blinked in white at the bottom of the green screen. A shade over four hundred million dollars at the prices that were registered on the screen. They seemed to enlarge every time the profit column blinked.

"Joe! Get Hogan on the phone. I want to sell ten thousand more contracts."

"You are crazy, Sam! It's a day to buy, not sell."

Sam picked up a tan phone and pushed a button, then handed the phone to Glassmann. "Here. This rings right to Hogan's desk. See if you can get him on the phone. He won't leave the pit for me."

Joe reached for the phone reluctantly and put it to his ear. "Sam, I doubt if he'll come to the phone for the Virgin Mary. The man has to be buried with orders. I've been there when things like this happen. He's the best, and everybody wants him to fill their orders."

Joe put up his hand. Somebody had answered. Sam stood up and brushed specks of cigar from his vest. He felt a surge of energy shoot through him. He whispered. He didn't know why, but he whispered, "Who answered the phone?"

Joe's head remained still, more like he was listening, but his eyes looked up, and he whispered back as if they were sharing a common secret, "Some girl answered and said, "Hold on." Jesus Christ! You should hear the noise."

Sam reached for another phone and pushed the far button, then yanked the earpiece from its cradle. He grimaced and immediately pulled it from his ear.

Christ, he thought, how could anybody think in such pandemonium? It sounded like a lynch mob on the radio turned up as far as it would go.

After four minutes of waiting, a male voice said impatiently, "Who is it?"

"Joe Glassmann. Who's this?"

"Frank Hammer, Joe. What do you need? And hurry up. We're swamped."

Joe fumbled to speak quickly. "What are chances of talking to Hogan?"

The voice was sharp. "Slim to none, and that's optimistic. Anything else?"

Sam cut in with a stern voice. "Frank, this is Sam Ross. I need to talk to Hogan."

"Yes, Mr. Ross. I've talked to you before...Board of Trade...when we were handling your Bond business."

Sam pushed out his chest as if he were conducting a board meeting. "I remember, son, and it's very important that I speak to Hogan--NOW!"

There was a short pause, and Sam felt his cheeks puff with authority. "Well, no disrespect, Mr. Ross, but I don't think he'd come out of the pit to talk to the President of the United States. I'm standing thirty feet from the pit, and there is nothing in front of me but a wall of human beings trying to get orders into the pit."

Sam felt a slice of anger cross his face, but this was the man called "HAWK" he was trying to reach, not some ass-kissing politician who would jump at the chance to talk

to him. He bit the end of his cigar off and spit it into the waste basket at the side of his huge desk. He knew Hammer would hang up the phone if he became nasty or even offered him a bribe to get Hogan. He spoke politely. "Well, can you get a message to him in any way? It's extremely important, Frank."

A frustrated voice sighed on the other end of the line. "I'll try, Mr. Ross, but I can't promise you how long it will take me to reach him, and I can't promise you what he'll do once he gets your message. What's the message? I'll try."

Sam moistened his lips and spoke clearly. "Tell Hogan that Mr. Ross wants to sell ten thousand contracts of December S & P's."

Sam held the phone away from his ear while he waited for Hammer to answer. "Would you please repeat the message, Mr. Ross. I think I misunderstood you."

"TELL HAWK THAT I WANT TO SELL, S-E-L-L, TEN THOUSAND CONTRACTS OF DECEMBER S & P's." Sam heard only noise, then Frank spoke with professional control. "Is Mr. Glassmann on the line?"

Joe moved nervously in his chair. "I'm here, Frank." Frank raised his voice. For a moment Sam thought it was Hogan. The voice was stern and candid. "It's not easy for me to hear--too much noise. I know you're using Michael's private phone, but no offense, how do I know it's really you and not two crackpots?"

Sam was impressed with the straight question but noticed that Joe's face had turned crimson with a shade of blue in the neck. "Jesus Christ, Frank. It's really me, and I'm really with Sam Ross."

Frank hesitated a moment. "What's Hogan's middle name, Joe?"

Joe snapped again, "Martin."

The voice said calmly. "What was his father's name?"

Joe snapped out, "Patrick, Goddammit."

"What was his mother's name?"

"Clair, come on, Frank!"

Sam was amused with the interrogation. "What was his grandfather's name?"

Joe took the phone away from his ear and looked at Sam with exasperation.

Sam smiled and motioned for him to answer. "Martin was his grandfather's name."

A hesitation. "His grandfather's legendary name?"

Sam saw Joe's face turn from an angry red to a cement gray in a second. He looked past Sam with a sense of alarm that Sam didn't understand.

Then he spoke quietly into the mouthpiece. "Frank, his grandfather's nickname was "'The Ghost of Kildare-The Deceptive One'."

"I'll get the message to Hogan. He knows how to reach you?"

Sam responded. "You are on my direct line, Frank. He just has to pick it up, and I'll answer. How long will it be, Frank?"

"At least fifteen minutes, maybe not at all." The line and noise came to an abrupt death.

Sam squeezed his lips together and looked at the phone he held in his hand, then gently placed it back in its cradle. He smoothed his white hair back with the palm of his left hand, trying to regain a little dignity that he had so abruptly lost with one of Hogan's loyalists. Senators, Congressmen, members of the Cabinet treated him with the utmost respect. He had to smile at the polite discipline and alertness Frank Hammer had expressed. His calm and quick screening of the call and his candid reply that Hogan might not call him back.

Then he frowned and looked over at Joe. He moved his head slightly to establish perspective.

Joe simply nodded, wrinkled his nose, and switched off a button on the phone he held in his hand.

Sam let his eyes narrow. "Joe, who is The Ghost of Kildare, The Deceptive One?"

Joe's shoulders drooped and he leaned back in his chair relaxing as he let out a billow of air. His old eyes looked up to meet Sam's.

Sam felt an uncomfortable chill flow through him with both Joe's look and his next words. "It's a long story, Sam. But I think 'The Ghost of Kildare' is your new partner, the man called HAWK--The Deceptive One."

* * *

Michael's shirt had been ripped, and he had accidentally caught an elbow below the right eye, causing a slight swelling. Bo's back was to him, and they stood with their feet firmly planted on the second step leading down into the pit. They passed orders back and forth over each other's shoulders to be filled or endorsed. The system was working well, and all of their orders were receiving fair prices, as fair as could be under the circumstances. Between the two of them, Michael estimated they had filled close to thirty thousand contracts, a record for Michael, certainly for Bo, and no doubt for the Exchange. Further, there was still two hours to trade.

Few had survived the catastrophic break. A number of brokers had thrown up in the pit, and Michael had heard that the toilets were being used for vomiting as well. Michael saw one broker crying, and other faces mirrored the look of death. They were broke--more than broke. What had taken them years to build financially had been mysteriously yanked from them in four days. They would die a slow death. Most would not survive. The strong-willed brokers would make a comeback, the ones with more guts than brains. But this type of shock would raise doubts in even the strongest men. Was a second try worth the emotional trauma? Was there such a thing as reincarnation?

Shit, Michael thought. It would take months, even years for some of these men to pull out of their lives of fantasy and realize they were broke. The realization wouldn't

set in until they lost their homes and cars and were bartending at night to pay for the staples of life. Then, maybe then, they would realize that they were broke and the dream was over, but still, they would think rich. Just the strong would make it back--it was possible. Some would get faith in God. Some would lose what faith they had. Some would sink into despair and kill themselves, or worse, live on earth as doomed men stinking of negativism, blaming the world for unfair punishments. Others would learn to laugh it off and say, "Hey, it was fun while it lasted."

His joy for his own good fortune was overshadowed by the financial death of many of his friends. But in the end, he thought, the acceptance of life on life's terms was man's own responsibility. How a man dealt with the taste of victory and defeat was purely up to the man: he could live again, or he could die.

A shout came. "Hawk!"

Michael's peripheral vision was at its sharpest. He recognized the jacket, and his ears heard the voice of Frank Hammer.

He reached out his hand to receive an order from Frank but received a message written on a yellow order instead.

"Sam Ross and Joe Glassmann want you to SELL them 10,000 DEC contracts at the market i.e. SELL 10,000 DEC at MKT. Any questions, call them." HAM

Michael couldn't believe what he read, and yelled back to his protege, "FRANK!"

Frank was still squeezed on the top shelf between a mass of screaming brokers.

He looked into Frank's perplexed face and shouted, "IS THIS FOR REAL?"

Frank shrugged his shoulders, cupped his hands over his mouth and shouted over the noise. "THAT'S EXACTLY WHAT WAS SAID. THEY'RE WAITING TO HEAR FROM YOU."

Michael put one finger in the air to Frank, making sure he stayed where he was. He moved closer to Bo and asked, "How are you doing?

The pit smelled, so did Bo, so did he. Bo yelled over his shoulder, "I'm barely keeping up. Still have one hundred orders to endorse but keeping up with the orders coming in."

A hand reached through the mass of bodies and poked an order in Michael's face. He opened it and read: "SELL 50 DEC S&P's MKT."

His eyes caught Larry Larson on the top step with both hands raised, palms in. He shouted, "LARCENY, I'M SELLING YOU FIFTY."

Larson took no offense at Michael's nickname for him. He was a thief, but a small one. He responded, "I'm bidding one hundred lower, Hawk. I think there are higher bids in the pit."

"I don't care. I'm not shopping, just give me the price."

"TWO THIRTY-NINE, EVEN MONEY."

"YOU GOT FIFTY." Both checked with the flick of a finger and a high five in the air.

Michael waved his hand at Hammer, whom he could hardly see through the throng of brokers. He yelled, "FRANK, COME DOWN HERE!"

"HOW?"

"USE FUCKING DYNAMITE. JUST GET DOWN HERE," he said in a stern, stentorian voice.

To Bo he said, "I'm leaving you with Hammer for five minutes."

Bo turned and looked at Michael with panic in his eyes. "You can't leave me now, Asshole." He held out his hands filled with crumpled orders. "Look at the paper I have to endorse."

Michael had to smile. Bo had colored orders sticking out of six different pockets of his trading jacket plus what he held in his hands. "You look like a flower pot, Bo. Hammer will take my place, you won't be alone."

Bo's face paled. "JESUS CHRIST! YOU PICK A HELL OF A TIME TO TAKE A SHIT."

"I'll be right back."

"SHHHIIIITT!" Bo yelled.

Frank pushed the final human obstacle out of his way. Michael said, "Frank, I've got six hundred fifty to sell a hundred higher and four hundred to buy scale down starting a hundred fifty lower. Just keep pace with the orders coming in. I'll be back in five minutes."

Frank spoke with confidence. "You got it."

Michael pushed and ducked and squeezed his way out of the pit and threaded his way through clerks and runners to his desk. "MARY ELLEN, GIVE ME THAT TAN PHONE." Michael's mind raced, as he calculated in a split second where the market was in relationship to where it had broken from. One ring and the phone was picked up.

Glassmann spoke first, "Mike!"

He allowed a sharp edge of anger to cut through the phone. "Don't Mike me. With all disrespect intended, tell me you two assholes are drunk and just want to see a crazy man go over the edge. What's this about selling ten thousand contracts?"

Mike heard Sam Ross clear his throat. "Michael, the market is falling out of bed. I just thought we should help it along."

He screamed into the phone. "HELP IT ALONG? DOES THE MARKET LOOK LIKE IT NEEDS ANY HELP FROM YOU TWO?" He squinted at the noise around him. "This is the blood bath we've been waiting for. It's the ROLLOVER. The longs are literally puking in the pit. The computer traders are selling. The program traders are selling. The Japs are selling. The Europeans are selling, even the Communists are selling. The only buyer is Stanley the cab driver, and that's because he does what he says he's going to do."

A moment of silence hung heavily, then Glassmann spoke up, "Who is Stanley the cab driver?"

Michael snapped back quickly: "He's a guy who taught me to finish the job I set out to do, and that's what I'm going to do. Today's volume of trades will be close to double its previous record. That means all the longs are just about out. There should be one or two more drives to the down side, and that's it. When the stubborn longs finally give up, there won't be a sell order in the pit, and it will jump three thousand points before you can fart. I'm buying in our short position at two thirty, maybe sooner, depends on the action."

He looked around for something dry to wipe his face. "Hold on, you two."

Then he looked down his row of phone clerks. "Mary Ellen, do you have a towel or something down there? Something dry?" She slid open a drawer and pulled out one of Bo's terry-cloth towels and threw it to him. "Bless you, girl. Remind me to give you a bonus."

He wiped his face, his hair and the back of his neck, then the earpiece on the phone, which was dripping from his sweat. He stuck the towel in his belt and continued with Mo and Curly.

"Okay, I'm back."

Ross spoke. "What's this about double volume and..."

Michael interrupted. "Joe, you explain the market technicalities to Sam. I have fifteen more seconds to talk to you, and I'm going to tell you what I'm going to do. On the next break I'm buying in my short position plus the shorts in our partnership account, Sam--unless you've changed your mind about being partners."

Ross's voice was caustic. "That's an insult, Michael."

Michael's voice leaped into the phone. "No more of an insult than pulling me from the pit on the busiest day in the history of the Exchange and busting my balls by telling me to sell ten thousand contracts. You know I'm about to buy back our position. If you want to sell more contracts, call your own clearing house, or Merrill Lynch, or some other broker, but I'll guarantee they won't be answering their phones for a week. I'm the only crazy bastard in the country who will talk to you two lunatics. It's my way or no way--and if you don't like it, sue me and tell the judge I only made you five hundred million in seventy-two hours."

Sam backed off. "Okay. You're the boss. We're partners, it's your play. What are you going to do?"

Michael looked up at the Dow Averages--1810. "Goddamn, the Dow is making new lows again. I'm buying in all of our shorts soon. What's our total? How many shorts do you have, Joe?"

A quick hesitation, then the answer came, "Two thousand."

"Sam, we have five thousand, right?"

There was a long wait. Michael's voice croaked as he screamed into the phone, "COME ON MAN, HOW MANY? I HAVE TO KNOW HOW MANY TO BUY!!!"

Finally, Sam said quietly, "Ten thousand."

Michael closed his eyes and lowered his head. "I didn't hear that right, Sam. Say again!"

"Mike, partner, you and I have ten thousand shorts."

Michael gasped for air. He eyed a can of Coke sitting on the phone desk, grabbed, it and took a gulp. "You sold another five thousand contracts of December S & Ps?"

Sam responded proudly, "I put my faith in you, boy, and you came through. We're short ten thousand contracts!"

Michael's mind worked like a computer. Son of a bitch, the amount was staggering. His mind blew a fuse at six hundred million dollars.

"You there, Mike?"

"Yeah, I'm here."

"Well?"

Michael's voice was horse and rough. "Okay, *partner*, I'll tell you what. Give Joe Glassmann two thousand contracts, and you and I split eight thousand contracts--four thousand each. No hesitation or find another partner. That gives Joe four thousand contracts also. And I'll tell you why so there's no subconscious resentment on your part. You wouldn't have met me if it wasn't for Joe, and Joe Glassmann gave me my first job at the Exchange. Neither of us would be talking right how if it wasn't for Joe Glassmann. You there, Joe?"

Sam spoke. "You made the bastard cry, he can't talk. It's a deal, two thousand to Glassmann, that's four thousand each. That's fair with me."

He spoke quickly. "He's a Jew. He'll get over it. I'm buying twelve thousand contracts plus what I'm short. Talk to you after the close." Not waiting for an answer, he handed the phone back to Mary Ellen. He took another swig of Coke and headed for the pit oblivious to the noise and confusion.

He patiently waited until the market broke through 230.00, then Michael began buying up every offer that hit the pit. He bought a thousand contracts every one hundred points down as the market continued to break. He had bought over 14,000 contracts by the closing bell and a cash realization of over eight hundred million dollars.

The next day the market closed higher. The rollover came to a screeching halt, and the market began its move up again. It had not violated the 66 per cent break mark, which simply meant that the market had been overbought at high prices. Michael expected the market would now be able to retrace its trail and eventually make new highs, but it would take years. More importantly, he had become a wealthy man overnight, and he realized he had help from a Power greater than himself to make this all happen. He must not abuse what had so generously been given to him.

The FBI collected over 1500 photos of brokers making what appeared to be illegal trades. They had twenty-eight rolls of recorded conversations and enough hard evidence to accelerate their painstaking investigation into the sanctioned corruption at the Exchanges. The end was now in sight.

FORTY-THREE

The Philosopher

Michael signed the last check, leaned back in his easy chair, and stared down at the impressive stack of bank drafts.

The mansion was quiet. Maria and the children had retreated to their rooms hours ago. From his desk in the lake room, he looked out the expanse of windows into brief illuminations from far-off lightning. Otherwise there was only darkness. His feet could feel the vibration of the thundering waves as they pounded the metal and concrete sea wall, then rolled south to find a more vulnerable, unprotected area. He loved the feeling, the natural power that reminded his three-million-dollar, titanic mansion who the Boss Lady was.

He amused himself with the thought: what others considered chaos, he understood as order--balance. Water created and balanced life. The powerful lake was like life itself. She would find a weakness in the soul of terra, bang at it until it fortified itself, or tear at it until it became part of her. Dead as plotted soil, alive as part of something greater. Live with barriers, or die and live again--with no barriers. He smiled at the analogy.

The hot, dry summer had finally given way to cooler temperatures and brief periods of fierce storms. He sensed a new storm entering the city from the west. The pressures of warm air meeting cool air angered the lake. Like man, Michael knew that she would rest only when the pressures equalized.

He leaned forward and thumbed through the stack of checks. The break in the market had produced profits of 16.3 million dollars in the various accounts he had set up for families and institutions that he knew needed a financial boost.

Legitimate hungry and distraught people had never been hard for Michael to find. All a man had to do was open his eyes. Hunger of mind, body, and spirit was all around. He knew that wealth could change a person, narrow his vision. He must never forget where he had come from and where he could return, if he abused his good fortune.

A hundred and forty-seven checks in all. Delinquent mortgages and college tuition--paid in full. Money to poor families to cover current debt and additional money to relieve financial pressures for years to come. Donations to halfway houses throughout the city, legitimate nursing homes, anonymous self-help organizations, philanthropic groups, priests, nuns, rabbis, ministers who dealt with the poor, and large donations to VA hospitals and Viet Nam organizations. The black man, the whites, the tan, the yellow, the red, the young, the old, all would share in the windfall. Four checks would be held out, the others would be turned over to his attorneys, Martins and Rosen, for proper distribution.

There were so few competent and honest administrators. He would not tempt or trust them by placing large amounts of money in their hands without his personal control. This money was earmarked for people in need. It was not meant for administrative salaries and overhead costs. Over and above the checks written, Martins and Rosen would set up trusts. With Michael's authorization, the funds would be distributed from there.

He flipped through the other four checks: 326 thousand, one each for Bollan "Bo" Lynch, John "Snake" Adams, and Clarence "Bear" O'Leary. Michael had placed another 180 thousand dollars of winnings in a trust fund that would be invested properly to reduce the upcoming tax liabilities. This would leave them each a healthy pension fund. If handled properly, the trust funds would grow over the years and provide a sizable retirement for them. He knew that taxes and financial security were not priorities with the three men. He had taken it upon himself to set up a long-term financial structure for them.

A crack of lightning riveted his attention again to the lakeside windows. The storm was moving in fast. He pushed himself away from his desk and went to the double-wide glass terrace doors and opened them full peak. A gust of cool lake air billowed the screen doors and caught him straight on.

He felt strength flow through him as he flung open one of the screen doors and walked out onto the expansive, slate terrace to face the wrath of the oncoming storm. This was power, he thought. And his mind turned to dwell upon the third woman in his life. A woman of infinite earthly power. So gentle, She could ease apart the petals of the smallest flowers in spring. So ferocious, She could destroy a city with a sneeze. Time would tell whether or not mankind could anger Her to the point of total earthly destruction. Man was indeed poking at her, testing her patience with the poisons they were spraying into Her nostrils and the crap they were pumping into Her lakes and rivers and great seas.

He said out loud, as if he were apologizing for his brothers' mistakes: "You just don't treat a Special Woman like that. Forgive us!"

A snap of electricity buried itself in the lake a mile from shore. He saw and heard the fierce white rollers as they headed for land, and he smiled as the man-made barrier halted their advance directly in front of the mansion. The rain began to fall. He lifted his arms to greet the cleansing drops that soaked his face and the wind that tousled his hair and pulled at his sweater. "You are all powerful, and I love you." He spoke both to Nature and to his Creator, or were they one and the same?

In the midst of the electrically charged turmoil that surrounded him, he felt a sense of the infinite, a sense of strength and purity. This kind of experience always reassured him that there was an Ultimate Power in the universe. He felt the warmth of inner peace flow through his body. His arms lowered as another jagged arrow lanced the black sky.

Michael's mind drifted into a shallow state of meditation as he continued to watch the storm intensify. Nature's siblings battled with each other as the storm snapped and stung the great waters of Lake Michigan. The lake became frustrated, reaching with white hands into the electric air, sometimes grabbing a jagged arrow from the heavens and

pulling it like a hot iron into her reaching arms. She would remain angry long after the raucous bully from Heaven moved on to the east to terrorize others.

His mind eased back to reality, and he looked around. He hadn't remembered moving off the terrace and down the path to the gazebo. Nor did he sense the presence of another body standing to his right about eight feet away. His head snapped and he automatically stooped to reach for his ankle holster. As he bent he remembered the Mauser was locked in the bottom drawer of his desk. He didn't walk around his own house wearing a goddamn gun.

Bo's voice sounded quickly, above the pouring rain. "Hold on, Mike. It's just me." A flash over the lake revealed his smiling face. He wore a dark rubber rain slicker and Snake's Cubs baseball cap. Rain water fell from its bill.

Michael stood straight up and leaned against the railing of the gazebo. "Jesus Christ, Bo, don't you ever knock?"

Bo's face was in darkness again. "Wasn't sure it was you, standing out in the rain with your hands in the air like you're praying or talking to somebody. For all I knew you were some loony-tunes who escaped from the fifth floor of the Manteno Mental Hospital."

Michael took one more look at the lake, blessed himself, stepped down from the gazebo, and headed for the house. "Come on, dickhead. You scared the shit out of me!"

He heard Bo laugh. "Didn't know that was possible."

He turned and waited for Bo, who was scouring the open area of the lawn down to the lake. Bo turned and double-timed to catch up. He said comically, "Sorry, didn't mean to shake you up. I'm point man tonight--just had to see who the lunatic was standing in the rain talking to the lake."

While walking up the lawn, Michael reached around Bo's shoulder and gave him a squeeze. "I'm going to give you and your boys your winnings tonight. I'll meet you in a few minutes at the coach house."

Bo nodded and walked around the south end of the house. Michael stepped onto the terrace and turned once again toward the lake. His eyes squinted into the falling rain. He was going to utter a prayer but decided his powerful Creator knew his needs better than he did. He blessed himself again and entered the lake room, leaving the rolling thunder behind him.

* * *

The storm passed quickly, leaving a warm, Indian-summer breeze and the fresh smell of damp fall in the air. Michael stopped on the stone path leading to the coach house and picked up a maple leaf that had floated to the ground in front of him. Amber light from a line of lamp posts allowed him to examine the multicolored leaf as he twirled it with his thumb and forefinger.

Life and death. Life and death, he muttered to himself. Most death was ugly, but not so for the maple leaf. It had served its purpose for its brief life, taking in toxic air as food and giving mankind back the oxygen he needed for his own life. Job completed, the leaf died a beautiful death. A death that motivated people to drive a thousand miles to take a photograph, or paint a picture, or maybe just to pick from the ground and collect.

He spoke in a whisper: "The beauty of death to a leaf. Man doesn't die with such dignity and grace..." He kissed the maple leaf, laid it back gently on the ground, and finished his sentence, "...because man takes without giving. Most men live a life unworthy of the colors of nature. Despite earthly wealth and power, man gives in to the inevitable law that dictates the same end for all mankind. In all his pomp and earthly splendor, in all his frivolous worries and titanic concerns, the rich and the poor, the good and the bad, the mean and the just, the casket is lowered into the ground, and man simply becomes dessert for worms. Justice to all and to all a good night!"

The thought amused him as he looked at the four checks he had in his left hand and reassured himself that life was short. Like the maple leaf, poison had to be taken in and turned into something good. Money was neither good nor evil. The man holding the money determined its essence. He hoped the two million dollars he had for his men would produce good things for their world. Maybe it would enrich and give them confidence-- renewed confidence, which had been stripped away by a lying government and a far-off war. Ultimately, he would have no control over the decisions Bo Lynch or Bear O'Leary or Snake Adams made with their new-found wealth. But, he thought, at least the money would give them an opportunity to make decisions without financial pressure. Right or wrong, no man should be denied that opportunity. He continued on to the coach house.

He walked past the four-car garage attached to the quaint habitat. All four doors were closed, but he knew that behind one was the white van that housed Adams's arsenal. Behind another were three powerful dirt bikes and two snowmobiles in case there was a need to chase down somebody in the ravines. The third door probably held Bo's Pontiac Firebird, and God only knew what was behind the fourth door. The way the men had wired the estate with sensors, cameras, and other hi-tech equipment, he presumed this stall had been turned into a receiving room for all of their equipment.

He knocked once and walked in. The room had the sweet smell of cherry wood crackling on the small hearth in the corner. He scanned it quickly. Bo sat near the fireplace reading a thick blue book. Both Adams and O'Leary sat at the wooden picnic table in the middle of the room. Adams was working on his wristwatch receiver, which vibrated if any of the trip wires or pressure sensors were activated. Bear was paging through a thick law book.

Two automatic pistols and a rifle with a night scope were lying at the end of the table next to a cleaning cloth and small can of gun oil. Although the cottage had electricity, the only light came from two Coleman lanterns and the fireplace. He accepted the idiosyncrasy as some type of precaution for a power shortage and the split second it would

take for the generator to kick in. The room was exceptionally clean and well kept. The cot in the corner, where the night watch rested, was made up tight and tidy. He suspected the two beds in the loft were just as neat.

Adams was quiet as usual. Bear was the first to speak. "What's up, Mike? Any problem? Bo said you wanted to see us."

Michael walked behind Snake to the fireplace, picked up a piece of cut oak, and flipped it gently onto the top of the cherry wood. He sensed pressure in the room. Only Bo knew about the money, although he didn't know how much. The other two didn't like being kept in suspense.

He picked up a smaller piece of cherry wood and placed it crosswise on the crackling oak, then turned and walked to the end of the table where the guns were. He removed the guns from the table and set them on the bench next to Bear; at the same time he saw Snake watch his hands. He smiled and said, "Don't worry, John. I haven't come to bury Caesar."

With that statement, he placed the four envelopes in front of him and slid them down the waxed, polyurethane table top, where they were stopped by a bottle of Wild Turkey 101 and a can of Miller beer, in front of Snake and Bear.

Snake stopped working on his watch, and Bear closed the law book. Both merely stared at the envelopes as if they were forbidden to touch. Michael felt good, but he wasn't sure how these unique men would take the gift, especially Adams.

Snake looked up at him with suspicion in his eyes. "What's this, Mike? They look like checks. Are we finished?"

Bo interrupted and pushed himself out of his chair. "Finished hell, Asshole. Open the goddamn thing." Bo picked up the envelopes, pulled out his, flipped one to Bear, and laid the other back down in front of Snake. The fourth envelope, the one for the 'Nam halfway house, Hill-112, he left in the middle of the table. Bo proceeded to open his. "Open 'em, Jerkoffs. They're not goddamn grenades."

Bear picked up the envelope and tore it open. Snake reached down to his boot and pulled out a nine-inch throwing knife and slit his envelope.

Michael watched Bear squint his eyes as he looked at the check, then he reached around behind to a small wooden coffee table for a pair of half-glasses. The dark rims hung on his thick, black nose, making him look like a college professor. He examined the check carefully. His nostrils flared as he sucked in a deep breath.

Snake turned the check cautiously in his hands, then held it up in front of the Coleman lantern, searching for a flaw.

Bo didn't know how much Michael had made them, but his exclamation indicated he thought it was a much lower figure. "Jesus H. Christ." He sat back down with a thud in the cane chair by the fireplace.

Both Snake and Bear spoke at the same time. "What's this?"

They looked at each other. Then, in a whisper, Bear said, "What's this all about, Mike?"

Michael kept the emotion out of his voice. He was excited for them but wanted their reaction first. With his foot, he pulled out a small stool that was hidden under the table and lowered himself onto it. "Remember those account forms I had you guys sign a few months ago?"

He leaned forward on the table, weaving his fingers together, and rested on his elbows. He forced all emotion from his face. He needed to muster a bit of psychology here. He wanted the gift to be a character builder, not a payoff. In fact, he didn't want it to be a gift at all. He wanted them to realize they had worked and waited for this a long time.

"Those forms gave me the discretion to trade a commodity account for you men. So I did! We were lucky and caught a nice move in the market, and what you have there is your cut of the pie."

Bear peered over the top of his glasses, and his lips tightened, curling down at the corners, as he regarded Michael with a cocked head. "Three hundred twenty-six thousand dollars is more than a piece of pie. Are you kidding?"

Michael returned the same serious look but made sure his eyes penetrated Bear's. He wanted it understood that it was market money and not an ass-kissing gesture. "That's right. Three hundred twenty-six thousand dollars. No kidding!"

Michael heard Bo moan to himself, "I'm rich. I'm fucking rich!"

Michael went on. "Plus another one hundred eighty thousand each which is in the hands of my attorneys. That money will be used to set up a trust fund. They will take care of your taxes on the gain and see that you pay the least amount possible. The balance will be invested for your retirement. You have to sign the trust papers and give us limited power of attorney to use the remaining one hundred eighty thousand. If for some reason you want to handle the money yourself, let me know and I'll draft another check for a hundred eighty grand."

Snake snapped out, "Is this some type of gag?"

Michael's voice was firm. "I don't gag with money, John. That is, unless I jam it down someone's throat. You earned this money. It took you guys a long time to get it, but you earned it."

Michael watched as Snake turned his knife with long, nervous fingers. "What do ya mean we earned it? We didn't earn shit."

Michael was relieved to see him place the knife on the table and run his fingers through his cropped hair. His mumble was almost inaudible as his hand left his hair and rubbed his forehead. "What's this all about, Mike?"

Bear took his glasses off and laid them on the table next to the jug of Wild Turkey. His eyes and lips were tight with suspicion. "Mike, nobody gives money like this

to guys like us unless they want something in return." He looked at the check and shook his head. "This kind of money tells me you want something pretty big, pretty ugly."

Michael saw Snake agree with a quick emotionless look and nod, then he asked, "What's the job, Mike?"

He looked at both men with disbelief. He felt his shoulders droop as his mind raced into an angry area, but he spoke softly. "The only job I want you men to do is win a war. The war you have going on between yourselves and the rest of society. I want nothing in return for something you richly deserve and have had to wait so long for. I'm not the government, I'm not the Mafia, or the IRA, or your banker, or lawyer. I want nothing except for you guys to get your acts together. Live in harmony with the life that's passing you by."

Snake raised his head to look at him. His eyes were curiously sad. "You make no sense, Mike."

He leaned forward on his elbows and spoke as a brother. "I make no sense because you don't understand me. You don't understand the way I think. That doesn't matter. All you have to know is that in every man's life there comes an opportunity to grab hold of something good. That something will allow you to feel the warmth of the sun on your face again. It will allow you to go and do the things you want to do. It can accelerate the good in you, or it can accelerate the bad in you; that is your choice. This money, your money, will give you that opportunity. There are no catches. You can take the money and walk out that door."

The room was silent. The men were listening, but were they hearing? Michael's mind took another tack. He decided to sail windward, use a language they understood. His voice took on strength. "How long were you guys in Viet Nam? How many combined tours of duty?"

The men were quiet as he went on. "Snake, how many tours?"

Adams looked from the check to Michael and back to the check. Again he was having trouble finding words and seemed confused.

Michael persisted. "How many tours, John?"

With a snap of frustration, Snake's words slashed. "I don't know, Mike, goddammit, a long time."

Michael persisted. "How many years, John?"

Snake's eyes were misting. He looked back and a drop fell from his eye onto the check. "Four years for Bo and me. Three and a half for Bear."

Michael slammed his palm down on the table, making the Coleman lantern flicker and the bottle of Wild Turkey jump. "Eleven and a half years you three spent in a jungle fighting for a country who scorned you and whose government was ready, willing, and able to lay the guilt of, God only knows how many, deaths on your shoulders."

He rested a moment while his mind caught up with his tongue. Then he said as a matter of fact, "You guys didn't kill anybody."

Michael heard Bo's chair squeak as he turned to look at him. Bear and Snake also looked up at him. He repeated the last statement. "You guys didn't kill anybody! *The politicians killed those people.* They just let eighteen and twenty year old kids pull the trigger for them. So get rid of the guilt that binds you to the past."

He had their attention; they were hearing now. "And while you were pulling the trigger for the politicians, the rich kids went to school to become doctors, and lawyers, and politicians, and bad guys, and commodity brokers and stock brokers. Well, now you've been paid just a portion of what your effort in 'Nam was worth to *me*. Just a small portion."

He leaned back in his chair and pointed to the checks. "You want to know where that money came from? It didn't come from me!" They were listening. Bear was tracing the pink scar on his face with his finger, and Adams's eyes had bowed to the table again.

Michael reached for the last envelope on the table and opened it. "I'll tell you where the money came from." He tossed the envelope aside and threw the 860-thousand-dollar check for Hill-112 in front of Bear and Snake. They both studied the check. Now Bear rubbed his eyes. Bo turned again to stare into the fire. Snake looked away, and Michael reached over and picked up the check.

He explained with coolness, "The two million three hundred seventy-eight thousand dollars that sits in this room came from those doctors and lawyers and engineers and politicians, and crooked stock and commodity brokers. The men *you* allowed to go to school while *you* were each blowing away hundreds of commies in North Viet Nam, and pulling poisoned bamboo sticks and shrapnel from your own bellies."

He felt his jaw muscles tighten. He held the check for the halfway house in front of him and shook it. "Guns don't win wars in America anymore. Money, clear thinking, and a sense of purpose wins the wars. Now you guys finally have a chance to fight back. The same protestors who spit at you when you returned have just paid a small portion of their dues." He flipped the check back down in front of Snake.

The room was quiet. He let his words sink into the scared souls of his men. Thirty seconds passed before he spoke again. "Bear?"

Bear looked up with glassy eyes.

Michael leaned forward. "That scar on your face? It's a knife wound, right?"

Bear shook his head. "Machete."

Michael spoke emphatically. "Well, Dr. Smith from Toledo just sent you a half million and wants to thank you for fighting his fight for him and taking that injury for him."

He looked in Bo's direction. Michael thought to himself that this meeting was turning into an encounter--the bringing up of the past, the resentments, the hurt, the hate. "Bo, the pain of losing several toes and that football size scar on your chest may have been worth it; you just received a check from Attorney Jones from L.A. telling you how much he appreciates your fighting his war for him while he went to school."

Then Michael looked at Snake, whose head he still had to penetrate. "Snake?"

Adams didn't move. "Snake, your injuries are still bleeding inside. Your wounds are deep and still aching. They are so obvious I can feel them. Psychiatrist Brown from N.Y. just sent you a check thanking you for carrying his load along with your own through the jungle. He says he's sorry he couldn't have been there with you."

As an afterthought he decided it was time to soften the conversation and return the men to the present. He spoke with a tone of irony. "In fact, all three, Dr. Smith, Attorney Jones, and Psychiatrist Brown are all sorry they couldn't have been there with you fellows. But do you know what they're a hell of a lot sorrier about?"

Michael's voice rose in unison with the heads in the room. Snake was back with it as he wiped his eyes with the back of his plaid shirt and looked at Michael. Michael felt his cheeks pull back in a smile as he said, "They are goddamn sorry they ever played the commodity market. They didn't intend on paying you fuckers back, so we *took* the money from the stingy bastards."

He felt the pressure ease. The three warriors smiled at Michael's last comment. Suddenly Michael saw Snake's knife raise high in the air, and in a flash it descended. Michael jumped back, tipping over his stool in the process. He thought, son of a bitch. I pushed him too far.

But Snake was still sitting there holding onto the handle of the knife with the blade implanted in the table. Between the blade and the table were his check along with the 860-thousand-dollar check for the Nam House, Hill 112.

Bo had sprung to his feet and now held a log poker ready to club Snake. "You crazy bastard. What the fuck are you doing?"

Snake's mood had swung the other way, and for the first time since Michael had met the man, he heard humor in his voice. "I just want to make sure that if that door opens again these two checks don't blow into the fireplace. That would really piss me off."

Bear had leaned back with his huge pink palms out, thinking the knife was coming his way. "Snake, you have a funny way of holding onto your money."

Bear reached back and opened a cupboard and pulled out three clean jelly jars. He placed them on the table, reached back again, and opened a small refrigerator, pulling out three cans of Miller and a can of pop.

He flipped the can of pop to Bo, uncorked the Wild Turkey, and poured the three jelly jars half full of the 101-proof whiskey. He slid a jar and a beer down to Michael and raised the brown liquor in front of him. "Here's to Dr. Smith, Attorney Jones, and Shrink Brown."

A sense of pride filled the room. Michael could feel a total illumination, exhilaration. Something strong, that certainly wasn't in the room when he entered. He felt he had pulled them together and himself with them. He grabbed the jelly jar and raised it to clink with the other two in the middle of the table. A pop can clinked into the toast with

a comment from Bo. "Go ahead, ya fuckers. Hope you all end up alkies and don't ask me to sponsor you. You're on your own you drunken sots."

Relief filled the room as anxiety seeped away. Bo left to walk the grounds, and Michael stayed for an hour, finishing the bottle of Wild Turkey and five beers.

A truth had been established. More importantly, there was a bonding of friendship amongst men who had lived half their lives in the dark tunnels of their own minds. Michael knew they could find a way out so they, too, could taste the rain and smell the fresh fall air. A sense of peace--of purpose--permeated the room; it flowed through them all. Thunder in the distance told him another storm was headed into the city from the west.

* * *

Bear threw another oak log on the fire and listened to the rain pound the slate roof. He looked down at the crackling fire, then turned to Snake, who had uncorked another bottle of Wild Turkey. As he nursed his drink, he stared at the two checks on the table, still pinned down with his knife.

Bear lumbered over and sat across from Snake. "Well, what do you think?"

Snake's thin lips pursed in thought as he raised his eyes to meet Bear's. Bear had never seen him ever come close to relinquishing his animal image until tonight. Hogan had pulled him apart enough in a gentle way to help heal past wounds and plant new ideas for growth.

Bear felt that because neither had expected the money, this was the first time they had been taken off guard. It wasn't the money as much as Hogan's words. His psychological ploys and maneuvering were what made his visit so effective.

They didn't know this man Hogan. Who the hell was he? A guy just didn't hand out two million dollars to a handful of Viet Nam vets without wanting something in return. But Hogan said there were no contingencies except for helping the men at Hill-112's halfway house. They could leave at any time. His only personal request was that they stay with him until the trouble had passed. Hell yes, they would stay. They would protect his family and try to keep their leader alive.

Bear asked himself the question: Was Hogan a liar? A manipulator? A buyer of loyalty? He didn't think so. The man called life as he saw it. He didn't mince words. He was direct and firm and controlled. He was a good, honest man in a dirty world. Son of a bitch. What was his angle? Then Bear thought, maybe there is no angle. Maybe the man was just a leader of men, asking only for loyalty.

One thing Bear sensed from his own experience, and something he had seen on rare occasions in Hogan's eyes, was that the man was capable of turning his warm generosity to cold, brutal strength. Although stronger and a trained killer, Bear thought, he would not want to be the one who crossed the man called Hawk.

412

He thought Michael's only handicap was that he was counting on the government to get Zitello, the fat German-Swede called Peterson, and his underbosses Conti and Ruzzo. Bear knew different.

The government couldn't be trusted. Somebody would pay somebody in Washington to tell who was leaking information, and they would come for Hogan and keep coming. He was a dead man. Unless Hogan's adversaries were hit first.

"What do I think about what?"

Bear looked through the dim lantern light. Snake was slouched in his chair with his left arm hanging over its back and his right twirling a half a jam jar of brown whiskey.

Bear ran his finger down the white scar to his chin and smiled at Hogan's charade about the Doctor and Lawyer and Psychiatrist paying for the slash that almost cut half his face off. "What do you think about Hogan?"

Snake took his arm from the back of his chair and cupped his drink. "I don't know. The man's either insane, which doesn't seem to be the case, using us, which seems unlikely because of his concern for our buddies at 112, or he's completely on the level. That seems like more of a possibility. Doesn't take him long to get to the point, does it? Seems he knows exactly what we're thinking. He should have been a priest!"

Bear grunted and spoke with a deep, concerned voice. "Tell ya one thing. He's going to get a second opportunity to be a priest if we don't do something about the bad guys before they decide to take him out."

Snake looked up at Bear. His eyes were reddened from the booze and half-closed. His thin chin jutted out, and Bear saw the jaw muscle tighten. He knew the look.

"Bear, this money makes it even more important that we go ahead with our original plans. Our plans for Zitello and Peterson remain the same. Hogan said he didn't want the money to change us, and it's not." He drooped his head for a moment of thought, then looked back at Bear and said, "Anybody who hands me a check for three hundred twenty-six thousand dollars and says, 'Thanks for all you've been through, don't worry about me, just take good care of yourself and your friends,' is going to get the best I've got."

Bear took a swallow of beer and said, "I agree, but I think we have to move fast before they hit Bo or Hogan. We can't wait a year for the government to act with their bullshit legal process. We have the advantage now. They don't know who we are, how we work, or how many there are of us. Bo's sober now. He can carry his own weight, and he's got Zitello near crazy. As far as I'm concerned, Hogan's the guy we're being paid to protect, so let's do one thing and protect him--our way and now!"

There was one knock, and the door opened. Bo sauntered in, took off a black poncho, shook the water from it, and hung it on a wooden peg by the door. Bear watched him as he walked around a counter top and poured a cup of black coffee. He finally spoke. " All's quiet outside! You guys okay?"

Bear had grabbed a legal pad and pencil from the table behind him and said, "Bo, ya know those floor plans Pete Lewis gave you for Zitello and Peterson's office?"

Bo sipped the steaming coffee and walked to a pine bookcase on the far side of the room. He produced a manila folder and took a seat next to Snake. "He didn't give 'em to me. I swiped them, then I copied them. Lewis was showing Mike and me where the computer and telephone lines were and where all the lines veered off to private terminals that the phone and computer companies know nothing about. The Feds have the two broads, Winters and McFadden, trying to tap the secret terminals."

He placed the folder on the table and pulled out two sets of floor plans, one marked *Z* the other marked *P*. Then he asked with a cool tone, stripped of emotion, "We going through with it?"

Bear looked at him with question. "What do you say?"

Bo looked down into the black coffee. "I don't know that we have a choice. If they get me, and they've already tried once, they'll get Mike too. We have to control the war. We know where they are, and we know they don't expect us. They think they're dealing with an honorable, peaceful man in Hogan. They will use that to their advantage. They don't know that our honor among each other was derived from and built on eliminating scumbags before they eliminated us. Hogan said money and a sense of purpose wins wars today, not guns. Well, we seldom use guns, but we have all three now: money, guns, and purpose. If it comes down to it, we have the ability to recruit men from the Hill. As far as I'm concerned..." Bo sipped the steaming coffee, "...whoever hits first is going to be the winner. I vote for elimination--total."

Bear watched his two friends. "What about Mike? He wants to quarterback the team. He made it clear he wants to call the plays."

Bo pulled the knife from the table and placed it to his lips. "He's going to have to sit out this game. As sharp as he is, I'm not going to wait around for some slime-bag to put a bullet in the back of his head. I'll take the heat for what we do. He's forgiving--I think!"

Bear looked at Snake. Their eyes met. Bear felt his own body stiffen for combat, and a smile painted Snake's sinister face. Bear took the knife from Bo and slammed it back into the checks. He placed his hand on top of the knife handle. Snake followed, placing his on top of Bear's. Bo reached over and did the same, and all three said in unison, "done."

FORTY-FOUR

Dirty Laundry-October 28,1987

Three twenty-dollar gold pieces shuffled back and forth in his pudgy left hand, as Karl Peterson squeezed the ivory doorknob with his right. He mocked the brass nameplate that read "TONY ZITELLO." His fat lips curved down as he slowly studied the wheat leaves mixed with corn stalks and husks and shafts of grain. They were all cradled in the arms of Ceres, the Roman goddess of grain, and had been hand carved on Zitello's heavy oak door.

The magical sound of the clinking gold coins was interrupted by a short chime that sounded from his fifty-thousand-dollar Rolex. He didn't bother to look. He knew it was ten o'clock. No time to be changing diapers for some Italian, chickenshit bastard. A couple of warm broads and a hot-tub bath were waiting for him at his downtown penthouse. Instead, here he was talking this paranoid wimp down out of a tree.

Before he pushed through the heavy door, he looked back down the long hall to the outer office where his two bodyguards, Gunter Schmidt and Dieter Wolf, had been instructed to wait. Poor excuses for protectors, he thought, one with half a hand and two ear phones. The other, still with wires in his jaw from injuries inflicted by--by--the name lodged in his throat--Hogan, the son of a bitch. Was there no competence left in the world except for himself? Fuck 'em. He'd have two new men in three weeks, and the Rodent and the Albino would be on their way back to Germany. Let 'em go back and work for the Russians. They were no good to him if they couldn't take out Hogan.

The coins shuffled faster, and he felt the fat sacks around his eyes pull together in scorn as he caught the nameplate once again. He mumbled to himself, "The coward guinea son of a bitch. I paid for this door and everything else the wop prick owns." In anger he flung open the heavy door, slamming it into the wall.

He felt his thick shoulder bump against the door jamb as he entered. He quickly looked around the lavish office and found Tony standing by one of the eight massive windows that looked out at a dismal, rainy Chicago. Tony turned abruptly, as if a gun had exploded behind him. "Jesus Christ, Karl, you coulda knocked. Ya scared me."

Peterson's hand worked the coins harder, and he felt anger and heat rise within him. "I don't have to knock in the places I own! Now, what is it this time, Zitello?"

Peterson saw the quarter-bottle of Chivas on the bar, then looked back at Tony's bloodshot eyes. He avoided him and searched the rest of the office. He became more infuriated at each piece of expensive sculpture his eyes settled on. It was through his power and money that the bastard was able to afford such extravagance.

His angry eyes came back to Zitello. He studied the pathetic bastard. Since the close of the market, the jerk had consumed a bottle of Scotch, plus twenty lines or more of cocaine, and his hands still shook. By this time, he should be well on his way to oblivion from the booze and cocaine intake, but not tonight. What was the matter with the spineless twerp?

The only noises in the room were the shuffling coins and his own heavy breathing. He felt a clamminess in the air as he looked around the room again. Despite Zitello's expensive taste and lavish decor, the room looked as if it had been burglarized. It smelled of sweat, too, like a locker room. As he lumbered to the bar, his sharp words sliced the stagnant air. "What a mess, Zitello. What's the matter with your air conditioning? Must be a hundred in this room." He poured three fingers of Chivas into an empty glass, downed it in one gulp, and poured three fingers more. Zitello didn't look at Peterson when he talked. "I dunno, air and phones went dead 'bout a half hour ago. Probably the storm!" Peterson watched Tony stumble toward his desk. Straw-lines marked the pile of cocaine, telling him that much more had already been drawn. Tony leaned and sniffed two lines through a rolled hundred-dollar bill.

"Didn't you check it out, Asshole? The air conditioning and phones have nothing to do with each other." Tony looked up with red, bulging eyes and said with irritation, "How am I supposed to check anythin' out with the phones not workin'? And I'm not leavin' the office for nothin'."

Alarm etched every line and feature of Zitello's face. His words were slurred, disjointed, as he attempted to speak and navigate. "Karl, we gotta stop this shit now, or at leas' cut back. We're skimmin' an' washin' too much, too fas'. Two million this week already. Six mil' the week of the crash. Three times that las' month and now you wan' me to *step it up even more*! Jesus Christ, Karl, I'm only one man, outta twenty guys movin' cash through the market fer ya. Why ya layin' so much shit on me? People are lookin' at me funny in the pit. 'Specially Hogan's men. They all know what I'm doin'. Is becoming too obvious. Lynch is *still* all over my ass when I make a trade--I thought you were gonna take him out?"

The sliding coins picked up speed. Peterson felt blood rush to his face at Hogan's name, and his words exploded: "SHUT THE FUCK UP. We own the goddamn pits, and we make the rules, not Hogan and not Lynch."

He tried to control his scorn. "None of the men in the other pits seem to be complaining. We did go after Lynch, last week. But the bastard's either clever or he was tipped off. We'll get 'em, Tony. He'll be off your back--and soon!"

He placed the gold coins in his suit pocket, plunked one ice cube into his tumbler of scotch, thumped past Tony, and plopped into the black-leather couch. He watched the rain streak the wall of windows, which gave the city an ugly distortion. He detested rain. In fact he detested all storms--rain, wind, snow--made him feel uneasy.

Peterson's presence brought more heat into the room, and he felt perspiration begin to seep from his forehead and cheeks, a familiar irritation he had come to accept over the years from his rich appetite. His face grew sullen as he watched Zitello hurry to the bar, swallow the rest of his drink, and pour another, almost emptying the bottle. He returned and sat across from him in a complementary black-leather chair. "Listen, Karl..."

His own words came quick and sharp. "No, you listen, asshole. You're getting paranoid. I've been over this with you before. There is nobody, *nobody*, looking at you funny--because they're all skimming and bagging trades off your orders and off our other men in the pits. We are their livelihood!"

He rested his heavy body back in the soft couch and loosened his tie. With a diabolic smile, he said, "Everybody's entitled to pad their pockets a bit, don't you think? Buy nice cars and live in fancy houses and take trips around the world and have a small savings account off shore."

Zitello was quiet. His head rolled as if it were too heavy for his shoulders. He jerked to a standing position, almost falling, then sat back down.

Peterson forced himself to relax. Excitement wasn't good for his blood pressure. He felt the fat loosen on his face and hang like slabs of soft lard. "Who do you think is feeding the leeches? We are, Tony! We give up a little bit to the weasels in the pits so they will keep their mouths shut, can keep up their life styles, and brag that they are financial wizards. We bag and move the big money and give them the pennies and nickels."

A flash of fear assailed Tony. "Karl, somebody's watching us...gonna...gonna rat on us. I just feel it."

"Who's watching? Who's gonna chirp, Tony? And to whom?"

Tony's head twisted and rolled, like he was retarded. His eyes were dilated, the size of black olives. "I don't know who, but they'll tell the Exchange, the government,...they'll even tell God. I don't know."

Peterson's voice pushed out loud again. "OF COURSE YOU DON'T KNOW. You're seeing and hearing ghosts because of all that white powder you snort."

He felt drops of sweat run down his cheeks. Anger began to twist and turn inside his body like a rabid rat in a small cage, but he tried to stay calm with the Italian prick because he was such a strong producer. That is, until recently. Until Lynch came down on him, and Hogan--that son of a bitch. He swirled the scotch. "Tony, money and power are God, and I have both. My people *are* the Exchange. I'm the top man, the one who sits at the head of the table on all the major Exchange committees, *and* at both Exchanges. I *own* the powers in the government who are supervising us. I instruct *them*. They don't tell *me* what to do. *My* people warn me if anybody starts making waves in Washington. I pay over thirty million a year for their friendship, a mere pittance compared to what I move and take in. Tony, I've set up an organization that's invincible."

Tony's head drooped forward, his long, black hair spilling onto his face. "I thought it was only five million for the Washington support."

Peterson felt the warmth of the scotch. He thought he'd better switch to a lower gear. If it was up to him, he'd have had Zitello thrown off a building like Hogan's buddy, O'Neal, or better yet, blow his brains all over his dashboard like Al Josephson. But right now he needed the slime bag. He was still valuable. He laundered too much money in the big pits. To get rid of him yet wouldn't be good business.

He spoke in a softer tone. "It *was* five million until that asshole in New York got caught trading off information before it hit the streets. Dumb bastard didn't cover his ass-- had no network. So, pressure was put on our Washington friends by the SEC. And in their own diplomatic, greedy way they decided to up the ante. Of course, we only show a half million in political contributions to the media. That's nice and respectable."

He mumbled to himself. "Can you imagine people actually believe that we get our political power for only a half million dollars? Shit, a half million wouldn't buy a bologna sandwich in Washington."

Tony's eyes were at half mast and his mouth hung loose. "Karl, I'm scared shitless with the amount of dirty cash were runnin'. A few of the other boys are too. We think we should cut back. And what about Hogan? I know he's up to somethin', I can smell it. There are guys in the pit who jus' watch me all day. *I know they're Hogan's men.*"

As he heard the name of Hogan, Peterson felt his blood run hot again. He tried in vain to lean forward in the soft couch, but his heavy bulk held him back. "Fuck Hogan. He's a dead man. He tried to break up our Brotherhood before, and we buried him. This time he goes into the ground in pieces, Hogan and Lynch both. No more about those motherfuckers.

"As far as guys watching you in the pits, they're watching you because they admire you. There are new guys coming and going every day from the pits. What gives you the crazy idea they're looking at you for any other reason than admiration?"

His fat lips sucked at the scotch, and his jowls shook as the burning liquid traveled down his throat. "If my grandmother came down here and stood next to you, she would be suspect in your mind. You give ol' granny a trade for a couple thousand dollars, and she would give you a kiss and probably a blow job on top of it."

He waved his hand in the air. "If you have some new guys in the pits, go over to them and give 'em a coupla good trades and watch them come back the next day for more. Pretty soon you own them. It's just like dope, Tony, give 'em a little and they'll be back for more. You should know that better than anybody. You sell and use enough of the junk!" Peterson looked over toward Tony's desk and saw the lines of dream dust. "You know how it is, Tony, trust me!"

The perspiration ran from his face and began to trickle down his neck and back. He was talking to a blank face but continued.

"What do you think, Zitello, the new guys are Feds? We'd know they were coming before they had their application for membership in. The government isn't going

to spend millions for memberships and fifty million more trying to figure out our puzzle when they can send the money to Central America and let the CIA buy a country. Hell, they haven't any idea what goes on here and never will. We've got the best game in the world going, AND I CONTROL IT!"

He finally made it off of the couch and grabbed a bar towel from the mahogany credenza. He wiped his face vigorously, then the back of his neck.

He sat back down and said, "Listen Tony, we can't cut back now, not with the record volume of outside business flooding the pits. We push now...the S & P's, the bonds, the beans, the Eurodollars, the Swiss franc, the yen, wherever there is big customer volume. We push hard while the business is here. Besides, I have my instructions from the Man in New York that he wants us to double our cleaning for him. I negotiated an additional three per cent for the added laundry."

Tony leaned close; his breath smelled like rotten eggs and nearly overwhelmed Peterson. "Jesus Christ, Karl. It's not your ass, it's..."

Peterson threw the bar towel on the couch and with the back of his right hand slapped Tony in the face, leaving a cut that mimicked the large ring he wore on his thick little finger. He knew his composure was gone again, but he couldn't help it: he angered quickly. With his fat hands, he grabbed Zitello by his sweaty shirt, pulling him half out of his chair. He hissed through his teeth, "Listen, you guinea, it's nobody's ass. ARE YOU LISTENING TO ME?" He threw Zitello back into the chair and felt his eyes slant in hate.

Tony began to sob, nodding his head yes. He wiped the blood from his cheek with the back of his hand.

He watched Zitello with disgust. He had to calm himself, or he would kill the man. He spoke with more control. "We'll get the job done at both Exchanges. We're going into three more pits next month to take care of the overflow. Your quota won't go up much."

Tony inched back in his chair, out of Peterson's reach. He spoke in a low, little boy's, scared voice. "Much, shit! I'm tellin' you Karl. I'm over my quota now. Too obvious. Too much pressure. Too many eyes watchin'."

Zitello lifted himself from his chair, rubbing his injured cheek, and stumbled to the bar. He poured the rest of the Chivas. Fumbling, he opened another bottle and filled his glass until it overflowed and dripped from the marble bar top onto the oriental rug. He grabbed the drink, sloshing it over his hand, and didn't seem to notice as he threw half of it into himself.

Peterson saw danger signs. "Tony, how much did you make last year from our operation? Eleven, twelve million? Most of it in your island accounts?"

Tony leaned on the bar with both elbows. His head sagged as he mumbled, "about four hundred thousand, according to my tax return."

Peterson said, "What do you think the Man in New York would think if he found out you didn't want to wash his clothes any more, or if he found out you pissed away

seven million dollars to Hogan in a stupid trade he tricked you into making with him? How about our friends in Washington? They don't take kindly to having a brother leave the fold or lose his nerve."

Tony abruptly turned from the bar and walked to the window, groping furniture as he stumbled along. He pressed his forehead against the glass and looked out at the crying metropolis. "Fuck the Man and fuck Washington. Can' a man get tired? Can' a man get burned out?" He stopped talking for a second. "And can' a man get scared? I jus' wan' out!"

Peterson set his half-empty tumbler down on the massive, antique coffee table, pulled the three heavy coins from his pocket again, and began the obsessive shuffling. He had to get out of here before he killed the whiny little wop. Tony was on the edge, and he couldn't talk him down. He struggled to get off the couch again, then strolled to within a foot of Tony, placing his left arm on his shoulder. He stared at the back of Tony's head. His black hair was matted, wet, and oily.

His words came out soft but clear. "You can't get out, Tony, I own you. Once you're in, you're in to stay, so don't give me any more 'I wanna get out' shit."

He let his heavy hand slide down. He gathered some thoughts. "Hey, come on, Tony. I'm sorry for the slap. You just shouldn't anger me like that. You know it doesn't take much for me to blow my top. Why don't you take some time off? A month, two months. Whatever you want. Go to the islands and count your money. Drink rum and ball your brains out. I'll have Jasper Pozzi fill in for you. He's maturing, and he's ready for the big numbers. I'll cover your ass with my people and tell the Man you need an overdue rest." Peterson paused, then turned and rumbled toward the door, clinking the coins together as he walked.

Tony said, "Karl?"

He stopped in mid-stride and forced his thick neck up so his head was looking at the dark, wood moldings that framed the ceiling. "Yeah, Tony?"

His voice cracked, and Zitello said quietly, "I'm sorry, Karl!"

Peterson opened the door. 'Sorry' was a word for weaklings, and he didn't need cowards working for him. "Yeah, sure, Tony. Me too."

Peterson left the door standing open as he walked into the dark outer office. No air conditioning. The largest commodity exchange in the world with no cool air. He pulled out his handkerchief and wiped his face. His thoughts mimicked the conversation. "*A few of the other boys are scared too.*" Spineless, gutless Italians, he mumbled as he strode through the office. If only he had a few more good Swedes and Germans he could put to work instead of having to count on Sal Ruzzo's Italians and Jews. Then he could own the Exchanges, he could own the government, the world. Some day his own men would be ready, and everybody would bow to him and kiss his ring like the Pope. Power and money were the only two things that mattered in this world--at any cost. He'd show Hogan, too, him and his bunch of classless, Irish bastards. "It won't be long now, Hogan."

He stopped as he entered the large outer office. His bodyguards were nowhere in sight. His angry voice bounced off the walls. "SCHMIDT...WOLF! Where the hell are you?" Goddamn them.

He walked to the reception desk and looked down at the bronze name plate of the receptionist. "SAMANTHA WINTERS," he read. He'd fuck the blond-haired beauty someday soon, with or without her permission, the pompous bitch. All women were bitches. He'd fuck her to death.

His thoughts were interrupted by a sweeping noise just inside the entrance. "Schmidt?" No answer. He felt the prick of a shiver in the small of his back. The only sound was the rubbing of the coins. He stood still. His eyes scanned the dark office. Then he spoke with irritation to cover his uncertainty. "Wolf, you son of a bitch, is that you?"

Still no answer. "Who's there, goddammit?"

As he squeezed the coins tight in his hand, the clinking stopped. His heavy eye lids squinted into the dim light. A large figure emerged from the side office by the exit door. A black giant holding a long, narrow broom.

The man's words came slowly. "Just the janitor, mista."

Whew! Just the janitor, he thought. He looked closer. The black man was huge, bigger than he was. Even in the dim light he could see a wide, white scar that reached from the bottom of his left ear to the corner of his mouth.

Peterson puffed out his chest and with false courage said, "Well, what the fuck are you doing here so late? Where are the two men who were waiting for me?"

The black man stood still as stone, just watching him. "I din' see no men. An'...an it's only 'leven a' clock, mista. I works all night long in this here buildin'. This here's ma fust week. Still gettin' the lay o' the land, know what I mean?"

He sensed the man was too big to be a janitor. Maybe a leg breaker or something worse, but he wasn't going to challenge the monster's credentials.

Goddamn them, Schmidt and Wolf. They must have gone down to the bar. Total incompetence. He stood straighter. "I think you better move your black ass out of this office and into another one. We have this office cleaned during the early evening so none of you bastards can come in here and steal us blind. Now move your ass, blacky."

Peterson watched as the huge man picked up his pail and mop, vacuum cleaner, desk polish, broom, a couple of cans of cleaning solution and place everything in a large laundry cart.

Again came the slow, almost musical words. "I'm a leavin', sir. Jus' hope I don' get in no trouble for not cleanin' this office."

Peterson noticed that the laundry cart was bulging. The bastard probably had it filled with typewriters and other office equipment. "Hey, black boy. What do you have in that there cart of yours?"

The man stopped and looked back at Peterson as the cart was partially through the door. The man's eyes told Peterson not to ask any more questions. "Jus' gots myself a whole lots of dirty laundry and a whole lots of filthy garbage, Mista Peterson."

The black man began to hum a tune that Peterson had heard before, but he didn't remember the words. The thick, glass doors closed behind the ape as he pushed his bulging, laundry cart through and hummed the familiar song.

Maybe he is a janitor, Peterson thought, he's sure dumb enough. But then the right side of his face began to twitch and the coins moved fast in his hand. The black bastard had called him by his name, "Mista Peterson." How did he know his name? Goddammit, where were his two men? He'd have their asses. They sure as hell weren't worth two grand a week for protection. His whole body shuddered with uneasiness. He locked the office doors and swayed with effort to the elevators. The coins continued their incessant clinking. His last thought before he reached the elevator was, that *fucking Hogan*!

No phones, no air conditioning. He hoped the elevators were working. He'd hate to have to walk down thirty-eight floors. The shuffling coins echoed through the marble hall as he pushed the down button. Zitello, the black man, and his two irresponsible body guards had unnerved him. He needed a good drink, a hot bath with two gorgeous hookers, a few snorts of white love dust, and a couple hours of fucking and sucking that would soothe him.

The door opened immediately, almost as if the elevator had been waiting for him. His lungs pushed out a gust of air. He began to step forward before the doors were completely open. He stopped abruptly.

Another janitor and his yellow vinyl laundry cart occupied the elevator. The man was tall and thin, dressed in a khaki janitor's outfit, and a Cubs baseball cap. He chomped hard on chewing gum, which pronounced every muscle in his face. The casual look on his face was friendly but strange as he stared out at Peterson. An inner voice told him not to enter the elevator, but the thought erased itself when the janitor's convincing sound beckoned him forward.

The smooth, clear voice was more of a welcome than a threat. "How ya doin', buddy'?...Better grab it while you can...long walk down to the main floor." He popped his gum and spoke again, holding the elevator button so the door would remain open. "All the rest of the elevators are out, partner. Storm blew out most of the condensers and relays for the building. Don't know how long it'll take to fix. You a Cubs fan? Next year's the year for 'em!"

Peterson looked at the large, yellow cart half filled with crumpled papers. A canvas tarpaulin was neatly folded and hung over one end of the cart. He felt the corners of his mouth curl down. His eyes moved back to study the janitor. He had taken his Cubs cap off and was tracing the red C with his finger. The man's short, sandy hair was wet as if he'd just come in from outside.

Now the gum-chewing janitor spoke with irritation. "Come on, mac, you ridin' down, or can I be on my way? I got to dump all the shit in this cart outside, and it's pouring. Then I got six more floors to finish before I go home. In or out, buddy!"

The gold started shuffling again. He wasn't going to walk thirty-eight floors down. His mind sensed suspicion but his heavy body demanded the pleasure of a quick ride to the lobby.

He stepped into the elevator and pressed his back against the side wall next to the man. The doors closed. He disliked being around ignorance, first Zitello, then the big, black janitor, now this guy, all assholes--all losers.

He thought to himself, just not my night. Then said with feigned authority and indignation, "you watch your mouth, boy, or I'll have your goddamn job. I'll get on any elevator in this building whenever I please. No jerkoff like you is going to tell me, 'On or off, buddy.' I own this building, and..." It took a moment for him to realize that the elevator was not moving.

His jowls drooped as he reached over and pushed the lower-lobby button. Still the elevator remained motionless. He looked at the rest of the buttons. Suddenly, fear attacked him, like a knife slicing through his spine. The only button that had been pushed was for the thirty-eighth floor, and the on-off toggle switch was in the off position.

His head snapped to the man who stood to his side. The man had replaced his cap, but the bill was in the back, like a baseball catcher's. His eyes, no longer casual, were wide and icy like chips of black glass. The sound of the sliding coins in his hand stopped for a moment, then started again, shuffling quicker, much quicker, as if the magic of gold rubbing together would ward off evil.

He pushed the "Door Open" button, the lobby button, the toggle switch. The elevator didn't move. His mind raced, became frantic. He pushed and pounded at the buttons. There was no sound except the sound of gold rubbing gold.

Peterson's eyes looked up to meet a face stripped of emotion. The man took the gum from his mouth and flipped it into the laundry cart. He gently pushed the cart with his foot a short distance to the other side of the elevator and stood to face Karl about three feet away. Peterson shivered, and felt his lower lip begin to quiver. His face twitched out of control. The man's frigid eyes glassed over, and he looked like a poisonous snake ready to strike.

Peterson fumbled for words. He tried to sound tough, in control. "What...what do you want? Money? Do you know who I am, you idiot?"

He couldn't think. Sweat ran into the corners of his eyes as his head jumped out of control, up and down, over and around, looking for a way out.

The man spoke softly, intelligently: "I know perfectly well who you are, Mr. Peterson."

He tried to move to his right. Out of nowhere came the man's hand and grabbed him around his throat. The grip was paralyzing. He tried to kick out and defend himself

with his hands, but his arms and legs had gone limp from the man's crushing grip. Yet, his three-hundred-pound bulk didn't fall. In fact, the man's strength pushed his body so hard against the wall his feet lifted off the ground. What was happening? Who was this man? His voice choked out the words, "I can make you RICH!"

The cold voice seared Peterson's mind. "I am rich, Fat Man. I'm rich with friends, and it is my understanding you have threatened to hurt two of my friends. It is also my understanding you would even go so far as to kill my two friends. Shame on you, Mr. Peterson."

The grip tightened. The Swede gasped for air as his wind had been cut off. He tried to shake his head no. He choked out the words "No, I wouldn't do..."

The words came in a whisper. "Ever hear of Bo Lynch, Mr. Peterson? Ever hear of 'Hawk' Hogan, Mr. Peterson?" At Hogan's name, the gold coins fell from Peterson's hand. He heard them hit the tile floor and begin to roll around the elevator. His mind was dulled from lack of oxygen. Hogan? This was one of his men? It couldn't be, not the honest, pacifist Hogan. Had he underestimated him?

The man's grip relaxed, and Peterson felt his feet touch the floor. Before he had time to slump further, everything blurred, and the Fat Man felt a sharp pain slice his throat. His head slammed against the elevator wall. The sounds that registered in his mind told him that the crackle of cartilage was from the razor edge of the man's hand, not a knife.

As his knees hit the floor, blood filled with particles of white he'd coughed up splashed in front of him. He felt his body teeter and begin to fall forward, but it was halted by his enemy's strong arms, which wrapped around his head like an octopus. In a fraction of a second Peterson felt the hands tighten and twist. The crack that shot through his mind sounded like a dry tree limb snapping.

His eyes were open when his head hit the floor of the elevator, but everything seemed strange. There was no pain, yet he knew he was dying. His body was cold, completely numb, as if it had been frozen. His last thought before he died was that he was the King. How could this happen to the King? Who would do this to the King? Not Hogan?

His eyes wouldn't move, but they focused on a twenty-dollar gold piece not three inches from his head. The gold piece sat like a shiny island in a red sea of his own blood. He wanted to hold the gold coin, but his hands just quivered. The island of Blood-Gold began to fade as the lights dimmed and blackness took over his mind.

The last thing he heard before he died was, "Regards from Bo Lynch and 'Hawk' Hogan, Mr. Laundry Man."

* * *

Tony leaned his face up against the cold window again and rolled it from side to side. His eyes closed; the drink slipped from his hand to the plush rug, unnoticed.

424

Heavy rain deluged the city, and lights along the Chicago skyline dotted the darkness. Although it was distorted through the thick wet glass, Tony thought the city was pretty at night. He felt better. The booze and dope were well on their way to sending him into to the colored dreams of sweet delirium. He'd finish the bottle of scotch, snort a little more cocaine, and sack out here tonight. Everything was going to be all right. He'd take a long vacation. The night waves of the Islands swirled in his mind as he turned and slid to the floor. He could feel the warm ocean water wash over him, and he could taste its salt. A scrim of dreamy magic covered him, and he closed his eyes. He would rest for a moment.

In his semi-conscious state he sensed a presence in the room. His words were slurred. "Karl, that you?" His eyes remained closed. There was no answer, no sense of motion in the room, just the presence, and it was closer, standing over him.

His drugged mind tried to separate the real from the onslaught of crooked dreams that smoked through his brain. "Who's here? That you, Karl?" he asked again. Without warning, his head was snapped back and something was placed on his mouth. Instantly, he felt a piercing pain on the left side of his head that pricked his senses alive. A muffled scream rushed through the black caverns of his mind. He realized the scream had come from himself, and he opened his eyes. Was this a bad dream? Where was he? It had to be a dream! A nightmare!

There was a flow of warm fluid running down his cheek onto his silk shirt. The pain grew stronger, as did his senses. He felt the side of his face and knew the warm fluid was blood. He pushed himself to a sitting position and looked down at his hand. It was soaked with a dark, thick fluid. His hand moved back to his face, this time higher, and horror shot through his body when he realized the blood was coming from the area of his head where his left ear used to be. Another scream; again it was muffled.

He felt sick and began to retch, but his mouth wouldn't open. It--it was taped shut. Slowly, with what little consciousness he had left, he raised his head to see the blurred figure of a black giant. Deep, drugged voices of his soul told him that his world was about to come to an end and there was nothing he could do about it; he couldn't even offer money. He began to choke on his own vomit, and he felt tears running down his cheeks. Please, don't hurt me. Another pain shook his body; he knew his right ear had been severed; then something was placed over his head and tied tight around his neck. It must have been plastic. The blue, warm waters of the Caribbean that moments before had flowed over his tired body were replaced with the black flood of death. His mind began to drift downward into a dark abyss. The plastic sack was filling with blood and tears. His choking and lack of air were bringing on his own death.

Why? Why was he dying? Why were they killing him? He felt a spasm rock his body as something sharp entered his neck. His mind went blank. The dark waters stopped flowing. The rain stopped falling. His body stopped working. Tony Zitello was dead.

* * *

Seven minutes after Tony Zitello, Karl Peterson and his two bodyguards were eliminated, a black giant and a tall man wearing a Cubs baseball cap lifted two yellow laundry carts into a white van parked on the side street just west of the Exchange. Both men followed the dirty laundry into the back of the van and closed the doors behind them. A tape was slipped into the cassette player on the dashboard, and Louis Armstrong put the words to the tune the black man was humming. "Mac the Knife" seemed to echo through the dismal streets of Chicago as the van began to move slowly. Turning east on Jackson, it crept down the wet street and into traffic like a white cat. Fierce rain slashed down on the cold city, trying in vain to cleanse its sins away, and the music played on:

> *...Oh the shark bites, with his teeth, dear, and he*
> *shows them pearly whites...*

FORTY-FIVE

The Ninth Bullet

Pete's mouth felt like paste and tasted of sour coffee. His quick eyes and photographic mind reviewed, categorized, and filed over three thousand pages of the agents' reports. He had listened to thirty hours of incriminating tape conversations. He had also played back the tapes containing his own illegal deal-making with the eight brokers who were going to give him twenty cents on the dollar for his multimillion-dollar, bogus tax loss. There was no doubt that the balance had tipped. The doom of the commodity brokers was now in his hands.

He rubbed his tired eyes. They felt like sandpaper. He shook his head and asked himself the question: human nature?--No, just rationalized, donkey greed, he thought.

During the crash in the market, the commodity system of trading, which had been nurtured for decades to become a confusing network of genius client fraud, had broken down momentarily to become simple, obvious theft, and he and his agents had been there to slip the noose over the brokers' heads. The precaution and use of intermediary bagmen to move laundered and skimmed money to clean accounts had been ignored. As the market swings increased, he saw how the panic had taken over and all discipline eroded.

That was what usually happened to novice crooks. If a man's hand wasn't slapped early in his career as a thief, his reach would eventually extend beyond his grasp; all caution would be abandoned, and his hand would be cut off. A professional crook never deviated from his method of operation if it worked and kept him out of jail. The problem with most of the broker groups under investigation was that they had rationalized their behavior for so long that skimming from customer orders, tax evasion, and general bogus trading procedures had become an accepted way of life. Unlike a true con-man, the brokers had no back door to escape through. Pete had never met a professional thief, caught in the act, who said, "Gee, I didn't know I was doing anything wrong." He would bet a year's pay that when the brokers were read their rights, they would merely say, "I didn't know I was doing anything wrong. Everybody does it!"

Pete struggled against his own misgivings. A lot of nice guys were going to be indicted. Guys who were not, in the true sense of the word, crooks. If the Exchange officials hadn't been corrupt themselves, maybe these guys would have played the game straight and probably been able to make as much money as they were stealing. Except for the boys who worked for the mob. They bagged and cleaned more money than the mind could comprehend. They were the slime he was after, and they were the ones he would get.

He leaned forward, closed his eyes, and cradled his forehead in his palms. He remembered Max Leonard's words, *"We make our own rules down here--we are the law."* He had poor Max by the balls. And Pete knew when that happened, the mind and body were soon to follow. Max was one of a number of brokers who were buying the phony tax losses from Pete and paying him under the table or with skim money. They had also used Pete, Pete Alexander, as a bagman, slipping him points from customer orders as a down payment for the tax scam. None of the money would come from their own pockets.

He whispered to himself, as if Max were sitting next to him, "Son of a bitch, Max. You can make three, four hundred thousand a year legally. Why can't you be satisfied with that? Why don't you take the twenty cents on the dollar you're giving me, get a good tax attorney, and pay a few bucks to the IRS instead of going down the crooked road? Dumb bastard. Been cheating so long you don't even know it's cheating."

Pete looked at his watch. 7:26 a.m. Another night without sleep. He had scheduled himself to watch the soybean pit today and wondered if he could trust himself to doze for an hour. He decided against it. Once his head hit the pillow, he'd be gone for at least three hours.

He stood and stretched, walked to the bathroom, took a long drink of water, and splashed cold water on his face, feeling the stubble of whiskers. The image staring from the mirror revealed a tired, pale face with blue eyes. The whites around the eyes were laced with thin, red webbing. Gray lines spread from their corners. "And I thought this was going to be easy. I'd rather be blowing drug dealers' brains out on the streets of New York than busting guys like Max." Befriend and betray, he thought to himself.

A sharp blast from the phone snapped Pete's head in the direction of the kitchenette. He wiped his face as he walked toward the phone. He grabbed it on the second ring. He sensed fear in the shaky voice. "Pete, this is Samantha!"

He paused. She was supposed to contact him by phone only in extreme emergencies. "Is your phone clean, Sam?" He should know better, she was a professional, but panic brought on carelessness, and he sensed trouble.

Her voice was controlled; nevertheless, he heard the tremor. "I'm in the lobby of the Exchange at a pay phone. I've been calling all over for you. He's gone, Pete. So is Zitello, so are his two bodyguards. Their personal office doors were wide open, usually locked..."

An alarm went off inside him. "Hold on, Sam. Slow down. Who's gone? What office doors?"

Silence. He could tell she was trying to pull herself together. "Peterson, Zitello, Schmidt, and Wolf have not shown up for work. I arrive early every morning--about four thirty, to field and record calls. It's about the only time I have to snoop around. Peterson is usually here by five thirty with his two ginzos, and Zitello has been sleeping in his office for the past month like a drugged hermit. He comes out during market hours and returns

at closing. He's been an emotional mess since Bo Lynch started pushing him around in the pit, and he's heavy, *real* heavy, into cocaine."

Pete's words were calm. His head was clear. "Hold on, Sam. Maybe they're all just out for breakfast, or took a day off, or..."

She interrupted abruptly and said emphatically, "Pete! They are gone! There is something happening that we know nothing about. When I arrived this morning I checked Peterson's and Zitello's offices. Both doors were wide open. They are always locked. Lights were on where they shouldn't be, and both safes were standing wide open and empty, like somebody was in a hurry or just didn't care who noticed."

His mind quickly computed, calculated, and dissected the vague information, but it came up blank. "Maybe they were skimming too much from the mob and the mob took 'em for a ride."

Samantha's voice came quick, with more control. "Not a chance, Pete. Conti is already in the office, and he's frantic. The first thing he did was call Ruzzo. He's on his way in from Lake Geneva. Jake Edwards is in Miami, waiting to hear further from Conti. Apparently, Conti received a phone call last night telling him his laundry operation had been closed down at the Exchanges. I heard him relay that much to Edwards before he shut the office door."

Pete rubbed his temples. "Maybe they just sensed trouble and got the hell out. Maybe one of our people showed their hand and they ran for cover."

Samantha had the answers. "I doubt it. The consequences for running from the mob are too great. Besides, Peterson's too obsessed with the need for power to run, and he's too smart to take Zitello and his two buffoons with him even if he did split."

"Pete," Samantha said softly, "one other thing. There were blood stains in Zitello's office."

Pete felt his forehead furrow as he said, "Blood stains?"

"Yes, on the rug near one of the windows; not much and not very noticeable, but I'm sure it was blood. It looked like it might have been diluted, probably with a spilled glass of scotch."

Pete scratched his head with his free hand and tried to tie together what he was hearing. It didn't make sense. He spoke quickly. "I need more information, Sam."

"Pete, there was an empty bottle of scotch plus a fresh bottle on the bar and two tumblers. One tumbler was on the coffee table; the other was on the floor by the window, next to the stain. I grabbed both glasses and dabbed at the stain with my handkerchief for the lab before anybody showed up this morning."

"Any signs of a struggle?"

"None. Zitello's office is always a mess, but there was no apparent sign of a fight."

He said hopefully, "The room was bugged wasn't it?"

She popped back, "Bugged with the best equipment we have, K-23's, direct from CIA headquarters. Real, hi-tech, spy toys!"

"Never heard of a K-23--must be the new kid on the block. Go on."

He heard her sigh. "I hid four microphones where even you couldn't find them. All K-23's, all smaller than an eraser head. No wires, no batteries, just a tiny microwave transmitter that bounces voice vibrations from Zitello's office to a receiver I hid behind the bottled-water dispenser outside of his office. I pick up the tape every night and send it to the lab, where they decode and reproduce every word spoken in the office. I did the same in Peterson's office."

"And? Did you get anything?"

Pete heard her blow through her lips as if trying to catch her breath; then she spoke in a frustrated tone. "Pete, only the most sensitive detector could pick up the place where the K-23's were hidden. All four microphones had been detected and sprayed with some kind of polyurethane. Any conversation in Zitello's office after the spray job will be lost to us."

He felt a jab of irritation. "Jesus Christ, talk about a clean sweep. Who are we dealing with, our own people?"

"I don't know who's playing games with us, Peter, but whoever it is, they're clean, fast, and invisible. I'm scared to death."

She waited for instructions, but Pete's mind was unable to come up with any answers. "Okay, Sam. Go on back to work and just do your job. Act normal and see if you sense any further panic develop. If Peterson or Zitello show up, get to me A.S.A.P."

For a while she considered, then she gave him a half question. "If they didn't take off on their own, and if the mob had nothing to do with it, do you think...?" Then she stopped before she went on. "Do you think Michael?...I mean Hogan, uh...?"

Creases angled in toward the corner of his eyes as he finished the sentence for her, "Do I think Michael could have had anything to do with their disappearance?"

He could read Samantha like a neon billboard. He had seen her flush when Michael's name was mentioned in conversation. She was crazy about the shrewd Irishman. On the other hand, when Sam's name came up in talking to Michael, he had been as cool as fresh snow, always business. Pete had trouble reading Michael but remembered the occasional flow of ice cross his face. That scared him.

"Sam, I don't know what to think. I don't even know if the four jerks are even missing. As far as Mike goes, I believe he could and would do most anything to combat what he considers to be evil forces or a threat on his life. I believe he is capable of accomplishing almost anything he sets out to accomplish. He's like water. He seems to be able to emotionally and psychologically seek the same level that surrounds him. If he's in a high-pressure situation, he tunes himself to the pitch of the pressure. If he is in a casual atmosphere, he levels off on that plateau. If he is in a violent situation, he responds as such, and--I imagine when he is in a loving situation, he flows with nature."

Samantha's silence revealed more to Pete than if she had spoken. "Sam, call me here on your lunch break. Let me know what's going on up there. I'll talk to Michael and see if he can give me any clues as to what's going on--if anything really is going on. He's honest with me. Don't call Lorenzo or Simpson. If need be I'll make those calls. The police haven't been notified, have they?"

Her voice was almost tinged with sarcasm. "Are you kidding? They want nothing to do with cops. There would be too many questions. Conti will sweep this away before the weekend if there is a problem. I'll call you at noon."

His mind was sorting and filing quickly now. "Be careful, Sam. If Conti or Ruzzo feel caged, they'll snap out, so be on guard."

Pete spoke to Samantha slowly, feeling his way. She confided in him, and he needed her support. He also needed Michael's trust. He walked around the small kitchenette area with the phone and sat at one of the bar stools that cozied up to the counter. "Sam, I want you to listen to me as a friend and confidant." He hesitated, not sure if he should even open his mouth. Then, he decided there was too much at stake not to speak his piece. "We have a terrific investigation going here, and we are going to land a lot of big fish as long as we keep our heads and our emotions on line with the way we were trained."

How was he going to be subtle about what he was about to say? "We are putting years into this project and have already uncovered more than we anticipated. I have become very close to Michael. He is a good man, honest, strong, and unusually cunning."

Samantha's voice had taken on a different pitch. Pete heard the tremor return. "What's your point?"

He took the phone from his ear for a brief second, leaned his head back in thought, then said, "My point is that he is also dangerous. I don't mean to you or me, but the man is becoming stronger by the day. He has a terrific amount of money behind him now. He has soldiers who are dedicated to him and can get his hands on hundreds more, and he is revered by thousands. Politically, his new partner, Sam Ross, can pull almost any string he needs in Washington, and knowing Michael, it won't take him long to move into the same circles as Ross. In his own suave way, it's just a matter of time before he woos the allegiance of honest politicians. He is becoming as strong as a Mafia don with the big exception that he gives without reservation and he makes his money legally. Sam, he has the ability to heal good people--and he has the ability to kill bad people."

Samantha interrupted, her voice spiced with irritation. "And you call that dangerous, Pete? If that's dangerous, I'd like to know a few more men like Michael."

Pete felt his own mind somersault with confusion. "Sam, I've never known a wealthy, powerful man who wasn't dangerous."

Her sharpness cut through the phone. "Well, maybe you are about to meet one, Pete. Michael will only strike out at people who threaten his family, his friends, and lastly himself. He doesn't go looking for trouble. He doesn't take from or exploit people; he

gives to them. No wonder he is gaining popularity and strength." She slowed, then said almost in a whisper. "He's a very unusual man, Pete!"

Pete's counsel was falling on deaf ears. He backed up the conversation. "Okay, Sam. I agree. He is a great guy, and you are right. I've never met anybody quite like him either. Just watch your personal attachment to the man."

Her words had bite. "Is that professional, FBI advice, or friendly advice?"

"Both. I want the two of you safe and sound when the gunfire stops. Enough about Michael. Is there anything else?"

He knew her mind was still on Michael. Her voice was controlled, almost tight. "Yes, one more thing."

He looked at his watch. 8:05. "What is it?"

"I'm not sure if it's anything, but Colleen said Ruzzo walked in on her the other night when she was working on their main computer. She was pulling out client names and accounts and searching for holding companies which accepted laundered trades. She said he was furious with her for tampering. She told him she had been instructed to check the computer every night for proper menu readouts by the computer company because it had been jamming up."

Pete gritted his teeth and swore to himself, remembering the granite warning Michael had delivered to both Simpson and Lorenzo if anything happened to either Samantha or Colleen. He asked, "Did Ruzzo believe her?"

Her voice had lost its sharp edge. "No, Ruzzo called the computer company the next morning and one of our men, Vince Angeleri, was alerted. He intercepted the call and assured Ruzzo that Colleen had been instructed to do just that."

"And?"

"And, that's it. Nothing else has been mentioned, but she's damn scared of Ruzzo now that she's aroused his suspicion. And Pete, he's a mean bastard! I guess he roughed her up a little."

"She's okay?"

"He just slapped her a few times. She's fine. Just scared."

Pete hugged the phone between his right shoulder and cheek as his mind worked fast. He reached over on the counter top for his new .45 Magnum. He pinched his lower lip with his teeth as he popped the special clip holding eight bullets and pulled on the breech, releasing the ninth bullet. "Son of a bitch. I think we had better pull her out."

She didn't hesitate. "No, not yet Pete. She said she is just about there. She has broken a number of the codes and should have read-outs within a week or two."

He checked the clip and slammed it back into the butt end of the gun, checked the safety, and placed it gently back on the counter. He had a gut feeling he would be back in action soon. "I don't give a shit about Peterson and Zitello, but if anything happened to either of you two, I'd..."

"Don't worry about us. She'll be okay. She was just shaken by the incident. They still have no idea who I am. I have to go now, or I'm going to be missed. Talk to you around noon."

"You be careful, Sam. I'm going to take my attention off Michael and put it on Colleen until she's out of there."

"No, Pete, don't do that. I'll call the central office and have another agent keep an eye on her. Michael needs you."

He felt a flash of panic. "NO! Don't do that, I don't want Simpson or Lorenzo to know there is any trouble. I'd rather pull her out today, or watch her myself."

Her voice was suspicious. "What's your hangup with Simpson and Lorenzo? That's not like you to fear what they think."

He stood the butt end of the .45's ninth bullet on the counter. He'd said enough. He thought he should end the conversation but added, "I'm afraid they'll panic if they find out either of you are in trouble."

"Panic! Why would two of the strongest men in government panic because one of their female agents is getting a little heat?"

He scratched his head and said, "Sam, Hogan told them that he was holding them personally responsible for both yours and Colleen's safety. If anything happened to either of you, because of their indiscretion in placing you in a dangerous situation, he would deal with them. By now they know he's a man of his word. Instead of four missing people, you can add two politicians to the list. So, keep a lid on this until we get Colleen out of there."

Her voice took on a edge of admiration, and she laughed heartily. "Michael told them that?"

"You know how he can be with words. It wasn't a statement or a threat, Sam. It was more like a promise. He was very clear about everything. He didn't approve of you working close to Peterson. He didn't approve of Colleen working close to Conti and Ruzzo."

She laughed again. "I guess I should be mad at the chauvinist beast, but I'm not. Does he think we spent two years of FBI training to sell lingerie at Sears? He doesn't have much faith in lady FBI agents, does he?"

Pete stared at the thick bullet. "I really don't know what Michael thinks or how he thinks. I do know he doesn't trust anybody but himself and a handful of men around him. I would like to think that I would be included in that handful."

The other end of the phone suddenly went silent. Pete figured Samantha probably had the same wish. Then she spoke quietly, with reservation. "I...I have to go Pete. I'll call you later."

Pete held the phone in his hand for a moment, then placed it back on the receiver. He picked up the powerful new .45, released the safety, slid the bridge back then forward, allowing a bullet from the clip to enter the chamber. He then pushed a tiny button on the side of the weapon and the clip slid out. He took the ninth bullet from the counter and

pushed it into the clip to replace the chambered bullet. He said to himself, "If a cat has nine lives, I may need you, number nine."

FORTY-SIX

The Clouded Sun

Michael picked up the large manila envelope that sat on the edge of his desk. The big black letters read, **MICHAEL HOGAN-PERSONAL AND CONFIDENTIAL**, the words *personal* and *confidential* highlighted and circled in red. He threw it back on the desk; he would get to it after the close of the market.

The market was about to open; 8:13 a.m. He grabbed his kelly-green trading jacket and was headed out of his office when the phone rang. He halted for a short moment, deciding whether to go back and answer the call or continue on. Then he realized it was his private line to which only Lewis, Ross, Glassmann, Maria, Bo, and Samantha had the number. A brief look at his watch told him he had a few seconds. He quickly returned to his desk and grabbed the phone.

"Hogan here!"

Pete's voice was stern, and Michael immediately sensed something was wrong. "Mike, I'll just keep you a moment, but I have to know something."

Michael raised his head to the golden streaks of sunshine that had briefly cut holes through the rain clouds that had shrouded the city for a week, then he sat on the edge of his desk. "What's up, Pete?"

A moment's pause wasn't like Pete. He was usually quick and to the point. "Where were you last night, Mike?"

His lips pursed and he said, "I was with you until nine, Amigo, then I went home. Ask Charlie Taft. I think he is finally able to keep up with me."

"You didn't go out after that?"

He felt his eyebrows arch. "I had no reason to go out."

Another quick question. "Any phone calls?"

"Sure I had phone calls, and a long swim, and a walk on the beach, and popcorn, and a few cans of beer, and a nice evening with my family--for a change. Why the third degree? And why aren't you in the soybean pit?"

He heard Pete's voice turn up a notch. "Forget the bean pit for a minute. Samantha called me and said Peterson, his two men, and Zitello are missing. Do you know anything about that?"

Michael watched the rising sun as it played peekaboo through the tall metal buildings and dark clouds. He placed his trading jacket on the desk next to the manila envelope and walked around to his chair. "What do you mean missing?"

435

"That's just what she said, 'missing.' They're usually there early in the morning, and there has been no sign of them today. She also found blood spots in Zitello's office, both Peterson and Zitello's office doors were wide open, as were their empty safes."

Michael reached over a pile of papers and the morning *Journal* and picked up the sealed envelope that had been placed on his desk sometime during the night. He held it in front of him, weighing its contents with one hand, then he began to open it. "Maybe they all just decided to take a vacation."

Another snap from Pete. "BULLSHIT, vacation. Samantha said Conti is running around like a crazy man quizzing everybody regarding their whereabouts, and if they had seen anything unusual."

Michael replied bitingly, "So who gives a shit?" He emptied the contents of the large envelope onto his desk. What he saw stopped the breath in his throat as though a valve had been turned off in his lungs: a large diamond ring and three twenty-dollar gold pieces, he recognized as Peterson's; four Rolex watches, one heavy with diamonds; four grotesque Polaroid pictures of Peterson, Zitello, Schmidt, and Wolf, all dead, all without ears; at least five hundred thousand in cash; two address books, and numerous bank statements from dozens of American and Canadian accounts. His dogs had gone hunting during the night and brought him back a bone. "Jesus Christ!" He thought he said this to himself.

"Mike, 'Jesus Christ' what? Do you have any clues? Any ideas?"

He gathered his thoughts quickly. "Yeah, Pete, Yeah."

"You do?"

He corrected himself immediately, "No, no clues." His mind worked fast, not wanting to lie to Lewis. "I'm uh...just thinking about the market. As of the moment you called me I had no knowledge of anything concerning the matter. Let me do some checking, and I'll call you back."

"Mike, this could mean my job if their disappearance is in any way connected to you..." Then he said sarcastically, "for whom I am supposed to watch and be responsible?"

Michael turned the Rolex watches in his free hand. Dried blood covered the gold bands and crystals. He felt a coldness flow through him at the thought of Peterson.

His speech slowed as if he were drugged. "You afraid that Simpson will retire you, Pete?"

Pete blazed back, "Retire, my ass. I'm history if there is trouble in the Windy City. Any trouble at all. I'm the coordinator of the investigation, and you know as well as I that Simpson is just waiting for me to screw up."

Michael was mesmerized by the small, dead fortune that lay motionless in front of him. He pushed one of the gold coins with his fingernail, and for a split second he remembered the sliding noise they used to make as Peterson obsessively slid them back and forth in his meaty hand. He pushed the heavy coin again, saying silently to himself, "Al Josephson, that's for you." He pushed another coin. "Tim O'Neal, that's for you." And

a third coin slid on the desk with the flick of Michael's finger and fell to the floor. He imagined the coin falling into the fires of hell. "Fat Man, these coins will melt fast where you're going."

He resurfaced from his inner thoughts. His words were soft. "Pete, I hope Simpson shit-cans you."

Frustration echoed through the phone. "Thanks, Mike, my good friend. Fifteen years of five-star undercover work down the drain because of some fat thief in Chicago and a few dumb-ass commodity brokers."

His attention not on Pete, he continued to toy with the envelope's contents on his desk. He touched the five tightly wrapped packets of money and ran his thumb up the side of one stack of bills, revealing a blurred one hundred as the bills flapped by like a cartoon in slow motion.

He felt calm, relaxed. No more Peterson? He couldn't believe it. It had all happened so quickly he hadn't had time to analyze it, and he was in no hurry to do so. All he knew was that four evil men were no longer living. He said quietly, "If Simpson fires you, you can work for me, Pete. I think I'm going to need a good in-house attorney."

Pete's words were sudden and raw and very angry. "TALK TO ME, MIKE! You sound like you've been smoking pot. Stop playing with my head."

Michael pushed the trinkets of death aside and returned his attention to Pete. "Sorry, Pete, I'm not fucking with you on purpose. I'm serious. If Asshole fires you, you come and work with me. You know you're getting sick of playing cops and robbers. I can see it in your face. The burnout time for a good cop has got to be about the same as it is for a good pit broker. It's time for both of us to run our business from a desk. Besides, we are after the same thing."

"Yeah? What's that, Mike?"

Michael pondered a moment, then he said, "The truth! A just way of life! Satisfaction and reward for a day's work! Picking up someone else's litter from the streets. Picking someone up out of the gutter and brushing him off. A family life, or girl friend. Someone you can share your life with, your ideas, your fantasies--your love."

"You have that, Mike?"

A brief sense of sad realism flowed through him, and his eyes dropped to the edge of his desk. "Yeah, Pete. I have all that, right at my fingertips, but I don't take advantage of it--and that's my fault. I'm always looking for another mountain to climb, and life goes by as I make plans to scale another mountain wall."

"Well," Pete, now calmed, said, "maybe we should both climb the rest of this mountain and sit for awhile and enjoy the view."

"That sounds enticing. You know, I've always watched my footing as I climb but seldom stop to see the beauty. Maybe we should round up as many bad guys as we can right now, and get the rest from behind a big, white desk perched on the top of the mountain."

Pete, his words tempered now, sighed into the phone. "I don't know if either of us can ever change much, Mike. Once a mountain lion, always a mountain lion. But it sounds like a good idea. We'll explore it further after we catch a few of the bad guys. Call me if you get any word on Peterson and Zitello. I'll be at the condo. I'm passing on the bean pit today until I find out what's going on."

The phone was quiet for a moment; then Pete spoke. "I'll be honest with you--give me your word..."

Michael shrugged. "I've always been honest with you."

Irritation shot through the phone as Pete yelled, "You *haven't* always been honest with me."

Michael was patient, even amused. "Yes I have."

"You don't always tell me all you know or what your next move is going to be," Pete answered.

Michael pursed his lips and looked at the mouthpiece of the phone. "You're not my boss, or my wife, or my mom, or God. You're my friend who I met six months ago and you work for the government who I don't trust any farther than I can pee. It's not you I don't trust, Pete. It's your superiors, and you're required to report everything you see and hear to them. I give you what you need for the investigation, and you act on that. It's your case, and it should earn you a citation rather than a demotion. You deal with pompous, political, self-serving bastards. If you think for one moment I want them knowing my personal business, you're goofy. You take care of the investigation, the indictments, the trials, the plea bargaining, and I'm going to get the guys you miss, just the mean ones, not the little guys. Now, that is something I haven't told you."

In a mocking voice Pete fired back, "You going to take care of guys like Peterson and Zitello and Schmidt and Wolf? Do we have a new cowboy in town? A new vigilante? How are you going to be sure they are guilty?"

Michael said, "It's their call. I'll deal with anybody at anytime playing by their rules on their turf. I'll know they are guilty the same way you know the New York drug dealers are guilty when they laugh at you on their way out of court because some unethical, unscrupulous lawyer is able to make a mockery of our justice system by twisting a few ambiguous laws. Give me a break, Pete. I know the guilty ones!"

"Well, it's a real pleasure knowing the next John Wayne."

Michael looked at the stack of money and smiled. He knew Pete agreed with him because of his frustrations with the spineless court system in New York, which mirrored the rest of the country. But he was still a cop and had to stick up for what he had been conditioned for. And that certainly wasn't letting Michael Hogan go out and seek justice on his own.

When he didn't speak, Pete went on. "Okay. You told me something about your intentions, now I'll tell you something I know, but you have to promise me you won't get excited and that you'll let me handle it my way."

Michael readjusted in his chair and gathered his face into a frown. "What do you have?"

"Your word first. You won't interfere!"

"You have my word, no interference."

Michael felt a creeping uneasiness flow through him. "Samantha said Colleen may be in a bit of a jam with Ruzzo."

"What kind of jam?"

"It seems Ruzzo caught her playing with their private computer late one night. She was searching for the codes that would bring up information to nail their asses: phony bank accounts, trading accounts, holding companies, foreign and domestic assets, names, addresses..."

Michael's voice lifted in a shout. "Get them the fuck out, Pete, I mean it."

"Colleen just wants another week, Mike."

"She doesn't have that long. I know how they think and act." He felt his own panic begin to swell in his mind. "Get both the girls out, Pete. If Colleen had a run-in with Ruzzo, and if Peterson is missing, things are going to get goddamn hot around those offices, and everybody will be suspect. You don't know them like I do. They'll kill her, Pete."

A long sigh told him Pete had other ideas. "I'm going to have to take my attention off of you for a short time and keep an eye on Colleen until I can get her out."

Michael shouted, "Get her out now!"

Pete's defense surfaced quickly. "I can't, Mike, Simpson has to pull her out. Any change in tactics goes through him along with my blessing, Lorenzo's two cents, and Colleen's agreement. It's called protocol."

Michael's lips were tight as he pronounced each word emphatically, through clenched teeth. "I don't give a rat's ass about *protocol*. The girl is in danger; both girls are in danger. I'm sure Ruzzo knows that the two of them room together at Sandburg Village condos, and if he doesn't, it won't take him long to put two and two together and find out."

"Mike, take it easy, I'll get them out, Colleen first. It's just going to take a few days. Both girls have been trained for situations like this, they will be all right. Trust me!"

Michael couldn't think straight when he was angry; nobody could, but he knew it. "Pete, this has nothing to do with *trust*. You can stick their FBI training in your ass. You can't snip the wings of a canary, put it in a cage with a hungry cobra, and expect it to survive."

"Okay, I'll get her out as soon as I can. You'll be on your own for a few days, just you and Charley Taft. Watch yourself."

"Don't worry about me. I'm better off alone than with Charley Taft; besides, I have Lynch to hold hands with if I think I need company. Just get those two beauty queens out of danger." He brought the phone close to his mouth and spoke through his teeth. "And

another thing--if Simpson gives you any shit, you can tell the arrogant son of a bitch that if anything happens to either Colleen or Samantha, I will come to Washington and castrate the self-righteous bastard--then I'll kill him. AND YOU KNOW I MEAN IT!

Michael knew that would end the conversation. His last comment had shaken an already-nervous Pete "Alexander" Lewis.

"And this assignment was supposed to be a piece of cake. It's a goddamn punishment. I'll call you later, Mike, and take it easy. Remember, no interference."

"You have my word." Michael hung up the phone and swung around in his chair to gaze at the rising sun. Heavy, dark clouds were beginning to hush the morning light. Another gloomy day was about to descend upon Chicago.

Michael whirled in his chair and picked up the trading-floor phone. A female voice answered. "Nancy, give all my orders to Ned White. I'm not coming in today." Without giving an explanation, he hung up and turned again to stare at the gray city, to clear his mind, to think and to plan.

FORTY-SEVEN

Swift Justice

"Evil flourishes when good men do nothing." The words played over and over in his mind.

Michael stared at the large manila envelope and the contents that lay in front of it. How swift, he thought. In what he estimated took only minutes, four evil men had been eliminated. The government would have taken years and millions of dollars of taxpayers' money to bring these men to justice. Michael was sure the attorneys, who would have been paid millions, would have struck deals to get the four scum off with little or no punishment. That presupposed that they would even be caught and judged at all. How swift was the justice of the sword, the justice of the streets to men who were beyond redemption.

He remembered the arguments of his father and grandfather. His father would sit calmly smoking his pipe, speaking with a soft voice defending the legal systems and the power of negotiation. Michael was a little boy, but remembered looking through the slats of the stairway and seeing his grandfather's red face, pulsating with anger and pointing his finger at his son, Michael's father, swearing that, "Violence begets violence, and the only way to rid a neighborhood of mad dogs is to kill them, not talk to them!"

He remembered how his own eyes bulged with fear as his grandfather stood and took out a small, black gun from his dark wool jacket and shook it in front of his father, saying with his thick Irish brogue, "Patrick, this is the only justice for us. This is swift justice. Justice that lasts forever. Words won't win our war, my visionary son."

Now, Michael rested his head back on the tufted pillow of his chair and closed his eyes. He found all of his emotions agreeable, calm and relaxed. The picture of Patrick and Martin Hogan arguing in the small room below where he hid on the stairs took form like a photographer's picture as if it had been pulled from the final phase of processing. Dripping from the water wash, the picture slowly appeared. He could see his mother's floral shawl neatly hung by the door, the glow of the crackling fire, the bottle of brown whiskey with no label sitting on a small, round table. He could see the intensity in his grandfather's eyes and could smell the sweet cherry smoke of his father's pipe and his thin face which never lost its calm.

The picture faded as the intercom buzzed, pulling him back to the present. He reached over and pressed the red button. "Yes, Margaret?"

A jovial voice announced, "Mr. Hogan, Mr. Bo Lynch has arrived. He said you are expecting him."

"Yes, Margaret. I called for him. Send him in, please."

He released the red button. His mind still trying to pull itself from the past. "Violence begets violence. The only way you rid a neighborhood of mad dogs is to kill them, not talk to them!" He agreed with his grandfather, and his own plan was beginning to take form.

The knock came with false authority, and Bo entered the office, head down, as if he were looking for something on the floor. As usual he had a two days' growth of beard, and his brush-cut hair was longer than usual. He still wore his trading jacket, no tie, a tan cotton shirt, and what looked like a rather expensive pair of dark-brown slacks plus his usual grubby tennis shoes.

Michael smiled to himself. What a character. Instead of outfitting himself fully in one sitting, as Maria made sure Michael did, Bo would buy one new item at a time until he had a full outfit. By that time the first article of clothing would have to be replaced because of the time lapse in purchases.

Still looking for nothing on the floor, Bo asked, "You wanted to see me?"

Then he looked up. His eyes were solemn but determined, clear and alert. He was sober.

"Pot of coffee on the bar or Coke in the 'fridge'."

Bo closed the door and walked to the bar, where he poured three coffees into fourteen-ounce styrofoam cups.

Michael watched him pour four heaping teaspoons of sugar into two of the coffees and two teaspoons each of Coffee-Mate into the sugared coffee. He left one black. Corralling all three cups in his thick hands, he strolled to the desk. He placed the black coffee in front of Michael and set the other two on the manila envelope at the front edge of the desk. Then he sat down with a heavy grunt in an arm chair facing Michael.

He took a sip of one of his coffees and pulled his cheeks back at its heat, showing his neat, white teeth. Bo avoided Michael's stare. His eyes first looked to the ceiling, then out the window, and then to the desk. A stalking amusement mapped his face as he glared at the articles in front of him.

Michael watched him for a moment, missing nothing in Bo's expression and attitude. He asked cynically, "Two coffees, Bo?"

Bo looked down at the cups and shrugged. "If it's worth doing, it's worth overdoing. I don't do much of anything in moderation, Mike, you know that. If one's good, why not two or three?"

Michael toyed with a yellow chart pencil, pressing the eraser to his lips as he analyzed Bo and his nonchalant expression. Then he reached down with the end of the pencil and picked up a diamond-studded, blood-stained Rolex. He held it up in front of Bo by the thick, gold band. "Then again, if it's worth doing, why not do it in fours? I don't suppose you know anything about this?" he asked as he motioned to the articles on his desk.

Bo looked surprised, almost insulted. "Sure I do. I did it--*we* did it!"

Michael felt his own expression change to surprise at Bo's matter-of-fact honesty. He flipped the Rolex back on the desk, and it clunked with a heavy thud among the other three watches. "All four of them, Bo?"

He said with a sense of pride. "I told you, Mike. I have trouble with moderation, and I like to do things in even numbers. You know, two, four, six, eight, fifty, one hundred. It's kind of a fetish with me."

Michael picked up the four Polaroid pictures of the dead bodies. All four powder-gray faces had the same expression of surprise and death. "You killed them and stole the watches and the money and the gold coins?"

Bo sipped his coffee. "Stole, shit! We killed the fuckers. They won't be telling time or spending money anymore. The money and jewelry were a bonus. We just wanted the documents that were in the safes."

Michael's head moved ever so slightly, but he let the corners of his eyes glare at Bo. "Just like that? You killed them?"

Bo stared back at him, and his automatic response revealed an air of offensive conquest. "Just like that. It was self-defense!"

Michael placed the chart pencil back in a brass cup that housed a dozen others. He was amazed at Bo's casual response and questioned, "Self-defense?"

"Yeah, self-defense. They were going to come after you and me. They made that known. They bragged about it. We just hit them first. That's self-defense with a twist."

Michael spoke calmly. "A big twist. Do you think that taking out one slob underboss and three pawns is going to keep Conti and Ruzzo and Jake Edwards and God knows who else from coming after us?"

Bo reached over and pulled a pencil from the brass holder and stirred his coffee. "Hell, no, I don't. I know they'll come for us, but we sure as hell slowed down their aggression. For the first time in twenty years these assholes are trying to figure out what happened. They have no idea who did this. We buy time to see what their next move is going to be, and we temporarily close down their laundering operation. After you called me from the floor, Frank Hammer said Peterson's desk looked like a Chinese circus. None of the brokers wanted to handle the big orders. I think Raulf Hoge finally agreed to give it a try, but that moron can't count to ten without missing a few numbers. Zitello was their main man, and all the rest of their good brokers are swamped in the other pits."

Michael watched as Bo finished one coffee and started on the other. He lifted himself from his chair and went back to the bar. He spooned two more heaping teaspoons of sugar in the coffee, then lumbered back to his chair. "Are you upset, Mike?"

Michael ignored the question. He turned his chair slightly and rubbed his chin in thought. "What did you do with the bodies, Bo?"

"They're gone. You don't have to know the details."

Michael swiveled his chair and looked deep into Bo's eyes. A coldness ran through his body and was immediately replaced with the heat of anger. Their eyes met, and Bo's

cocky expression changed to one of caution. Then Michael snapped out: "Listen, as long I'm paying the rent and paying Snake and Bear a handsome salary, I expect to know what's going on. You guys are paid to protect my family and myself, not kill for me. I call the shots, all of them, not you!"

He saw that Bo was taken by surprise and had stopped in mid motion from taking another swallow of coffee. "We...we were protecting you, Mike. We didn't think you would go along with it."

Michael snapped back. "I've been honest with you from day one. I expect the same respect. If you can't give that to me, then get the fuck out of my life. Now where are the goddamn bodies? I'm not just curious; I have some planning to do myself."

Bo flinched and said, "What's left of them is on the floor of the lake, twenty miles off Kenosha."

"What do you mean, 'what's left of them'?"

Bo looked away. "They all left this world with a grenade in their mouths and their hands taped to their head. No head, no hands for identification. The fish will take care of the rest."

Michael sucked in some air around him and slowly shook his head. "Jesus Christ, Bo. You guys are brutal bastards."

Bo's wide shoulders drooped slightly. "You are wrong, Mike. We're sensitive guys. We have feelings. What we did was only business. They were bad men, and now they're gone. They were dead before they left the building. Since it was business, we were nice to them. They died quick. Had we been angry, we would have allowed them to experience the full horror of their death. That would have been personal. You weren't included because we wanted you to have an alibi in case anything went wrong, and we knew you would nix the idea. Those guys were garbage and did a hell of a lot worse things by selling dope and laundering money than we did by eliminating them."

Michael felt not so much anger as a terrible gulf of confusion about the whole ordeal. This was wrong, or at least he thought it was wrong, yet, very simply, justice had been served. His breathing was shallow, and he knew his stone look was beginning to bother Bo.

"How about your alibis, Bo?"

Bo relaxed again and shifted his body in the chair. "We have a hundred guys at Hill-112 who would vouch for our being there if we needed an alibi, but I really don't think an alibi will be necessary. No bodies, no evidence, no case!"

Michael felt his face muscles relax but still spoke in a stern tone. "You tell Moe and Curly that we are either a team and I'm the quarterback or to find another game. If I want a bad guy knocked out of the game, I'll make that decision, understood?"

Bo nodded his head yes. "Understood. Then you're not upset with what we did? You're just upset because we didn't tell you?"

Michael felt a warmth cross his face and knew Bo saw it. "No, I'm not upset. You were playing by their rules. Their laws. You just scored first. But it's not over. More will come."

"We know that, and we'll be ready for them."

"When they finally find out who's responsible, they'll probably hit the house, if they plan to get us all. I want something wired in the house that will alert me of any intrusion at the same time you are alerted. I'm in on the next play, Bo. It's my fight. You can help protect my family and watch my back, but I'm not going to hide under my bed while you're doing dirty work for me."

Bo opened his mouth to protest. Michael held one finger up. "Understand?"

Bo sat back and simply nodded.

"Okay, you better get back and give Hammer a hand in the pit, and while you're at it, both you and Frank give Raulf Hoge a tough time. Without Zitello, there is going to be complete havoc in the Peterson camp, and Hoge's mind works counter clockwise. Check and recheck trades made with him. Tell him you sold to him when you bought from him; tell him you bought when you sold; throw a raft of out-trades into him. Just rattle his cage. I'll call McGiven and have a few of his men do the same thing. I want them fucked up with bad trades for weeks."

Bo rose from the chair and stood, his face calm. "Anything else?"

Michael thought back to his conversation with Pete and hesitated before he spoke. He had given his word not to interfere.

"Maybe...I'm not sure yet."

Bo cocked his head. "What is it, Mike?"

"Colleen McFadden may be in some trouble with Ruzzo and Conti. She was caught fooling with the computer, and I know Winters will be watched closely because of Peterson's disappearance. They could be in trouble."

He saw Bo look down at him with a "so what?" look on his face. The two girls were the government's responsibility, but Bo kept his thoughts to himself. "Those broads better get their pretty asses to safe ground. You can bet Conti and Ruzzo will be looking over their whole staff. Both men are like scared rats right now, not to mention what they'll get from the big bosses. Both in Chicago and New York."

Michael rose and looked Bo in the eye as a brother would. "That's why I want you to keep the pressure on Peterson's pit brokers. You foul up their laundry operation for awhile, and they won't have time to look over their staff for a snitch. Maybe we can buy a week or two for Lewis so he can pull Colleen out of that office. I may have two of you guys keep your eyes on McFadden and Winters."

He saw the disapproval in Bo's expression. "For how long, Mike?"

"For as long as it takes."

Bo's strong face flushed with anger. "That's bullshit and you know it. Two of us are supposed to baby-sit a couple of federal broads? And how about watching the house? We can't be in two places at one time!"

"You leave Bear with me at the house, and I'll take care of everything else." He stopped and dropped his head in thought. "Bo, I have to think this thing through. Then I'll let you know exactly what to do. But I'm going to put you close to McFadden regardless."

Bo shook his head no but said, "Okay, pal, it's your call. I'll check in with you after the market." He started toward the door and turned. "Say, you wouldn't happen to have some chocolate around here, would you?"

"Chocolate?"

"Yeah, when a guy stops drinking he craves sweets to replace all the sugar that the booze had in it."

Michael smiled and opened the bottom drawer of his desk, where he found an old basket Margaret had given him the previous Easter. He rummaged through the green and pink fake grass and came up with a small bag of M & M's and a chocolate-covered Easter egg. He flipped them to Bo at the door. "Here. Go crazy!"

Bo showed a wide grin. "Great. Thanks. Later, Mike."

He grinned back. "Yeah, Bo. Later."

FORTY-EIGHT

Alone With Ghost's Eyes

The screeching tires sounded like alarms in Colleen's ears as she circled the concrete pillars of the underground parking lot in her gray '86 Cutlass. Thank God she was almost to her apartment, she thought. Damn! There must be a thousand parking stalls, and each level looked alike in the dim lighting. Where was the blue section?

She pushed the car forward, accelerating for a short stretch, then braking for the turns. Her eyes moved quickly from the black, rubberized concrete path to the rear-view mirror to the digital clock on the dashboard. 10:08 p.m.

Thank God! There was the first blue pillar. She made a sharp right, looked in the rear-view mirror one more time, and turned hard to the left into her parking stall. The car screeched to a halt, cockeyed in the parking space. She could hear her heart beating fast, and she was breathing as if she had just run up ten flights of stairs. Her hands were clammy, and she saw that they were shaking.

She pushed a few strands of auburn hair away from her eyes and rested her head on the steering wheel as she slipped the car into park and turned off the engine. She was getting paranoid. Ever since being caught by Sal Ruzzo in the computer room, she had been on edge.

Her head jerked up at the sound of another car. Her breath came faster as she looked over her left shoulder to see a green BMW move past her slowly. Her ears caught the sound of loud music and laughter as the green auto moved on. She sighed and closed her eyes. Come on, Colleen. Snap out of this. Nobody is after you, she assured herself, hesitantly and with deep-seated reservation.

"I did it," she whispered to herself. "I finally did it." She had broken the last code and pulled over fifty pages of criminal data from the computer. Not only would this break Ruzzo and Conti's backs and their organization, it would mean a nice promotion for her.

She checked the side mirror, opened the door of the Cutlass, and dragged her heavy briefcase and purse across the front seat. As she hurried to the elevator, she looked over her shoulder. She could hear protesting rubber against smooth concrete on another level, but she could see nobody behind her. Damn! Was her worry all in her head? She was sure she had been followed from the Exchange, but her mind had been scrambled lately, thinking there was a boogie man around every corner.

She pushed her hair back again and tucked it behind her ear, automatically half-glancing over her shoulder as she walked. A hot, steamy shower and a glass of white wine were what she needed. The automatic doors leading to the elevators opened in front of her.

The magnetic security key slipped in and turned easily, calling for an elevator. While she waited for the lift, she looked back through the glass doors and saw her own reflection. She looked a mess.

Turning back, she heard her voice echo in the small waiting area. "Come on. Come on." She hit the chrome doors with her left hand as if it made a difference to the patient, unperturbed speed of the elevator. Her eyes drifted with fake curiosity around the small hall. On the far wall, stenciled in blue letters, was the placard, "SANDBURG VILLAGE RESIDENTS ONLY." A pair of tube ashtrays stood as midget sentries between the elevators, and an antique bench had been bolted to the floor just inside the glass doors.

She closed her eyes and sighed with relief when she heard the ding of the oncoming elevators. The wide doors began to open, and she was about to step in when a rotund man with a wide, sardonic grin stumbled toward her with both hands outstretched. She screamed and jumped back, swinging her briefcase and purse in front of her. They caught only air.

"Hey, Baby," he said. "Don't be so hostile. Jus' going for a drink. Wanna come?"

Her fright now turned to disgust, and she pushed past the blubbering drunk. She felt like giving the burly sot a knee to the groin, but it wasn't his fault she was so keyed. She pushed floor 27 and leaned her head against a picture of Chicago's finest dining and shopping places, which hung tight to the wall.

She was alone in the elevator. *Alone*, she thought. What a terrible word. Being a computer wiz and trained cryptanalyst, she played with words. The word *alone* spelled backwards was *enola*. Scrambled another way it was *lonea* or *noela*. Three pretty words, names for little girls, but the word *alone* was a scary word, and how well she knew it.

The elevator stopped at the thirteenth floor, and she moved to the back and froze as the doors opened. A young couple entered. The man obviously saw alarm on her face and said, "Good evening," as he pressed floor 18. She remained silent until they stepped out on 18, then she let out a long exhalation of air. She was *alone* again.

She looked at her wristwatch. 10:17. Please be home tonight, Samantha. Don't stay at the Federal Building until 11:00. I need somebody to talk to. I'm so alone. I need someone.

The elevator bell sounded, and the red numbers above the door showed floor 27 as the doors slid open. Almost there, she said to herself.

She hurried out and down the long hallway, fumbling for the keys in her purse as she moved. As she walked, she blubbered nervously. "I'm not going back there. No way. I'm calling in sick tomorrow and never going back. I have all the information Simpson wants, and that's it."

She could smell the corruption and danger in the office. She remembered the meanness in Sal Ruzzo's eyes as he grabbed her in the computer room and slapped her

hard in the face. She could still feel the numbness in her right cheek. The man wanted to kill her. She wasn't going back.

How different this investigation was from Operation Graylord. Danger was almost non-existent with most of the judges and clerks. But Michael Hogan had been right. The FBI had underestimated the criminal activity at the Exchanges. They underestimated the amounts of money being stolen, the amounts of money being laundered, and they had grossly underestimated the dangerous men they were dealing with. Simpson should have given Hogan the manpower he asked for.

She turned the corner and headed for apartment 2742, halfway down another long hall. Her feet moved faster with each step. She felt her hair begin to fall into her eyes again, but she didn't bother to push it back. She would be safe in a moment.

She hoped Sam was home. She needed to talk. A barrage of negative thoughts assaulted, like piranhas ripping at her mind. Dammit, Colleen, act like an agent, not a schoolteacher. This is all part of the job and a job well done. She had all, and more, that Simpson would need for convictions. Major, RICO convictions.

She smiled nervously and a sense of pride flowed through her shaking body at the thought of what she was carrying in her briefcase. The names of banks, both foreign and domestic, bogus accounts, names, and addresses. She had even been able to pull out the names of over four hundred businesses where the laundered money had gone. Car washes, restaurants, bars, auto-repair shops, bakeries, pizza companies, tire companies, toy stores, dress shops, almost every type of business imaginable. She had the real-estate purchases that had been made during the past five years. Billions of dollars' worth. U.S. citizens were upset because the Japanese were buying up American real estate. If they only knew it was a fraction of what the Mafia owned and controlled. Simpson, Lorenzo, and probably she too went to Mafia-owned barbers and hairdressers.

Finally; she was standing, puffing heavily, in front of 2742. She automatically looked back down the hall; it was empty. Except for the slamming of a door a few corridors away, the hall was silent. The key trembled in her fingers as she inserted it in the bolt lock. There was no evidence of forced entry, she was relieved. She spoke the words silently. God, Samantha, be home.

As the door opened, she saw only an alley of light from the hall that lined itself through the apartment like a dim, straight road ending at blowing curtains that covered the sliding patio doors. Her figure was silhouetted in the stream of light.

Why was the patio door open? Had Samantha forgotten to close it? Had she herself forgotten to close it before she left this morning? Twenty-seven floors up, nobody could break in, unless they came from the balconies on either side, and she knew both those neighbors. From above? Damn, Colleen. You are sick! You are scared! You are paranoid! The thoughts twisted and writhed within her.

She pulled the keys from the door, set her briefcase and purse down on the floor, kicked the door shut with her foot, then heard it click and lock shut. Home at last, she

thought. She knew Samantha wasn't home yet but called anyway to make herself feel better, "Sam?"

The room was now dark except for the city lights, which moved like eerie eyes with the blowing, sheer curtains. Another time, another place, the lights would probably be romantic or pretty. Tonight they looked like roaming ghost's eyes. She shivered and realized the room was cold as she reached for the light switch by the door. Nothing! No lights. She flipped the switch a half dozen times. Nothing. Now she felt the cold move inside her body, but not from the chilly air coming off the lake. Fear like the quick, hot touch of the devil shot through her. Why were the patio doors open, and why were the lights out?

With her foot she slid the briefcase and her purse under a long table close to the door. Her eyes tried to adjust to the darkness. "Sam?" There was no answer. She was alone again. Alone with ghost's eyes, but now she hoped she was alone. If Samantha wasn't here, she didn't want anybody here.

As she moved to her left, she reached back and gently placed her keys on the table. The keys slid from the table's edge and landed on the tile floor, sounding like a bag of change being emptied into a tin can.

Her body was cold, both inside and out, yet sweat was forming on her face as she inched toward the bedroom where she kept her gun and badge. Oh, God! Was she over-reacting? Maybe! Probably! She hoped so!

She mustered as much courage as she could and reached for an end-table lamp by the couch. She squeezed the button under the shade. It, too, was out. No light. She pulled her hand back and continued on toward the bedroom, quicker this time, almost there. She had to get to her revolver.

Her eyes were having a hard time adjusting to the dark. She hurried now, bumping into a small table and knocking something to the floor. She paid no attention as she turned the corner into her bedroom and ran to the bureau of drawers that held her gun. In her frenzy, she pulled too hard on the drawer, and it came flying out, dumping everything on the floor. She fell to her knees and ravaged frantically, through lingerie, jewelry tidbits, and other personal items. No gun. No wallet. No badge. She was almost hysterical. As she began to search under the dresser, she heard a noise to her right.

She turned slowly. A confusing rush of dread whirled inside her as she saw large, heavy, black shoes standing beside her. As her eyes moved up the long dark slacks in total panic, she saw the blur of a fist that caught her on the left cheek and sent her head to the bedroom floor. A scream clawed in her throat. Her mind was filled with floating ghost's eyes, and she realized that whoever had hit her had now clamped her mouth shut with his hand. The powerful hands lifted her by the head. She felt her feet flail as they left the floor.

Another punch to the face sent her mind past the ghost's eyes into blackness. What little sense she had left told her she had been caught. She was going to die. A black veil covered her thoughts, and she stopped struggling.

FORTY-NINE

The Black Angel

Pete's eyes roamed the underground garage, watching for anything suspicious. He chewed on the last bite of a Big Mac and took a swig of Coke to wash it down. The souped-up purple VW was anything but inconspicuous, but it wouldn't arouse suspicion as far as belonging to the Feds. The Bug looked more like it belonged to the punk world with decals of flowers covering the hood and trunk and orange flames flowing along all four fenders. The rear seat and engine had been removed and replaced with a 1967, 289 Mustang, Pepper engine.

He reached back and patted the chrome air filter and said, "good boy," as if he was trying to make friends with a temperamental bulldog.

He shoved the final four french fries in his mouth when the antiquated car radio pinged. He grabbed it swiftly and said, "Delta One."

The man's voice on the other end answered, "Delta One." A short hiss of static prefaced the communication. "This is Delta Two. Subject is leaving Exchange parking lot in her gray Cutlass heading north on LaSalle Street." Another blip of static.

Pete held the phone close to his mouth and pressed the talk button stopping the static. "I read you, Delta Two, but can hardly hear you with this Joe-Friday radio. Does she have any company?"

Static, then he heard, "No, she's alone, and I haven't seen any strays follow."

Pete saw a slow-moving vehicle approach. "Delta Two, hold on one moment." Pete raised his head as he watched a yellow town car pass by Colleen's parking space. An old man, hardly able to see over the wheel, continued on toward the next level.

"Okay Number Two." Static. "Delta Two?" More static. He tapped on the mouthpiece. "Son of a bitch, Duffy, do you read me?"

The static was broken. "Pete, you're fading fast. I can hardly hear you. Let me clear a few of these tall buildings."

Pete sighed with frustration. A big drug-transport bust in South Chicago had taken all the dependable cars from the Feds garage, and the Delta group ended up with two old beaters. "Delta Two, follow at a safe distance and keep your eyes open for foreign companionship. Make sure she enters the garage here, and you park down the street and wait for an all-safe. I'll pick her up here. Do you read?"

"Ten-four, Delta One. You're coming through better now. I'll bring 'er home safe and sound, then she's all yours." Static filled the line and then nothing.

He looked at the radio and swore. The radio was at least fifteen, twenty years old, out of date and unreliable. The commodity investigation hadn't been a priority amongst the higher-ups at the Federal Building, except for Lorenzo.

He looked in the McDonald's bag. There were always a few stray fries at the bottom. He reached in and found two that had escaped. He should have bought a quarter-pounder too. He was still hungry.

His dinner these days was never before 10:00 p.m., tonight was no exception. His watch told him that Colleen should be about another seven minutes before she squealed into her parking stall, which was located four cars in front of him.

He hadn't told her he would be watching. This was the first time he had worked one on one with her, and he didn't know her moves. The last thing he needed was to have her wave to him and blow his cover as it had happened once in New York. That simple wave of the hand by an agent in the Big Apple had signalled seven unmarked federal cars to crash an arms warehouse prematurely. How trained, federal agents could screw up so much was beyond comprehension.

His head turned as another auto squealed around one of the blue posts and headed for the exit. A red Corvette with a lead-footed blond sped past the parked cars in front of him.

He scanned the dim parking lot again, and his eyes settled on the black plumbing van that had been parked close to the elevator since he had arrived thirty minutes ago. Although it looked harmless enough with the name *Reliable Plumbing Contractors*, Oak Brook, Illinois, vans were always suspicious. He picked up the binoculars on the seat next to him and tried to get the license number. A car to his right was in the way of his view, so he quietly stepped from the VW and stood in the shadows of a concrete column. He moved about four feet in front of the VW and picked up the license number PLUMR 6.

Original, he thought. Vanity, plumber plates, truck #6. He eased back into the VW and checked his watch. 10:02. He picked up the car-radio speaker, changed frequencies, and pressed the talk button twice and waited through the static for the control center to answer.

A female voice spoke with authority. "You call it, Delta."

Pete sighed at the corny response. "This is Delta One. I need a license check on Illinois plates P-L-U-M-R-Sixer."

"One moment, Delta One...say, what kind of phone are you calling in on?"

"It's a twenty-year-old Early Bird radio, not a car phone, now just get the plate number for me, will you, please?"

His eyes continued to roam the garage for signs of motion, and his ears perked for any unusual noise. The voice returned.

"Delta One, P-L-U-M-R-Sixer is registered to Reliable Plumbing, 782 Harlow, Oakbrook, Illinois."

"Whose name is on the registration?"

There was a pause and more static, then the voice came back, "Angelo Barnetti."

Angelo Barnetti. Had he heard that name before or not? His mind raced quickly through the files of his memory. No, the name was new to him, close to a few names in New York, but he knew of no Angelo Barnetti.

"How long will it take you to check Reliable Plumbing or Barnetti and tell me if one of their trucks has been dispatched to Sandburg Village?"

"I'm not sure, Delta One. I have three phone numbers with the registration. I'll make the calls and get right back to you."

"Ten-four." Pete threw the radio mouthpiece on the passenger seat next to the binoculars, along with an extra clip he had been loading for his weapon, then he looked at his watch. 10:06.

He yawned and shrugged the tightness from his shoulders. Colleen would be out of Ruzzo's office by the end of the week and he could get off this stake-out. Then he thought, maybe he should have told her he was watching her back so she would feel more at ease. But then again, he had told the agent in New York the same thing and the guy blew it with a simple, innocent wave. No, he was right not to have told her. She would just have to sweat out the loneliness that went with the job.

In the distance he heard squealing tires. He listened, and the squealing became louder, still far off, but louder. Christ, somebody's in a hurry, he said to himself. 10:08.

Pete's radio pinged and he jumped on it. "Delta One."

"Yo, this is Delta Two. Your package is delivered as promised. No problems, no strangers, but she sure is in a hurry."

The squealing was loud and close. "I think I have her, Number Two. Park down the street and give me the same playtime as the last ten nights, fifteen minutes. If you don't hear from me, it's a green light and move your ass, but I'll probably be back with you in eight or nine minutes and you can go home to Mama."

More static, then the remainder of a chuckle. "Let's go for a clean drop. I have a Scrabble game planned with a brunette tonight."

"Ten-four, Romeo."

He put the speaker back on the seat and watched as the gray Cutlass, leaning on its left tires, moved quickly around a blue column and made a sharp turn into the parking stall one hundred feet from where Pete sat.

He winced at the sharp noise of the squealing tires. What was her hurry? He waited for her to leave the auto that was parked half in the stall next to hers. He hoped her neighbor had a small car, she had only left him about six feet in which to park. What's she waiting for? His shoulders tensed.

The door of the Cutlass finally opened, and Colleen slid from the car. Pete relaxed and checked the time again. 10:10. He would wait until she was on the elevator before he followed.

He watched as she looked back from where she had flown in. She looked nervous. Her face appeared haggard, and her usual impeccable hair arrangement was loose and falling.

"Tough day at the office, Colleen?" he said in a whisper.

He scanned the garage quickly and immediately returned his gaze to Colleen. Her pace was more hurried now, and she ran to the elevators. Something was wrong. She was scared. He felt for his new .45, still there. Always there. What the hell was she so tense about?

He watched as she pushed through the glass doors of the elevator waiting area and decided to catch her and calm her down. This wasn't an illegal arms bust; it was simple white-collar crime, and so what if she knew he was there? He could let his guard down on this one. Nobody was going to hurt McFadden, in spite of what Hogan thought about Ruzzo and Conti.

As he opened the VW door, a ping came from the car radio. He grabbed it and said, "Delta One here."

More static then the female voice from headquarters. "Pete. You have a bad radio. I've been having trouble getting through to you..."

"No shit, 'bad radio.' Two tin cans and a long string would be better than this dildo." She continued, this time with concern. "You also have a big problem with that Reliable Plumbing truck." A cold, invisible finger traced his spine and twisted in the small of his back. "The third phone number I called was Angelo Barnetti's home. According to him, all his trucks are in. They only do business in the western suburbs, and if one of his trucks is at Sandburg Village, it was stolen sometime after five-thirty this evening."

Pete felt his body go limp. He saw Colleen pounding on the elevator doors inside the glass enclosure. "Rose, call Larry Duffy, Delta Two, he's right down the street and tell him to..." He realized he was speaking into static. He pressed the speaker button and tapped the mouth piece. "Rosie? Hello, headquarters." Static filled the tiny VW cabin. "Son of a bitch." He threw the phone onto the floor and left the purple car door open as he raced for the elevators.

He drew his .45 as he ran, then he saw the green light appear above the elevators. He screamed and heard his own words echo through the garage. "Colleen, wait." She didn't hear him. But he saw that she stepped back as if she had seen something frightening. Pete saw a man come at her out of the elevator with both hands extended. Pete was about 150 feet away, squatted and ready to blow a hole through the man's right temple when he saw him stumble and head for the glass doors. Colleen had entered the elevators, and Pete saw the green light go off. She was on her way up. "Goddammit!" He shouted out loud.

His mind moved faster than his body, giving it direction. He reached into an inside pocket of his black windbreaker and pulled out a thick silencer, custom made for the .45 he carried. If he had to fire his weapon, he didn't need a thousand residents screaming in the halls and jumping off balconies.

He rounded the plumbing van quickly and opened the passenger door, dodging and ducking and waving the .45 like an excited fish after food. Nobody there. He moved to the rear of the van and reached around to pull open the wide handle. Damn! Locked. He steadied himself and fired one of his heavy-load bullets into the lock, replacing it with a hole the size of a golf ball. Only a loud spit was heard, but the power of the bullet swung one of the rear doors open. A quick look inside and he was satisfied that all occupants were elsewhere, dissatisfied that he didn't know where.

"Son of a bitch." They could only be in one place. Colleen and Samantha's apartment. He had forgotten about Sam. He raced from the van toward the glass doors and the elevators beyond. He turned as he ran and spit another bullet into the rear right tire of the van. At least they would be without transportation unless they had planned another route of escape.

The drunk man grabbed his jacket as Pete ran through the automatic glass doors. "You wanna go get a drink with me?" A back kick caught the man in the solar plexus, and he went to his knees gasping.

Pete never looked back. He quickly pulled a master security key from his pocket and inserted it into the key slot. Six elevators; one of them should be on the parking level.

He looked up at the location board above the elevator Colleen had entered. It had stopped at Floor 13. Now what, he thought. Then he saw the numbers move again and stop at 18. He sighed. Must have been another tenant, he hoped. He punched the buttons again. "Come, you slow bastard."

The stairs, where were they? He saw the stairwell door just outside the glass doors and let his mind catch up with his crazed reflexes. Running up twenty-seven floors would turn him to Jello; that wasn't a good idea.

Finally he heard the ding and saw the green light of the elevator next to the one Colleen had taken. Before the doors opened he looked up to see how far she had gone. The red lights indicated floor 27. She was on her way to her apartment.

The doors opened, and a group of seven yuppies were hooting it up. "Out!" he hollered. "Out now! FBI." They stood motionless for a moment then Pete cradled his weapon so all could see. "OUT, Assholes!" They ran like rabbits. Pete stepped in and pushed floor 27. Then, 26. He'd have to waste three seconds by getting off on 26 and running up one floor. He'd control his entry to the 27th floor from the stairwell, a better idea than being met by a shotgun as the doors opened on 27. He hoped Colleen walked slow.

He watched the numbers click by slowly 6-7-8-9. At 10 it stopped and the doors opened. He reached in the back pocket of his jeans and pulled his badge. Two elderly ladies both carrying white poodles stood ready to enter. "FBI, ladies. Take the next train." He left them with their mouths wide open and both poodles barking.

Come on you slow bitch, move! 22-23-24-25-26 and the elevator stopped. He squeezed through the opening door and dashed to the stairwell on his left. Through the door, three steps at a time and around two posts brought him to the twenty-seventh floor.

Before he opened the door, he rested a moment and dropped his eyelids. Count your shots, two in the garage left seven. Slowly he turned the metal door handle and opened the heavy fire door. The hall was empty. He stepped through and peered down the long carpet that led to Colleen and Samantha's apartment. He raced the length of the hall. Just as he was nearing the junction that would lead him to 2742, a door opened and a pretty black girl stepped into the hall.

Pete flashed his badge and said, "FBI, honey, get back in your apartment and stay there." She didn't hesitate. As he passed he caught the subtle smell of jasmine. Ah! If all life could be that sweet, he thought.

He stopped and peered quickly around the corner. 2742 was about halfway down on the left. He eased over to the far wall, the side the apartment was on, and crept like a cat closer to his objective.

He stopped next to the apartment door, gun raised, and listened. Nothing. He released his left hand from his weapon and held it out in front of him. It was steady. Then he felt his forehead, warm but not wet. He was under control. As he inched closer to the door preparing to place his ear on it, something told him to look right.

The apartment door to 2743 about eight feet away was cracked about three inches and opening slowly. Pete raised his weapon and pointed it at the opening, expecting it to swing open and gunfire to erupt. The door moved like a tired turtle and Pete saw a sandy, brush head emerge. Son of a bitch. It was Bo Lynch.

The whisper sounded like it came through a megaphone. "Hi, Pete!"

Pete's lips pursed to say something, but nothing came. He hissed out, but still no words formed except in his head. Bo Lynch. Goddammit. So much for no interference from Hogan.

Bo whispered again. "Hi, Pete."

Pete's anger pushed out his words. "Hi, Pete, my ass, what the hell are you doing here?" he whispered back.

Bo's head stuck out the door, and he looked up and down the hall like a little boy playing Hide and Seek. Pete would have shot it off if he didn't have more important business. Bo whispered again. "Lease-option."

Pete shook his head and said quietly through his clenched teeth. "Lease-option, what?"

Bo grinned as if he had just pulled a fast one, opened the door, and stepped quickly across the hall on the same side as Pete. "I leased this place," motioning with his head to 2743, "for six months with an option to buy. Great apartment, twenty-eight hundred square feet, ten-grand sound system, heated water bed, even has a jacuzzi."

Now Pete felt perspiration forming on his forehead. "You idiot. Get the hell out of here. You're not supposed to interfere."

Bo looked hurt. "I'm not interfering--I live here. Just thought I'd say hello. Go on with your business. Just pretend I'm not here." Bo began to step back across the hall to his apartment then whispered again, "Oh, Pete, you better be careful of the half-ton of baboon muscle inside."

Pete's eyelids fell with frustration, and he took his right hand from his gun and wiped it on his jeans. "How many?"

"Three. They came from the apartment above, landed on the patio, and jimmied the balcony door. They are big fuckers, too, *real* big."

Pete looked down at the green carpet. Now what? Seven shots left and a crazy man for a back-up. He looked up at Bo who was as casual as he would be waiting for a bus.

"How do you know there are three of them and how they entered?"

Bo raised his eyebrows and whispered, "I watched 'em."

"From where?"

Bo put his finger to his lips, and mouthed almost inaudibly, "my secret."

Pete had a tough time keeping his voice low. "Your secret, my ass."

Bo feigned a hurt look again and responded quickly but quietly. "Yeah, fuck it, I'd rather be in my jacuzzi, but if you don't do something soon the girl's ass is going to be in pieces or lying on the street in front of Sammy Wong's Steak House twenty-seven floors down."

Pete didn't know why he was carrying on this conversation with the lunatic. But the bastard seemed to know more than he did, and word had it that Bo could take care of himself. Pete didn't doubt that, by the looks of Bo's scarred face and hands and his carefree attitude about danger. A perfect Hogan soldier.

Pete hesitated then said reluctantly, "How long has she been in there?"

Bo looked at his watch, tapped it, then raised it to his ear. Then looking back at Pete, he said, "four minutes, twenty-two seconds."

Pete felt the sudden leash of fear. "Did you hear any shots?"

Bo frowned and stepped back across the hall, coming close to the other side of the apartment door. He shook his head. "No they'll torture her first then throw her off the balcony, make it look like a suicide. That's the way they always do it--suicide--you should know that. She'll go right through Sammy Wong's restaurant canopy at about seventy-eight miles per hour.

Pete felt his body grow rigid along with his jaw. "Okay, Asshole. You stay out of it. I'm going in." Pete readied himself in front of the door to kick it in. He took a deep breath, concentrated on the door between the handle and the dead bolt. The kick had to be accurate, or he'd break his ankle and the door wouldn't budge.

Bo's words hit him like a stubbed toe. "You'll never do it that way."

Pete tensed and looked at Bo with total disgust. "What do you mean, I'll never do it. I've kicked in a hundred doors before."

Bo pointed to the dead bolt and whispered, "Two inch dead bolt, metal on both sides, takes up to eight hundred pounds of pressure. Unless you're into Zen, you can muster only three hundred and eighty pounds of pressure in a kick, maximum. You sure you don't want to try out my jacuzzi before you try this?"

Pete ignored the mockery. He was trapped. Bo knew he needed him. Bo knew Hogan had given his word not to interfere. Bo knew Pete couldn't kick in the door. "I'll shoot the goddamn thing open then."

Bo said casually, "That's a good idea, but there's a better way and you won't have to waste your bullets...Do you want my interference?"

Pete lowered his gun. "What do you suggest?"

Bo came close to Pete and spoke softly. "The hinges."

Pete felt his face wrinkle. He couldn't believe this. It was like a TV show. A federal agent about to be killed and Bo acting as if he was shopping for a new shirt. "The hinges?"

"Yeah, the hinges can only stand about two hundred pounds of pressure each. You concentrate on the middle of the door, and a good kick can rip the door off its hinges in one second."

Bo's eyes weren't those of a crazy man but a man with complete confidence. Pete reluctantly inquired, "How do you know?"

Bo smiled. "I've done it a hundred times before! You want to try it, or do you want me to do it?"

Pete looked Bo over. He wore a dark, plaid shirt that hung outside his olive green pants with large pockets. "Do you have a gun?"

Bo looked insulted. "I don't need a *gun*! For those jerk-offs inside?" He motioned with his thumb to Colleen's apartment.

Suddenly there was a crash inside the apartment, and Pete motioned to Bo to go ahead and kick it in.

Pete saw nothing but a blur and heard a blood-curdling yell as Bo's foot made a complete circle, sweeping over Pete's head and landing exactly where he had indicated. The door was knocked from its hinges and fell three feet into the dark room. Another blur, and Bo had entered the room and disappeared.

Pete rolled into the apartment and came to a squat position, moving quickly to his left, out of the hall light. His eyes saw only black. He heard two spits from a silenced gun. One bullet broke a piece of glass to his right, the other made no sounds. Must have entered the wall. He returned two shots of his own in the direction of the enemy's sound. Shit, no hit. No falling noise.

Where was Colleen? Stay down, girl, if you're still alive, he thought to himself. Another spit and the bullet caught the collar of his jacket. But this time he saw the blue

flash and fired two rounds four inches apart just below the place he had seen the flash. He heard a gasp, followed by a heavy thud that knocked over a table and lamp on the other side of the living room. Good, one down.

The room was quiet and dark. Only the curtains moved. How many more rounds left before he needed another clip? That's if he had time to re-load. Three rounds left and two enemies. He had to make his shots accurate, and in the dark.

His eyes were adjusting but slowly. What now? With two enemies left, Colleen and God only knew what Bo was up to. He could think of only one thing to do and it never worked, but he said it anyway: "This is the FBI, throw down your guns..."

Before he was able to complete what the Law called Proper Announcement, there were three more muffled shots, this time from his left. One of the shots ripped through his right thigh, and he did everything he could not to scream. It felt like a hot poker was pressed through his leg just below his ass. He gritted his teeth, put the .45 in his left hand, and fired one shot; then he rolled to his right and pushed himself up against the back of the couch.

His face muscles were locked in pain as he squeezed at the wound with his free hand. The pain took the breath from him, but he couldn't yell out, couldn't let his enemy know he was hurt. Son of a bitch. He felt the back of his pants begin to soak with blood. He looked around and could hardly see past his own body. The bastards could be standing right over him and he wouldn't know it.

Two shots remaining. If he moved any farther to his left, he would be in the light of the door. He didn't even know where the third bastard was. One down near Samantha's bedroom on the far side of the apartment. The one who shot him was on the opposite side of the room, and Pete knew he was in a very vulnerable position near the door. The sour taste of bile climbed menacingly up into his throat. Swallowing was nearly impossible, and the pain was forcing its way upward through his body, like a slashing knife. He had to take his chances. Roll through the light of the door and get around the couch.

His eyes were adjusting, and he spotted a dark object on the floor about three feet away, part of a broken figurine. As he reached the pain intensified. Finally he had it in his hand. He flung it over his head and waited for it to hit the floor by the moving curtains. It crashed on the tile, and Pete rolled across the smashed door. Spits of gun fire shattered a patio door; then the gunman realized the diversion and riddled the door. As he rolled, bullets followed him across into more darkness. He pushed himself around the couch and rested his head.

Goddamn, how did I get into this mess? Just another routine day at the office. A nice easy white-collar investigation. No danger, early hours, fine dining, a walk in the park, a piece of cake, a piece of ass was more like it--his ass, and it had nearly been blown off.

He heard a groan and saw the dark figure of the man he had shot lying about twelve feet away. The large clump moved. He was still alive but apparently out of commission.

He knew he had to move. He felt around the couch, then on top of the couch. He pulled back his hand when he felt something silky and sticky. What the hell was that? His mind categorized the article and immediately told him he had just touched someone's hair. He felt again. The hair was long and soft where it wasn't wet--wet with blood. Goddamn! It was Colleen! He groped further, feeling for her neck. His fingers traveled gently down the face, feeling bumps where there shouldn't be bumps. He came to the chin and went four inches further to the neck and felt the weak pulse. She was alive but not very healthy.

An immediate surge of angry heat cut through him. What had the bastards done to her? He felt her face again. It felt more like bubble wrap or pumpkin skin than a woman's face. He nudged her gently. She moved slightly and uttered an unconscious, "Nooo."

At the sound of her moaning, two more spits from the other side of the room smacked into a glass-top coffee table in front of him, and he yelled automatically as small chips of glass sprayed into the side of his face. He blinked to make sure his eyes were all right, but could feel blood begin to trickle down his cheeks from the razor-sharp glass.

Where in the hell was Delta Two? He should be here by now. Then he realized that, although it seemed like an eternity, fifteen minutes hadn't elapsed since he last talked to Delta Two, and he probably hadn't received the green light from headquarters because of the goddamn radio equipment.

He lifted and fired one shot toward the kitchen, from where he thought the last shots were fired. He waited and watched for movement, then saw a large bulk move quickly through the door leading to Colleen's bedroom. His mind propelled, and in a millisecond told him, it's your ninth bullet. The trigger squeezed as the body disappeared into the bedroom, but instead of hearing a thud he heard a loud snap, like a tree limb being broken. Then he heard the thud. His mind tried to decipher the noise but didn't have the seconds it took to register the possibilities. All his mind told him was that another enemy was down.

He pulled himself up on one knee, fighting against the increasing pain in his thigh. He listened to nothing. Was there a third man, or had Bo been mistaken? He extracted the empty clip and reached in his pocket for another. Where was the extra clip? He felt all the pockets of his windbreaker. "Damn," he said out loud. He had left the clip on the seat of the VW when he was loading it.

All of a sudden his peripheral vision caught a movement by the open door. His back-up? Please be there, Delta Two--but get out of the fucking light. "Duffy?"

There was no answer from the man standing in the open door. The light from the hall made it impossible for Pete to see the face. All he knew was the man was not his

backup. This man was tall, with wide shoulders, slicked-back hair, and wore a dark trenchcoat.

The black image standing in the doorway reminded Pete of an old artist's rendering of judgment day, and the black angel you had to pass before you could enter the eternal light beyond.

"Duffy?" He knew his voice was questioning in vain. It was hope he was uttering, not curiosity. This was the third enemy. Pete was a dead man if it were. Then he thought he'd try it by the book again, but he was ready to dive at the slightest motion of the man in the doorway.

"This is the FBI, ..." Shit, he thought sarcastically, he really had these guys by the balls now! "This is the FBI, drop your guns!"

There were no shots. The man in the door was motionless, like a statue. Pete's tension rose a few more increments at the sight of the black angel of death who evidently had no concern for his own life. How would he know that Pete was out of bullets? He couldn't. He just didn't care. A goddamn Ninja. Pete blinked the blood from his eyes thinking he may be seeing things. Maybe the pain was bringing on delirium. No, the stone figure remained, but his head began to move as if he were analyzing the room. Pete yelled out again. "FBI, Stop..."

Then Pete saw the profile as the head dipped to look in the direction of Samantha's bedroom. Pete's body went limp, and his gun dropped from his hand hitting the rug with a thud.

The granite jaw, the tight curled lips, the hawk-like nose were unmistakable. Pete relaxed, closed his eyes, and wiped blood from his face. He winced at feeling the prick of glass that was implanted in his right cheek. "Mike?" No answer. He had stepped into the room, and Pete felt a cold stare touch him, then go beyond him to the moving curtains.

The voice finally spoke a loud warning, "Bo, the balcony!"

Out of nowhere, a shadow, too fast for Pete's eyes, shot from Colleen's bedroom through the open patio door. He heard a loud yell, identical to the yell Bo had made when he crashed down the apartment door. This time it was a crunching noise of what Pete's mind knew to be bones breaking and a loud expulsion of bubbling wind.

From the balcony, Pete heard Bo's words ring out to the cool night. "Over the side with you, shitbag."

The long, fading scream told Pete that in a matter of three seconds Bo had taken Michael's directions, acted, disabled the third man, and thrown him twenty-seven floors into the black, cold night.

The next few moments escaped him as he filled with the realization that he had cheated death one more time. He squeezed hard at his wound, trying to stop the bleeding. Dim lights washed the room. He looked up to the open kitchen area to see Michael walk slowly toward him. His eyes were as dark as the trenchcoat he wore, his face cold and as

unforgiving as the wind that blew in from the black lake. Pete had seen the look before, but infrequently. It was the look of an animal after one of its newborn had been threatened.

Pete was on his knees and was about to greet him when Michael pulled an automatic from his pocket and aimed it directly at his head. All computers jammed in Pete's head. Pain and pressure did strange things to a man's mind, and Pete thought he was seeing things. Words jumbled together in his mouth as he put his hands in front of him in protest. The sound of two loud shots made Pete's reflexes do what his mind was unable to comprehend. He lunged forward toward the couch and Colleen McFadden. Michael was going to kill him, but *why*?

FIFTY

First Kill

Michael drew the black Astin-Martin to a screeching halt about four car lengths beyond the front entrance of the Sandburg Village condos. He made a quantum leap out of the car and into the plush lobby. The security guard left his station and hurried toward him protesting, "Hey buddy, you can't leave your car unattended there. Not even for a minute."

Michael kept walking and felt his eyes toughen as he stared at the guard. He watched the false authority melt from the man's face when he looked into his eyes.

The guard stopped abruptly and blubbered, "You really shouldn't park..."

Michael had anticipated the protest from the guard and pulled out a crisp one-hundred-dollar bill. His eyes quickly caught the guard's name tag, *Bill Phillips*.

As he hurried by the short, overweight man, he handed him the C-note and said politely, "Here, Bill, watch that car for me, will you please?"

As he stepped into an open elevator and pushed floor 27 with his left hand, he heard the guard come to life, "Yes, sir!" He sounded like a private in the army.

Michael's mood was calm, controlled. He had learned to anticipate, not to expect. He held the Mauser tight in the right pocket of his black trenchcoat. Think, but live one second at a time, he told himself. Too many variables in projecting. Too many deceptive conclusions. He'd let his reflexes take over his behavior. It had to be action, reaction just like in the trading pit.

He thought of the phone call from Bo telling of the three phony plumbers coming into Sam and Colleen's apartment. He had been unnerved briefly and had to step outside to become part of the cool air that chilled the city. He knew that his abrupt departure from the dinner party didn't set well with Maria, but he was sure her perceptive powers picked up the importance of his leaving. She was a Sicilian woman. She understood and accepted her man.

He was tempted to wish the elevator to move faster, but fate knew no time. Neither did the Great Power of Life that moved with him. He would yield to the Almighty Power and simply follow the direction of his spirit.

The elevator stopped on 10 and the door opened to two blue-haired ladies holding identical white poodles. The scowl on their faces reminded him of grade-school teachers who had been in the system too long.

They looked at Michael's stern face, and both stepped back, not forward toward the lift. He said softly, but with no apology in his voice, "Another will be along shortly, girls."

As the doors closed he heard one exclaim, "I'll bet he's another FBI man!"

How Bo knew the three men had entered the girls' condo from the twenty-eighth floor when he was supposed to be in the apartment across the hall, Michael didn't know, nor did he care. His information had been very precise. Three big men, dark mechanics' suits, driving a plumbing contractor's van, and wearing ski masks. It all made sense. Colleen had reached too far into the rathole.

There were no more interruptions to the twenty-seventh floor, and within a minute he was standing with his back to the wall outside Samantha and Colleen's smashed door. Bo's work, he figured. He heard a number of silenced shots in the room and glass breaking. Then a quick, painful yell, which sounded like it came from Pete.

Now was the time to make his move. But what kind of move? Roll inside the room shooting in all directions like they did in the movies? No, too costly. He knew Pete was in the apartment, and he was sure Bo and Colleen were as well. He hoped Samantha hadn't come home too early. At that thought his guts churned.

He shook her beautiful image from his mind. He instructed himself to be calm. Tighten and control the mind, don't speculate. Live one second at a time. React as if it may be the final reaction of this life.

He looked up and saw two couples standing in the open doorways of their apartment with curiosity written on all four faces. He felt his face harden as he looked into each of their eyes and motioned for them to get back. They immediately retreated into their apartments.

He was surprised the hall wasn't teeming with gapers, but yuppies usually went out to eat. This was the dinner hour for most of them; then they partied until midnight or later.

Another spit from a large-caliber gun drew his attention back to the open door. Within two seconds of the muffled shot he heard the unmistakable snap of a broken neck. Bo had at least one man down.

His reactions told him to move. The only light in the apartment was coming from the hall lights. If he moved into view, maybe he would be able to divert the attention of the enemy, and Pete and Bo could finish the job. He covered his eyes with his left hand for a few seconds to prepare them for a dark room. The thumb of his right hand released the safety on the Mauser, which he still held tight in his right pocket. A strange thought occurred to him as his eyes rested in darkness. Maria had given him the expensive, black trenchcoat for his birthday and would be furious if he came home with bullet holes in it. She'd be even more furious if he came home dead.

He released the crazy thought and stepped into the doorway. He saw his own shadow cast into the room like a black silhouette, making him look larger than he was. Pete was hunched down in front of the couch, and it appeared as if someone was lying on the couch. His voice sounded controlled but in pain when he called, "Duffy?"

Michael didn't answer. If there was a question in Pete's mind, maybe there was question in the enemies' minds also. Nobody wanted to kill one of their own men, and he knew that the slightest hint of confusion in the apartment would give Bo enough time to make his kill.

There was a hint of desperation in Pete's next announcement, "This is the FBI, Drop..." A short hesitation, and Michael heard him repeat the empty words, "This is the FBI. Drop your guns!"

Michael remained silent as his eyes narrowed to study the room. He looked for motion. Someone was lying beyond Pete moving slightly, not entirely out of commission. Michael had heard the snap of bones; he figured that was a second man. Where was the third?

A gust of wind blew the curtains apart. The city lights in all areas of the balcony were evident except one. There Michael could see the dark shape of a large man.

A futile plea came from behind the couch. "FBI. Stop!"

Michael paid no attention to Pete's handbook words. He stepped into the room. He turned to the left, in the direction he sensed Bo was lurking, and said, "Bo, the balcony!"

Michael stepped to his left, into darkness and toward the open kitchen area, to the circuit breakers. At the same time, he saw Bo move like a ghost from Colleen's bedroom through the open balcony. The waving curtains remained blowing as if he had passed right through them. A powerful attack yell from Bo was followed by a sickening crack. Michael suspected chest bones.

As Michael's eyes watched the rest of the room, his left hand found the circuit box.

From the balcony came a drowning, fading scream. Bo answered some words of departure for the man he had just killed.

Michael pushed the breakers back and forth, and a few tipped-over lamps turned on, filling the room with a dull light.

He saw the blood on Pete's confused face as he tried to lift himself. Michael felt his face turn to ice as he pulled the Mauser from his pocket and aimed it just to the right of Pete's left ear. Pete dove forward onto the couch as Michael cracked off two quick shots, then a third.

The wounded man behind Pete with a ski mask on had come to a sitting position, raising a short-barreled, pump shotgun toward Pete's back. Michael watched over the bridge of the Mauser as the man's head snapped back and his body slammed to the floor ten feet behind Pete.

Michael's eyes felt like lasers watching to see if the man moved. Three more shots would be on their way if the bastard as much as twitched. He didn't. He had killed his first man. He felt nothing at first. Then anger. Tonight he had killed a man and Bo had killed two. They had killed for a governmental agency that was so ingrained in doing everything

by the bureaucratic book that it thought nothing of placing its agents' lives in needless jeopardy. How impotent this government was with its rules and regulations. How omnipotent an enforcer who played by the simple rules of the street.

He saw the curtains move, but his senses said the motion was not from the wind. He swung the Mauser to the ghostly motion.

Bo stepped back inside. His face was calm until he saw Michael with a gun raised toward him, then a bloody hand came up quickly in front of him. He bellowed, "Whoa, amigo, me friend!" Michael lowered the Mauser and placed it back in his trenchcoat. He forced his thoughts to cool. "Is the place clean, Bo?"

Bo motioned to Colleen's bedroom with his hand that held two small, bloody pieces of flesh--ears. "Pete shot the guy in there in the back of the head with his bazooka. I broke his neck when he fell into the room, didn't know he was already dead. His face is all over the bedroom, and I have his ears. The sweep squad will find most of his brains in his ski mask."

Bo motioned to the dead man behind Pete. "I don't see much life there." Then his thumb, accompanied with a smile, pointed over his shoulder. "And there's a limo parked in front of Sammy Wong's Steak House, twenty-seven floors down, with 250 pounds of slime imbedded in its roof. That's all three bad guys. Three up, three down."

Michael motioned with his head, indicating the man behind Pete. "Check that scum out over there, Bo."

He saw that Pete had taken a bullet in the leg. He pulled a white dishtowel from a kitchen handle, then walked around a small dinette set. He felt and heard the crunch of broken glass under his feet and stepped to the couch near Colleen. She was coming to and beginning to moan. He handed the dishtowel to Pete and said, "You look like hell. You better sit down before you fall down." Pete said nothing as he took the towel and pulled himself up onto a soft, cushioned chair.

Michael turned his eyes to what used to be a pretty face. Now distorted, ugly, and bloody with swollen lumps of broken bones, her face would never be very pretty again. The thought sickened him. Once more, he felt the heat of anger begin to build in him but he held it down, under control.

He turned back to Pete. He had wiped some of the blood from his face and was wrapping the towel tight around his upper thigh. Michael picked up a phone that had fallen to the floor and handed it to Pete with a frigid order. "Get her to the hospital."

Pete looked up at him. Without saying it, Michael knew Pete was telling him that he was not the enemy. He punched in a series of code numbers and waited. With a disheartened tone, he said, "Yeah, this is Delta One. Find out where Delta Two is and pass me through to Control."

Michael's eyes roamed from Colleen to Bo to Pete. After fifteen seconds had crept by, he finally said, "Why don't you just call an ambulance, Pete?"

Pete looked at him with embarrassment and covered the mouthpiece. "Procedure, Mike. Just procedure."

Michael shook his head with disbelief, and Bo echoed his own thoughts while he tried to pull the ski mask from the dead intruder. "Your fucking procedure doesn't work, Lewis. Your procedure gets good people killed. It sucks!" Bo struggled with the limp head as he continued. "The race is to the swift, Pete, and a half dozen phone calls for an ambulance isn't very swift."

As Bo yanked the ski mask off the man's head, he said, "Nice shot, Mike. Two in the forehead and one in the neck. Good thing you didn't have to follow procedure before you fired or good ol' Pete would have had a hole in his back the size of a watermelon. Maybe you should have called Maria first and asked her if it would be all right if you saved Pete's life."

Michael saw the frustration in Pete's eyes at Bo's comment. This was the truth, and Pete knew it.

Pete's attention came back to the phone. "Yeah, Joe. This is Lewis. I need an ambulance for one of our agents and a sweep team to clean up...Sandburg Village 2742...Colleen McFadden...She's been beaten pretty bad...No, we...I hit them all, two inside the apartment and one lying on top of a limo in front of Sammy Wong's Steak House. Total three, all eliminated...I don't know. I haven't had time to check her over, but they messed up her face bad...Okay. You had better get in touch with the locals and tell them it's a federal case, otherwise they'll be licking their chops to kick us out of Chicago...tell them we could use their support...just try to keep them off my back until I clean up here."

The next comment brought Pete's eyes in focus with Michael's. "No, I'm alone...Yeah, I got all three of them...took a slug in the thigh and a little glass in the face...No, I'll drive over to the hospital myself...Yeah, see you at St. Luke's."

Michael watched Pete as he set the phone in its cradle. Then he lifted his eyes back to Michael. He motioned to the body next to Bo. "Thanks, Mike. I owe you."

Michael eased off a bit. "You helped me out in the garage when we first met, remember? I helped you out here tonight. You owe me nothing. We do for each other, Pete, as many times as it takes, as long as it takes. You're supposed to be watching my back. You want no interference because of procedure, and I end up watching your back."

"Well, thanks anyway."

Michael waved him off, turned, and saw that Bo was now attending to Colleen. He had propped her head up on a pillow and was speaking soft, encouraging words that Michael had never heard from him before. Bo had gotten a cold, wet towel and was dabbing Colleen's puffed face. His words were almost inaudible, gentle and hushed, like a father whispering peaceful promises to a whimpering child. Maybe this incident would have a good effect on Bo. Maybe he would realize that Viet Nam vets weren't the only people who felt the wrath of evil men.

His attention turned back to Pete. The question caught in Michael's throat. "How about Samantha? She's not..."

Bo was now standing next to him. "She's not here, Mike. Probably still downtown."

Michael's facial muscles loosened. He felt his body drain of adrenalin to the point that he even felt a bit faint. He looked at the blowing curtains and said to Pete, "Make sure Sam's okay, will you Pete? Put her someplace safe."

"I'll take care of it, Mike." Bo's face was as calm as if he had just finished an ice-cream cone.

"Nice job, Bo," Michael said.

"Hey, Brother, nice job yourself. Two in the forehead and one in the neck. That's dead. You're catching on fast!"

Pete had picked up the phone and punched in his code again. "Delta One. Pass me through to Samantha Winters at the Federal Building...Department of Audits and Investigation."

Michael had turned to leave but stopped to wait for an answer. Life re-entered his body when he heard Pete speak. "Sam, this is Pete. How's it going there? Good...say, I'm going to have a car pick you up in a half hour..."

He hesitated and sighed in answering her question. Then he said, "Yes, there was a problem, and Colleen's been hurt. She'll be okay, but they roughed her up pretty good. Joe will pick you up in half an hour." He hesitated again, and then his eyes met Michael's. He said slowly into the phone, "I haven't seen him. I think he's at a dinner party...No, I'll call him...Yes, I promise...Yes, I'll tell him to meet us at the hospital...I'll call him when I hang up from you...Okay, soon as I finish up here." He replaced the phone.

Michael heard sirens and knew they were close. He turned to leave, and Pete interrupted. "You had better give me the Mauser, Mike."

Michael spun and glared. Pete didn't waste any time answering the look of hate. "I need the Mauser for my story. Forty-five slugs all over the place and three Mauser bullets in a man's head. It won't fit unless I report the Mauser was my second gun. You're at a dinner party, remember? And Bo's sitting in a jacuzzi someplace. Unless you both want your picture all over the *Tribune* and *Times*, and a whole lot of aggravation from downtown, you'd better give me your gun and get the hell out of here. The press usually arrives three minutes after the first squad car."

Michael stared at Pete as he pulled the Mauser from his pocket, wiped it clean with his trenchcoat, and placed it on the table next to the door. His stare turned to a glare again. "I want it back! Whether you know it or not, there's going to be a war."

He looked down and saw Colleen's briefcase. He picked it up and placed it next to the Mauser. "This is probably what that garbage was looking for. When Colleen looks into a mirror, do you think she'll think it was worth it?"

He saw Pete's agitation. He also saw his pain and knew it wasn't coming from his wound. "Mike?"

Michael's eyes softened. He felt his friend was trying to reach out. "What, Pete?"

Pete's head drooped with dejection as he looked over at Colleen. "Forget it. Maybe I'll see you at St. Luke's."

Michael spoke over his shoulder as he left the apartment. "You can count on it, Pete. Come on, Bo, we have some planning to do. Simpson and a few others are going to pay for this."

A heavy gust of cold lake air blew through the patio doors, following Michael from the room as if he had brought the wind with him.

FIFTY-ONE

One Year Later, November, 1988
Friday the Thirteenth, 6:00 A.M.

The four thick tires of the red Ferrari splashed wet slush high in the air as Max Leonard sped down Wells Street and pulled to a sliding halt in front of Louie Roma's Restaurant. He gripped the leather steering wheel tightly and saw his own white knuckles staring back at him. His hands shook so badly he grasped them as in prayer and held them in his lap. He said to himself, if there is a God, make this not be true.

Pulling air into his lungs was a major effort. For a brief moment, he watched the smooth, hypnotic swish of the windshield wipers catch the melting snow as it hit the warmed glass. Although almost soundless, their rhythmic motion echoed through his panicky mind like a banging window in the wind.

He had to move--get out of the small confines of the Ferrari. He had to get more information. Son of a bitch. I gotta get out of here. He slid the gearshift easily into park, yanked the keys out of the ignition, and pulled his leather collar tight to his thin neck. As he swung the door open, a bus rumbled by, splashing his car and him with gray blotches of slush. The elevated train, which rolled overhead, drowned out his loud curses.

As he rounded the front of the Ferrari, his expensive leather shoes slipped from beneath him, and he went down on one knee, ripping a hole in his two-hundred-dollar pants. Holding onto the Ferrari for support, he looked to the gray sky and announced another curse to the great city of Chicago. With total apathy, another passing bus answered his curse, and more slush splashed his way.

He stepped up on the curb, ignoring the black and white NO PARKING-LOADING ZONE sign and headed for the front door of the restaurant. His thoughts became vocal. "It's all a big mistake...the phone call from Morrie Franko last night was an error...no truth to it...bad information, everything is okay...Pete Alexander is not a federal agent...can't be, just can't be!" But something deep inside the blackest rivers of his mind told him this early breakfast meeting would be short and would confirm Franko's findings that Pete Alexander really was a federal agent. What am I going to do? Fear had him in her clutches.

Looking up Wells Street, he saw a bank clock rotate slowly, informing the city that it was 6:08 a.m. and the temperature was 33º. His body shivered from both cold and fear. The words trembled as they slipped from his mouth, "This isn't true. God, make it not true."

He had to stop for a moment, or he was going to pass out. He pressed his back up against the wet concrete wall just outside Roma's Restaurant and closed his eyes, opening his mouth to pull air into his lungs. Pete Alexander--a friend. A distant fellow, but a nice guy and a friend. Not a federal agent. "Maybe he was a Fed, but not now. No way!"

Max brought his trembling hands up and covered his face momentarily. He felt the wet snow mix with his own sweat and run down his cheeks to his neck. A sharp, cold shiver shook the upper part of his body. He took his hands away and looked at them, expecting to find blood, or pus, or worry, or fear, or something ugly. There was only sweat and water. All of his internal apprehensions were banging around inside of him like black golf balls with teeth.

He pushed himself away from the cold cement and said out loud, "Come on Max, this has all got to be one bad, dream." Everything was going so well. A new six-hundred-thousand-dollar home for his family in Barrington, two new eighty-thousand-dollar automobiles, a beautiful hooker girl friend who lived in his secret downtown condo, and a half-million-dollar home on Lake Geneva which he had acquired by taking a loss from another broker who quit-claimed the lake home over to him. Sure it was illegal. He guessed tax-fraud. But who cared? Everybody did it.

Then he felt the blood drain from his face. He had boasted to Pete how smooth and easy a tax dodge was accomplished. Max had made, or bagged, eight hundred thousand last year. The Murphy brothers shared a commodity account with a five-hundred-thousand-dollar loss in it. Max made numerous trades in the bean pit that lost him five hundred thousand to the Murphy boys. That's when they gave him the home. Easy. Their house was worth much more than five hundred thousand, and they needed money, not a tax loss. With the profits from Max, their account broke even for the year. His income was reduced to three hundred thousand, which he was able to cover with other tax dodge programs, and he had a new lake house he didn't have to pay taxes on. A five-hundred-grand asset the Government had helped him pay for.

In his conversation with Pete about the trade, he remembered his exact words, *Fuck the IRS. My money is my money, and the government isn't getting a dime. The IRS will never catch on to our tax schemes. They're too complicated for them, and if we ever get audited we pay a few bucks and their incompetent auditors go away feeling they are the victors.*

He remembered Pete quizzing him on the Geneva house. He had told him the house would never come up because it had been quit-claimed to Max from the Murphy brothers and the deed was never recorded. So, for all practical purposes the house was still in the seller's name but owned by Max.

Now, Max could hardly open the door to the restaurant, he was shaking so badly. As he walked through the doors, he said again, "Don't let this be true."

He walked quickly through the dim lounge area, which would be teeming with brokers in less than six hours, through the bar and into Roma's breakfast area.

The room was basically empty. Still too early for the majority of brokers to be in the city. He quickly spotted the big frame of Chuck Nicolelli and Scott Bradley, who were sitting at a large table at the far end of the restaurant. Morrie Franko and Ted Terrin flanked Nicolelli and Bradley. The other three brokers involved with buying Pete's so-called tax losses were vacationing in the Islands.

In seconds he was sitting, trying to pour himself a cup of black coffee, but it was spilling. Bradley reached over and took the jug of coffee, gave him a new cup and saucer, and poured for him. Max fumbled for a stainless-steel flask and splashed a healthy shot of vodka into his coffee. He finally looked around the table, forced a nervous smile, and said, "Things look pretty grim, eh?"

The table was quiet for a good minute until Franko broke the silence. "Max, you are the guy who introduced us to the bastard. You are the guy who set up all the luncheons. You are the fucking guy who came to us with the tax scam to pay Alexander twenty cents on the dollar, and under the table no less, for his defunct New York textile company. Then we go and pay the bastard five grand apiece in skim trades for a hundred thousand worth of losses he had taken in the market. A real goddamn bonus!"

Max tried to control his breathing. His chest was jerking, and he could hear the thud of his heart in his head. A barrage of other unfriendly, undefined emotions touched areas of his mind that had been virgin areas of thought until now.

He heard his voice crack as he countered Franko. "Don't go blaming this on me, Morrie. You were the one who instructed everybody to keep our eyes open for an easy mark so we could hide money from the IRS."

Franko's eyes were fire red as he leaned forward in his captain's chair. Max saw that he was unshaven, and his long, brown hair was a mess, as were the expensive clothes he wore. It looked as though he had slept in them, if he had slept at all. "Max, you're the prick who brought us a federal agent to do business with. It was your goddamn, big, Jew mouth that boasted of having friends who were looking to fuck the government out of millions of tax dollars."

Franko sat back and extended both palms out in a mocking gesture and said sarcastically, "and, of course, you obliged when the weasel took you under his black wing and said, "Sure, Max, I can help all your friends. Just speak into my hidden recorder, set up a few meetings so I can get them all on tape, and we'll make a deal that all of us can get something out of. Max, you didn't even check 'em out."

Max felt a dribble of urine wet his undershorts as he forced a feeble defense. "How do you know he's a Fed, Morrie? Who says your information is correct?"

Franko slammed the table with his fist, and the silverware chimed its discomfort in being reorganized.

Tim Bradley shushed him. "Keep it down, Morrie! Keep it down!"

Max saw that Franko didn't bother to take Bradley's suggestion and slammed his fist again. "My information happens to be reliable, Asshole. It came from the man supposed to be the next Chairman of the Board of Governors, Noel Brown."

Max relaxed, leaned back, ran his fingers through his wiry hair, and gave a loud sigh. Franko looked away and remained quiet for a moment as he pinched his whiskered chin in thought.

Max jumped and his wide eyes shot to Charlie Nicolelli when Nicolelli said, "Morrie, where did Brown get his information?"

Max looked back at Franko, hoping he would say a reporter from the *Enquirer* or the *Star*, but no such luck.

Franko took his hand from his chin and stared back at Max as if Max had asked the question. He hissed the words, "Senator Richards, who we conveniently manipulated and gave an honorary placement as one of the elite Board of Governors, phoned me yesterday."

Scott Bradley interrupted. "Why'd the Senator call you?"

Franko gave Bradley a hateful look. "Because I'm head of the Trading Conduct Committee, asshole. In case you forgot, you are the ones who elected me to that prestigious position so I could cover everybody's cheating ass. I'm the guy who tells the media, the government, the Exchange committees, the CFTC, my wife, my mom, and any other deaf person I can find that everything is clean in the trading pits."

Max was glad Bradley had temporarily taken the attention off of him. He sipped at his coffee hoping the vodka would work fast.

Bradley seemed cool as he continued to test Franko's knowledge, with caution. "So what did Richards say to you?"

Max noticed Franko's left eye twitch as he said, "The prick threatened us, saying that if there was any truth to there being a federal agent investigating illegal trading practices on the Exchange floors, he would be the first to back the Feds. He said that he and a number of other Exchange officials who have been kept in the dark about floor activity will go to the wall for us if there is nothing to the investigation. But if there is any sign of widespread skimming or laundering, he and his small group will resign and do what they can to close down the Exchanges. Needless to say, he was incensed."

Max saw Ted Terrin lean beneath the table and heard him snort at a small gold container he had been holding in his hand. When his head bobbed back to face the group, he placed the gold toothpick container on the table and said, "The good Senator is going to have to search hard to come up with a handful of clean board members. I only know of three or four who have been kept in the dark, and I'm not so sure they're all that clean. Besides, I thought Richards was on our side."

Franko snapped at Terrin. "Listen, Dopehead. Nobody, and I mean nobody, is going to be on our side if we're exposed. Senator Richards is a politician. Although he claims he's on the side of free enterprise, the Commodity Exchanges being the last frontier

of big business without government interference, he's strictly on his own side. The side of money and votes. Since we backed him with heavy contributions from our political fund, he felt it an honor to be invited to join us as one of the thirty-one prestigious Board of Governors. It was an ego trip for him and a whitewash job by us."

Max anxiously watched as Franko rubbed his angry eyes and rolled his neck from side to side. Then Franko looked around the table and said with a tone of defeat in his voice, "What business skimming as much cash as we do on a daily basis would ever ask a government official to sit on their board? The asshole only saw what we wanted him to see, and the public thought it was great that our questionable commodity institution would open their doors to one of their endeared Senators. Richards was only window dressing on the part of the Exchange. Good for his ego. Good for our image. But now, the prick is hearing and seeing a few facts unfold in front of him, and he's afraid his hands may have gotten a little dirty. You can be sure that if he feels his future as a powerful politician is threatened, he'll start to dig beneath the surface and find out what we are all about. If that happens, he'll pull every trick in the book to regain his clean image that the Commodity Exchanges may have tarnished. You can bet he'll call for reforms and probably even propose a move to have the SEC regulate us. And that, gentlemen, will be the end of our little game. And that, gentlemen, is, right now, the least of our problems, thanks to Max."

Max had gulped his coffee and felt the vodka warm him. He asked sheepishly, "Did Senator Richards tell you where he got his information? Maybe it's just a rumor. I just can't believe Pete's a Fed. Doesn't make sense...I just..."

Franko interrupted sharply. "You can't believe it? Well you have your head in your ass, Max. I didn't get a word in with Richards. As soon as he was finished with his almighty threats, he hung up on me. It was ten o'clock at night. I was taken by complete surprise, drunk, and half numb from that white powder when he called. He began the conversation with a threat and ended it that way. It took me awhile to put it all together. All I remember are the words 'federal agent in the pit.'"

Max's eyes turned to Bradley, then to Nicolelli. He was confused. Bradley spoke softly. "How do we know it's Pete Alexander? It could be any number of guys. New brokers come and go every day."

Max looked at all the faces, hoping for a reprieve. Bradley's statement made sense. How could anybody be sure Pete was a Fed? Nicolelli merely stared blankly into his untouched orange juice. Terrin poured a few shots of booze into a half cup of coffee from a gold flask that matched his cocaine container. There was no apparent alarm in his face, and his eyes gave off a look of sleepy boredom. Franko had slouched in his chair, leaned his head back, and looked at a slow-moving Casablanca fan rotating above the table.

Franko sighed and spoke, with a tone more of despair than of anger. His voice was quiet as he watched the fan. "First, I called Jeff Weisen, our know-it-all Exchange attorney, who usually has all the first-hand gossip from Washington. Without throwing up a bunch of red flags, I just asked him if he had word of any type of investigation going on

at the Exchanges. The arrogant bastard was upset because I woke him up, then said he had heard rumors but assured me if the rumors had been based on fact he would be the first to know and I would have been the second to know. He's another egomaniac with his head in his ass. One of the biggest legal thieves in Chicago with a three-hundred-thousand-dollar retainer from the Exchange plus five times that in kickbacks."

Bradley mumbled, "He's not so clean. If I were him I think I'd be a little more concerned."

Franko looked disgusted. "The son of a bitch is so well insulated nobody will ever be able to touch him. We stand in the pits with our asses hanging out, actually writing down our dirty trades on paper and trading cards, and he sits in his office collecting cash dividends for selling classified information. He's too smart not to hide that cash someplace in Europe. We're the assholes. We're the dummies!"

Franko dropped his head and rested it in the palms of his hands, then continued. "I made four more phone calls, one each to Bob Travis, Charlie Cullis, and Paul Sinclair. All three in charge of important Exchange committees. They had heard nothing--they said don't worry about it--we were covered. If any waves had been made, our Washington man would have let us know. It was all a bunch of bullshit. They didn't know anything because they don't give a damn. All of them are covered and covered well.

"Then I called that bimbo, Ms. Cohen, who thinks her shit smells like strawberry jam, and sits with her thumb in her ass at all the board meetings, criticizing everything and everybody. You know what Ms. Perfect Bitch told me?"

Max realized he was biting his cheek. He could taste blood.

Franko stirred his coffee with his finger. "Ms. Cohen told me that she had heard this rumor six months ago from a goddamn clerk who works in one of the law enforcement offices at the Federal Building."

Nicolelli shot out a question. "Why didn't the bitch say something? She's not so lily white either."

Franko mimicked Trudy Cohen with his lips turned down shaking his head. "She said, 'Well, I didn't think anything of it, Morrie. You know, there are always rumors!' She's probably fucking the clerk and promised not to tell. The dumb bitch. Another mistake, juggling the ballot box, and allowing her elected to the Board of Governors, just for the sake of women's lib." Franko shook his head. Disbelief replaced disgust. "Most of our mistakes have gone unnoticed, but electing her was a major mistake. We'll all pay for the cunt's stupidity."

Ted Terrin took a long drink of coffee laced with booze and said with a lack of concern, "Nothing like protecting our image. We invite a Senator to join us at the round table so we can dress up our public image, control the ballot box. Then we let a dumb broad sit with us in order to win the support of the few females who thread the industry. We think we can throw pigs into a pile of shit and tell the government and the public it's

a tuxedo the pig is wearing around--just smells a little--and they are supposed to believe us?"

Franko insisted, "They believed us for a long time, Ted, but now, it smells worse than a little. We're all about to get our asses burned."

Franko sighed and went on. "My last call was to Washington." Then he added with sarcasm, "to our Big Man at the Agriculture Department. He didn't know squat..."

Nicolelli interrupted. "He's an ostrich, as long as he's guaranteed his monthly retainer from the Exchanges he's not going to risk putting his neck on the line for us."

Max had relaxed slightly and poured another cup of coffee as he listened to Franko. "Don't kid yourself, Nico. He's getting kickbacks like everybody else. That son of a bitch was goddamn scared at the thought of a Fed snooping around in the pits. He said he'd do some checking and get right back to me. Within an hour, he called back and told me that one of his buddies at the Justice Department, a guy he's been paying off, reluctantly told him there has been an investigation going on and it was being conducted by the FBI and the U.S. Attorney's Office in Chicago. The federal agents in charge of the investigation are two men by the names of Andrew Golden, who works out of the Federal Building and Peter A. Lewis, who works the trading floor operation."

Max's heart stopped as he watched Franko's eyes turn to him again. Franko wasn't a handsome man to begin with, but the cruel look he had taken on made him look like an angry monkey with his narrow eyes, puffed cheeks, and small chin. A spasm of fear rushed through Max, and he felt his hands begin to shake again.

Franko said with emphasis, "I presume the *A* stands for *Alexander*, Max?"

Max looked away. He wanted to get up and run but to where? He gathered enough nerve to lean forward on one elbow. "Listen, Morrie. Just because his middle initial is *A* doesn't mean it stands for Alexander. It could stand for anything...uh Andrew or Anthony or..."

Ted Terrin came alive again speaking with a "don't-give-a-shit" attitude. "Or it could stand for Alice or Agnes or Arlene, or maybe it stands for Arresting officer."

Franko spewed out at Max, "You find out, Max. You find out what's going on. I'm not going to jail because of your fuck-up. None of us are."

Max pushed back his chair and looked at all the faces. All but Terrin's had the look of dry ice without the gas. Terrin's red hair had disappeared beneath the table again for another snort.

I'll talk to Pete this morning. I...I...promise. This has to be a mistake...just has to a big mistake."

Max turned and tripped over his chair as he backed from the table and hurried from the restaurant. God, what have we done? What have I done? This can't be happening to me. It's all a big mistake. He heard his own words: "Please, God, please."

FIFTY-TWO

Friday the Thirteenth, 9:10 A.M.

Pete stood on the top step of the Soybean pit and read the note that had just been handed to him. His guts rolled like rocks in his stomach as he read the thirteen words. He looked at the time: 9:13, and it was the thirteenth of November. He wasn't a superstitious man, but in this case the number thirteen didn't mean he or Max had won the lottery. He read the note again:

> Meet me in the men's room on the second floor.
> Important - please. Max.

He crumpled the note and stuffed it in his trading jacket, then stared off into oblivion, feeling a strange remorse. Max had found out the game of chance was over. He could feel it like he could feel a slap in the face. It wasn't like Max to send "Please" notes to anybody. No, Pete's cover had been blown. It didn't take a genius to figure that out. It was just a matter of time before some lame-brain in Washington opened their mouth for a thirty-minute fuck or a few thousand dollars. He was surprised his cover had been protected for as long as it had, but he would play out his hand just in case he was wrong.

Could he be wrong? Maybe Max had knocked up his girl friend or was a homosexual or had killed somebody. Pete sighed, placed one foot on the next step down, and stared at the scuffed oak decking of the floor.

He filled his lungs and shook his head in despair. Pete owed it to Max to meet and try to explain. Jesus Christ, why was he feeling guilty? It was Max who was playing the dirty game and didn't let the customers' emotion get in the way of ethics. Why should he, Special Agent Pete Lewis, feel guilty for doing his job? He had done no wrong.

Then he analyzed his last thought and came to the realization that he was also wrong. But that was his job. "Befriend and betray" was the slogan of all government law enforcement agencies, barring none. No questions asked. As far as fair play went, the end always justified the means, without exception. Bullshit, he thought to himself.

How many times had he done this before? Fifty, seventy, one hundred times? As an undercover cop, he had to win the confidence of those he was pursuing. But Max Leonard was different. A lovable little man with a nice family, good upbringing, pretty girl friend--even if she was a hooker. Pete stopped thinking before he went so far as to admit to himself that Max had become a friend.

He checked out at the trading desk, headed to the second floor, and within three minutes had descended the two flights of stairs to where he was to meet Max.

As he stood in front of the men's room he glanced at his wristwatch. Eight minutes had passed since he had received the note. He ran his hand down the patch on the right side of his trading jacket, activating the tape recorder, then began to push through the door but stopped. He turned and walked back to the heavy marble railing that circled the first-floor foyer.

People were rushing into the building, some running, some stopping at the cigar stand for a newspaper or pack of gum or candy bar. When was the last time he had a candy bar? He couldn't remember. For most of the scurrying bodies life was pretty simple: get up, kiss the wife and kids, catch the commuter train or subway or bus. When was the last time he had been on a bus? He couldn't remember.

His thought continued as he watched one girl drop her petite brown-bag lunch. She couldn't have much more than an apple and a few crackers in that bag. Then she hurried on her way again. When was the last time he kissed a girl? He couldn't remember, but it had been too long.

He figured the majority of the people he was watching made between thirty-five and sixty-five thousand dollars a year. They would put their day in, catch a ride to the suburbs, kiss the wife and kids, maybe go to a ball game or movie. He couldn't remember when he had last seen a ball game or a movie or eaten an ice-cream cone, either.

He turned and leaned his rear against the marble railing and thought ninety per cent of the people who scurry around hallways and through buildings like this all day long, all over the world, were the ones who made the earth turn. Nine per cent tried to stop or hinder that harmony by cheating and killing and raping society. And one per cent tried to keep the harmony of life in balance. He was part of that one per cent who, by destiny or choice, he didn't really know, tried to keep the order in balance and keep the nine per cent from growing larger, like cancer. What a lousy job, a losing battle.

He pushed himself from the rail and said quietly, "If all else fails, Lewis...fuck it! Let's go see Max."

He pushed open the door cautiously. "Max?" There was no answer. "Max Leonard? You in here? It's Pete!"

The washroom was well lit but small. A sink and mirror, two urinals and four toilets. Three green doors stood ajar. The fourth was closed. "Max? You wanted to see me?"

Pete heard a slight rustling in the fourth stall, and the door swung open. Max appeared slowly, his face the color of copy paper, his eyes red and dilated. Pete knew he had been snorting cocaine, and it looked as if he had done quite a bit. He appeared to have been crying as well. The scent of whiskey drifted through the air of the small room.

Pete approached him with caution. "Max, you look like hell. What's the matter?"

Max leaned back against the wall, still wearing his tan leather jacket, not his usual bright trading jacket. His droopy, dark-circled eyes just stared at Pete.

Pete spoke softly. "What's the problem, man?"

Max braced himself against an old porcelain sink, still mute. Pete noticed drool roll slowly from the left corner of his mouth. His eyes were merely slits.

Pete looked around the small auxiliary washroom, hearing only the hum of two fluorescent lights and said, "Max, you're into the powder early today. What's on your mind? What's the problem? Talk to me, man!"

How much "candy" had Max taken? It appeared to be quite a bit, and he wasn't a heavy user. Pete had seen the effects a thousand times. Max was in trouble.

He stepped forward when he thought Max was going to fall. Then, Max screamed, "YOU USED ME!"

Pete stopped abruptly and looked at this pathetic friend. Be cautious, Lewis, he reminded himself. Emotions lead to carelessness, but then as quickly he changed his tune. The hell with the training manual, he added.

The glazed eyes poked holes into Pete, and Max yelled again. "YOU USED ME, PETE!"

Pete sighed, bit his top lip and thought. Okay, let's lay down our cards. "What do you mean, Max?"

Max came off the wall and staggered a step forward, his head bobbing. "You're a Fed, Pete, a fucking Fed."

Pete was quiet as he watched Max try in vain to wipe the spit from his chin. He caught the lower part of his cheek with his hand, but the spit remained, and with every word more saliva rolled from his mouth. With every word, Pete felt his own character shrink.

"How could you do this to me, Pete? You set me up. You became my friend. No-- I became your friend. Then, you weaseled your way into my life, my perfect life, and you used me."

He fell back against the bathroom wall and began to roll his head. "How could you do it, Pete...PETER A. LEWIS? Isn't that your name?"

Pete's eyes closed at the disclosure of his real name, and he turned to lean against one of the urinals. No words came.

Out of the corner of his right eye he saw Max reach into his heavy coat, and Pete froze. Not a gun, Max, please. It's not worth it!

Just as Pete was about to drop for his ankle pistol, a pint of whiskey emerged from the jacket, and Max took a long gulp, draining the bottle. Then he threw it at Pete. His aim was way off. Pete moved slightly backwards as the empty pint whistled by and crashed against the far wall.

His attention returned to Max when he heard the sad tone. "We were friends, Pete." He saw Max's mouth curl down and tears begin to run down his cheeks to the corners of his mouth, where they had no trouble reaching his chin. "We were good friends. I befriended you. I brought you into my home. My wife thought you were sent from Heaven to straighten my bad habits out. My kids loved you, man! I loved you like a

brother. We ate dinners together. *We bullshitted together.* We...We...I thought..." The tears came faster.

It had been a long time since Pete had felt something other than freezone pump through his calloused heart. His eyes were now fastened to the floor, looking beyond the tiny, black-and-white checker-board tile, and into his thoughts. *This is the price I have to pay for $46,380.22 a year salary. No amount of money was worth this type of pain.*

His heart ached, and he felt a heavy hurt in his throat. He wanted to tell Max that everything would be okay. That he would erase the tapes--but he couldn't. His eyes came up to meet Max, who was barely standing. He was slumped between the last urinal and the tile wall, just staring down. The tears now dripped like a clock ticked, steady and forever.

Pete felt the urge to do something, to say something. Never had this happened to him before, and now he was afraid for Max. The jovial little man had never shown Pete this side of him. Maybe Max had never seen it himself. "Max...Max, will you listen to me?"

It was a grumble but understandable, "Fuck you!"

Pete placed his hand in front of him, unconsciously trying to emphasize or initiate some type of communication. "Max, listen to me. Yes, I am a federal agent, and my name is Peter A. Lewis."

"What's the *A* stand for, Pete? Asshole?"

Pete took the slight insult as a way to ease closer to Max. "Yes, Max. My middle name is Asshole."

Max's eyes glanced up, and Pete noticed the slightest trace of amusement. Pete made a minute step forward. He just wanted to hold Max and tell him everything would work out. "And Max, I feel like a complete asshole. I had a job to do. How was I to know I would run into a guy like you? A guy I have a deep feeling for!"

He inched closer to Max. Max didn't move. Just leaned against the wall and stared at the floor with glassy eyes.

"Remember the first day I was in the pit, Max, and you gave me a winning trade? Then you invited me to lunch?"

Max's mouth moved slightly. "That was my first mistake."

Pete jumped on it. "No, it wasn't, pal. You had been making mistakes for years. You just didn't know it."

Pete saw Max push himself from the wall and turn his back, leaning one hand on the cold tile. He was calming down, and Pete wanted to talk him down even further. "Max, do you think I showed up here by chance? That I had nothing better to do than walk by the Exchange and decide I would go in and see if I could catch somebody cheating?"

"What the fuck are you doing here, Pete?"

Pete was within three feet of Max's back. His mind computer had been fouled by the emotional overload. "I'm here because you asked to see me, Max. But right this

moment, I'm here to save you from a whole lot of grief. Grief that you're just beginning to get a taste of."

Max turned and looked him in the eyes. His complexion matched the ivory-colored tile that covered the wall behind him. His breath smelled of booze and rotten eggs. Without looking twice, Pete noticed that Max had wet his pants. The poor bastard was really scared. His kinky black hair clumped in bunches, uncombed, making his thin face look ever thinner. The tears kept coming.

Pete was tempted to reach out, but not yet. Instead, he pulled a handkerchief from his pocket and handed it to Max. "Here, wipe the snot off your face."

Max obliged and said, "You didn't answer me, Pete. What are you doing here, really? Who is going to be able to fix this mess? That's all I want, to have this mess straightened out. I've got a wife and kids and a mom and dad and..."

Pete put his finger to his mouth, "Shhh." he didn't want to lose him now. He took a deep breath and began to explain. "Max, I'm an undercover agent for the FBI. Have been for a long time. The Justice Department has received thousands of complaints from disgruntled commodity customers claiming fraud, corruption, theft, you name it. I was elected to come to Chicago and investigate." That was about as much as he could say without blowing the investigation wide open.

"What did you find?"

Pete weighed his words. "I found that there is a lot of cheating going on. It doesn't take a federal officer to figure that out."

Max's eyes were red, but the tears had stopped. "And what about me and the other guys who made the tax deal with you?"

He nodded, keeping his voice calm. "There's a lot of that going on also."

Max looked down at his feet, a slight glare from the humming, fluorescent lights lit up a round balding spot on the back of his head. "What's going to happen to me, Pete?"

Pete didn't answer at first. He wanted to be gentle with Max. He liked the man too much to hurt him any more than he already had been hurt. "I'm not sure, Max. What happens to you is really going to be up to you."

"What do you mean?"

"I mean that the government isn't after the minnows. They are after the big fish. You are just a minnow who wanted to be a shark. I guess all of us have that same desire once in a while."

Max's words were mumbled. "Jesus Christ, what's my wife gonna say? My kids? My mom? My..."

Pete interrupted quickly. "Max, the imagination is a holy thing because it has no limits. Where an artist uses his imagination to his own human limits, a common man can find it self destructing. Try not to project or imagine. Leave that to the artists of the world. Just step easy, a day at a time, and stay out of trouble. Maybe you should take some time off. Spend it with your family. Be honest with your wife. It will be a long time before

anything happens, so try to block it out of your mind. You screwed up and got caught, but the punishment won't be nearly as bad as you will imagine it will be. I've checked your record. You've never been in trouble before. If you want to talk, I'll give you a number where I can be reached twenty-four hours a day. I'll be glad to talk to your wife and explain things to her. It's not the end of the world, even though it will seem that way. We can talk anytime you want."

The voice was pitiful. "Off the record, no tapes, no cameras or whatever you guys use?"

"Completely off the record, Max. We'll talk as friends, if that's possible." Pete then grabbed Max and hugged him tight. Max's arms hung limp, but Pete kept a tight grip on the man. "You're going to be all right, my friend. Just be cool and don't let your buddies rattle your cage. I will pull as many strings as I can to clean this thing up with as little pain as possible for you and your family, okay?"

Finally, Pete felt the frail arms rise and come behind him squeezing back. "Okay, Pete," Max said. Pete felt the lump in his throat grow. What a cesspool job, he thought. As he broke from Max, he held him by the shoulders.

Tears welled in Max's eyes again. "Pete, two questions!" He blew his nose with Pete's handkerchief then wiped his eyes. "You like this kind of work?"

The words burned at Pete's soul like a searing iron. He felt his lips part, and he stared beyond Max, beyond the tile wall, beyond the Exchange and the City of Chicago to the dirty alleys of New York City and the heartless drug pushers.

"Pete?"

"Yeah, Max?"

"Do you like this work?" he repeated.

He forced his mind back to Max's searching eyes. "No, Max. Not this kind of work. What's your second question?"

Max's spaniel eyes were sad. "How do I really know you're a federal agent?"

Pete smiled at him. "Is there a doubt in your mind, Max?"

"Not really, but I just wondered if you carried a badge."

Pete took his hands from Max's shoulders and bent down to pull up his pant leg. He rose quickly and produced a gold badge with the large letters FBI and a black Beretta. "Proof enough, Max?"

He watched Max gulp hard and stumble around him to the sink, where he splashed water on his face. As he looked in the mirror and wiped his face on two paper towels, he spoke. "I look a mess." Then he turned and faced front again. "I never would have believed it in a million years. Then last night I got the call from Franko..." Alarm suddenly painted his face. He was about to betray his friends again.

Pete saw the panic and put both hands up. "That's okay, Max. We can hash over everything later and see how we can get you out of this with the least amount of damage.

We don't have to talk about it now. Let's just go someplace quiet and have a cup of coffee, and I'll drive you home."

Max turned and looked at himself in the mirror again. "Jesus Christ, what a mess. I'm really buzzed. I'll take you up on the coffee, but not around here. Certain people will be looking for me. A few cups of coffee, and then I'll drive home."

They walked out together. Pete put his arm around Max's thin shoulder and squeezed. "Everything is going to work out okay, you'll see." Then he said to himself, at least I hope so.

FIFTY-THREE

Bermuda Jade
December 23, 1988

Tony Lorenzo stood grinning in front of a mahogany conference desk as if posing for a picture. His hand was resting atop reams of subpoenas ready to be issued to brokers and commodity firms at both Chicago Exchanges.

"Congratulations, Michael. Thanks to you we are on our way to breaking *the* largest investment scam in the history of the United States."

Michael sat, unimpressed, legs crossed, listening patiently. He simply nodded, knowing praise was dangerous to most men. Lorenzo continued in a more serious tone. He motioned with his hand toward Pete, who sat next to Michael. "I am required to take chances, as is Agent Lewis here. We are paid by the government to keep crime in our designated areas under control, be it white, blue, or black-collar crime. That's what we do for a living, and sometimes it seems like we're fighting a losing battle." He hesitated and looked down at the subpoenas. "I don't really know if I would have taken the chance you did if I were a civilian." He looked up at Michael with warmth in his eyes. "So, in case nobody has thanked you for your help, and since I don't know when I will be transferred out of this district, I will take this opportunity to thank you for doing something we couldn't have done alone. We accomplished in eighteen months what it would have taken a good five years to accomplish without you. You have my personal thanks."

Michael looked over at Pete, who returned his stare and shrugged his shoulders. He let his eyes move back to Lorenzo. "How many subpoenas are there, and when will they be served?"

Lorenzo picked up one of the packets of stapled papers about a half inch thick and looked at it quickly. "Two hundred eighteen subpoenas in all, with more to follow. They will be served some time after the first of the year."

Michael pressed him, feeling a sense of urgency. "How long after the subpoenas will the indictments come out?"

Lorenzo walked from the stack, looking a little discouraged, probably because Michael hadn't been impressed with his complimentary acknowledgment. He sat on the edge of his massive desk and said, "I imagine we'll have indictments ready in six to eight months."

Michael noticed that Lorenzo was more serious now. He must have realized Michael wasn't after thanks or gratitude. "It's going to take a lot of man hours and a lot of manpower to sift through the volumes of records we subpoena."

Michael bit his left cheek, feeling the sting as he looked down at the plush carpet. He thought for a moment, then said, "How many indictments do you think you'll serve?"

Lorenzo stood. He pushed his arms in front of him and turned his palms toward the ceiling. "I have no idea, Michael. Maybe fifty."

Impatience flew through his mind like an angry shark looking for food. "Fifty? That's it? Two hundred and eighteen subpoenas and only fifty indictments?"

Lorenzo raised one eyebrow and lowered the other in a frown. "Fifty is good for the first round. The most I've ever served at one time prior to this investigation is twenty-- two, and that was to a very large corporation. Fifty will lead to fifty more, then fifty more until we get almost everybody. We'll look under every rock, Mike, don't worry."

Michael's thoughts were ahead of Lorenzo. "I'm not worried, if they have it coming; the ones you miss, I'll get."

Lorenzo analyzed the last statement and then said, "You know my door is always open to you, but there are some things I won't be able to help you out of, Michael."

Michael smiled and said, "That's all right, Tony. I'll pay for my own parking tickets."

Lorenzo turned and walked to his desk, then looked back at Michael. "Well, you just try to keep everything clean or I'm of no use to you whatsoever!"

Michael sighed and ran his hands through his hair. He expected but didn't like government cop-outs. His eyes zeroed in on the bridge of Lorenzo's nose. Then he spoke with a soft voice. "I'm straight with you, Tony, and I expect the same from you. First you tell me your door is always open to me, then, you add conditions to your welcome! You can either assist me when I need it or you can't. You either make a commitment or you don't. You take two simple words, *try* and *clean*, and make them abstract and ambiguous. A strong man doesn't even have the word *try* in his vocabulary. He substitutes the word *will*. The man simply will get the job done. For another man, the word *try* means 'maybe'! On the other hand, *clean*, for one man, means the absence of dirt or evil; for another man, *clean* is anything goes that accomplishes a mission. For the Feds, the end justifies the means, that's clean." He hesitated for a moment, uncrossed his legs, and ran his long fingers down the crease of his Italian-made slacks. "I made you a promise, Tony, and I fulfilled that promise. I pointed out the bad guys to the government, and you didn't care what means I used to get you the information needed to indict dirty brokers. Now, I'll promise you something else. I won't do anything the government wouldn't do to accomplish the balance of my mission." He felt the coldness travel through him as his eyes watched Lorenzo closely.

Pete shifted his weight in his chair and said bluntly with annoyance in his voice, "Let's move this conversation along, boys, and screw the semantics!"

Michael continued to rub the creases in his slacks and watched with cold eyes as Lorenzo glanced at Lewis, then back at him. Lorenzo's expression had lost its authority

as his lips sagged with exasperation. Michael sensed the same thought was going through all three minds--the government had no limits, therefore, Michael declared no limits!

He saw that Lorenzo was satisfied with letting Pete's impatient mood end Michael's challenge for an argument. He continued in a peaceful tone . "Okay, Mike, I'd appreciate it if you would give me the benefit of the doubt once in a while. Let's not argue; we still have a lot of work to do, and right now we need each other." He breathed out heavy. "The balance of this investigation won't deviate from other government probes. The government will push hard for the initial indictments, then they will pull back their manpower and let the domino effect take place. Plea bargaining, deal making, scare tactics, you know how the law works..."

Not worth a shit, Michael said to himself. Law, order, guilt, innocence, right, wrong were all distant cousins when it came to the American Justice System. They lived in separate valleys, seldom to cross each other's paths. Whoever had the most money, power, and influence would be the winners in the government's chess game--justice would play a small part. Talk about pre-arranged trades in the trading pits. The government did the same thing in the halls of the Federal Building before trials. The deals were already made before the attorneys walked into the court room--the fix!

Lorenzo continued his speech. "...It's going to take years to bring everybody to trial. With a case of this magnitude we could see a five to ten-year stretch from start to finish. Hell, it's already been over two years, and we're just getting to the subpoenas."

Michael looked at Lewis, who had echoed the same words in an earlier conversation. The law books he had read also indicated the length of time it took to bring a man to justice. It was crazy! He said with disgust, "That is absurd, Tony. Ten years to bring corrupt men to justice--if there is such a thing in your system. What you consider a victory, I consider an insult, a travesty."

He saw Lorenzo shake off the comment as he said, "Mike, this case, unfortunately, will be so devastating to the commodity markets that it will break the industry. Its credibility and any positive image it had will be crushed. The days of the open outcry and floor brokers are numbered. The days of the commodity scams are history. Sure, the trickery will continue for awhile longer, but the industry's death is at hand. At least twenty per cent of the commodity industry will fall as a result of our sting operation, maybe more. That's four to six hundred brokers, brokerage firms, clerks, not to mention the accountants, attorneys, and politicians."

Lorenzo sat down in his high-back leather chair, abruptly placed both hands in front of him, and weaved his fingers together. "What do you think the reaction will be at the Exchanges?"

Michael looked out the window. The swirling snow soothed his impatient mood. "They will naturally defend themselves to the hilt, claiming the government is full of shit, and say it's a few rotten apples, not the whole bushel. They will tighten floor rules and regulations, fine, suspend, and eject a number of sacrificial lambs in an attempt to maintain

their image as an honest, free-market industry. They will fight like mean rats to protect their self-governing status. Without the ability to make and change rules and regulations on their own, and with the possibility of an effective government watchdog in their back yard, the whole network of corruption would break down. You'll see some of the big shots resign as directors of the Exchange and get out while they can. You'll also see a number of companies go belly-up--bankrupt. Without the present system, they can't function."

He brought his attention back from the wild outside weather and focused on Lorenzo's thin mustache. "The Exchanges will go on full alert, policing the pits, the offices, the curbs, the bars, and the toilets. They will open old files of brokers with trading violations and re-evaluate them. The brokers who have little or no Exchange clout will be sacrificed. They will probably outlaw dual trading, which has been criticized for years as a means of cheating the public. They will precede the inevitable and try to make it look like it is the Exchange Governors' idea to tighten disciplinary screws and not the government regulators'. They will never admit that their past negligence is what forced stricter government intervention and a restructure of the rules and regulations. Yes, a ban on dual trading will be a must. Exchange spokesmen will publicize the fact that they will no longer stand for the abuse of dual trading. The Exchanges will come out with statements saying they will go to any lengths to protect the revered customer. Therefore, a ban on dual trading, curb trading, and any other minor infraction they can think of, will be instituted. The Exchanges and their attorneys are so used to deception they believe their own lies. They will do anything to save their almighty asses, and to keep the government from putting a hard-nose Federal regulator in charge. The last thing they want is for anybody to see how they really work."

Lorenzo asked, "Do you think by letting the SEC govern the commodity markets, as well as the stock market, that the corruption would be stifled?"

The blowing snow mesmerized him, flakes of truth in a city of lies. "Tony, you know as well as I that the SEC will have their feet in the door within three years. That's pure logic; it's pure politics. If you push this investigation as hard as you say you're going to, there will be too much pressure on the politicians not to let the SEC take a shot at watchdogging the commodity markets."

"Do you think it will work?"

Michael pursed his lips and shook his head. "No! You know what I think of government agencies. They are either incompetent bureaucrats, or they are as corrupt as the animals they stalk. No, I think the broker will be replaced by the computer. I think the Exchanges will eventually produce larger electric bills than they do volume, and the value of memberships will go to zero. I think the investigation will land lots of small fish, a few big fish, but as usual, the piranhas will get away. When the SEC does step in, their job will be minimal. The Exchange is killing itself. It's just a matter of time."

Lorenzo placed both hands palms down on his desk, breathed deeply, and said, "Well, the piranhas won't get away if I have anything to say about it."

Michael spoke with curiosity. "Tony, just for my own information. When your prosecutors are preparing to go to trial, how do you plan on finding a jury who will be able to understand the crimes that the defendants are being accused of?"

Lorenzo looked at Michael as if there were something wrong with the question. "Jury selection will be no different for these cases than any other case."

Michael nodded. "You think twelve common people who know nothing about commodity jargon, hand signals, shouting, yelling, pushing, shoving, will be able to understand in a few weeks what it takes years for the professionals to learn?"

"I...I really never thought about it, Mike. But I'm sure our prosecutors will have that under control."

"I hope you're right. Otherwise you may as well conduct the proceedings in Latin, because no juror will understand a damn thing, and you can bet the defense attorneys will take full advantage of that."

Lorenzo dismissed the insight with a wave of his hand and said, "Leave the jury up to the prosecutors. We're out of it at that point."

Michael looked at his watch and motioned to Lewis that it was time to go. He remained silent as he stood up from his chair and put on his raccoon jacket. Lorenzo rose from his chair and stroked his chin. Something was on his mind.

"Michael...uh, just out of curiosity and off the record, did you ever hear any rumors as to what may have happened to Mr. Zitello, Mr. Peterson, and his two associates?"

Michael kept his face emotionless, as he always did when he was verbally challenged, but he welcomed the question. "I've heard a number of rumors, Tony."

Lorenzo searched him with his detective eyes. "Such as?"

He allowed a slight smile to appear on his face. "Probably the same rumors you've heard, that they were all skimming more than their share of laundered money and a few boys from New York took them for a long ride. I heard they found out the Feds were on to them, so they left town and are now living in South America." For effect, he hesitated, then said, "and I also heard that a clandestine group working for the government just got sick of 'em and killed 'em."

Lorenzo smoothed his mustache, then tucked his hands under his armpits. "I like that last rumor the best, don't you?

Michael let his smile remain as he buttoned his heavy coat. "I don't really give a shit about them, but the idea of a covert group of good guys killing bad guys does lend more imagination and intrigue to the stories going around."

Lorenzo gazed hard at him. "And I don't imagine you ever heard much about the whereabouts or disappearance of Salvano Ruzzo?"

Michael knew Lorenzo was toying with him and was enjoying the social interrogation. As long as he didn't have to pull the trigger, Lorenzo had been done a big favor by having a few of the big boys eliminated. "I heard the same rumors, Tony."

Lorenzo walked from around his desk and buttoned the top two buttons of his dark suit. "It must have been a coincidence, Michael, that the same night Salvano Ruzzo disappeared from his heavily guarded mansion in Lake Geneva, John Simpson crawled into bed only to find that his sleeping partner for the night was a coral snake. How do you think a Brazilian coral snake got all the way from Brazil to downtown Washington, D.C., up thirty-nine floors to a penthouse, past four seasoned bodyguards, and into Mr. Simpson's bed?"

Michael was enjoying the game and played along, letting his body rock slightly and his eyes roll in thought. "I haven't heard too many rumors regarding Mr. Simpson's bed partners, but I do know that snakes are amazing creatures and will travel a long distance and fight many obstacles just to keep a date with one of their kind. Maybe it was a blind date, and after traveling all that distance the snake was probably disappointed in what he found."

Lorenzo walked to the window. "How do you think a Brazilian coral snake could get past the guards and into his bedroom?"

Michael saw Pete shrug his shoulders and push out his lower lip with a "who knows?" look on his face. "Remember, Tony, the snake has been around longer than the cockroach--since the beginning of time, according to the Bible. It developed virtues available to, but not usually found in most men. They're called perseverance and patience. The snake that Simpson went to bed with probably had both." With a slight squint of the eye and a sideways movement of jaw, he continued. "Snakes not only have a cunning mind, they also have the physical ability to snatch and patiently swallow a rodent five times their size. They have the ability to smooth out like syrup and squeeze under a door with less than a half inch between the bottom of the door and the floor. And I'll bet you a bottle of scotch that Mr. Simpson's carpeting is a gaudy red and black and white floral, the same color as a Brazilian coral snake. Four big bodyguards probably are trained to watch for big, bad guys with guns, not a tiny piece of moving carpet."

Lorenzo stood silent with his back to Michael and Pete. He knew Lorenzo was sorry he had brought up the subject of Simpson. Michael motioned to Pete that they leave. As they moved toward the door, Michael added, "There is one thing you neglected to mention, Tony, in your hypothesizing."

Still facing the window, Lorenzo asked, "What's that, Michael?"

"You neglected to mention that both Ruzzo and Simpson's misfortune took place exactly one year from the date that Colleen McFadden was beaten to a pulp. There may be some connection there. You should check it out--Merry Christmas, Tony. Pete and I have business to attend to, then I have a raft of shopping to do."

Michael winked at Pete, and they both reached the double wooden door when Lorenzo spoke.

"Mike?"

Michael turned and looked into a stern but pale face, "Yes, Tony."

He noticed a slight twitch of Lorenzo's right eye. "Hypothetically, why don't you think I received one of those snakes? After all, I was somewhat responsible for what happened to Colleen also."

He softened his look and said, "Tony, those snakes are a pretty good judge of character. You admitted Colleen should be pulled away from Ruzzo. It was Simpson who forced her to stay. Besides, you don't have carpeting in your home; you have hardwood floors throughout, and your bedroom door fits flush to the floor. Merry Christmas, Tony!" He laughed to himself. Lorenzo would wonder for a long time how Michael knew the details of his home when he had never been there.

As he reached for the door handle, Michael turned back. Lorenzo's face had lost most of its color. The smile had left Michael's face. He spoke with strength in his voice. "And, Tony, if *you* ever need *me* for anything, my door is always open also--regardless of the circumstances."

* * *

Pete stopped Michael on the second floor landing and asked, "Off the record and of course hypothetically, how would the snake find its way to Simpson's bed?"

Michael's lips parted in a smile, something he hadn't felt like doing in a long time. "Beats the hell out of me, Pete. Something about a snake having an acute sense of smell, and Simpson wears a very distinct and expensive aftershave lotion called Bermuda Jade. Hypothetically, I imagine you could starve a coral snake for a month or two then give him a mouse for dinner with a drop of Bermuda Jade on his hairy little cheeks. Then, you could starve the snake for another month and put a mouse wearing the Bermuda Jade on the other side of the room. The snake will find the mouse, believe me! Then one more month and put the mouse outside, same thing--dead mouse, happy snake. After eight to ten months, the snake relates the Bermuda Jade to food--and that son of a bitch will crawl all the way to Washington, D.C. for lunch."

He turned to walk down the remainder of the stairs, and he felt Pete's tight grip on his arm. His eyes were slanted in doubt. "How did the snake get into the house?"

Michael noticed Pete's cautious attitude and he let the smile fade from his face. "Maybe the man who trained the snake is like the snake, and can kill things larger than himself, and can go undetected by blending into the surroundings he finds himself in, and squeeze through small places, and can smell and hear like an animal. Hypothetically, it could have been a man like that who was able to gain entrance into Ruzzo's and Simpson's fortresses."

Michael turned, stepped forward and walked down the marble stairs. "By the way, Pete. How is Simpson doing?"

"He's on indefinite leave of absence from the Bureau. Physically he's fine but the company psychiatrist has doubts whether he'll ever be able to serve with any reliability in

government again. It seems he's still a basket case, suffers from insomnia, and when he does sleep, he wakes up hysterical because of the nightmares about Brazilian coral snakes."

They hit the foyer together. Both men gathered their winter jackets around their necks, seeing the wild snow fly outside.

They walked quickly to the automatic doors when Michael said, "If the dummy would change the color of his carpet and his brand of cologne, he would probably sleep better. By the way, Pete, what would you like for Christmas?"

Pete didn't answer for a moment. Then he spoke with a tone of humor. "I don't want aftershave lotion, if that's what you're asking--especially Bermuda Jade! How about a mongoose?...Yeah, I think I'd like a mongoose for Christmas!" The electric door opened, and a blast of winter air slapped Michael in the face. He raised his head and breathed the cold air deep into his lungs, feeling its energy. He walked with his good friend toward the State Street shopping district and a few hours of mindless browsing.

FIFTY-FOUR

Subpoena and Deal
Tuesday, Jan. 17, 1989, 11:00 p.m.

Pete turned on the dome light of the purple Volkswagen and read the name out loud to his partner, Larry Duffy. "Theodore Terrin. His trading symbol is TITS, and he works for a broker syndicate group called Coast to Coast Commodities, Inc.. After Terrin, we visit two more guys, and we're finished for the evening."

He looked over at Duffy, who was trying to stretch his stocky body, but a simple adjustment was a major task in the small VW compartment. "Christ, Lewis! What made you pick this piece of shit to serve subpoenas?"

Pete glanced back down at the papers he was studying and said, "Since they put a cellular phone in for me, I've grown kind of attached to the little beast. Look at that engine, Duff. I can do wheelies in this little bug."

Duffy groaned with discomfort. "You might be able to do wheelies, but you have a hell of a time just trying to find the room to fart."

He rolled down the window and stuck his head outside. "Smells good out here, Pete. Somebody's fireplace is working overtime!" Pete felt the cold air touch his cheeks and inhaled deeply, savoring the scent of burning cherry wood on a cold night. What a luxury, to sit around a dark room with the glow of a crackling fire, a soft woman to keep him company, and a bottle of expensive brandy, not necessarily in that order. Get it out of your mind, Lewis. Your job is a destroyer of such dreams, not a promoter.

Duffy pulled his head in. "Nice neighborhood. Don't any of these guys live in the brownstones? Christ. These homes must all go for a half-mil plus."

Pete spoke without looking up. "Terrin paid six hundred seventy-five thousand bucks for this joint. He got a steal. They were asking seven-fifty."

Duffy sniffled once and said in a drone of irony, "You mean the prick didn't pay full price?"

Pete tried to concentrate on the subpoena and grunted, "Maybe he had a bad day in the market."

Duffy continued to thrash around, cradling the small car back and forth as if two teenagers were screwing in the back seat. Pete looked up and said, "Stop rocking the goddamn boat, will ya Duffy? You're making me sick."

Duffy ignored him and continued to jockey for comfort. "This is what you call a constipation, Lewis. For Christ sake, when is this guy supposed to be home?"

Pete refolded the subpoena, slipped it into his jacket, and glanced up the street. "This might be him coming now. We'll let him get in the house first, then we'll serve him. You want to be the good guy, or do you want the job of Devil's Advocate?"

Duffy exhaled with frustration from being forced to conform to the tiny box they sat in. "I'll be the bad guy. I'm in that frame of mind after sitting in this shitcan. Besides, you're getting too soft with these crooked bastards."

Pete let the crack slide. "Okay, you're the bad ass with TITS Terrin. Jesus. What a nickname." He squinted through the small windshield as low-riding headlights approached with speed. A black Corvette pulled onto a tiled drive, which led two hundred feet to a large, white colonial house. Two or three rooms on the main floor were lighted and one on the second floor. The Corvette slowed and disappeared around the north corner of the house. He could see the exhaust billow and disappear into the cold air. He was probably waiting for the garage door to open.

When the exhaust disappeared and he saw a dim light go on near the far end of the house, he said, "Okay Duff. Let's go see what Mr. Terrin has to say. You're the bad guy, and remember, we need names--as many names as we can get. Put the pressure on him. Let's go."

Pete was out of the VW and around the front of the car when Duffy whispered in desperation. "How do I get out of this sardine can?"

Without looking back, Pete said, "Use a shovel, you nitwit!"

The walk to the house was half a football field. A light frost and shallow covering of snow had Duffy's 230-pound bulk slipping as he walked in his heavy leather shoes. Pete looked back at him and grumbled, "Told you to wear sneakers, Nutsy."

Duffy rebuffed Pete. "Why don't we just use the goddamn sidewalk?"

"Because we'd have to walk a half mile to get to it."

Pete pushed an ivory doorbell button surrounded with what looked like a very expensive brass frame, which complemented the rest of the hardware on the door. He rang the bell again. The chimes sounded like an overzealous altar boy at the Consecration of Holy Mass.

A foyer light went on, and the door was unlocked and opened quickly. He immediately caught the stale draft of alcohol, and he could see in Terrin's red eyes that he had been drinking and probably snorting most of the day. His face wrinkled and moved from side to side as he tried to focus his eyes and look over Pete's shoulder at Duffy. "Pete!...Pete Alexander!...Whadya doing in Barrington this time of night?"

Pete had already given his introduction four times earlier in the evening. He began again. "Ted, this isn't a social call. My name is Pete Lewis, and I am an FBI agent. This is Larry Duffy. He is with the U.S. Attorney's Office on special assignment with the FBI. We would like to speak with you for a moment."

He watched as Terrin hesitated and groped to understand. "You guys both Feds?"

Pete pulled out his badge and held it up eight inches from Terrin's face. Duffy's badge and picture ID flipped out right over Pete's shoulder. "We're both Feds, Ted. Can we talk?"

Terrin's eyes drooped and blinked in drunken, slow motion. His speech was slow. "I knew you were a Fed, Pete. Known it for a couple a months. Guess I been waitin' for ya to ring my door bell." He licked his dry lips and said with a carefree slur, "Fuck it, Pete. I can take a joke. Come on in."

He stepped back, swinging the door open, and with an exaggerated hand motion, welcomed them both into his house. "Never let it be said that Ol' TITS Terrin wasn't cordial to the Federal Government."

They stepped inside, and Terrin closed the door. The foyer was as large as Pete's bedroom, and Terrin motioned for Pete to follow him. "I'm gonna have a drink, Pete. You and your buddy, what's his name, want beer, booze, coffee?"

Pete blew into his hands, trying to hurry the warmth. He followed Terrin toward the kitchen. "No thanks, maybe next time, Ted." Next time, he thought. Next time he saw Terrin would be in a court room and after that, jail. For some reason, the thought disturbed him as he looked around the magnificent house and its expensive furnishings. The asshole had the world by the balls. He could make millions just filling orders in the pit, but greed had crept into the arena, and Terrin had been caught up in the "gimme more" philosophy.

Terrin's country kitchen was the size of Pete's whole condo with a breakfast room, two pantries, a bath, and a green house extending out from the back of the house.

Terrin motioned to a round, dark, oak table with six captain chairs and said, "Have a seat, guys. I'm gonna have a beer. Sure you won't join me?"

Duffy spoke with harsh, government authority. "Terrin, we don't want beer, we don't want coffee, we just want to talk to you, and we haven't all night."

Pete sensed someone behind him and turned in a start as he heard a female voice. "Ted?"

Pete nodded to a pretty little brunette wearing a pink cashmere robe tied at the neck. She spoke with a tone of hostility. "Ted, what's going on? Don't you think it's a little late to be having a party?"

Pete caught Duffy's eyes change to enforcer as his large bulk turned to look at the girl. He spoke with no apology in his tone. "Maybe you should join us, Mrs. Terrin. My name is Larry Duffy, from the U.S. Attorney's Office, and this is Chief Investigator Pete Lewis, of the FBI."

Pete watched the brunette's face grow pale, changing in seconds from hostile, to emotionless, to fearful. She looked at Terrin. His back was to her as he pulled a beer from the commercial Sub-Zero refrigerator. Then she looked back at Duffy. His face had arranged itself into a federal scowl. "What's going on, Ted?"

Terrin turned, shut the refrigerator door, and took a deep breath as he popped open a can of Budweiser. He took a gulp of his beer and licked his lips nervously. "I'm not sure, Kim. Just have a seat, and let's see what good ol' Pete has to say."

Pete hands rested on the table, motionless, like empty gloves. His thoughts clashed against each other. Many of the agents he knew reveled in this type of face-to-face dialogue. After years of investigation he understood his fellow agents had the right to go into a home and scare the shit out of an alleged suspect, but this type of work wasn't for him. He wanted to go after the home breakers, not the home makers. He would kill a drug pusher in a minute, but he felt sympathy for Terrin and his family. He knew what kind of pain they would experience during the next few years. The fear, the uncertainty, the humiliation, and worst of all, the power of the imagination that would lead them out of today and into the nightmare of tomorrow. He might as well get the show on the road. "Ted, you are in a lot of trouble!"

Duffy couldn't wait to interject with a threatening voice. "Goddamn right you're in trouble!"

Pete ignored Duffy and looked over at Kim Terrin, who had taken the comment very seriously. Her face was plagued with fear and total bewilderment. Her eyes flashed from Pete to Duffy and back again to Pete.

His attention moved to Terrin. He paused. There was no easy way to say this. Yet he had to make his words effective to set the stage for pulling more information from Terrin. "Ted, we have gathered a boat load of incriminating evidence that could put you and a good number of other brokers in jail for a long time."

He saw Kim Terrin jerk a breath inward. She spoke with a quivering voice. "TED! What is this all *about*?"

Terrin scratched his head and tried to shake off her worry. "Just a few bad trades, Kim, that's all. Uhh...it's nothin' bad."

Duffy spouted out, "It's more than that, buddy boy."

Pete looked at Duffy, telling him with his eyes to go easy, but he pushed with the immediate need to let the wife know the severity of what was happening. As difficult as it was, she had to know the truth, and he knew he would need her support later. "Mrs. Terrin--and Ted, it's more than a few bad trades we're talking about. We are speaking of major trading violations. Possible mail and wire fraud, tax fraud, violations of the Commodity Exchange Act, and there is a good possibility Ted could be charged with conspiracy under RICO, which is simply the acronym for Racketeer Influenced and Corrupt Organizations Law. If indicted, tried, and found guilty under RICO, you are going to spend the better part of the rest of your youth in jail. And if you go to jail, Ted, you won't be young when you come out, even if it's just for a few years. You age like a dog in jail, believe me. I've seen a lot of men go in young and come out old, and I hope that scares you, because that's what you're facing."

Terrin leaned back and regarded the wooden beams crossing the ceiling. Then he looked at Pete. "Pete, where do you come off telling me I committed a crime? I'm just a broker trying to make a living."

Duffy leaned his heavy frame forward for more emphasis.

Pete saw the government eyes speak before the mouth. "An honest living, Mr. Terrin? Or is your living derived primarily at the cost of the customer? We have information that points to the latter, so don't give us any drivel about you just trying to make an honest living."

Terrin looked offended. "Hell. I just do my job. I'm reliable, show up every day, fill a lot of customer orders, trade some for myself..."

Duffy cut him off gruffly. "Have you ever skimmed or shaved points from customer orders? Have you ever used bagmen to filter through points that should have gone to the customer?"

Duffy's words were effective. The room was graveyard still. Pete thought Kim Terrin had stopped breathing, and Terrin was nervously licking at his lips. Finally, he ran his fingers through his red hair the wrong way, making it stand straight up. Then, he spoke. "Everybody picks off a little here and there. If you're going to come down on me, you better come down on ninety per cent of the brokers at the Exchange."

Duffy persisted. "Is that a yes, Mr. Terrin?"

"Well, hell! Yes...no, I don't know. What am I supposed to say?"

Pete caught his eye and said. "You just have to tell the truth, Ted. We have taped breakfast and lunch conversations where you admit fraudulent dealings. You made a deal with me to buy phony losses from a bogus New York company and pay me cash for the purchase under the table. You also made a deal to buy a portion of my trading losses and pay me back under the table. That's conspiracy to commit fraud, Ted, not jay-walking."

Terrin said, "I should have an attorney here. I don't need this crap. I haven't even been served with a subpoena yet. I should have an attorney."

Pete reached into his jacket and produced a stapled packet of papers and flipped it onto the middle of the table. "There is your subpoena, Ted. We're checking every trade you made for the past five years, who you made them with, and who they traded with. We'll also be checking your withdrawals, your deposits, your taxes, your bank accounts, your wife's bank accounts, your kids', both your parents'. We'll check on your house payments, car payments, credit card payments. We'll even find out if you paid cash for your dog and where that cash came from. We'll know in one hundred twenty days how many dollars you made, how you made them, who paid you, how much you spent, how much you saved, and how much you invested."

Pete looked at Kim Terrin, whose eyes had filled with tears. This was always the hard part of the job, he thought. The innocent bystander watching the empire crumble in seconds. "I'm sorry, Mrs. Terrin!"

She looked from her husband back to Pete, and her eyes were asking him to stop the nightmare. Not yet, he thought, this was just beginning. "Ted, do you know who we are? We're the Federal Bureau of Investigation. We investigate, and we find things--things that nobody else in the world can find, we find. When I was in the trading pit, that was your back yard, and you ripped me apart, but now you are in my back yard, and if you want, I can cut you apart piece by piece, your present, your past, and your future."

Duffy cut in. "And we can do it with or without novocaine." Pete folded his hands in front of him, trying to avoid Kim Terrin's stare. "I would suggest you find yourself a good criminal attorney tomorrow. We're not here tonight to arrest you, Ted. We're just here to serve the subpoena and talk to you while we still can."

Terrin's brow perked at the scent of a deal. Pete was amused. As drunk as Terrin was, he had the instincts of a gambler and could smell a deal coming. Pete gave Duffy a quick look, which said, takeover!

Duffy looked bored but puffed himself up ready to slash away like a true G-Man. He spoke gruffly, "One thing both of you should know, if you are tried under the statutes of RICO, Mr. Terrin, the government will seek harsher penalties than it would for a straight fraud case, and that includes seizure of assets and all profits earned through'your alleged illicit trading activities."

He paused for effect. "The government will take everything you own, Mr. and Mrs. Terrin."

Kim Terrin shoved back her chair hard, stood abruptly, and slammed her hand down in front of Ted. She had held up quite well, Pete thought, but she had heard enough. Now it was her turn to play a card for the government. Come on, girl, he thought to himself.

He didn't realize such a petite thing could shout so loudly. "I'VE HEARD ENOUGH. TED, WHAT HAVE YOU DONE? WHAT ARE YOU DOING? I PUT UP WITH YOUR DRINKING AND CAROUSING...AND, AND...LATE HOURS, AND NOW THIS???" She slammed her hand down again and Pete flinched. "YOU TELL THESE MEN YOU ARE INNOCENT OR TELL THEM YOU ARE GUILTY AND FIND OUT HOW YOU CAN GET OUT OF IT AS FAST AND AS SAFE AS POSSIBLE. DO YOU HEAR ME???" Sobbing now, she turned and walked to the sink, where she stopped for a moment. Pete saw spasms of fear and emotion shake her body. She turned on a gold faucet, splashed cold water on her face, and dried off with a fancy hand-towel.

She sniffled a few times and turned back toward Terrin. "You tell these men what they want, Ted, then you pray to God they don't decide to put you in jail and the children and me out on the street." She opened her mouth to say more, but no words came. She turned and hurried from the kitchen.

Terrin sat motionless, one hand around the beer can, the other holding his head up.

Pete sighed quietly. Duffy shrugged his thick shoulders. Finally after a good two minutes of silence, Terrin looked up at Pete and said, "Okay, what's the deal?"

FIFTY-FIVE

Pit Moles
Friday, January 20, 1989

Michael glanced over the top of the *Journal* and looked into Maria's large, dark eyes. "Have you seen the headlines?"

She lifted her dark eyebrows and brushed her long, black hair back with the side of her hand. "Not yet, you've been hogging the paper."

He smiled at her. "I'll read it to you. The headline reads:

> *"Pit Moles: FBI Sting Operation in Chicago Staggers Two Commodity Exchanges: Government Probe of Trading May Implicate 150 Brokers, Aims for Top: Taping Lunch Conversations Reveals Whole-Scale Corruption."*

Michael peered over the newspaper to see if Maria was still interested. She was watching him with waiting eyes and a coquettish smile. "Read on, Michael. You've been waiting for this for five years."

He winked at her and continued.

> *"This was a sting operation aimed at proving what many investors have long feared about Chicago's commodity industry. For nearly two years, a handful of federal agents put on brightly colored trading jackets and waded into the turbulent pits at the nation's two largest commodity futures exchanges, the Chicago Board of Trade and the Chicago Mercantile Exchange. There, they secretly taped hundreds of conversations between traders in the process of accumulating evidence of widespread shady dealings that cheated the public. The federal investigation, the largest ever of futures commodity trading, is sending shock waves through Chicago's investment community. Traders are stunned by its broad scope: numerous subpoenas have been issued, and federal authorities predict that as many as fifty indictments will result.*
>
> *"The scope of the investigation, one law-enforcement official says, 'is huge, the largest ever to hit the world's financial markets.' Two officials say indictments could be*

> *threatened against as many as five hundred individual traders, brokers and executives. Suspects could face charges of mail fraud, wire fraud, racketeering and trading-law violations to mention a few..."*

Michael lifted his eyes again and looked at Maria. Head cocked, her raven-black hair lay loose on her right shoulder, partially covering the white-on-white silk kimono she wore. "Is that it?" she asked.

He wrinkled his nose, flirting with her, and heard the crackle of the fire in the hearth. "No, there are about ten columns more. Would you like me to continue?"

She nodded yes.

"I'll skim it for you." He continued reading.

> *"The investigation covers trading violations in the Board of Trade's popular soybean and Treasury bond pits and in the Mercantile's S & P and currency pits. In a brief statement, Andrew Golden, who recently replaced John Simpson as Assistant to the Director of the FBI, said, 'Federal investigators sought and acquired evidence of such questionable practices as "bucket trading, skim trading, prearranged trading, curb trading, and bagging trades'"--transactions that cheat investors by failing to execute their trades at the most favorable price. Mr. Golden also stated that among numerous other trading violations, he had acquired evidence that indicated a large-scale money-laundering operation. All evidence is now being processed by agents to determine just how far the laundering operation extends.*

> *"Both Exchanges issued statements saying that they 'have no knowledge of surveillance activities of any nature being conducted on the trading floors and that if there is such an investigation going on, the financial world should know that it is pure nonsense to think that any more than a handful of violations by a few brokers would result from the government probe.*

> *"A spokesperson for the Mercantile Exchange said, 'There is no industry in the country that is policed as well as the commodity industry by its own members. Our self-governing privilege has inspired our membership to protect the invested dollars of our customers, and any covert action on the part of the government to destroy that image is gross irresponsibility and a miscarriage of justice'".*

Michael felt Maria's presence as she stood next to him. "I've heard enough, dear." Her hands wrapped around his neck, and she kissed his forehead, then his cheeks. "I think, as usual, you've accomplished what you started out to accomplish, Michael."

He folded the newspaper and placed it next to him on the couch. "Not everything, my *bella donna*. You know what I've been planning all these years. The FBI has just helped to clear the way."

She sat down next to him on the couch, and he smelled her fresh womanhood mixed with a touch of an elegantly intriguing fragrance. He put his arm around her and pulled her close. She cuddled, letting her hand reach through an open area of his terry-cloth robe. She gently ran her long fingernails up the front of his chest and down to his stomach, where her tantalizing nails lingered and played. "You're shrewd, Michael," she said, "and I love you."

He shivered with excitement, pulled her close, and kissed her cheek, then reached around and moved her long, black hair away from the side of her perfect face and kissed her ear, her neck, and her mouth. Her eyes closed as she rolled her head back on her shoulders. Her hand moved lower, and he came quickly alive. He uttered quietly into her ear, "If the children are all in bed, maybe we should call it an early evening."

She turned her head and kissed him, shallow at first, running her tongue over his lips, then deep, with love, more than spontaneous passion.

He gently broke and looked into her inviting eyes. "The children?"

She rattled off the litany of a watchful mother. "The twins are in bed, the girls are staying with friends, Patrick and Martin are with Bo in the coach house watching *Revenge of the Nerds*, Parts one, two and three, and Mary went to bed shortly after the twins."

His eyebrows lifted as Maria moved her hand lower and teased at his ready desire. "We're alone, then?"

She cocked her head back to look into his eyes. "As alone as it gets around here."

Michael kissed her and stood up quickly. "Good, let's play house. You go to the kitchen and cut up some fruit and cheese. I'll go up to the bedroom, light a fire, put some fifties and sixties music on, and meet you in the jacuzzi."

He saw her eyes light up. His words had nudged her excitement. "And a bottle of wine?"

He grinned. "Make it champagne, just like the old days!"

She joked, showing her perfect white teeth. "Just like the old days, except then it was Schlitz beer and Mrs. Fischer's potato chips in that old claw-footed bathtub."

He was at the library door when he looked over his shoulder, feeling Maria's extraordinary sensuality. "Even then, it was champagne and caviar to me, my beauty. Don't tarry, dear, or I'm liable to forget what I'm doing, take a cold shower, and go to bed."

A pillow followed him out of the room with an excited voice, "Give me seven minutes."

"That's too long!"
"Four minutes, then."
"You're on. Four minutes."

* * *

Hot air from the wall vent blew on the back of Pete's neck. The heat felt good as he sat in his condominium with his feet propped up on the coffee table, finishing an egg-salad sandwich and sipping on a lukewarm Coors.

Randy Harris was relaxed in a soft chair watching TV. He wore a white tee-shirt displaying the thick, black letters FBI on the front. He listened closely to the six o'clock news as anchorman Harvey Williams expounded on the day's activities in the financial world:

"The colorful and sometimes questionable commodity futures industry was rocked today by the revelation that for the past two years federal agents have been posing as traders and gathering information on illegal trading activity that could lead to as many as two hundred indictments.

"Attorneys from both Exchanges had little comment except that both were in agreement that they knew nothing of a government investigation until a few days ago.

"Traders scrambled throughout the day trying to piece together details of how their insular world could have been penetrated by undercover agents."

Pete pressed the remote control and switched to another channel. An attractive blond was halfway through her broadcast:

"...U.S. Attorney Anthony Lorenzo stated that subpoenas were handed out freely at both Exchanges asking for all membership and trading records from 1983 to the present. The voluminous records would enable investigators to search for fraudulent trading practices.

"According to Lorenzo, investigators are setting their sights high. 'We hope to target top-level executives, clearing firms, and broker syndicates who specialize in bagging and skimming the invested capital of the public,' he stated.

"Whatever the outcome, the investigation promises to shake the futures industry, provoke calls for regulatory reform, and raise questions in many minds about the ethics of the people who handle investors' money. Many are asking the question: 'Who is supposed to be the watchdog for these high-wheeling commodity brokers?'

"This is Nancy Bennett reporting to you live from the trading floor of the Chicago Mercantile Exchange for Eyewitness News Channel Three."

Lewis pushed the remote control, and a nice-looking black man holding a microphone stood in front of what looked to be the Federal Building:

"...the so-called commodity investor scam has apparently gone beyond the simple cheating by a few brokers in a few trading pits. According to a government source, the

sting operation, called Skim-Trim, which has been developing for over two years, follows the alleged market fraud all the way to the top officials who govern the Exchanges...and possibly even further. Executives of the Mercantile Exchange and Chicago Board of Trade could not be reached for comment, and the attorneys for both Exchanges indicated they would make a statement regarding the allegations after reviewing the subpoenas and other information provided by the government.

"Now, let's take you inside the Federal Building, where Carol Tucker is standing by to bring you a news conference about to begin with U.S. Attorney Anthony Lorenzo. This is Steve Kent reporting from outside the Federal Building."

The camera shifted to an empty podium with a four-foot circular plaque displaying Lady Justice with her blindfold on, holding her scales and the words "United States Justice Department" flowing around the perimeter. The large plaque was flanked by the flags of the United States, state of Illinois, and city of Chicago.

In the background, Pete heard the off-camera crew say, "They're coming now." The mobile camera blurred for a moment, then focused its attention on the corner of the room, where Pete saw six men enter. The first man was one of Lorenzo's bodyguards. The second man was Andy Golden, new Assistant to the Director of the FBI. The third man was Tony Lorenzo, then another bodyguard, and two assistant attorneys.

Lorenzo took the podium, retrieved a folded piece of stationery from his suit coat, and looked up at the group of reporters. His face looked different to Pete. He looked younger. He had shaved off his thin mustache for this, one of his few TV appearances. He was going for image. Pete said out loud, "Looks good, Tony!"

Lorenzo began to speak. Pete and Harris both leaned forward. Pete pushed the volume a notch higher.

"Ladies and gentlemen of the press, this is going to be brief as we all have a lot of work to do. For the past few weeks we have been issuing subpoenas to various brokers at the Chicago Board of Trade and the Chicago Mercantile Exchange. This morning we handed out over two hundred subpoenas to brokers, clerks, and commodity brokerage companies.

"After a two-year investigation we have found that the lax rules and regulations administered by Exchange officials and committee members have been abominable, and we have enough hard evidence in our possession that we feel warrants further investigation into the possible criminal activity of the members of both Exchanges, therefore, the issuance of the subpoenas today. When I receive more information, I will call another press conference and keep you all informed."

Pete watched Lorenzo begin to move from the podium, and a reporter asked quickly, "Attorney Lorenzo, do you consider this the largest financial investigation in U.S. history?"

Pete saw Lorenzo stop and look at Andy Golden standing next to him. Andy nodded, and Lorenzo moved back to the podium.

"Under normal circumstances I try to refrain from answering questions because the investigation is ongoing, and much information is still being processed. The last thing I want is for innocent people to be hurt by misconstrued statements."

Lorenzo took a drink of water and continued:

"Since the magnitude of this probe will affect the city of Chicago and its people, I will deviate for a moment from protocol and answer a few questions which are not directly related to the case. Your question again, Miss?"

The female reporter's persistent voice sounded again. "Do you consider this the largest financial scandal in the history of the United States?"

"I'm not calling it a scandal, I'm calling it an investigation."

"I'm sorry sir, let me rephrase the question. Is this the largest investigation of customer fraud in the history of the U.S.?"

"It's certainly the largest for me!"

Pete heard a tumult of questions being fired at Lorenzo, and the U.S. Attorney pointed one finger at a reporter.

From far off a voice spoke.

"Is it true that the FBI planted a mole, an agent in the pits, to gather information?"

"That is already news. The answer is yes."

The same male voice quickly asked another question. "Was there more than one mole assigned to the investigation?"

"I have no comment on that."

A female voice bellowed above the mob. "Mr. Lorenzo, is it true that the government had an inside informer, a member of the Exchange who guided your investigation?"

Immediately Pete felt the hair stand up on the back of his neck. With reflex actions he reached out, spilling the Coors on the coffee table as he zeroed his eyes in on Lorenzo. Don't give Hogan away, Lorenzo, he said to himself. He saw Andy Golden's blurred image stir with apparent nervousness. As if he had expected the question, Lorenzo's cool composure diverted, yet answered the question.

With a smile he said, "I assure you that our investigation is purely federal. If our suspicions are correct and there is wide-scale theft at the Exchanges, there will be plenty of brokers who will want to talk to us in order to help their own status with the government. This was a highly secretive investigation, and to rely on any single broker or member of the Exchange would have been imprudent on our part.

"Now, please excuse me. I have given you more information than usual because of the magnitude and possible consequences of the investigation."

Pete took a deep breath and released it slowly. Hogan would be found out soon enough without the help from a local news conference that would go national within a few hours. He commended Lorenzo's handling and dismissal of the question. The least bit of

hesitation or glance in the wrong direction would have alerted the fine-tuned suspicions of the media.

Pete sat back and rubbed his eyes as the TV channel cut for a commercial.

His thoughts focused on Michael, and he hardly noticed Harris get up from his chair and go to the refrigerator.

"Pete, you want another beer?"

He was oblivious to Randy's question. Ideas in his mind were rolling around like tumbleweeds looking for a corner to lodge. Hogan had fulfilled his promise to the Feds, and the government was doing its best to keep his name out of the spotlight. The investigation had gone smoothly, no major glitches except personality and ego problems between Hogan and Simpson. Otherwise no apparent tricks, at least he didn't think so--but something was rolling around inside of him that didn't fit. Why did he feel uncomfortable? Then he thought, shit, he had been trained to be suspicious, and he tried to dismiss his skepticism as his sixth sense going awry.

"Pete?"

His eyes moved slowly to Harris. "What?"

"Would you like another beer?"

"Sure, thanks." He pushed the button on the remote control and turned down the volume of the TV. He heard two cans pop open, and Harris set another can of Coors next to the one he had spilled in a moment of anxiety.

He felt Harris's eyes on him. "Well, Pete, what do you think?"

He looked up, blinked a few times to clear his eyes and said, "I think we have a lot of guys by the balls, and we're going to have a lot more."

Harris probed. "Do we walk or stay?"

He thought for a moment. "I'm already gone as of a month ago. A Washington leak let my name slide into Morrie Franko's hands, and he took no time blowing my cover at the Board of Trade. Golden wants me to leave Kane and Tully hidden for a while longer to see what else they can uncover."

Harris plopped down in his chair and threw one leg over the arm. His Harvard-law-student look had not changed much in the past eighteen months. He still was clean shaven and combed his sandy hair neatly to the side. "What are you going to do with Fitzsimmons and me?"

Pete took a long swig from his fresh beer and said, "You will probably come out in the open. We'll leave Fitz where he is for the time being. We're going to need your testimony, and when the Exchanges see that I wasn't the only Fed fishing, that it was a government team effort, they may be more likely to cooperate with us, not to mention the brokers we indict."

Pete looked back at the TV and saw Morrie Franko being interviewed. He grabbed for the remote control and its volume button. "Goddamn, it's Franko. Let's see what that birdbrain has to say."

Franko was nearly through with a statement:

"...So let 'em come. We've taken on the government before--and won every time. People think because some of us brokers make a lot of money, we make it illegally. We make our money because we can put up with pressure that ninety-nine per cent of the population can't live with, and we're not afraid to take a chance. We don't want to be like the rest of the sheep in the country and that upsets the government because they feel they can't control us. Well, let 'em come, lady, we're not afraid of the jerks."

A female reporter continued her probe: "Mr. Franko, when the word came out today that hundreds of subpoenas were handed out and that at least one federal agent had been working undercover in the trading pits, what was your reaction?"

Franko sneered at the camera as he said, "My first thoughts were that the government can't do a decent job stopping the real criminals, so in order to cover up their own failures, they are trying to make a big issue out of a few unrelated trading violations at the Chicago Commodity Exchanges. They think nothing of throwing away millions of dollars of taxpayers' money in order to cover up their own inadequacies in other areas of corruption."

"Mr. Franko, one more question. Were you aware of a federal agent posing as a trader in the pits?"

Franko's face tightened with anger. Pete felt a sardonic grin form on his face.

"Lady, I found out a few months ago that there might be a G-Man snooping around. Then I found out who the bozo was, and believe me when I tell you he was typical government, he just stood in the pit and gawked. He was clumsy and didn't understand what was going on. When he did make a trade, he lost money, and half the time he didn't know if he was buying or selling. The whole pit had him picked as a loser, but he kept coming back every day with more money. Nobody had to cheat to make money off of that dope, and I'm sure the government and the taxpayers will pay dearly for that insanity."

"Thank you, Mr. Franko, and good luck. Now to another trader with another story.

Now Pete's face drooped into a scowl as Harris burst into laughter. "Hey, Pete! Franko called you a clumsy bozo, a loser, and a dope. You really impressed those guys."

Pete's head faced the TV, but his eyes moved to meet Harris's. He said with a vile voice, "Wait till Franko sees my next move, then we'll see who the dope is." His eyes returned to the TV. "Let's see whose side this guy is on!"

A haggard-looking broker with bags under gentle eyes stood ready to speak.

The female voice said, "Mr. Norm Wilson, trades...where, Norm?"

"I trade at the Mercantile Exchange, basically in the S & P's and currencies. I'm a spreader. I trade for myself."

"A spreader?"

"Yeah, you know, I buy one product or month or option and sell another."

The female voice expressed the lack of understanding of her TV audience by saying jokingly, "That sounds like French to me."

Norm Wilson was cool. "It's not French, Miss, but it is a bit complicated if you're hearing it for the first time. I just buy one item for one price and sell another item for a different price and hope the prices move my way. It's usually a safer way to trade with less risk than taking an outright buy or sell position."

"Tell me, Mr. Wilson, what is your feeling about this government probe?"

Norm Wilson looked around, as though to see if anyone was listening. Pete knew his nerves were reacting to the question as millions of people watched him, and numerous brokers mulled around behind him. Wilson answered the question.

"I think it's a good thing. It's about time somebody took notice of the crap that goes on down here. I bust my tail trying to make a few bucks, and others walk in every day, take no risk, and walk out with their pockets filled with money. That's not fair, and that's all I'm going to say."

"Mr. Wilson, one more question, please. Do you think the government had an inside man other than the federal agent or agents who may have directed this sting operation?"

Again Pete felt the surge of panic shoot through him. Don't say Hogan, please Wilson, he said to himself. He felt the quick pound of his heart against his ribs as his body tightened.

A cruel smile edged onto Wilson's face, mimicking a Cheshire Cat as it looked at a struggling mouse it held in sharp claws. The look was out of character for the man, Pete felt, but the smile remained as he spoke.

"It would take a special type of man to do that, and I don't think there is a man like that at either Exchange...No, I think this sting operation was strictly government and that it was kept a close secret until just recently. No brokers or members of the Exchanges were in on the investigation in my opinion."

His smile remained as if he knew a secret and wasn't going to tell.

"Thank you, Mr. Wilson. This is Jean Woods coming to you from Chicago's financial district now returning you to our studios."

Pete turned the TV on mute and took another swallow of beer. 'Bozo! Incompetent! Dumb!'...You prick, Franko. I have you on tape buying a bogus tax loss from an FBI agent, and you are calling me a bozo? Well, fuck you!

The voice broke into his thoughts. "Hey Lewis."

He looked up at Harris, who was stepping over half a dozen newspapers and Colonel Saunders Chicken buckets on his way to the door. "I have to split, buddy. You know where I'll be if you need me. Thanks for the chicken and the beer."

He felt some of the pressure seep from him. "Okay, Harris, stop by Bozo's Circus anytime for a good laugh."

Randy laughed and closed the heavy door firmly behind him.

Pete finished his beer, slipped off his shoes, leaned back, and rested his feet on the coffee table. He stared at the ceiling in thought. Something was wrong. It wasn't just today. He had the feeling for months, but he couldn't put his finger on it. Was it the fact that Hogan had become strong and not weak because of the government crackdown? He felt a nagging in his guts. Everybody was eating out of Michael's hand. A major part of the puzzle was missing, and he expected Michael held the pieces and the last trump card. You sly bastard, Hogan, what's your secret? What's your next play? The questions drilled at him, boring into his mind.

Fuck it, he said to himself and turned the TV audio back on, flipping the channel until he found something other than news. Mr. Ed was on Channel 9. That was about as stimulating and philosophical as he could handle right now. A talking horse made a hell of a lot more sense than what he had seen and heard in the past two years.

He leaned his head back and closed his eyes to the theme song of "Mr. Ed."

> *"A horse is a horse of course of course, and no one can*
> *talk to a horse, of course, that is, of course, unless the*
> *horse is the famous Mr. Ed!"*

Adjusting his head on the cushion, he let his mind drift. Even in his semiconscious state, his thoughts churned until they brought forward the dark, icy eyes of Michael Martin Hogan. Although brief, and almost undetectable, Pete had seen the presence of cold, venomous deception in his friend, and the thought nagged at his senses and would not go away. He slept, but his dreams were too real. He was standing in the middle of a frozen lake, the black ice cracking, and Michael Martin Hogan standing on shore smiling at him. He knew panic as he fought to keep his footing, but exhaustion overtook his panic, and he let his mind yield to a dark, cold sleep.

> *The theme song played on: "Go right to the source and*
> *ask this horse, he'll give the answer that you endorse.*
> *He's always on a steady course. Talk to Mr. Ed!"*

FIFTY-SIX

Indictments And The Great Deception
Six Months Later: Thursday, August 3, 1989

Carlo Santini watched the CNN News broadcast as he sat in the study of his Long Island, New York home. A frown carved deep into his face. Ornery, Atlantic rollers slammed at the Long Island shoreline, adding to the banging words of danger that reverberated in his head from the large-screen television.

As he listened to the news of the forty-six commodity-broker indictments, he mentally scolded himself and his son-in-law. Goddamn you, Michael. You're going to get my beautiful daughter and my grandchildren killed. I should have stopped you long ago. Why didn't I stop you? I knew you were holding hands with the Feds. You should know better. I should know better.

He felt his face stiffen as the newscaster announced a standby interview with the Assistant Chief of the FBI, Andrew Golden.

Carlo knew Golden. He had met him at Maria and Michael's wedding, at one of his grandchildren's christenings, and again at a deposition held in New York City when Golden was leading a task force against organized crime. He didn't like the man--but then, he didn't like any government official, even the ones he owned.

If only Michael had confided more in him. Maybe he could talk to a few of the Chicago Families. Maybe he could swap favors with the Families. Hell, the Tarracino Family owed him a big favor.

Then he thought, No, if the Mafia bosses in Chicago or New York find out that Michael Hogan was responsible for turning one of their largest laundry operations into a root-beer stand, he, Carlo Santini, could do nothing. Business was business, and the code of the Cosa Nostra came even before family. The younger generation of mob soldiers had seen to that. The family was not sacred any longer as it had been in the old days. Besides, Michael was an outsider. He was not Sicilian. There would be no favors.

He listened as the arrogant interviewer, John Morvitz, from CNN, spoke to Andy Golden, broad-shouldered federal man with droopy, hound-dog eyes that matched his brown suit.

"We are here in Washington with the Assistant Director of the FBI, Andrew Golden, to see if Mr. Golden can clear up some of our curiosities as to what in the world is actually happening to the high-rolling Chicago Commodity Exchanges.

"Mr. Golden, first of all, I want to thank you for taking this time out of your busy schedule to help clarify just what is going on in Chicago. *Forty-six indictments* served at

virtually the same time to one group of individuals is almost mind boggling. Will there be more indictments, or is this a one-time shot--a flash in the pan?"

Carlo felt his face harden as he saw the intensity and powerful authority in Golden's deceiving, sleepy eyes.

"Mr. Morvitz, this is just the beginning. There will be many more indictments. I assure you this is not a one-time shot or a flash in the pan. Our allegations against the forty-six commodity traders indicted yesterday are based on evidence that they systematically cheated thousands of customers. This will be the most sweeping financial fraud investigation in history."

"Do you expect any of the forty-six to cooperate with the government, or will they stick to their so-called code of silence, as many brokers have indicated?"

"Twenty-four of those charged have already agreed to come forward and cooperate with us, and most of them have signed civil-consent decrees barring them for life from ever holding a membership at any Exchange."

"Obviously the cooperation of the twenty-four will play an important role in making the government's case."

"Our case is made, Mr. Morvitz. The testimonies of the twenty-four will implicate dozens of other traders who allegedly play dirty pool with customer funds, but our case does not hinge on their testimonies."

"Mr. Golden, What are some of the charges being made against those indicted?"

Carlo felt a tightening in his chest. He clutched at his sweater, then pulled a gold pill box from his pocket and placed a nitroglycerin tablet under his tongue. Eyes riveted to the TV screen, he listened as Golden continued.

"Our undercover operation has revealed a wide range of abuses of federal racketeering, tax and commodity laws. We are talking whole-scale grand larceny. We believe our allegations will prove that a large percentage of the broker population is involved in customer fraud as a result of many highly sophisticated trading schemes."

"Mr. Golden, you have indicted some very wealthy men, and a few of them are quite powerful. Do you think you will lose some of your federal punch when you see these men file into the courtroom with the shrewdest and most cunning criminal attorneys in the country?"

Even through the TV screen Carlo saw Andy Golden's ears turn red; nevertheless, the super-agent remained in control, letting his voice take on more authority than anger.

"Mr. Morvitz, first of all, we haven't even begun to go after the big boys yet. The forty-six brokers who were indicted are merely pawns for the so-called bosses. Secondly, these men can walk into the courtroom with whomever they would like to defend them.

"We have indicted forty-six brokers. The total counts they have to defend themselves against is one thousand, four hundred eleven. That means that the grand jury found one thousand, four hundred eleven reasons to bring these men to trial. That's over fourteen hundred counts of fraud on which they have to prove their innocence. We feel we

have the evidence to prove all violations were knowingly and willingly committed; that is, defrauding the customer to benefit themselves. As far as I'm concerned, they're going to need good attorneys!"

Carlo shifted his weight in his chair as he watched Andy Golden's face. He thought to himself, the FBI man was like a rock, a big one, with brains and balls. I hope you know how to take care of my son-in-law and his family, you bastard.

He knew it was Michael who had led the pit operation. Who else could it be? The Feds didn't have the pit savvy to pull a commodity sting without a man like Michael. Besides, he was a close friend of Andrew Golden's. They were old college buddies. Michael was a natural for the job. Carlo took his eyes off the TV and rubbed his chin in thought. But Michael was clever. He wouldn't lay his life on the line, especially for the government. He certainly wouldn't place his family in jeopardy, unless--unless he was planning something. He placed one finger on his upper lip as his mind spun quickly in reverse. He remembered vividly that in 1983, Michael had vocally, and in writing, condemned the Exchange's hierarchy for tolerating "gross, unorthodox and corrupt trading practices." Those words Carlo had read in the *New York Times*. Then, he remembered how nobody, including the government, had come to Michael's defense. The two men who did side with him supposedly committed suicide. Michael claimed they had been silenced-- murdered. Others who sided with him had either been bludgeoned, threatened, or financially ruined. Michael survived. How? He didn't know how, but his elusive, fearless son-in-law had survived and had told him that he would live to fulfill a promise. Carlo's eyes widened with total incredulity. Mother of God, he thought, a vendetta, Michael was living to fulfill a goddamn vendetta!

Carlo's mouth dropped open as his blood pressure and surface body temperature simultaneously rose. The beat of his heart reverberated in his head. He hastily shoved another white pill under his tongue. *Madon'*! That's what this was all about! Just as Michael's grandfather had done seventy years earlier in Ireland, and as he, Carlo, had done to the men who had killed his father in Sicily, Michael Hogan was avenging the deaths of his two friends who had been killed and his other friends who had been beaten. But then, he thought, those men were not family. Why was Michael taking their misfortune so seriously? His mind considered all the possibilities that surged through his head. Then a thought caught like a kite in a tree. He knew the answer. A true Godfather had internal strength as well as physical and mental strength. It didn't matter if he was Siciliano or Irish. The Sicilian Godfathers, in the old days, gave and protected others out of kindness, asking only for loyalty in return. It was that loyalty that had built the strongest survival organization in the world--the Cosa Nostra.

He leaned back and felt a smile crawl across his face. That's what the proud bastard is doing. He's forming his own organization to avenge his friends' misfortune, to protect others, and to make correct those situations and people who are obviously evil. He will be the judge and executioner.

The smile vanished when the thought of Maria and his six grandchildren entered his mind. As much as he admired Michael for his gallant efforts, the man didn't know what he was doing, who he was going up against. The money, the power, the numbers of soldiers. He had to talk to Michael. He had to warn him.

He looked at his wristwatch. 4:48 p.m. 3:48 in Chicago. All the markets had closed. Michael should be in his office.

As he reached for the phone, he heard John Morvitz ask Andy Golden a question that left his hand hanging in the air just above the phone.

"Mr. Golden, is it true that you had an insider working with the government? A broker, a man who helped with the investigation?"

Carlo felt his hands turn clammy as he looked into the eyes of the U.S. Government, who couldn't be trusted, friendship or no friendship. His mouth went dry as he slowly lowered his hand to the phone and listened for Golden's answer.

"Sure, we had inside help..."

Carlo's heart stopped beating for what seemed like too long.

"...as a matter of fact it was one of the Exchange's Board of Governors, Senator Richards, who came forward and vowed his support when he found out we were conducting an investigation. Numerous brokers have also come to us since they were subpoenaed last January and have furnished us with information."

Carlo held his breath as Morvitz persisted with arrogance.

"I'm talking about an insider from the beginning. A top-flight broker who knew where to point the finger, who to go after, where to look. How about training of the agents? You just didn't send federal agents into the confusion and havoc of the trading pits and expect them not only to learn how to trade properly, but to sort out fourteen hundred eleven charges against forty-six brokers...and all this in less than eighteen months?

"Come on, Mr. Golden, your men may be intelligent and the top law-enforcement investigators in the world. But I've known men who are geniuses at finance and it has taken them years to figure out the machinations in the trading pits. That's if they are lucky enough to even get close to becoming part of the confusion. You must have had an inside man, Mr. Golden."

Carlo would have punched the arrogant Morvitz right then and there, and later he would have had his kneecaps shot off. He saw that Golden was unruffled. Carlo realized any other behavior would have disclosed certain secrets Golden wanted kept in the hush. And a "no comment" or "not at liberty to discuss the topic" would have gone as an affirmative to the shrewd reporter.

Golden spoke calmly, but his eyes showed a distinct dislike for either Morvitz or the question he was asking. "Mr. Morvitz, the FBI has not been working on this investigation for just eighteen to twenty-four months. We began this probe five years ago. Our agents have read all the manuals written on commodities, taken courses in commodity

brokerage training, have reviewed files over and over, and practiced amongst themselves in ready for their experience in the pits."

Carlo was surprised to see Golden smile and say,

"You said, yourself, Morvitz, that the brokers had a code of silence by which they lived. You also said that numerous brokers stated that our agents were incompetent in their trading and obviously unable to understand the chaotic dynamics of trading in general. As you say, if there was an inside man working for the government, he would have to be a top flight broker, which means he would probably have an annual income of close to one million plus. You tell me, Mr. Morvitz, would you jeopardize that type of annual income for your government? You would have to be crazy!"

Morvitz and Golden stared at each other for a moment, then without realizing what he was saying, Morvitz casually stated, "Maybe money means nothing to the man. Maybe he has an ulterior motive--I guess we'll know more later, right, Mr. Golden?

"I want to thank you for your time, Assistant Director Golden. I wish you the best of luck in your further investigation of the Chicago Commodity scam.

"This is John Morvitz reporting from the Federal Building in Washington, D.C. returning you to our studios in New York."

Carlo let out a long-awaited gasp, and his chin fell to his chest. He lifted his head, closed his eyes, and breathed deeply through his nose. Then he reached for the phone and dialed a Chicago number.

* * *

The ping of his private line, as soft as it was, jarred Michael as he dozed on his office couch. He blinked a few times as the fog drifted from his mind. He looked down and saw that he still wore his kelly-green trading jacket. He must have passed out after the market closed. Two nights without sleep, working with Lewis, Lorenzo, and Golden, had finally caught up with him. He realized it was his private line ringing, and his body moved faster than his sleepy mind.

"Hello, Hogan here." His head cleared quickly as the voice on the other end spoke with caution.

"Michael, this is Carlo."

He pushed his bottom lip forward in thought. "Carlo? Papa Carlo?"

"Yes, Michael, It's Papa Carlo! Is your phone clean?"

His eyes wrinkled both in surprise and suspicion. He hadn't talked to Carlo for months. "Yes, this line has a scrambler. What's the problem?"

He listened to Carlo's voice ease through the phone cautiously, feeling his way. "I have been watching your FBI friend, Andy Golden, on national news. It looks as though you have hit the long ball for the government."

He leaned up against the edge of his desk, knowing there was going to be more to the conversation than a news update. "I helped them get a running start, but you knew that!"

Carlo's voice began to move faster, more like the Sicilian he knew. "Michael, you are a target. As soon as your enemies find out it was you who tipped the scales, you're a dead man."

He knew Carlo and knew how to handle him. With control, with conviction, and with respect. "Papa Carlo, you can't find fault in my actions because I did what I had to do. I know you're concerned about the family..."

Carlo's voice rose as he cut him short. "You're damn right I'm concerned about the family. You have no idea who or what you're up against. If your enemies have to, they will send one hundred men after you. These young punks have no respect for the family. They kill anybody and everybody."

He had to slow Carlo before his imagination took hold of the conversation. "Slow down, Carlo! What I have done for the government is done, and what I did was right, and..." He cut himself short for a moment, not sure if he should disclose any more to Carlo. He decided to continue. "...what I am going to do will be just. The Feds were going to show up regardless of me; I only pushed things along."

Silence. Michael's suspicion rose. It wasn't like Carlo Santini to avoid an argument, to keep quiet when the family was involved. Michael decided to wait him out. Thirty seconds walked by slowly before Carlo spoke. He said in a whisper, "I know, Michael!"

Michael turned and eased himself into his desk chair. He picked up a framed photograph of himself and the family with the lake in the background. He looked closely at all of their beautiful, smiling faces. His face was solemn, both in the photograph and now. "What do you know, Carlo?"

"I know why you pulled this stunt, all in the shadowed name of law and order and honesty and justice!"

His fingers traced across the faces of his family. "I'll admit I let my government help me clean up the commodity industry, Carlo. You can't criticize me for that."

Carlo's voice took on a cunning, knowing tone. "I'm not criticizing you, Michael, but I know that your efforts with the government to clean up the commodity industry was purely a smoke screen for a more personal, more powerful motive."

Michael placed the picture back on the desk and returned his attention to the wisdom of his father-in-law. "I agreed to help the Feds, and that's what I did, Carlo."

"Yes, but your helping them was not your primary motive, was it, Michael?"

He felt his lips tighten, then part slightly. His voice revealed nothing. "And what was my primary motive, Carlo?"

Again there was a pause before Carlo spoke. Then he said, "You used the government, Michael. You were cunning and shrewd..." His voice hushed "...and, oh, so

patient you were! You waited for the government to come to you. You played every card perfectly, and the Feds didn't even know they were playing cards. I have to hand it to you, Michael. You knew every move they were going to make. Shrewd, son, deceptive and shrewd."

"Carlo, what are you trying to say?"

Carlo spoke with a tone of victory in his voice. "Your primary motive, Michael...it's simple. You weren't out to help the government. Instead, you recruited them to help you!"

He leaned back in his chair and smiled. The Sicilian scoundrel was cunning, and Michael wondered just how much Carlo had figured out. He would play cat 'n' mouse with his father-in-law for a few minutes more to see if he was fishing or if he had actually discovered Michael's diversion. "I recruited them?" His smile remained.

"Your enemies killed two of your close friends, beat up several others, tried to ruin you, and probably would have eventually killed you. You knew the Exchange officials couldn't be trusted. They were your enemy. You tried to get the government involved, but they didn't give you the time of day in 1984. You called your good friend Andy Golden, the only politician you knew, but political strength hadn't materialized as a federal agent yet for Andy. So you waited. You knew you needed time, time to get yourself strong with money and physical strength. You gathered information, you stole information, you sent letters to Congressmen, Senators, all government agencies, and mailed them from all over the country, giving specific examples, photocopies of bogus trades made by corrupt brokers. You planted seeds in your friend Joe Glassmann's mind, knowing that it would take a political figure like Sam Ross to place everything under the government's microscope. Your friendship with Glassmann enabled you to get close to Sam Ross. You filled his orders, made him a ton of money in the market, and he couldn't wait to have you as his honest, Irish-Catholic partner. You were in--you had the political contact you needed to fill your royal flush. You stayed quiet and clean so your enemy would think they had scared you into submission. You planned it all with the cleverness of a champion chess player...Checkmate, World of Corruption and Arenas of Greed--Hogan is here!"

Michael pushed back his chair, lifted his feet up onto his desk, and listened to Carlo with amusement, yet with respect. "When did you figure all this out, Carlo?"

"Michael, it has taken me a long time to get to know you." He paused a moment, and Michael waited patiently. "I was looking in the wrong areas, comparing your peaceful philosophy of life with that of your father. At first, I was only able to know small bits about you, but I have always been able to see in your eyes the frustration and rage you harbored in the darkest part of your soul because of what happened to your friends. I know your antagonism for our government and its phony politicians, and I also know that your philosophy of 'live and let live' would allow you to ignore the corruption in the market and let time eventually cut the thieves' throats. Your cooperation with the government and your connection with Sam Ross fooled me, Michael--until about thirty minutes ago."

"What happened thirty minutes ago, Papa Carlo?"

Michael thought he heard a sigh, then a chuckle. "Thirty minutes ago, I watched one of the strongest men in government law enforcement, your good friend, Andrew Golden, professionally worm his way around the question of whether or not the Feds had an inside man. He protected your identity and would have lied to protect you. The government is indebted to, responsible for, and protecting a man who used them to accomplish his main objective."

"And what was my...?"

Carlo quickly answered his question before it was asked. "Your objective, my boy, was to go after the men who killed your buddies. You did just that. You took out Peterson, Zitello, Ruzzo, and God knows how many more. You fulfilled your promise, your vendetta, all with the sanction of your government." Carlo chuckled as he went on, "That's something I've never been able to do. Have the Feds give me a green light to kill a group of men."

Michael said softly, "They were evil men and deserved to die!" The statement filled him with satisfaction. Although he felt the smile leave his face at the thought of those he had eliminated, he believed with his whole being that his actions had been justified.

"I don't doubt that, Michael, but to have the sanction and immunity from the government is not an easy task!

"You set the Government up perfectly, all for the sake of a vendetta. A promise to your friends that you would personally even the score. In the meantime, God smiles on you and he sends you wealth. Through your deceptive ways, you set up a partnership with a man named Sam Ross, who is mesmerized by your cool, intelligent honesty, and who is connected to the strongest political figures in the country. You planned it all.

"While that's happening, you surround yourself with an unsavory group of jungle fighters who are among the toughest, most loyal soldiers in the world, and who are trained in silent kill rather than shotgun kill."

"How do you know all this, Carlo?"

The proud, sage voice spoke in a whisper. "I know because I am a Sicilian and vendettas run in our blood as does the patience and planning to perform those vendettas-- even if it takes a lifetime. Vendettas were not invented by or limited to Sicilians. It seems you have such blood running through your veins also, Michael. The blood of a Godfather."

Michael was silent. He closed his eyes a moment while his thoughts gathered. Carlo had figured out a good portion of the deception, but even *his* shrewd mind would never figure out the total illusion Michael had performed.

When Carlo spoke again, a humorous tone crept in. "And to think for all these years, I thought my daughter had married a puritan, an aging altar boy who wouldn't lift a finger for the sake of violence. As I said, I thought you were like your father, Patrick, a man of peace through negotiation at any cost, but that's what you wanted me to see-- that's what you wanted everybody to see! The truth is, I was really looking in the wrong

direction. Finally I fit the pieces together. You show the world your father's face, but you wear your grandfather's soul. Peace, yes, but through violent persuasion if necessary."

Michael corrected Carlo. His voice was sharp. "I have no intention of changing my philosophy, Carlo. I'm not advocating violence, but I will allow it if evil men will not be reasonable. I consider a human life to be very sacred, despite the evil that fills many minds."

He listened as Carlo countered quickly. "Dear boy, violence, killing, beatings, personal hardship are by-products of your philosophy. They are all necessary not only for survival, but also for you to reach your goals and make your reputation grow as a man who administers effective justice for his friends who are subservient to and exploited by others. There is no turning back, Michael. No turning back!"

He felt the challenge. "How do you know what my philosophy and goals are when I'm not sure myself?"

He heard Carlo scoff at his last question. "Come on, Michael, you are talking to a master. I know you well enough now to know that your plans have been well thought out. You have counseled with no one except maybe your dead grandfather. Doesn't legend call him 'The Deceptive One, The Ghost of Kildare'? A very intriguing tag. You have to be deceptive. Many times you have to be a ghost in order to be a leader...a Godfather. You've already proven your unusual ability to deceive the government by twisting their metal coating, to stretch and bend them to your wishes without becoming suspect."

Michael drew his feet in and down from the desk; then he turned in his chair. A soft summer rain had begun to fall on the city. The urge to hang up and go stand in the rain was strong. The drops from Heaven were like food to him.

Carlo's patience dwindled as he waited for Michael to speak.

"Michael, are you still there?"

He spoke in a hush. "It's raining, Carlo!"

The voice was harsh. "So what?"

Michael swiveled back to his desk. "So nothing. You wouldn't understand."

Again came the voice, softer now. "Michael, destiny, along with your cooperation, has charted your course. At one time you had a choice to become a poet, a monk, or a husband and father, but it's too late to turn back now. You have chosen to be a leader of men. Sure, you can have poetry in your heart and the solitude of a monk in your soul, and a beautiful wife and children in a warm home, but whether you like the title or not, you have chosen to become a...Godfather. There are those who need your help and guidance."

Michael felt a wave of satisfaction. His secret was known--by Carlo, a man he could trust and a man who would support his decision. But he had to make his true plan clear to the man who had the potential of becoming a Mafia don himself.

His tone turned serious. "Carlo, my intentions are not criminal, nor are they directed toward profit or territorial domain. It's true, I do intend to serve others who are being exploited. To serve the poor, the sick, the old. No charge, no favors for my services.

Just my encouragement and protection. It's a good philosophy with swift justice. No procedure or protocol or due process. Just an analysis, judgment, and affirmative action."

"And you will make the judgment?"

"I will consider both sides of a disagreement. If a man plucks another man's eye out, maybe he had good reason."

The voice was velvet smooth. "If he doesn't have good reason?"

Michael let a coldness come into his voice. "Then I shall ask that he replace the plucked eye with one of his own."

"If he refuses?"

Michael felt the frame of his family's picture. He felt no emotion. "He won't refuse Carlo! His choice will be his eye or his life!"

Now, Carlo was silent. Michael could hear his shallow breathing through the phone. What was he thinking? Then he said, "So, you're going to be a modern-day Robin Hood with 'an eye for an eye' philosophy?"

Michael turned again to look at the rain. Watching it made him feel good. If only he could be washed by the clean drops.

Carlo continued. "You know, Michael, the Mafia was formed in Sicily during the seventeenth century. Not unlike your own organization, the Mafia unified under the leadership of men like your grandfather and yourself to combat corruption and to protect their innocent, weak friends. It was very popular and the leaders were good men, God-fearing and humble, as you are."

His words went on slowly, carefully. "It was not until later that the criminal elements crept in and eventually turned what began as a benevolent, protective union into a union of men, bound to each other by an iron oath of fidelity, who turned to greed, murder and corruption. They represent today the very tyranny the organization was founded to fight against."

After a moment, Carlo said, "Maybe the Mafia needs a new man on the street to remind us..." He corrected himself. "...to remind them where they came from and what the original purpose of their organization was."

Michael's voice was stern, but controlled and confident. "I have no quarrel with the Mafia, Carlo. But if they interfere with my program, I will deal with them!"

He heard Carlo clear his voice and hesitate before speaking. "Of course, you fucked over the government about as well as I've seen it done by one man before. You may as well see how your luck runs with the Mafia." He paused again, then went on. "I don't have to tell you to be careful, Michael. If you carry out your plan as perfectly as you did with the Feds, you'll earn respect, but chances are, you'll get a bullet in the head first. How is your protection? Can I help? I have some good men I can send you."

"I have my soldiers, Carlo." Michael said quickly. "Men who can't be bought and can leave me at any time without being killed. We also have a code of silence, and that is our only requirement for living a peaceful life if they leave."

A question niggled at Carlo. "Are they loyal?"

Michael snapped back. "More loyal than you can imagine. They have found a war they have a chance of winning. I have given them a reason to live, a purpose. The opportunity to do good for themselves and others without arousing their violent natures."

"How many soldiers do you have?"

Michael sensed sarcasm but remained cool. "I have three councilmen who will aid me in determining the validity of the requests which come to us and to determine whether a punishment is in order for the person who brought about the injustice. These three men also have the responsibility of protecting my family."

With less sarcasm, Carlo inquired, "Are they qualified?"

"More than you know!"

"Any other soldiers? Three won't get the job done."

He began his explanation. "I have bought the three homes that adjoin my property, adding six more acres to the estate. Eight additional men will be chosen at some time in the future, no hurry for that. They will occupy the three homes and will be responsible for carrying out the orders of the four-man council. I'm also trying to persuade Pete Lewis to join me as my in-house attorney."

"The FBI man?"

"He's a good man, Carlo, and can be trusted. Our feelings on most things coincide. He's a genius attorney. His mind is as fast and accurate as his weapon, and he has the federal contacts which I need."

Carlo snapped out. "Sorry, Michael. I don't like that idea. Once a Fed, always a Fed."

Suddenly he wished the conversation was over. He turned to watch the rain. "It's not your decision, Carlo. Besides, he's a maverick and probably won't last long with the Bureau once he's back in New York. He has some apprehensions, but he'll come around because he sees the efficiency and logic in swift justice. He will close his eyes at some of our behavior, but he'll squeeze the trigger if necessary."

"Have you been called on for help from outsiders yet?"

"Dozens. Father Tiffin called me a few months ago and asked that I help finance a new tile roof for the church to the tune of a hundred and fifty thousand dollars."

"And?"

"I was surprised at the request, and in so many words, I told him a new roof had been placed on the church only five years ago. He said the parishioners decided the roof should be tile to match the new rectory and convent."

"You agreed?"

Michael felt anger flow with his words. "I agreed like hell! I told Father Tiffin he had his head in his ass and that spending one-point-two million on a new rectory for three priests and a new convent for four nuns was totally irresponsible. I added that I would be happy to help in renovating the church, rectory, and convent into dormitories for the old

people, poor, and homeless. I added that I would burn the one hundred fifty thousand in my fireplace before I would give it to him for a new tile roof as a memorial to him. I called him an arrogant hypocrite who preached a lousy sermon and practiced what he preached even worse. He hung up on me."

Laughter erupted through the phone. "You don't deviate much from your principles, do you?"

"I do what I believe in, Carlo. And a new roof on top of a new roof is insane, when not six miles away are Hispanics, blacks, and old people starving and dying. What happened to the old priest who wore sandals with the frayed black cassocks and three-day growth of beard, who shared his meager dinner with a different poor family every evening, rain or snow?"

"You are a visionary, Michael. This is America, and the Church is as selfish and as full of greed as our government is."

Michael had heard the word *visionary* used before in reference to him and momentarily scolded himself for allowing his inner feeling to enter into the conversation. What he felt inside should stay there. It would be dangerous to allow others to get too close to him. With Carlo, he was safe, but others would be looking for inner weakness.

Carlo probed further. "What other requests have you encountered?"

Michael took a deep breath and switched the phone to his left ear. "Do you remember Mrs. Manelli?"

"Maria's friend, the one whose husband died of cancer, and lives on the west side of Chicago with a bunch of kids?"

"Right. Well, Maria asked if I would talk to her. She said Mrs. Manelli was afraid to call me herself. She didn't want to bother me."

Michael paused, recalling Mrs. Manelli's exact situation. "Maria said she needed help, so naturally I was happy to help if I could. It seems that after her husband's death there was quite a bit of debt. They have no money, their insurance was minimal, and the excess debt was something like sixty-three thousand dollars owed mainly to one very wealthy doctor...a Dr. Bowman. She had asked him to reconsider the debt and she would try to pay him one hundred dollars a month. He demanded full payment. He said he didn't have fifty years to wait for her bill to be paid, and told her to sell her house to pay the bill--he didn't make it a practice to work for nothing. He then proceeded to file a lawsuit against her and was about to take her house. That's when she came to me."

The voice was eager. "And of course you helped! Did you pay the debt?"

Michael shook his head with both despair and disgust. "Carlo, my heart breaks for people like Mrs. Manelli. Through no fault of her own, the poor woman has never owned more than one dress and has to take the bus wherever she goes. Then her husband, who was a fine man, ups and dies on her, and she is left with four kids and this huge debt to Dr. Bowman."

"And you did what?"

Again he felt the anger which he remembered so well. "I personally made an appointment with Dr. Bowman. When I finally was able to see him, I told him I was a friend of Mrs. Manelli's and I thought he should reconsider dropping the lawsuit and accept the one hundred dollars per month as she promised him. He asked me to leave and said the lawsuit would stand until the bill was paid in full. I asked him to please reconsider, that it would be to his advantage if he did, and it would certainly ease Mrs. Manelli's financial burden. He evidently didn't hear me."

Carlo's voice was hurried. "What did you do to the prick?"

Michael's lips formed into a cruel smile at the memory. "I cut off the small finger of the fucker's right hand and jammed it in his ear. Then I asked him if he could hear me. The man was hysterical but nodded yes. I told him that if the lawsuit for sixty-three thousand wasn't dropped by noon the next day and a cashier's check for twenty-four thousand written to Mrs. Manelli wasn't in her hands by two o'clock the same afternoon, I would be back to cut off both of his hands. The twenty-four thousand was the amount of insurance money he had already been paid by Mrs. Manelli. I also told him if he called the police I would kill him."

Carlo was silent except for the long, slow, deliberate exhale. "You obviously made your point with the good doctor!"

He felt his eyes narrow with satisfaction. "By two o'clock the next afternoon, everything had been taken care of. The doctor even added interest to the twenty-four thousand. I guess he realized he wouldn't be much of a doctor without his hands."

"Would you have done it, Michael?"

"What's that, Carlo?"

"Cut off his hands?"

"Carlo, without my intervention, four out of five of the doctors who treated Mr. Manelli either dropped the bill entirely or cut the bill dramatically. Dr. Bowman is greedy. He was one out of five doctors who had no sympathy, no feelings, a self-righteous, egotistical prick. You're goddamn right I would have cut off his hands, maybe his balls, too."

Humor and sarcasm tinged Carlo's words. "That's very Christian, Michael."

Michael nodded his head in agreement. "You're right, Carlo. The doctor should have been more Christian. His greed cost him his little finger and could have cost him a lot more."

Carlo laughed. "I mean it wasn't very Christian what you did to the doctor."

"I helped a poor woman, Carlo. A woman who couldn't turn to the law, to the church, to the doctor. By law and the courts of man, she owed sixty-three thousand dollars, or pay the consequences. If I'm alive long enough, I'll see that people like Mrs. Manelli get at least one break in life. I'll go visit the doctors and lawyers and politicians and try to deal with them in a reasonable way. If I find greed, then I'll deal with them in a more influential way. Besides, the way I read it, Christ said to take care of the poor, the

homeless, the naked, the hurting people. I've never read where he said step aside from those who thrive on the misfortunes of others."

"I'm not a religious man, Michael. I don't know about that stuff."

"I'm not religious either, Carlo. Do you know why? Because religion was made by man--finite, error-prone man--but I do believe in a powerful Spirit who directs me. Until I sense that Spiritual Presence placing His hand on my shoulder telling me to slow down, I will continue."

Carlo asked yet another question. "Does anybody else know of your government manipulation with the purpose of fulfilling a vendetta and starting your own covert group of supermen?"

"I expect Maria knows. She thinks like her father." Michael could almost see Carlo smile. "Other than that, it's just you and me, Carlo, and I would appreciate it if it stayed that way."

How about your business? Aren't you afraid it will suffer?"

"Suffer? The whole commodity industry as we've known it for a hundred years is history. I'm leaving the trading floor in a few weeks and will be working from the office. I've already begun selling my memberships, and I'm encouraging all other brokers who are close to me to do the same. Cash in, and lease memberships until the smoke clears."

He went on more slowly. "As far as my business goes, Sam Ross and I are buying up as many computer companies who process commodity trades as possible. We feel that within five years the open-outcry auction system which has been obsolete for over a decade will become computerized. There is no question that the romance of screaming brokers will be replaced shortly by the hum of a computer. The acceleration of trading information, honest execution of orders, and prompt, technical read-outs alone will force computerization.

"Ross is going to push Washington for SEC intervention, and he expects the SEC to be regulating the stock-index markets within two years. Once their foot is in the Exchange door, they will force the door open, and the CFTC will be defunct. No more defunct than they are now, but officially they will cease to be. The brokerage companies that go broke because of the government sting, Ross and I will buy and computerize."

Carlo was evidently thinking. The phone was silent. When he spoke, his voice was full of praise. "My hat is off to you, Michael. Especially the way you manipulated the grand manipulator, the U.S. Government. They played right into your hands. You cleaned up the garbage that hurt you, and you did it with their blessing. You pointed out your enemies to the federal agents. Those enemies and the credibility of the commodity Exchanges will be ruined.

"You'll bring down one of the largest financial industries in the world just because they pissed you off by killing a few of your buddies, and at the same time you're making

plans to replace the doomed floor brokers with state-of-the-art computers. And you did it all with a straight face."

Michael lifted his eyes to the window and watched the tears of rain run the length of the window. He rocked back and forth in the soft, leather chair. His face and mind remained calm. "I was angry, Carlo, not much to smile about. Tim O'Neal and Al Josephson were damn good men, and Peterson had them killed. The Exchange backed Peterson's complaints against me because the Board of Governors, along with their Washington counterparts, were afraid their kickbacks would surface. They knew I would fuck up their network of corruption, so they came at me hard. I voiced then that I would go to any lengths to avenge the deaths of O'Neal and Josephson and I would take both Exchanges down if I had to...We're all gamblers; let the chips fall where they may.

"The Exchanges had turned dirty. They had to pay for running from the truth by siding with the scum who were killing my friends and the industry. They didn't take me seriously. I couldn't do it myself, and I knew the government moved like an elephant in a mudhole when it came to investigating one man's complaint about murder or theft, so I concocted a plan which worked. It took a few years, but the Feds finally came running and couldn't wait to lend a helping hand if I'd be their inside man. You know the rest if you've been watching TV."

Carlo jumped in as a true Sicilian, wanting the final word. "Letting the Feds think it was their idea to bust the Exchanges and take the public credit for a successful, well - planned investigation, of course!"

Michael broke in. "Of course! Now, I want my name left out of this mess as long as possible. Until I feel comfortable with the men around me and the money behind me."

He stopped rocking and smiled as he remembered the original luncheon at the Union Club that had started the ball rolling, two and a half years earlier. "Ya know, Carlo, I didn't think Glassmann and Golden would ever invite me to lunch. Finally after about ten thousand letters to the Justice Department, plus those from truly disenchanted customers, the government finally contacted me. I had a choice: either play the tough, arrogant, self-centered broker encouraging the government to pursue the investigation, knowing they would uncover everything I pointed to, or just let the Exchange die a slow corrupt death. I was too impatient and played the roll of an egocentric prick, agreeing to work with the Feds under certain conditions. They virtually gave me carte blanche."

The voice was hearty. "Neat, Michael, very neat! Will you need my assistance in any way?"

"Just your support, Carlo."

"They will come for you!"

"I'll be waiting for them."

"I'm sure you will, son...I'm sure you will! Be careful!"

He had enjoyed this conversation, but now he felt tired. "*Ciao*, Carlo. I'm glad you know. It was getting heavy carrying all this around by myself. It's good that you can help me carry the weight."

"*Ciao*, Michael. Call me anytime and you'll have whatever you need within hours. Weapons, men whatever you need."

"*Grazie*, Papa, I'll keep in touch."

Michael heard the distant phone disconnect, and he placed his own phone back on its receiver.

The rain came down harder. The tears on the window had turned to one full flow of rippling water. He felt himself relax. His mind had been living in a silent movie, but now Carlo knew of his deception; soon others would know. Everything was falling together. He had done nothing wrong. He had just let the government do his dirty work.

Then he felt his eyes pull tight, and his lips pushed out in thought. He would have many enemies. When would they strike? He felt a thrill slowly ripple through him. Come for me anytime, boys. I'll be waiting for you. Then you'll know The Deceptive One has returned.

FIFTY-SEVEN

The Dark Side of the Moon
One Year Later: August 19, 1990

Michael wiped his wet, black hair and smoothed it back with a heavy, terry-cloth towel. His three-hour workout with Snake, followed by a brisk two-mile swim, and a period of meditation relaxed his mind as well as his body. He felt good. He felt strong, as he walked by the gazebo toward the house and jumped the four tile steps to the slate terrace which led to the lake-room.

He stripped the red-nylon swimming suit from his body and hung it to dry on the handle of a brown Jordan terrace chair, something Maria would raise hell with him about if she saw it. He smiled. But she and the children were spending the summer on Long Island. She would never know about his crass actions. He dried himself, wrapped the towel around his waist and breathed deep into the dusk of the dog-day summer evening.

Once inside, he stopped to admire the amber haze that filled the windowed room with the final rays of the day's Golden Guardian. He blessed himself in thanksgiving and continued on through the room.

As he passed his desk and headed toward the bar, the phone rang. He stopped and without turning, heard a warning bell sound in his head. He didn't know why, but his instincts turned to suspicions. He saw the fifth button on the phone blinking. His twenty-four-hour secretary had a message. He breathed easy, but his senses had been alerted.

"This is Hogan!"

The female voice spoke swiftly and efficiently. "Mr. Hogan, I have a man on hold who insists on talking to you."

"Did he tell you his name?"

"He won't give his name, sir!"

He was patient with the young voice. "Then just take a message and tell him I'll return his call on Monday."

"He says it's important." She hesitated briefly and continued. "He says that he's a friend of Mrs. Manelli's."

Michael looked at the clock on the table. 7:07 p.m.. He bit his lower lip in thought and looked out at the lake. "You have him on hold?"

"Yes I do, sir!"

He had helped Maria's friend, Mrs. Manelli, and had received numerous calls from her friends who were having difficulties. This could be another call for assistance,

yet he felt an uneasiness push through his body. Only one way to find out, he thought. "Put the call through, Miss."

He was startled at the gravel voice that spoke. "Is this Mike Hogan?"

He felt his forehead wrinkle and was silent for a moment, then spoke calmly. "Yes, this is Hogan."

The voice had a west-side, dese-and-dose, Italian accent. "You're the man who helped my friend, Anna Manelli?"

He thought for a moment, recalling the name, the face, the date, and the situation. Anna Manelli...Doctor Bowman, the man with the missing little finger. "Yes, I did Mrs. Manelli a small favor. What can I do for you?"

The voice was muffled, almost indecipherable." You did my friend, Anna Manelli, a big favor, and you don't know it, but you did me a favor some years back. Now, I return the favor."

Michael's curiosity grew along with his suspicion. To ask the man's name would be amateur. If the throaty voice wanted his name known, he would disclose it. Besides, it didn't matter. The conversation was about information, not names. He spoke with a stern voice. "I don't do favors for favors in return!"

"If you're going into the type of business I think you are, you had better change your game plan, Mr. Hogan, and accept favors."

Michael didn't speak. He'd let the man continue, but he felt his senses pique like a lion looking at a dead zebra hanging from a tree, smelling not only food but an unfamiliar scent of something threatening. Something deadly. A chill traced his spine.

The deep voice spoke, and Michael felt his skin turn colder at the man's words. "They are coming for you tonight, Mr. Hogan!"

Michael forestalled an immediate reaction. His eyes caught the gold rays filtering through the room and felt their power. This is what he'd been waiting for. Did the voice scare him? He didn't know. He didn't think so. This was more intriguing than scary. Why would a man be calling and warning him of a personal assault? He spoke softly. "Who is coming tonight?"

"Trick or treaters, Mr. Hogan, but they won't be coming with grocery bags looking for candy. They will be armed with explosives and automatic weapons."

He felt the icy fingers trace his spine again. "How many men?"

"There will be eight, all coming by boat. One man will stay with the boat. The others will come to fulfill a contract on you and your family."

Michael felt anger pour through his veins now turning the original chill to heat, heavy heat. Carlo Santini was right. The new generation of hoods had no respect for family. "When will they come?" His words were terse and quick.

The voice was low, intimate. "Tonight...late!"

Keep calm, he told himself, anger is not a friend--it clouds the mind. A thousand thoughts sped through his mind, and for a split second he felt fear, something he hadn't felt

in a long time, but then he remembered his family was safe with Carlo. He was alone with his men, his disciplined, fighting men. His mind slowed to a run. He needed more information, and without insulting the man by indicating he might be a liar, he said cautiously, "How do I know your information is accurate?"

The gruff voice became strong. "If the people I work for knew I was making this phone call, I'd be dead in thirty minutes. I don't like the men I work for. They have no feelings. No respect. And it was you who helped Anna Manelli and saved my life once."

Michael still felt the heat push his heart faster, but the last statement made him frown in question. "How did I save your life?"

The deep voice hesitated, then became more gentle. "The man in the white van, the one with the Cubs baseball cap. The man with ice in his eyes could have killed me when he ran our car off into your ravine. He could have killed me easily, and I knew he would have if...if somebody hadn't instructed him to simply destroy the car. I presume it was your orders not to have my partner and me killed. For that, I return the favor."

Michael remembered the black limousine his men had destroyed, and he remembered telling Bo precisely not to kill anyone. "If you're telling me the truth, you're taking a big chance in calling me, and I will be indebted to you."

"You have already fulfilled your indebtedness to me, Mr. Hogan. Besides, even this warning probably won't keep you alive. The eight men who are being sent have killed stronger, more fortified men than you. They take their professionalism very seriously, and are the best my bosses can hire."

Michael felt a sinister smile zig-zag across his face as he thought of his small band of protectors. Each one of them could kill eight men in minutes without using an automatic weapon. They would have to send ten times eight to make it a contest. Then the grin softened as he reminded himself that he would be going into the most important contest of his life, and not to get cocky and underestimate the enemy as they had underestimated him. To be strong he would have to stay humble! A wild ego was like a wild stallion. It would lead to carelessness, which would be deadly. There would be only first and second place in this race--and the ones who came in second would be dead.

The man spoke again, more as a confidant than an informer. It was his turn to ask a question. "What will you do?"

Michael's mind had cleared. He was already setting his plans into motion by pulling the Mauser from the bottom drawer of his desk. He was amused with the question. The man wasn't asking what his strategy was going to be; he was asking where Michael was going to run and hide. "Well, my friend, I plan to take a cold shower and then sit for awhile in my whirlpool. Then I plan to take another cold shower." He felt his voice turn cold. "And then I am going hunting!"

The voice was silent and Michael continued. "If your people come for me tonight, I suggest you not be with them, and if your information is correct, you may be looking for a new employer at a later date. If the heat gets too intense in your camp, you obviously

know how to get in touch with me. Just tell my secretary you are a friend of Anna Manelli's. I'll know who it is."

"My information is correct, Mr. Hogan, and don't forget, the system works because of returned favors, not money and power alone."

"I'll remember that. Thank you." The line went dead.

He sat at his desk and noticed that the lake-room had lost its golden glow from the setting sun. Clouds had evidently covered the sun's final departure from Chicago. He lifted his head and smelled the warm air drifting through the screens: more rain was coming. He sensed the storm as did the birds and the flowers.

He leaned back and rubbed the barrel of the Mauser. He extracted the clip, examined it, and slammed it back into the handle of the gun. Water still dripped from his hair onto his shoulders and down his back.

His thoughts were collating like an old IBM computer shuffling punch cards into piles of facts mixed with strategy. Should he call Lewis and include him in the turkey-shoot, or should he let his own men handle the evening? He decided it might be an insult to his men if he brought Lewis in on a job that should be awarded to Snake, Bear and Bo.

He picked up the phone and pressed a red button, the direct line to the coach house.

Bear's voice was gentle and intelligent. Michael thought to himself that Bear's clarity in both speech and thought would never give him away as a two-hundred-fifty-pound man from the ghetto. He sounded more like an attorney.

"Yes, Mike, any problem?"

"Rumor has it that we're going to be hit tonight, Bear."

There was a short silence, then Bear said calmly, "Do you have details?"

"Eight professionals armed with automatic weapons and explosives." He studied the Mauser. "They are coming in by boat some time after dark--I expect after midnight, when the lake clears of boaters. Seven will hit the estate; one will stay with the boat."

He heard no emotion in Bear's voice. "Is your information accurate?"

Michael toyed with the Mauser. "I think so but can't be sure."

Bear responded as a knowledgeable commando. "Well, this is what we've been waiting for, Mike. Full alert, zero tolerance?"

"You got it brother! Zero tolerance. Kill anybody who enters the property." Michael looked at the desk clock and date: 7:28, August 19, 1990. "And Bear, keep in mind, tonight is the dark side of the moon. It's going to be pitch black. And...there is a storm coming."

"How can you tell?"

"It's in the air, I can smell it!"

He could almost see the white scar stretch in a smile as Bear spoke. "Good! Both will work to our advantage. We're used to living on the dark side of the moon, and the rain will make the enemy jumpy. These guys are used to shooting people in the head at close

range and stuffing them into a car trunk, not slopping through slick ravines and shooting at something they can't see. This time of year the foliage is well grown, and that's our type of fighting terrain. They won't get within a hundred yards of the house. We'll know how many there are, their approximate weight, and their exact location ten seconds after they hit the shore line."

He knew the value of the words. "Okay. The three of you meet me in the library in forty-five minutes to go over our strategy!"

Bear hesitated a moment, and Michael heard the question in his own voice. "What's the matter, Bear?"

"Uhhm...John and I will meet with you, but...Bo went to an AA meeting."

Michael yelled into the phone. "AN AA MEETING? We've been trying to get him to a meeting for three years, and he picks tonight to finally break the ice?"

Bear spoke in defense of Bo. "No, he's been going fairly regularly to Hill-112 and the VA hospital, but it seems tonight he has to speak...He said he had to give his story and speak on humility."

Michael's temper cooled quickly, and in the midst of a sigh he said, "Well, if he's giving a talk on humility, you can be sure it will be a short meeting!"

Bear laughed and said, "See you in forty-five minutes. We'll turn on all the pressure grids and electric eyes. Bo should be home by 10:30. We'll be ready for our friends!"

The phone went dead, and Michael walked to the open windows overlooking the lake. The breezes had picked up, and he heard the oak trees begin to talk. Thunder in the distance told him the Heavens would be full of nasty rascals within hours. He spoke in a whisper. He spoke a prayer. "If it is indeed Your wish that I serve Your people in this questionable way, show Your approval in tonight's conflict."

He blessed himself and walked to the bar, where he pushed the bottle of scotch to one side and reached around the bar for a can of diet pop from the refrigerator. As he leaned on the bar, he shook his head, and a smile came to his face. He recalled Bear's words. "Bo Lynch is giving a talk on humility tonight." Michael thought, that's funny Bo, but get your humble ass back here after your humble speech so we can kick the best professionals right into hell.

He turned and pressed three buttons on an elaborate sound system, and the whine of bagpipes blasted an Irish tune, "Brennan on the Moor," throughout the house and through the open windows for the whole estate to appreciate. He slicked back his hair with his hand, picked up the Mauser from the bar, and headed toward the spiral staircase and the hot tub that awaited him. He puffed with strength at the sound of the pipers playing the inspiring tune of his father's homeland, "The Legend of Willie Brennan"-or was it truly "The Legend of Martin Hogan"?

EPILOGUE

The time was 2:08 a.m., July 22, 1990, exactly seven hours after the man named The Deceptive One had been contacted by Anna Manelli's friend. The muffled sound of dual turbo engines powered a fifty-two foot Bertram luxury yacht through the inky waters of Lake Michigan.

The storm had come out of nowhere. Rain fell hard, and the lake was angry with the powerful vessel of evil that sliced through her rough surface. The white breakers slammed against the hull of the strong boat as if they were alive and determined to keep the powerful ship from entering sacred waters.

Against the perpetrators' wishes, the yacht had to be anchored two hundred yards from the shore line because of the hysterical waters and torrential rains that pelted the seven Latino assassins. They cursed nature as they stepped into a fourteen-foot Whaler with their heavy weaponry. Another man stayed with the yacht.

At 2:28 a.m. the seven men, all dressed in various dark colors, slipped from the Whaler thirty feet from shore. They forced their way through the protesting undertow toward the concrete sea wall that fortified the land in front of the dimly-lit, ghost-white mansion. A strange, whining noise chanted from the house. An uneasiness wormed its way through each of the Latinos at the realization that it was the sound of bagpipes clashing with the banging cymbals of nature.

The men stood for a moment in the stinging rain glancing at each other. Then one man motioned, and they all turned to inspect the expansive, rising lawn, flanked by two steep and heavily wooded ravines. The Whaler was pulled onto a sandy beach just south of the sea wall. A strong gust of wind came from nowhere and yanked the Whaler from its mooring. The killers watched through the mockery of laughing lightning as their vehicle of escape tumbled like a piece of thin plywood down the beach and broke up on a large pile of rocks. Distracted only momentarily, they turned to observe the terrain and check their weapons.

Lightning pierced through one of heaven's keyholes, filling the black night with the temporary brilliance of shining chrome.

The seven, unimpressed, began their ascent toward the mansion. Three entered the ravines to the north, three to the south, and one man, the leader, moved cautiously toward a gazebo that sat in the middle of the lawn that sloped upward to the eerie mansion. The bagpipes played louder.

As the men moved away from the roaring lake, their movements were picked up immediately by buried pressure grids and hidden microwave motion and direction sensors, pinpointing each of the enemies' positions.

Fluorescent green screens of computerized wristwatches were studied closely by four men wearing black who were placed at different positions throughout the estate. The men all wore electronic, night-vision glasses and watched the amber silhouettes of their enemies approach with quick staccato motion.

At 2:37 a.m. an aluminum arrow sliced the air and entered an enemy's neck, pinning him to a solid oak pillar of the gazebo. An automatic weapon fell from his hand as death came instantly. A jagged sword of lightning spit fire at the gazebo, revealing the limp body to the angry lake. The loud clap deafened and shook the Latinos.

At 2:39 a.m. a loud roll of thunder accompanied the snapping of neck bones from the north ravine. The killer, who just six hours earlier had delivered a talk on humility, whispered the holy words"...*And the courage to change the things I can*!"

The time was 2:43 a.m. The three men in the south ravine had spread out and struggled to pull themselves up the steep hill that led to the open grassy area two hundred feet from the terrace of the mansion. As one intruder reached the top and pulled himself onto the open area, a flash of lightning momentarily blinded him. He had expected his vision to clear, but it immediately dimmed in death as a machete wielded by a black man sliced off his head. The black man, mistaken for ravine foliage, moved as fast as the lightning; and in the same motion, he threw a twelve-inch boot-knife forty feet. The knife entered the left temple of another enemy and imbedded in his brain. Thunder applauded, and the bagpipes played on.

One perpetrator had found better footing and had reached the terrace. He tried to muffle his anxious jerks of breath. Sweat and mud from his face, mixed with the rain, dripped from the Latino's chin as he stepped cautiously into the safety of the mansion's dark shadows. Suspicion engulfed him as he sensed he wasn't alone. As his head began to turn, the nervous finger on the trigger of his machine pistol tightened. A foot snapped out of the darkness and crushed the man's nose, sending cartilage and numerous other bones into his brain. A hand reached out and caught the man's weapon before it hit the slate terrace. The muffled words of a slogan were heard only by the killer: "*Live and let live*...or die, motherfucker!"

The only gunshots fired were at 2:47 a.m. by the man with the features of a hawk who stalked the north ravine. As the storm raged, claps of thunder drowned out four sharp cracks from a Mauser. Two bullets to the heads of each of the remaining enemies quelled the storm. His allies of nature were satisfied and the pipers played on.

The captain of the Bertram peered through the rain soaked windshield. He had seen no flashes of gunfire, only lightning. Something had gone wrong. He looked at his watch. 3:13 a.m. They should have been back by now. Sweat ran from his tight Latin face. The storm had unnerved him. This was a different type of storm, one that he had never seen before. It seemed as though it had a personality; it seemed alive, almost human, and it wasn't friendly. He picked up a hand radio and pressed a black button three times,

hoping to hear from the men on shore. His tough face turned gray and twitched with confusion and fear at the static return from the hand radio.

Behind him the man who moved and swam like a deadly snake had slipped on board as unobtrusively as a giant slug, and with a split-second snap, the captain's head faced the opposite direction of his body. The man's eyes were wide, and reflexes made them blink with surprise, but they were dead.

The anchor was pulled, and the storm eased as the thin man with ice in his eyes pulled the Bertram close to shore, where seven bodies were lifted onto the yacht. A Chicago Cubs equipment bag containing eight grenades, duct tape, and C-4 plastic was also placed on the yacht.

At 3:33 a.m. the Bertram set out north for Kenosha, and a white van crept through the winding streets of Chicago's wealthy North Shore in the same direction as the yacht. The half-million dollar Bertram would sink twenty miles off Kenosha along with the eight assassins. Only eight sets of amputated ears would be left from the massacre, and they would be sent to the man who had ordered the contract kill. The criminal Boss would then know there was a new game in town!

The huge black man with the long, white scar on his face who drove the van was surprised that just two miles from the mansion the streets were dry. There had been no storm except near the mansion. His mission was to pick up the Ice Man, after the Bertram and its crew slept with the fish.

The time was 6:13 a.m. when the van pulled back onto the estate property. The black man and the man called Snake went immediately to the mansion for a meeting in the lake-room.

The tall man with the features of a hawk, along with his sober and "humble" friend, welcomed their two associates. They sat and listened to a cunning plan that had been developed through one hundred years of blood lines.

As the earth moved to meet the morning's golden globe of power and light, a clandestine union of friendship and loyalty was formed. The Chalice of the East blessed the union with arrows of bright strength. The group would be called IUSTICIA DE NATURAS--Justice of Nature.

A NOTE ABOUT THE AUTHOR

William Fitzgerald was born and reared in Rockford, Illinois. He graduated with a BA degree in Philosophy and Psychology from The University of Dayton, did graduate work at Loras Collage in Dubuque, Iowa and Loyola University in Chicago, Illinois. The author acknowledges that his education received from St. Joseph's Prep School, Bardstown, Kentucky, was one of the turning points in his life. Mr. Fitzgerald spent eighteen years as a Commodity 'Pit' Broker and was a member of The Chicago Mercantile Exchange, The Chicago Board of Trade, The International Monetary Market and The Mid-America Commodity Exchange. He and his wife live in Florida with their children.

Grateful acknowledgment is made to the following for the reprinting of excerpts of previously published material:

Final Countdown" by Europe. Copyright 1986, CBS Inc. "Good Golly Miss Molly." Words and music by Ottis Blackwell and Marascalo. Copyright 1958. "Theme From Mr. Ed. "Cats in the Cradle", words and music by Harry and Sandy Chapin. Copyright 1974, 1987 by Story Songs. The Chicago Tribune, The Wall Street Journal, Barrons, Time and News Week magazines.

3 1382 00203 8359

AS   PS 3556 .I843 A88 1990

Fitzgerald, William Edward.
   Arenas of greed

#23086913   1/94